INTRODUCTION TO GOVERNMENTAL AND NOT-FOR-PROFIT ACCOUNTING

Sixth
Edition

INTRODUCTION TO GOVERNMENTAL AND NOT-FOR-PROFIT ACCOUNTING

Martin Ives
New York University

Laurence Johnson
Colorado State University

Joseph R. Razek
University of New Orleans (retired)

Gordon A. Hosch
University of New Orleans

PEARSON

Prentice
Hall

Pearson Education International

Library of Congress Cataloging-in-Publication Data

Introduction to governmental and not-for-profit accounting / Martin Ives ... [et al.].—6th ed.
  p. cm.
  Rev. ed. of: Introduction to governmental and not-for-profit accounting / Martin Ives,
Joseph R. Razek, Gordon A. Hosch. 5th ed. c2004.
  Includes bibliographical references and index.
  ISBN-13: 978-0-13-236635-9 (casebound)
  ISBN-10: 0-13-236635-5 (casebound)
  1. Fund accounting. 2. Finance, Public—Accounting. 3. Nonprofit organiza-
tions—Accounting. I. Ives, Martin. II. Ives, Martin. Introduction to governmental
and not-for-profit accounting.
  HF5681.F84R39 2009
  657′.835—dc22

2007048020

AVP/Editor-in-Chief: Eric Svendsen
VP/Editorial Director: Jeff Shelstad
Product Development Manager: Ashley
  Santora
Editorial Project Manager: Kierra
  Kashickey
Editorial Assistant: Mauricio Escoto
Senior Marketing Manager: Jodi Bassett
**Associate Director, Production
  Editorial:** Judy Leale
Production Project Manager: Kerri
  Tomasso

Permissions Coordinator: Charles Morris
Senior Operations Supervisor: Arnold
  Vila
Operations Specialist: Michelle Klein
Cover Design: Rob Aleman
Cover Illustration/Photo: Getty
  Images, Inc.
Composition: Aptara
Full-Service Project Management: Thistle
  Hill Publishing Services, LLC
Printer/Binder: Courier/Westford
Typeface: Times Ten Roman

Credits and acknowledgments borrowed from other sources and reproduced, with permission, in this textbook appear on appropriate page within text.

Pearson Education LTD., London
Pearson Education Singapore, Pte. Ltd
Pearson Education, Canada, Ltd
Pearson Education–Japan

Pearson Education Australia PTY, Limited
Pearson Education North Asia Ltd
Pearson Educación de Mexico, S.A. de C.V.
Pearson Education Malaysia, Pte. Ltd.

PEARSON
Prentice
Hall

10 9 8 7 6 5 4 3 2 1
ISBN-13: 978-0-13-236635-9
ISBN-10: 0-13-236635-5

Brief Contents

Contents

Preface

This basic-level text on governmental and not-for-profit financial accounting and reporting is easy to read, comprehensive, practical, and up-to-date. It is fully illustrated with material drawn from actual governments, not-for-profit entities, hospitals, and universities. It has been updated to cover newly issued GASB standards, such as those on post-employment health care benefits and statistical reporting. The chapter on financial statement analysis takes the student beyond the preparation of financial statements and into the *implications* of the data contained in the statements.

This text is written for the college student (both accounting and public administration majors) and for practitioners. To permit use by different types of readers, its 15 chapters cover not only the specialized financial accounting and reporting standards applicable to the public and not-for-profit sectors, but also the basic processes of business-type accounting. Most of the chapters relate to governmental accounting, but those who have not had a course in basic accounting can start with Chapter 15 on the fundamentals of accounting and draw selectively on the governmental, not-for-profit, health care, and financial statement analysis chapters. Because of its flexibility, this text can be used by:

1. Accounting majors who wish to learn the fundamentals of governmental and not-for-profit accounting in either a full semester or less than a full semester.
2. Public administration majors who have had no accounting training but who need a basic understanding of general, governmental, not-for-profit and health care accounting, financial reporting, and financial statement analysis.
3. Persons employed by governmental and not-for-profit organizations, including the federal government, health care entities, colleges and universities, and voluntary health and welfare organizations.
4. Persons preparing for the Uniform Certified Public Accountant (CPA) examination and for civil service and the Certified Government Financial Manager (CGFM) examinations.
5. Persons who wish, on their own, to learn about the financial accounting and reporting practices of governmental and not-for-profit organizations.

FEATURES OF THIS EDITION

Use of "Real World" Examples

To prepare for the practice of accounting, auditing, and financial management, students need both a good conceptual background in accounting theory and an understanding of its application in the real world. In writing this sixth edition, we therefore increased our use of illustrations based on financial statements issued by actual organizations. For example, our Chapters 9, 10, and 14 on governmental financial reporting and financial statement analysis use the actual 2005 financial statements prepared by Grafton, Wisconsin. Because Grafton is relatively small (population 11,310), the student can readily visualize the transactions leading to its financial statements.

Similarly, chapters 13 and 14 on hospital accounting and statement analysis are illustrated with current financial statements of Hudson Valley Hospital Center, and Chapter 12 on not-for-profit accounting has Fordham University's financial statements. (Both of these entities are in New York State.) Chapters 4 through 8, which cover fund level governmental accounting, are also illustrated with financial statements taken from state and local governments throughout the country. Further, the text contains many illustrations of specific transactions and events, covering such entities as the U.S. Social Security Administration, New York City, and People Allied to Combat Hunger.

Revised Chapter on Budgeting

We revised Chapter 3 on governmental budgeting extensively by reducing coverage of budget preparation and incorporating a discussion of the budgetary accounting journal entries and the scheme of revenue and expenditure classification. We believe this change will give accounting and public administration students a better sense of the relation of budgeting and budgetary control to governmental accounting and financial management. Chapter 4 builds on the material in Chapter 3 by adding a simple series of revenue and expenditure transactions to the basic budgetary journal entries, and Chapter 5 covers many transactions that affect General and Special Revenue Funds.

Revised Discussion of Government-Wide Financial Reporting

Financial reporting is covered in two chapters. Chapter 9 covers financial reporting in general, fund-level financial reporting, management's discussion and analysis, and GASB *Statement No. 44* on economic condition (statistical section) reporting. Chapter 10 covers the government-wide financial statements and the adjustments needed to prepare them.

To simplify presentation of the changes brought about by GASB *Statement No. 34,* we continued to separate the discussion of accounting *within the funds* from financial reporting. We did this because the current financial resources measurement focus and modified accrual basis of accounting continue to be used to account *within* the governmental-type funds and for *fund-level* financial reporting. As a result, Chapters 4 through 8 (covering fund accounting) deal exclusively with the manner in which accounting data are accumulated and reported at the fund level.

Because GASB *Statement No. 34* was in the process of implementation when the previous edition of this text was published, Chapter 10 of the text was written from an early implementation perspective. Now that government-wide financial statements are being prepared routinely, we rewrote that chapter to describe how conversion from fund-level financial statements to government-wide statements takes account of both opening balances and transactions during the year. The conversion process is described in simple terminology and is fully illustrated.

Coverage of Not-for-Profit and Hospital Accounting

This text provides extensive coverage of the unique aspects of accounting and financial reporting for not-for-profit entities, including not-for-profit hospitals. Chapter 12 covers accounting for the various types of contributions received by not-for-profit entities, as well as the requirements established by the Financial Accounting Standards Board for reporting by net asset classification. We also simplified this chapter's coverage of fund accounting. Chapter 13 covers matters relevant to not-for-profit and governmental hospitals, including accounting for patient service revenues, malpractice claims, and investments. We also added a section on accounting for contributions received through hospital foundations. The section on hospital financial reporting is based on guidance provided by the AICPA Guide on *Health Care Organizations,* and, as previously noted, is illustrated with the financial statements of an actual hospital.

Expanded Discussion of Pension Processes and Accounting

To provide the student with a broader perspective on pension trust funds, we expanded Chapter 8 to cover more completely the work of the pension actuary and pension accounting for the sponsoring government itself. This chapter also covers the new GASB standards on other postemployment benefits.

Chapter on Financial Statement Analysis

Accounting and public administration students need to understand not only how accounting information is gathered and reported, but also how it is used. We introduced a full chapter on financial statement analysis in the previous edition and felt that the subject was sufficiently important to do so again. Chapter 14 starts with a discussion of financial statement analysis indicators that are generally applicable to governmental, not-for-profit hospital, and other not-for-profit organizations. It then illustrates the calculation of the indicators for a not-for-profit hospital and a government, using the same "real world" financial statements used in Chapters 9 and 10 (Village of Grafton) and in Chapter 13 (Hudson Valley Hospital Center).

Continuing Problems

This text has three "continuing problems" for instructors who like to reinforce the discussion of accounting principles with problems that carry throughout the text. One problem, called Leisure City, is designed to emphasize fund accounting. It starts at the end of Chapter 5 and covers fund-level accounting and financial reporting in Chapters 5 through 8. The other two, called CoCo City and Croton Village, also cover fund-level accounting transactions, but they are designed primarily to emphasize fund-level and government-wide financial reporting. They are presented at the end of Chapters 9 and 10 and are developed so that portions of each problem can be assigned, as appropriate, with Chapters 2 through 10.

Other Features and Changes

All chapters of this text have been updated to incorporate relevant changes in accounting and financial reporting standards issued by the Governmental Accounting Standards Board, the Financial Accounting Standards Board, and the Federal Accounting Standards Advisory Board since preparation of the previous edition. In updating the text, we also considered the material in the relevant AICPA Audit and Accounting Guides and the GASB Implementation Guides. In addition, we added current illustrations of accounting and financial reporting issues, simplified and clarified the material wherever possible, and updated the questions, exercises and problems. Above all, we tried to continue the approach taken in the first edition—to write the text in clear, readily understood language.

Ancillary Package

To assist you in the classroom, the solutions manual and test item file are available for download by registered faculty at the Instructor Resource Center at www.prenhall.com.

ACKNOWLEDGMENTS

We sincerely appreciate the help of the many members of the professional community, students, and faculty in preparing this edition and previous editions of this text. In particular, we thank:

Those who assisted us in obtaining the actual financial statements and other material that we used to make governmental and not-for-profit accounting and financial reporting come alive. They include Mr. Paul Styduhar, Village of Grafton, Wisconsin; Mr. Mark Webster, Hudson Valley Hospital Center; Mr. Hugh Dorrian, City of Columbus, Ohio; and Mr. John Lordan, Fordham University. We also thank them for taking the time to answer questions we had regarding those statements. We made extensive use of the financial statements prepared by the Village of Grafton and the Hudson Valley Hospital Center, and we particularly thank all those involved in preparing those statements.

Those who reviewed and commented on drafts of chapters or helped us resolve matters requiring clarification. They include Mr. David Bean, Mr. Kenneth Schermann, and Mr. Wesley Galloway of the Governmental Accounting Standards Board; Ms. Wendy Comes of the Federal Accounting Standards Advisory Board; Ms. Carol Block of Larimer County, Colorado; and Mr. David Agee, a governmental accounting consultant.

The people at Prentice Hall: Eric Svendsen, editor-in-chief; Kierra Kashickey, editorial project manager; Judy Leale, senior managing editor, production; and Kerri Tomasso, production project manager. And, Angela Williams Urquhart and the staff at Thistle Hill Publishing Services.

And most of all, our wives, Eunice Ives, Nancy Johnson, Cordelia Razek, and Kathy Hosch, who encouraged us in this undertaking and reminded us (gently or otherwise) when it was time to eat.

MI

LJ

JRR

GAH

About the Authors

Martin Ives, **MBA, CPA, CGFM, CIA,** serves as the Distinguished Adjunct Professor of Public Administration at New York University's Wagner Graduate School of Public Service. Before entering the academic world, Mr. Ives was Vice Chair and Director of Research of the Governmental Accounting Standards Board, First Deputy Comptroller of the City of New York, Deputy Comptroller of the State of New York, and a member of the Federal Accounting Standards Advisory Board.

In addition to this text, Mr. Ives is the author of the textbook *Assessing Municipal Financial Condition*, coauthor of the textbook *Government Performance Audit in Action*, and coauthor of *Program Control and Audit* and *Financial Condition Analysis and Management*. He has also written chapters for books on auditing and municipal finance, has authored over 25 articles for the *Journal of Government Financial Management*, the *Journal of Accountancy*, the *Internal Auditor*, and other professional journals, and has spoken to numerous professional and civic organizations.

Mr. Ives was founding president of the Albany chapter of the Institute of Internal Auditors, president of the Capitol District Chapter of the American Society for Public Administration, and a member of the founding board of the Association of Government Accountants' Certified Government Financial Manager program. He has received many honors and awards including the Public Service Award (Fund for the City of New York); the Governor Charles Evans Hughes Award (Capitol District chapter of the American Society for Public Administration); and the S. Kenneth Howard Award (Association for Budgeting and Financial Management). He has also been voted Adjunct of the Year by the students at NYU's Wagner Graduate School.

Laurence E. Johnson, Ph.D., CPA (inactive), CISA, is Associate Professor of Accounting at Colorado State University, Fort Collins. He received his bachelor and master's degrees in business from Northern Arizona University. Professor Johnson has public accounting experience with KPMG, where he worked extensively on the financial statement audits of the City of Phoenix, Arizona. Later, he received his Ph.D. with an emphasis in governmental accounting from Texas Tech University.

Professor Johnson has published articles dealing with governmental accounting and auditing issues in the *Journal of Accounting & Public Policy, Research in Government and Nonprofit Accounting, Research in Accounting Regulation,* the *Journal of Public Budgeting, Accounting, and Financial Management,* and the *CPA Journal,* among others. A member of the Colorado State University accounting faculty since 1990, Professor Johnson has taught financial accounting and auditing courses at the undergraduate and graduate levels. He is a member of the American Accounting Association, the Colorado Society of CPAs, and the Government Finance Officers Association.

Joseph R. Razek, Ph.D., CPA (inactive), recently retired from the University of New Orleans as the Energy Accounting and Tax Conference Professor of Accounting. A graduate of Ohio Wesleyan University, Dr. Razek received his master's of business administration from the University of Michigan and his doctorate from the University of Illinois. He is a certified public accountant and was a certified government financial manager. Dr. Razek has consulted for many governmental and not-for-profit organizations.

Dr. Razek has published articles in the *Accounting Review, Government Accountants Journal, Accounting Historians Journal, Nonprofit World* and other professional journals. He has also coauthored many chapters in governmental accounting handbooks, as well as a textbook on managerial accounting. Cited by his students as a dedicated and innovative teacher, Dr. Razek received several teaching awards. He taught governmental and not-for-profit accounting and health care accounting at both the graduate and undergraduate level and was a member of the Society of Louisiana CPAs' Health Care Task Force.

Gordon A. Hosch, Ph.D., CPA, received his bachelor's degree from the University of New Orleans, a master's degree from the University of Arkansas, and his doctorate in accounting from Louisiana State University in Baton Rouge. He has served as chairman of the Department of Accountancy and the KPMG Professor of Accounting, and is currently Professor Emeritus and Graduate Programs Coordinator in Accounting at the University of New Orleans. He has public accounting experience with KPMG and has served as a faculty intern with the Department of Agriculture's National Finance Center.

Dr. Hosch has served as a member of the Louisiana Society of CPAs Governmental Accounting and Auditing Committee. He has made presentations to various organizations including the American Society of Women Accountants, the American Software Users Group, the U.S. Navy, and the Internal Revenue Service. He has received the Lifetime Membership Award and the Educator of the Year Award from the Louisiana Society of CPAs and numerous teaching awards, including the University of New Orleans College of Business Outstanding Alumnus Award. His publications have appeared in the *Government Accountants Journal* and other journals. In addition, he has coauthored numerous chapters in governmental accounting handbooks. He has also reviewed numerous textbooks and papers during his career.

CHAPTER

1

GOVERNMENTAL AND NOT-FOR-PROFIT ACCOUNTING ENVIRONMENT AND CHARACTERISTICS

Chapter Outline

After completing this chapter, you should be able to:

- Describe the characteristics of governmental entities.
- Describe the characteristics of not-for-profit organizations.
- Describe the governmental and not-for-profit organization environment.

- Describe the users and uses of accounting information.
- Define the term generally accepted accounting principles (GAAP).
- Describe the jurisdictions of the accounting standards-setting bodies.
- Describe the objectives of governmental and not-for-profit entity financial reporting.
- Describe the unique characteristics of governmental and not-for-profit organization accounting and financial reporting.

Significant changes in accounting and financial reporting by state and local governments, the federal government, and not-for-profit organizations have occurred within the past 15 years. For example, as a result of new accounting and financial reporting requirements developed by three separate standards-setting bodies:

- State and local governments began implementing a new financial reporting model in 2002—a process that was only recently completed.
- The federal government issued its first ever set of audited consolidated financial statements, covering the fiscal year ended September 30, 1997.
- Not-for-profit organizations also began issuing statements based on a new financial reporting model, starting in 1995.

Accounting standards-setting is an ongoing process, however, and changes beyond those enumerated above have occurred and are being considered in response to many knotty problems. For example, a recently issued standard concerning state and local government accounting for postemployment health care benefits will provide data about the costs of and obligations created by the benefits. The emergence of new types of financial instruments has created a need for guidelines to ensure both uniform accounting and appropriate disclosure of risk. And federal accounting standards-setters continue to grapple with the best way to report on Social Security, Medicare, and similar benefits.

Accounting and financial reporting matters have hit the media with great frequency during the past decade. Many have concerned corporate financial reporting scandals. But there are media articles about governmental accounting as well, such as the consequences of declining stock market values on the status of governmental pension funds.

State, local, and federal government consumption expenditures account for nearly 20 percent of the gross domestic product. The issues affecting both sides of their accounting ledgers are no less consequential than those affecting business enterprise accounting.

GOVERNMENTAL AND NOT-FOR-PROFIT ORGANIZATIONS

It is not always easy to distinguish among governmental, not-for-profit, and for-profit organizations. The distinction lies less in the functions these entities perform than in the details of how they are organized, governed, and financed. For example, hospitals may be for-profit, not-for-profit, or governmental organizations. A hospital is not necessarily a governmental one just because it was financed partly with tax-exempt debt issued by a governmental agency. An entity is not necessarily a not-for-profit one just because it was created under a state's not-for-profit corporation law.

Governmental entities include the following:

- Federal government
- General-purpose political subdivisions (such as states, counties, cities, and towns)
- Special-purpose political subdivisions (such as school districts)
- Public corporations and bodies corporate and politic (such as state-operated toll roads and toll bridges)

Other organizations created by governments by statute or under not-for-profit corporation laws are governmental if they possess one or more of the following characteristics: (1) their officers are popularly elected or a controlling majority of their governing body is appointed or approved by governmental officials; (2) they possess the power to enact and enforce a tax levy; (3) they hold the power to directly issue debt whose interest is exempt from federal taxation, or (4) they face the potential that a government might dissolve them unilaterally and assume their assets and liabilities.[1]

Not-for-profit organizations exhibit certain basic characteristics that distinguish them from business enterprises. Not-for-profit entities (1) receive contributions of significant amounts of resources from resource providers who do not expect equivalent value in return; (2) operate for purposes other than to provide goods and services at a profit; and (3) lack ownership interests like those of a business enterprise.[2] As a result, not-for-profit organizations may get contributions and grants not normally received by business enterprises. On the other hand, not-for-profit organizations do not engage in ownership-type transactions, such as issuing stock and paying dividends. Four broad categories of not-for-profit organizations are covered in this text: voluntary health and welfare organizations, health care organizations, colleges and universities, and other not-for-profit organizations.

GOVERNMENTAL AND NOT-FOR-PROFIT ENTITY ENVIRONMENT

Governmental and not-for-profit organizations operate in a social, legal, and political environment different from the environment of for-profit business enterprises. As a result, users of their financial statements have somewhat different needs than do users of business enterprise financial statements. These environmental differences have caused accounting standards-setters to develop accounting and financial reporting requirements for governmental and not-for-profit entities that sometimes differ from requirements for business enterprises.

The Governmental Accounting Standards Board (GASB), the accounting standards-setting body for state and local governments, suggests that the major environmental differences between government and business enterprise relate to: organizational purpose, sources of revenue, potential for longevity, relationship with stakeholders, and role of the budget.[3] Some of these factors apply as well to differences in the environments

---

[1]For further discussion, see American Institute of Certified Public Accountants, *AICPA Audit and Accounting Guide, Health Care Organizations* (New York: AICPA, 2006), p. 2; and Martin Ives, "What Is a Government?" *The Government Accountants Journal* (Spring 1994), pp. 25–33.

[2]Statement of Financial Accounting Concepts No. 4, "Objectives of Financial Reporting by Nonbusiness Organizations" (Stamford, CT: Financial Accounting Standards Board, 1980), para. 6.

[3]"Why Governmental Accounting and Financial Reporting Is—and Should Be—Different," Governmental Accounting Standards Board (2006).

between not-for-profit entities and business enterprises. In the discussion that follows, we combined some of these factors and added another to show their potential consequences for accounting and financial reporting.

Organizational Purposes

Business enterprises exist to enhance the wealth of their owners. Because income is quantifiable and can be measured in monetary terms, business enterprise financial reporting focuses primarily on earnings and its components. A corporation might be considered an attractive investment if its revenues have exceeded its expenses consistently, and investors can look forward to continued growth in the bottom line.

In sharp contrast, governmental and not-for-profit entities exist to provide services to their constituents. They generally try to accumulate a reasonable surplus of financial resources to cushion against economic contraction and to provide for emergency needs. But they do not operate to maximize inflows over outflows. Indeed, if a local government were to accumulate large operating surpluses, many taxpayers would soon complain that they were being overtaxed.

For governmental and not-for-profit organizations, reporting whether inflows exceeded outflows is only part of the picture. The challenge to financial reporting lies also in demonstrating *accountability* for the resources entrusted to these organizations. When used in the broad sense of the term, accountability embraces not only probity and legal compliance, but also efficiency in delivering services and effectiveness in accomplishing program results. The GASB encourages state and local governments to report on outputs (including cost per unit of service) and outcomes (program results) to supplement their annual financial reporting. The federal government already requires federal agencies to prepare an annual *Performance and Accountability Report,* which encompasses both financial and performance reporting.

Sources of Revenue and Relationship with Stakeholders

Business enterprises derive virtually all their revenues from exchange transactions, generally involving specific products or services, between willing buyers and sellers. Governments, on the other hand, obtain most of their revenues from taxation—wherein taxpayers involuntarily transfer resources for a basket of services that may or may not bear a direct relationship to what the taxpayer wants or needs. Many not-for-profit entities obtain significant resources from voluntary donors who expect no product or service in exchange, but who are nevertheless concerned with whether their donations are achieving their intended purposes.

Taxes and donations are unique to governmental and not-for-profit entities and hence require special accounting standards appropriate to those transactions. Equally important, the nature of taxes and donations creates relationships with the providers of those resources that emphasize the accountability aspects of financial reporting, discussed in the preceding section.

Financial reporting for business enterprises means reporting to owners and lenders, who can divest themselves of their investments if they choose to do so. For business enterprises, accountability to their major resource providers—the consumers of their products and services—is direct and immediate. A consumer who doesn't like the product or service simply will not buy it again. But involuntary taxpayers may not be in a position to benefit directly from the services provided by the taxes they pay, nor are they likely to be able to move from the jurisdictions where they reside as readily as investors can sell equity securities. Donors often are not in a position to see for themselves the results of their contributions. The need for, and means of, demonstrating accountability take on added significance because of the nature of the relationship between these entities and their stakeholders.

Potential for Longevity

Business enterprises are at risk of going out of business for many reasons, such as global competition, emerging products, changing consumer tastes, inefficiencies, and recession. Not-for-profit organizations face similar risks. Business enterprises may also go out of business by being bought out by other enterprises. However, because of the power to tax and the nature of their services, general-purpose governments rarely go out of business and are not bought and sold like business enterprises.

As a result, governmental accounting standards-setters have tended to take a longer-term perspective than their business enterprise counterparts in developing accounting measurements for certain types of transactions. One notable difference concerns the standards for pensions and other postemployment benefits.

Role of the Budget and Legal Requirements

Business enterprises are free to provide only those goods and services they believe will enhance their profits. They cannot usually be required to provide goods and services against their will, and if they cannot cope with the legal or social environment, they are free to leave the market. Their spending decisions may or may not be subject to budgets, but if they are, the budgetary amendment process is relatively simple. Commercial organizations also can borrow money when convenient, subject only to requirements of lenders and investors.

Governmental entities, on the other hand, are required by law (constitution, charter, or statute) to provide certain services. For example, most city charters provide for police and fire protection. Managers cannot refuse to provide these services because of cost or because they believe their residents do not deserve them.

Most of the resources obtained by governmental entities come from taxes, higher-level government grants, and borrowing. Spending decisions made by the federal government, states, and general-purpose local governments are based on budgets that have the force of law. Budgetary appropriations typically cannot be exceeded without specific legislative approval. Generally, resources provided by higher-level governments must be used only for the specific purposes designated by that government. Most governmental borrowings are constrained by law as to purpose, quantity, and timing. Amounts borrowed may be subject to specific limits, such as value of real property in the jurisdiction. New bond issues may require approval by the electorate or by a higher-level government.

Many not-for-profit organizations derive most of their resources from donor contributions, which may be subject to restrictions either as to what they can be used for, when they can be used, or whether they must be maintained in perpetuity. Recipient organizations are legally bound to adhere to these donor restrictions.

Because of these factors, internal accounting for governmental and not-for-profit organizations generally focuses on the controls needed to ensure legal compliance. Such accounting tends to be conservative in nature, designed to make sure that spending amounts authorized by the legally adopted budget are not exceeded and that expenditures meet the purpose limitations of a bond issue or the spending restrictions imposed by grantors and donors. Although recent changes in external financial reporting emphasize entity-wide reporting, standards continue to require that financial statements show the distinction between unrestricted and restricted resources.

USERS AND USES OF ACCOUNTING INFORMATION

Persons both internal and external to organizations use accounting information. In establishing financial reporting standards, accounting standards-setters emphasize the needs of external users (those not directly involved in the operations of the reporting entity) because they do not have ready access to the entity's information.

Resource providers, oversight bodies, and service recipients are the major external users of governmental and not-for-profit entity financial reports. Resource providers include taxpayers; donors and potential donors; investors, potential investors, and bond-rating agencies (which provide data to investors); and grant-providing organizations, such as higher-level governments. External oversight bodies include higher-level governments and regulatory agencies. Service recipients include citizen advocate groups. Internal oversight bodies, such as boards of trustees, also are major users of financial data.

Users of financial reporting might seek answers to the following types of questions:

- What is the likelihood of the repayment of short-term and long-term debt?
- What is the entity's ability to continue to provide a particular level of services?
- Does the entity have sufficient resources to provide a cushion against revenue shortfalls caused by economic downturns?
- Does the entity use its resources consistent with the budget and with the requirements of legal and regulatory restrictions?
- Is the entity efficient and effective in using resources?
- Is the entity's ability to use its available resources restricted in any way?

ACCOUNTING PRINCIPLES AND STANDARDS

Rules guiding accounting and financial reporting are referred to as *generally accepted accounting principles (GAAP)*. The American Institute of Certified Public Accountants defines this term as follows:

> [T]he consensus at a particular time as to which economic resources and obligations should be recorded as assets and liabilities by financial accounting, which changes in assets and liabilities should be recorded, when these changes should be recorded, how the assets and liabilities and changes in them should be measured, what information should be disclosed and how it should be disclosed, and which financial statements should be prepared.

> Generally accepted accounting principles encompass the conventions, rules, and procedures necessary to define accepted accounting practice at a particular time. The standard of "generally accepted accounting principles" includes not only broad guidelines of general application, but also detailed practices and procedures.[4]

---

[4]*Statement No. 4*, "Basic Concepts and Accounting Principles Underlying Financial Statements of Business Enterprises" (New York: AICPA, 1970), paras. 137 and 138.

Establishing Generally Accepted Accounting Principles

The origins of GAAP can be traced back to the period just after the 1929 stock market crash, when attempts were made to formulate accounting principles. Many criticized the earliest statement of principles as being little more than a codification of then current accounting practices. Continued concerns with the way in which accounting principles were being established led to the formulation of the Financial Accounting Standards Board (FASB) in 1973 and then to the Governmental Accounting Standards Board (GASB) in 1984. Seven members are appointed to each of these bodies by the Financial Accounting Foundation (FAF), an entity whose members are appointed by certain professional accounting and financial organizations. Advisory councils to both the FASB and the GASB are composed of individuals representing organizations concerned with the activities of the standards-setting bodies. The GASB-FASB structure is shown in Exhibit 1-1.

The FASB and the GASB are charged with establishing and improving standards of accounting and financial reporting within their respective areas of jurisdiction. The GASB's jurisdiction includes all state and local governmental entities, including government-sponsored colleges and universities, health care providers, and utilities. The FASB establishes standards for all other entities, including not-for-profit colleges and universities and health care providers. Under this arrangement, it is possible for the two boards to establish different accounting and reporting standards for similar transactions of similar entities, such as hospitals. Although this situation occurs sometimes, the two boards cooperate with each other to keep differences to a minimum.

The Federal Accounting Standards Advisory Board (FASAB) was established in 1990 to develop accounting standards and principles for the federal government by the three officials who have prime responsibility for federal accounting and financial management. They are the U.S. comptroller general, the director of the Office of Management and Budget (OMB), and the secretary of the Treasury. Its 10 members include six public (nonfederal) members and representatives of the offices of the three sponsoring officials and the Congressional Budget Office. FASAB proposals become GAAP for federal agencies if neither the comptroller general nor the director of OMB objects.

Standards promulgated by the three boards are GAAP by virtue of the due process used by the boards in developing them and the authority accorded them by the American Institute of Certified Public Accountants (AICPA). The due process used in developing the standards includes using task forces, holding public hearings, issuing "exposure drafts" of proposals for comment by interested parties, and carefully considering those comments before issuing the standards. Auditors may not express unqualified opinions on financial statements if they violate standards issued by the applicable board.

EXHIBIT 1-1	Relationship Between the FASB, the GASB, and the FAF

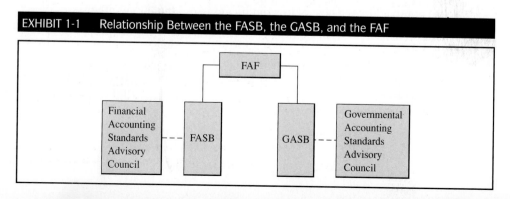

GOVERNMENTAL ACCOUNTING IN PRACTICE:
Accounting Standards in a Political Environment

The Governmental Accounting Standards Board (GASB) establishes accounting standards, but it has no enforcement powers. Several institutions, however, play a major role in enforcing GASB standards, including the governments themselves, the accounting profession, and the credit-rating agencies. Recent experience in Connecticut and Texas illustrate this point.

The state of Connecticut passed a law in the early 1990s requiring that its budget be balanced in accordance with generally accepted accounting principles. (This is unusual because GASB standards apply to financial reporting, not budgeting.) Each year, however, the state legislature delayed implementing the law because it chose not to raise the taxes or to cut the expenditures needed to achieve GAAP balance. As a result, the state ran up annual deficits when measured in accordance with GAAP. Then, in 2007, the legislature passed a bill giving the *state comptroller* the authority to establish GAAP for *financial reporting*. Someone had the bright idea that, if the

standards don't fit the situation, all you need to do is change the standards!

Governor M. Jodi Rell, deeply concerned that the bill would jeopardize Connecticut's credit rating, promptly vetoed it. The governor felt that credit analysts and municipal bond buyers wanted to see financial statements that followed uniform accounting standards set by an independent standards-setting body. Right on, Madam Governor!

But not everyone thinks the way Governor Rell thinks. Some officials in Texas were bothered by the implications of a new GASB standard that requires financial statement recognition of expenses and liabilities for employee postemployment health care benefits. (We discuss this standard in Chapter 8.) So Texas enacted a law in 2007 giving the state and its local governments the option to ignore the standard. We assume the auditors and the credit-rating agencies will take a dim view of those who choose to ignore the standard.

SOURCE: *New York Times,* articles by Mary Williams Walsh, May 18, June 2, and July 8, 2007.

Hierarchy of Accounting Principles

Because the standards-setting bodies deal with large workloads and because they may choose not to address a host of less significant issues that might otherwise come before them, the AICPA has adopted a *hierarchy* of accounting principles. The hierarchy allows a practitioner to look to less authoritative guidance issued by the board with jurisdiction (or its staff) and to guidance given by other bodies in the event the board with jurisdiction has not issued guidance on a particular matter. To illustrate, the following hierarchy, ranked from most authoritative to least authoritative, applies to state and local governments:

Level I: GASB Statements and Interpretations
           AICPA and FASB pronouncements that GASB Statements or Interpretations have made applicable to state and local governmental units

Level II: GASB Technical Bulletins
AICPA Industry Audit and Accounting Guides and AICPA Statements of Position that are made applicable to governmental units by the AICPA and cleared (not objected to) by the GASB

Level III: Consensus positions of a GASB-organized group of accountants that attempts to reach consensus positions on governmental accounting issues
AICPA Practice Bulletins made applicable to governmental units by the AICPA and cleared by the GASB

Level IV: GASB Staff Implementation Guides
Current practices widely used by governmental units

Level V: Other accounting literature, including GASB Concepts Statements and AICPA and FASB pronouncements that are not made specifically applicable to governmental entities

OBJECTIVES OF FINANCIAL REPORTING

All three standards-setting bodies issue *concepts statements* on the objectives of financial reporting in their areas of jurisdiction. (Concepts statements are not standards, but they articulate the framework within which the boards are developing standards.) The three statements on objectives of financial reporting show both similarities and differences, which reflect the differing environments of the entities to which the standards apply. The governmental accounting standards-setting bodies, in particular, emphasize the need for data to help financial report users assess accountability.

State and Local Government Financial Reporting

The GASB statement of reporting objectives for state and local governments calls for financial reporting to assist in fulfilling government's duty to be publicly accountable and to help users assess that accountability. To meet those objectives, financial reporting needs to provide data to show whether current-year revenues were sufficient to pay for current-year services, to demonstrate whether resources were obtained and used in accordance with the legally adopted budget, and to help users assess the entity's service efforts, costs, and accomplishments.

In addition to helping users evaluate the entity's operating results for the year and assess the level of services that can be provided by the entity, financial reporting that follows GASB objectives also discloses an entity's ability to meet its obligations as they come due. Financial reporting should accomplish the latter objective by providing information about financial position and condition and about physical and other nonfinancial resources with useful lives that extend beyond the current year, and by disclosing restrictions on resources and risk of potential loss of resources.

Federal Government Financial Reporting

FASAB objectives for federal financial reporting cover budgetary integrity, operating performance, stewardship, and systems and controls. The objectives state that financial reporting should assist in fulfilling the government's duty to be publicly accountable for monies raised through taxes and other means and for their expenditure in accordance with the government's budget. Financial reporting also should assist report users in: (1) evaluating the entity's service efforts, costs, and accomplishments and its management of assets and liabilities; (2) assessing the impact on the nation of the government's operations and investments and how, as a result, the nation's financial condition has changed and may change in the future; and (3) understanding whether financial management systems and internal accounting and administrative controls are adequate.

Not-for-Profit Organization Financial Reporting

The FASB's financial reporting objectives for not-for-profit organizations focus on information useful to present and potential resource providers, as well as other users, in making rational decisions about allocating resources to those organizations. Such information helps in assessing (1) the services provided by the entity and its ability to continue to provide them, (2) how the entity's managers discharged their stewardship responsibilities, and (3) the entity's performance, including its service efforts and accomplishments. Not-for-profit entities should provide information about their economic resources, obligations, net resources, restrictions on the use of resources, and liquidity.

UNIQUE ACCOUNTING AND FINANCIAL REPORTING CHARACTERISTICS

Several characteristics are unique to governmental and not-for-profit organization accounting and financial reporting. These characteristics flow primarily from the environmental factors discussed earlier. The characteristics are introduced here and described in greater detail in other chapters of this text.

Use of Fund Accounting

Fund accounting is perhaps the most distinctive feature of governmental and not-for-profit organization accounting. For many years, fund accounting provided the foundation both for internal accounting control purposes and for external financial reporting by these entities. In response to concerns expressed by financial report users about the complexity of fund-based financial reporting, however, the reporting emphasis shifted away from funds and to the entity as a whole. Nevertheless, general-purpose government organizations and many special-purpose government organizations continue to use fund accounting, and the GASB requires both entity-wide and fund-level reporting. The FASB does not require not-for-profit organizations to use fund-based reporting, but does not preclude such reporting provided the entity complies with the FASB requirements for entity-wide reporting.

Fund accounting segregates an entity's assets, liabilities, and net assets into separate accounting entities based on legal restrictions, donor-imposed restrictions, or special regulations. Fund accounting is a convenient control mechanism to help ensure that resources are spent for the intended purposes—like using separate cookie jars for food, rent, clothing, and so on.

Because each fund is a separate accounting entity, each must have a set of *self-balancing accounts;* that is, the total of the assets of a particular fund must equal the total of its liabilities and fund balance (or net assets). Thus, the accounting records of a particular fund must identify the unique resources of that fund and the claims to those resources, as distinguished from all other funds.

Entities that use fund accounting generally maintain a General Fund or an Unrestricted Current Fund, whose resources can be used for any purpose designated by the governing body. In addition, they use separate funds to account for the acquisition and disposition of resources whose use is restricted in some manner (generally by law, regulation, or donor requirement) to specific purposes.

Incorporation of Budgets into Accounting Systems

A unique feature in governmental fund accounting (applicable not only to state and local governments, but to the federal government as well) is the use of budgetary accounts in the accounting system for certain types of funds. In federal government accounting, two accounting tracks operate side by side. State and local governments incorporate budgetary accounting to a somewhat lesser extent, but it is nevertheless pervasive. The requirement for incorporating budgetary accounting into governmental fund accounting systems demonstrates the importance of ensuring that legally adopted budgets are not exceeded.

Measurement Focus and Basis of Accounting

As you know, business enterprises use the *accrual basis of accounting,* as distinguished from the cash basis of accounting, when they prepare financial statements. Basis of accounting is a term that refers to *when* assets, liabilities, revenues, and expenses are recognized as such in an entity's financial statements. Under the accrual basis of accounting, revenues are recognized when they are earned, not necessarily when cash is received; and expenses are recognized when they are incurred, not necessarily when cash is paid. Not-for-profit organizations, including not-for-profit hospitals, and the federal government also use the accrual basis of accounting in financial reporting.

State and local governments also use the accrual basis of accounting when they report on their business-type activities. For their basic governmental functions, however, state and local governments use a unique, hybrid-type basis of accounting, called the *modified accrual basis of accounting.* Further, when using this basis of accounting, they measure only inflows and outflows of *current financial resources,* rather than all economic resources. The accounting implications of this measurement method and focus are discussed in Chapters 2 through 6 and the financial reporting implications are covered in Chapters 9 and 10.

Entity-Wide and Fund-Level Reporting

Does the use of funds in governmental and not-for-profit internal accounting influence external financial reporting? For many years, the answer to that question was Yes. Recently, however, the financial reporting focus turned toward the entity as a whole. The change in emphasis came about for practical reasons. Entities with many types of funds and reporting on a fund basis often issue financial statements that may look complex and may not be readily comprehensible because of the number of details included. State and local governments issued financial statements with 10 or more columns, and many not-for-profit organizations issued statements showing each group of funds layered one atop another in a "pancake" format.

To make financial reporting more useful, accounting standards-setters emphasize the need for financial reporting on the entity as a whole. Specifically:

- State and local governments report on two levels: a government-wide level that distinguishes only between "governmental" and "business-type" activities, and a fund level that reports on individual funds. Although the fund-level financial

statements are prepared on the same basis of accounting used within the funds, the government-wide financial statements are prepared using the full accrual basis of accounting.
- Not-for-profit organization financial statements are required to "focus on the organization as a whole." Within those statements, they need to report on three classes of net assets: those that are unrestricted and those that are either temporarily restricted or permanently restricted by donors.

Review Questions

Q1-1 Describe the characteristics that distinguish not-for-profit organizations from business enterprises.

Q1-2 Identify the various types of entities that constitute governmental organizations, and describe the characteristics of other organizations that, when created by governments, are also considered to be governmental entities.

Q1-3 Identify and briefly explain three major environmental characteristics of governmental and not-for-profit organizations.

Q1-4 Illustrate the kinds of restrictions placed by laws on the ability of governments to use resources, and by donors on the ability of not-for-profit entities to use resources.

Q1-5 Who are the users of governmental and not-for-profit entity accounting information and for what purposes might they use that information?

Q1-6 What are the jurisdictions of the accounting standards-setting bodies: GASB, FASAB, and FASB?

Q1-7 Why is a hierarchy of generally accepted accounting principles needed?

Q1-8 List the three ways identified by the GASB in which financial reporting can help users assess governmental accountability.

Q1-9 List three objectives of not-for-profit organization financial reporting.

Q1-10 List three unique characteristics of state and local governmental accounting as contrasted with business enterprise accounting.

Cases

C1-1 Croton Hospital was a not-for-profit entity. Because it experienced financial difficulties, the county in which the hospital was located assumed control of Croton's assets and liabilities. The county executive appointed all five members of the hospital's new board of trustees. The hospital's chief accountant, who was not replaced, continued to use the same accounting principles and financial reporting used before the county takeover. Explain the position the county comptroller should take regarding Croton's accounting and financial reporting.

C1-2 State law provides that all cash not immediately needed by school districts to finance current operations be forwarded to the counties in which the school districts are located. The law also requires that county treasurers place these resources in a separate fund and invest them on behalf of the school districts. Because Contra County is experiencing some financial problems and to provide some badly needed resources to the county, the county treasurer tells the county administrator that he plans to invest the school district funds in "junk bonds" yielding 9 percent interest. He will credit the "normal" rate of return

(5 percent) to the school districts and the remaining 4 percent to the county itself. Explain the position the county administrator should take on the treasurer's proposal.

Exercises

E1-1   (Characteristics of not-for-profit and governmental entities)
The mayor of a large city approaches a group of citizens and suggests that they form an organization to provide social, educational, and recreational programs for local youth. The group agrees and forms an entity called the Community Youth Organization (CYO). The group also chooses a board of directors, and the board hires an executive director and several staff members. CYO's activities are financed entirely by grants from the city and many of CYO's programs are held after-hours in the high school. Is the CYO a not-for-profit or a government organization? Why? What changes in characteristics would be needed to change it from one type of entity to the other?

E1-2   (Accounting standards-setting bodies)
Three accountants started talking about hospitals. One said he was treated at a not-for-profit hospital, another said she was treated at a county hospital, and the third said he had just returned from the hospital run by the U.S. Veterans Administration. They wondered why three different bodies established accounting standards for hospitals. Give reasons for and against the existence of three accounting standards-setting bodies.

E1-3   (Accounting standards-setting procedures)
Several not-for-profit organizations use television campaigns to obtain pledges to contribute cash. Some people think that not-for-profit entities should recognize pledges as revenues when the cash is actually received. Others would recognize revenues when the pledges are made, subject to a provision for amounts not likely to be collected. Based on that scenario, discuss (a) the need for an accounting standards-setting body, (b) the qualifications members of that body should possess, and (c) the procedures that body should adopt in establishing accounting standards.

E1-4   (Objectives of financial reporting)
FASB Concepts Statement No. 1, *Objectives of Financial Reporting by Business Enterprises,* says that the primary focus of business enterprise financial reporting is "information about an enterprise's performance provided by measures of earnings and its components." Contrast the notion of "performance" in business enterprises with that of not-for-profit and governmental organizations, and discuss how the difference might affect the nature of financial reporting among the various types of entities.

E1-5   (Objectives of financial reporting)
The FASAB said that financial reporting should assist users in understanding whether financial management systems and internal accounting and administrative controls are adequate. (See subsection on federal government reporting on pp 9–10.) Why do you think the FASAB established this objective? How might this objective be implemented in financial reporting?

2

THE USE OF FUNDS IN GOVERNMENTAL ACCOUNTING

Chapter Outline

Ethics Case

Exercises

Problems

After completing this chapter, you should be able to:

- Understand the nature and purpose of fund accounting and identify the major fund categories used in governmental accounting.
- Compare and contrast the current financial resources measurement focus and modified accrual basis of accounting with the economic resources measurement focus and accrual basis of accounting.
- Understand the relationship between governmental budgeting and accounting within governmental-type funds.
- Identify the fund types used within each of the major fund categories, describe the function of each fund type, and give examples of when each fund type is used.
- Understand the measurement focus and basis of accounting used by each fund type.
- Identify the financial statements used by each fund type.

As noted in Chapter 1, state and local governmental accounting differs from business enterprise accounting in three major respects. State and local governmental accounting: (a) uses separate funds to account for its activities, (b) focuses on flows of current financial resources and uses a modified accrual basis of accounting in some funds, and (c) incorporates budgetary accounts into the financial accounting system for some funds. In this chapter, we discuss the nature of fund accounting and describe the various types of funds used in state and local governmental accounting. We also introduce the concept of the current financial resources measurement focus and modified accrual basis of accounting. We introduce budgetary accounting in Chapter 3 and discuss the fund types and accounting within each fund type in Chapters 4 through 8.

FUND ACCOUNTING

Funds as Subdivisions of an Entity

You are already familiar with the *entity* concept. As you know, the *reporting entity* defines the boundaries of a particular financial reporting unit by describing *whose* assets, liabilities, revenues, expenses, and equities are included in its financial report. If a parent company, such as General Motors, exercises control over its legally separate subsidiaries, the financial activities of all those units are consolidated for financial reporting purposes.

Although it is defined in a somewhat different manner, this notion of reporting entity applies as well to state and local governments. New York City's 2006 financial report, for example, covered not only the activities of the legally constituted government of New York City, but also the activities of more than 20 separate legal organizations (such as the Health and Hospitals Corporation) for which New York City is financially accountable. In this context, New York City is called the primary government and its constituent legally separate entities, which are public authorities or public benefit corporations, are called component units. We will return to this aspect of the reporting entity in Chapter 9.

In state and local governmental accounting, however, there is an additional dimension to the reporting entity. For internal accounting purposes, the primary government itself is disaggregated—subdivided—into separate fiscal and accounting entities, called funds. Each fund has its own assets, liabilities, net assets, and inflows and outflows of resources. Funds are the basic building blocks of governmental accounting and financial reporting.

The formal definition of a fund is:

> . . . a fiscal and accounting entity with a self-balancing set of accounts recording cash and other financial resources, together with all related liabilities and residual equities or balances, and changes therein, which are segregated for the purpose of carrying on specific activities or attaining certain objectives in accordance with special regulations, restrictions or limitations.[1]

In this definition, the term *fiscal entity* refers to the separate budgetary nature of funds that have only spendable financial resources, and the term *accounting entity* refers to a separate financial unit that is treated as an entity for accounting purposes. Some types of funds also have capital assets, which—in fund accounting terms—are nonspendable, nonfinancial resources.

Why Governments Use Fund Accounting

Governmental entities must comply with legal requirements set forth in constitutions, city charters, statutes, local ordinances, and so forth. Because their day-to-day activities are guided by budgets proposed by the executive branch and enacted into law by the legislative branch, internal accounting systems are needed to ensure compliance with budgetary spending limits. Funds have traditionally provided a basic control mechanism for ensuring compliance with legal restrictions on the use of governmental resources. Indeed, most funds are established pursuant to specific legal requirements.

To illustrate: If the legislature wants to segregate gasoline taxes from other revenues to ensure a steady flow of resources that can be used only to repair roads, it may establish a dedicated fund to record receipt of the taxes and their subsequent expenditure. If the citizens vote to approve a bond issue for a new firehouse, segregating the bond proceeds in a dedicated fund helps ensure that they are used for no other purpose. If the legislature wishes to demonstrate its intent to dedicate resources to the repayment of the debt, it may create a fund for that purpose. A dedicated pension trust fund that accumulates employer and employee contributions and the related earnings helps ensure that the resources will be used to pay pension benefits when employees retire.

Is fund accounting absolutely necessary? Not to the extent it is used in practice. Many governments can readily accomplish the purposes of fund accounting by establishing separate accounts for restricted resources within a single accounting and fiscal entity. In fact, there is no consistency among governments in the extent to which they create funds. Some governments use many more funds than others, even though they perform the same functions. Further, excessive use of funds—for example, earmarking

---

[1] *GASB Codification of Governmental Accounting and Financial Reporting Standards* (GASB Cod.) Sec. 1300, "Statement of Principle—Fund Accounting Systems" (Norwalk, CT: GASB, 2006).

a particular type of tax to finance one purpose, a particular fee for another purpose, and so on—is considered a poor practice because it reduces a government's flexibility in providing for citizen needs as priorities change. (We should also point out that fund accounting does not provide absolute assurance that dedicated resources will not be used for unauthorized purposes. This is why we used the term "helps ensure" in the preceding paragraph.)

On the other hand, some governments are quite complex because they are engaged in various business-type activities. The same business-type activity can be performed either by a department of a legally constituted government or by a specially created, legally separate entity for which a primary government is accountable. Thus, to some extent, one government will create a separate fund to accomplish what another will accomplish by creating a separate entity. Business-type activities may require different types of accounting systems to meet budgetary and other managerial needs. Creating separate accounting entities, such as funds, helps provide the control mechanisms and the separate financial reports needed to manage those activities.

Fund Categories

The funds used by state and local governments are grouped into three broad categories, based on their different characteristics: governmental, proprietary, and fiduciary. There are several types of funds within each broad category. The three fund categories are described below and the specific funds within each category are discussed later in the chapter.

State and local governments account for their basic services in the *governmental-type funds* category. Governmental-type funds account for the accumulation and spending of resources—primarily taxes and intergovernmental grants—that provide the public with day-to-day operating services, such as police, fire, education, sanitation, parks, and highway maintenance. Governmental-type funds are also used to account for resources legally earmarked for a particular governmental purpose and for the acquisition or construction of general governmental capital assets, such as roadways, maintenance depots, police stations, and firehouses. For example, a separate governmental fund may be used to account for the proceeds of debt sold to construct a new firehouse, and another fund may be used to accumulate resources to pay the debt service on those bonds.

One of the features of governmental-type funds is that their expenditures are likely to be controlled by budgets proposed by the executive branch of government and legally adopted by the legislative branch in the form of *appropriations*—authorizations to spend. The way governments prepare budgets and the legal status afforded them profoundly affects accounting within the governmental-type funds, as we shall see in the next section of this chapter and in Chapter 3. Although well-run governments do long-range planning, their annual budgets for day-to-day operations are short run in nature. They generally cover activities for only one year.

Proprietary-type funds are used to account for governmental activities that operate in a manner similar to private sector businesses in the sense that they charge fees for their services and want to measure whether their revenues will cover their expenses. Examples of such activities are municipal hospitals, electric and water utilities, mass transit facilities, lotteries, and central motor pools. Many of these activities are self-supporting because their fees are sufficient to cover their costs. Others (such as mass transit facilities) may receive subsidies from their parent government and some (such as lotteries) provide net revenues for the parent. When these business-type activities are performed by agencies within the legally constituted government, a separate proprietary fund is established. When the activities are performed by legally separate entities, these entities use what is called "proprietary fund accounting."

Governments use *fiduciary-type funds* to account for resources they hold in a trust or agency capacity for others. "Others" might be individuals, other governments, or private organizations. Because they are held for others, the resources in these funds cannot be used to support the government's own programs. Examples of situations in which a government might be acting in a trust or agency capacity include assets held on behalf of employees participating in governmental pension or postemployment health care plans, investment pools operated by a sponsoring government on behalf of other governments, and sales taxes collected by a state on behalf of county and city governments.

Financial Reporting with the Use of Funds

The balances and activities of the individual funds are displayed in individual fund financial statements. External financial reporting is guided by the requirements of GASB *Statement No. 34,* "Basic Financial Statements—and Management's Discussion and Analysis—for State and Local Governments" (1999). GASB *Statement No. 34* requires two sets of financial statements: *fund statements* and *government-wide statements.* The need for two sets of statements arises out of the different measurement focuses and bases of accounting used in the three fund categories, as discussed in the next section.

The fund set of statements is simply a presentation, in columnar form, of the account balances of individual funds, grouped by fund category. The government-wide set consolidates the funds into two groups of activities, governmental and business-type. In preparing the government-wide statements, adjustments are made to the fund statements so that all funds use the same measurement focus and basis of accounting. In addition, the Fiduciary Funds are removed from the consolidation because they do not support the government's own programs. (As you read Chapters 4, 5, and 6, keep in mind that certain adjustments will be needed to prepare the government-wide financial statements.) Chapters 9 and 10 describe how the financial statements are prepared.

MEASUREMENT FOCUS AND BASIS OF ACCOUNTING

In addition to the use of funds, another distinctive feature of state and local governmental accounting lies in the way inflows and outflows are measured in one of the fund categories—governmental-type funds. To grasp the implications of this notion, we first need to discuss the terms measurement focus and basis of accounting.

- *Measurement focus* refers to *what* is being expressed and *which resources* are being measured in reporting an organization's financial performance and position. For example, when a business enterprise focuses on measuring its net profit for the year, it takes account of transactions and events affecting both its financial and capital resources. If it wants to know how its activities affected its cash balance, it considers only the transactions that increase or decrease cash.

- *Basis of accounting* is a *timing* concept. It relates to *when* the assets, liabilities, revenues and expenses (or expenditures) are recognized (recorded) in financial statements. Basis of accounting and measurement focus are considered together, because timing of recognition helps achieve what one is trying to measure. For example, using the accrual basis of accounting provides the most accurate measure of an entity's net profit.

Application to Proprietary-Type and Fiduciary-Type Funds

How do the concepts of measurement focus and basis of accounting apply to the three categories of funds discussed in the previous section? We said that proprietary-type funds are used to account for governmental activities that operate in a manner similar to commercial business enterprises. Their accounting is also similar to commercial business enterprise accounting. The managers of governmental business activities are concerned with whether revenues are sufficient to cover costs. Therefore, the accounting system needs to take account of transactions and events that affect *all* the economic resources available to the activity—financial and capital. GASB literature refers to this measurement focus as the *economic resources measurement focus.*

To determine whether revenues are sufficient to cover costs, accounting measurements in proprietary-type funds are made using the accrual basis of accounting. This means that, in the proprietary-type funds, revenues are recognized in the period they are earned, even if cash has not been received. Expenses are recognized when assets are consumed or when liabilities are incurred, even if cash has not been paid. Capital assets, for example, are depreciated to allocate their costs over their estimated useful lives. Because of the passage of time, unpaid interest on borrowed capital is accrued when financial statements are prepared even if it is not yet due to be paid.

Fiduciary-type funds also use the economic resources measurement focus and the accrual basis of accounting.

Application to Governmental-Type Funds

To account for the basic day-to-day activities in the governmental-type funds, however, governments use a unique, hybrid measurement focus and basis of accounting. This unique accounting measurement process within the governmental-type funds is primarily the result of a basic purpose of the accounting system—to provide data needed for managing the budget. Departmental budget officers and the government's central budget office need to know the amount of *financial* resources available for current spending. The central budget office also needs data to help monitor actual performance against the current year's budget and to plan future years' budgets.

Let's look at the big picture first, taking the perspective of the central budget office. The governmental budget process is spending oriented, cash oriented, and short run in nature. Budgetary thinking runs something like this:

- If a government needs to acquire capital assets, its budget may provide for raising financial resources by selling long-term bonds. When the financial resources are spent, the capital assets are not available for future spending, unless they are sold.
- The government needs cash to pay principal and interest on the bonds, but depreciating assets doesn't produce cash. Instead, financial resources to pay the principal and interest must be raised primarily through taxation.

- Taxes will produce cash for the current budget period only to the extent the taxpayers pay in a timely manner. Taxpayers that don't pay in time to pay the government's bills don't produce budgetary revenues.
- On the other hand, if liabilities are incurred during a year because employees earn, say, vacation pay, but the accrued vacation pay will be paid in the form of cash on retirement, the current year's budget need not raise taxes to finance it.

Now let's look at budget management from the perspective of the city police department's budget officer. Assume the police department is authorized to spend $60,000 to acquire supplies and $80,000 to acquire police sedans. If the department has spent $50,000 to acquire supplies, it has only $10,000 left to buy additional supplies. If it has spent $60,000 to buy two police sedans, it has only $20,000 left to buy another sedan. For *budgetary management* purposes, the relevant information is not the inventory of supplies or the depreciated value of the sedans; rather, what is relevant is the fact that the police department has $10,000 of financial resources left to acquire more materials and $20,000 of financial resources left to buy another sedan.

Accounting within the governmental-type funds has evolved historically as an accommodation to budgetary needs. As a result, the measurement focus and the basis of accounting used within the governmental-type funds tend to be oriented toward current spending. It is more cash based than accrual based.

To provide data on the amount of financial resources available for current spending, governmental-type funds use a *current financial resources measurement focus,* rather than the economic resources measurement focus. To facilitate making measurements when focusing on flows of current financial resources, governmental-type funds use a *modified accrual basis of accounting,* rather than the accrual basis of accounting. The effect of the difference in measurement focus is that neither capital assets nor long-term liabilities are recorded in the governmental-type funds. Further, the combined effect of the differences in measurement focus and basis of accounting is that accrual accounting is *modified* in the governmental-type funds to record only those accruals that affect near-term financial resource inflows and outflows.

We will discuss the accounting measurement implications of the current financial resources measurement focus and modified accrual basis of accounting in the governmental-type funds at length in Chapters 4 through 6. For now, here are a few basic concepts:

- ***Revenue recognition.*** When accrual accounting is used, revenues are recognized when they are earned. When governments modify accrual accounting for purposes of recognizing revenue in governmental-type funds, tax revenues such as property taxes are recognized when they are measurable and available. *Measurable* refers to the ability to state the amount of revenue in terms of dollars. *Available* means collectible within the current period or soon enough thereafter so it can be used to pay the bills of the current period. "Soon enough thereafter" is interpreted in the accounting standards to mean no more than 60 days after the accounting period ends. So, for example, property taxes levied for the year ended December 31, 2008, are recognized as revenue for 2008 if they are expected to be collected by the end of February 2009.
- ***Expenditure recognition.*** Three types of expenditures are included in operating statements prepared for governmental-type funds: capital asset acquisitions;

current operating items, such as salaries and utilities; and debt service (payments of debt principal and interest).

- **Expenditures versus expenses:** Under the economic resources measurement focus, expenses (a resource consumption notion) are recognized when assets are consumed or liabilities are incurred. In governmental-type funds, however, the measurement focus is on decreases of financial resources, called expenditures. When financial resources are spent to acquire capital assets under the economic resources measurement focus, there is no effect on the operating statement; the effect occurs in the form of depreciation expense as the assets are consumed. But, when financial resources are used to acquire capital assets under the financial resources measurement focus, expenditures are reported in the operating statement because the entity's financial resources have decreased.

- **Modifications to accrual accounting caused by measuring flows of "current" financial resources:** The term *current* in the current financial resources measurement focus causes accrual accounting to be modified in governmental-type funds. For many items, such as salaries, utilities, and professional services, payment of the liability is normally made in a timely manner from available financial resources. Just as is done in accrual accounting, unpaid liabilities should be recorded and expenditures should be recognized for these services when incurred—without regard to the extent to which resources are currently available to liquidate the liabilities. Some liabilities, however, do not require liquidation with current financial resources; for those liabilities, modified accrual accounting introduces exceptions to accrual accounting rules. To illustrate, under modified accrual accounting, expenditures and liabilities for compensated absences are recognized when the liabilities *mature* (that is, when they come due for payment as a result of employee resignation or retirement), rather than when earned by the employees. Other exceptions relate to claims and judgments, interest on long-term debt, pensions, and post-employment health care benefits.

- **Bond proceeds and debt repayment.** When business enterprises receive resources from the sale of bonds, they credit a liability account called "bonds payable" that is reported in the balance sheet. When governments sell what are known as *general obligation* bonds, they record the bond proceeds in governmental-type funds as an inflow of current financial resources and credit an operating statement account called "other financing sources." When the debt is repaid, business enterprises record the repayment as a reduction of the liability. In governmental-type funds, however, repayments of bond principal are reported as expenditures because they result in outflows of financial resources.

As the foregoing illustrations indicate, the current financial resources measurement focus/modified accrual accounting basis is generally consistent with the way governments budget. However, accounting and financial reporting to accommodate budgetary needs does not mean that capital assets and longer-term obligations are ignored. If they were ignored, there would be a potential for misrepresentation. Therefore, as previously noted, governmental financial reporting standards require two sets of financial statements. The fund-level statements are based on the standards for accounting *within* the funds, so statements prepared for governmental-type funds use the current financial resources measurement focus and modified accrual basis of accounting. For government-wide financial reporting, the data in the governmental-type funds are aggregated and adjusted to the economic resources measurement focus and accrual basis of accounting. Capital assets and bonds payable are reported in the government-wide statements.

Tables 2-1 and 2-2 summarize the measurement focus, basis of accounting, and broad category of activities embraced within the three fund categories. Table 2-3 lists the specific fund types within each category and shows the measurement focus and basis of accounting applicable to each fund type. An overview of these funds and examples of individual fund financial statements are presented in the remainder of this chapter.

TABLE 2-1   Fund Categories

	Governmental-Type Funds	*Proprietary-Type Funds*	*Fiduciary-Type Funds*
Focus	Current financial resources	Economic resources	Economic resources
Activity	General government activities	Activities financed by user fees	Resources held for others
	Legally dedicated resources		

TABLE 2-2   Cash, Accrual, and Modified Accrual Bases of Accounting

	Cash Basis	*Accrual Basis*	*Modified Accrual Basis*
Record revenue:	When cash is received	When revenue is earned	When measurable and available
Record expenses (expenditures):	When cash is paid	When expense is incurred	Generally when expenditure is incurred (with specific exceptions)
Applicable fund category:		Proprietary, Fiduciary	Governmental

TABLE 2-3   Summary of Accounting Procedures Within Funds

Fund Type	*Category*	*Measurement Focus*	*Basis of Accounting*
General	Governmental	Current financial resources	Modified accrual
Special Revenue	Governmental	Current financial resources	Modified accrual
Debt Service	Governmental	Current financial resources	Modified accrual
Capital Projects	Governmental	Current financial resources	Modified accrual
Permanent	Governmental	Current financial resources	Modified accrual
Enterprise	Proprietary	Economic resources	Accrual
Internal Service	Proprietary	Economic resources	Accrual
Pension Trust	Fiduciary	Economic resources	Accrual
Investment Trust	Fiduciary	Economic resources	Accrual
Private-Purpose Trust	Fiduciary	Economic resources	Accrual
Agency	Fiduciary	Economic resources	Accrual

Source: Adapted from GASB *Statement No. 34,* "Basic Financial Statements—and Management's Discussion and Analysis—for State and Local Governments" (Norwalk, CT: GASB, 1999), Table B-2, p. 151.

GOVERNMENTAL ACCOUNTING IN PRACTICE
Current Financial Resources versus Economic Resources

As discussed in the narrative, the GASB requires preparation of two sets of financial statements: a fund set and a government-wide set. The required reconciliation of the two sets of statements shows how the current financial resources measurement focus and modified accrual basis of accounting (used in preparing the fund set) produces accounting measurements that differ from the economic resources measurement focus and accrual basis of accounting (used in preparing the government-wide set).

The following reconciliation, adapted from New York City's 2005 financial statements, accounts for a net difference of $3,513.6 million between the two sets of statements. Notice that the major differences in the two sets of operating statements relate to accounting for (a) the acquisition and depreciation of capital assets and (b) the issuance and repayment of long-term debt. (Numbers are in thousands of dollars.)

Governmental Funds report capital outlays as expenditures. However, in the government-wide statement of activities, the cost of those assets is allocated over their estimated useful lives and reported as depreciation expense. The amount by which capital outlays e ceeded depreciation in the current period is:

Purchases of capital assets	$3,110,766	
Depreciation expense	(2,366,576)	$744,190

The net effect of various miscellaneous transactions involving capital assets and other (i.e., sales, trade-ins, and donations) is to decrease net assets

	(706,473)

The issuance of long-term debt (e.g., bonds, capital leases) provides current financial resources to governmental funds, while the repayment of principal of long-term debt consumes the current financial resources of governmental funds. Neither transaction, however, has any effect on net assets in the government-wide statements. The net effect of these differences in treating long-term debt and related items is:

Proceeds from sales of bonds	(10,952,314)	
Principal payments of bonds	7,467,096	
Other	(121,785)	(3,607,003)

Some expenses reported in the government-wide operating statement do not require use of current financial resources and, therefore, are not reported as expenditures in governmental funds.

	(386,990)

Revenues in the government-wide operating statement that do not provide current financial resources are not reported as resources in the funds

	442,671

Difference between net change in fund balances for governmental-type funds reported in fund statements and change in net assets for governmental activities reported in government-wide statements

	$3,513,605

Source: Adapted from Comprehensive Annual Financial Report, the City of New York, NY, for the fiscal year ended June 30, 2005.

GOVERNMENTAL-TYPE FUNDS

As previously mentioned, governmental-type funds are used to account for basic day-to-day operating services provided by the governmental unit, and for resources earmarked for particular governmental functions. These funds use a current financial resources measurement focus and the modified accrual basis of accounting. Specifically, the governmental-type funds are the General Fund, Special Revenue Funds, Debt Service Funds, Capital Projects Funds, and Permanent Funds. Table 2-4 summarizes the purposes of each fund type and gives examples of their use. Fund-level financial statements prepared for governmental-type funds are the balance sheet and the statement of revenues, expenditures, and changes in fund balances.

The General Fund

Although the specific number and type of funds used by a governmental unit are determined by the particular operations of that unit, every governmental body must at least have a *General Fund*. Technically, this fund is a Residual Fund—it is used to account for all governmental operations not accounted for in some other fund. In reality, however, the General Fund encompasses the basic day-to-day operations of a governmental unit. Unless some legal, contractual, or managerial reason requires separate accounting for an activity, it is recorded in the General Fund.

General Funds obtain most of their resources from taxes on real property, general sales or specific types of sales, and personal and corporate incomes. They may also obtain intergovernmental grants for specific programs such as education and public assistance. Licenses, fees, and fines are also generally recorded in the General Fund. These resources are expended for basic operating programs, such as police and fire suppression services, trash removal, parks and cultural activities, traffic control, road maintenance, and the general administrative functions of government. The General Fund may also be used to acquire nonmajor items of equipment, including police

TABLE 2-4 Purposes of Governmental-Type Funds	
Fund Type	*To Account For:*
General	General operations of government; any activity not accounted for in another fund
	Examples: Police department, fire department
Special Revenue	Resources legally designated for specific purposes and separately reported
	Examples: A dedicated hotel-motel tax, a dedicated motor vehicle tax
Debt Service	Resources dedicated to pay principal and interest on general obligation debt
	Examples: Sales tax or revenue transfer to service general obligation bonds
Capital Projects	Resources dedicated to acquiring or constructing major capital facilities
	Examples: Construction of a city hall or bridge
Permanent	Resources legally restricted so only earnings (and not principal) may be used to support governmental programs
	Examples: Public cemetery perpetual-care fund; public library endowment fund

sedans. In addition, resource transfers may be made from the General Fund to other funds to fully or partially finance the activities of those funds.

Assets found in the General Fund are primarily current financial resources and usually include cash, investments, receivables (such as unpaid property taxes), and receivables from other funds. In governmental accounting terminology, the receivables from other funds are referred to as *due from other funds*. If these receivables are not currently due, they are referred to as *advances to other funds*. Liabilities found in the General Fund are also primarily currently due to be paid. They typically include claims of various suppliers and payables to other funds. The latter items are referred to as *due to other funds*. As in the case of receivables, if these liabilities are not currently due they are referred to as *advances from other funds*. (Notice that the inclusion of long-term loans between funds is an exception to the general rule regarding current financial resources. The special treatment required in this case is discussed in Chapter 5.)

Fund balance (equity) represents the excess of assets over liabilities. Fund balance is separated into two components: unreserved and reserved. The *unreserved* portion is the net amount of resources available for spending. Net assets (or individual assets) not available for current spending are reported as being *reserved*.

The accounting equation for governmental-type funds is similar to that used in commercial accounting. The only difference is that the equity section is referred to as *fund balance* rather than owners' equity. This equation is stated as follows:

$$\text{Assets} = \text{Liabilities} + \text{Fund Balance}$$

General Fund Balance Sheet Compared with Business Entity Balance Sheet

Governments are required to prepare fund financial statements and government-wide financial statements. A simplified fund-level balance sheet for the General Fund is presented in Table 2-5. Carefully study this table and notice how the accounting equation is presented in the financial statement. For comparison purposes, the balance sheet of a business organization is shown in Table 2-5.

The most significant difference between fund-level financial reporting for governmental-type funds and commercial financial reporting results from the current financial resources measurement focus used by governmental-type funds. As previously stated, when fund-level balance sheets are prepared, governmental-type fund assets consist primarily of current financial assets (spendable resources). Business organizations, on the other hand, report long-term assets as well, such as property, plant, equipment, and intangibles, on their balance sheets. Governmental-type fund-level balance sheets report only current liabilities, whereas business organization balance sheets also report long-term liabilities, such as bonds payable.

Another difference between fund-level financial reporting for governmental-type funds and commercial organizations is that the latter use classified financial statements. The elements of the commercial financial statements usually are reported in subgroups that distinguish the current from the noncurrent assets and liabilities.

A third difference between governmental-type fund-level financial reporting and commercial reporting lies in the equity section of the balance sheet. In governmental-type funds, equity is reported as fund balance and separated between reserved and unreserved amounts. In business organizations, equity is reported as contributed capital and retained earnings.

TABLE 2-5	General Fund Balance Sheet Compared with Corporate Balance Sheet

The City of Angusville General Fund Balance Sheet December 31, 2009		Cool Wheels Co., Inc. Balance Sheet December 31, 2009	
Assets		*Assets*	
Cash and investments	$576,000	Current assets:	
Taxes receivable (net of allowance for uncollectible accounts, $3,000)	89,000	Cash and investments	$ 50,000
		Accounts receivable (net of allowance for uncollectible accounts, $3,000)	135,000
Due from other funds	50,000	Inventory	145,000
Total assets	$715,000	Prepaid expenses	34,000
Liabilities		Total current assets	364,000
Accounts payable	$123,000	Property, plant, and equipment:	
Due to other funds	75,000	Land	100,000
Accrued liabilities	100,000	Buildings (net of accumulated depreciation, $55,000)	150,000
Total liabilities	298,000	Equipment (net of accumulated depreciation, $14,000)	45,000
Fund balance		Total property, plant, and equipment	295,000
Reserved	—	Intangibles:	
Unreserved	417,000	Patents	30,000
Total fund balance	417,000	Total assets	$689,000
Total liabilities and fund balance	$715,000	*Liabilities*	
		Current liabilities:	
		Accounts payable	$ 35,000
		Accrued expenses payable	55,000
		Dividends payable	10,000
		Total current liabilities	100,000
		Long-term liabilities:	
		Bonds payable	300,000
		Total liabilities	400,000
		Owners' Equity	
		Contributed capital	150,000
		Retained earnings	139,000
		Total owners' equity	289,000
		Total liabilities and owners' equity	$689,000

General Fund Operating Statement Compared with Business Entity Operating Statement

The fund-level "income statement" for a governmental-type fund is called a *statement of revenues, expenditures, and changes in fund balance.* Because governmental units do not usually operate to make a profit, the concept of income is not important. Throughout this text we will use the term *operating statement* to refer to the statement of revenues, expenditures, and changes in fund balance. Governmental fund operating statements are presented in the following format, with details shown for each caption, as appropriate. The net change in fund balance is added to or subtracted from the beginning-of-period fund balance to arrive at the end-of-period balance.

Revenues
− Expenditures
= Excess (deficiency) of revenues over expenditures
± Other financing sources and uses, including transfers
± Special and extraordinary items
= Net change in fund balance
+ Fund balance at beginning of period
= Fund balance at end of period[2]

Revenues usually available for use by the General Fund include taxes, licenses and permits, and fines and forfeitures. Expenditures generally are associated with the services and supplies used in the various operating departments and are reported on the operating statement by function. Examples of these functions include general government, public safety, and recreation and parks.

An example of an operating statement of a governmental General Fund and the income statement of a business is shown in Table 2-6. Notice that the General Fund operating statement includes other financing sources (uses). These increases and decreases in fund balance are not revenues or expenditures. In the General Fund, they consist mainly of transfers (transfers of resources between funds). Transfers in are transfers received by a fund from other funds, whereas transfers out are transfers from a fund to other funds. The technical aspects of transfers are discussed in Chapter 5. At this point you just need to be aware that fragmenting a government into separate pots of financial resources, called funds, often results in transfers of resources from one fund to another.

The major difference between the fund-level operating statement for the General Fund and a business organization results from the difference in measurement focus and basis of accounting. Notice, for example, that the Cool Wheels operating statement, which is prepared using the economic resources measurement focus and the accrual basis of accounting, shows depreciation expense but no capital outlay expenditures. By contrast, the City of Angusville operating statement, which is prepared using the current financial resources measurement focus and the modified accrual basis of accounting, shows no depreciation but does show capital outlay expenditures. This point will be explained in greater detail in a later chapter.

A second difference between the operating statement of a governmental-type fund and the income statement of a business organization is the presence of transfers from other funds. Transfers affect the operating results and changes in net assets of the individual governmental-type funds. Although transfers among related companies occur in commercial enterprise, they are eliminated in the preparation of consolidated financial statements, because they do not affect the enterprise as a whole. (When governmental organizations prepare government-wide financial statements, the interfund transfers offset each other, as discussed in Chapter 10.)

---

[2]GASB Cod. Sec. 2200.156 (adapted).

TABLE 2-6   General Fund—Statement of Revenues, Expenditures, and Changes in Fund Balance Compared with Corporate Income Statement

The City of Angusville General Fund Statement of Revenues, Expenditures, and Changes in Fund Balance For the Year Ended December 31, 2009		Cool Wheels Co., Inc. Income Statement For the Year Ended December 31, 2009	
Revenues		*Revenues*	
Income taxes	$ 990,000	Net sales	$988,000
Property taxes	900,000	Other revenue	10,000
Licenses and permits	550,000	Total revenues	998,000
Fines and forfeits	250,000		
Miscellaneous	92,000	*Expenses*	
Total revenues	2,782,000	Cost of goods sold	450,000
		Salaries expense	280,000
Expenditures		Depreciation expense	175,000
Current:		Interest expense	25,000
General government	550,000	Other expenses	20,000
Public safety	990,000	Total expenses	950,000
Human services	780,000	Net income	$ 48,000
Health	300,000		
Recreation and parks	50,000		
Capital outlay	100,000		
Total expenditures	2,770,000		
Excess of revenues over expenditures	12,000		
Other Financing Sources (Uses)			
Transfers in	50,000		
Transfers out	(40,000)		
Total other financing sources	10,000		
Net change in fund balance	22,000		
Fund balance at beginning of year	395,000		
Fund balance at end of year	$ 417,000		

A third difference between business reporting of operations and that of governmental-type funds is the treatment of equity. Ending fund balance is reconciled with beginning fund balance on the operating statements of governmental-type funds. Although some commercial organizations use this form of reporting, the majority reconcile beginning and ending retained earnings on a separate statement—either a retained earnings statement or a statement of changes in owners' equity.

Finally, commercial operating statements often are prepared under what is called the single-step approach; that is, total revenues less total expenses. The operating statements for governmental units contain several levels of aggregation. They are similar to multiple-step income statements sometimes used by business organizations.

Special Revenue Funds

Special Revenue Funds are used to account for the proceeds of specific revenue sources (other than trusts for individuals, private organizations, or other governments, or those used for major capital projects) that are legally restricted to be spent for a particular purpose. The accounting treatment of these funds is identical to that of the General Fund. The primary difference between the two types of funds lies in the scope of activities recorded in each.

As a general rule, Special Revenue Funds should be used only when legally mandated, such as by law or city charter. The main purpose of separating these types of activities from those of the General Fund is to maintain control over the collection and use of specific sources of revenue. For example, assume that a tax on gasoline is specifically dedicated to highway maintenance. Generally, the law establishing the tax requires establishment of a Special Revenue Fund. This separation makes it easier for a governmental unit to account for the dollars collected from the gasoline tax, as well as the expenditures for highway maintenance. If these resources were commingled with other revenues and expenditures, it would be more difficult to demonstrate accountability for the money collected and its use. Special Revenue Funds might also be used to account for hotel-motel taxes earmarked for specific purposes, parks admission fees earmarked to support parks maintenance, and higher-level government grants that must be used for community development.

A governmental unit can have several Special Revenue Funds. Usually the law requires that separate records be maintained for the activity of a Special Revenue Fund. Each of these funds is treated as a separate accounting entity for record-keeping purposes.

The types of assets and liabilities found in Special Revenue Funds are generally the same as those found in the General Fund. Because the accounting for Special Revenue Funds is identical to that of the General Fund, the comments made regarding the fund balance in the discussion of the General Fund are also relevant here. The balance sheet and the statement of revenues, expenditures, and changes in fund balance for Special Revenue Funds are similar to those shown for the General Fund in Tables 2-5 and 2-6.

Generally, the sources of revenue for Special Revenue Funds are taxes, rents and royalties, fees, and intergovernmental grants. Expenditures from these funds are usually for services and supplies specifically identified by the law establishing the particular fund. The current financial resources measurement focus and modified accrual basis of accounting are used for each Special Revenue Fund.

Debt Service Funds

Debt Service Funds account for the accumulation of resources for paying principal and interest on general long-term debt. This type of fund can be used also to pay long-term liabilities resulting from debt-like commitments, such as installment purchase contracts and lease-purchase agreements. Debt to be serviced by proprietary fund revenues is not general long-term debt, so resources accumulated for that purpose should be reported in the appropriate proprietary fund rather than in a Debt Service Fund.

Debt Service Funds should be used when legally mandated or when financial resources are being accumulated for principal and interest that comes due in future years. In the absence of those situations, debt service payments may be made directly from general revenues on an annual basis, and accounted for in the General Fund. A single Debt Service Fund should be used for all general long-term debt whenever possible. In many instances, however, each debt issue may require the establishment of a separate Debt Service Fund.

Debt Service Fund resources come most often from transfers from the General Fund (or other funds), income from the investment of resources held by the fund, and taxes assessed specifically to service the debt. Debt Service Fund expenditures generally result from payment of principal and interest on the debt. Debt Service Funds follow the modified accrual basis of accounting.

As a result of these types of transactions, the assets of Debt Service Funds usually consist of cash, investments, and sometimes receivables. The liabilities are generally for matured interest and principal that have not yet been paid. It is important to understand that the long-term liability for principal not currently due is not reported in the Debt Service Fund balance sheet. The fund balance therefore represents the resources available to service (pay principal and interest on) the debt. Debt Service Fund balance sheets and statements of revenues, expenditures, and changes in fund balance are similar to those presented for the General Fund in Tables 2-5 and 2-6.

Capital Projects Funds

Capital Projects Funds account for receipt and disbursement of resources used to acquire major capital facilities through purchase or construction. A Capital Projects Fund should be used to account for capital outlays financed from general obligation bond proceeds, and must be used whenever legally required. A Capital Projects Fund is not used to account for capital assets acquired by an Enterprise Fund, an Internal Service Fund, or trust funds for individuals, private organizations, or other governments. A Capital Projects Fund is also not used for capital assets purchased directly with current revenues of the General Fund or a Special Revenue Fund.

Generally, a separate Capital Projects Fund is used for each project. When a bond issue is involved in the financing, a separate fund is used for each bond issue. Using a separate fund provides better accountability for expenditures made with the proceeds of a bond issue.

Projects usually accounted for in these funds include construction of bridges, a new city hall, and acquisition of assets that involve long-term financing. Examples of the types of acquisitions that usually do not require the use of a Capital Projects Fund are purchases of automobiles, furniture, and minor equipment.

The balance sheet of a Capital Projects Fund is similar to that presented for the General Fund in Table 2-5. Assets normally found on the balance sheet of a Capital Projects Fund include cash, investments, receivables, and amounts due from other funds or governments. Liabilities include accounts payable and amounts due to other funds or governments for services and materials associated with the construction projects (or to construction companies if the projects are completed by outside contractors). Because Capital Projects Funds use a current financial resources measurement focus, neither the capital assets acquired with Capital Projects Fund resources nor long-term debt used to finance those resources are shown on the balance sheet of a Capital Projects Fund.

The statement of revenues, expenditures, and changes in fund balance for a Capital Projects Fund is similar in format to the General Fund operating statement shown in Table 2-6. Often, however, the amounts shown as other financing sources will be greater than the amounts shown as revenues in a Capital Projects Fund. This is because proceeds from the sale of bonds and transfers from other funds, both of which are classified as other financing sources, tend to be larger than federal and state grants and investment income, the common revenue sources for Capital Projects Funds. Expenditures are usually limited to amounts related to the capital projects and include construction and engineering costs. Because Capital Projects Funds are governmental-type funds, they follow the modified accrual basis of accounting.

Where are the capital assets acquired with Capital Projects Fund resources shown? Where is the long-term debt used to finance those assets reported? Because governmental-type funds use a current financial resources measurement focus, capital assets and long-term liabilities are not shown in fund-level financial statements. They are instead reported in the government-wide financial statements, which are prepared using the economic resources measurement focus and the accrual basis of accounting. To accumulate these data for government-wide reporting, this text (Chapter 10) suggests use of a Capital Investment Account Group.

Permanent Funds

Permanent Funds are used to report resources that are legally restricted so that only the earnings generated by the principal, and not the principal itself, may be used to support programs that benefit the government or its citizens. Permanent Funds do not include private-purpose trust funds, which are fiduciary-type funds discussed later in this chapter.

An example of a Permanent Fund is a perpetual-care public cemetery fund, whose resources generate revenues to maintain the cemetery. Another example is an endowment made to a public library, where the endowment must be maintained in perpetuity, and the income generated by the endowment must be used to purchase library books.

Financial statements prepared for Permanent Funds are similar to those shown in Tables 2-5 and 2-6. Assets of Permanent Funds generally include cash and investments. Liabilities might include amounts due to other funds. Permanent Fund revenues generally include investment income (interest, dividends, and net increase or decrease in the fair value of investments). Distributions of revenues to the fund designated as the beneficiary of Permanent Fund earnings—usually a Special Revenue Fund—are reported as transfers out.

PROPRIETARY-TYPE FUNDS

Proprietary-type funds are used when a governmental unit handles its financial operations in a manner generally similar to that of business enterprises. Activities that use proprietary fund accounting and reporting charge user fees for their services and focus on determining operating income and changes in net assets (or cost recovery). Examples of such activities include the operation of electric and water utilities, airports, mass transit facilities, golf courses, and central motor pools. Although sometimes subsidized by transfers (often from the General Fund), these activities are financed by user charges that at least partially cover operating and capital costs. As a result, accounting principles followed by proprietary-type funds are similar to those followed by commercial organizations; that is, they use an economic resources

TABLE 2-7	Purposes of Proprietary-Type Funds

Fund Type	To Account For:
Enterprise	Resources used to supply goods and services, for a fee, to users external to the governmental unit
	Examples: Municipal airport, municipal electric utility
Internal Service	Resources used to supply goods or services, based on cost reimbursement, within the governmental unit
	Examples: Central motor pool, central purchasing function

measurement focus and the accrual basis of accounting. Accrual-basis accounting provides governmental units with accurate measures of revenues and expenses to help in developing user charges, as well as cash flow information to help determine any subsidy needed to run an activity.

The two types of proprietary funds are Enterprise Funds and Internal Service Funds. Table 2-7 summarizes the purposes of these funds and gives examples of their use. Financial statements prepared for proprietary funds include a statement of net assets or balance sheet; a statement of revenues, expenses, and changes in fund net assets or fund equity; and a statement of cash flows.

Enterprise Funds

Enterprise Funds may be used to account for any activity whose products or services are sold for a fee to external users, such as the general public. Enterprise Funds *must* be used if any one of the following criteria is met:

- The activity is financed with debt that is secured solely by a pledge of the net revenues from the activity's fees and charges.
- Laws or regulations require that the costs of providing services, including capital costs (such as depreciation or debt service), be recovered through fees and charges, rather than with taxes.
- The activity's pricing policies set fees and charges that are designed to recover its costs, including capital costs (such as depreciation or debt service).

Operations accounted for in Enterprise Funds may include municipally owned utilities, mass transit facilities, toll roads and toll bridges, airports, parking facilities, and lotteries. Generally a separate fund is established for each type of activity. (As discussed in Chapter 9, some of these business-type activities may be organized as public authorities or public benefit organizations, legally separate from the parent government. When that happens, they use enterprise-type accounting, but are reported as separate "component units," rather than as Enterprise Funds of the parent government.)

The balance sheet of an Enterprise Fund is shown in Table 2-8. Notice that the balance sheet is prepared in classified form. A *classified balance sheet* presents the assets and liabilities so as to distinguish between those that are current and those that are noncurrent (or long term). *Current assets* include cash and items that will be converted to cash or used up in operations within 1 year. *Noncurrent assets* generally include land, buildings, and equipment. *Current liabilities* are debts that are due to be paid within 1 year. *Noncurrent liabilities* are debts that will be paid later than 1 year in the future.

Table 2-8   Enterprise Fund—Balance Sheet

The City of Angusville
Enterprise Fund
Sewerage and Water Fund
Balance Sheet
December 31, 2009

Assets

Current assets:

Cash	$ 650,000	
Receivables (net of allowance for uncollectibles of $8,000)	547,000	
Due from other funds	75,000	
Inventory of parts and supplies	155,000	
Total current assets		$ 1,427,000
Restricted assets:		
Customer deposits	879,000	
Current debt service account	500,000	
Total restricted assets		1,379,000
Noncurrent assets:		
Advances to other funds	300,000	
Property, plant, and equipment		
(net of accumulated depreciation, $2,400,000)	8,500,000	
Total noncurrent assets		8,800,000
Total assets		$11,606,000

Liabilities

Current liabilities:

Accounts payable	$ 235,000	
Due to other funds	100,000	
Accrued liabilities	77,000	
Accrued vacation and sick leave	90,000	
Total current liabilities		$ 502,000
Liabilities payable from restricted assets:		
Customer deposits	879,000	
Accrued interest	500,000	
Total liabilities payable from restricted assets		1,379,000
Noncurrent liabilities:		
Bonds payable		7,890,000
Total liabilities		9,771,000

Net Assets

Invested in capital assets, net of related debt	610,000	
Unrestricted	1,225,000	
Total net assets		1,835,000
Total liabilities and net assets		$11,606,000

Also, notice the presence of *restricted assets.* These assets represent resources set aside for some particular use that results from a contractual (such as a debt covenant), legal, or regulatory restriction. Showing certain assets as restricted (such as cash held in a separate account to pay debt principal and interest, pursuant to a debt covenant) lets the reader know that the resources are not available to pay other current liabilities. Depending on the circumstances, the restricted assets may be offset by liabilities that will be satisfied either from those resources or by net assets. In Table 2-8, the related liabilities are labeled "Liabilities payable from restricted assets."

Finally, notice that the balance sheet shown in Table 2-8 is presented in the traditional balance sheet format, where assets equal liabilities plus net assets. Proprietary fund balance sheets may also be shown in a net assets format, where assets minus liabilities equal net assets (called a statement of net assets). Net assets should be displayed in three major components, where applicable: invested in capital assets, net of related debt; restricted; and unrestricted. The components of net assets are discussed in Chapter 7.

The operating statement for Enterprise Funds is presented in multistep format, with a separate caption for operating income (or loss) and a reconciliation between beginning and end-of-period net assets or fund equity. The general format for this statement (with details shown, as appropriate) is as follows:

Operating revenues
− Operating expenses
= Operating income (or loss)
± Nonoperating revenues and expenses
= Income before other revenues, expenses, gains, losses, and transfers
+ Capital contributions
± Special and extraordinary items
± Transfers
= Increase (decrease) in net assets
+ Net assets at beginning of period
= Net assets at end of period[3]

Operating revenues earned by Enterprise Funds usually result primarily from user charges. Enterprise Fund operating expenses depend on the type of operations but usually include the cost of services, supplies used, utilities, depreciation, and so forth. Notice particularly the charge for depreciation. Because Enterprise Funds use the economic resources measurement focus and accrual basis of accounting, depreciation must be included as an expense. Nonoperating revenues and expenses might include investment revenue and interest expense. Capital contributions might include grants from higher-level governments to acquire capital assets and contributions from developers. *Extraordinary items* are transactions and events that are unusual in nature and occur infrequently, such as a loss from a flood. *Special items* refer to transactions and events within the control of management that are either unusual in nature or occur infrequently, such as a large one-time revenue from the sale of capital assets. Transfers include subsidies received from another fund. A statement of revenues, expenses, and changes in fund net assets is illustrated in Table 2-9.

Because Enterprise Funds use the economic resources measurement focus, operating statements do not report important data on financing sources and capital asset

---

[3]GASB Cod. Sec. 2200.167 (adapted).

TABLE 2-9 Enterprise Fund—Statement of Revenues, Expenses, and Changes in Fund Net Assets

The City of Angusville
Enterprise Fund
Sewerage and Water Fund
Statement of Revenues, Expenses, and Changes in Fund Net Assets
For the Year Ended December 31, 2009

Operating revenues:		
Charges for services		$2,400,000
Operating expenses:		
Personal services	$980,000	
Contractual services	370,000	
Depreciation	620,000	
Materials and supplies	176,000	
Other	101,000	
Total operating expenses		2,247,000
Operating income		153,000
Nonoperating expenses:		
Interest expense		125,000
Income before capital contributions		28,000
Capital contributions		100,000
Increase in net assets		128,000
Net assets at beginning of year		1,707,000
Net assets at end of year		$1,835,000

acquisition. Therefore, an additional financial statement—a statement of cash flows, illustrated in Table 2-10—is prepared for Enterprise Funds. Discussion of how cash flow statements are prepared is beyond the scope of this text. You should be aware, however, that cash flow statements prepared for governmental Enterprise Funds differ from their commercial counterparts in two ways: (a) they report four classifications of cash flow (operating, investing, noncapital financing, and capital and related financing activities), rather than three; and (b) they are prepared on the direct method (showing, for example, the purposes of cash flows for operating purposes), rather than the indirect method.

Internal Service Funds

Internal Service Funds are used to account for providing goods or services within the governmental unit, or to other governmental units, on a user-charge, cost-reimbursement basis. The main reasons for establishing this type of activity include (1) reduced cost of obtaining goods or services from purchasing in volume and (2) improvement in the distribution of goods or services within the governmental unit. Typical Internal Service Funds are those that account for supplies distribution, motor pool operations, data processing, and printing services.

Because Internal Service Funds are classified as proprietary-type funds, the accounting system used for these funds is designed to accumulate the total cost of the goods or services provided. Therefore, similar to Enterprise Funds, the economic

TABLE 2-10   Enterprise Fund—Statement of Cash Flows

The City of Angusville
Enterprise Fund
Sewerage and Water Fund
Statement of Cash Flows
For the Year Ended December 31, 2009

Increase (Decrease) in Cash		
Cash flows from operating activities:		
Cash received from vehicle rentals to departments	$2,390,000	
Cash paid to suppliers for goods and services	(560,000)	
Cash paid to employees	(980,000)	
Net cash provided by operating activities		$850,000
Cash flows from capital and related financing activities:		
Purchase of equipment	(720,000)	
Interest paid on capital debt	(125,000)	
Capital contributions	100,000	
Net cash used from capital and related financing activities		(745,000)
Net increase in cash		105,000
Cash at beginning of year		545,000
Cash at end of year		$650,000
Reconciliation of operating income to net cash provided by operating activities:		
Operating income		$153,000
Adjustments to reconcile operating income to net cash provided by operating activities		
Depreciation	$620,000	
Decrease in accounts receivable	262,000	
Increase in due from other funds	(50,000)	
Increase in inventory of parts and supplies	(40,000)	
Decrease in accounts payable	(50,000)	
Decrease in accrued liabilities	(30,000)	
Decrease in accrued vacation and sick leave	(15,000)	
Total adjustments		697,000
Net cash provided by operating activities		$850,000

resources measurement focus and full accrual basis of accounting are used. Using full accrual accounting enables compilation of the total cost of goods or services provided, leading to the calculation of user charges based on cost per unit of product or service or total cost for a specific job.

The Internal Service Fund bills the funds receiving the goods or services (often, the General Fund), and this amount is treated as a revenue of the Internal Service Fund and as an expenditure (expense) of the other funds. A separate fund is used for each identifiable unit because the accumulation of costs of goods or services provided must be specifically associated with revenues earned from providing the goods or services.

Financial statements prepared for Internal Service Funds are similar to those prepared for proprietary funds, shown in Tables 2-8, 2-9, and 2-10.

FIDUCIARY-TYPE FUNDS

Fiduciary-type funds are used to account for assets held by a government in a trust or agency capacity for others (individuals, other governments, or private organizations). Because they are held for others, these resources cannot be used to support the government's own programs. The fiduciary fund category includes Pension (and other employee benefit) Trust Funds, Investment Trust Funds, Private-Purpose Trust Funds, and Agency Funds. Trust Funds are distinguished from Agency Funds generally by the existence of a trust agreement that affects the degree of management involvement and the length of time the resources are held. Table 2-11 presents a summary of the fiduciary-type funds, showing the purpose and examples of each.

Pension (and Other Employee Benefit) Trust Funds

The most widely used and often most significant Trust Funds are *Pension (and other employee benefit) Trust Funds*. These funds account for resources required to be held in trust for members and beneficiaries of public employee defined benefit and defined contribution pension plans, health care and other postemployment benefit plans, and other employee benefit plans. (*Defined benefit pension plans* guarantee specific benefits on retirement. *Defined contribution plans* do not guarantee specific benefits; instead, benefits are based on periodic contributions to the plans and the earnings on them.)

Investment Trust Funds

Some governments sponsor investment pools, wherein they invest and manage resources belonging both to the sponsoring government (the *internal* portion of the pool) and to governments that are external to the sponsoring government (the *external* portion of the pool). The internal portion of these investment pools is reported as assets of

---

TABLE 2-11   Purposes of Fiduciary-Type Funds

Fund Type	*To Account For:*
Pension Trust	Resources held in trust for employee retirement plans and other employee benefit plans
	Examples: Defined benefit pension plan, postemployment health benefit plan
Investment Trust	Resources of an external investment pool managed by a sponsoring government
	Examples: Financial reporting of the portion of an external investment pool that belongs to other governments
Private-Purpose Trust	Resources of all other trust arrangements maintained for benefit of individuals, other governments, and private organizations
	Examples: Unclaimed (escheat) property, such as bank accounts, investment accounts, and other property held pending claim by rightful owners
Agency	Resources held in a custodial capacity that must be disbursed according to law or contractual agreement
	Examples: Sales or property taxes collected by a government on behalf of another government, Social Security taxes withheld from employees and kept separately pending distribution to the federal government

---

GOVERNMENTAL ACCOUNTING IN PRACTICE
How Many Funds Do Municipalities Have?

The numbers and types of funds used by municipal governments have nothing to do with the size of the government. Rather, the fund structure depends primarily on how a government is organized, how it is financed, what services it provides, and how many Special Revenue Funds it decides to establish. For example, the Village of Grafton, WI (population 11,310) has 20 governmental-type funds, but the City of New York (population 8,143,197) has only 14. Grafton's governmental-type funds include 10 Special Revenue Funds (including funds captioned "library," "aquatics," "recreation," and a cemetery). New York operates without a single Special Revenue Fund, but its financing structure is much more complex than Grafton's, so it maintains 9 Debt Service Funds.

Grafton has an Enterprise Fund (a water and wastewater facility), but New York City has no Enterprise Funds. On the other hand, New York City has a large number of specially created public benefit corporations that engage in business-type activities and are reported separately as part of its reporting entity. Grafton also has a Permanent Fund (for perpetual care of a cemetery), but New York City does not. Grafton provides pension benefits for its employees through a state-operated pension plan, so it has no Pension Funds. But New York City operates its own pension system and has 5 very large Pension Funds and 9 pension-related "variable supplements funds."

---

the funds for which the investments were made. The external portions, however, are reported in *Investment Trust Funds,* another type of Fiduciary Fund.

Private-Purpose Trust Funds

Private-Purpose Trust Funds are used to report all other trust arrangements under which the principal and income are held for the benefit of individuals, other governments, and private organizations. An example of a Private-Purpose Trust Fund is an Escheat Property Fund. *Escheat property* is private property that reverts to a governmental entity in the absence of legal claimants or heirs. Many governments have laws that enable a rightful owner or heir to reclaim such property into perpetuity if the claimant can establish a right to it.

Agency Funds

Agency Funds are used to account for resources held by governmental units in a purely custodial capacity. They generally involve only the receipt and subsequent disbursement, after a short period of time, of assets held for individuals, private organizations, or other governments. Agency Funds may be used also to account for resources belonging both to other governments and the custodial government. For financial reporting purposes, however, only the resources belonging to other governments are reported in an Agency Fund. Assets held for the reporting government, pending distribution within the reporting government, should be reported in the appropriate governmental or proprietary fund.

An example of an Agency Fund is a *Tax Agency Fund,* wherein the reporting government collects taxes (such as sales taxes or property taxes) both for itself and as agent for other governments. The resources are held for a short period of time in an Agency Fund, which serves as a clearing account, pending distribution to the appropriate government. Agency Funds are also used to account for deposits made by contractors when submitting bids on construction contracts.

It is possible to use one Agency Fund to account for several agency relationships, provided there are no legal restrictions. However, due to the legal problems that exist in situations involving trusts, a separate fund generally is used for each individual trust.

Reporting on Fiduciary-Type Funds

For the Trust Funds, governmental entities are required to prepare a statement of fiduciary net assets and a statement of changes in fiduciary net assets. These funds should be reported using the economic resources measurement focus and the full accrual basis of accounting, except for certain liabilities of defined benefit pension plans and postemployment health care plans. Agency Funds have no "net assets." Instead, all resources held are equal to the liabilities to be paid from the resources in the Agency Fund statement of fiduciary net assets. A statement of changes in fiduciary net assets is not prepared for Agency Funds.

A statement of fiduciary net assets for a Pension Trust Fund is shown in Table 2-12. Assets usually found in a Pension Trust Fund statement of fiduciary net assets include

TABLE 2-12   Pension Trust Fund—Statement of Fiduciary Net Assets

The City of Angusville
Pension Trust Fund
City Employees' Retirement Fund
Statement of Fiduciary Net Assets
For the Year Ended December 31, 2009

Assets		
Cash		$ 5,000
Receivables		50,000
Accrued income		25,000
Investments, at fair value:		
Bonds	$18,000,000	
Common stock	6,000,000	
Total investments		24,000,000
Office equipment and furniture (net of accumulated depreciation of $10,000)		75,000
Total assets		24,155,000
Liabilities		
Accounts payable	20,000	
Accrued expenses	35,000	
Total liabilities		55,000
Net Assets		
Held in trust for pension benefits		$24,100,000

TABLE 2-13   Pension Trust Fund—Statement of Changes in Fiduciary Net Assets

The City of Angusville
Pension Trust Fund
City Employees' Retirement Fund
Statement of Changes in Fiduciary Net Assets
For the Year Ended December 31, 2009

Additions		
Contributions:		
Member contributions	$2,500,000	
Employer contributions	2,500,000	
Total contributions		$ 5,000,000
Investment income:		
Net appreciation in fair value of investments	875,000	
Interest	550,000	
Dividends	450,000	
Total investment income		1,875,000
Total additions		6,875,000
Deductions		
Benefits paid	4,375,000	
Administrative expenses	200,000	
Total deductions		4,575,000
Change in net assets		2,300,000
Net assets available for benefits:		
Beginning of year		21,800,000
End of year		$24,100,000

cash, investments, and receivables (including interest receivable). Liabilities usually include accounts and refunds payable. The net assets of the Trust Fund represent the amount held in trust for pension payments to retirees, current employees, and their beneficiaries.

Table 2-13 shows the statement of changes in fiduciary net assets for a Pension Trust Fund. Notice that this statement is called a Statement of Changes in Fiduciary Net Assets, thus linking it with the Statement of Net Assets. Typical additions to plan net assets are contributions and investment earnings, which include interest, dividends, and net increase (or decrease) in the fair value of investments. Typical deductions are benefits paid to retirees, refunds of contributions, and administrative expenses.

Review Questions

Q2-1   Define *fund* as the term is used in governmental accounting.

Q2-2   What is the purpose of fund accounting?

Q2-3   List the three categories of funds used in governmental accounting and describe the types of activities accounted for in each category.

Q2-4   Describe the difference between *economic resources measurement focus* and *current financial resources measurement focus.* Which measurement focus is used in each fund cagtegory?

Q2-5   How has governmental budgeting influenced the measurement focus and basis of accounting used in the governmental funds category?

Q2-6   Compare the timing of revenue and expense or expenditure recognition using the *accrual basis of accounting* with that using the *modified accrual basis of accounting.* Which basis of accounting is used in each fund category?

Q2-7   List the governmental-type funds and briefly describe the use of each.

Q2-8   The controller for the City of Walla Walla recently made the following comment: "At a minimum, we could run city government with the use of only one fund." Do you agree with this statement? Why or why not?

Q2-9   Why are there no capital assets in governmental-type funds?

Q2-10 List the proprietary-type funds and briefly describe the use of each.

Q2-11 Why do proprietary-type funds use full accrual accounting?

Q2-12 List the fiduciary-type funds and briefly describe the use of each.

Q2-13 Discuss why Agency Funds do not have a fund balance.

Cases

C2-1   A large city has been financing all of its services through the property tax and the sales tax. As the cost of services has been increasing, the city has found it necessary to raise its tax rates. A special commission appointed by the mayor suggests that it would be possible to reduce the property tax rate by charging residents a monthly fee to cover the costs of collecting and disposing of trash and garbage. The mayor likes the suggestion and decides to implement it. Describe the fund accounting implications of adopting that suggestion.

C2-2   Each department in a large city maintains its own fleet of vehicles. The cost of purchasing and maintaining the vehicles is financed through the General Fund. One day, the mayor walks past the parking lot of the Parks Department and notices that many vehicles are not being used. The mayor calls her finance commissioner into the office and says: "Couldn't we save money by setting up a central motor pool and requiring each department to use a pool vehicle whenever they need one?" The finance commissioner replies: "Yes, that will save us lots of money, but we will need to change our accounting system a bit to handle it." Discuss the fund accounting implications of the finance commissioner's reply.

C2-3   During a heated campaign for mayor of Hoschkosh, an unsuccessful candidate boasted that he would "do away with all the special interests in government. I will abolish all the Special Revenue Funds and merge that money with the general operating resources of the city." You are the successful candidate in that race and now the local press is pressuring you to respond to the campaign promise of that other candidate. How would you respond to the press?

Ethics Case

EC2-1 To fulfill a campaign promise, the new mayor of Cordelia is looking for ways to finance an increase in the level of police protection without raising the city's property tax rate. He reads the city's financial report and notices that the Capital

Projects Fund has a large fund balance. He discusses the fund balance with his finance commissioner, who says: "The fund balance is high because the city voted to sell bonds last year to finance construction of new firehouse. The architect just finished the design of the firehouse and we are about to award a constructon contract." The mayor responds: "Forget the firehouse. I promised to put more police patrols on the street. Let's use the bond proceeds to hire more police officers." How should the finance commissioner respond to the mayor?

Exercises

E2-1   (Fund categories)
State which category of funds (governental-type, proprietary-type, or fiduciary-type) would be used for each of the following purposes:
1. To accumulate resources to pay the pension benefits of a city's employees.
2. To construct a firehouse.
3. To pay the salaries of the city's police officers.
4. To provide a new bus service for the city's residents based on fares designed to cover all service costs.
5. To provide a central purchasing service for all city departments, to be financed by charging the departments for the cost of the supplies plus a small fee to cover the cost of the service.

E2-2   (Identification of funds, measurement focus, and basis of accounting)
For each scenario shown in problem E2-1, state which fund type would be used and which measurement focus and basis of accounting would be used within each fund type.

E2-3   (Identification of funds through examples)
For each of the following situations, indicate which fund would be used to report the transaction.
1. A city made payments to a contractor on a major bridge project.
2. The Department of Streets purchased materials to be used to repair potholes.
3. A city paid salaries to the employees of its Fire Department.
4. The state Tax Department collected sales taxes on behalf of several large cities in the state.
5. A city accumulated resources in a fund to pay principal and interest on its general obligation bonds.
6. A city acquired land for bridge approaches as part of the project mentioned in part (1).

E2-4   (Identification of funds through examples)
For each of the following situations, indicate which fund would be used to report the transaction. (Note: Several of the transactions require using more than one fund.)
1. A city-owned water utility sent bills to the city for water provided to city departments.
2. The city's mass transit facility received an operating subsidy from the city and a construction grant from the federal government.
3. The city sent out property tax bills to pay for the day-to-day city operating activities.

4. The city sold bonds to constuct new roads—a major capital project.
5. The city used tax resources to pay for new police sedans. (The city classifies the purchase of all sedans as "minor capital items," to be paid from tax resources, rather than the sale of bonds.)
6. The city paid principal and interest on a bond issue from resources accumulated for that purpose.
7. The city's centralized printing facility billed the city's Tax Department for printing tax forms.
8. The city levied a special hotel tax dedicated to beautifying its downtown shopping area.

E2-5 (Identification of funds through examples)

For each of the following situations, indicate which fund would be used to report the transaction. (Note: Several transactions require using more than one fund.)

1. A city-owned airport sent bills to various airlines.
2. The fund that operates a central motor pool sent bills at the end of the month to all city agencies that used the motor pool.
3. A county received cash from three school districts in accordance with a state law that requires counties to invest temporarily idle cash on behalf of all school districts in the county.
4. A state sent bills for $50 to all residents who owned motor vehicles. The revenues were dedicated to a special road improvement program.
5. A city sent a check for $3 million to a fund that accumulates resources for the purpose of paying postemployment health care benefits to its employees.

E2-6 (Use of funds)

The mayor of New West Norwalk wants to simplify the accounting system used by the town. He approached you with the following task: Reduce the number of individual funds used in our governmental-type funds. How might you achieve this purpose?

E2-7 (Use of funds)

For each of the following situations, write a short paragraph describing a specific set of circumstances that would require use of the funds listed.

1. An Investment Trust Fund
2. An Agency Fund
3. A Special Revenue Fund
4. A Capital Projects Fund
5. An Internal Service Fund
6. An Enterprise Fund

E2-8 (Matching—general terminology)

Match the terms on the left with the descriptions on the right by placing the appropriate letter in the space provided (use each letter only once).

_I_	1. Governmental fund type	a. Cash payment or incurrence of liability for services in a governmental-type fund
_F_	2. Fund categories	
_G_	3. Definition of a fund	b. Collectible within the current period or soon enough thereafter (within
_J_	4. Economic resources	
_E_	5. Basis of accounting	

_C_   **6.** Recognition of revenue when resources are available and measurable

_E_   **7.** Available

_A_   **8.** Expenditure

_B_   **9.** Current financial resources

_H_   **10.** Agency Fund

60 days) to be used to pay the liabilities of the current period

c. Modified accrual

d. Measurement focus for governmental-type funds

e. Refers to the timing of the recognition of assets, liabilities, revenues, and expenses or expenditures

f. Governmental, proprietary, fiduciary

g. A fiscal and accounting entity with a self-balancing set of accounts

h. Example of a fiduciary-type fund

i. Type of fund that accounts for general governmental operations

j. Measurement focus for proprietary-type funds and fiduciary-type funds

E2-9   (Fill in the blanks—general terminology)

1. A _____ is a fiscal and accounting entity with a self-balancing set of accounts.
2. The current financial resources measurement focus is used for _____ funds.
3. The basis of accounting refers to the _____ of the recognition of revenues and expenses (expenditures).
4. Accounting measurements in the General Fund are based on the _____ measurement focus and the _____ basis of accounting.
5. Accounting measurements in proprietary-type funds are based on the _____ measurement focus and _____ basis of accounting.

E2-10 (Fill in the blanks—general terminology)

1. A governmental unit may have _____ (one or more than one) General Fund.
2. Accounting for a _____ Fund is the same as that of the General Fund.
3. _____ Funds are used to account for the receipt and disbursement of resources used to acquire major capital facilities.
4. Payments of principal and interest on general obligation governmental debt are generally recorded in a _____ Fund.

E2-11 (Use of funds)

The city council asked you to explain why the accounting records for proprietary-type funds use a different basis of accounting than those of governmental-type funds. Write the explanation that you would provide to the council.

E2-12 (Fill in the blanks—general terminology)

1. Three fund financial statements required for proprietary-type funds are _____, _____, and _____.
2. The two funds included in the proprietary-type funds are _____ and _____.
3. The basis of accounting used for proprietary-type funds is _____.
4. Assets that are limited in use for a specific purpose are generally referred to as _____.
5. Transactions and events within the control of management that are either unusual in nature or occur infrequently are referred to as _____.

E2-13 (Matching—use of funds)

Using the following codes, indicate which description best fits the funds listed by placing the code in the space provided.

GF   General Fund
SRF   Special Revenue Fund
CPF   Capital Projects Fund
DSF   Debt Service Fund
EF   Enterprise Fund
ISF   Internal Service Fund

  _EF_ **1.** Services are provided to the general public and the costs of providing the services are financed by user charges.

  _DF_ **2.** Resources are accumulated to pay principal and interest on general long-term debt.

  _GF_ **3.** Accounting for the police department activities.

  ISF **4.** Goods or services are furnished to other segments of the governmental unit on a user charge basis.

  SRF **5.** Resources are dedicated to a particular purpose.

  CPF **6.** Expenditures are made by the city's streets department.

  _EF_ **7.** An "operating income" figure is computed.

E2-14 (Difference between expenditures and expenses)

Based on the information shown below, calculate for the year ended December 31, 2008: (a) the total amount of expenditures that would be recognized when using the current financial resources measurement focus and modified accrual basis of accounting, and (b) the total amount of expenses that would be recognized using the economic resources measurement focus and accrual basis of accounting.

Salaries, paid in cash during 2008	$ 3,000,000
Salaries, applicable to 2008, due to be paid January 5, 2009	20,000
Utility bill, applicable to 2008, due to be paid January 10, 2009	10,000
Equipment, acquired at the beginning of 2008 and having an estimated useful life of 10 years	200,000
Payment of principal on long-term debt on December 31, 2008	100,000
Payment of interest on long-term debt on December 31, 2008	40,000

E2-15 (Summary of general reporting)

Following is a listing of codes for several types of funds. Indicate next to each fund financial statement the code of the fund for which the financial statement must be prepared.

GF   General Fund
EF   Enterprise Fund
PTF   Pension Trust Fund
CPF   Capital Projects Fund
ISF   Internal Service Fund
AF   Agency Fund

  _____ **1.** Balance sheet (or statement of net assets)

  _____ **2.** Statement of revenues, expenditures, and changes in fund balance

  _____ **3.** Statement of cash flows

  _____ **4.** Statement of fiduciary net assets

_____ **5.** Statement of revenues, expenses, and changes in fund net assets
_____ **6.** Statement of changes in fiduciary net assets

Problems

P2-1   (Discussion of the nature of the three fund categories)
Identify and describe the three fund categories used in governmental accounting. For each category, discuss the broad purposes and illustrate the purposes by identifying several specific fund types. Also, describe the measurement focus and basis of accounting used in making accounting measurements within each category.

P2-2   (Identification of activities with funds and identifying funds with the appropriate measurement focus and basis of accounting)
Bacchus City is a small city in the southeastern United States. Because of its colorful history and fine restaurants, it is a tourist destination. It is located on a major river and is vulnerable to flooding in the spring. As a result, it is surrounded by a system of levees. In addition to many fine, old homes, it has a number of parkways connecting various parts of the city. Bacchus City uses separate funds to account for the following activities:
1. The city's day-to-day operating activities
2. Sources of financing and expenditures related to the construction of an office building
3. Payment of debt service on long-term bonds issued to build the office building
4. A central activity that acquires supplies and sells them to the various city agencies
5. A city-owned utility that buys and sells electricity to its residents
6. A fund that accumulates resources to pay pensions to city employees
7. An activity that invests funds on behalf of two small neighboring cities
8. Disposition of sales taxes collected by the city on behalf of the county where it is located

Required: For each of the activities listed, state (1) the type of fund that Bacchus City will use, (2) the measurement focus and basis of accounting of each fund, and (3) the fund-level financial statements required for each fund.

P2-3   (Conceptual section review)
Answer each of the following questions.
1. A city operates a municipal health clinic that provides outpatient care for children. It charges fees for services to those who can afford to pay, bills the state for Medicaid-eligible patients, and subsidizes the clinic to the extent necessary. What type of fund is most suitable for this activity? Why?
2. A state maintains a central printing activity that provides services to all departments. For example, it prints the state budget document, the annual financial report, all the tax forms, and all license documents. What type of fund is most suitable for this activity? Why?
3. Several small governmental units decided to pool their resources to build and operate a regional airport. What type of fund would you recommend for the airport? Why?

4. A city decides to dedicate resources to improving the appearance of its downtown business area. Among other things, it adds 2 percent to its hotel occupancy tax and earmarks it for that purpose. What type of fund is most suitable for this activity? Why?

P2-4 (Conceptual section review)
Answer each of the following questions.
1. Explain how the fund balance of a governmental-type fund represents available spendable resources.
2. Special Revenue Funds, Capital Projects Funds, and Debt Service Funds are similar in nature. Explain this similarity.
3. Why do governmental units use Special Revenue Funds, Capital Projects Funds, and Debt Service Funds?

P2-5 (Identification of activities with particular governmental-type funds)
Using only the governmental-type funds, indicate which would be used to record each of the following transactions and events. Some transactions require the use of more than one fund.

GF General Fund
SRF Special Revenue Fund
DSF Debt Service Fund
CPF Capital Projects Fund
PF Permanent Fund

____ 1. The city transferred cash to the fund used to accumulate resources to pay bond principal and interest.
____ 2. The city received its share of a state sales tax that is legally required to be used to finance library operations.
____ 3. The city sent property tax bills to homeowners to help pay for day-to-day operating costs.
____ 4. The city paid for five fire engines, using resources accumulated in a fund to pay for major capital projects.
____ 5. The city received a grant from the state to build an addition to the city hall.
____ 6. The city received the proceeds of general obligation bonds to finance the construction of a new police station.
____ 7. The mayor was paid his monthly salary.
____ 8. Expenditures for the operation of the Police Department were recorded.
____ 9. After completing construction of the new police station, the city had $60,000 left in the fund. The city charter requires that any such assets be transferred to the fund that pays the debt service on the bonds.
____ 10. Parks admissions fees, dedicated for use in day-to-day maintenance of the city park system, were collected.
____ 11. The city has a financing policy that calls for transferring a portion of its general tax revenues each year to the fund that accumulates resources for capital construction. The purpose of the transfer is to reduce the need for borrowing. The city transferred $800,000 to that fund.
____ 12. The city paid a contractor who had completed a report on the potential for improving police deployment as a way to reduce the crime rate.

___ **13.** The city workers were paid their weekly salaries.

___ **14.** The city retired some of its outstanding bonds, using monies accumulated for that purpose.

___ **15.** A federal grant was received to help pay for the cost of constructing the new city hall.

___ **16.** The city received a donation from a taxpayer, with the stipulation it be invested and kept in perpetuity, so that the income from the investments could be used to buy library books.

___ **17.** The city received income from the investments made in part (16).

P2-6 (Identification of activities with particular governmental- and proprietary-type funds)

Using the governmental- and proprietary-type funds, indicate which would be used to record each of the following events.

GF	General Fund
SRF	Special Revenue Fund
DSF	Debt Service Fund
CPF	Capital Projects Fund
PF	Permanent Fund
EF	Enterprise Fund
ISF	Internal Service Fund

_EF_ **1.** Bonds were issued by the fund used to account for providing water to the residents of a municpality.

_GF_ **2.** The fund that finances the city's basic day-to-day operating activities lent $50,000 to the fund that will provide city agencies with supplies on a user charge basis.

_EF_ **3.** The city-operated utility that provides electricity to the residents of a municipality billed the city for electricity provided to city agencies.

_RF_ **4.** The city charter required all hotel taxes to be accounted for in a separate fund dedicated to maintaining the downtown business district. Hotel tax collections for the period were $500,000.

_GF_ **5.** Salaries were paid to the city's police officers and firefighters.

_PF_ **6.** The state lottery, which operates like a business entity, sent a check for its net revenues (after paying lottery prizes) to the state. The state will add these revenues to general state revenues as part of the state's program for financing elementary and secondary education.

DSF **7.** Interest and principal on the city's general obligation debt was paid, using resources accumulated specifically for that purpose.

_GF_ **8.** The fund that finances the city's day-to-day operating activities transferred cash to the fund that pays principal and interest on outstanding debt.

CPF **9.** The city sold general obligation bonds to buy land as part of a city hall expansion program.

ISF **10.** The city's central motor pool billed each city department for use of vehicles.

SRF **11.** The state established a highway beautification program, to be financed by dedicating a new motor vehicle license fee for that purpose.

_PF_ **12.** A wealthy taxpayer donated securities to a village, stipulating that the donation be kept in perpetuity, and that the resulting investment income must be used solely to help support the activities of the village library.

SRF   **13.** The state-operated toll road collected tolls of $1 million.

PF   **14.** The village maintains a perpetual-care public cemetery fund. Income from that fund was transferred to the fund that accumulates resources dedicated to maintaining the cemetery.

P2-7   (Transactions involving all funds)

Indicate which fund(s) would be used to record each of the following events by the city, county, or state referred to in the transaction. Use the following codes:

GF   General Fund
SRF   Special Revenue Fund
DSF   Debt Service Fund
CPF   Capital Projects Fund
PF   Permanent Fund
EF   Enterprise Fund
ISF   Internal Service Fund
PTF   Pension Trust Fund
ITF   Investment Trust Fund
PPTF   Private-Purpose Trust Fund
AF   Agency Fund

____ **1.** The city made a contribution to the employees' retirement fund.

____ **2.** Taxes that are dedicated to street repairs were collected. The ordinance establishing the tax requires a separate accounting for these monies.

____ **3.** The contractors who were building a bridge were paid.

____ **4.** General governmental revenues were transferred to the fund that accumulates resources to retire general long-term debt.

____ **5.** The salary of the chief of police was paid.

____ **6.** The central supplies fund sent out bills (covering the cost of the supplies plus overhead) for supplies provided to the Police and Fire departments and to the city airport.

____ **7.** The city received a gift from a citizen to be held in perpetuity. The investment income must be used to provide free concerts in city parks.

____ **8.** Bonds were issued to finance construction of an office building.

____ **9.** The Police Department purchased three police sedans, using general tax revenues. (The purchase was not considered to be a major capital project.)

____ **10.** Sales taxes were collected by the state Tax Department. One-half of the collections was deposited in the fund that accumulates resources to finance day-to-day operating activities, and one-half was held for remitting to other governments on whose behalf the state collects taxes.

____ **11.** The city sold some of its excess office equipment. The proceeds were to be used for general city operations.

____ **12.** General obligation bonds were retired, using monies accumulated in a fund used solely for that purpose.

____ **13.** The county bus system, accounted for as a separate fund, sold bonds to finance a bus depot.

___ **14.** The city uses a separate fund to account for its central purchasing function. Supplies were purchased by this fund.

___ **15.** A citizen donated securities to the city, stipulating that the principal amount must remain intact and that the income must be spent to provide free food to the elderly at the city-operated senior citizen centers.

___ **16.** The village treasurer received property tax revenues and deposited them to the credit of a fund dedicated solely to the operation of the village library.

___ **17.** The county treasurer distributed to school districts the school districts' shares of the earnings from investments made by the county-operated investment pool.

P2-8   (Implications of differences in measurment focus and basis of accounting)

1. Explain the meaning of *measurement focus* and *basis of accounting.*
2. Discuss the difference between the *economic resources measurement focus* and the *current financial resources measurement focus.* Describe how using the two measurement focuses results in different accounting treatments for the acquisition and subsequent use of capital assets.
3. Discuss the difference between the *accrual basis of accounting* and the *modified accrual basis of accounting.* Describe how using the two bases of accounting result in different accounting treatments for the recognition and measurement of property tax revenues.

P2-9   (Justification for using different meaurement focuses and bases of accounting)

1. Discuss the justification for using the economic resources measurement focus and accrual basis of accounting by a municipally operated water utility.
2. Discuss the justification for using the current financial resources measurement focus and the modified accrual basis of accounting in the General Fund.
3. Discuss the advantages and disadvantages of using the current financial measurement focus and the modified accrual basis of accounting in the General Fund.

P2-10 (Statement preparation—General Fund)

Using the following data, prepare a statement of revenues, expenditures, and changes in fund balance for the General Fund of Harlan County for the year ended December 31, 2009.

Miscellaneous revenues	$ 180,000
Licenses and permits revenues	2,000,000
Education program expenditures	2,000,000
Public safety expenditures	4,000,000
Transfers to other funds	1,500,000
Property tax revenues	7,000,000
Welfare program expenditures	2,100,000
State and federal grants	4,000,000
Parks program expenditures	750,000
Highways program expenditures	900,000
Transfers from other funds	700,000
Fund balance at beginning of year	1,500,000

P2-11   (Multiple choice)

1. Which of the following fund types of a governmental unit has (have) current financial resources as a measurement focus?

	General Fund	*Enterprise Fund*
a.	Yes	Yes
b.	Yes	No
c.	No	No
d.	No	Yes

2. In which fund should the proceeds of a federal grant made to assist in financing the future construction of a police training facility be recorded?
   a. General Fund
   b. Special Revenue Fund
   c. Capital Projects Fund
   d. Enterprise Fund

3. In which fund should the receipts from a special tax levied to pay principal and interest on general obligation bonds issued to finance the construction of a city hall be recorded?
   a. Debt Service Fund
   b. Capital Projects Fund
   c. Enterprise Fund
   d. Special Revenue Fund

4. Several years ago, a city established a fund to retire general obligation bonds issued for the purpose of constructing a new police station. This year the city made a $50,000 contribution to that fund from its general revenues. The fund also realized $15,000 in revenue from its investments. The bonds due this year were retired. This year's transactions require accounting recognition in which fund(s)?
   a. General Fund
   b. Debt Service Fund and Special Revenue Fund
   c. Debt Service Fund and General Fund
   d. Capital Projects Fund and Debt Service Fund

5. Which fund should be used to account for the activities of a central motor pool that provides and services vehicles for the use of municipal employees on official business?
   a. Agency Fund
   b. Enterprise Fund
   c. Internal Service Fund
   d. Special Revenue Fund

6. Which fund would recognize a transaction in which a municipal electric utility paid $150,000 for new equipment out of its earnings?
   a. Enterprise Fund
   b. General Fund
   c. Capital Projects Fund
   d. Special Revenue Fund

7. Which of the following funds of a governmental unit records the acquisition of a fixed asset as an expenditure rather than as an asset?
   a. Internal Service Fund
   b. Pension Trust Fund
   c. Enterprise Fund
   d. General Fund

8. Which of the following funds of a governmental unit use the modified accrual basis of accounting?
   a. Internal Service Fund
   b. Enterprise Fund
   c. Pension Trust Fund
   d. Debt Service Fund

9. Under the modified accrual basis of accounting for a governmental unit, revenues should be recognized in the accounting period in which they _____.
   a. Are earned
   b. Become available and measurable
   c. Are earned and collectible
   d. Are collected

10. Which fund would account for fixed assets in a manner similar to a for-profit organization?
   a. Enterprise Fund
   b. Capital Projects Fund
   c. Permanent Fund
   d. General Fund

(AICPA adapted)

P2-12 (Multiple choice)

1. In which fund should the fixed assets of a central purchasing and stores department organized to serve all municipal departments be recorded?
   a. Enterprise Fund
   b. Internal Service Fund
   c. General Fund
   d. Capital Projects Fund
   e. Debt Service Fund

2. Which fund would a city use if it had a separate fund to hold and then remit to an insurance company the lump sum of hospital-surgical insurance premiums collected as payroll deductions from employees?
   a. General Fund
   b. Agency Fund
   c. Special Revenue Fund
   d. Internal Service Fund
   e. Private-Purpose Trust Fund

3. Which fund would be used to account for the activities of a municipal employee retirement plan that is financed by equal employer and employee contributions?
   a. Agency Fund
   b. Internal Service Fund
   c. General Fund

    d. Pension Trust Fund

    e. Private-Purpose Trust Fund

4. A transaction in which a municipal electric utility issues bonds (to be repaid from its own operations) requires accounting recognition in which fund?

    a. General Fund

    b. Debt Service Fund

    c. Capital Projects Fund

    d. Enterprise Fund

    e. Internal Service Fund

5. Which fund should be used to account for the operations of a public library receiving most of its support from property taxes levied for that purpose?

    a. General Fund

    b. Special Revenue Fund

    c. Enterprise Fund

    d. Internal Service Fund

    e. None of the above

6. In which fund should the liability for general obligation bonds issued for constructing a city hall and serviced from tax revenues be recorded?

    a. Enterprise Fund

    b. General Fund

    c. Capital Projects Fund

    d. Special Revenue Fund

    e. None of the above

7. To provide for the retirement of general obligation bonds, a city transfers a portion of its general revenue receipts to a separate fund. In which fund should the city account for receipt of the transfer?

    a. Public-Purpose Trust Fund

    b. Internal Service Fund

    c. Capital Projects Fund

    d. Special Revenue Fund

    e. None of the above

8. Which fund should be used to account for the operations of a municipal swimming pool receiving the majority of its support from charges to users?

    a. Special Revenue Fund

    b. General Fund

    c. Internal Service Fund

    d. Enterprise Fund

    e. None of the above

9. A city collects property taxes for the benefit of the sanitary, park, and school districts (all of which are legally separate governmental units) and periodically remits collections to these units. Which fund is used to account for this activity?

    a. Agency Fund

    b. General Fund

    c. Internal Service Fund

    d. Private-Purpose Trust Fund

    e. None of the above

10. Bay Creek's municipal motor pool maintains all city-owned vehicles and charges the various departments for the cost of rendering those services. In which of the following funds should Bay Creek account for the cost of such maintenance?

a. General Fund
b. Internal Service Fund
c. Special Revenue Fund
d. Enterprise Fund
e. None of the above

(AICPA adapted)

P2-13   (Financial statements used in governmental accounting)
Indicate which of the following fund financial statements generally would be prepared for each of the funds listed.

BS   Balance sheet (or statement of net assets)
SRECFB   Statement of revenues, expenditures, and changes in fund balance
SRECFNA   Statement of revenues, expenses, and changes in fund net assets
SCF   Statement of cash flows
SFNA   Statement of fiduciary net assets
SCFNA   Statement of changes in fiduciary net assets

___ **1.** General Fund
___ **2.** Special Revenue Funds
___ **3.** Debt Service Funds
___ **4.** Capital Projects Funds
___ **5.** Permanent Funds
___ **6.** Enterprise Funds
___ **7.** Internal Service Funds
___ **8.** Pension Trust Funds
___ **9.** Investment Trust Funds
___ **10.** Private-Purpose Trust Funds
___ **11.** Agency Funds

P2-14   (Comparison of financial statements)
Review the balance sheet and the operating statement for the General Fund (Tables 2-5 and 2-6) and the balance sheet and the operating statement for the Sewerage and Water Fund (Tables 2-8 and 2-9). Identify the major similarities and differences between each type of statement.

CHAPTER

3

BUDGETARY CONSIDERATIONS IN GOVERNMENTAL ACCOUNTING

Chapter Outline

After completing this chapter, you should be able to:

- Identify three types of budgets used by governmental units.
- Recognize that budgets of governmental units are legal documents.
- Understand the steps involved in preparing a budget.
- Discuss the contents of a budget document.
- Calculate the millage rate used by a governmental unit.
- Explain how budgets are used to control operations of governmental units.
- Understand the relationship between governmental budgeting and accounting.
- Prepare budgetary general journal entries.
- Prepare revenues and appropriations subsidiary ledgers.

Chapter 1 notes that commercial organizations are driven by one overriding goal, maximization of profits, whereas governmental units have many goals, all of which are considered important by their supporters and all of which compete for scarce resources. For example, a governmental unit may support police protection at the expense of street maintenance. Or it may determine that it will use available monies to support public housing, even though it needs to finance a program of economic development.

Whereas commercial organizations are governed by boards of directors and managers who generally hold similar views as to what and how activities should be conducted, governmental units are governed by elected bodies representing diverse constituencies. By their very nature, governmental units are faced with disparate goals and a high level of political competition for financial resources. The budgetary process provides for the orderly allocation of resources and reduces, to some extent, political influences.

A budget is a formal estimate of the resources that an organization plans to expend for specified purposes during a known time interval (typically, a fiscal year) and the proposed means of acquiring these resources. The budget conveys the activities the organization plans to undertake and how the organization expects to finance these activities. The budget thus acts as a standard against which efficiency and effectiveness can be measured. The budget represents public policy in that its adoption implies certain objectives, as well as the means of accomplishing these objectives, as determined by the legislative body. In addition to serving as a framework for operations, the budget often acts as a legal document for certain types of organizations, principally governmental units. Indeed, the budget has the force of law in most local governments. This means that revenues can be raised only from authorized sources (with legal maximum amounts specified) and that expenditures can be incurred only for authorized purposes and in amounts not to exceed authorized maximums, known as "appropriations."

Even if not required by law, the use of a budget is strongly recommended. The GASB, for example, expresses the need for budgets in the following principles:

1. An annual budget(s) should be adopted by every governmental unit.
2. The accounting system should provide the basis for appropriate budgetary control.
3. Budgetary comparisons should be presented as required supplementary information for the General Fund and for each major Special Revenue Fund that has a legally adopted annual budget.[1]

In this chapter we discuss budget laws, some types of budgets, the budget process, and budgetary accounting.

BUDGET LAWS

States usually have laws governing budgetary activities of local governmental units located within their borders. These laws deal with types of budgets to be prepared, funds required to have budgets, public input into the budgetary process, and the means of putting the budget into effect.

To encourage fiscal responsibility, the budget laws of nearly all states require a balanced budget. Generally, a budget is considered balanced if proposed expenditures do not exceed estimated monies available for the budget year. This latter amount is the sum of fund balances at the beginning of the year and estimated revenue. A few states take a more conservative approach to balanced budgets and define them as ones in which estimated revenues of the budget year equal or exceed the proposed expenditures of that year.

Despite these laws, a "fudge factor" often is associated with the balanced budget concept. For example, in some states the chief executive may be required to submit a balanced budget, but the legislative body is not required to adopt a balanced budget. In addition, under many balanced budget laws true "balance" can be avoided by not budgeting for certain expenditures that are attributable to the current period but not required to be paid in cash until subsequent years, such as pensions and postemployment health care benefits. Nonetheless, balanced budget requirements in government, even if imperfect, undoubtedly benefit taxpayers.

TYPES OF BUDGETS

Nonbusiness organizations prepare several types of budgets. They develop short- and long-term operating budgets and capital budgets and, in many cases, they prepare cash forecasts.

---

[1]GASB Cod. Sec. 1100.111

Operating Budgets

Operating budgets (also known as current budgets) are general-purpose budgets used by organizations to formalize their activities of a given period, usually a fiscal year. Virtually all governments prepare annual operating budgets for the General Fund and the more significant Special Revenue Funds. The budget document typically displays actual revenues and expenditures for the prior year and the current year to date, and the anticipated revenues and proposed expenditures for the budget year.

A budget provides information on the specific purpose of and services performed by each operating unit. It also provides information, for example, on (1) personnel and salaries, (2) proposed bond issues, (3) proposed methods of reducing costs, and (4) the cost of operating specific facilities and providing specific services. Because the budget is a highly visible legal document, great care should go into its preparation. In addition to using the budget for control purposes, a government should use it, along with the annual financial report, as a means of presenting its "story" to the public.

Capital Budgets

Capital budgets (also known as capital programs) articulate the plans of expenditures, and the means of financing these expected expenditures for long-lived or "capital" assets, such as land, buildings, and equipment. They usually cover a 4- to 6-year period. Many organizations maintain a "running" or "continuous" capital budget, adding a future year and dropping the earliest year when annual revisions are made. In fact, governments typically incorporate the current year of the capital budget into the operating budget for a fiscal year. Capital budgets are especially helpful when an organization needs to determine when and if it will be necessary to incur debt.

Cash Forecasts

Cash forecasts predict the amounts of cash to be received and expended during a particular period. Governmental units are likely to receive a large percentage of their revenues in an uneven manner during the year while their expenditures are generally spread out evenly over the year, possibly leading to cash shortages and surpluses at various times. Governments should develop cash forecasts to anticipate cash shortages and surpluses and thereby facilitate orderly short-term borrowing and investing. A cash forecast is shown in Table 3-1.

APPROACHES TO BUDGETING

Budgets are many and varied according to their intended purpose. Budgets can serve as contracts (legal documents), control mechanisms, means of communication, planning tools, and bases for the creation of short- and long-term policies. Depending on their intended usage, they can be prepared under one of several approaches: object of expenditure, performance, program and planning-programming budgeting, or zero-based budgeting. Budgets prepared under each approach differ as to what type of information they present and as to how expenditures are aggregated. Today, many departments or agencies within governmental units use the object-of-expenditure approach, so we illustrate the object-of-expenditure budget in this text.

The Object-of-Expenditure Approach

Under the object-of-expenditure approach (also known as the traditional or line-item approach), budgets are prepared to show, as line items, every category of expenditure

TABLE 3-1   Sample Cash Forecast

Wolverine City
General Fund
Cash Forecast
Second Quarter, 2008

	April	May	June	Quarter
Beginning cash balance	$ 12,000	$ 10,500	$ 16,350	$ 12,000
Cash receipts:				
Property taxes	$ 13,000	$ 28,000	$ 230,500	$ 271,500
Sales taxes	95,000	97,000	96,000	288,000
Fixed asset sales	500	1,000	3,000	4,500
Fines and penalties	15,000	15,000	18,000	48,000
License fees	5,500	3,000	1,600	10,100
Total cash receipts	$ 129,000	$ 144,000	$ 349,100	$ 622,100
Cash available[a]	$ 141,000	$ 154,500	$ 365,450	$ 634,100
Cash disbursements:				
Personal services	$ 56,000	$ 58,000	$ 57,500	$ 171,500
Travel	2,500	4,000	11,000	17,500
Operating expenses	32,000	36,000	35,500	103,500
Equipment	10,000	30,000	25,000	65,000
Transfers to Capital Projects Funds	130,000	—	82,000	212,000
Transfers to Debt Services Funds	—	—	50,000	50,000
Total disbursements	$ 230,500	$ 128,000	$ 261,000	$ 619,500
Minimum cash balance	10,000	10,000	10,000	$ 10,000
Total cash required	$ 240,500	$ 138,000	$ 271,000	$ 629,500
Excess (deficiency) of cash available over cash required	$ (99,500)	$ 16,500	$ 94,450	$ 4,600
Financing:				
Tax anticipation notes	$ 100,000	—	—	$ 100,000
Repayment of notes	—	$(10,000)	$(90,000)	(100,000)
Interest	—	(150)	(800)	(950)
Net financing	$ 100,000	$(10,150)	$(90,800)	$ (950)
Ending cash balance	$ 10,500	$ 16,350	$ 13,650	$ 13,650

[a]Before financing.

to be made during the year, described in terms of the physical good or service to be obtained by the government. Performance or program data may be included with an object-of-expenditure budget to support the various appropriation requests. The object-of-expenditure budget is well suited to the typical method of budget preparation, that is, by department.

Let's consider the types of expenditures government departments must make to operate. All departments need the services of their employees, electricity and water, and operating supplies, so at a minimum departmental budgets require appropriations for *current operating* items such as personal services, utilities, and materials and supplies. Additionally, payments made for temporary employees, for example, might require a contractual services appropriation.

Some departments, such as Police, Fire, and Streets, are "capital intensive" in that they particularly need motor vehicles and other special equipment for daily operations. Automobiles, firetrucks, dump trucks, and the like ordinarily last for several years. In any given year, however, a department might need to purchase vehicles to replace those that have worn out and/or to expand operations. Thus, government department budgets often include *capital outlay* appropriations for vehicle and equipment purchases. Additionally, many government departments lease photocopy machines and similar equipment. If the leases in question are capital leases, lease payments are chargeable to a *debt service* appropriation. (Payments for operating leases would be charged to a contractual services appropriation.) To summarize, a department budget always includes appropriations for a variety of current operating items (objects) and might also have appropriations for capital outlay and/or debt service objects. A portion of an object-of-expenditure budget is shown in Table 3-2.

THE BUDGET PROCESS

The budget process is a continuous cycle, wherein evaluation of this year's performance significantly influences next year's budget. The process itself can be broken down into the following steps, the order of which may vary among organizations:

1. Prepare budgetary policy guidelines.
2. Prepare the budget calendar.
3. Prepare and distribute budget instructions.
4. Prepare revenues estimates.
5. Prepare departmental (or program) expenditure requests.
6. Prepare nondepartmental expenditure and interfund transfer requests.
7. Prepare a capital outlay request summary (if appropriate).
8. Consolidate departmental expenditure requests, nondepartmental expenditure and interfund transfer requests, capital outlay requests, and revenues estimates. Submit to the Chief Executive Officer (CEO) for review and revision.
9. Prepare the budget document.
10. Present the budget document to the legislative body.
11. Hold public hearings on the budget.
12. Record the approved budget in the accounts.
13. Determine the property tax (millage) rate.

Budgetary Policy Guidelines

At the outset of the budgetary process, the CEO, the budget officer, and members of the legislative body should discuss the policies to be followed when preparing the budget. During these discussions, fiscal conditions of the current year should be reviewed, along with the prospects for the following year. In addition, the following points need to be considered:

1. The level of revenues collected to date and the level of revenues likely to be collected during the remainder of the year.
2. Possible increases or decreases in current taxes and fees, and ideas for new taxes and fees.

TABLE 3-2	Sample Object-of-Expenditure Budget

Orleans Levee Board
FY 20X9 Budget Presentation
Airport Safety

Acct. #	Account Name	Previous Actual FY 20X7	Approved Budget FY 20X8	Proposed FY 20X9
5410	Office supplies	$ 345	$ 1,572	$ 500
5411	Copier supplies	0	0	0
5412	Computer supplies	0	0	0
5431	Janitorial supplies	130	562	262
5432	Medical supplies	0	750	50
5433	Safety apparel and supplies	5,158	0	5,295
5434	Clothing supplies	8,129	10,875	10,000
5435	Police supplies	1,227	5,050	2,000
5436	Fire-fighting supplies	4,507	9,980	6,000
5437	Sodding/herbicides/fertilizer	0	0	0
5440	Improvements—other than buildings	0	0	0
5441	Hardware supplies	210	1,044	300
5442	Mounted patrol	0	0	0
5443	Dive team supplies	0	0	0
5451	Boat/motor/trailer—GOS	0	0	0
5452	Autos/trucks—GOS	8,447	7,706	9,000
5453	Tractors and grass cutters	120	0	0
5461	Buildings	36	0	0
5471	Airfield/runways/taxiway	0	0	0
5472	Bridges/floodgate/floodwall	0	0	0
5473	Grounds	0	0	0
5474	Levees	0	0	0
5475	Emergency supplies	0	0	0
5476	Fountain and pool supplies	0	0	0
5477	Piers, catwalks, bulkheads	0	0	0
5481	Miscellaneous equipment	0	0	0
5482	Autos (parts)	1,809	1,808	1,900
5483	Boats, motors, trailers	49	0	0
5484	Heavy construction equipment	0	0	0
5485	Office equipment—furniture	0	0	0
5486	Police	0	0	0
5487	Radio communications	194	0	0
5488	Recreational	0	0	0
5489	Tractors and grass cutters	0	0	0
5490	Trucks and trailers	0	0	0
5491	Hand tools and minor equipment	273	0	0
	Total material and supplies	$30,634	$39,347	$35,307

Source: A recent budget of the Orleans Levee Board.

3. Current and future economic conditions, as well as any possible developments that might affect the revenues or expenditures of the following year (e.g., a plant closing or the loss of a federal grant).
4. Items due the following fiscal year that might require an unusually large expenditure, such as the repayment of a bond issue.
5. The status of current-year revenues and expenditures and the possibility of a surplus (or deficit).

An analysis of these issues provides insight into potential financial problems a government may face during the following year. From the discussions of these issues, budgetary policies satisfactory to the legislative body, the CEO, and other affected parties should emerge. These policies should cover, at a minimum, the following:

1. Types of programs and services to be emphasized and deemphasized.
2. Changes in capital spending.
3. Permissible increases or decreases in taxes and fees.
4. Permissible merit salary increases.
5. Permissible cost-of-living adjustments.
6. Inflationary adjustments to be used.

The budgetary policies should be disseminated, in the form of *budgetary policy guidelines,* to all persons responsible for preparing and reviewing the various segments of the budget.

The Budget Calendar

For the budgetary process to proceed in an organized manner, certain deadlines must be met. A budget calendar formalizes all key dates in the budgetary process and often is specified by a government's laws. The calendar itself can be a simple listing of dates or it can be more complex (for example, a flowchart). At a minimum, it should list the steps of the budgetary process and the dates on which each of the various steps must be finished. More elaborate calendars often list who is responsible for each step and what data must be provided by whom and to whom. If each person involved in budget development is aware of when his or her budget input is due and if the time allotted to each task is reasonable, the process should proceed fairly smoothly. A sample budget calendar is shown in Table 3-3.

Budget Instructions

To disseminate the budgetary policy guidelines and to assist the various subunits in the preparation of their expenditure requests, a set of budget instructions should be prepared and sent to each person responsible for a segment of the budget. These instructions should be distributed with sufficient lead time to provide these persons sufficient time to prepare their budget requests properly.

In addition to copies of the forms and worksheets to be used, the budget instructions should contain the following:

1. A budget calendar.
2. A copy of the budgetary policy guidelines.
3. A statement summarizing the organization's anticipated fiscal condition for the following year.
4. A statement of specific policies to be followed when preparing expenditure requests.
5. A set of inflationary guidelines to be used in estimating the future costs of equipment, supplies, and so on.

TABLE 3-3	Typical Budget Calendar for a December 31 Fiscal Year
July 6	Departments receive instructions for the preparation of the budget.
August 15	Departmental expenditure requests are returned to the budget officer.
September 6–21	Departmental hearings are held with the mayor.
October 1–8	Review and preliminary presentation is made to the city council.
October 9–31	Budget is reviewed and finalized by the mayor.
November 5–18	Budget printing and production take place.
November 20	Mayor formally presents the budget to the city council.
November 21–December 15	City council conducts public hearings.
December 18	City council formally votes on the budget.
December 20–30	Budgetary information is entered into the computer.
January 1	New fiscal year begins.

6. Specific instructions on how each form and worksheet should be completed.

7. Instructions on where to seek help and clarification of any ambiguities.

Revenues Estimates

A key part of the budgetary process is determining the total amount of resources available for spending in the coming fiscal year. This determination requires the responsible individuals to:

1. Estimate probable fund balance in each fund at the end of the current year

2. Project revenues expected to be realized during the budget year

3. Summarize the estimates in a statement of estimated revenues (and transfers-in), such as the one illustrated in Table 3-4

Departmental Expenditure Requests

Expenditure requests should be prepared by each department, agency, or other subunit of the government. These documents show the total expenditures of the prior year, the total estimated expenditures for the current year, and the proposed amounts of expenditures for the budget year. Detailed supporting schedules for each major object of expenditure should accompany these requests. Such schedules help answer questions that may be raised by the budget officer, the CEO, or the legislative body.

Expenditure requests serve a number of purposes. First, they enable the CEO and the legislative body to evaluate the performance of each subunit. They also enable persons making budgetary decisions to determine the propriety of each request in terms of the goals of the entire organization, as opposed to the individual subunits; and when resources are limited, they enable these persons to allocate resources to those activities of each subunit that best serve the organization as a whole.

Finally, expenditure requests force department heads and other managers to take a close look at the objectives and the current levels of activity of their subunits and to determine whether operational improvements are possible. If managers wish to expand the scope of the activities of their subunits, they must be able to justify the additional expenditures.

TABLE 3-4 Statement of Actual and Estimated Revenues (and Transfers-In)

Fund: General
Date: September 15, 2008

Prepared by ____PNW____
Approved by ____LVT____

Acct. #	Source	2007 Actual	Jan.–Aug. 2008 Actual	Sept.–Dec. 2008 Est. Act.	Total 2008 Est. Act.	2008 Budget	2009 Budget	Remarks
1110	Property tax	$3,246,575	$1,384,300	$1,940,700	$3,325,000	$3,325,000	$3,550,000	Reassessment of property
1112	Liquor tax	355,240	235,650	124,350	360,000	354,000	480,000	International Exposition
1114	Sales tax	1,864,680	1,252,840	857,160	2,110,000	2,200,000	2,650,000	Same as above
1116	Royalty payments	385,000	245,000	120,000	365,000	375,000	300,000	Decline in gas production
1119	Fines and penalties	84,610	63,450	30,000	93,450	92,000	100,000	International Exposition
1121	Rental charges	8,500	6,500	3,500	10,000	9,500	11,000	Same as above
	Subtotal	$5,944,605	$3,187,740	$3,075,710	$6,263,450	$6,355,500	$7,091,000	
2010	Transfer from Enterprise Fund	122,000	—	145,000	145,000	145,000	150,000	Major events
	Total	$6,066,605	$3,187,740	$3,220,710	$6,408,450	$6,500,500	$7,241,000	

The following process should be applied to each line item when preparing departmental expenditure requests:

1. Determine the total amount of the expenditure for the past year and project the amount of the expenditure for the current year.
2. Apply inflation and cost-of-living factors and other allowances for "uncontrollable" factors to each current-year expenditure. This will result in a "stand-still" expenditure request.
3. Identify those activities to be expanded, scaled back, or discontinued. Identify any new activities that, if funded, will commence the following year.
4. Adjust each proposed expenditure for the changes in the type and level of activities identified in step 3.
5. Prepare a justification for each new activity or each increase in the level of an existing activity. Include in this justification the effect that not adopting, or increasing the level of, the activity will have on the organization.
6. Prepare a budgetary worksheet for each type of expenditure (personal services, contractual services, materials and supplies, etc.). The formats of the worksheets will vary with the type of expenditure being projected, although each worksheet should show the prior-year, current-year, and projected budget-year level of expenditures for each line item.
7. Summarize the information from each worksheet on the expenditure request.

Preparing a Budgetary Worksheet

Let's look at the steps involved in preparing a budgetary worksheet using the personal services (payroll) object of expenditure as our example. The heart of a personal services budget is the *position classification plan,* which lists all authorized position titles within a department and their corresponding salaries. From the plan, past and current personnel costs can be identified. The positions expected to be occupied during the budget year should be recorded on the personal services worksheet, along with the past, current, and projected rate or salary attached to each position.

Employee (fringe) benefits should be treated as a separate item, although they can be combined with salaries and wages on the budgetary worksheet. The simplest approach to handling this item of cost is to determine the total expenditures for the prior year or the current year to date and to divide this amount by the total payroll to obtain the employee benefit cost per payroll dollar. This ratio can then be used when determining the full cost of new positions or existing positions at new salary levels.

Employee benefits (Social Security, vacation pay, sick pay, and so on) are generally a function of salaries, so this method usually provides accurate data. However, the cost of certain benefits, such as paid dental insurance, may be fixed; that is, it may be the same for all employees regardless of salary level. Hence, those benefits may be budgeted based on an estimated amount per employee.

Other personal service costs that must be considered are overtime, shift differentials, and requests for temporary help. For example, on certain holidays it is sometimes necessary to ask police officers to work overtime to handle the crowds of parade watchers. In addition, some cities hire students to perform special tasks, such as street repairs, during the summer. These costs are usually known well in advance and can easily be determined by multiplying projected hours by appropriate pay and fringe benefit rates.

Table 3-5 shows a personal services budgetary worksheet for a police department. Notice that the worksheet explains the calculations made to develop requested

TABLE 3-5 Personal Services Worksheet

Fund: **General**
Function: **Public Safety**
Department: **Police**

Prepared by ___PE___
Approved by ___PRT___
Date: *September 15, 2008*

Code	Position Title	Prior-Year Actual			Current-Year Est. Actual			Budget Request[b]			Remarks
		No.	Rate[a]	Amount	No.	Rate[a]	Amount	No.	Rate[a]	Amount	
101	Chief	1	$51,300	$ 51,300	1	$54,000	$ 54,000	1	$59,474	$ 59,474	
102	Captain	2	44,888	89,775	2	47,250	94,500	2	52,324	104,648	
104	Lieutenant	4	38,475	153,900	4	40,500	162,000	4	42,903	171,612	
105	Detective	2	32,063	64,125	2	33,750	67,500	2	35,753	71,506	
106	Sergeant	5	29,925	149,625	5	31,500	157,500	5	33,369	166,845	
108	Police Officer	12	25,650	307,800	12	27,000	324,000	14	28,602	400,428	Two new positions[c]
	Total	26		$816,525	26		$859,500	28		$974,513	

[a]Includes employee benefits, which are budgeted at 13.5% of salaries and wages. This rate is 1% higher than the current rate because of an expected increase in the FICA rate (6%) and the state unemployment tax rate (.4%). The prior-year rate is 11.1% of salaries and wages. Actual salaries for the current year are expected to equal the amount budgeted.

[b]Includes a cost-of-living factor of 5.0% plus an additional merit increase of $2,000 each for the chief and captains.

[c]*Justification for new positions:* In the latter part of the current year, an area of 4 square miles was annexed. To provide an adequate level of protection in this area and the original parts of the city, an additional patrol unit is necessary. If this additional unit is denied, the annexed area containing 562 residents will receive inadequate police protection or the entire city will receive a lower level of protection due to the overextending of available personnel and equipment. In either case the level of crime can be expected to rise significantly if the additional unit is not approved.

TABLE 3-6   Departmental Expenditure Request

Fund:	General			Prepared by	BER
Function:	Public Safety			Approved by	PRT
Department: Police				Date: September 15, 2008	

Code	Object	Prior-Year Actual	Current-Year Budget	Current-Year Est. Actual	Budget Request
100	Personal services	$816,525	$859,500	$859,500	$ 974,513
200	Travel	4,600	4,800	4,800	5,350
3-600	Operating	60,500	61,600	61,450	62,350
700	Equipment	62,470	66,500	65,800	87,100
	Total	$944,095	$992,400	$991,550	$1,129,313

Narrative: The Police Department maintains law and order in the community. Major departmental expenditures are for personnel, operating, and equipment. Because of the increased area of the city, the department must add two police officers and an additional police cruiser. In addition, it must replace three police cruisers that have reached the end of their useful lives. Finally, the department must upgrade its communication system because of a recently passed law requiring that police departments throughout the state maintain comprehensive networks that are integrated into the state system.

amounts and justifies certain increases on the basis of expanded operational responsibilities.

When the worksheets for the various objects of expenditure are complete, summary information is transferred from these forms to the departmental expenditure request document. This schedule contains, at a minimum, the title of each object of expenditure, the level of prior- and current-year expenditures, and the requested level of expenditures for the budget year. It also may include a column in which the amount actually appropriated by the legislative body is recorded.

Some organizations summarize the requested level of expenditures by activity (e.g., vice squad, juvenile control, traffic control, and so on) and include this summary in a supplementary schedule. Such information can help the CEO and the members of the legislative body make judgments on the costs and benefits of specific activities. An expenditure request for a Police department is shown in Table 3-6.

Nondepartmental Expenditure and Interfund Transfer Requests

Nondepartmental expenditures are expenditures that do not relate to any one specific department or activity. Instead, they benefit the organization as a whole. Examples of nondepartmental expenditures include utility and maintenance costs of buildings used by several departments or programs (such as a city hall), interest on long-term debt, certain pension costs, and liability insurance premiums for city-owned vehicles. In addition, many organizations budget an amount to cover possible revenues shortfalls, emergencies, or contingencies (such as cleaning up after a flood). An interfund transfer is a movement of existing resources from one fund to another as necessary for operating purposes. Interfund transfers are classified separately from revenues and expenditures.

Amounts budgeted for nondepartmental expenditures and interfund transfers usually are determined by the budget officer or the CEO. A nondepartmental expenditure and interfund transfer request is shown in Table 3-7.

TABLE 3-7 Nondepartmental Expenditure and Interfund Transfer Request

Fund: General
Date: September 15, 2008

Prepared by ____CCW____
Approved by ____LVT____

Code	Object	Prior-Year Actual	Current-Year Budget	Current-Year Est. Actual	Budget Request	Remarks
730	City dues	$ 1,500	$ 1,500	$ 1,500	$ 1,500	
810	Repairs	—	—	3,000	20,000	Damage to city hall from dust storm
850	Legal settlements	150,000	120,000	210,000	200,000	Uninsured portion of damage claims
925	Audit fees	12,000	15,000	15,500	18,000	Inflation
930	Legal services	35,000	35,000	40,000	40,000	Inflation
950	Advertising	2,000	2,500	2,450	8,000	Promote International Exposition
970	Res. for contingencies	205,000	180,000	180,000	165,000	
980	Transfer to Debt Service Fund	500,000	500,000	500,000	1,300,000	Bond issue
	Total	$905,500	$854,000	$952,450	$1,752,500	

SERVICE EFFORTS AND ACCOMPLISHMENTS

Many organizations supplement their budget requests with data showing what they expect to accomplish during the year. These kinds of data are consistent with the current trend toward managing for results and service efforts and accomplishments reporting. The following data are typically provided for each of the major functions performed by a department:

1. Description of the function.
2. Inputs (service efforts)—numbers of personnel (and dollar amounts) and amounts of materials, supplies, and equipment needed to accomplish the function.
3. Outputs—quantities of services expected to be performed (e.g., number of lane miles of road expected to be maintained during the budget year).
4. Outcomes—the results expected to be achieved during the budget year (e.g., 85 percent of the lane miles will be rated as "very good" or better as a result of efforts made during the budget year).

Information presented on service efforts and accomplishments should, at a minimum, cover the past year, current year, and budget year. The performance measures (i.e., anticipated outputs and outcomes) should be used by departmental managers and the chief executive of the governmental unit to monitor performance during the year and to report to the public at year-end.

BUDGETARY REVIEW

The departmental expenditure request documents are submitted to the budget officer, along with the worksheets and any other supporting materials. The budget officer or a member of the staff determines whether each expenditure request document has been properly prepared and whether each requested item is appropriate, justified, and realistic. If the budget officer believes that the expenditure request documents have been properly prepared and that each item is appropriate, justified, and realistic, the budget officer incorporates the revenues estimates and expenditure requests into the budget summary. The budget summary is then forwarded to the CEO. The CEO reviews the information and prepares recommendations for the legislative body. A budget summary is shown in Table 3-8.

Determining whether expenditure request documents have been properly prepared is a relatively simple procedure. It consists primarily of ascertaining that all requested information has been provided, that the arithmetic on each form is correct, and that no errors have been made when transferring information from one form to another.

Determining whether each requested item is justified, realistic, and appropriate is more difficult. The budget officer must determine the need for each activity and level of service, the validity of the assumptions underlying each budgetary calculation, and whether each requested item falls within the budgetary guidelines. If a requested item exceeds these guidelines, the budget officer must determine why and whether the additional request is justified.

The budget officer should have close contact with department heads, program directors, and other persons responsible for preparing expenditure requests. A budget

TABLE 3-8   Budget Summary

Fun City General Fund
Budget Summary Fiscal Year 2009

Estimated Revenues

Property tax	$ 3,550,000	
Liquor tax	480,000	
Sales tax	2,650,000	
Royalty payments	300,000	
Fines and penalties	100,000	
Rental charges	11,000	$ 7,091,000

Appropriations

Administration:			
Personal services	$435,000		
Travel	22,400		
Operating expenditures	85,800		
Equipment	24,600	$ 567,800	
Fire:			
Personal services	$665,104		
Travel	12,500		
Operating expenditures	235,000		
Equipment	146,250	1,058,854	
Parks:			
Personal services	$215,573		
Travel	1,850		
Operating expenditures	82,350		
Equipment	72,300	372,073	
Police:			
Personal services	$974,513		
Travel	5,350		
Operating expenditures	62,350		
Equipment	87,100	1,129,313	
Streets:			
Personal services	$314,646		
Travel	1,150		
Operating expenditures	103,360		
Equipment	146,000	565,156	
Nondepartmental:			
City dues	$ 1,500		
Repairs	20,000		
Legal settlements	200,000		
Audit fees	18,000		
Legal services	40,000		
Advertising	8,000		
Reserve for contingencies	165,000	452,500	4,145,696
Excess of revenues over appropriations			$ 2,945,304

Other Financing Sources (Uses)

Transfer from Enterprise Fund	$ 150,000	
Transfer to Debt Service Fund	(1,300,000)	(1,150,000)
Excess of revenues and other sources over expenditures and other uses		$1,795,304
Estimated fund balance—January 1, 2009		1,000,000
Estimated fund balance—December 31, 2009		$ 2,795,304

officer who believes that a request is questionable should meet with the person who prepared the request to resolve the matter. If the matter cannot be resolved at this level, the person preparing the request should have the right to appeal to the CEO.

In most governments, the budget officer is responsible for ensuring that the total proposed expenditures do not exceed total budgeted resources (the sum of estimated revenues plus fund balance expected at the end of the current year). Because the total expenditure requests often exceed budgeted resources, even after the screening process discussed previously, and because of balanced-budget requirements, the budget officer is usually forced to decide which requests should be included in the budget document without modification and which requests should be reduced or eliminated.

The final review of the expenditure requests is made by the CEO. The data from the various subunits should be presented to this executive in summary form, with supporting materials readily available. The purposes of the final review are (1) to obtain the input of the CEO into the budgetary process, (2) to act as a court of last resort for disputes between the budget officer and the persons preparing the expenditure requests, and (3) to enable the CEO to prepare specific budget recommendations before submitting them to the legislative body.

A sound approach to the final review is to have each person responsible for preparing expenditure requests brief the CEO on those requests and provide supporting data or evidence that the CEO can use when presenting the budget to the legislative body. If the CEO has been involved in the budgetary process from its inception and if all differences between the views of the budget officer and those of the persons responsible for preparing the expenditure requests have been resolved, this final review can be a positive experience.

THE BUDGET DOCUMENT

After completion of the final review, the budget officer assembles the budget requests, the revenues projections, and the CEO's recommendations into a comprehensive budget document, which is presented to the legislative body. The magnitude of a budget document can range from one to several volumes, depending on the organization's size and complexity. At a minimum, a budget document should contain the following elements:

1. A *budget message,* which, in general terms, discusses the following:
    a. The fiscal experience of the current year
    b. The present financial position of the organization
    c. Major financial issues faced during the past year and ones expected during the budget year
    d. Assumptions used when preparing budget requests (e.g., expected rate of inflation)
    e. Significant revenues and expenditure changes from the current year's budget
    f. New program initiatives and anticipated accomplishments during the year
    g. Significant budgetary changes resulting from the proposed new program initiatives, such as increased numbers of personnel and new debt issues
    h. The future economic outlook of the organization

2. A *budget summary,* which lists the total budgeted revenues by source, and lists the total budgeted expenditures by program or department and for the organization as a whole
3. *Detailed supporting schedules,* among which should be the following schedules:
   a. Estimated revenues by source
   b. Departmental and nondepartmental expenditure requests
   c. Budgeted fixed charges such as the repayment of debt
4. A *capital projects schedule*
5. *Detailed justifications of the budgetary recommendations*
6. *Supplementary information,* such as
   a. Departmental budget request worksheets
   b. Departmental work programs
   c. Pro forma balance sheets for each fund, as of the beginning and the end of the budget year
   d. A cash forecast
   e. A schedule of interest payments, sinking fund contributions, and bond issues and retirements
7. Drafts of appropriation and tax levy ordinances or acts

LEGISLATIVE CONSIDERATION AND ADOPTION OF THE BUDGET

The completed budget document is sent to the legislative body, which reviews, modifies, approves, and adopts it. Before approving the budget document, the legislative body usually conducts administrative hearings. In some cases the budget document is furnished to a legislative finance or ways-and-means committee for review and comment.

At a designated meeting, the CEO formally presents the budget document to the legislative body. This presentation should include a general overview of the contents of the budget document, a discussion of the assumptions made when preparing the budget document, and a discussion of any major financial difficulties that the organization will face during the budget year. The revenues estimates and budget requests should also be reviewed, as should the justification for each new or nonroutine request.

Many organizations are required by law to hold public hearings on the budget. Citizen input to budgetary decisions is obtained by allowing interested parties to offer their views on the budget to the legislative body. The process of budgetary approval is expedited if copies of the budget document (or a summary) are disseminated to the members of the legislative body and to the public in advance of public hearings and the formal presentation. If the users of the budget document are allowed a reasonable amount of time to digest its contents, issues of concern can readily be identified and the public hearings and deliberations of the legislative body will proceed more smoothly.

When the budget hearings conclude, the legislative body completes its deliberations, makes any modifications to the budget document it believes are necessary, and enacts a final appropriation ordinance or, in the case of a state, appropriation act. The purpose of this ordinance or act is to establish a spending ceiling for the budget year and to authorize the organization to make the expenditures listed in the budget.

After the appropriation ordinance or act has been passed, the budget document is returned to the organization, where the budgeted amounts are entered into the accounts. Most governmental units also publish their approved budget.

PROPERTY TAX LEVY

After approval of the budget, the legislative body must raise revenues necessary to finance the budgeted expenditures. The collection of many types of revenues does not require frequent action on the part of the legislative body. These revenues are usually the result of past actions (e.g., license fees, sales taxes, income from investments, and so on). Other revenues measures, however, require legal action more frequently, the most common example being property taxes.

Two approaches can be used to determine the taxes to be assessed on each piece of property. Under the first approach, the assessed value of the property (less any exemptions) is multiplied by a flat rate, which is "permanently" fixed by law. Under the second and more common approach, the property taxes are assessed on the basis of a government's fiscal need (subject to legal limits).

Before an organization using the second approach can send tax bills to the property owners, it must determine a tax (millage) rate that, when applied to the assessed valuation of the property, will provide the desired amount of revenue. This amount is usually shown as part of the revenues estimates in the budget. Although simple in concept, the second approach can become complicated because of (1) uncollectible or delinquent taxes and (2) property exempt from taxation (such as land belonging to religious organizations) and exemptions due to the military service, age, physical condition, and economic status of the owner, and the use of the property as a homestead. This last exemption can be particularly costly to taxing organizations. In Louisiana, for example, the homestead exemption is applied to the first $75,000 of the current market value of any piece of property used as the principal residence of its owner.

Using this approach, Fun City would compute its tax (millage) rate as follows:

Amount to be collected (from Table 3-8)	$ 3,550,000
Estimated uncollectible property taxes (assumed)	4%
Required tax levy ($3,550,000/.96)	$ 3,697,917
Total assessed value of property (assumed)	$ 80,000,000
Less: Property not taxable (assumed)	(2,000,000)
	$ 78,000,000
Less: Exemptions (assumed)	
Homestead	$ 1,000,000
Veterans	500,000
Old age, blindness, etc.	900,000
	2,400,000
Net assessed value of property	$ 75,600,000

Tax (Millage) Rate = Required Tax Levy / Net Assessed Value of Property
= $3,697,917 / $75,600,000
= .0489

In this example, the property tax will be levied at the rate of $4.89 per $100 of net assessed valuation. If the tax rate is expressed in mills (thousandths of a dollar), it will be 48.90 mills. Thus, the owner of a piece of property with a net (after exemptions) assessed value of $200,000 will be required to pay property taxes of $9,780 ($200,000 × .0489).

USING BUDGETARY INFORMATION

One purpose of budgets is to provide a measure or "standard" against which actual results can be measured. If, for example, a department has spent 50 percent of its personal services budget after only 4 months have elapsed, there is a strong possibility that it will have insufficient budget authority to complete the year. Why did this occur and what action needs to be taken? Thus, by comparing actual expenditures with budgeted appropriations, managers, legislators, and other decision makers can judge the organization's financial performance and can take corrective action when necessary.

A good budget, however, is more than a statement of anticipated revenues and expenditures. It is also a statement of anticipated accomplishments and priorities. Therefore, as suggested previously, the budget also should be used to control program performance.

Many governments produce monthly statements for internal use that detail budgeted and actual expenditures, by object, and the remaining amount available for spending. This latter piece of information is particularly important to organizations that are subject to antideficiency laws (laws that make the overspending of one's budget an act subject to civil and/or criminal penalties), as well as to those managers whose performance is judged, in some measure, by whether they meet their budgets. In addition, knowledge of this amount is helpful to organizational personnel when they plan the activities of their work unit for the remainder of the fiscal year. If the spending rate is greater than originally planned, their unit must curtail its activities or ask for a supplemental appropriation from the legislative body. If the remaining amount available for spending is higher than originally planned, the unit can expand its activities.

An example budgetary control report (budget comparison) is illustrated in Table 3-9. In addition to showing the budget for the current month and the year to date, it shows (1) actual expenditures incurred for these periods; (2) differences between budgeted and actual expenditures (called variances), in both absolute numbers and as a percentage of budget; and (3) amounts that can be spent for the remainder of the year without exceeding the budget. If the amount spent is less than the amount budgeted, a favorable (F) variance is shown. If the amount spent is more than the amount budgeted, an unfavorable (U) variance is shown.

The budgetary control report in Table 3-9 is presented in one of several possible formats and is based on the 2008 (current-year) budget. For example, some organizations include the following month's budget in the budgetary control report. Regardless of the format used, the report should meet the organization's needs, all users should be able to understand the report, and use of the report should be strongly encouraged by the government's management and legislative body.

To control program performance, budgetary control reports should be supplemented with budgetary performance reports. Anticipated performance set forth in the submitted budget should be used to develop measures of actual performance. When this is done, anticipated performance (expressed in terms of expected quantities of outputs and outcomes) becomes a benchmark for measuring what actually happens during the year. The resulting reports (usually prepared monthly, but no less frequently than quarterly) help department managers and the chief executive to manage for results. When also used to report to the public, budgetary performance reports help governmental managers demonstrate accountability.

TABLE 3-9 Budgetary Control Report

Fund: General
Function: Public Safety
Department: Police

Prepared by RGS
Date: September 30, 2008

| Year to Date | | | | | | Current Month | | | | Available |
Budget	Actual	Variance	% Budget	Code	Object-of-Expenditure	Budget	Actual	Variance	% Budget	for Spending
					Contractual Services					
$ 75	$ 60	$ 15(F)	20	301	Advertising	$ 8	$ 10	$ 2(U)	25	$ 40
1,200	1,300	100(U)	8	310	Printing	133	120	13(F)	10	300
6,000	6,200	200(U)	3	320	Vehicle maintenance	667	645	22(F)	3	1,800
4,200	3,900	300(F)	7	330	Communication	467	378	89(F)	19	1,700
150	180	30(U)	20	350	Dues and subscriptions	17	21	4(U)	24	20
225	200	25(F)	11	360	Postage	25	30	5(U)	20	100
450	550	100(U)	22	370	Telephone	50	35	15(F)	30	50
300	300	—	1	380	Professional services	33	0	33(F)	100	100
$ 12,600	$ 12,690	$ 90(U)			Subtotal	$ 1,400	$ 1,239	$ 161(F)	12	$ 4,110
					Supplies and Materials					
$ 825	$ 850	$ 25(U)	3	401	Office supplies	$ 92	$ 97	$ 5(U)	5	$ 250
3,525	3,595	70(U)	2	410	Building maintenance	392	370	22(F)	6	1,105
7,875	7,750	125(F)	2	420	Fuel	875	825	50(F)	6	2,750
$546,375	$563,430	$17,055(U)	3		Grand total	$60,708	$63,386	$2,678(U)	4	$165,070

Budgetary comparisons also appear in external annual financial reports. The Governmental Accounting Standards Board (GASB) requires that annual financial reports include budgetary comparison statements or schedules for the General Fund and each major Special Revenue Fund with a legally adopted budget. These schedules should show (1) the original adopted budget, (2) the final appropriated budget, and (3) actual revenues and expenditures on the budgetary basis of accounting.[2]

CLASSIFYING REVENUES AND EXPENDITURES

The budget has tremendous influence on government financial operations in general and on some of the particulars of government accounting practices. Indeed, a long-standing convention in government accounting is that budgetary and accounting systems should be integrated and use common classifications and terminology as much as possible.

In this section, we introduce the classification system widely used by governments for both budgeting and accounting. The classification scheme for revenues is fairly simple. In contrast, the classification scheme for expenditures is more complex, due to the need for accountability—and thus control—over spending.

Revenue Classification

Revenues should be budgeted and accounted for at a minium by (1) fund and (2) source within that fund. Typical sources of revenues include taxes, charges for services, fines and forfeits, fees for licenses and permits, interest on investments, and intergovernmental revenues (grants received from other governments). Many governments also subclassify revenues within a larger source, such as property taxes and sales taxes within the "taxes" source classification.

The total amount of any particular revenues source may be accounted for in a single fund or in several funds. For instance, a portion of property taxes may be earmarked to finance "general government" operations, such as public safety, while another portion of the property tax is intended to finance library operations. If the library is accounted for in a Special Revenue Fund, for instance, that portion of property tax proceeds designated for library operations is budgeted and accounted for in the appropriate Special Revenue Fund, while the general government portion of property taxes is budgeted and accounted for in the General Fund.

Practice varies as to the mechanics of recording revenues apportioned among funds. In some governments, the General Fund initially accounts for all property tax receipts and subsequently transfers the proper share to the Special Revenue Fund. In other governments, the General Fund and Special Revenue Fund each account only for their respective shares of total property tax revenue.

Expenditure Classification

Governments are strictly accountable to their citizens for monies spent to achieve governmental objectives. The need both to be accountable and to demonstrate accountability leads governments to use up to five levels of subclassification in budgeting and accounting for expenditures. This extensive detail provides structure for

---

[2]GASB Cod. Sec. 100.111.

budget development and enables accumulation of expenditure data in various combinations to facilitate reporting and analysis.

Before examining the specifics of the expenditure classification system, it is useful to understand the concept of the *legal level of budgetary control.* This refers to the level of subclassification within the expenditures budget at which expenditures cannot legally exceed budgeted amounts. The level of control is defined in budgetary or organizational terms, for example, by fund (the highest level), by government department (an intermediate level), or by "object of expenditure" (a low level). Should it become necessary or desirable to spend more than the total appropriation at the legal level of control, permission for the additional spending must be obtained from the governing body (for example, the city council) in the form of a budget amendment. In this manner, the legal level of budgetary control promotes accountability over spending.

The five expenditure classification levels and an example of each are as follows:

Fund	the General Fund
Function/Program	Public Safety
Organizational Unit	Police Department
Activity	Neighborhood Patrol
Object	Personal Services (i.e., Payroll)

The *fund* classification level is obvious and needs no further explanation. *Functions* and *programs* are almost synonymous from a practical standpoint. A function is a group of related activities intended to accomplish a major government responsibility; a program is a group of activities directed toward attaining specific objectives. *Organizational unit* refers to specific departments of the government (Fire, Police, Administration, etc.). The *activity* subclassification is largely self-explanatory. Examples of activities within a Fire Department are fire prevention and fire suppression. Examples of Police Department activities include patrol and crime investigation.

Finally, the *object* ("object-of-expenditure") classification refers to the physical description of items purchased or services received; for example, personal services (payroll), contractual services such as rent payments, materials and supplies, debt service, and capital outlay. The object-of-expenditure classification is particularly important from a budgetary standpoint because, as we noted earlier, many governments develop their budgets by department and then by object codes within each department. Indeed, individual line items generally are the "building blocks" of a budget. Also, individual expenditures usually are made at the object level, so comparing budgeted amounts with actual expenditures in terms of objects-of-expenditure is particularly useful for control.

Although this multilevel classification system is somewhat complex, it is not as intimidating to work with as it may seem at first. This is because the lower level subclassifications "roll up" into higher level subclassifications. For example, all the object-of-expenditure amounts within any specified activity will define the budget for that activity. In turn, the sum of the budgeted amounts for all the activities within a department define that department's total budget, and so forth. Table 3-10 presents a diagram of the expenditure classification "roll-ups."

Finally, note that particular reporting situations rarely require that all five classifications be employed simultaneously. For example, external financial reporting requires

TABLE 3-10   Diagram of Expenditure Classification "Roll-Up" Relationships

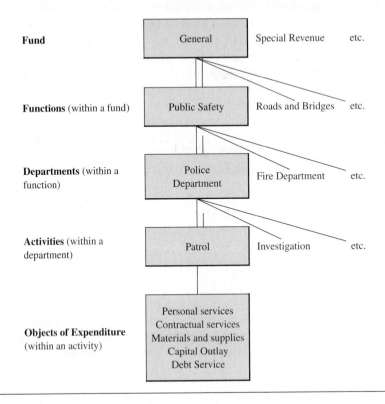

only that expenditures be classified by fund, function/program, and character.[3] Similarly, an internal analysis of the Fire Department, for example, would focus on expenditures by organizational unit, activity, and object of expenditure.

A practical consequence of the legal level of budgetary control is that it determines the extent to which a government manager may use discretion in determining the amounts and purposes for which expenditures are incurred. A high level of budgetary control affords a manager considerable spending discretion, while a low level grants the manager minimum flexibility in making spending decisions.

To illustrate, if a government has defined the legal level of control at the fund level, a manager has the authority to allocate the fund's total appropriation as she sees fit among the various operations (e.g., functions and departments) accounted for within that fund. For example, should circumstances require, the city manager could reallocate part of the Fire Department's appropriation to the Police Department

---

[3]In external fund-level operating statements, governments must classify expenditures by "character" according to whether they are *current operating, capital outlay,* or *debt service* in nature. Classifying by character is readily accomplished by aggregating capital outlay and debt service expenditures according to object code. The remaining expenditures (such as for personal services and supplies) represent *current operating* items. In very small governments, the operating statement may present current operating expenditures by individual object code within functions/programs. Larger governments usually report current operating expenditures only at the function/program level.

within the General Fund without seeking legislative approval. The Fire Department would have less spending authority and the Police Department would have more such authority, but the overall General Fund appropriation would remain unchanged.

If the legal level of budgetary control is established at, say, the department level, the department executive has authority to allocate the department appropriation to various activities as he sees fit but may not incur expenditures in excess of the department appropriation. For example, the fire chief would decide how much of the Fire Department appropriation should be spent for fire prevention activities versus for fire suppression activities and the objects of expenditure within each activity. However, the chief could not legally spend more than the appropriation made for the Fire Department.

If a government establishes the legal level of budgetary control at the object-of-expenditure level within each specified activity, a department manager has minimal flexibility to redirect spending. For instance, the fire chief might wish to hire as full-time a temporary employee who is particularly capable. The cost of the temporary employee presently is charged to the Fire Department's contractual services appropriation but would be chargeable to the department's personal services appropriation if the employee were hired full time. Because the legal level of budgetary control is at the object level, the chief cannot reallocate some of the contractual services appropriation to the personal services appropriation to provide for the new full-time hire without seeking the necessary budget amendment.

BUDGETARY ACCOUNTING

The importance of the budget in government accounting is epitomized by *budgetary accounting*—the formal recording of budget components within the accounting system to facilitate financial control. Budget and actual information is recorded in the general ledger; ledger balances are used to develop reports for managerial review.

In its simplest form, budgetary accounting involves recording (1) *estimated revenues,* for comparison with actual revenues, and (2) *appropriations,* to monitor expenditures. To illustrate, assume that the city council of Tiny Town has approved the budget shown in Table 3-11 for its General Fund.

TABLE 3-11 Illustrative Operating Budget		
Tiny Town *General Fund Budget* *January 2008*		
Estimated Revenues		
Property taxes	$900,000	
Miscellaneous	100,000	$1,000,000
Appropriations		
Salaries	$700,000	
Materials	190,000	
Police cars	100,000	990,000
Budgeted Increase in Fund Balance		$ 10,000

At the beginning of the fiscal year, Tiny Town makes the following General Fund entry:

1. Estimated revenues   1,000,000
       Appropriations   990,000
       Budgetary fund balance   10,000
   To record the FY 2008 budget.

To best understand this entry, it is useful to decompose it into two parts. First, Tiny Town could record estimated revenues in this manner:

2. Estimated revenues   1,000,000
       Budgetary fund balance   1,000,000
   To record estimated revenues for FY 2008.

The debit to estimated revenues predicts the effect, in isolation, that *actual* revenues will have on the fund balance at the end of the year—that is, actual revenues are predicted to be $1,000,000 and, by themselves, would increase fund balance by $1,000,000. Likewise, Tiny Town could record its planned expenditures—that is, its budget appropriation—as follows:

3. Budgetary fund balance   990,000
       Appropriations   990,000
   To record appropriations for FY 2008.

This entry in essence identifies the amount of fund net assets (fund balance) that Tiny Town plans to spend during fiscal year 2008. That is, expenditures are predicted (authorized) to be $990,000 and, by themselves, would reduce the fund balance by that amount.

The $10,000 credit balance in the budgetary fund balance account—from entry 1 or from the combined effect of entries 2 and 3—indicates that Tiny Town expects a budget surplus for the year.[4] That is, if actual revenues and expenditures prove to be exactly as budgeted, the ending actual fund balance will increase by $10,000 (actual revenues of $1,000,000, less expenditures of $990,000 = $10,000). Conversely, if appropriations exceed estimated revenue, the resulting *debit* balance in the budgetary fund balance account would signal that Tiny Town anticipates a budget deficit for the year.

In practice, the budgetary entry normally is prepared in compound form, as shown at entry 1. Note that at the end of the fiscal year the budget will have served its purpose. Accordingly, Tiny Town will reverse the budgetary entry as part of the year-end closing process, leaving only "actual" account balances in the general ledger.

Control Relationships

The purpose of recording estimated revenues and appropriations is to establish financial reference points for budget administration. At any time during the year, government officials can compare the balance of estimated revenues with that of actual

---

[4]Some writers and practitioners prefer to credit Unreserved fund balance, rather than Budgetary fund balance, when recording the budget. The authors of this text do not recommend this practice because it (a) creates the appearance of increases or decreases in actual fund balance before changes actually occur; (b) may mislead unsophisticated preparers and users of financial reports; and (c) needlessly confuses budgetary accounting with financial accounting.

revenues to see whether actual revenues are meeting expectations. Similarly, the balance of expenditures can be compared at any point with the appropriations balance as a check on spending.

Encumbrances

In practice, budgetary accounting also incorporates *encumbrance* entries to account for the effect on the available appropriation of items *ordered* by a government but not yet received. Recall that a business entity ordinarily makes three entries related to the purchase and use of supplies: one entry to record the liability for the purchase, a second to record payment of the liability, and a third entry (or series of entries) to record supplies used. Businesses do not make formal accounting entries to record items on order. In contrast, from a government budgetary perspective, a portion of the appropriation effectively is "used up" or *encumbered* at the point a government orders supplies—even though the supplies have not yet been received. Thus, a government may make four entries related to the purchase and use of supplies: The first entry encumbers the appropriation for the cost of an order placed with a vendor, a second entry records the liability for the purchase, a third records payment of the liability, and a fourth entry (or series of entries) records supplies used.

At the point it issues a purchase order, a government expresses its intent to incur an expenditure (a reduction of net assets). From a financial accounting standpoint, the expenditure is not recognized until the related liability is incurred, typically when the ordered materials are received. From a budgetary accounting standpoint, however, the purchase order uses up a portion of the appropriation. The government gives formal accounting recognition to the order by recording an *encumbrance* equal to the purchase order amount. If Tiny Town were to issue a purchase order for $1,000, the entry to record the encumbrance would be this:

Encumbrances	1,000	
Budgetary fund balance reserved for encumbrances		1,000
To record encumbrance for purchase order.		

The encumbrance (debit) reduces the net available appropriation. The "budgetary fund balance reserved for encumbrances" is in effect a placeholder for the ensuing liability. When the open purchase order is fulfilled (i.e., ordered items are received), the encumbrance entry is reversed and an expenditure is recorded. Assuming that the cost of goods received equals the cost of goods ordered, Tiny Town would make the following two entries:

Budgetary fund balance reserved for encumbrances	1,000	
Encumbrances		1,000
To reverse encumbrances.		
Expenditures	1,000	
Cash (or Vouchers Payable)		1,000
To record expenditure for purchased materials.		

Thus, at any time, the available appropriation equals the *total appropriation* less the *encumbrances balance* less the *expenditures balance*. Note that the purpose of recording encumbrances is to provide control over an appropriation characterized by expenditures that are unpredictable as to timing and/or amounts, or in cases in which a single appropriation supports geographically dispersed activities. In contrast, some appropriations are drawn down by expenditures in predictable patterns, (for example, monthly payments on a photocopier lease). For such appropriations, encumbrances serve no worthwhile control purpose and need not be recorded.

Dealing with Detail

Recall that the purpose of budgetary accounting is to facilitate financial control by enabling government managers to compare actual revenues with estimated revenues and expenditures with available appropriations. We have discussed the basic general journal entries associated with budgetary accounting. As we have seen, though, governments prepare budgets and record actual transactions in considerable detail. Thus, our remaining task is to understand how this detail is recorded and summarized in the accounting system in a way that is useful for monitoring day-to-day operations. Government accounting systems achieve these objectives (1) through the use of detailed general ledger accounts and (2) by posting the entries to revenues and appropriations subsidiary ledgers. Each general ledger account, of course, is posted only with the activity that applies to that account. In contrast, the subsidiary ledgers are posted with activity from related accounts (i.e., estimated revenues versus actual revenues, and appropriations versus encumbrances plus expenditures) to provide budget-to-actual comparisons.

Now we will illustrate the accounting for the detail comprising total estimated revenues and the total appropriation. Assume the following additional background information for Tiny Town: Tiny Town's government performs only one function, public safety, administered through one department, Police, and accounted for in a single fund, the General Fund. The legal level of budgetary control is the object level. This scenario is, of course, highly simplified from reality for ease of illustration. Refer again to Tiny Town's January 2008 budget in Table 3-11. Estimated property tax revenues are $900,000 and estimated miscellaneous revenues are $100,000. The appropriation includes two current operating line items, $700,000 for salaries and $190,000 for materials, and a capital outlay line item, $100,000 for purchase of four police cars. Actual events and transactions for January 2008 are as follows:

Date

January 2	The budget is recorded.
3	$500,000 of property taxes are received in cash.
8	Two police cars are ordered at an estimated total cost of $46,000.
12	The first two cars are received at an invoiced cost of $45,000.
15	Miscellaneous revenues totaling $103,000 are received in cash.
16	The second two police cars are ordered at an estimated total cost of $54,000.
21	The second two police cars are received with an invoice for $55,000.
22	Remaining property taxes of $399,500 are received in cash.
25	Materials are ordered with an expected cost of $190,000.
28	The ordered materials are received, along with an invoice for $188,000.
31	Payday for Tiny Town's employees is the last day of the month; salaries of $700,000 are paid.

Here is how the Tiny Town transactions are recorded in general journal form and how the entries affect the Revenues ledger (Table 3-12) and Appropriations ledger (Table 3-13):

TABLE 3-12   Illustrative Revenues Ledger

Tiny Town
General Fund
Revenues Ledger
January 2008

Source: Property Taxes

Date	Item	Estimated Revenues Dr	Actual Revenues Cr	Difference Dr (Cr)
2	Budget	900,000		900,000
3	Cash Receipts		500,000	400,000
22	Cash Receipts		399,500	500

Source: Miscellaneous

Date	Item	Estimated Revenues Dr	Actual Revenues Cr	Difference Dr (Cr)
2	Budget	100,000		100,000
15	Cash Receipts		103,000	(3,000)

Jan. 2	Estimated revenues—property taxes	900,000	
	Estimated revenues—miscellaneous	100,000	
	Appropriations—salaries		700,000
	Appropriations—materials		190,000
	Appropriations—police cars		100,000
	Budgetary fund balance		10,000
	To record the budget in the general ledger.		

Note that the debit items in the above entry are posted by revenues source in the Estimated Revenues column of the Revenues ledger and the credits to appropriations are posted by object of expenditure in the appropriations columns of the Appropriations ledger on page 84. (The credit to the Budgetary fund balance is not posted to either subsidiary ledger.) The balance column of the Revenues ledger now shows debit balances of $900,000 for property taxes and $100,000 for miscellaneous revenue, indicating that no actual revenues have yet been received. In the Appropriations ledger, the Available Appropriations column shows balances for each object of expenditure as of January 2 equal to the full appropriations for those objects. That is, the appropriations have not yet been reduced by encumbrances and/or expenditures.

Jan. 3	Cash	500,000	
	Revenues—property taxes		500,000
	To record receipt of property taxes in the general ledger.		

The credit to revenues from this entry is posted by source to the *actual* revenues column of the Revenues ledger; the resulting $400,000 balance indicates that this amount of property tax revenues remains to be realized to meet the budget estimate.

Jan. 8	Encumbrances—police cars	46,000	
	Budgetary fund balance reserved for encumbrances		46,000
	To record encumbrance for purchase of police cars.		

TABLE 3-13   Illustrative Appropriations Ledger

Tiny Town
General Fund
Appropriations Ledger
January 2008

Object Code: Personal Services

Date	Item	Appropriation Cr	Encumbrances Dr	Encumbrances Cr	Expenditures Dr	Available Appropriation Cr
2	Budget	700,000				700,000
31	Payroll				700,000	0

Object Code: Materials

Date	Item	Appropriation Cr	Encumbrances Dr	Encumbrances Cr	Expenditures Dr	Available Appropriation Cr
2	Budget	190,000				190,000
25	Order materials		190,000			0
28	Receive materials			190,000		190,000
28	Record expenditure				188,000	2,000

Object Code: Police Cars

Date	Item	Appropriation Cr	Encumbrances Dr	Encumbrances Cr	Expenditures Dr	Available Appropriation Cr
2	Budget	100,000				100,000
8	Order 2 vehicles		46,000			54,000
12	Receive 2 vehicles			46,000		100,000
12	Record expenditure				45,000	55,000
16	Order 2 vehicles		54,000			1,000
21	Receive 2 vehicles			54,000		55,000
21	Record expenditure				55,000	0

The debit to encumbrances from the January 8 entry on page 83 is posted to the Encumbrances column of the Appropriations ledger for the Police Cars object. The resulting $54,000 balance in the Available Appropriation column shows that this is the amount of the Police Car appropriation remaining for future spending.

Jan. 12	Budgetary fund balance reserved for encumbrances	46,000	
	Encumbrances—police cars		46,000
	To reverse encumbrance for purchase of police cars.		
	Expenditures—police cars	45,000	
	Vouchers payable		45,000
	To record purchase of police cars.		

Notice that the credit to encumbrances in the first entry above, when posted to the Encumbrances column in the Appropriations ledger for Police Cars, reverses the encumbrance previously posted. Reversing the encumbrance restores—momentarily—the available Police Car appropriation to the original $100,000 amount. The debit to expenditures from the second entry above, when posted to the expenditures column, reduces the available Police Car appropriation to $55,000. Notice that, whereas the available appropriation balance was $54,000 on January 8 after the encumbrance was recorded, the available appropriation balance on January 16—after the initial police car purchase is complete—is $55,000 because the actual cost of this purchase is $1,000 less than initially expected.

Jan. 15	Cash	103,000	
	Revenues—miscellaneous		103,000
	To record collection of miscellaneous revenue.		

The credit to miscellaneous revenue, when posted to the Actual Revenues column of the Revenues ledger on page 83, swings the current balance from the original $100,000 debit amount to a credit of $3,000. The credit nature of this balance signifies that actual miscellaneous revenues exceeds Tiny Town's budgeted amount for January 2008.

Jan. 16	Encumbrances—police cars	54,000	
	Budgetary fund balance reserved for encumbrances		54,000
	To record encumbrance for purchase of police cars.		

The debit to encumbrances from the above entry is posted to the Encumbrances column of the Appropriations ledger object account for Police Cars. The resulting $1,000 credit balance in the Available Appropriation column shows that, at the time the second police car order is encumbered, Tiny Town still has $1,000 of Police Car appropriation available for future spending.

Jan. 21	Budgetary fund balance reserved for encumbrances	54,000	
	Encumbrances—police cars		54,000
	To reverse encumbrance for purchase of police cars.		
	Expenditures—police cars	55,000	
	Vouchers payable		55,000
	To record purchase of police cars.		

As with the January 12 entries, the credit to encumbrances from the first entry above reverses the encumbrance previously posted in the Appropriations ledger. Reversing the encumbrance raises the available Police Car appropriation temporarily to $55,000. The debit to expenditures from the second entry above zeroes out the available police car appropriation for January. The unanticipated $1,000 extra cost of the second order of police cars absorbed the remaining appropriation in its entirety.

Jan. 22	Cash	399,500	
	Revenues—property taxes		399,500
	To record receipt of property tax revenue.		

As with the January 3 entry, the credit to revenues in the above entry is posted to the "actual" column of the Revenues ledger account for Property Taxes. The resulting $500 debit amount in the balance column shows that, to this point, actual property tax revenues are less than estimated property tax revenues by $500.

Jan. 25	Encumbrances—materials	190,000	
	Budgetary fund balance reserved for encumbrances		190,000
	To record encumbrance for purchase of materials.		

The debit to encumbrances in the above entry, $190,000, is posted to the Encumbrances column of the Appropriations ledger account for the Materials object. The zero balance in the Available Appropriation column as of January 25 signifies that Tiny Town has used up its entire January appropriation for materials with this order.

Jan. 28	Budgetary fund balance reserved for encumbrances	190,000	
	Encumbrances—materials		190,000
	To reverse encumbrance for materials purchased.		
	Expenditures—materials	188,000	
	Vouchers payable		188,000
	To record purchase of materials at June 30.		

Posting the credit to encumbrances in the first of the above two entries to the Appropriations ledger reverses the encumbrance of January 25, resulting in the temporary restoration of the available Materials appropriation to $190,000. The $188,000 debit to expenditures in the second entry above, when posted to the Expenditures column of the Appropriations ledger, reduces the Available Appropriation to a balance of $2,000. This signifies that Tiny Town will end January 2008 with $2,000 of the Materials appropriation remaining available for spending.

Jan. 30	Expenditures—personal services	700,000	
	Cash		700,000
	To record disbursement of payroll at month end.		

Finally, the end-of-month payroll entry is posted by object to the Expenditures column of the Appropriations ledger in the Personal Services account. Observe that this expenditure was not preceded by an encumbrance. Recall that, in practice, encumbrances should be recorded only when doing so serves a meaningful control purpose. In this illustration, Tiny Town chooses not to record encumbrances of the Personal Services appropriation because payroll tends to be predictable. That is, "drawdowns" of the Personal Services appropriation result only from monthly payroll expenditures, the dollar amounts and timing of which are known for the fiscal year.

We see from this illustration how the Revenues and Appropriations ledgers provide useful information about actual account balances compared with budgeted amounts. For instance, after Tiny Town ordered the first pair of police cars, the expenditures ledger showed that the remaining available appropriation was $54,000. However, because the invoiced cost of these cars was $45,000 instead of the $46,000 originally encumbered, the remaining available appropriation increased from $54,000 to $55,000. As a result, Tiny Town was able to specify better-equipped cars when it placed the second order. The appropriation for police cars was neither overspent nor underspent for the month. Likewise, the personal services appropriation was neither overspent nor underspent; the materials appropriation was underspent by $2,000. Similarly, the Revenues ledger shows that, although actual property tax revenues were $500 under the budget estimate, miscellaneous revenues exceeded the budgeted amount by $3,000, more than offsetting the shortfall in property taxes.

How Much Expenditure Classification Detail Is Enough?

Recall from previous discussion that, in practice, many governments use up to five levels of expenditure classification (fund, function/program, department, activity, and object of expenditure), but that much of the account coding is automatic because of computerization and the fixed "roll-up" relationships among the various subclassification levels. For the sake of simplicity, in this text generally we will follow the convention of presenting expenditure journal entries (and posting Appropriations ledgers) with a single level of subclassification, usually by function, with the additional subclassifications and subsidiary ledger postings being assumed.

In the preceding example for Tiny Town, however, expenditures were subclassified by object code to illustrate the Appropriations ledger because of the simple nature of the example. That is, Tiny Town had only one fund, the General Fund, performed a single function, Public Safety, through a single department, Police. If we applied our function level of subclassification convention to the Tiny Town illustration, the debit items of all expenditure journal entries would have been captioned as "Expenditures—Public Safety."

ADDITIONAL ASPECTS OF BUDGETARY ACCOUNTING

We conclude this chapter with brief discussions of three additional facets of budgetary accounting often encountered in practice. These are (1) situations in which the amount of an encumbrance differs from the amount of the related expenditure, (2) receipt of partial orders, and (3) budgetary interchanges.

Encumbrances Not Equal to Expenditures

We noted earlier in the chapter that, when an encumbrance is removed, the reversing entry is for the amount of the purchase order. The entry to record the expenditure, however, is for the amount of the invoice: the "actual" cost of the materials or services received. Often, these two amounts are equal.

As the Tiny Town illustration demonstrates, however, the invoice cost of an order can differ from the estimated cost on the purchase order. It is not unusual, for example, to have a price change between the time an order is placed and the time the materials or services ordered are received. In such a situation, the encumbrance amount reversed out is the original amount of the purchase order and the expenditure is recorded for the actual (invoice) amount.

If there is a difference between the amount of the purchase order and the invoice amount, the unencumbered balance of the appropriation is automatically adjusted because the outstanding encumbrance is replaced by an expenditure for the actual amount of the purchase.

To illustrate, assume that a city's appropriation for materials is for $100,000 and that a purchase order is issued for materials costing $34,000 (see Table 3-14). The balance of the appropriation, at the time the order is placed, is shown on the left. The effect of three different "actual" invoice amounts is shown on the right. Notice the following:

1. Regardless of the amount of the invoice, the encumbered amount (the amount of the purchase order) is reversed out when the purchased materials arrive or the services ordered are provided.

	When Purchase Order Is Sent to Vendor	Case 1 Actual Invoice Is $34,000	Case 2 Actual Invoice Is $33,000	Case 3 Actual Invoice Is $35,000
TABLE 3-14 Effect of Different Invoice Amounts on an Unencumbered Balance				
Appropriations—materials	$100,000	$100,000	$100,000	$100,000
Expenditures—materials	-0-	34,000	33,000	35,000
Unexpended balance	$100,000	$ 66,000	$ 67,000	$ 65,000
Amount encumbered for materials	34,000	-0-	-0-	-0-
Unencumbered ("free") balance— available for the purchase of additional materials	$ 66,000	$ 66,000	$ 67,000	$ 65,000

2. If the amount of the invoice equals the amount of the purchase order (Case 1), recording the expenditure does not alter the unencumbered balance.
3. If the amount of the invoice is smaller than the amount of the purchase order (Case 2), the unencumbered balance is increased by the amount of the difference.
4. If the amount of the invoice is greater than the amount of the purchase order (Case 3), the unencumbered balance is decreased by the amount of the difference.

Receipt of Partial Orders

When only a portion of the items ordered is received, such as when ordered items are back-ordered or scheduled for phased delivery, the encumbrance amount should be reversed out in the proportion that the quantity of items received represents in relation to the total quantity ordered. For example, assume a government orders 10 barrels of street-patching tar at $100 per barrel. The resulting encumbrance is recorded at $1,000. If, say, six barrels of tar are received in one delivery, the amount of the encumbrance to be reversed is $600 (6 × $100) and the invoice cost of the six barrels is recorded as an expenditure. At a later date, when the government receives the remaining four barrels of tar, the remaining $400 of encumbrance relating to this order will be reversed and the actual cost of the four barrels will be recorded as an expenditure.

Budgetary Interchanges

Sometimes events that were not anticipated when the budget was prepared occur, and they require unplanned expenditures. To provide the budgetary authorization for these expenditures, appropriations are sometimes transferred from other activities. To make this transfer, a portion of the unexpended appropriation of one or more activities is reduced and the appropriation of the activity making the unplanned expenditure is increased.

Assume, for example, that a fire engine belonging to Windy City is destroyed by a tornado and must be replaced immediately. Assume also that it will cost $150,000 to replace the vehicle. The City Council is aware that the Fire Department has a number of budgeted but unfilled positions and that it is unlikely to spend a portion of its appropriation for salaries. As a result, the City Council reduces that department's appropriation for salaries by $150,000 and increases its appropriation for capital equipment by the same amount. The entry to record this *budgetary interchange* at the object level is:

Appropriations—salaries	150,000	
Appropriations—capital outlay		150,000

To record budget interchange in response to tornado damage.

The Fire Department now has the budgetary authority to purchase a new fire engine. It cannot, however, fill all of its vacant positions unless it receives budgetary authority to do so.

CLOSING COMMENTS

The budget holds unique importance in government and its importance is manifested by the amount of effort that governments expend in preparing budgets. Governments' obligation to demonstrate budgetary compliance in the name of accountability underscores the significance of budgetary accounting. Budgetary accounting includes recording the original budget as expressed in estimated revenues and appropriations and in recording/reversing encumbrances as purchase orders are issued/fulfilled. Budgetary accounting also involves preparing Revenues and Appropriations ledgers to aid in budgetary control during the budget execution phase. Budgetary interchanges are another important dimension of budgetary accounting.

It should be evident that maintaining the necessary accounting records for both budgetary data and actual transactions requires a lot of bookkeeping. Fortunately, in practice, much of the bookkeeping is done with the benefit of information technology. Thus, having introduced the rationale and procedures for recording budgetary detail in the accounting system, we will illustrate the use of Revenues and Appropriations ledgers selectively in following chapters of this text. Our principal purpose is to address the substance of the accounting issues presented in the following chapters so sometimes we will "assume away" the detailed record keeping required in actual practice. Finally, we save the discussion of a couple more aspects of budgetary accounting, budget amendments and use of allotments, for following chapters.

Review Questions

Q3-1 What is a budget? What purpose(s) does it serve?

Q3-2 Identify three types of budgets prepared by state and local governments.

Q3-3 Identify various approaches to budget preparation. Which approach is most common in practice?

Q3-4 What is the purpose of a cash forecast? How can it assist in the smooth functioning of a government?

Q3-5 List the steps involved in preparing a budget.

Q3-6 Name three types of supplementary information that should be included with budget requests.

Q3-7 What information should be contained in a set of budgetary instructions?

Q3-8 What is the purpose of a budget calendar?

Q3-9 What is a capital budget? Why should it be prepared for several years beyond the budget year?

Q3-10 What is the purpose of a budgetary review? By whom should it be performed?

Q3-11 What is a millage rate? How is it determined?

Q3-12 What is a budget *appropriation*?

Q3-13 What are three typical types of departmental expenditures?

Q3-14 What is meant by the term *legal level of budgetary control*? Cite some examples.

Q3-15 Does the balance in the *estimated revenues* account represent an asset? Why or why not?

Q3-16 What information is conveyed by the *budgetary fund balance* account?

Q3-17 Identify five typical sources of revenues received by local governments.

Q3-18 Identify the various subclassifications of expenditures used in governmental budgeting and accounting.

Q3-19 What is the purpose of *encumbrances* in governmental accounting?

Cases

C3-1   The City of Toth produces monthly budgetary control reports. The amount shown in the budget column is one-twelfth of the annual budget. Over lunch, two department heads were discussing this report. The first manager said, "I like the idea of using one-twelfth of my annual budget each month. My costs are constant throughout the year. I can usually find small savings and show favorable variances each month." The second manager disagreed. "I don't like it. Most of my costs are incurred during Carnival and around Christmas. As a result, I always have unfavorable variances in March and December regardless of what I do. It is especially upsetting because employee performance appraisals are made in April and the council looks especially hard at our March results."

What is the problem with the way these control reports are prepared? What do you think should be done to make the reports more reflective of the actual performance of the departments?

C3-2   You have just been elected to your state legislature. One piece of legislation on your desk is a proposed law requiring all governmental units in the state to prepare balanced budgets. In this bill, balanced budgets are defined as ones in which expected resources available at the beginning of a fiscal year (beginning fund balance plus estimated revenue) must equal or exceed that year's appropriations. A fiscally conservative legislator from a rural county attached a rider to the bill deleting this definition of balanced budgets and substituting one in which budgets are balanced only if estimated revenues equal appropriations. Would you vote for this rider? State your reasons. Why might feelings vary on this issue between legislators from large cities and those from rural counties?

Ethics Case

EC3-1 During lunch, the director of Streets and Parkways of Thor City made the following comment: "For the past 10 years, I deliberately overstated my labor and equipment needs by 20 percent when preparing my budget request. I figure that the city council will cut it by 10 percent and I can use the other 10 percent as slack. If there is money left over, I can always find a way to spend it." Do you consider this behavior to be ethical? If not, what steps might you, as budget director, take to cut down on this "padding"?

Exercises

E3-1 (Discussion of uses of budgeting)

Rex, a budget officer, conducted a class for nonaccounting managers and program directors on the subject of budgets. Rex began the class discussion by asking, "What are some of the uses of a budget?" One manager replied, "Planning." Another said, "Evaluating performance." Still another suggested, "Coordinating activities." "What about implementing plans?" inquired another. "Or communicating them?" added still another. "Don't forget motivation," one manager warned from the rear of the room. "I'm on the school board," commented another, "and we use it to authorize actions." Finally, one manager asked, "Can budgets do all that?" "Yes," Rex responded, "all that and more."

Required: 1. Define the term *budget*.

2. Select any four of the uses suggested by the managers and explain how a budget might accomplish each of the four uses selected.

(IIA adapted)

E3-2 (Budgeting cash disbursements)

The City of Amboy is preparing its cash forecast for the month of July. The following information is available with respect to its proposed disbursements.

Items vouchered in July	$650,000
Estimated payments in July for items vouchered in July	50%
Items vouchered in June	$400,000
Estimated payments in July for all items vouchered in June	70%
Estimated payments in July for items vouchered prior to June	$50,000
Items vouchered in June but returned in July before payment was made	$20,000

Required: What are the estimated cash disbursements for July?

E3-3 (Budgeting cash receipts)

The City of Saltus is preparing its cash forecast for the month of May. The following information is available with respect to its sales tax collections.

Sales tax rate	5%
Estimated retail sales in May	$2,000,000
Actual retail sales in April	$1,500,000
Estimated payments by merchants to city in May of sales taxes collected in May	20%
Estimated payments by merchants to city in May of sales taxes collected in April	70%
Estimated payments by merchants to city in May of sales taxes collected prior to April	$10,000

Required: Compute the estimated cash receipts from sales tax collections in May.

E3-4 (Determination of property tax rate)

The legislative body of Pandora County just approved the 2008–2009 fiscal year budget. Revenues from property taxes are budgeted at $800,000. According to the county assessor, the assessed valuation of all of the property in the county is $50 million. Of this amount, however, property worth $10 million belongs to either the federal government or to religious organizations and therefore is not subject to property taxes. In addition, certificates for the following exemptions have been filed:

Homestead	$2,500,000
Veterans	900,000
Old age, blindness, etc.	600,000

In the past, uncollectible property taxes averaged about 3 percent of the levy. This rate is not expected to change in the foreseeable future.

Required: 1. Determine the property tax rate that must be used to collect the desired revenues from property taxes.

2. How much would the levy be on a piece of property that was assessed for $100,000 (after exemptions)?

E3-5   (Estimating the fund balance at the end of the year)

At the end of the preceding year, the General Fund of the Atlas Township School Board had a fund balance of $800,000. Revenues and expenditures of the current year are expected to be as follows:

	Year-to-Date Actual	Remainder of Year Estimated
Revenue		
Property taxes	$1,250,000	$500,000
Out-of-township tuition	50,000	20,000
Share of lottery receipts	100,000	50,000
State grants	500,000	—
Expenditures		
Salaries	$ 875,000	$450,000
Fringe benefits	90,000	40,000
Operating expenses	588,000	240,000
Equipment	110,000	50,000
Transportation	15,000	10,000
Debt service	100,000	100,000

Required: Determine the projected year-end fund balance for this fund.

E3-6   (Multiple choice)

1. What is a key difference between budgets prepared by governmental units and by commercial organizations?

a. Budgets prepared by commercial organizations must be approved by a governing body, whereas those prepared by governmental units need no approvals.

b. Budgets prepared by governmental units are legal documents, whereas those prepared by commercial organizations are not.

c. Operating, capital, and cash budgets are prepared by governmental units, but only operating budgets are prepared by commercial organizations.

d. Budgets prepared by commercial organizations are formally recorded in the organizations' operating accounts, whereas those prepared by governmental units are not.

2. Which of the following is not included in a cash budget?
   a. Personal services
   b. Redemption of bonds
   c. Utilities
   d. Depreciation
3. Who prepares a nondepartmental expenditures request?
   a. The department heads as a group
   b. The auditor
   c. The city council
   d. The CEO or the budget director
4. To provide government officials with maximum flexibility in making operating decisions, the legal level of budgetary control should be set at which level?
   a. Object of expenditure
   b. Departmental
   c. Function/Program
   d. Fund
5. Which of the following is not a basic rule to follow when using budgets?
   a. The budget must be presented in a positive manner.
   b. The budget must have the support of top management.
   c. Managers must only be held responsible for revenues and costs over which they have a degree of control.
   d. The budget must be prepared by top management.
6. A continuous capital budget
   a. Is used only by commercial organizations.
   b. Covers a specific period but is continuously updated.
   c. Is also known as a line-item budget.
   d. Is valid over a range of activity, rather than just one level.
7. What approach to budgeting is most commonly used by governmental units?
   a. Zero-based budgeting approach
   b. Planning-programming-budgeting approach
   c. Flexible budgeting approach
   d. Object-of-expenditure approach

E3-7 (Behavioral aspects of budgeting)
The operating budget is a common instrument used by many organizations. Although it usually is thought to be an important and necessary tool for management, some managers and researchers studying organization and human behavior criticize its use.

Required: 1. Describe and discuss some benefits of budgeting from the behavioral point of view.
2. Describe and discuss some criticisms leveled at the budgetary process from the behavioral point of view.
3. What solutions do you recommend to overcome the criticisms described in part (2)?

(CMA adapted)

E3-8 (Budget laws)

Every state has a law or laws regulating its own budgetary practices and those of its local governmental units. Check the law(s) of your state to determine the following:

1. Are budgets legally required by local governmental units, such as cities and counties, in your state?
2. For what funds must budgets be prepared?
3. Must governmental budgets prepared in your state be "balanced"? If so, what does your state law consider to be a "balanced" budget?
4. What legal provisions are made for public input into the budgetary process in your state?

E3-9 (Budgetary Fund Balance)

Compute the debit or credit, if any, to be made to the Budgetary Fund Balance for Grove County's General Fund under each of the following three assumptions:

a. Budgeted revenues and expenditures each are $30,000,000.
b. Budgeted revenues are $30,000,000 and budgeted expenditures are $32,000,000.
c. Budgeted revenues are $34,000,000 and budgeted expenditures are $32,000,000.

E3-10 (Budgetary accounting)

Parrytown's General Fund budget for fiscal 2009 includes estimated revenues by source and appropriations by function as follows:

Estimated Revenue		_Appropriations_	
Property taxes	$2,000,000	Administration	$ 425,000
Sales taxes	720,000	Public Safety	1,300,000
Licenses and permits	120,000	Streets	630,000
Fines and forfeits	8,500	Parks and recreation	367,000

Required: Is Parrytown projecting a budgetary surplus or a deficit for 2009? Prepare the general journal entry to record the 2009 budget.

E3-11 (Relationship between budgetary fund balance and actual fund balance)

The Village of Albert's Alcove recorded the following budgetary journal entry at the beginning of fiscal 2009:

Estimated revenue	5,000,000	
Appropriations		4,950,000
Budgetary fund balance		50,000

Required: At the end of fiscal 2009, what would be the effect on ending actual unreserved fund balance, assuming that:

a. Actual revenues are equal to estimated revenues but appropriations exceed expenditures by $7,000?
b. Actual revenues are equal to estimated revenues and appropriations are equal to expenditures?
c. Actual revenues exceed estimated revenues by $4,000 but appropriations are equal to expenditures?
d. Actual revenues are less than estimated revenues by $3,000 but appropriations exceed expenditures $3,000?

e. Actual revenues exceed estimated revenues by $2,000 but appropriations exceed expenditures by $6,000?

E3-12 (Encumbrance journal entries)

Reggieville Township ordered materials and supplies for its Fire Department at an estimated cost of $16,700. The ordered goods were received with an invoice for $16,700. Prepare the journal entries necessary to record these events and transactions within the General Fund. Assume Reggieville credits cash when expenditures are incurred. Subclassify your encumbrance and expenditure entries by the Public Safety function.

E3-13 (Encumbrance journal entries)

Assume the same facts as in E3-12 except that the ordered goods were received with an invoice for $17,000. Prepare the journal entries necessary to record these events and transactions.

E3-14 (Encumbrance journal entries)

Assume the same facts as in E3-12 except that the ordered goods were received with an invoice for $16,500. Prepare the journal entries necessary to record these events and transactions.

E3-15 (Encumbrances and partial orders)

On October 1, 2009, the City of Highland placed an order with the Ajax Sand & Gravel Co. for 1,000 tons of cinders to be spread upon Highland's streets during winter storms. The estimated cost of the cinders was $10 per ton, delivered. Ajax delivered 800 tons of cinders to Highland's Road Maintenance Yard on October 20 along with an invoice for $8,000. Ajax delivered the remaining 200 tons of cinders on November 1 along with an invoice for $2,000.

Required: Prepare the General Fund journal entries necessary on October 1, October 20, and November 1, 2009. Subclassify your encumbrance and expenditure entries by the Road Maintenance function.

E3-16 (Budgetary interchange)

The town council of the Town of Pedregon has received an increasing number of complaints from citizens about the poor condition of some of the streets following an exceptionally harsh winter. In response, the town council directed that the Public Safety appropriation be reduced by $500,000 to support an increase in the town's Streets and Bridges appropriation.

Required: Prepare the entry necessary to record this budgetary interchange.

Problems

P3-1 (Budgeting revenue)

The following information relates to the prior- and current-year revenues of the General Fund of the Village of Nimbus:

	2007 Actual	Jan. – Sept. 2008 Actual	Oct. – Dec. 2008 Est. Act.	2008 Budget
Property taxes	$5,436,720	$4,084,000	$1,400,000	$5,504,000
Interest and penalties	38,486	22,800	15,000	38,000
Sales taxes	872,680	454,500	445,000	900,000
Fines and penalties	64,842	39,240	30,000	70,000
Share of lottery receipts	—	54,250	175,750	225,000
License fees	9,650	7,540	2,460	10,000

Additional information:

1. Because of a reassessment of commercial property, property taxes are expected to increase by $400,000 in 2009.
2. Interest and penalties and license fees are expected to remain constant over the next several years.
3. Because of an increase in the sales tax from 4 percent to 5 percent and the expectation of several large conventions in 2009, sales tax revenues are expected to increase by 20 percent.
4. Because of the conventions mentioned in part (3), fines and penalties should rise by 10 percent in 2009.
5. Because of the lottery's success in its first few months of operation, city officials expect the board's share of the lottery receipts to double in 2009.

Required: Using Table 3-4 as a guide, prepare a statement of actual and estimated revenues for 2009. Assume the 2009 budget is prepared by applying the additional information furnished in the problem to the estimated actual revenues for the full calendar year 2008, and is rounded to the nearest $1,000.

P3-2   (Budget summary)
Using your answers from the preceding problem and the following information, prepare a budget summary for the General Fund of the Village of Nimbus for fiscal year 2009. Assume that fund balance at the beginning of 2009 is $2,607,241.

1. The Village has three departments: Public Safety, Administration, Streets and Parkways.
2. Budgeted expenditure data pertaining to the Public Safety, Administration, and Streets and Parkways departments for fiscal year 2009 are as follows:

	Public Safety	Administration	Streets and Parkways
Personal services	$1,115,000	$1,450,000	$1,846,285
Travel	10,000	20,000	1,850
Equipment	650,000	100,000	80,900
Operating expenses	85,000	60,000	36,450

3. Budgeted non-departmental items are comprised of a $1 million transfer to the Debt Service Fund and a $50,000 transfer to the Venus Park Fund.

P3-3   (Budgetary journal entry)
The city of Bolsa Grande adopted the fiscal 2009 operating budget for its General Fund as follows:

Estimated Revenues

Property taxes	$ 9,500,000
Sales taxes	1,835,000
Fines and forfeits	65,500
Intergovernmental	1,455,250
	$12,855,750

Appropriations

Administration	$ 2,250,000
Public Safety	4,770,500

Parks and Recreation	1,150,000
Streets	3,435,000
Libraries	900,000
	$12,505,500

Required: Prepare the general journal entry to record the budget at the beginning of fiscal 2009.

P3-4 (Budgetary accounting)

The events and transactions listed below took place in the General Fund of Tessietown during fiscal 2009.

Required: Prepare the necessary general journal entries.

1. The annual budget was originally adopted as follows:

Estimated Revenues

Property taxes	$1,600,000
Fines and forfeits	150,000
Intergovernmental	475,000
	$2,225,000

Appropriations

General government	$ 210,000
Public safety	1,580,000
Streets	395,000
	$2,185,000

2. Purchase orders were issued for goods and services with the following estimated costs:

General government	$ 210,000
Public safety	1,450,000
Streets	395,000
	$2,055,000

3. Revenues were received in cash as follows:

Property taxes	$ 855,000
Fines and forfeits	117,000
Intergovernmental	295,000
	$1,267,000

4. Items on order were received with these costs (cash paid):

	Estimated	*Actual*
General government	$ 165,000	$ 163,500
Public safety	719,000	720,100
Streets	135,000	134,000
	$1,019,000	$1,017,600

5. The Tessietown city council directed that $120,000 of the Public Safety appropriation be reappropriated to the Streets function in a budgetary interchange.

6. Additional revenues were received in cash as follows:

Property taxes	$742,000
Fines and forfeits	37,000
Intergovernmental	181,000
	$960,000

7. Items on order were received with these costs (cash paid):

	Estimated	*Actual*
General government	$ 45,000	$ 45,000
Public safety	693,700	691,250
Streets	234,800	235,350
	$973,500	$971,600

P3-5   (Revenues and appropriations subsidiary ledgers)
Prepare the revenues and expenditures subsidiary ledgers for the 2009 events and transactions of Tessietown listed in P3-4. What are the balances for each individual source of revenues after transaction 7? What are the available appropriations for each function after transaction 7?

P3-6   (Journal entries and subsidiary ledgers)
The events and transactions listed below took place in the General Fund of Quiet City during fiscal 2009.
Required: Prepare the necessary general journal entries.

1. The General Fund annual operating budget was adopted as follows:

Estimated Revenues

Property taxes	$2,550,000
Charges for services	400,000
Miscellaneous	175,000
	$3,125,000

Appropriations

Administration	$ 465,000
Public safety	1,860,000
Roads and bridges	930,000
	$3,255,000

2. Purchase orders were issued for goods and services with the following estimated costs:

Administration	$ 465,000
Public safety	1,860,000
Roads and bridges	930,000
	$3,255,000

3. Revenues were received in cash as follows:

Property taxes	$2,005,000
Charges for services	248,000
Miscellaneous	65,000
	$2,318,000

4. Purchase orders were fulfilled with the following estimated and actual costs:

	Estimated	Actual
Administration	$ 265,000	$ 263,500
Public safety	902,000	902,000
Roads and bridges	776,000	776,000
	$1,943,000	$1,941,500

5. Additional revenues were received in cash as follows:

Property taxes	$535,000
Charges for services	155,000
Miscellaneous	111,000
	$801,000

6. Purchase orders were fulfilled with the following estimated and actual costs:

	Estimated	Actual
Administration	$ 200,000	$ 201,000
Public safety	948,000	947,000
Roads and bridges	154,000	153,500
	$1,302,000	$1,301,500

P3-7 (Revenues and appropriations subsidiary ledgers)
Prepare the revenues and expenditures subsidiary ledgers for the 2009 events and transactions of Quiet City listed in P3-6. What is the balance for each revenues source after transaction 6? What is the available appropriation for each function after transaction 6?

4

THE GOVERNMENTAL FUND ACCOUNTING CYCLE

An Introduction to General and Special Revenue Funds

Chapter Outline

Learning Objectives

Recognizing Revenues and Expenditures

Illustrating the General Fund Accounting Cycle
  Background Information
  The Basic Illustration: Journal Entries and Financial Statements
  The Extended Illustration: Journal Entries and Financial Statements

Control Accounts and Subsidiary Ledgers

Closing Comments

Summary Problem

Review Questions

Case

Ethics Cases

Exercises

Problems

After completing this chapter, you should be able to:

- Compare the objectives of fund accounting with those of commercial accounting.
- Understand how the accounting cycle of a governmental unit differs from that of a commercial organization.
- Understand the basic nature of the General Fund and Special Revenue Funds.
- Prepare the budgetary journal entry at the beginning of the fiscal year.
- Prepare basic operating entries for revenues and expenditures during the fiscal year.
- Prepare closing entries at the end of the fiscal year.

■ Describe and prepare the financial statements for the General Fund and Special Revenue Funds.

■ Understand how control and subsidiary accounts are used in an accounting system.

The General Fund is the most significant single fund maintained by state and local governments. This fund records many of a government's most important transactions and also serves as a catchall for revenues and expenditures not required to be recorded in other funds. Functions accounted for in the General Fund include general administration, public safety (police and fire protection), street maintenance, and other day-to-day operations of the governmental unit.

Special Revenue Funds account for specific revenues that must be spent for particular purposes. Generally accepted accounting principles do not require governments to use Special Revenue Funds except when legally required; for example, by local law. When governments use Special Revenue Funds, they do so to provide some assurance that the resources are used only for the designated purposes. From a procedural standpoint, the accounting for General Funds and Special Revenue Funds is identical. Governments will have only one General Fund but often have multiple Special Revenue Funds. The scope of operations accounted for in a government's General Fund, though, is broader than the scope of operations accounted for within any particular Special Revenue Fund of that government.

A good example of Special Revenue Funds used in practice is found in Colorado local governments. Proceeds from the Colorado lottery, by law, are shared among Colorado towns and cities and must be spent for open-space preservation, such as land acquisition. The state operates the lottery and distributes the local governments' shares of these proceeds. The local governments, in turn, account for the receipt and expenditure of lottery proceeds in Special Revenue Funds to help ensure that these monies are spent only as intended. Other examples of Special Revenue Funds include those that account for gasoline tax proceeds (often restricted for road maintenance), earmarked sales taxes, and state and federal grants. Table 4-1 shows that the use of Special Revenue Funds varies considerably in practice.

This chapter introduces the General Fund accounting cycle. The knowledge of General Fund events and transactions—and how they are recorded—that you develop from studying this chapter and Chapter 5 will help you understand the accounting procedures presented in later chapters.

As with commercial accounting, an objective of governmental accounting is to convey to a reader of financial statements a picture of what happened in the past. The reader can use this information as input for making decisions. Governmental accounting, however, also is concerned with ensuring compliance with legal restrictions; that is, the budget. Thus, a distinguishing feature of the governmental accounting cycle is that it formally integrates the budget into the accounting records while the commercial accounting cycle does not. The end products of both accounting cycles are financial statements. Table 4-2 compares the objectives and activities of the two accounting cycles.

The financial statements prepared for each individual governmental fund include a balance sheet and a statement of revenues, expenditures, and changes in fund balance (often called an "operating statement"). Governments also prepare budget-actual comparison statements or schedules for their General Funds and the Special Revenue Funds that have legally adopted annual operating budgets.

TABLE 4-1   Special Revenue Funds in Practice

This table shows the number of Special Revenue Funds maintained by 10 randomly selected municipalities (populations 100,000–110,000) from around the United States. The table also shows the (self-descriptive) names of selected Special Revenue Funds for each municipality. Notice from the fund names the diversity of purposes for which governments use Special Revenue Funds.

Municipality	No. of Special Revenue Funds	Names of Selected Funds
Cambridge, MA	6	Community Development Block Grant; School Assistance; Community Preservation Act
Clarksville, TN	8	Police Special; Cemetery and Other; Parks
Clearwater, FL	4	Special Programs; Community Redevelopment Agency; Local Housing Assistance
Costa Mesa, CA	13	Special Gas Tax; Air Quality Improvement; Traffic Impact Fees
Green Bay, WI	17	Lambeau Field; Police Grants; Transit Operations
McAllen, TX	6	Miscellaneous Government Grants; Park Development; Hotel Occupancy Tax
Peoria, AZ	6	Public Transit; Section 8 Housing; Other Grants
Provo, UT	14	Library; Arts Council; Winterfest
Waterbury, CT	6	Food Service; Waterbury Development Agency; Recreational Programs
West Covina, CA	23	Traffic Safety; Recreation Programs; Inmate Welfare

Source: Recent Comprehensive Annual Financial Reports

TABLE 4-2   Fund Accounting versus Commercial Accounting

Fund Accounting Objectives	Commercial Accounting Objectives
• To show the financial position of the organization's funds • To show the results of operations of the organization's funds • To show changes in the financial position of the organization's funds • To show compliance with legal restrictions	• To show the financial position of the firm • To show the results of operations of the firm • To show changes in the financial position of the firm

Fund Accounting Cycle	Commercial Accounting Cycle
• Record the budget in the accounting records • Record transactions for the period • Prepare closing entries • Prepare fund financial statements and schedules	• Record transactions for the period • Prepare closing entries • Prepare financial statements

RECOGNIZING REVENUES AND EXPENDITURES

As Chapter 2 indicates, the modified accrual basis of accounting evolved largely in response to budgetary considerations. Government budgeting, in turn, focuses on near-term liquidity. Indeed, the emphasis on near-term liquidity characterizes the "modifications" that differentiate the modified accrual accounting basis from the "full" accrual accounting basis.

Recall that, under the modified accrual concept, governments recognize revenues at the point that revenues are *measurable* and *available*. The measurability attribute means that governments must know with reasonable certainty the dollar amount of an asset inflow in order to recognize that inflow as revenue. The availability attribute means that an asset inflow must occur within the current period or soon enough thereafter to pay the bills of the current period. The availability criterion is intended to ensure that recognized revenues produce liquid spendable resources.[1]

Applying the measurable and available criteria in practice means that certain sources of revenues are accrued in advance of receipt while others are recognized upon receipt; that is, on a cash basis. Property taxes are a prominent example of a revenue source that is susceptible to accrual because they are measurable before they are received by the government: A government levies property taxes on the (known) assessed value of taxable property within its jurisdiction. Once the millage (tax rate) is determined (usually, when the budget is approved) the assessed amount of property taxes is calculated, by individual parcel of property, and in total.

Because they are not measurable in the sense that property taxes are, sales and income taxes are generally recorded when received in cash; for financial reporting purposes, accruals are made to the extent that uncollected taxes meet the measurable and available criteria. Interest on investments is typically accrued. Sources of revenue that normally are not considered measurable until received in cash include fines and forfeits and various fees, such as those for recreation, licenses and permits, building inspections, and parking.

Recall, too, that under the modified accrual basis of accounting, the basic principle is that an expenditure should be recognized at the point a liability is incurred. Salaries are generally recorded when paid; for financial reporting purposes, an accrual is made for salaries earned but unpaid. Other expenditures of an "operating" nature, such as professional services and purchases of supplies, are recorded at the time the related liabilities are incurred because the liabilities require current settlement in cash.

ILLUSTRATING THE GENERAL FUND ACCOUNTING CYCLE

The next section of this chapter presents a very simple example of the basic activities occurring within the accounting cycle of the General Fund. These activities are (1) recording the budget, (2) recording selected "actual" revenue and expenditure transactions in the general ledger and subsidiary ledgers, (3) closing the accounts, and (4) preparing the

---

[1] Inflows of liquid resources not available for current-year expenditure—for example, prepayments of next year's property taxes by property owners—are recorded initially as *deferred* revenues and carried on the balance sheet. In the subsequent fiscal year, when the resources become legally available to finance operations of that fiscal year, the deferred revenues balance is reclassified to revenues.

fund financial statements. We do not illustrate postings to general ledger accounts but do illustrate the postings to the revenues and appropriations subsidiary ledgers. Subsidiary ledger postings are keyed with the number of the corresponding general journal entry.

Background Information

Assume that the Town of Arthursville is established effective January 1, 2009, in a highly populated but previously unincorporated area of Major County. The town will observe a calendar fiscal year. In its first year, Arthursville budgets three sources of revenues: property taxes, charges for services, and fines and forfeits. The town government is organized to provide three "current operating" functions: administration, public safety, and street maintenance. The budget provides an appropriation for each of these functions and an appropriation for debt service. To simplify the illustration, the administration and street maintenance appropriations cover goods and services (which are encumbered) and the public safety appropriation covers salaries (which are not encumbered).

Arthursville employs a "voucher" system. Governments prepare vouchers in the process of approving expenditures for subsequent payment. In addition to documenting approval for payment, a voucher specifies the account(s) in which the debit side of the journal entry is to be recorded; the credit side of the entry is always to "vouchers payable." The term *vouchers payable* has the same meaning in governmental accounting that the term *accounts payable* has in business accounting—current trade liabilities that normally are settled with cash payments in 30–60 days.

The Arthursville scenario is constructed so that the General Fund has insufficient cash to pay the entire vouchers payable balance. This does not result from bad budgeting or unauthorized spending, but simply from differences in the timing of cash receipts relative to cash disbursements. To provide a straightforward example of the accounting cycle, we first assume that the fiscal year ends before the town remedies the cash shortage. Then, to add more realism, we extend the illustration to assume that, during the fiscal year, the town borrows money on a short-term note payable to pay the vouchers payable balance in full.

The individual events and transactions to be recorded within the General Fund are summarized below.

Basic Illustration:
Record legally adopted budget (item 1)
Levy property taxes (item 2)
Issue purchase orders (item 3)
Collect revenues in cash (items 4 and 6)
Receive purchased items and record expenditures and vouchers payable for
   purchased items and salaries (items 5 and 7)
Close the accounts and prepare the financial statements (item 8)

Extended Illustration:
Borrow cash on a short-term note payable (item 9)
Pay off the short-term liability (item 10)
Accrue the liability for interest on the note payable (item 11)
Close the accounts and prepare the financial statements (item 12)

TABLE 4-3	Illustrative Operating Budget

Town of Arthursville
General Fund
Operating Budget
Fiscal Year Ending December 31, 2009

Estimated Revenues		
Property taxes	$1,800,000	
Charges for services	150,000	
Fines and forfeits	125,000	$2,075,000
Appropriations		
Administration	$ 209,000	
Public safety	1,440,000	
Street maintenance	420,000	
Debt service	1,000	$2,070,000
Budgeted Increase in Fund Balance		$ 5,000

The Basic Illustration: Journal Entries and Financial Statements

The 2009 operating budget for the General Fund is presented in Table 4-3.

1. At the beginning of the fiscal year, the following journal entry records budget amounts in the accounting system:

Estimated revenues—property taxes	1,800,000	
Estimated revenues—charges for services	150,000	
Estimated revenues—fines and forfeits	125,000	
Appropriations—administration		209,000
Appropriations—public safety		1,440,000
Appropriations—street maintenance		420,000
Appropriations—debt service		1,000
Budgetary fund balance		5,000

To record General Fund budget for 2009.

and the revenues ledger (Table 4-4) and appropriations ledger (Table 4-5) are posted accordingly.

2. The town levied the property taxes provided for in the budget, resulting in the entry immediately below. Taxes receivable are, of course, an asset of the General Fund.

Property taxes receivable	1,800,000	
Revenues—property taxes		1,800,000

To record the 2009 property tax levy.

3. The town issued purchase orders for goods and services, with the following estimated costs.

Administration	$208,000
Street maintenance	420,000
	$628,000

TABLE 4-4   Illustrative Revenues Ledger

Town of Arthursville
General Fund
Revenues Ledger
Fiscal 2009

Source: Property taxes

Entry no.	Item	Estimated Revenue Dr	Actual Revenue Cr	Difference Dr (Cr)
1	Budget	1,800,000		1,800,000
2	Property tax levy		1,800,000	0

Source: Charges for services

Entry no.	Item	Estimated Revenue Dr	Actual Revenue Cr	Difference Dr (Cr)
1	Budget	150,000		150,000
4	Cash receipts		117,000	33,000
6	Cash receipts		38,000	(5,000)

Source: Fines and forfeits

Entry no.	Item	Estimated Revenue Dr	Actual Revenue Cr	Difference Dr (Cr)
1	Budget	125,000		125,000
4	Cash receipts		95,000	30,000
6	Cash receipts		30,000	0

Recall from Chapter 3 that open purchase orders use up resources from a budgetary standpoint, so available appropriations are reduced by recording encumbrances as follows:

Encumbrances—administration	208,000	
Encumbrances—street maintenance	420,000	
Budgetary fund balance reserved for encumbrances		628,000

To record encumbrances for issued purchase orders.

4. The Town of Arthursville received cash consisting of $855,000 in property tax collections, $117,000 in charges for services, and fines and forfeits revenues of $95,000. Note that in the following entry, because the property taxes had been accrued previously, the property taxes receivable account is credited. In contrast, the town recognizes the charges for services and fines and forfeits revenues on receipt of cash.

Cash	1,067,000	
Property taxes receivable		855,000
Revenues—charges for services		117,000
Revenues—fines and forfeits		95,000

To record cash receipts.

TABLE 4-5   Illustrative Appropriations Ledger

Town of Arthursville
General Fund
Appropriations Ledger
Fiscal 2009

Function: Administration

Entry no.	Item	Appropriation Cr	Encumbrances Dr	Encumbrances Cr	Expenditures Dr	Available Appropriation Cr
1	Budget	209,000				209,000
3	Order materials		208,000			1,000
5	Receive materials			100,000		101,000
	Record expenditure				101,000	0
7	Receive materials			108,000		108,000
	Record expenditure				108,000	0

Function: Public Safety

Entry no.	Item	Appropriation Cr	Encumbrances Dr	Encumbrances Cr	Expenditures Dr	Available Appropriation Cr
1	Budget	1,440,000				1,440,000
5	Record expenditure				730,000	710,000
7	Record expenditure				708,000	2,000

Function: Street Maintenance

Entry no.	Item	Appropriation Cr	Encumbrances Dr	Encumbrances Cr	Expenditures Dr	Available Appropriation Cr
1	Budget	420,000				420,000
3	Order materials		420,000			0
5	Receive materials			250,000		250,000
	Record expenditure				248,000	2,000
7	Receive materials			170,000		172,000
	Record expenditure				170,000	2,000

Debt Service

Entry no.	Item	Appropriation Cr	Encumbrances Dr	Encumbrances Cr	Expenditures Dr	Available Appropriation Cr
1	Budget	1,000				1,000
11	Record expenditure				417	583

5. The town incurred salary expenditures of $730,000 on its public safety function. In addition, purchased items were received, with these costs:

	Encumbered	Actual
Administration	$100,000	$101,000
Street maintenance	250,000	248,000
	$350,000	$349,000

The first following entry reverses outstanding encumbrances for the encumbered costs of the items received; the second following entry records expenditures and vouchers payable at their actual costs.

Budgetary fund balance reserved for encumbrances	350,000	
Encumbrances—administration		100,000
Encumbrances—street maintenance		250,000
To reverse encumbrances for ordered items received.		
Expenditures—administration	101,000	
Expenditures—public safety	730,000	
Expenditures—street maintenance	248,000	
Vouchers payable		1,079,000
To record expenditures.		

6. Additional cash receipts were as follows:

Property taxes	920,000
Charges for services	38,000
Fines and forfeits	30,000
	988,000

resulting in an entry similar to that at item 4.

Cash	988,000	
Property taxes receivable		920,000
Revenues—charges for services		38,000
Revenues—fines and forfeits		30,000
To record cash receipts.		

7. Public safety salary expenditures were $708,000. Also, supplies and services were received under the remaining purchase orders and invoices were received, as listed below:

	Encumbered	Actual
Administration	$108,000	$108,000
Street maintenance	170,000	170,000
	$278,000	$278,000

so encumbrances are reversed, with this entry:

Budgetary fund balance reserved for encumbrances	278,000	
Encumbrances—administration		108,000
Encumbrances—street maintenance		170,000
To reverse encumbrances for ordered items received.		

Note from the appropriations ledger (Table 4-5) that, after posting the preceding entry, the outstanding encumbrances balances are now zero for the administration and street maintenance functions. The zero balances signify that, at this point, all goods ordered have been received. (Chapter 5 discusses accounting for encumbrances that remain outstanding at fiscal year end.) The expenditures are recorded, with this entry.

TABLE 4-6   Illustrative Year-End Preclosing Trial Balance

Town of Arthursville
General Fund
Preclosing Trial Balance
December 31, 2009

Account	Dr	Cr
Estimated revenues—property taxes	$1,800,000	
Estimated revenues—charges for services	150,000	
Estimated revenues—fines and forfeits	125,000	
Appropriations—administration		$ 209,000
Appropriations—public safety		1,440,000
Appropriations—street maintenance		420,000
Appropriations—debt service		1,000
Budgetary fund balance		5,000
Cash	2,055,000	
Taxes receivable	25,000	
Vouchers payable		2,065,000
Revenues—property taxes		1,800,000
Revenues—charges for services		155,000
Revenues—fines and forfeits		125,000
Expenditures—administration	209,000	
Expenditures—public safety	1,438,000	
Expenditures—street maintenance	418,000	
	$6,220,000	$6,220,000

Expenditures—administration	108,000	
Expenditures—public safety	708,000	
Expenditures—street maintenance	170,000	
Vouchers payable		986,000
To record expenditures.		

8. Now, let us complete the basic illustration by assuming that the fiscal year ends with the preceding transaction and that the General Fund accounts are ready to be closed. The preclosing trial balance for the Town of Arthursville General Fund as of December 31, 2009, appears in Table 4-6. The first closing entry reverses the budgetary entry made at the beginning of the fiscal year:

Appropriations—administration	209,000	
Appropriations—public safety	1,440,000	
Appropriations—street maintenance	420,000	
Appropriations—debt service	1,000	
Budgetary fund balance	5,000	
Estimated revenues—property taxes		1,800,000
Estimated revenues—charges for services		150,000
Estimated revenues—fines and forfeits		125,000
To reverse the General Fund budgetary entry for 2009.		

TABLE 4-7   Illustrative Year-End Postclosing Trial Balance

Town of Arthursville
General Fund
Postclosing Trial Balance
December 31, 2009

Account	Dr	Cr
Cash	$2,055,000	
Taxes receivable	25,000	
Vouchers payable		$2,065,000
Unreserved fund balance		15,000
	$2,080,000	$2,080,000

This entry removes all budgetary balances from the general ledger. Only actual balances remain open. The next entry closes actual revenues and expenditures to actual (unreserved) fund balance.[2]

Revenues—property taxes	1,800,000	
Revenues—charges for services	155,000	
Revenues—fines and forfeits	125,000	
Expenditures—administration		209,000
Expenditures—public safety		1,438,000
Expenditures—street maintenance		418,000
Unreserved fund balance		15,000

To close the revenue and expenditure accounts
at fiscal year end.

This entry shows that actual unreserved fund balance, $15,000, is $10,000 more than the town anticipated when the budget was prepared. As we will see in more detail from the financial statements, the "extra" fund balance arises from a combination of actual revenues exceeding estimated revenues and total actual expenditures being less than total appropriations.

The General Fund's postclosing trial balance is illustrated in Table 4-7.

The Statement of Revenues, Expenditures, and Changes in Fund Balance for the General Fund of the Town of Arthursville appears in Table 4-8. Table 4-8 explains the change in fund balance from zero at the beginning of the year to $15,000 at year end. This statement "articulates" with the balance sheet in that the ending fund balance of $15,000, derived on the Statement of Revenues, Expenditures, and Changes in Fund Balance, is the amount necessary to make the balance

---

[2]Mechanically, the closing process may be achieved through any of several combinations of closing entries. For example, actual revenues may be closed against estimated revenues with any difference being debited or credited to unreserved fund balance. Similarly, expenditures may be closed against appropriations, again, with any difference debited or credited to unreserved fund balance. However, closing the accounts in such a manner can create confusion. Accordingly, the authors of this text recommend the straightforward practice of first reversing the budgetary entry and then closing actual revenues against expenditures with any difference between revenues and expenditures being debited or credited to unreserved fund balance.

TABLE 4-8	Illustrative Statement of Revenues, Expenditures, and Changes in Fund Balance

Town of Arthursville
General Fund
Statement of Revenues, Expenditures, and Changes in Fund Balance
For the Year Ended December 31, 2009

Revenues, by source	
Property taxes	$1,800,000
Charges for services	155,000
Fines and forfeits	125,000
	2,080,000
Expenditures, by function	
Administration	209,000
Public safety	1,438,000
Street maintenance	418,000
	2,065,000
Excess of revenues over expenditures	15,000
Fund balance, January 1, 2009	0
Fund balance, December 31, 2009	$ 15,000

sheet "balance." As the balance sheet (Table 4-9) shows, the General Fund has total assets of $2,080,000 versus total liabilities of $2,065,000, or net assets of $15,000. The General Fund's net assets are represented by total fund balance.

The balance sheet reveals that the General Fund is in an illiquid situation: The $2,065,000 current liability, represented by vouchers payable, exceeds the General Fund's available cash of $2,055,000. Further inspection of the balance sheet shows that the cash shortage occurs because $25,000 of taxes receivable

TABLE 4-9	Illustrative Balance Sheet

Town of Arthursville
General Fund
Balance Sheet
December 31, 2009

Assets	
Cash	$2,055,000
Taxes receivable	25,000
Total assets	$2,080,000
Liabilities	
Vouchers payable	$2,065,000
Fund Balance	
Unreserved	15,000
Total liabilities and fund balance	$2,080,000

TABLE 4-10   Illustrative Budgetary Comparison Statement

Town of Arthursville
General Fund
Statement of Revenues, Expenditures, and
Changes in Fund Balance—Budget and Actual
For the Year Ended December 31, 2009

Revenues	*Budget*	*Actual*	*Variance Favorable (Unfavorable)*
Property taxes	$1,800,000	$1,800,000	$ 0
Charges for services	150,000	155,000	5,000
Fines and forfeits	125,000	125,000	0
	2,075,000	2,080,000	5,000
Expenditures			
Administration	209,000	209,000	0
Public safety	1,440,000	1,438,000	2,000
Street maintenance	420,000	418,000	2,000
Debt service	1,000	0	1,000
	2,070,000	2,065,000	5,000
Excess of revenues over expenditures	5,000	15,000	10,000
Unreserved fund balance, January 1, 2009	0	0	0
Unreserved fund balance, December 31, 2009	$ 5,000	$ 15,000	$10,000

remain to be collected at fiscal year end. In short, ending fund balance is positive because of accrued revenues, but the liquidity of the fund is negative because accrued revenues have not yet been realized in cash. This set of circumstances easily can occur in practice and is a reason that governments typically prepare cash forecasts, as discussed in Chapter 3. (In practice, governments must antici-pate that some accrued revenues never will be collected. We introduce account-ing for uncollectible property taxes in Chapter 5.)

Finally, the Statement of Revenues, Expenditures, and Changes in Fund Balance—Budget and Actual, often referred to as the *budgetary comparison statement,* appears in Table 4-10. Budget amounts for this statement are taken from the Revenues and Appropriations subsidiary ledgers.

The variance column of this statement explains why the General Fund's ac-tual ending fund balance is $15,000 when the budget plan called for a year-end fund balance of $5,000 (a total $10,000 favorable variance). First, the town of Arthursville recognized $5,000 more revenue than was budgeted because of un-expectedly high charges for services revenue. By itself, the effect of the revenue variance is to increase actual fund balance by $5,000 compared with budget. Sec-ond, the town incurred expenditures less than appropriations for three items ($2,000 for public safety, $2,000 for street maintenance, and $1,000 for debt service), an aggregate favorable expenditure variance of $5,000. The favorable expenditure variance also has the effect of increasing actual fund balance by $5,000 compared with budget. Taken together, the two favorable variances comprise the total $10,000 amount by which the actual fund balance of $15,000 exceeds the budgeted fund balance of $5,000.

The Extended Illustration: Journal Entries and Financial Statements

Now, to add a bit more "real world" complexity to this illustration, we extend the illustration by assuming that additional transactions occurred between the preceding transaction 7 and fiscal year end. Specifically, the General Fund borrowed cash on a note payable, paid the vouchers payable balance in full, and recorded accrued interest in the General Fund's general ledger. These are transactions 9, 10, and 11 in the following discussion.

9. Note that the temporary cash shortage was caused by the town's inability to collect all the taxes receivable in sufficient time to pay all its bills. State law allows the town to borrow short-term in anticipation of the collection of taxes. These borrowings are called *tax anticipation notes*. The town expects to receive all the taxes by February 28, 2010, so the town sells $25,000 (the full amount of the taxes receivable) of tax anticipation notes on September 1, 2009. The note is payable February 28, 2010, with interest at the rate of 5 percent per annum. Because the liability is short term, it is recorded as a General Fund liability. The entry to record the borrowing is as follows:

Cash	25,000	
Tax anticipation notes payable		25,000
To record borrowing on tax anticipation note.		

10. Arthursville disburses cash to pay the General Fund vouchers payable balance in full:

Vouchers payable	2,065,000	
Cash		2,065,000
To record payment of vouchers payable.		

11. The borrowing on the note took place on September, 1, 2009, so, at year end, the town is liable for four months' interest (assuming a 360-day year). Using the Principal $\times$ Interest Rate $\times$ Time Period formula for interest, the interest amount is $417 ($25,000 principal $\times$ 5% per year $\times$ 4 months = $417. The liability for the accrued interest is a General Fund liability, so the following entry is made:

Expenditures—debt service	417	
Accrued interest payable		417
To record interest accrued on note payable at year end.		

    Recall from Chapter 3 that governments' external fund-level operating statements must report expenditures classified, at a minimum, by *character* (current operating, debt service, and capital outlay) and by *function/program* within the current operating character classification. At the conclusion of the basic illustration, Arthursville's General Fund operating statement (Table 4-8) presented only "current operating" expenditures, subclassified by function. The above entry signifies, however, that Arthursville's General Fund operating statement now will include a Debt Service expenditure character classification.

    After journal entries 9, 10, and 11, the preclosing trial balance is as shown in Table 4-11. Observe that there is no longer any vouchers payable balance. Items

TABLE 4-11   Year-End Preclosing Trial Balance (Adjusted)

Town of Arthursville
General Fund
Preclosing Trial Balance
December 31, 2009

Account	Dr	Cr
Estimated revenues—property taxes	$1,800,000	
Estimated revenues—charges for services	150,000	
Estimated revenues—fines and forfeits	125,000	
Appropriations—administration		$ 210,000
Appropriations—public safety		1,440,000
Appropriations—street maintenance		420,000
Budgetary fund balance		5,000
Cash	**15,000**	
Taxes receivable	25,000	
Tax anticipation notes payable		**25,000**
Accrued interest payable		**417**
Revenues—property taxes		1,800,000
Revenues—charges for services		155,000
Revenues—fines and forfeits		125,000
Expenditures—administration	209,000	
Expenditures—public safety	1,438,000	
Expenditures—street maintenance	418,000	
Expenditures—debt service	**417**	
	$4,180,417	$4,180,417

that differ from the preclosing trial balance in the basic illustration (Table 4-6) appear in boldface type.

12. The books are closed at the end of the fiscal year. The budgetary general ledger reversing entry is the same as that in the first part of this illustration. For convenience, we repeat it here:

Appropriations—administration	209,000	
Appropriations—public safety	1,440,000	
Appropriations—street maintenance	420,000	
Appropriations—debt service	1,000	
Budgetary fund balance	5,000	
Estimated revenues—property taxes		1,800,000
Estimated revenues—charges for services		150,000
Estimated revenues—fines and forfeits		125,000

To reverse the General Fund budgetary entry for 2009.

The next entry closes actual revenues and expenditures to unreserved fund balance:

Revenues—property taxes	1,800,000	
Revenues—charges for services	155,000	
Revenues—fines and forfeits	125,000	
Expenditures—administration		209,000

Expenditures—public safety	1,438,000
Expenditures—street maintenance	418,000
Expenditures—debt service	417
Unreserved fund balance	14,583

To close the revenue and expenditure accounts
at fiscal year end.

The postclosing trial balance is presented in Table 4-12.

The town prepares the financial statements for the General Fund. Table 4-13 presents the Statement of Revenues, Expenditures, and Changes in Fund Balance. Observe

---

TABLE 4-12   Postclosing Trial Balance (Adjusted)

Town of Arthursville
General Fund
Postclosing Trial Balance
December 31, 2009

Account	Dr	Cr
Cash	$15,000	
Taxes receivable	25,000	
Tax anticipation notes payable		25,000
Accrued interest payable		417
Unreserved fund balance		14,583
	$40,000	$40,000

TABLE 4-13   Illustrative Statement of Revenues, Expenditures, and Changes in Fund Balance (Adjusted)

Town of Arthursville
General Fund
Statement of Revenues, Expenditures, and Changes in Fund Balance
For the Year Ended December 31, 2009

Revenues, by source	
Property taxes	$1,800,000
Charges for services	155,000
Fines and forfeits	125,000
	2,080,000
Expenditures	
Current operating	
Administration	209,000
Public safety	1,438,000
Street maintenance	418,000
Debt Service	417
	2,065,417
Excess of revenues over expenditures	14,583
Fund balance, January 1, 2009	0
Fund balance, December 31, 2009	$ 14,583

TABLE 4-14   Illustrative Balance Sheet (Adjusted)

Town of Arthursville
General Fund
Balance Sheet
December 31, 2009

Assets	
Cash	$15,000
Taxes receivable	25,000
Total assets	$40,000
Liabilities	
Accrued interest payable	$ 417
Tax anticipation notes payable	25,000
Total liabilities	25,417
Fund Balance	
Unreserved	14,583
Total liabilities and fund balance	$40,000

that expenditures are classified by character and, within the current operating character classification, by function.

We see from Table 4-13 that, in the extended illustration, fund balance at the end of fiscal 2009 is less than ending fund balance in the basic illustration. This, of

TABLE 4-15   Illustrative Budgetary Comparison Statement (Adjusted)

Town of Arthursville
General Fund
Statement of Revenues, Expenditures, and
Changes in Fund Balance–Budget and Actual
For the Year Ended December 31, 2009

Revenues	*Budget*	*Actual*	*Variance Favorable (Unfavorable)*
Property taxes	$1,800,000	$1,800,000	$ 0
Charges for services	150,000	155,000	5,000
Fines and forfeits	125,000	125,000	0
	2,075,000	2,080,000	5,000
Expenditures			
Administration	209,000	209,000	0
Public safety	1,440,000	1,438,000	2,000
Street maintenance	420,000	418,000	2,000
Debt service	1,000	417	583
	2,070,000	2,065,417	4,583
Excess of revenues over expenditures	5,000	14,583	9,583
Unreserved fund balance, January 1, 2009	0	0	0
Unreserved fund balance, December 31, 2009	$ 5,000	$ 14,583	$9,583

course, is because total expenditures in the extended illustration exceed total expenditures in the basic illustration by the amount of accrued interest, $417. The balance sheet and the budgetary comparison statement prepared at the end of the extended illustration appear in Tables 4-14 and 4-15, respectively. The balance sheet presents total assets and liabilities that are greatly reduced from those presented at the conclusion of the basic illustration (Table 4-9) because, in the extended illustration, the town settled the vouchers payable liability by paying cash. Also, in the budgetary comparison statement, notice that the increase in total expenditures in the extended illustration due to the interest accrual changes the amounts of certain variances, subtotals, and totals.

We conclude this chapter by discussing the use of control accounts with subsidiary ledgers.

CONTROL ACCOUNTS AND SUBSIDIARY LEDGERS

In the illustration earlier in this chapter, the town of Arthursville debited the current asset account, Taxes receivable, for $1,800,000, the full amount of the 2009 tax levy. The total taxes receivable balance, of course, consists of many smaller amounts receivable from individual property owners. In practice, it is necessary for governments to maintain records of the specific property taxes levied on—and paid by—individual property owners. In this manner, governments can identify taxpayers who are in arrears on some or all of their property tax liabilities.

Maintaining a separate general ledger account for each piece of taxable property within a governmental unit is not practical. This would result in a general ledger having from hundreds to many thousands of individual taxes receivable accounts and would be unworkably cumbersome. (The same problem would confront a business that maintained separate accounts receivable accounts in its general ledger for each of its many customers.)

The practical solution to this problem is for governments to maintain a general ledger *control account* supported by a subsidiary ledger similar in nature to those we introduced previously. The control account records *aggregate* increases and decreases in property taxes receivable, while the subsidiary ledger captures the increases and decreases in taxes receivable by individual taxpayer in what are called "subsidiary accounts" or "subaccounts." The subsidiary ledger for property taxes receivable often is called a "tax roll."

In practice, a tax roll will include, for each piece of taxable property, details such as the legal description of the property, address of property, type of property (in cases in which undeveloped property is taxed at a rate different from that for developed property), name of property owner, and assessed value.

Table 4-16 illustrates a simplified tax roll. Assumed amounts are posted to this subsidiary ledger corresponding to entry 2 (property tax levy) and entries 4 and 6 (cash receipts) from the Arthursville illustration presented previously. It shows the property tax amounts receivable from individual property owners comprising the total property tax levy of $1,800,000 and the property tax collections from individuals for the year which aggregate to $1,775,000. It also identifies F. Chopin as being among the taxpayers who are in arrears on some or all of their individual property tax liabilities. As further explained in Chapter 5, the town may impose interest

TABLE 4-16 Town of Arthursville Tax Roll

Town of Arthursville
Tax Roll 2009

Taxpayer	Item #	Levied	Collected	Dr (Cr) Balance Due
J. Bach	2	$ 2,500		$ 2,500
	4		$ 1,250	1,250
	6		1,250	0
J. Brahms	2	3,000		3,000
	4		1,500	1,500
	6		1,500	0
F. Chopin	2	4,000		4,000
	4		2,000	2,000
	6		0	2,000
E. Grieg	2	2,600		2,600
	4		1,300	1,300
	6		1,300	0
F. Mendelssohn	2	3,500		3,500
	4		1,750	1,750
	6		1,750	0
W. Mozart	2	8,000		8,000
	4		4,000	4,000
	6		4,000	0
J. Strauss	2	2,700		2,700
	4		1,350	1,350
	6		1,350	0
A. Sullivan	2	1,800		1,800
	4		900	900
	6		900	0
etc.		etc.	etc.	etc.
Totals		$1,800,000	$1,775,000	$25,000

and/or penalties on property owners who are in arrears on property tax payments. At the extreme, the town may foreclose on property for which taxes have not been paid.

CLOSING COMMENTS

This chapter illustrates some of the basic events and transactions that normally take place within the governmental accounting cycle of the General Fund and Special Revenue Funds of governmental units. General journal entries we presented included the revenue "source" classifications and the appropriations/expenditures "functional" classifications. For the most part, this is the level of detail that we will illustrate in following chapters.

We provided examples of the financial statements that governments prepare for individual funds at the end of the fiscal year. These include the balance sheet, the statement of revenues, expenditures, and changes in fund balance ("operating statement"), and the budgetary comparison statement.

We also introduced vouchers payable in this chapter. In practice, most governmental units use a voucher system for all expenditures, including salaries. However, as we proceed in this text, sometimes we will dispense with recording vouchers payable prior to recording cash disbursements, for the sake of simplicity. That is, we will assume the immediate payment of cash when expenditures are incurred.

Additionally, this chapter illustrated a short-term borrowing transaction. (Governmental units also borrow long term, usually by selling bonds. When bonds are issued, fund-level entries are made in the fund receiving the proceeds of the bond issue, usually a Capital Projects Fund. Long-term borrowings are discussed in Chapter 6.) Finally, we discussed governments' use of control accounts and subsidiary ledgers to reduce the degree of detail they must maintain in their general ledgers.

The basic concepts presented in this chapter will apply to several of the following chapters. Of course, we will build on the material presented here as we introduce some of the additional complexities that characterize actual practice.

Summary Problem

This problem reviews the concepts in this chapter. If you have any questions as you review the problem, turn back to the appropriate sections and reread the material.

On December 31, 2008, the city council of Surf City approved the budget shown in Table 4-17.

Among the accounting policies of Surf City are the following:

1. All purchases of supplies are encumbered.
2. Other expenditures do not require encumbrances.
3. Control and subsidiary accounts are maintained for property taxes receivable.
4. Vouchers are used to record all purchases.

TABLE 4-17 Annual Budget		

Surf City
General Fund Budget
For the Year Ended December 31, 2009

Estimated Revenues		
Property taxes	$900,000	
License fees	50,000	
Fines	40,000	
Service charges	10,000	$1,000,000
Appropriations		
Salaries	$700,000	
Supplies	200,000	
Other	89,000	
Debt service	1,000	990,000
Budgeted Increase in Fund Balance		$ 10,000

The opening, or budgetary, entry is

Estimated revenues—property taxes	900,000	
Estimated revenues—license fees	50,000	
Estimated revenues—fines	40,000	
Estimated revenues—service charges	10,000	
Appropriations—salaries		700,000
Appropriations—supplies		200,000
Appropriations—other		89,000
Appropriations—debt service		1,000
Budgetary fund balance		10,000

To record estimated revenues and appropriations for FY 2009.

The operating entries are as follows:

Property taxes receivable—control	900,000	
Revenues—property taxes		900,000

To set up receivable for FY 2009 property taxes.
(Note: Subsidiary accounts are not shown here.)

Encumbrances—supplies	200,000	
Budgetary fund balance reserved for encumbrances		200,000

To record encumbering of Purchase Order No. 1426.

Cash	100,000	
Tax anticipation notes payable		100,000

To record issuance of tax anticipation notes.

Cash	900,000	
Property taxes receivable—control		900,000

To record collection of FY 2009 property taxes.

Budgetary balance fund reserved for encumbrances	200,000	
Encumbrances—supplies		200,000

To record receipt of supplies ordered under Purchase
Order No. 1426.

Expenditures—supplies	195,000	
Vouchers payable		195,000

To record expenditure for supplies purchased under Purchase
Order No. 1426. (Note: The supplier delivered the entire order,
and reduced the price by $5,000.)

Cash	96,000	
Revenues—license fees		47,000
Revenues—fines		38,000
Revenues—service charges		11,000

To record collection of nonproperty tax revenues, FY 2009.

Vouchers payable	195,000	
Cash		195,000

To record payment for supplies purchased under Purchase
Order No. 1426.

Expenditures—salaries	700,000	
Expenditures—other	89,000	
Cash		700,000
Vouchers payable		89,000

To record expenditures for salaries and other items during FY 2009.

Vouchers payable	89,000	
Cash		89,000

To record payment of outstanding FY 2009 vouchers.

Expenditures—debt service	1,000	
Tax anticipation notes payable	100,000	
Cash		101,000

To record repayment of tax anticipation notes, with interest.
(*Note:* The amount of interest on the note is assumed.)

The closing entries are as follows:

Appropriations—salaries	700,000	
Appropriations—supplies	200,000	
Appropriations—other	89,000	
Appropriations—debt service	1,000	
Budgetary fund balance	10,000	
Estimated revenues—property taxes		900,000
Estimated revenues—license fees		50,000
Estimated revenues—fines		40,000
Estimated revenues—service charges		10,000

To close budgetary accounts for FY 2009.

Revenues—property taxes	900,000	
Revenues—license fees	47,000	
Revenues—fines	38,000	
Revenues—service charges	11,000	
Expenditures—salaries		700,000
Expenditures—supplies		195,000
Expenditures—other		89,000
Expenditures—debt service		1,000
Unreserved fund balance		11,000

To close nonbudgetary accounts for FY 2009.

After closing entries have been posted, the postclosing trial balance will appear as shown in Table 4-18. The resulting fund financial statements are shown in Table 4-19.

TABLE 4-18 Postclosing Trial Balance

Surf City
General Fund
Postclosing Trial Balance
December 31, 2009

	Debits	Credits
Cash	$11,000	
Unreserved fund balance		$11,000
	$11,000	$11,000

TABLE 4-19   Fund Financial Statements

Surf City
General Fund
Balance Sheet
December 31, 2009

Assets		Liabilities and Fund Balance	
Cash	$11,000	Unreserved fund balance	$11,000

Surf City
General Fund
Statement of Revenues, Expenditures, and Changes in Fund Balance
For the Fiscal Year Ended December 31, 2009

Revenues		
Property taxes	$900,000	
License fees	47,000	
Fines	38,000	
Service charges	11,000	
Total revenues		$996,000
Expenditures		
Current operating		
Salaries	$700,000	
Supplies	195,000	
Other	89,000	
Debt service	1,000	
Total Expenditures		985,000
Excess of Revenues over Expenditures		
and Net Change in Fund Balance		$11,000
Fund balance, January 1, 2009		-0-
Fund balance, December 31, 2009		$11,000

Review Questions

Q4-1   What is the major distinction between the accounting cycle of a commercial business and the accounting cycle of a government fund?

Q4-2   What is the minimum number of Special Revenue Funds you would expect a local government to have?

Q4-3   What are some similarities and differences between a General Fund and a Special Revenue Fund?

Q4-4   Which financial statements do governments prepare for their General Funds?

Q4-5   Do the differences between full accrual accounting and modified accrual accounting apply to revenues, expenditures, or both? Explain.

Q4-6   Provide some examples of revenues (revenue sources) that governments normally accrue in advance of receiving cash. What revenue sources do governments normally record at the time cash is received?

Q4-7   If the debits to Estimated Revenues are less than the credits to Appropriations in the budgetary journal entry made at the outset of the fiscal year, does the government expect actual fund balance to increase or decrease during the year? Explain.

Q4-8 When a government levies property taxes, what accounts are debited and credited? When a government collects property taxes, what accounts are debited and credited?

Q4-9 What is a voucher? What purpose(s) does a voucher serve?

Q4-10 For a General Fund or a Special Revenue Fund, what does a credit balance in the unreserved fund balance account at the end of the year signify? What does a debit balance signify?

Q4-11 What are some arguments in favor of maintaining a budgetary fund balance account separate from the actual, unreserved fund balance account?

Q4-12 For a General Fund, does a credit balance in the unreserved fund balance account at the end of the year necessarily mean that the fund has sufficient cash to pay its liabilities in full? Why or why not?

Q4-13 What is a tax roll? What purpose(s) does a tax roll serve?

Q4-14 Assume that, in its first year of operation, a General Fund has expenditures equal to appropriations and estimated revenues in excess of actual revenues. Will the actual fund balance at year end be less than, equal to, or greater than the budgetary fund recorded at the beginning of the year? Explain.

Case

C4-1 Because of lax tax collections, the City of Bliss has run out of money on several occasions. Upon reviewing this situation, the new finance director noticed that most purchases of goods and services are actually for less than amounts encumbered for these purchases. As a result, he requested that, when removing encumbrances, only the actual amount of the purchase be reversed out, not the entire amount encumbered. Using this method, he reasoned, will provide a "cushion" that can be used to make up any shortfall that might arise by the end of the year.

Do you think this accounting practice is sound?

Ethics Cases

EC4-1 The newly elected mayor of Wherever noticed that in the recently enacted budget of that city's General Fund, revenues exceed expenditures by $15,000. Later that year, after a hurricane caused a large amount of damage, she ordered the city's finance officer to write a check for $15,000, on the General Fund, to an emergency relief fund. Because of the unexpected nature of the hurricane, no appropriation had been made to cover this transaction. When confronted by the press, she pointed out that the General Fund was only required under the balanced budget laws of the state to "break even" and that she could not, in good conscience, allow the city to retain idle monies when people needed help.

From an accounting standpoint, did the mayor do the right thing? From an ethical standpoint?

EC4-2 You are the finance director of Bloomfield City. Recently, the voters of your city approved a special property tax to finance the purchase of books and software for the local library. The day the first receipts from this new tax arrived, you ate lunch with the mayor. After finishing his second piece of pie, the mayor suggested that you record the proceeds of this tax in the General Fund. "I know that this is a dedicated tax, but we need the money now to pay for the new computers and police cars we just purchased. This fall, when sales tax collections peak, we will buy some books and software for the library. If sales tax collections are down, the library patrons will just have to reread the old books." Assuming that the mayor is a reasonable person, how would you respond to his comments?

Exercises

E4-1 (Budgetary entries)
The city council of Alhambra approved the following budget:

Estimated Revenues		
Property taxes	$160,000	
Fines and fees	25,000	
Service charges	15,000	
Licenses	10,000	$210,000
Appropriations		
Salaries	$100,000	
Materials and supplies	60,000	
Capital outlay	40,000	200,000
Budgeted Increase in Fund Balance		$10,000

Required: Prepare the budgetary entry necessary at the beginning of the fiscal year.

E4-2 (Budgetary entries)
The budget for the Perlita Park Fund is as follows:

Estimated Revenues	
Property taxes	$2,400,000
Greens fees	600,000
Camping fees	400,000
Fines and permits	200,000
Appropriations	
Wage and salaries	$1,600,000
Grass seed	200,000
Animal food	200,000
Operating supplies	400,000
Outside services	600,000
Repave driveways	200,000
Move locomotive	50,000
Construct shelters	300,000

Required:
1. Prepare the entry to record the approved budget at the beginning of the year.
2. If this year is the park's first year of operation, how much should the fund balance contain at the end of the year if actual revenues and expenditures are as planned?

E4-3   (Closing entries)

The ledger of the General Fund of the City of New Rachel shows the following balances at the end of the fiscal year:

Estimated revenues	$300,000
Appropriations	285,000
Budgetary fund balance	15,000
Revenues	300,000
Expenditures	285,000

Required: Prepare closing entries.

E4-4   (Closing entries)

At the end of FY 2009, the following balances were found in the ledger of the Green Creek Library Fund:

Estimated revenues	$800,000
Appropriations	750,000
Budgetary fund balance	50,000
Revenues	780,000
Expenditures	760,000

Required: Prepare closing entries. What was the net effect on Unreserved fund balance?

E4-5   (Complete budgetary cycle)

The board of supervisors of Delaware County approved the following budget for FY 2009:

Estimated Revenues		
Property taxes	$66,000	
Traffic fines	40,000	$106,000
Appropriations		
Salaries	$80,000	
Supplies	12,000	
Other	8,000	100,000
Budgeted Increase in Fund Balance		$ 6,000

Transactions for FY 2009 were as follows:

1. Mailed property tax bills amounting to $66,000 at the beginning of the year.
2. Collected property taxes of $66,000 in cash during the year.
3. Purchased supplies for $12,000.
4. Paid salaries of $80,000.
5. Collected traffic fines of $40,000.
6. Purchased a membership in the Kenner Country Club for Sheriff Lee in recognition of his services to the county. The cost of the membership was $8,000.

Required: Prepare journal entries to set up the budgetary accounts, to record these transactions, and to close the budgetary and nonbudgetary accounts. Do not make entries to record encumbrances.

(E4-6) (Complete budgetary cycle)

The city council of Avalon approved the following budget for FY 2009.

Estimated Revenues

Property taxes	$150,000	
Fines and penalties	40,000	
Service charges	10,000	$200,000

Appropriations

Salaries	$100,000	
Supplies	30,000	
Equipment	65,000	195,000
Budgeted Increase in Fund Balance		$ 5,000

In FY 2009, the following transactions took place:

1. Mailed property tax bills for $150,000 at the beginning of the year.
2. Collected property taxes of $150,000 during the year.
3. Purchased equipment for $60,000.
4. Purchased supplies for $34,000.
5. Collected fines and penalties of $38,000 and service charges of $7,000 in cash.
6. Paid salaries of $98,000.

Required: Prepare journal entries to set up budgetary accounts, to record these transactions, and to close the budgetary and nonbudgetary accounts. Do not make entries to record encumbrances.

E4-7   (Complete budgetary cycle)

The board of supervisors of Oraibi Township approved the following budget for FY 2009:

Revenues

Licenses	$10,000	
Fines	5,000	
Parking	3,000	
Parade permits	2,000	
Gas royalties	20,000	$40,000

Appropriations

Salaries	$25,000	
Materials	10,000	
Equipment	3,000	38,000
Budgeted Increase in Fund Balance		$ 2,000

Actual Revenues

Licenses	$11,000
Fines	7,000
Parking	3,000
Parade permits	2,500
Gas royalties	19,500

Actual Expenditures

Salaries	$24,000
Materials	8,000
Equipment	5,000

The township does not use encumbrances. All expenditures are paid in cash. Assume that property tax bills totaling $150,000 were mailed at the beginning of the year.

Required: 1. Prepare the budgetary entry.
2. Prepare operating entries. (Do not record encumbrances.)
3. Prepare closing entries.

E4-8 (Encumbrances)
In February, the City of Golders Green ordered a fire engine, for which the manufacturer quoted a price of $120,000. The machine arrived the following month, along with an invoice for $120,000.

Required:

1. Make the appropriate journal entries to record setting up the encumbrance, the removal of the encumbrance, and the expenditure and the liability to the vendor.
2. Assume that the actual cost of the fire engine was $125,000. Would your entries be the same as in the preceding question? Why?

E4-9 (Encumbrances)
On January 10, the City of Wynnewood issued a purchase order to its stationery supplier for $50,000. On March 20, the stationery arrived, along with an invoice for $50,000, which was immediately approved for payment. The invoice was paid on April 15.
Required: Prepare the entries necessary to record setting up the encumbrance, the arrival of the stationery and approval for payment of the invoice, and the payment of the invoice.

E4-10 (Encumbrances)
On April 25, the City of Bryn Mawr ordered supplies with a quoted price of $80,000. On May 15, one half of the supplies arrived, along with an invoice for $40,000. On June 6, the other half of the supplies arrived, accompanied by an invoice for $42,000. Both invoices were paid at the end of the month of arrival. Assume that there are sufficient resources in the appropriation to pay both invoices and that invoices are approved for payment upon receipt of the accompanying goods or services.

Required: 1. Prepare entries to record setting up the encumbrance, the arrival of the supplies in May and June and approval of the invoice, and the payment for the supplies.
2. What effect, if any, will the second invoice have on the balance of the appropriation?

Problems

P4-1 (Discussion question on governmental accounting)
Governmental accounting gives substantial recognition to budgets, with those budgets being recorded in the accounts of the governmental unit.

Required: 1. What is the purpose of a governmental accounting system, and why is the budget recorded in the accounts of a governmental unit? Include in your discussion the purpose and significance of appropriations.

2. Describe when and how a governmental unit records its budget and closes it out.

(AICPA adapted)

P4-2 (Complete set of entries and statements)

The following transactions apply to the FY 2008 operations of Arctic City:

a. Revenues were estimated at $150,000. Appropriations of $145,000 were made.

b. Property tax bills totaling $120,000 were mailed at the beginning of the year. During the year, the entire amount was collected. Fines and penalties collected amounted to $28,000.

c. Supplies worth $33,000 were purchased during the year. Salaries paid amounted to $100,000, and utilities for the year amounted to $9,000. The Board does not use encumbrances. All expenditures were paid in full and in cash during the year.

Required:

1. Prepare journal entries to record the transactions.
2. Post the entries made in part (1). (Use T-accounts.)
3. Prepare a preclosing trial balance.
4. Prepare closing entries.
5. Post the entries made in part (4).
6. Prepare a postclosing trial balance.
7. Prepare, in good form, a balance sheet and a statement of revenues, expenditures, and changes in fund balance for FY 2008. Assume that the fund balance at the beginning of the year was zero.

P4-3 (Beginning balances, complete set of statements)

The December 31, 2007, postclosing trial balance of the General Fund of the City of Pompano was as follows:

	Debits	Credits
Cash	$500	
Accounts receivable	300	
Vouchers payable		$400
Unreserved fund balance		400
	$800	$800

a. The city council estimated revenues for FY 2008 to be $1,500 and expenditures to be $1,450.

b. The city's outstanding voucher payable, due to a contractor for remodeling city hall, was paid in March.

c. Service charges of $800 were collected during the year.

d. The Provo Bread Company paid the city $300 it owed for repairs to a fire hydrant because of damage done by a runaway delivery truck.

e. Speeding tickets, which resulted in fines of $500, were issued to tourists en route to the city. The fines were paid in cash.

f. Salaries of $1,000 were paid to the mayor and the city clerk. Supplies costing $125 were purchased for cash.

g. A used traffic light was purchased from the City of Clarkson for $150, to be paid the following year.

Required:

1. Prepare journal entries to record the listed transactions in the General Fund.
2. Post these journal entries to the ledger. (Use T-accounts.)
3. Prepare a preclosing trial balance.
4. Prepare closing entries and post to the ledger.
5. Prepare a postclosing trial balance.
6. Prepare, in good form, a balance sheet and a statement of revenues, expenditures, and changes in fund balance.

P4-4   (Multiple choice)

1. Which of the following revenues can be recorded when levied (when bills are mailed), rather than when actually received?
   a. Fines
   b. Property taxes
   c. Service charges
   d. Licenses and permits

2. Which of the following events causes the Estimated revenues control account of a governmental unit to be debited?
   a. Budgetary accounts are closed at the end of the year.
   b. The budget is recorded.
   c. Actual revenues are recorded.
   d. Actual revenues are collected.

3. Which of the following accounts of a governmental unit is debited when a purchase order is approved?
   a. Encumbrances
   b. Budgetary fund balance reserved for encumbrances
   c. Vouchers payable
   d. Appropriations

4. When a police car is received by a governmental unit, the entry on the books of the General Fund should include a debit to which of the following?
   a. Appropriations—police cars
   b. Expenditures—police cars
   c. Encumbrances—police cars
   d. Unreserved fund balance

5. Which of the following terms refers to an actual cost, rather than an estimate?
   a. Expenditure
   b. Appropriation
   c. Budget
   d. Encumbrance

6. In approving the budget of the City of Troy, the city council appropriated an amount greater than expected revenues. What will be the result of this action?
   a. A cash overdraft during the fiscal year
   b. An increase in outstanding encumbrances by the end of the fiscal year
   c. A debit to Budgetary fund balance
   d. A necessity for compensatory offsetting action in the Debt Service Fund

7. Which of the following is a budgetary account?
   a. Expenditures—supplies
   b. Appropriations
   c. Revenues—property taxes
   d. Vouchers payable

8. If estimated revenues exceed appropriations, closing the budgetary accounts must include which of the following entries?
   a. A debit to Estimated revenues
   b. A debit to Revenues—control
   c. A debit to Budgetary fund balance
   d. A credit to Budgetary fund balance

9. Entries similar to those for the General Fund may also appear on the books of a municipality's _____.
   a. Enterprise Fund
   b. Private Purpose Trust Fund
   c. Agency Fund
   d. Special Revenue Fund

10. What type of account is used to earmark a portion of the appropriation to record the contingent obligation for goods ordered but not yet received?
    a. Encumbrance
    b. Expenditure
    c. Obligation
    d. Budgetary fund balance reserved for encumbrances

11. Authority granted by a legislative body to make expenditures and to incur obligations during a fiscal year is the definition of _____.
    a. An appropriation
    b. An authorization
    c. An encumbrance
    d. Budgetary fund balance reserved for encumbrances

(AICPA adapted)

P4-5   (Complete set of entries; breakdown of revenue and expenditure accounts) The city council of Masonville approved the following budget for its General Fund on December 31, 2008:

Revenues	
Property taxes	$ 85,000
Service charges	35,000
Parking meters	15,000
Fines and penalties	10,000
Liquor licenses	5,000

Appropriations

Salaries	$100,000
Supplies	20,000
Equipment	15,000
Motor scooters	10,000

FY 2009 is the first year of operation for this city. As a result, there are no balances in the accounts as of January 1, 2009. Assume that the city uses encumbrances and a voucher system to record all expenditures, except for salaries. During 2009, the following transactions took place:

a. FY 2009 tax bills were mailed to the property owners.
b. Ordered supplies expected to cost $20,000.
c. The supplies arrived, along with an invoice for $19,000; the invoice was paid immediately.
d. Paid salaries of $97,000 for the year.
e. Ordered equipment costing $15,000.
f. Collected property taxes for the year, in full. Collections of service charges were $33,000.
g. Four motor scooters were ordered from a local dealer, who had submitted a bid for $10,000.
h. Parking meter revenues for the year were $18,000, and receipts from the issuance of liquor licenses amounted to $2,000.
i. Collections from fines and penalties were $9,000.
j. The equipment ordered arrived, along with an invoice for $15,000; the invoice was paid immediately.
k. The motor scooters arrived; because of a change in specifications, the dealer asked the city to pay an additional $500 over the amount bid. The city agreed to this additional cost and promptly issued a check for $10,500 to the dealer for the motor scooters. Before issuing the check, the city made a budgetary revision—it increased the appropriation for motor scooters by $500 and reduced the appropriation for supplies by the same amount.

Required: 1. Prepare appropriate journal entries to record the budget and these transactions (including the budgetary interchange).
2. Post the entries and prepare a preclosing trial balance.
3. Make closing entries and prepare a postclosing trial balance.
4. Prepare, in good form, a balance sheet and a statement of revenues, expenditures, and changes in fund balance.

P4-6   (Prior balances, encumbrances, complete cycle)
The city council of Watford approved the following budget for the General Fund for FY 2008.

Revenues

Property taxes	$50,000	
License fees	10,000	
Fines and penalties	15,000	
Parking meters	5,000	
Federal grants	20,000	$100,000

Appropriations		
Salaries	$50,000	
Materials	20,000	
Motorcycles	24,000	
Interest	1,000	95,000
Budgeted Increase in Fund Balance		$ 5,000

The postclosing trial balance for the fund, as of December 31, 2007, was as follows:

	Debits	Credits
Cash	$ 5,000	
Due from federal government	10,000	
Vouchers payable		$ 8,000
Unreserved fund balance		7,000
	$15,000	$15,000

Transactions for FY 2008 include the following:
a. FY 2008 property tax bills were mailed to the property owners: $50,000.
b. Ordered two new motorcycles at an estimated total cost of $24,000.
c. Received a check for $30,000 from the federal government to cover 2007 and 2008 federal grants. (Hint: Record the FY 2008 grant as Revenues.)
d. Borrowed $15,000 from the Canal Bank for 6 months in anticipation of tax receipts.
e. Ordered materials costing $20,000.
f. Paid vouchers outstanding at the end of 2007: $8,000.
g. License fees for 2008 were $9,500. Fines and penalties were $16,000.
h. The motorcycles arrived, along with an invoice for $23,400.
i. Parking meter revenues for 2008 were $6,500.
j. Repaid loan to bank, along with accrued interest of $900.
k. The materials arrived, accompanied by an invoice for $19,500.
l. Paid the outstanding voucher for $23,400 to the vendor who supplied the motorcycles.
m. Salaries for the year were $50,000.
n. Property taxes received during the year were $50,000.

Required: 1. Prepare journal entries to record the budget and these transactions.
2. Prepare a preclosing balance.
3. Prepare closing entries.
4. Prepare a postclosing trial balance.
5. Prepare a balance sheet and a statement of revenues, expenditures, and changes in fund balance for FY 2008.

P4-7 (Journal entries and subsidiary ledgers)
Prepare the general journal entries to record the following General Fund transactions and events of Mercury Township for the fiscal year ended December 31, 2008. Also, prepare revenue and appropriations subsidiary ledgers and make the necessary postings thereto. Assume that Mercury Township vouchers all expenditures prior to payment. When you have finished your work, refer

to your subsidiary ledgers to answer the following questions as of the end of fiscal 2008:

a. What are the General Fund revenue variances by source? In total?

b. What is the remaining available appropriation for the General Government function? The Public Safety function? The Recreation function? The General Fund in total?

1. The annual budget for the General Fund was adopted as shown below and budgetary amounts were entered into the accounting system.

Estimated Revenues

Property taxes	$400,000
Licenses and permits	200,000
Fines and forfeits	25,000
	$625,000

Appropriations

General government	$ 70,000
Public safety	450,000
Parks and recreation	90,000
	$610,000

2. Property taxes were levied in the budgeted amount.

3. Purchase orders were issued for goods and services with the following estimated costs:

General government	$ 70,000
Public safety	450,000
Parks and recreation	90,000
	$610,000

4. Cash receipts were as follows

Property taxes	$345,000
Licenses and permits	168,000
Fines and forfeits	17,000
	$530,000

5. Items on order were received with the following encumbered and actual costs:

	Encumbered	*Actual*
General government	$ 45,000	$ 43,500
Public safety	350,000	348,000
Parks and recreation	44,000	43,100
	$439,000	$434,600

6. Additional cash was collected as follows

Property taxes	$ 50,000
Licenses and permits	33,000
Fines and forfeits	7,000
	$ 90,000

7. Additional items on order were received with the following encumbered and actual costs:

	Encumbered	Actual
General government	$ 25,000	$ 25,700
Public safety	100,000	101,400
Parks and recreation	46,000	42,300
	$171,000	$169,400

P4-8 (Preparation of financial statements)
Based on the information in the preceding problem, prepare the balance sheet and the statement of revenues expenditures and changes in fund balance—budget and actual for Mercury Township's General Fund for fiscal 2008. Assume that the beginning unreserved fund balance was zero.

P4-9 (Closing entries and financial statements with beginning balance in fund balance)
Below is the September 30, 2008, adjusted trial balance for Hubbub City's General Fund. (Encumbrance balances already have been reversed to zero.) Based on this information, prepare (1) entries necessary to close the general ledger accounts, (2) a statement of revenues, expenditures, and changes in fund balance, (3) a balance sheet, and (4) a statement of revenues, expenditures, and changes in fund balance—budget and actual.

Account	Dr	Cr
Accrued interest payable		$ 800
Appropriations—general government		158,500
Appropriations—parks and recreation		175,000
Appropriations—public safety		446,000
Appropriations—economic development		30,500
Budgetary fund balance	$ 10,000	
Cash	35,600	
Estimated revenues—property taxes	500,000	
Estimated revenues—intergovernmental	150,000	
Estimated revenues—charges for services	100,000	
Estimated revenues—fines and forfeits	50,000	
Expenditures—general government	150,500	
Expenditures—parks and recreation	170,500	
Expenditures—public safety	441,000	
Expenditures—economic development	27,000	
Note payable		10,000
Property taxes receivable	67,200	
Revenues—property taxes		497,000
Revenues—intergovernmental		154,000
Revenues—charges for services		99,000
Revenues—fines and forfeits		48,000
Unreserved fund balance		62,000
Vouchers payable		21,000
	$1,701,800	$1,701,800

P4-10 (Relationship between encumbrances and free balance; appropriations ledger)
The city council made an appropriation to the police department of $100,000
for the purchase of supplies, equipment, and vehicles.

a. The department placed an order for 10 motorcycles, estimated to cost
$5,000 each.

b. The department placed an order with Owen Supply Company for crime
prevention supplies; the estimated cost of the order was $30,000.

c. The motorcycles arrived in good condition, along with an invoice for
$50,000.

d. An order was placed for radio equipment; estimated cost was $10,000.

e. The supplies ordered in part (b) arrived, along with an invoice for $32,000.

f. The radio equipment was received in acceptable condition; actual cost was
$9,000.

g. The department purchased a new firearm for $250 cash, on an "emergency"
basis, directly from a local dealer; no order had been placed.

Required: 1. Prepare an appropriations ledger. Use columns for Appropriations, Encumbrances (Dr. and Cr.), Expenditures, and Available
balance.

2. What was the free balance at the end of the period?

THE GOVERNMENTAL FUND ACCOUNTING CYCLE

Additional Transactions of General and Special Revenue Funds— Introduction to Permanent Funds

Chapter Outline

After completing this chapter, you should be able to:

- Understand the significance of legal requirements to the accounting for property taxes.
- Prepare journal entries for the various aspects of property tax accounting.
- Understand the basic principle for recording expenditures and recognize several important exceptions to this principle.
- Understand reservations and designations of fund balance.
- Understand the four types of interfund activity and prepare journal entries for each type of activity.
- Prepare journal entries for budget revisions and allotments.
- Understand the accounting for acquisition and disposition of long-lived assets within governmental-type funds.
- Prepare journal entries to account for purchases and uses of inventory.
- Understand the basic accounting and financial reporting for Permanent Funds.

This chapter presents topics that expand upon the fundamentals of General Fund and Special Revenue Fund accounting introduced in Chapter 4. As such, the material we cover here will extend your knowledge of General Fund and Special Revenue Fund accounting to include most of the routine transactions found in practice.

Up to this point, the illustrations in this text have incorporated simplifying assumptions. We have assumed that all property taxes levied are collected and all encumbrances are reversed by the end of the fiscal year. In reality, of course, taxpayers are sometimes unable or unwilling to pay their taxes or taxes are collected too late for the government to treat them as revenues of the year for which they were assessed. Likewise, it is common for encumbrances to remain outstanding at the end of the fiscal year or to be reversed if the underlying purchase orders are canceled. The discussions in this chapter address these and other "real world" complexities. The major topics presented include property tax accounting, other taxes and grant revenues, certain aspects of expenditure accounting, fund balance presentation, interfund transactions, and additional aspects of budgetary accounting. The chapter also includes an "other issues" section and a review of fund financial statements. It concludes with a discussion of the basic accounting and financial reporting for Permanent Funds.

PROPERTY TAX ACCOUNTING

A number of situations can affect the accounting for property taxes. For example:

- Property tax laws may stipulate that taxes receivable become delinquent and thus subject to interest and penalties if not collected as of a specified date.
- Uncertainty may exist over how much of the property tax levy the government ultimately will collect.
- Governments may exercise the right to seize properties for nonpayment of taxes.
- Assessments on certain properties may require adjustment after taxes have been levied.

These issues, along with tax discounts and deferred property taxes, are discussed in this section.

Property Tax Laws

The largest source of revenue for most local governments is property taxes. The importance of this revenue source is underscored by the fact that the laws of local governments typically specify the property tax "calendar" for those governments. A property tax calendar identifies the dates on which property taxes are to be levied, become due, and become delinquent. Delinquent tax balances are subject to interest and/or penalties in many cases. Moreover, government property tax laws typically provide that the government can foreclose property for which back taxes are due and sell such property to enforce collections. The property tax calendar and related laws establish the normal sequence of property tax events and transactions, which we illustrate next. Table 5-1 presents the property tax calendar appearing in a recent financial report of the City of Reno, Nevada. (Notice that Washoe County, Nevada, administers the tax collection effort for Reno. This is a common practice and avoids undue duplication of effort.)

Basic Property Tax Entries

Chapter 4 introduced the journal entry to record the property tax levy. For example, if the General Fund property tax levy for a fiscal year was $1,000,000, the entry was

Property taxes receivable	1,000,000	
Revenues—property taxes		1,000,000
To record property tax levy.		

TABLE 5-1   Example Property Tax Calendar

City of Reno, Nevada
Notes to Financial Statements
June 30, 2006

Note 4: **Property Tax**

Washoe County is responsible for the assessment, collection and subsequent distribution to the City of property taxes. Property taxes are billed in July of each year. They are due in installments by the third Monday in August and the first Mondays in October, January, and March.

In the event of delinquent payments, the County Treasurer must assess a 4% penalty on the first installment, a 7% penalty on two installments, 11% on three installments, and a 16% penalty if all four installments are delinquent. In the event of nonpayment, the County will file a lien against the property on the first Monday in June.

If delinquent taxes and penalties are not paid after two years from the date of the lien, the County Treasurer will obtain a deed to the property and may sell the property to satisfy the lien.

Two modifications are needed to make this entry represent actual practice: First, the asset initially needs to be classified as "current," as opposed to "delinquent," so the debit caption will read "Property taxes receivable—current." Second, it is necessary to provide for uncollectible property taxes.

The standard practice for accounting for uncollectible property taxes is to recognize revenue at the net expected collectible amount. This procedure anticipates that a certain portion of the taxes levied will not be collected and is consistent with the short-term liquidity focus of fund accounting. Using past experience and predictions of future economic conditions, finance officials can estimate what percentage of the total taxes will be uncollectible. This forecasting is possible even though, at the time of the levy, it is not known which particular tax receivables will prove to be uncollectible.

When property taxes are levied, the Property taxes receivable—current account is debited for 100% of the levied amount to establish accounting control over property taxes receivable. Revenues—property taxes is credited for the amount of taxes expected to be collected and a contra asset account, Allowance for uncollectible taxes—current, is credited for the difference, the predicted total uncollectible amount. At such time as a specific property tax receivable is deemed uncollectible, the Allowance for uncollectible taxes account is reduced with a debit and the receivable in question is written off with a credit.[1]

We now present an extended illustration of property tax accounting. The effects of the following journal entries are summarized in Table 5-2. Assume that a city's property tax levy for 2008 is $1 million and that experience shows that about 4 percent of the taxes levied will not be collected. Therefore, a credit of $40,000 to the allowance account is necessary and revenues should be recognized net of the uncollectible amount.

---

[1]Typically, property tax receivables are not written off while they are "current." Instead, as we will see, the decision to write off property tax receivables is made at some point after the receivables have become "delinquent." Establishing the Allowance for uncollectible taxes at the time the property tax levy initially is recorded is necessary, however, to ensure that revenues are not accrued in excess of total expected property tax collections.

Table 5-2 Summary of Property Tax-Related Journal Entries   Dr   (Cr)   T/R = Taxes Receivable

	Cash	Vouchers Payable	Current Taxes Receivable	Allowance for Uncollectible Current Taxes	Delinquent Taxes Receivable	Allowance for Uncollectible Delinquent Taxes	Interest and Penalties Receivable	Tax Liens Receivable	Property Tax Revenues	Interest and Penalty Revenues
Initial levy			1,000,000	(40,000)	0	0	0	0	(960,000)	0
Cash receipts	940,000		(940,000)							
Subtotals	**940,000**	**0**	**60,000**	**(40,000)**	**0**	**0**	**0**	**0**	**(960,000)**	**0**
Reclassify current T/R and allowance to delinquent			(60,000)	40,000	60,000	(40,000)				
Subtotals	**940,000**	**0**	**0**	**0**	**60,000**	**(40,000)**	**0**	**0**	**(960,000)**	**0**
Write off T/R					(4,000)	4,000				
Subtotals	**940,000**	**0**	**0**	**0**	**56,000**	**(36,000)**	**0**	**0**	**(960,000)**	**0**
Accrue interest, etc.							600			(600)
Subtotals	**940,000**	**0**	**0**	**0**	**56,000**	**(36,000)**	**600**	**0**	**(960,000)**	**(600)**
Reclassify delinquent T/R to lien status					(8,000)		(500)	8,500		
Subtotals	**940,000**	**0**	**-0-**	**-0-**	**48,000**	**(36,000)**	**100**	**8,500**	**(960,000)**	**(600)**
Additional lien costs	(300)	(3,200)						300		
Subtotals	**939,700**	**(3,200)**	**0**	**0**	**48,000**	**(36,000)**	**100**	**8,800**	**(960,000)**	**(600)**
Sell property	12,000							(8,800)		
Subtotals	**951,700**	**(3,200)**	**0**	**0**	**48,000**	**(36,000)**	**100**	**8,800**	**(960,000)**	**(600)**
Pay vouchers	(3,200)	3,200								
Ending balances	**948,500**	**0**	**0**	**0**	**48,000**	**(36,000)**	**100**	**0**	**(960,000)**	**(600)**

Assuming the use of a control account for property taxes receivable, the entry to record the property tax levy is:

Property taxes receivable—current	1,000,000	
Allowance for uncollectible taxes—current		40,000
Revenues—property taxes		960,000
To accrue fiscal 2008 property taxes net of		
4 percent estimated uncollectible.		

Now, assume that current property taxes are collected in the amount of $940,000. The collection will be recorded with this entry:

Cash	940,000	
Property taxes receivable—current		940,000
To record collection of property taxes in fiscal 2008.		

At this point, Property taxes receivable—current has a $60,000 total balance but an expected collectible, or net realizable, value of $20,000 ($60,000 − $40,000). At the date that uncollected property taxes become delinquent, the following entries are necessary to reclassify the current receivable and contra asset to delinquent status:

Property taxes receivable—delinquent	60,000	
Property taxes receivable—current		60,000
To reclassify delinquent taxes receivable.		
Allowance for uncollectible taxes—current	40,000	
Allowance for uncollectible taxes—delinquent		40,000
To reclassify the allowance for uncollectible		
taxes from current to delinquent.		

The effect of the two preceding entries is that the net realizable value of the remaining property tax levy is still $20,000, but the receivable and related contra asset that comprise this value have been reclassified to delinquent status.

Now, assume that delinquent property taxes totalling $4,000 are deemed uncollectible and will be written off. The write-off is accomplished with this entry:

Allowance for uncollectible taxes—delinquent	4,000	
Property taxes receivable—delinquent		4,000
To write off uncollectible delinquent property taxes.		

Note that the net realizable value of taxes receivable remains at $20,000, as shown in this analysis:

Property taxes receivable—delinquent	$ 56,000
Less: allowance for uncollectible taxes—delinquent	(36,000)
	$ 20,000

Many governments charge interest on the delinquent taxes or assess penalties against delinquent taxpayers. When this happens, a debit is made to a receivable account to recognize the additional claim against the taxpayer. An offsetting credit to a revenue account also is made. If penalties totaling $600 are assessed against delinquent taxpayers, the entry (assuming use of a receivables control account) is

Interest and penalties receivable	600	
Revenues—interest and penalties		600
To record assessment of late payment penalties.		

Some governments also establish an Allowance for uncollectible interest and penalties account. In most cases, however, the balance in the Interest and penalties receivable account is not large enough to warrant the extra effort involved in setting up an offsetting allowance. Assuming the latter case, if the accrued interest and penalties prove to be uncollectible, the preceding entry simply is reversed.

When back taxes are owed, a government will sometimes place a lien against a piece of property. A *lien* is the legal right to prevent the sale of a piece of property to satisfy a claim against the property's owner. Such property cannot be sold or transferred by its owner until the lien is removed.

When a lien is placed against a piece of property, existing receivable accounts are reclassified to an account called Tax liens receivable. To illustrate, assume that a lien is placed against a piece of property for which delinquent taxes total $8,000 and accrued interest and penalties are $500. The entry to recognize the lien in the general ledger is shown below.

Tax liens receivable	8,500	
Property taxes receivable—delinquent		8,000
Interest and penalties receivable		500
To reclassify property taxes, interest, and penalties receivable as a tax lien receivable.		

The net realizable value of Property taxes receivable—delinquent is now $12,000 because the preceding entry reduced the total Property taxes receivable—delinquent balance by $8,000 but did not change the balance in the Allowance for uncollectible taxes—delinquent account.

If it costs $300 to process and advertise the lien, this cost will be added to the tax lien receivable:

Tax liens receivable	300	
Cash		300
To record the cost of processing and advertising a tax lien.		

At this point, the property owner must pay the government $8,800 to have the lien against the property removed. In the meantime, the property owner probably has become liable for the subsequent year's property taxes and may be in a financial "downward spiral."

In extreme cases, if the property owner does not pay a lien, a government will exercise its right to seize the property and sell it to the highest bidder. After the taxes, penalties, and costs of the sale have been deducted, any remaining proceeds will be remitted to the now-former property owner.

Assume that the delinquent property is sold at auction for $12,000 and the auctioneer is paid $1,500, so the net proceeds of the auction are $10,500, an amount more than sufficient to settle the lien in full. The excess of net proceeds over the lien balance is paid to the former property owner, so the government records no "gain" from the tax sale. The following entries are made to record the sale and the amounts due to the auctioneer ($1,500) and the former property owner ($1,700):

Cash	12,000	
Tax liens receivable		8,800
Vouchers payable		3,200

To record forced sale of property to satisfy lien and
    amounts due to auctioneer ($1,500) and former
    property owner ($1,700).		

Vouchers payable	3,200	
Cash		3,200
To record cash disbursements related to tax sale.		

The analysis at Table 5-2 shows the effects of the preceding entries on the relevant accounts. Notice that the net realizable value of uncollected taxes "flowed" from the "current" classification into the "delinquent" and "lien" classifications. Also, $500 of the $600 interest and penalties receivable balance was reclassified into the lien balance. The lien amount was fully realized in cash from the tax sale. The last line of Table 5-2 shows that the total of property taxes and related revenues, $960,600, equals the sum of total cash receipts, $948,500, plus the net balance of taxes receivable—delinquent, $12,000, plus the balance of $100 in the interest and penalties receivable account.

Adjustments to the Allowance for Uncollectible Property Taxes

The purpose of estimating uncollectible property taxes when property taxes are accrued is to recognize revenues equal to the expected net realizable value of property taxes receivable. Thus, in the ideal case, collection of taxes receivable generates cash equal to recorded revenues. Sometimes, though, the initial estimate of uncollectible property taxes proves to be either too high or too low, so an adjustment is required during the fiscal year or at year end. If, for example, the allowance initially is too low, the net realizable value of taxes receivable on the books exceeds the amount of taxes that ultimately will be collected in cash. In such a case, the allowance account is credited (increased) and the revenue account is debited (decreased). (For simplicity, in this section we dispense with the current/delinquent suffix for the Allowance for uncollectible property taxes.)

To illustrate, assume that during the year city officials conclude that uncollectible property taxes will be $5,000 higher than previously anticipated. The adjusting entry is

Revenues—property taxes	5,000	
Allowance for uncollectible property taxes		5,000
To adjust the revenue and allowance for uncollectible property tax accounts due to increased estimate of uncollectible property taxes.		

This entry decreases revenues consistent with the downwardly revised estimate of the net realizable value of taxes receivable.

If, on the other hand, city officials conclude that uncollectible property taxes will be $5,000 lower than first anticipated, the reverse of the preceding entry is made, that is:

Allowance for uncollectible property taxes	5,000	
Revenues—property taxes		5,000
To adjust the revenue and allowance for uncollectible property tax accounts due to decreased estimated uncollectible property taxes.		

This entry increases revenues in keeping with the expected increase in the net realizable value of taxes receivable.

Property Tax Refunds

Governments are often required to make refunds of property taxes. These refunds can be due to errors in tax assessments or can arise from actions of the legislative body, such as the refunding of property taxes to businesses that hire a certain number of people locally (tax abatements). The amount of property tax revenues should be recorded net of any expected refunds.[2] The procedure used to record these estimated refunds is similar to the one just shown for recording estimated uncollectible property taxes—a debit is made to Revenues—property taxes and a credit is made to Allowance for property tax refunds.

To illustrate, assume that the city estimates that it will be required, for various reasons, to refund 5 percent of the property taxes levied ($1,000,000). The entry to record this estimate is

Revenues—property taxes	50,000	
Allowance for property tax refunds		50,000
To record allowance for estimated property tax refunds.		

When a refund is made, the allowance account is debited and Cash or Property taxes receivable is credited, as will be illustrated in the next section.

Over- and Underassessed Property Taxes

Taxpayers in virtually all jurisdictions have the right to appeal their property tax assessments and their tax bills may be adjusted on appeal. These adjustments, of course, increase or, more commonly, decrease the revenues of the government. To adjust for an overassessment, the Allowance for property tax refunds is debited (decreased) and the receivable account is credited (also decreased). If the taxpayer already paid his or her entire tax bill, a cash refund is issued.

To illustrate, assume that the taxes originally levied on several parcels of property are $350,000 and that upon appeals by the property owners, the taxes are lowered to $300,000. If the tax reduction takes place before the property owners pay their tax bills, the adjusting entry will be:

Allowance for property tax refunds	50,000	
Property taxes receivable—current		50,000
To adjust for successful appeals of the fiscal 2008 tax assessment.		

If, however, the property owners pay the original $350,000 assessment when due and successfully appeal the assessment later, the entry will be:

Allowance for property tax refunds	50,000	
Vouchers payable		50,000

To adjust for successful appeals of the
    fiscal 2008 tax assessment and record
    resulting liability for refund.		

In the case of underassessments, the receivable (and revenue) accounts are increased to cover the additional assessments. Assume, for example, that the property owners lose the appeal and are assessed an additional $75,000. The adjusting entry is:

Property taxes receivable—current	75,000	
Revenues—property taxes		75,000
To adjust for errors noted in the fiscal 2008 property tax assessment.		

Notice that the Allowance for estimated refunds is not affected by underassessments.

---

[2]GASB Cod. Sec. N50.115.

Tax Discounts

Sometimes governments allow cash discounts to encourage prompt payment of property taxes. Revenue losses from this practice are usually offset by reduced borrowings. Discounts should be treated as a reduction of revenue in the same manner as uncollectible accounts.

To illustrate, assume that a government levies property taxes of $600,000. To encourage the early payment of taxes, it offers a 2 percent discount for payment within the discount period. When taxes are levied, the entry is:

Property taxes receivable—current	600,000	
Allowance for discounts on property taxes		12,000
Revenues—property taxes		588,000
To record property tax levy net of estimated 2% discount for prompt payment.		

If the taxes are collected in the expected amount, the entry is:

Cash	588,000	
Allowance for discounts on property taxes	12,000	
Property taxes receivable—current		600,000
To record collection of property taxes net of discount.		

Any difference between the net estimated collectible amount of the tax receivable and actual cash receipts requires an adjustment to revenues. If discounts actually taken exceed the amount initially estimated by, say, $1,000, the government must make the following entry:

Cash	587,000	
Allowance for discounts on property taxes	12,000	
Revenues—property taxes	1,000	
Property taxes receivable—current		600,000
To record collection of property taxes net of discount.		

Deferred Property Taxes

Under the modified accrual basis of accounting, revenues are not "available" unless they are "collected within the current period or expected to be collected soon enough thereafter to be used to pay liabilities of the period."[3] The GASB specifies that, unless a government justifies a longer period, the period should not be more than 60 days.[4] Revenues expected to be collected after this period should be reclassified and reported as deferred revenues.

To illustrate, assume that at the end of 2008, a government determines that property tax revenues amounting to $250,000 will not be collected until the middle of 2009. Because the expected time of collection is more than 60 days past year end, the government must make the following entry:

Revenues—property taxes	250,000	
Deferred revenues—property taxes		250,000
To record deferral of property taxes expected to be collected in 2009.		

---

[3]GASB Interpretation No. 5, Property Tax Recognition in Governmental Funds.
[4]GASB Cod. Sec. P70.104.

At the beginning of 2009, this entry would be reversed, and the monies collected would be treated as revenue of that year, rather than 2008.

Payments in Lieu of Property Taxes

Governments sometimes receive payments from other governments, or from certain not-for-profit organizations, to reimburse them for revenues lost because these organizations are not required to pay property taxes. Amounts received may be based on amounts the governments would have received if the paying organizations had been required to pay these taxes or may be separately negotiated to cover certain governmental costs. Examples of payments in lieu of property taxes include impact payments made by the federal government to school districts near military installations and amounts paid by certain religious organizations and not-for-profit entities owning large amounts of real estate. Payments in lieu of property taxes are treated in the same manner as other tax revenues, except that they generally are identified separately.

ACCOUNTING FOR OTHER TAXES AND INTERGOVERNMENTAL GRANTS

Derived Tax Revenues (Taxpayer-Assessed Revenues)

Some governments collect taxes that are assessed by individual taxpayers in accordance with legal requirements. Examples include sales taxes and income taxes. Sales taxes paid by merchants are collected from their customers at a fixed percentage of the merchants' sales. Income taxes are levied on taxpayers' income, less certain deductions and credits. In both cases, the amount of taxes that must be paid is determined initially by the taxpayers, rather than the governments. Revenues from these taxes are known as derived tax revenues.

GASB *Statement No. 33* requires that derived tax revenues (formerly known as taxpayer-assessed revenues) be recognized in the accounting period in which the underlying exchange occurs and the resources are available.[5] As a result, an adjusting entry must be prepared at the end of each fiscal year to recognize derived tax revenues that will be received early enough in the following year (usually 60 days) to pay the bills of the current fiscal year. Fortunately, tax collections tend to be predictable over time and generally it is possible to make reasonable estimates of the amount of each tax that will be collected and when it will be collected.

To illustrate, assume that at the end of fiscal 2008 it is estimated that outstanding income taxes for this year, less estimated refunds and uncollectible amounts, amount to $500,000. $475,000 of this amount is estimated to be collected in the first 60 days of the following year. The adjusting entry is

Income taxes receivable	500,000	
Revenues—income taxes		475,000
Deferred income tax revenues		25,000
To record receivable for fiscal 2008 income taxes to be collected in 2009.		

Accounting for Grants

Grants received by governments frequently are restricted for specific activities. To maximize control over these resources, restricted grants often are accounted for in

---

[5]GASB Cod. Sec. N50.127.

Special Revenue Funds. Revenues from restricted grants, like those from other voluntary nonexchange transactions, are recognized in the period in which "all eligibility requirements have been met."[6] Meeting eligibility requirements usually requires the recipient government to make "qualifying" expenditures as specified by the terms of the grant. As a result, revenues from restricted grants usually are not recognized until qualifying expenditures have been incurred.

If grant proceeds are received before its eligibility requirements are met, Cash is debited and an offsetting credit to Deferred revenue, a liability account, is made to indicate that revenue is not yet earned. When qualifying expenditures take place, revenues are recognized in the amount of the expenditures.

To illustrate, assume that a city receives a grant for $500,000 to be used to supplement salaries of police officers. When the grant is received, the following entry is made:

Cash	500,000	
Deferred revenues—grants		500,000
To record receipt of grant.		

During the year, $300,000 is spent in accordance with the terms of the grant. The entries to record the expenditures and to recognize revenue from the grant are:

Expenditures—salaries	300,000	
Cash		300,000
To record payment of supplemental compensation to police officers.		
Deferred revenues—grants	300,000	
Revenues—grants		300,000
To record revenue from grant.		

The remainder of the revenue from the grant will be recognized the following year, when additional qualifying expenditures are made.

Governments often receive grants that they can spend on behalf of, or transfer to, a secondary recipient and for which they have "administrative involvement." For example, a state might receive a grant for security enhancements from the federal government, which it disburses to various cities. These grants are known as *pass-through* grants. They should be reported by the government as revenues and expenditures, usually in governmental-type funds. In those instances when a government serves only as a "cash conduit" for a grant (that is, it maintains no administrative involvement) the grant should be accounted for in an Agency Fund.[7]

IMPORTANT EXCEPTIONS TO THE GENERAL PRINCIPLE FOR RECOGNIZING EXPENDITURES

Under modified accrual accounting, the general principle regarding expenditures is that expenditures should be accrued if the related liabilities are to be paid promptly and in full from current financial resources.[8] Examples of such expenditures include

---

[6]GASB Cod. Sec. N50.901.
[7]Ibid.
[8]GASB Cod. Sec. 1600.119.

payroll (personal services), contractual services, and purchases of supplies and equipment.

The expenditure recognition principle is subject to a number of specific exceptions. These pertain to expenditures for

- Interest on long-term debt
- Compensated absences
- Claims and judgments
- Pensions and other postemployment benefits (OPEB)
- Special termination benefits
- Landfill closure and postclosure costs

These items should be recognized as fund liabilities and expenditures only to the extent that they are "normally expected to be liquidated with expendable available financial resources."[9] The GASB interpreted that phrase to mean that governments are normally expected to liquidate liabilities with expendable available financial resources to the extent the liabilities mature or come due for payment each period.[10]

To illustrate the compensated absences case, assume that a government allows its employees to accumulate vacation time and, on resignation or retirement, to receive cash for up to 30 days unused vacation time. Under modified accrual accounting, the amount reported as accrued vacation pay at the end of an accounting period would be the amount that has matured and is due to be paid to specific employees who resigned or retired as of the end of the accounting period. That accrual would generally be significantly lower than the liability under full accrual accounting, which would cover all employees whether or not they had resigned or retired. (The full-accrual amount of the liability would be reported in the governmentwide Statement of Net Assets, as discussed in Chapter 10.)

For another illustration, assume that, during 2009, various claims for damages are filed against a government that does not carry third-party insurance. Government officials estimated that the total liability represented by these claims ultimately will be $850,000. Of the claims filed, three were settled as of December 31, 2009, at a cost of $30,000. The government expects to pay these settled claims during January 2010. In this case, the amount "normally expected to be liquidated with expendable available resources" is only $30,000, not $850,000. The journal entry to record the expenditure and liability is

Expenditures—claims and judgments	30,000	
Accrued claims and judgments liabilities		30,000
To record liability for settled claims to be paid in January 2010.		

The remaining $820,000 would be recorded as an expense and a liability in the governmentwide financial statements, as explained in Chapter 10. We discuss accounting for interest on long-term debt in detail in Chapter 6 and discuss accounting for pension and OPEB benefits in Chapter 8.

---

[9]GASB Cod. Sec. 1500.108.

[10]GASB Cod. Sec. 1600.122.

FUND BALANCE PRESENTATION

As you have learned, "fund balance" equals the net assets of a fund, that is, the extent to which the total assets accounted for within a fund exceed total fund liabilities. We have previously applied the term "unreserved fund balance" to describe total fund balance. In practice, unreserved fund balance refers to the amount of a fund's net assets that is "free and clear" for future appropriation and expenditure as of fiscal year end. Now we extend our discussion of fund balance to reservations and designations of fund balance.

Reservations and Designations of Fund Balance

For a variety of reasons, it is seldom the case that the entire amount of fund balance is available for spending at a given time. Thus, governments use the *reservation* mechanism to distinguish between (1) net assets of a fund that are truly free and clear for future appropriation and (2) net assets that are not appropriable (spendable) for some reason. Reservations of fund balance, then, identify the extent to which net assets are not available for immediate appropriation, and why. Reservations or "reserves" are established generally by debiting the unreserved fund balance account and crediting a "Fund balance reserved for _____" account. Reserving a portion of fund balance in this manner has no effect on total fund balance; rather, it represents a reclassification of a portion of total fund balance from the status of "free and clear" to "not free and clear."

According to governmental GAAP, "use of the term reserve should be limited to indicating that a portion of the fund balance is not appropriable for expenditure or is legally segregated for a specific future use."[11] An example of the first use of reserves (to indicate to a reader of the financial statements that a portion of the fund balance is not appropriable for future expenditures) is the Reserve for inventories, which is discussed on page 160. An example of the second use of reserves (to indicate to the reader of the financial statements that a portion of the fund balance is legally segregated for a specific future use) is the Reserve for encumbrances. This reserve represents the amount of purchase orders outstanding at the end of the fiscal year.

Sometimes a government will set aside or "designate" a portion of its fund balance to inform the readers of its financial statements of tentative plans for the future use of financial resources, such as extra police protection for a special event or equipment replacement. These *designations* denote managerial plans rather than formal legal requirements. As a result, designations should be clearly distinguished from formal reserves of fund balance. Unlike fund balance reserves, they are subject to change at the discretion of the management, rather than the legislative body, of the government. If, for example, the mayor decides that a portion of the fund balance of the General Fund should be designated for equipment acquisition, there would be a debit to Unreserved fund balance and a credit to Fund balance designated for equipment acquisition.

Open Encumbrances

To this point in the text, we have assumed that all materials and services ordered during the fiscal year are received on or before year end. In reality, however, items ordered

---

[11]GASB Cod. Sec. 1800.142.

during one year often arrive the following year, especially when orders are placed close to the end of the first year. Recalling that encumbrances pertain to the appropriations (spending authority) of a specific fiscal year, the question arises as to the proper accounting treatment of encumbrances open at year end.

Very few governments outright cancel their open purchase orders at fiscal year end. Instead, the prevailing practice is for governments to accept in the following year any goods and service still on order at year end, as represented by open encumbrances. Thus, the financial reporting needs to convey to readers that purchase orders open at year end represent probable future claims against the fund's net assets. This is done either by reporting a reservation of fund balance equal to the amount of open purchase orders or through note disclosure of this amount. The mechanics of the reporting depend on whether year-end encumbered appropriations remain open or lapse.

Appropriations Remain Open

For budgetary purposes, some governments allow the encumbered portion of their unexpended appropriations at year end to remain open. For such situations, governmental GAAP require that a reservation of fund balance be reported equal to the amount of the open purchase orders.[12] This is accomplished with two entries: First, a closing entry is made to reverse out the encumbrances. The second entry establishes the necessary reservation of fund balance.

To illustrate, assume that a city has $50,000 of open encumbrances at year end and that, under its budget law, encumbered appropriations remain open. The first entry made by the city is

Budgetary fund balance reserved for encumbrances	50,000	
Encumbrances		50,000
To close outstanding encumbrances for 2008.		

This entry is necessary because, as we have noted, encumbrance entries are budgetary in nature and at the end of the year, all budgetary account balances must be closed.

The second entry is as follows:

Unreserved fund balance	50,000	
Fund balance reserved for encumbrances		50,000
To record reservation of fund balance for		
open encumbrances at year end.		

This entry reclassifies a portion of fund balance from "unreserved" to "reserved" status. The balance reported as "Fund balance reserved for encumbrances" signifies that $50,000 of the fund's net assets are "earmarked" for future expenditure even though the forthcoming liabilities (and expenditures) have not yet been recorded for financial accounting purposes.

At the beginning of 2009, the preceding entry will be reversed:

Fund balance reserved for encumbrances	50,000	
Unreserved fund balance		50,000
To reclassify fund balance reserved for		
encumbrances to unreserved fund balance.		

---

[12]GASB Cod. Sec. 1700.128.

This entry signifies an *apparent* $50,000 increase in fund net assets available for appropriation and expenditure. However, because the $50,000 appropriation remains open, the city's budgetary journal entry for the new fiscal year will include a "prior year" or "carryover" appropriation of $50,000. Thus, the "increase" in unreserved fund balance from the preceding entry will be offset immediately by the recording of the carryover appropriation.

Finally, encumbrances representing the open orders at the end of fiscal 2008 that will be charged to the carryover appropriation during fiscal 2009 are reestablished at the beginning of fiscal 2009 with this entry:

Encumbrances	50,000	
Budgetary fund balance reserved for		
encumbrances		50,000
To reestablish encumbrances open at end of 2008.		

Appropriations Lapse

If, under budget law, encumbered unexpended appropriations lapse, those appropriations become void as spending authority at the close of the fiscal year. In such a case, the expenditures relating to the open encumbrances will be charged to the appropriations of the following year and the following year's budget will be developed with "prior year" open encumbrances in mind.

The reporting options available to governments in this case are either (1) to present in the balance sheet a reservation of fund balance equal to the amount of the open encumbrances or (2) to disclose the amount of open encumbrances at year end in the notes to the financial statements (without reserving a portion of fund balance).

If a government chooses to present a reservation of fund balance, the year-end entries will be identical to those illustrated above for the case in which appropriations remain open. For convenience, we repeat them here:

Budgetary fund balance reserved for encumbrances	50,000	
Encumbrances		50,000
To close outstanding encumbrances for 2008.		

Unreserved fund balance	50,000	
Fund balance reserved for encumbrances		50,000
To record reservation of fund balance for open encumbrances at year end.		

Similarly, at the beginning of the new year, the government will make the same two beginning-of-year entries illustrated for situations in which appropriations remain open. These entries are repeated here for convenience:

Fund balance reserved for encumbrances	50,000	
Unreserved fund balance		50,000
To reclassify fund balance reserved for encumbrances to unreserved fund balance at the beginning of 2009.		

Encumbrances	50,000	
Budgetary fund balance reserved		
for encumbrances		50,000
To reestablish encumbrances open at the end of 2008.		

Now, however, the rationale for the first of the two preceding entries is this: Where appropriations lapse, the appropriation for the new fiscal year will provide for prior-year open encumbrances in addition to "new" spending. Thus, when the city's budgetary journal entry is made at the beginning of the new year, the $50,000 credit to unreserved fund balance in the first of the two preceding entries will be offset immediately by $50,000 worth of appropriations attributable to open encumbrances.

If the second option is chosen (note disclosure of open encumbrances), only the entry to close open encumbrances is made. That is, no reservation of fund balance for open encumbrances will be reported in the balance sheet; instead, the dollar amount of open encumbrances will be disclosed in the notes to the financial statements. At the beginning of the next year, an entry to reestablish open encumbrances will be made.

Canceled Purchase Orders

As does any organization, governments occasionally find it necessary or desirable to cancel outstanding purchase orders before the ordered goods or services are delivered. This may happen, for instance, because a government determines that it has sufficient quantities of some item on hand so that additional supplies on order will be excessive. When a purchase order is canceled, the entry that initially recorded the encumbrance in question is reversed. The effect of canceling a purchase order, of course, is to increase the available amount of the applicable appropriation.

INTERFUND ACTIVITY

Transactions between individual funds of a government are collectively referred to as interfund activity. Under GASB *Statement No. 34,* these transactions fall into one of four categories: *interfund loans, interfund services provided and used, interfund reimbursements* or *interfund transfers.*[13] Each of these transaction types is discussed in the following sections.

Interfund Loans

Interfund loans arise when one fund lends cash to another fund. The recipient fund recognizes a liability to the paying fund, and the paying fund recognizes a receivable from the recipient fund. When recording short-term receivables and payables (those due within 1 year), the terms *Due from other funds* and *Due to other funds* are used. When recording long-term receivables and payables (those due after 1 year), the terms *Advance to other funds* and *Advance from other funds* are used.[14] The amounts shown on the financial statements as Due from/to other funds and Advance to/from other

---

[13]GASB Cod. Sec. 1800.102.

[14]Where suitable, the account titles can refer to specific funds. That is, if a government has only a single short-term interfund loan, for example, from the General Fund to a Special Revenue Fund, the General Fund balance sheet would show "Due from Special Revenue Fund" and the Special Revenue Fund balance sheet would show "Due to General Fund." In practice, governments often have multiple interfund loans. When this is the case, they are reported in the aggregate using the more general terms "Due from Other Funds" and "Due to Other Funds." This same convention applies to Advances.

funds, for the government as a whole, should be equal at all times. The entries to record a short-term interfund loan from Fund A to Fund B (amounts assumed) are presented here:

Fund A records this entry

Due from Fund B	5,000	
Cash		5,000
To record loan to Fund B.		

while Fund B records the "reciprocal" entry

Cash	5,000	
Due to Fund A		5,000
To record loan from Fund A.		

If the loan from Fund A to Fund B is long-term rather than short-term, the following entry would be made in Fund A

Advance to Fund B	5,000	
Cash		5,000
To record long-term loan to Fund B.		

and Fund B would record this "reciprocal" entry

Cash	5,000	
Advance from Fund A		5,000
To record long-term loan from Fund A.		

Funds making long-term loans (Advances) to other funds also should record reservations of fund balance to inform readers of the financial statements that current financial resources are not available for spending. Thus, this entry is also necessary in Fund A:

Unreserved fund balance	5,000	
Fund balance reserved for interfund advance		5,000
To record reservation of fund balance for advance to Fund B.		

Interfund Services Provided and Used

As the name implies, *Interfund services provided and used* transactions occur when one government department sells goods to, or performs services for, another department of the same government for a price approximating market terms. These transactions result in the recognition of revenues and expenditures (or expenses) by the participating funds although they do not involve parties external to the government.

For example, a government department recognizes revenue when it provides services to outside parties. If, additionally, that department provides those same services to a different department of the same government, it is appropriate for the providing fund to recognize revenue. Similarly, when a government department obtains necessary services, it incurs an expenditure (or expense) regardless of whether the supplier is an outside source or another department of the same government.

To illustrate, assume that an Enterprise Fund (Water Utility Fund) provides water and sewerage services to the city hall of a local government. The departments of the government housed within city hall must have water and sewer services in order to function, so those departments will incur water and sewer expenditures regardless of the identity of the provider. Similarly, the Water Utility Fund exists to sell water and sewer services to *all* customers—primarily to the jurisdiction's residents, but also to the government itself. Thus, the billing from the Water Utility Fund to the General Fund will be recorded as follows (amounts assumed) in the respective funds:

Due from General Fund	150,000	
Sale of water and sewerage services		150,000
To record billing to General Fund.		
Expenditures—water and sewerage services	150,000	
Due to Water Utility Fund		150,000
To record billing from Water Utility Fund.		

Because these transactions involve the recognition of revenues and expenditures (or expenses), they are reported on the fund-level statement of revenues, expenditures (or expenses), and changes in fund balance (or fund net assets).

Interfund Reimbursements

In some instances, expediency may require that an expenditure (or expense) be paid in part or entirely by a fund other than the fund properly chargeable for the transaction. The repayment to the paying fund by the one properly chargeable for the transaction is an interfund reimbursement. For example, assume that the General Fund makes an expenditure of $25,000 for consulting services that benefit several funds. If the General Fund initially pays the entire bill and determines later that the amount allocable to the Auditorium Fund (a Capital Projects Fund) is $5,000, the following entries are made in the General Fund:

Expenditures—consulting services	25,000	
Cash		25,000
To record payment for consulting services		
that benefit several funds.		
Due from Auditorium Fund	5,000	
Expenditures—consulting services		5,000
To record reimbursement due from Auditorium Fund		
for consulting services paid for by General Fund.		

In turn, the Auditorium Fund records this entry:

Expenditures—consulting services	5,000	
Due to General Fund		5,000
To record expenditure for consulting services		
initially paid for by the General Fund.		

These entries shift $5,000 of expenditures from the books of the General Fund to the books of the Auditorium Fund. This ensures that the expenditure will not be recorded more than once and that the fund receiving the benefit will recognize the expenditure. At a later date, when the Auditorium Fund pays cash to the General Fund to settle the interfund liability, the "due from" and the "due to" balances are liquidated.

Interfund Transfers

Interfund transfers record "flows of assets (such as cash or goods) without equivalent flows of assets in return and without a requirement for repayment."[15] Interfund transfers account for the largest part of the interfund activity of most governments. A typical interfund transfer is a periodic debt service payment made by the General Fund to a Debt Service Fund. Other examples include (1) an operating subsidy from the General Fund to an Electric Utility Fund (Enterprise Fund), (2) a payment made by the General Fund to a Capital Projects Fund for its share of the cost of constructing a civic auditorium, and (3) a transfer of the residual fund balance of a Debt Service Fund to the General Fund after the principal and interest have been paid in full.

Interfund transfers should not be treated as revenues or expenditures (or expenses) by either fund involved in the transaction. Instead they should be reported as other financing sources (uses) for governmental-type funds in the statement of revenues, expenditures, and changes in fund balances. Proprietary-type funds should report these transactions after nonoperating revenues and expenses in the statement of revenues, expenses, and changes in net assets.[16] Reporting of these transfers was introduced in Chapter 2 and is illustrated further in Chapters 6 and 9.

To illustrate, assume that a city council directs the General Fund to transfer $8,000 to a Capital Projects Fund. The following entries are recorded in the respective funds to record this transfer:

Transfer out to Capital Projects Fund	8,000	
Cash		8,000
To record transfer to Capital Projects Fund.		
Cash	8,000	
Transfer in from General Fund		8,000
To record transfer from General Fund.		

Notice that transfers out and in also can be accrued before cash is paid. The entries to accrue transfers between the respective funds are:

Transfer out to Capital Projects Fund	8,000	
Due to Capital Projects Fund		8,000
To accrue transfer to Capital Projects Fund		
Due from General Fund	8,000	
Transfer in from General Fund		8,000
To accrue transfer from General Fund		

Later, the cash payment will liquidate the "due to" and "due from" balances.

Interfund transfers should net to zero among all funds within a government.

ADDITIONAL ASPECTS OF BUDGETARY ACCOUNTING

We now discuss some important aspects of budgetary accounting beyond those illustrated in Chapter 3. These include budget revisions and the use of allotments.

Budget Revisions

Sometimes budgets are revised during the year. Conditions such as disasters or economic contractions can cause serious shortages of actual revenues. If such events do

---

[15]GASB Cod. Sec. 1800.102.

[16]Ibid.

happen and a balanced budget is to be maintained, appropriations must be reduced. (Many city charters and state constitutions require a balanced budget.) Such adjustments are recorded by debiting Appropriation accounts, crediting Estimated revenue accounts, and "squeezing" any differences to Budgetary fund balance.

Assume, for example, that a city begins fiscal 2008 with the following budget:

Estimated revenues	$1,000,000
Appropriations	990,000
Increase in budgetary fund balance	$ 10,000

During the year, the city council concludes that revenues for the year will be $20,000 less than projected and votes to reduce appropriations by $15,000. The adjusting entry is:

Appropriations	15,000	
Budgetary fund balance	5,000	
Estimated revenues		20,000
To record revisions to 2008 budget.		

Alternatively, appropriations may need to be increased during the year, perhaps because an unusually heavy winter requires unanticipated extra spending for snow plowing and removal. Assuming no changes in estimated revenues, the entry to increase a budgetary appropriation by, say, $6,500, would be as follows:

Budgetary fund balance	6,500	
Appropriations		6,500
To record increase in appropriations made necessary by emergency snowfall removal efforts.		

Budget revisions should not be confused with budgetary interchanges (discussed in Chapter 3), in which resources budgeted for one purpose are later budgeted for another. When budgetary interchanges are made the overall amount budgeted does not change, as it does when budget revisions are made.

Allotments

To maintain closer control over departmental expenditures, some governments subdivide their appropriations into time-based *allotments*. Allotments are then encumbered and expended during the allotment period, which can be a month, a quarter year, or a half year. When allotments are used, the Appropriations account is retitled *Unallotted appropriations*. The budgetary entry is thus (amounts assumed):

Estimated revenues—various sources	5,000,000	
Unallotted appropriations—various functions		4,900,000
Budgetary fund balance		100,000
To record estimated revenues and unallotted appropriations for fiscal 2008.		

At the time the central budget office makes formal allotments to each department, Unallotted appropriations is reduced (debited) and an Allotment account is credited. Assuming a semiannual allotment period, the first period's allotment is $2,450,000, so the government makes the following entry:

Unallotted appropriations	2,450,000	
Allotments		2,450,000
To record allotment for first half of fiscal 2008.		

During each semiannual allotment period, the government will charge encumbrances and expenditures against the Allotment balance. In the same manner as for appropriations, allotments are monitored by means of subsidiary ledgers, which provide a running total of balances available for spending.

To illustrate in detail, assume that in fiscal 2008, $990,000 is appropriated to a government department. The department receives its spending authority in semiannual allotments of $495,000 and maintains the subsidiary ledger illustrated in Table 5-3. Assume that actual revenues and estimated revenues will be equal at $1,000,000 while actual expenditures will total $978,000. Encumbrance entries are excluded from the illustration for clarity.

At year end, the Revenues and Expenditures balances are closed to Unreserved fund balance in standard fashion. Notice in this illustration that the credit balance initially posted to the Unallotted appropriations account is *transferred in full* to the Allotments account *during the year* as the allotments are recorded.[17] Thus, to reverse the budgetary entry at the end of the year, the Allotments account is debited and the Estimated revenues account is credited, with any difference between these account balances being added to or deducted from Budgetary fund balance.

Jan. 1	Estimated revenues—various sources	1,000,000	
	Unallotted appropriations		990,000
	Budgetary fund balance		10,000
	To record budget for fiscal 2008.		
Jan. 1	Unallotted appropriations	495,000	
	Allotments		495,000
	To set up allotments for first half of fiscal 2008.		

TABLE 5-3   Subsidiary Ledger for Allotments

Date	Allotment	Expenditures	Remaining Balance
1/1	$495,000		$495,000
1/8		$ 75,000	420,000
3/15		200,000	220,000
5/17		150,000	70,000
6/25		60,000	10,000
7/1	495,000		505,000
7/15		200,000	305,000
9/26		75,000	230,000
11/15		100,000	130,000
12/18		30,000	100,000
12/29		88,000	12,000
	$990,000	$978,000	$ 12,000

---

[17]Should there be a revenue shortfall, however, the central budget office will not allot the full amount of the Unallotted appropriations to the departments.

Jan. 1–	Cash	500,000	
June 30	Revenues—various sources		500,000
	To record revenues of first half of fiscal 2008.		
	Expenditures—various	485,000	
	Vouchers payable		485,000
	To record expenditures of first half of fiscal 2008.		
July 1	Unallotted appropriations	495,000	
	Allotments		495,000
	To set up allotment for second half of fiscal 2008.		

As of July 1, the balance in Unalloted appropriations is zero.

July 1–	Cash	500,000	
Dec. 31	Revenues—various sources		500,000
	To record revenues of second half of fiscal 2008.		
	Expenditures—various	493,000	
	Vouchers payable		493,000
	To record expenditures of second half of fiscal 2008.		
Dec. 31	Revenues—various sources	1,000,000	
	Expenditures—various		978,000
	Unreserved fund balance		22,000
	To close revenue and expenditure accounts for fiscal 2008.		
	Allotments	990,000	
	Budgetary fund balance	10,000	
	Estimated revenues—various sources		1,000,000
	To close budgetary accounts for fiscal 2008.		

OTHER ISSUES

This section of the chapter addresses other aspects of General and Special Revenue Fund accounting. They include acquisition and disposition of long-lived assets, inventories, prepaid items, warrants, and escheats.

Acquisition of Long-Lived Assets

The various departments of a government accounted for within the General Fund (in particular) and Special Revenue Funds (to some extent) routinely purchase long-lived (capital) assets. Examples include purchases of vehicles by Police and Fire departments and various types of equipment by Street departments. What is the proper accounting treatment of such purchases? Under the *current financial resources* measurement focus employed in the governmental-type funds (the General Fund, Special Revenue Funds, Capital Projects Funds, and Debt Service Funds), purchases of capital assets are accounted for as expenditures. This is because, from the standpoint of their effect on the net assets of a governmental-type fund, an expenditure made to acquire a capital asset has the same effect as one made for, say, payroll: Both decrease the spendable financial assets of the expending fund.

It follows, then, that capital assets purchased by governmental-type funds are not accounted for within these funds and, thus, do not appear in their balance sheets. This accounting treatment is correct within these funds because capital assets are not financial in nature; that is, capital assets are not appropriable for future spending. For the purpose of control, however, many governments record capital assets in a memorandum set of records, such as a Capital Investment Account Group (CIAG). The mechanics of this process are described in Chapter 10.

To illustrate the treatment of capital assets in governmental-type funds, assume that equipment costing $975,000 is purchased by the General Fund of a government. The entry to record this purchase would be:

Expenditures—capital outlay	975,000	
Vouchers payable		975,000
To record capital expenditure in the General Fund.		

Disposition of Long-Lived Assets

Governments routinely dispose of property or equipment, either because the asset is no longer needed or because it has become obsolete or damaged. Such transactions require an entry in the General Fund (or the fund that financed the purchase of the asset) if the disposal leads to a cash receipt. In such cases, cash is debited and a "proceeds from sale of capital assets" account is credited. The proceeds from sale of capital assets account is presented in the fund operating statement as an Other Financing Source. To illustrate, assume that a government disposes of a fire engine, which originally cost $75,000, for $15,000. The entry to record this sale is:

Cash	15,000	
Other financing sources—proceeds		
from sale of general fixed assets		15,000
To record sale of a fire engine for scrap value.		

Government-wide financial reporting entries for the disposition of long-lived assets will be covered in Chapter 10.

Depreciation

No entries are made for depreciation within the General Fund, Special Revenue Funds, or other governmental-type funds because these funds are concerned with accounting for inflows and outflows of expendable financial resources, rather than determining net income. The depreciation concept is necessary for measuring net income; however, as such, it is not consistent with the current financial resources measurement focus applied to governmental funds. Depreciation in government-wide financial statements is discussed in Chapter 10.

Inventories
The Consumption Method

Some governments follow the same practice as commercial organizations when recording inventoriable items in governmental-type funds. They record these items as assets when purchased and as expenditures when "consumed." This method is known as the consumption method.

To illustrate, assume that during the year purchases of supplies amount to $8,000 and that supplies costing $6,500 are used. The entry to record the purchase of supplies is

Supplies on hand	8,000	
Vouchers payable		8,000
To record purchase of supplies in fiscal 2008.		

The entry to record the usage of supplies is

Expenditures—supplies	6,500	
Supplies on hand		6,500
To record usage of supplies in fiscal 2008.		

Under the consumption method, inventories are considered "spendable" assets because their eventual use will result in the recognition of expenditures. Thus, under this method, fund balance reserves are required only to the extent that a certain minimum amount of inventory must be kept on hand and is, therefore, not "spendable."

The Purchases Method

Many governments record purchases of materials and supplies as fund expenditures when those purchases take place, even though the items purchased might not be used until later in the year or the following year. Under this budget-oriented procedure, called the *purchases method,* inventories initially are treated in the same manner as fixed assets; that is, they are "written off" when purchased. However, governmental GAAP require that material amounts of inventories be reported in the balance sheet, so at year end, the balance of inventory must be recorded.[18] To illustrate, assume that supplies costing $10,000 are still on hand at the end of a fiscal year. The amount is assumed to be material, so this fact should be disclosed to readers of the financial statements. The appropriate entry[19] is:

Supplies inventory	10,000	
Fund balance reserved for supplies inventory		10,000
To record amount of supplies inventory at the end of fiscal 2008.		

At the end of the following year, the inventory accounts and the reserve account should be adjusted to reflect the balance on hand. For example, if the cost of the supplies inventory at the end of the second year is $14,000, the balance in the inventory and in the reserve account should be adjusted to this amount, as follows:

Supplies inventory	4,000	
Fund balance reserved for supplies inventory		4,000
To adjust supplies and reserve accounts to reflect the amount of supplies on hand at the end of fiscal 2008.		

---

[18]GASB Cod. 1600.127.

[19]In practice, many governments use the purchases method because they consider their year-end inventories to be immaterial. But suppose inventories are material? We believe there is a conceptual inconsistency between permitting the use of the purchases method option and the requirement to report material amounts of inventory in the balance sheet, because reporting the inventory could have the effect of converting the purchases method to the consumption method. We think the preferable way to use the purchases method and still comply with the requirement to report material amounts of inventory is to offset the debit to inventory with a direct credit to Fund balance reserved for inventory. This method avoids making an entry that would ultimately increase Unreserved fund balance. Some writers, however, prefer to offset the increase in inventory with a credit to an Other financing sources account.

If the amount of supplies inventory decreased rather than increased, the supplies account would be credited and the reserve account would be debited by the amount necessary to bring their balances down to the new level. Notice that only the reserve changes, not Unreserved fund balance, because no change in available spendable resources takes place.

Prepaid Items

Prepaid items (e.g., prepaid rent, prepaid insurance) typically are charged to expenditure accounts when payments are made. At the fund level, such items usually are not reported on the balance sheet on materiality grounds. If the government does decide to report prepaid items on the balance sheet, the purchases method, as discussed in the previous section on inventories, generally is used.

Warrants

Some governments require that, before a check can be written and payment made, a warrant be prepared. A warrant is an order, drawn by the appropriate authority, requesting the treasurer (or someone designated by that person) to pay a specified sum of money to a particular person or organization. Its purpose is to assist in the prevention of unauthorized payments. No journal entries are necessary when warrants are prepared.

Escheats

In most states, the assets of persons who die *intestate* (without a valid will) and without known relatives revert to the state (after a stipulated period of time, often 7 years). Such reversions are known as escheats. Escheats are initially recorded in a Private Purpose Trust Fund, pending claim by rightful owners. If not claimed within a statutory period, the resources are transferred to the General Fund (if cash or securities) or are recorded as assets under government wide reporting (if fixed assets). In either case, a liability is recorded at the same time for amounts reasonably expected to be claimed "to the extent that it is probable that escheat property will be reclaimed and paid to claimants."[20]

REVIEW OF YEAR-END FINANCIAL STATEMENTS

As introduced in Chapter 4, the financial statements prepared at year end for the General Fund and each Special Revenue Fund include a balance sheet and a statement of revenues, expenditures, and changes in fund balance. A budgetary comparison schedule also is prepared for the General Fund and certain Special Revenue Funds. GASB *Statement No. 34* requires that the original approved budget, as well as the final amended budget, be shown on the budgetary comparison schedule. For the sake of simplicity, however, generally we will assume that the original budget and final budget are identical. (Examples of year end statements are found in Tables 5-10, 5-11, and 5-12 on pages 170, 171, and 172, respectively.)

To make the budgetary comparison schedule meaningful, it must present actual data on the budgetary basis of accounting. Thus, if the budget is prepared on a non-GAAP basis (e.g., on the cash basis), actual data must be presented on the same accounting basis. In such cases, there necessarily will be inconsistencies in reported amounts between the budgetary comparison schedule and the statement of revenues, expenditures, and changes in fund balance.

---

[20]GASB Cod. Sec. E70.103.

For example, in Table 5-10, expenditures for supplies are shown as $154,500, the amount paid in cash and accrued. In Table 5-12, they are shown as $204,500. This difference is due to outstanding encumbrances of $50,000, which were charged against departmental appropriations but not expended by year end. A reconciliation of differences between the two statements should be provided, either on the budgetary comparison schedule or in the notes to the financial statements.

PERMANENT FUNDS

Permanent Funds are used to account for resources that are legally restricted in a manner that (1) only earnings on the principal of these resources can be expended, and (2) the earnings must be used to support programs that benefit the government or its citizens, as opposed to specific individuals, organizations, or other governments. Examples of Permanent Funds include perpetual care cemetery funds and endowments to public libraries, the income from which must be used to purchase books. Permanent Funds should be established only when a legal trust agreement exists or when required by law. When legal or contractual agreements requiring the use of Permanent Funds are not present, the resources in question should be accounted for in the General Fund or a Special Revenue Fund.

The assets of Permanent Funds generally consist of cash and investments, while liabilities generally consist of amounts due to other funds. Revenues of Permanent Funds generally consist of interest and dividends, as well as increases (or decreases) in the fair market value of the funds' investments. Periodic transfers are made to funds designated as beneficiaries of Permanent Funds, usually Special Revenue Funds, and are reported as transfers out.

Control of Fund Activities

The operations of Permanent Funds are controlled through applicable state laws and provisions of individual trust agreements. Therefore, the accounting system must be designed to provide information and reports that permit a review of this stewardship role. Unless legally stipulated, formal integration of the budget into the accounting system is not usually required. Activities financed by Permanent Funds are budgeted in the funds receiving the Permanent Funds' earnings (usually Special Revenue Funds). As with the other governmental-type funds, Permanent Funds follow the current financial resources measurement focus and use the modified accrual basis of accounting for determining the amounts and timing of the recognition of revenues and expenditures.

Accounting for Fund Activities

Assume that the estate of Dr. Jo Breaux makes a bequest to the City of Llanerch of $10,000,000. Under the terms of the bequest, the city is to purchase securities and to use the earnings on these securities to provide support for the municipal zoo. Because only the net earnings on the securities can be expended and these expenditures must support programs that benefit the city, a Permanent Fund, the Breaux Bequest Fund, is used to account for the use of these resources. Shortly after receiving the bequest the city invests it in government securities. The entries to record the bequest and the purchase of securities are

Cash	10,000,000	
Revenues—bequest		10,000,000
To record bequest from Breaux estate.		

Investments	10,000,000	
Cash		10,000,000
To record investment of fund resources.		

During the year, investment earnings of $500,000 are recorded. Of this amount, $400,000 is received in cash.

Cash	400,000	
Investment income receivable	100,000	
Revenues—investment income		500,000
To record investment income for year.		

A transfer of $350,000 is made to the Zoo Operating Fund, a Special Revenue fund. Entry in the books of the Permanent Fund:

Transfer out to Zoo Operating Fund	350,000	
Cash		350,000
To record transfer to Zoo Operating Fund.		

Entry in the books of the Special Revenue Fund:

Cash	350,000	
Transfer in from Breaux Bequest Fund		350,000
To record transfer from Breaux Bequest Fund.		

During the year, the Breaux Bequest Fund incurs the following operating costs:

Audit	$ 2,500
Investment fees	10,000
	$12,500

Assume that the investment fees are paid in cash, but the audit item is still open (unpaid).

Expenditures—audit	2,500	
Expenditures—investment fees	10,000	
Vouchers payable		2,500
Cash		10,000
To record operating costs.		

By the end of the year, the marketable securities increased in value by $2,000,000. Because investments are generally reported at fair market value, an adjustment to record this increase in value must be made. The adjustment is

Investments	2,000,000	
Revenues—net appreciation in fair market value		2,000,000
To record increase in market value of investments.		

Note: It is assumed the increase in the fair value of the investments will increase principal of the Permanent Fund. The support for the Zoo is the investment income ($500,000) minus the operating costs ($12,500).

At the end of the fiscal year, the following entries would be made to close the books of this fund.

Revenues—bequests	10,000,000	
Revenues—investment income	500,000	
Revenues—net appreciation in fair market value	2,000,000	
Transfer out to Zoo Operating Fund		350,000
Expenditures—audit		2,500
Expenditures—investment fees		10,000
Fund balance reserved for permanent fund corpus		12,000,000
Fund balance reserved for Municipal Zoo		137,500
To close revenue, expenditure, and transfer accounts		
to Unreserved fund balance.		

Table 5-4   Permanent Fund—Postclosing Trial Balance for the City of Llanerch

City of Llanerch
Permanent Fund
Breaux Bequest Fund
Postclosing Trial Balance
December 31, 2009

	Debits	Credits
Cash	$ 40,000	
Investment income receivable	100,000	
Investments	12,000,000	
Vouchers payable		$ 2,500
Fund balance reserved for permanent fund corpus		12,000,000
Fund balance reserved for Municipal Zoo		137,500
	$12,140,000	$12,140,000

TABLE 5-5   Permanent Fund—Balance Sheet for the City of Llanerch

City of Llanerch
Permanent Fund
Breaux Bequest Fund
Balance Sheet
December 31, 2009

Assets	
Cash	$ 40,000
Investment income receivable	100,000
Investments	12,000,000
Total assets	$12,140,000
Liabilities and Fund Balance	
Vouchers payable	$ 2,500
Total liabilities	2,500
Fund Balance	
Reserved for permanent fund corpus	12,000,000
Reserved for Municipal Zoo	137,500
Total fund balance	12,137,500
Total liabilities and fund balance	$12,140,000

TABLE 5-6 Permanent Fund—Statement of Revenues, Expenditures, and Changes in Fund Balance for the City of Llanerch

City of Llanerch
Permanent Fund
Breaux Bequest Fund
Statement of Revenues, Expenditures, and Changes in Fund Balance
For the Fiscal Year Ended December 31, 2009

Revenues		
Bequests	$10,000,000	
Investment income	500,000	
Net appreciation in fair market value of investments	2,000,000	$12,500,000
Expenditures		
Audit	$ 2,500	
Investment fees	10,000	12,500
Excess (Deficiency) of Revenues		
over Expenditures		$12,487,500
Other Financing Sources (Uses)		
Transfer out to Zoo Operating Fund		(350,000)
Net change in fund balance		$12,137,500
Fund Balance at Beginning of Year		-0-
Fund Balance at End of Year		$12,137,500

After closing entries are made, the postclosing trial balance appears as shown in Table 5-4. The resulting financial statements are shown in Tables 5-5 and 5-6.

SUMMARY PROBLEM ON THE GENERAL FUND

The city council of Catalina City approved the 2008 budget shown in Table 5-7 for that municipality's General Fund on December 31, 2007. The gross levy for fiscal 2008 property taxes is $1,828,125. Experience indicates that 4 percent of the property taxes levied are usually not collected. At December 31, 2007, the city has a $500 delinquent property tax receivable from a former property owner.

Among the city's accounting policies are the following:

1. All purchases of supplies and capital outlays are encumbered.
2. Expenditures for salaries, interest, and transfers to other funds do not require encumbrances.
3. Encumbrances lapse at the end of the fiscal year; however, the Reserve for encumbrances is shown on the year-end balance sheet.
4. A control account for property taxes receivable is used.

The postclosing trial balance of the General Fund of Catalina City, as of December 31, 2007, is as follows:

	Debits	Credits
Cash	$51,850	
Property taxes receivable—delinquent	500	
Allowance for uncollectible property taxes—delinquent		$ 400
Interest and penalties receivable	50	

Vouchers payable		8,000
Due to Frazer Park Fund		9,000
Fund balance reserved for encumbrances		20,000
Unreserved fund balance		15,000
	$52,400	$52,400

TABLE 5-7   Budget of Catalina City

Catalina City
General Fund
Budget
For the Year Ended December 31, 2008

Estimated revenues:		
Property taxes	1,755,000	
License fees	70,000	
Interest and penalties	40,000	
Income taxes	55,000	$ 1,920,000
Appropriations and transfers:		
Salaries	$585,000	
Supplies	220,000	
Capital equipment	975,000	
Transfer to Frazer Park Fund	20,000	
Transfer to Debt Service Fund	100,000	1,900,000
Budgeted increase in fund balance		$ 20,000

During fiscal year 2008, the following transactions take place:

1. Purchase orders outstanding at the beginning of the year are encumbered. They are for supplies and amount to $20,000.
2. The property tax levy is accrued along with an Allowance for uncollectible property taxes equal to 4 percent of the total levy. An allowance of $25,000 for property tax refunds also is established.
3. Property taxes are collected on time and in full in the amount of $1,335,000.
4. The former property owner is unable to pay her fiscal 2007 property taxes in full. She pays the $50 penalty and $100 of these taxes. The remainder of her account is written off.
5. The city council decides, in late August, that the Allowance for uncollectible property taxes is too low and orders the city's finance director to increase it by $10,000.
6. Protests filed against property tax assessments total $350,000. As a result, the assessments are lowered to $325,000. The affected taxpayers pay their adjusted tax bills in full.
7. The amount due to the Frazer Park Fund and the vouchers that were outstanding at the end of fiscal 2007 are paid.
8. Uncollected property taxes are reclassified from current to delinquent, as is the balance in the Allowance for uncollectible property taxes account.
9. Property taxes receivable of $35,000 are deemed uncollectible and are written off.
10. Penalties of $900 are levied against delinquent property owners.

11. Tax liens are placed against property on which the balance of taxes owed is $50,000. $500 of the $900 of penalties previously accrued apply to the liens.
12. Costs of processing and advertising the liens amount to $300. They are paid immediately.
13. In November, the properties on which liens were placed are sold for $120,000. The auctioneer submits a bill for $1,500. The auctioneer and the former property owners are paid in full.
14. Supplies and equipment ordered the previous year arrive. Actual cost is $19,500. Payment is made the following week.
15. A cash payment of $13,000, representing part of the fiscal 2008 contribution, is made to the Frazer Park Fund, $7,000 less than the budgeted amount. The city expects to contribute the remaining amount by the end of the fiscal year or shortly thereafter, so the balance of the contribution is accrued.
16. Supplies costing $200,000 are ordered on Purchase Order No. 1426.
17. New fire engines, expected to cost $975,000, are ordered on Purchase Order No. 1427.
18. One-fourth of the supplies ordered arrive, along with an invoice for $45,000. The invoice is paid the following week.
19. One-half of the supplies arrive, along with an invoice for $90,000. Payment will not be made until the following year.
20. Salaries for the year amount to $580,000. They are paid in cash.
21. In December, a transfer of $100,000 to the Debt Service Fund is recorded. Actual payment will be made the following year.
22. At the end of the year, it is determined that the balance in the Allowance for uncollectible property taxes account is too low. The allowance is raised by $5,000.
23. The city disposes of an old fire engine for $10,000.
24. The new fire engines arrive, along with an invoice for $975,000. The invoice is paid immediately.
25. Revenues from other sources, which have been collected but not yet recorded, are as follows:

License fees	$75,000
Interest and penalties	38,000
Income taxes	47,000

Income taxes are considered to be derived taxes. The city's finance director estimates that, in addition to the amount shown above, another $5,000 of income taxes will be collected early in the following year.
26. Supplies costing $10,000 are still on hand at the end of the year. Catalina City officials decide that the inventory should be reported in the financial statements as "supplies inventory."

For fiscal 2008, complete the following accounting tasks:

1. Prepare budgetary and operating entries for the General Fund.
2. Prepare a preclosing trial balance (Table 5-8).
3. Prepare closing entries.
4. Prepare a postclosing trial balance (Table 5-9).
5. Prepare appropriate financial statements (Tables 5-10, 5-11, and 5-12).

Table 5-8 General Fund—Preclosing Trial Balance for Catalina City

Catalina City
General Fund
Preclosing Trial Balance
December 31, 2008

	Debits	Credits
Cash	$ 283,000	
Property taxes receivable—delinquent	58,125	
Allowance for uncollectible property taxes—delinquent		$ 53,125
Interest and penalties receivable	400	
Income taxes receivable	5,000	
Supplies inventory	10,000	
Vouchers payable		90,000
Due to Frazer Park Fund		7,000
Due to Debt Service Fund		100,000
Encumbrances—supplies	50,000	
Unreserved fund balance		35,000
Fund balance reserved for supplies inventory		10,000
Budgetary fund balance reserved for encumbrances		50,000
Budgetary fund balance		20,000
Estimated revenues—property taxes	1,755,000	
Estimated revenues—license fees	70,000	
Estimated revenues—interest and penalties	40,000	
Estimated revenues—income taxes	55,000	
Appropriations—salaries		585,000
Appropriations—supplies		220,000
Appropriations—capital outlay		975,000
Budgeted transfer to Frazer Park Fund		20,000
Budgeted transfer to Debt Service Fund		100,000
Revenues—property taxes		1,715,000
Revenues—license fees		75,000
Revenues—interest and penalties		38,900
Revenues—income taxes		52,000
Other financing source—sale of general fixed assets		10,000
Expenditures—salaries	580,000	
Expenditures—supplies	154,500	
Expenditures—capital outlay	975,000	
Transfer out to Frazer Park Fund	20,000	
Transfer out to Debt Service Fund	100,000	
	$4,156,025	$4,156,025

The budgetary, or opening, entry is as follows:

Estimated revenues—property taxes	1,755,000	
Estimated revenues—license fees	70,000	
Estimated revenues—interest and penalties	40,000	
Estimated revenues—income taxes	55,000	
Appropriations—salaries		585,000
Appropriations—supplies		220,000
Appropriations—capital equipment		975,000
Budgeted transfer to Frazer Park Fund		20,000
Budgeted transfer to Debt Service Fund		100,000
Budgetary fund balance		20,000
To record the budget for 2008.		

Table 5-9   Postclosing Trial Balance for Catalina City's General Fund

Catalina City
General Fund
Postclosing Trial Balance
December 31, 2008

	Debits	Credits
Cash	$283,000	
Property taxes receivable—delinquent	58,125	
Allowance for uncollectible property taxes—delinquent		$ 53,125
Interest and penalties receivable	400	
Income taxes receivable	5,000	
Supplies inventory	10,000	
Vouchers payable		90,000
Due to Frazer Park Fund		7,000
Due to Debt Service Fund		100,000
Fund balance reserved for supplies inventory		10,000
Fund balance reserved for encumbrances		50,000
Unreserved fund balance		46,400
	$356,525	$356,525

Note:	Unreserved fund balance is computed as follows:	
	December 31, 2007, *total* fund balance ($20,000 + $15,000)	$35,000
	Add: Credit to unreserved fund balance from CE 3	61,400
	Add: Increase in fund balance reserved for supplies inventory	10,000
	December 31, 2008, *total* fund balance	106,400
	Less: Fund balance reserved for supplies inventory	(10,000)
	Less: Fund balance reserved for encumbrances	(50,000)
	December 31, 2008, *unreserved* fund balance	$ 46,400

The operating entries are as follows:

1a. Fund balance reserved for encumbrances   20,000
    Unreserved fund balance   20,000
      To remove reservation of fund balance for
        encumbrances open at end of 2007.

1b. Encumbrances—supplies   20,000
    Budgetary fund balance reserved for encumbrances   20,000
      To reestablish encumbrances for supplies ordered,
        but not received, in 2007.

2a. Property taxes receivable—current   1,828,125
    Allowance for uncollectible property taxes—current   73,125
    Revenues—property taxes   1,755,000
      To set up receivable for 2008 property taxes along
        with a 4% allowance for uncollectible property taxes.

2b. Revenues—property taxes   25,000
    Allowance for property tax refunds   25,000
      To set up an allowance for property tax refunds.

3. Cash   1,335,000
    Property taxes receivable—current   1,335,000
      To record collection of property taxes.

TABLE 5-10   Statement of Revenues, Expenditures, and Changes in Fund Balance for Catalina City's General Fund

Catalina City
General Fund
Statement of Revenues, Expenditures,
and Changes in Fund Balance
Year Ended December 31, 2008

Revenues		
Property taxes	$1,715,000	
License fees	75,000	
Interest and penalties	38,900	
Income taxes	52,000	$1,880,900
Expenditures		
Salaries	$580,000	
Supplies	154,500	
Capital equipment	975,000	1,709,500
Excess (Deficiency) of Revenues over Expenditures		171,400
Other Financing Sources (Uses)		
Transfer to Frazer Park Fund	(20,000)	
Transfer to Debt Service Fund	(100,000)	
Proceeds from sale of firetruck	10,000	(110,000)
Increase in unreserved fund balance		61,400
Fund Balance, December 31, 2007		35,000
Increase in fund balance reserved for supplies inventory		10,000
Fund Balance, December 31, 2008		$ 106,400

4. Cash   150
    Allowance for uncollectible property taxes — delinquent   400
        Interest and penalties receivable   50
        Property taxes receivable — delinquent   500
        To record collection of penalties and part of
        delinquent 2007 property taxes and to write
        off the remainder of the receivable.

5. Revenues — property taxes   10,000
        Allowance for uncollectible property
            taxes — current   10,000
        To increase fiscal 2008 allowance for uncollectible
        property taxes.

6a. Allowance for property tax refunds   25,000
        Property taxes receivable — current   25,000
        To adjust for protested 2008 tax assessments.

6b. Cash   325,000
        Property taxes receivable — current   325,000
        To record collection of 2008 property taxes previously
        under protest.

TABLE 5-11   Balance Sheet for Catalina City's General Fund

Catalina City
General Fund
Balance Sheet
December 31, 2008

Assets		
Cash		$ 283,000
Property taxes receivable — delinquent	$ 58,125	
Less: Allowance for uncollectible property taxes	(53,125)	5,000
Interest and penalties receivable		400
Income taxes receivable		5,000
Supplies inventory		10,000
Total assets		$ 303,400
Liabilities and fund balance		
Vouchers payable		$ 90,000
Due to Frazer Park Fund		7,000
Due to Debt Service Fund		100,000
Total liabilities		197,000
Fund balance reserved for supplies inventory		10,000
Fund balance reserved for encumbrances		50,000
Unreserved fund balance		46,400
Total fund balance		106,400
Total liabilities and fund balance		$ 303,400

7.   Due to Frazer Park Fund 9,000

  Vouchers payable 8,000

    Cash 17,000

  To record payment of liabilities outstanding
  at end of 2007.

8a.   Taxes receivable—delinquent 143,125

  Taxes receivable—current 143,125

  To reclassify fiscal 2008 property tax receivables from
  current to delinquent.

TABLE 5-12   Budgetary Comparison Schedule for Catalina City's General Fund

Catalina City
General Fund
Budgetary Comparison Schedule
Year Ended December 31, 2008

	Original and Final Budget	Actual	Variance— Favorable (Unfavorable)
Revenues			
Property taxes	$1,755,000	$1,715,000	$(40,000)
License fees	70,000	75,000	5,000
Interest and penalties	40,000	38,900	(1,100)
Income taxes	55,000	52,000	(3,000)
Total revenues	$1,920,000	$1,880,900	$(39,100)
Expenditures			
Salaries	585,000	580,000	5,000
Supplies	220,000	204,500	15,500
Capital outlay	975,000	975,000	0
Total expenditures	1,780,000	1,759,500	20,500
Excess (Deficiency) of Revenues over Expenditures	$ 140,000	$ 121,400	$(18,600)
Other Financing Sources (Uses)			
Transfer to Frazer Park Fund	(20,000)	(20,000)	0
Transfer to Debt Service Fund	(100,000)	(100,000)	0
Proceeds from sale of fixed assets	0	10,000	10,000
Total other financing sources (uses)	(120,000)	(110,000)	10,000
Net change in unreserved fund balance	20,000	11,400	(8,600)
Fund Balance at beginning of year	35,000	35,000	—
Increase in fund balance reserved for inventory		10,000	10,000
Fund balance at end of year	$ 55,000	$ 56,400	$ 1,400

Note: For budgetary purposes, encumbrances are considered to be the equivalent of expenditures. Thus, the actual amount of the expenditures for supplies on this schedule exceeds the corresponding amount shown on Table 5-10 by $50,000, the amount of open encumbrances for supplies at December 31, 2008.

8b. Allowance for uncollectible property taxes—current   83,125
    Allowance for uncollectible property
       taxes—delinquent   83,125
    To reclassify allowance for uncollectible
    property taxes from current to delinquent.

9. Allowance for uncollectible property taxes—delinquent   35,000
    Property taxes receivable—delinquent   35,000
    To write off uncollectible 2008 tax receivable.

10. Interest and penalties receivable   900
    Revenues—interest and penalties   900
    To record assessment of late payment penalties.

11. Tax liens receivable   50,500
    Property taxes receivable—delinquent   50,000
    Interest and penalties receivable   500
    To record tax lien.

12. Tax liens receivable   300
    Cash   300
    To record cost of processing and advertising tax lien.

13a. Cash   120,000
    Tax liens receivable   50,800
    Vouchers payable   69,200
    To record sale of foreclosed property, removal
    of lien, and expenses related to sale ($1,500).

13b. Vouchers payable   69,200
    Cash   69,200
    To record payment of expenses related to tax
    sale ($1,500) and payment to former property owner.

14a. Budgetary fund balance reserved for encumbrances   20,000
    Encumbrances—supplies   20,000
    To record receipt of supplies ordered in fiscal 2007.

14b. Expenditures—supplies   19,500
    Vouchers payable   19,500
    To record liability for payment of supplies
    ordered in fiscal 2007.

14c. Vouchers payable   19,500
    Cash   19,500
    To record payment of voucher.

15. Transfer out to Frazer Park Fund   20,000
    Due to Frazer Park Fund   7,000
    Cash   13,000
    To record fiscal 2008 contribution to Frazer Park Fund.

16. Encumbrances—supplies   200,000
    Budgetary fund balance reserved for encumbrances   200,000
    To record Purchase Order No. 1426 for 2008 supplies.

17.	Encumbrances—capital equipment	975,000	
	Budgetary fund balance reserved for encumbrances		975,000
	To record Purchase Order No. 1427 for new fire engines.		
18a.	Budgetary fund balance reserved for encumbrances	50,000	
	Encumbrances—supplies		50,000
	To record receipt of one-fourth of supplies ordered under Purchase Order No. 1426.		
18b.	Expenditures—supplies	45,000	
	Vouchers payable		45,000
	To record liability for payment of one-fourth of supplies received under Purchase Order No. 1426.		
18c.	Vouchers payable	45,000	
	Cash		45,000
	To record payment of voucher.		
19a.	Budgetary fund balance reserved for encumbrances	100,000	
	Encumbrances—supplies		100,000
	To record receipt of one-half of supplies ordered under Purchase Order No. 1426.		
19b.	Expenditures—supplies	90,000	
	Vouchers payable		90,000
	To record liability for payment of one-half of supplies received under Purchase Order No. 1426.		
20.	Expenditures—salaries	580,000	
	Cash		580,000
	To record salaries paid during fiscal 2008.		
21.	Transfer out to Debt Service Fund	100,000	
	Due to Debt Service Fund		100,000
	To record liability for fiscal 2008 contribution toward service of bond issue.		
22.	Revenues—property taxes	5,000	
	Allowance for uncollectible property taxes—delinquent		5,000
	To adjust property tax revenues for expected uncollectible amounts in excess of adjusted fiscal 2008 allowance.		

(Note: Because fiscal 2008 property taxes outstanding are past due at this point, the "delinquent" allowance is increased.)

23.	Cash	10,000	
	Other financing source—proceeds from sale of fixed assets		10,000
	To record sale of one surplus fire engine.		
24a.	Budgetary fund balance reserved for encumbrances	975,000	
	Encumbrances—capital equipment		975,000
	To record receipt of fire engines ordered under Purchase Order No. 1427.		
24b.	Expenditures—capital outlay	975,000	
	Vouchers payable		975,000
	To record liability for payment for fire engines received under Purchase Order No. 1427.		

24c.	Vouchers payable	975,000	
	Cash		975,000
	To record payment of voucher.		
25.	Cash	160,000	
	Income taxes receivable	5,000	
	Revenues—license fees		75,000
	Revenues—interest and penalties		38,000
	Revenues—income taxes		52,000
	To record fiscal 2008 revenues from various sources.		
26.	Supplies inventory	10,000	
	Fund balance reserved for supplies inventory		10,000
	To record amount of supplies inventory at end of fiscal 2008.		

The closing entries are as follows:

C1.	Appropriations—salaries	585,000	
	Appropriations—supplies	220,000	
	Appropriations—capital outlay	975,000	
	Budgeted transfer to Frazer Park Fund	20,000	
	Budgeted transfer to Debt Service Fund	100,000	
	Budgetary fund balance	20,000	
	Estimated revenues—property taxes		1,755,000
	Estimated revenues—license fees		70,000
	Estimated revenues—interest and penalties		40,000
	Estimated revenues—income taxes		55,000
	To close budgetary accounts the end of 2008.		
C2.	Budgetary fund balance reserved for encumbrances	50,000	
	Encumbrances—supplies		50,000
	To close outstanding encumbrances at the end of 2008.		
C3.	Revenues—property taxes	1,715,000	
	Revenues—license fees	75,000	
	Revenues—interest and penalties	38,900	
	Revenues—income taxes	52,000	
	Other financing sources—proceeds from sale of fixed assets	10,000	
	Expenditures—salaries		580,000
	Expenditures—supplies		154,500
	Expenditures—capital outlay		975,000
	Transfer out to Frazer Park Fund		20,000
	Transfer out to Debt Service Fund		100,000
	Unreserved fund balance		61,400
	To close operating statement accounts for 2008.		
C4.	Unreserved fund balance	50,000	
	Fund balance reserved for encumbrances		50,000
	To record reservation of fund balance for open encumbrances at the end of 2008.		

Review Questions

Q5-1 What is the purpose of a property tax calendar?

Q5-2 An Allowance for uncollectible taxes account normally is established when property tax revenues are accrued. What is the main purpose of this practice?

Q5-3 What is a property tax lien?

Q5-4 What are payments in lieu of property taxes?

Q5-5 Cite two examples of circumstances in which a government may find it necessary to record deferred revenues.

Q5-6 Name two types of derived tax revenues. When are these revenues recognized? Is a year-end adjusting entry necessary in order to recognize some of these revenues?

Q5-7 What is reserved fund balance? Designated fund balance? How do they differ?

Q5-8 What does the term *lapse* mean when referring to encumbrances outstanding at year end?

Q5-9 What two methods are used to account for open encumbrances at year end?

Q5-10 What journal entry should be recorded if a purchase order is canceled?

Q5-11 Identify four categories of interfund activities. Which type or types of interfund activity result in the recognition of revenues and expenditures (expenses)?

Q5-12 What is the difference between an amount described as "due from another fund" versus an amount described as an "advance to another fund"?

Q5-13 What is an allotment? Describe the purpose of recording allotments in the accounting system.

Q5-14 Why is depreciation not recorded within governmental-type funds?

Q5-15 What is the accounting treatment for inventories if the "purchases" method is used? When it is necessary to record a change in the level of inventories at year end, what entry is needed?

Q5-16 In what amount should the expenditures and liabilities related to compensated absences be recognized for a fiscal year?

Q5-17 Under what circumstances do governments use Permanent Funds?

Cases

C5-1 When reviewing the financial statements of Crescent City, Councilwoman Peggy Doubleton noticed that the city uses an Allowance for uncollectible property taxes. This seemed odd to her because the city had recently sold several acres of land that had been seized for nonpayment of property taxes. At the next council meeting, Councilwoman Doubleton moved that the city no longer use an Allowance for uncollectible property taxes. She argued that the city had the right to seize property for nonpayment of taxes. As a result it could eventually recover any lost revenue and did not need to provide for uncollectible property taxes. Furthermore, by eliminating this allowance, revenues would be raised by a substantial amount and additional services could be provided without incurring a deficit. Would you vote for Councilwoman Doubleton's motion if you were a member of the city council? Why?

C5-2   The City of Khatt recently received a $500,000 grant from the federal govern-
ment to operate a day-care center for 2 years. This grant was to be the only
source of funding for the day-care center. Feeling pressure to maximize revenues, the city's accountant credited a revenue account for the entire $500,000
when the check arrived. He explained to you that because the entire amount
was in the city's possession, it was "measurable and available" and, therefore,
should be treated as revenue. Do you agree? Why?

C5-3   Joe Babitt, a former executive of T-Mart, just started a term as mayor of Saulk
Center. For the past several days he has been looking for a way to keep his
campaign promise to increase services without raising taxes or service charges.
While lunching at the country club with the treasurer of T-Mart, the subject of
a recent sale and leaseback of one of T-Mart's stores came up. Following a
common practice in retailing, T-Mart erected a building and sold it to an investor. It then signed a long-term lease on the building. "Bingo! That's it,"
thought Mayor Babitt. "We can sell several of the city's buildings, as well as police cars, fire engines, and other vehicles, to investors and lease them back. That
will give us the revenues we desperately need. In addition, we won't need to
worry about depreciation or future capital outlays. Now I can concentrate on
fighting crime." Do you agree with Mayor Babitt? If not, what are the flaws in
his reasoning?

Ethics Cases

EC5-1 River City requires not-for-profit organizations owning real property and
personal property, like vehicles and construction equipment, to make payments in lieu of property taxes. Homes for People, a large, not-for-profit organization, owns several rental properties in the city's central business
district and operates a large fleet of trucks and bulldozers. Sy Sutter, the
city's assessor, is an active member of this organization. Recently, Sutter informed the director of Homes for People that that organization would no
longer be required to make payments in lieu of property taxes because of the
assistance it had provided the city in cleaning up after a recent hurricane,
thus saving the city a large sum of money. Sutter did not notify the city council of this action, reasoning that, "in the end, it will all balance out." Was this
action ethical? Why or why not? How could such an action be prevented in
the future?

EC5-2 An accounting professor purchased residential property in a certain city for
$72,000, the amount for which the property was assessed. Three years later, the
professor received a notice from the tax assessor that his property was now assessed for $150,000. The general opinion of several realtors, who were familiar
with the professor's neighborhood, was that the property was worth no more
than $120,000. With this information in hand the professor confronted the as-
sessor, who was sympathetic and suggested that the professor appeal his assessment at a hearing that was to be held for that purpose. As the professor was
leaving the assessor's office, a secretary stopped him and suggested that he not

proceed with this matter because "the appeal process could go either way and the board of assessors could (and sometimes did) raise appealed assessments by as much as 50 percent." That evening, the professor was called by a "politically connected" neighbor, whose property was considerably more valuable than that of the professor, and told him not to appeal his assessment because it could "hurt the entire neighborhood." Being a state employee and a nonnative of the city, the professor decided not to pursue the matter. Several months later, when working on a research project, the professor gained access to the city's property tax rolls and discovered that the neighbor's property was assessed for $80,000. Were these actions an ethical way to treat taxpayers? What might the city do to prevent such abuses?

Exercises

E5-1   (Uncollectible accounts—allowance method)
The City of Chalmette levied property taxes of $150,000 in fiscal 2008. Experience shows that 3 percent of these taxes will not be collected.
Required: 1. What is the appropriate entry to set up the receivable for fiscal 2008 property taxes if the allowance method is used?
2. Taxpayer Holmes, whose tax levy is $200, is unable to pay her property taxes. The city decides to write off her account. Make the entry necessary to record this event.
3. If the Holmes account is not written off until fiscal 2009, what effect will this have on the fiscal 2008 revenues? Why?

E5-2   (Prior-year encumbrances that remain open)
The City of Eleanor follows a policy of allowing encumbrances to remain in force until the goods are delivered or the purchase orders are canceled. At the end of fiscal 2008, supplies costing $10,000 have not been delivered. In March 2009, the supplies arrive, accompanied by an invoice for $12,000.
Required: 1. What entry or entries should be made at the end of fiscal 2008?
2. What entry or entries should be made at the beginning of fiscal 2009?
3. What entry or entries should be made when the supplies arrive?

E5-3   (Grant not used up by year end)
In July 2008, Crescent City received a federal grant of $120,000, to be used to purchase food for horses used by that city's mounted police. By year end, hay and oats costing $90,000 had been purchased by the city and eaten by the horses. In 2009, the remainder of the grant was spent on more hay and oats.
Required: 1. What entry should be made when the grant is received?
2. What entry or entries should be made when the hay and oats are received? Assume that the city pays for these goods as soon as they are received.

E5-4   (Interfund loans)
Make the necessary journal entry in each fund assuming the Red Fox City Council directs that $2,500 cash be *loaned* (*not* transferred) from Special Revenue Fund #1 to Special Revenue Fund #2.

E5-5 (Interfund transfers)

Make the necessary journal entry in each fund assuming the Red Fox City Council directs that $2,500 cash be *transferred* (*not* loaned) from SRF #1 to SRF #2 and that the physical transfer of cash takes place immediately (without first being accrued).

E5-6 (Accrued interfund transfers)

Make the necessary journal entry in each fund assuming the Red Fox City Council directs that the $2,500 transfer be accrued immediately (with cash to be physically transferred at a later date).

E5-7 (Treatment of inventories—purchases method)

At the end of fiscal 2007, the City of Kensington has a balance of $6,000 in its Reserve for supplies account. An inventory taken at the end of 2008 reveals that supplies valued at $7,000 are on hand. Kensington uses the purchases method to account for supplies.

Required: 1. What entry should be made at the end of 2008 to disclose this change in the amount of supplies inventory?

2. Suppose the inventory shows that supplies valued at $4,000 are on hand. What entry should be made to disclose this fact?

E5-8 (Multiple choice—General and Special Revenue Funds)

1. The budget of Colfax County shows estimated revenues in excess of appropriations. When preparing budgetary entries at the beginning of the fiscal year, an increase will be recorded in which of the following accounts?
   a. Budgetary fund balance
   b. Encumbrances
   c. Due from other funds
   d. Reserve for encumbrances

2. What are reversions of property of persons not leaving a will, and with no known relatives, to a state called?
   a. Reversions
   b. Escheats
   c. Entitlements
   d. Contributions

3. Which of the following involves a routine movement of cash from the General Fund to a Debt Service Fund, to provide resources to pay interest and principal on a bond issue?
   a. An interfund reimbursement
   b. An interfund loan
   c. An interfund service provided and used
   d. An interfund transfer

4. At the end of fiscal 2008, Carson City has outstanding encumbrances of $15,000. Although the city follows a policy of allowing outstanding encumbrances to lapse, it plans to honor the related purchase orders in fiscal 2009. The management of the city wants users of its financial statements to be aware of these outstanding purchase orders. Therefore, at year end, the city's accountant should take which of the following actions?

   a. Credit Appropriations.
   b. Credit Fund balance reserved for encumbrances.
   c. Credit Unreserved fund balance.
   d. Credit Budgetary fund balance
5. Which of the following revenues of the General Fund are usually recorded before they are actually received?
   a. License and permit fees
   b. Property taxes
   c. Fines and penalties
   d. Parking meter receipts
6. If the City of Castletown sells a surplus ambulance, the entry to record this sale on the books of the General Fund should include which of the following?
   a. A debit to Unreserved fund balance
   b. A debit to Encumbrances—capital equipment
   c. A credit to Other financing sources—proceeds from sale of general fixed assets
   d. A credit to a Vehicles fixed asset account
7. The town council of Bayou Brilleaux adopted a budget for fiscal 2008 that anticipated revenues of $750,000 and expenditures of $800,000. Which entry is used to record this budget into the accounts?

	Dr	Cr
a. Estimated revenues	750,000	
Reserve for deficits	50,000	
Appropriations		800,000
b. Estimated revenues	750,000	
Budgetary fund balance	50,000	
Appropriations		800,000
c. Appropriations	800,000	
Budgetary fund balance		50,000
Estimated revenues		750,000
d. Encumbrances	750,000	
Budgetary fund balance	50,000	
Appropriations		800,000

8. Which of the following will increase the fund balance of a government at the end of a fiscal year?
   a. Estimated revenues are less than expenditures and reserve for encumbrances.
   b. Revenues are greater than expenditures and encumbrances.
   c. Appropriations are less than expenditures and encumbrances.
   d. Appropriations are greater than estimated revenues.
9. What does a government record in its Fund balance reserved for encumbrances account?
   a. Expenditures that were made in the current year for which payment will be made the following year
   b. Current-year purchase orders that will be honored the following year

    c. Excess expenditures of the prior year that will be offset against the current-year budgeted amounts

    d. Unanticipated expenditures of the prior year that become evident in the current year

10. The budget of the General Fund of the City of Olde Glen shows an appropriation for capital equipment of $150,000. So far a fire engine, costing $50,000, has been received and paid for. Another fire engine, expected to cost $60,000, has been ordered and an encumbrance for this amount is outstanding. How much can the city legally spend for a third fire engine this year?

    a. $40,000

    b. $100,000

    c. $90,000

    d. $0

11. Which of the following accounts of a government is (are) closed out at the end of the fiscal year?

	Fund Balance	Estimated Revenues
a.	No	No
b.	No	Yes
c.	Yes	Yes
d.	Yes	No

12. Which of the following is an appropriate basis of accounting for the General Fund of a government?

	Cash Basis	Modified Accrual Basis
a.	Yes	Yes
b.	No	Yes
c.	No	No
d.	Yes	No

13. Which of the following is not included among the financial reporting requirements of the General Fund of a city?

    a. Balance sheet

    b. Statement of cash flows

    c. Statement of revenues, expenditures, and changes in fund balance

    d. Budgetary comparison schedule

E5-9 (Tax discounts and deferred property taxes)

The City of Snake River allows taxpayers who pay their property taxes by the end of the fiscal year to take a 3 percent discount for prompt payment. The city budgets, as Estimated revenues, the amount it actually expects to receive. During fiscal 2008 the city sent bills to property owners totaling $150,000 (gross amount). Two-thirds of the amount billed (less discounts) was received by the end of the year. The remainder, $50,000, will not be collected until the middle of the following year.

Required: 1. Prepare an entry recording the collection of property taxes in fiscal 2008.

2. Prepare a year-end adjusting entry recording fiscal 2008 property taxes expected to be collected in fiscal 2009.

E5-10 (Using the Internet in governmental accounting)

Many local governments post their Comprehensive Annual Financial Reports (CAFRs) on their Web sites. Visit the Web site of a government of your choosing and view the CAFR if it is posted. (If no CAFR is posted, choose another government). Locate the financial statements for the governmental funds and see whether interfund transfers are reported in the operating statements and whether amounts due to/from other funds are reported in the balance sheets. Also, see whether any advances to/from other funds are reported in the balance sheet. If advances to other funds are reported, is a portion of fund balance reserved for advances?

Problems

P5-1 (Theory problem on the basis of accounting)

The accounting system of the municipality of Kemp is organized and operated on a fund basis. Among the types of funds used are a General Fund, a Special Revenue Fund, and an Enterprise Fund.

Required: 1. Explain the basic differences in revenue recognition between the accrual basis of accounting and the modified accrual basis of accounting as it relates to governmental accounting.

2. What basis of accounting should be used for each of the following funds? Why?

- General Fund
- Special Revenue Fund
- Enterprise Fund

3. How should an entity account for fixed assets and long-term liabilities related to the General Fund?

(AICPA adapted)

P5-2 (Preparation of financial statements)

The commissioners of the Regents Park Commission approved the following budget. Assume that the Unreserved fund balance at the beginning of the year was $10,000 and that no encumbrances were outstanding and no supplies were on hand at the beginning or the end of the year.

Estimated Revenues		
Property taxes	$300,000	
Concession rentals	100,000	
User charges	200,000	$600,000
Appropriations		
Wages and salaries	$200,000	
Capital equipment	300,000	
Supplies	50,000	550,000
Budgeted Increase in Fund Balance		$50,000

During the year, actual revenues were

Property taxes	$300,000
Concession rentals	120,000
User charges	185,000

Actual expenditures were

Wages and salaries	$205,000
Capital equipment	290,000
Supplies	40,000

Required: 1. Prepare a statement of revenues, expenditures, and changes in fund balance.

2. Prepare a budgetary comparison schedule. Assume the originally approved budget and final budget are identical.

P5-3   (Journal entries for selected events and transactions)

Prepare the general journal entries necessary to record the following *selected* transactions of the General Fund of the City of Roxyville.

1. Property taxes of $4,000,000 were levied. The city estimates that 1.5% of the total levy will prove uncollectible and that taxes of $2,000,000 (gross) will be collected soon enough to qualify for a 2% discount period. (At the expiration of the discount period, taxes receivable will become delinquent. All collectible property taxes are expected to be collected during the current year or early in the next year.)

2. Property taxes of $1,800,000 (gross receivable) were collected within the 2% discount period. The remaining taxes are now past due.

3. Property taxes of $1,550,000 (gross receivable) were collected after the discount period expired along with late penalties of $3,400.

4. The city's Building Inspection Department, accounted for through the General Fund, did work for an expansion of the city's water utility operation, accounted for through an Enterprise Fund. The Building Inspection Department billed the water utility $10,250.

5. A $220,000, three-year loan was authorized and made from the General Fund to the Water Utility Enterprise Fund to provide interim financing for an expansion project.

6. A new paving machine for the Street Department (accounted for through the General Fund) was ordered: $32,000.

7. Payment of $600,000 of General Fund cash was authorized and made to provide permanent capital for a new Internal Service Fund.

8. The city council reviewed budget-to-actual operating results to date with the Finance Director and reduced the estimate of sales tax revenue by $24,000; correspondingly, the council decided that the government should plan to spend $20,000 less for street maintenance than previously budgeted.

9. The paving machine ordered at item 6 was received along with an invoice for $31,700. The invoice was vouchered for payment.

10. Schlok-O, a major retailer and property owner within the city, is withholding payment of property taxes pending appeal of the assessed valuation of its property for the current year. The city attorney's opinion is that Schlok-O ultimately will lose the appeal. However, the appeal action means that

property taxes that would normally already have been collected, $42,000, will probably not be received until well into next fiscal year.
11. Delinquent taxes receivable of $9,500 were written off as uncollectible.
12. It was discovered that the purchase of a copy machine, $3,850, previously recorded as an expenditure of the mayor's office (General Fund) was actually made to benefit the public library (Special Revenue Fund). The General Fund and the SRF maintain their cash accounts at separate banks. The date to transfer cash has not yet been set.

The following simplified balance sheets pertain to problems P5-4, P5-5, and P5-6.

Special Revenue Fund (SRF) #1 simplified balance sheet:		Special Revenue Fund (SRF) #2 simplified balance sheet:	
Cash	$30,000	Due from General Fund	$50,000
Fund Balance	$30,000	Vouchers payable	$5,000
		Fund Balance	45,000
			$50,000

P5-4 Assume the city council directs that $7,500 cash be *loaned* (*not* transferred) from SRF #1 to SRF #2.

Required: 1. Prepare the journal entry needed in each fund to record this transaction.
2. Prepare the simplified balance sheets for each fund after this transaction has been recorded.

P5-5 Assume the city council directs that $7,500 cash be *transferred* (*not* loaned) from SRF #1 to SRF #2 and that the physical transfer of cash takes place immediately (without first being accrued).

Required: 1. Prepare the journal entry needed in each fund to record this transaction.
2. Prepared simplified operating statements for each fund as they would appear after transaction 1 is recorded. Hint: Revenues and expenditures both will be zero for both funds, but one fund's operating statement will report an Other Financing Use and the other fund's operating statement will report an Other Financing Source.
3. Prepare simplified balance sheets for each fund after transaction 1 has been recorded.

P5-6 Assume the city council directs that a $7,500 transfer from SRF #1 to SRF #2 be accrued immediately (with cash to be physically transferred at a later date).

Required: 1. Prepare the journal entry needed in each fund to record this transaction.
2. Prepared the simplified operating statement for each fund as they would appear after transaction 1 is recorded. Hint: Revenues and expenditures both will be zero for both funds, but one fund's operating statement will report an Other Financing Use and the other fund's operating statement will report an Other Financing Source.
3. Prepare the simplified balance sheets for each fund after transaction 1 has been recorded.

P5-7 (Allotments)

The City of Belle Vista divides its appropriations into allotments, which are expended during the allotment period. In this city, allotments are made at the beginning of each quarter. In FY 2009, estimated revenues are $500,000 and unallotted appropriations are $480,000. A $20,000 increase is projected for the fund balance. Actual revenues are $500,000. The allotments for the year are as follows:

1st quarter	$150,000
2nd quarter	100,000
3rd quarter	130,000
4th quarter	100,000

Expenditures for the year are as follows:

1/8	$20,000	7/28	$30,000
2/2	80,000	8/16	40,000
3/15	40,000	9/14	19,000
4/18	35,000	10/15	10,000
5/20	45,000	11/18	30,000
6/15	20,000	12/22	35,000
7/12	50,000	12/30	5,000

Required: 1. Prepare journal entries to record the allotments, expenditures, and unallotted appropriations for each period, including the year-end closing entries.
2. Prepare a subsidiary ledger for the allotments, using the following format:
Date   Allotments   Expenditures   Remaining Balance

P5-8 (Complete accounting cycle of a General Fund)

The Sherwood Park commissioners approved the following budget for fiscal 2009 for that government's General Fund:

Estimated Revenues		
Property taxes	$85,000	
License fees	25,000	
Fines and penalties	35,000	
Sales taxes	25,000	
Federal grant	30,000	$200,000
Appropriations and Transfers		
Salaries	$80,000	
Supplies	40,000	
Capital equipment	40,000	
Transfers to other funds	20,000	180,000
Budgeted Increase in Fund Balance		$20,000

The park uses the allowance method of handling uncollectible accounts. An allowance equal to 15 percent of property taxes billed is recorded when the bills are sent. The park's accounting policies include the following:

1. All purchases of supplies and capital equipment are encumbered.

2. Expenditures for salaries and transfers to other funds do not require encumbrances.
3. Outstanding encumbrances lapse at the end of each fiscal year. Outstanding purchase orders that will be honored the following year, however, are reported on its financial statements.
4. Separate accounts are maintained for each taxpayer.
5. At the end of each fiscal year, all outstanding property tax receivables are reclassified as delinquent.
6. The park uses the purchases method to record the purchase and use of supplies. An inventory taken at the end of fiscal 2008 revealed that supplies costing $5,000 were still on hand.

The park has four property owners, whose taxes for fiscal 2009 are:

R. Hood	$40,000
F. Tuck	10,000
M. Marian	20,000
A. Adale	30,000
	$100,000

Encumbrances still outstan at the end of fiscal 2008 amounted to $10,000 and were for capital . The postclosing trial balance of the General Fund of Sherwember 31, 2008, is presented here:

	Debits	Credits
	$20,000	
	3,000	
	8,000	
urrent		$3,000
	5,000	
Vc		8,000
Fun		10,000
Fund inventory		5,000
Unres		10,000
	$36,000	$36,000

[Handwritten note overlaying the table: "Fund balance reserved for... = Non-Spendable ↓ Unassigned!"]

During fiscal 2009, the following transactions occurred:

1. Fiscal 2008 encumbrances for capital equipment were restored.
2. Tax bills amounting to $100,000 were sent to fiscal 2009 property taxpayers. Of the amount billed, $15,000 was not expected to be collected.
3. L. John left town suddenly. When he departed, his account was written off.
4. A. Adale paid his fiscal 2008 property taxes in full, along with a late payment penalty of $100.
5. R. Hood and M. Marian paid their property taxes on time and in full.
6. The capital equipment ordered in fiscal 2008 arrived, along with an invoice for $10,000. The invoice was paid immediately.
7. Supplies expected to cost $40,000 were ordered.
8. A transfer of $18,000 was made to the Hyde Park Fund. Of this amount, $10,000 was paid in cash. The remainder will be paid in the future.

9. All outstanding fiscal 2008 vouchers were paid.
10. The federal grant, $30,000, was received.
11. Salaries for the year were $80,000.
12. Five motorcycles, costing $8,000 each, were ordered.
13. One-half of the supplies arrived in August, along with an invoice for $25,000. The invoice was paid in October.
14. Three of the motorcycles arrived. The actual cost of $28,000 was paid immediately.
15. F. Tuck was unable to pay his property taxes. The account was written off.
16. A. Adale paid $25,000 of his fiscal 2009 property taxes. He hopes to pay the remainder next year.
17. Other fiscal 2009 revenues were

License fees	$25,000
Fines and penalties	40,000

    Sales taxes amounting to $25,000 were collected during the year. The Park's accountant estimates that another $5,000 will be collected in January 2010 and, therefore, is "available."
18. One-fourth of the supplies arrived, along with an invoice for $9,000.
19. By the end of 2009, only $20,000 of the federal grant had been spent. The remainder will be spent in the middle of 2010.

Required: 1. Prepare budgetary, operating, and closing entries for fiscal 2009 for the General Fund. Assume that outstanding purchase orders will be honored the following year and that supplies inventory at the end of fiscal 2009 amounts to $8,000.
  2. Prepare preclosing and postclosing trial balances for fiscal 2009.
  3. Prepare a balance sheet and a statement of revenues, expenditures, and changes in fund balance for fiscal 2009.
  4. Prepare a budgetary comparison schedule for fiscal 2009.

P5-9 (Journal entries and financial statement presentation—interfund transactions) Following are several transactions for the City of Mason's Manor:

1. The Water Purification Fund billed its customers for $124,000. Included in this amount were $12,000 to the General Fund (not encumbered by the General Fund) and $5,000 to the Electric Utility Fund. Both the Water Purification Fund and the Electric Utility Fund are Enterprise Funds.
2. A Special Revenue Fund lent a Capital Projects Fund $25,000, to be repaid in 9 months.
3. The General Fund made a permanent contribution of capital to the Civic Swimming Pool Fund, an Enterprise Fund. The amount of the contribution was $50,000.
4. The General Fund made its annual payment of $200,000 to a Debt Service Fund.
5. The General Fund paid $34,000 for consulting services. At the time the transaction was incurred, a debit for the entire amount was made to Expenditures—consulting services. Later a Capital Projects Fund paid the General Fund $9,000 for its share of the consulting costs.

Required: Prepare the journal entries necessary to record these transactions and to identify the fund or funds involved.

P5-10   (Errors in recording interfund transfers)

Recently, the General Fund of Felicity Village received monies from the following sources:

1. $10,000 from a Debt Service Fund when that fund was closed out after a bond issue was repaid.
2. $25,000 from the Library Fund, representing that fund's share of the cost of the annual audit.
3. $5,000 as a yearly contribution from the Royal Park Fund, to be used for general operations of the city.
4. $15,000 from the Regional Transit Authority (an Enterprise Fund) to be used to pay salaries of police riding on its buses in high-crime areas.
5. $50,000 from the federal government as a grant to fund a program for homeless accountants, of which the city already spent $35,000, with the remainder to be spent in the latter part of the following year.

Each of these receipts was recorded in the General Fund as a current revenue. Do you agree with this accounting treatment? If not, how should they be recorded?

P5-11   (Complete accounting cycle of a Permanent Fund)

In fiscal 2009, Henry Comstock made a gift to the City of Gold Hill. Under the terms of the gift, the city was to purchase securities and to use the earnings on these securities to purchase books on history for its library. Only the earnings on the securities can be expended.

During fiscal 2009, the following transactions occurred:

1. The city received the gift from Mr. Comstock, a check for $2,500,000.
2. Shortly after receiving the gift, the city purchased government securities for $2,500,000.
3. Investment income of $100,000 was received in cash.
4. A transfer of $85,000, cash, was made to the Library Fund, a Special Revenue fund.
5. Salaries of $7,000 were paid in cash during the year.
6. A payment of $6,000 was made to the General Fund to cover the cost of supplies ($2,000) and office space ($4,000).
7. The fund received a bill for its annual audit, amounting to $3,000, from Yerington and Company, CPAs, which it will pay next year.
8. Investment income of $50,000 was received in cash.
9. A transfer of $40,000 was made to the Library Fund. Of this amount, $30,000 was paid in cash. The remainder will be paid to the Library Fund next year.
10. Investment income of $25,000 was accrued at the end of fiscal 2009.
11. By the end of fiscal 2009, the marketable securities had increased in value by $40,000.

Required: 1. Prepare the journal entries necessary to record these transactions on the books of the Permanent Fund.
2. Prepare a balance sheet and a statement of revenues, expenditures, and changes in fund balance for the Permanent Fund.

P5-12 (Preparing financial statements from a trial balance)

Following is the preclosing trial balance of Prairie City at the end of fiscal 2009. Assume that at the beginning of the year no encumbrances were outstanding, that the Reserve for supplies inventory amounted to $4,000, and that the Unreserved fund balance was $21,000.

Prairie City General Fund
Preclosing Trial Balance
December 31, 2009

	Debits	Credits
Cash	$ 22,450	
Marketable securities	50,000	
Property taxes receivable	35,525	
Allowance for uncollectible property taxes		$ 18,000
Sales taxes receivable	8,500	
Due from state government	16,000	
Supplies inventory	7,000	
Vouchers payable		12,275
Due to other funds		13,400
Advances from other funds		35,000
Encumbrances—contractual services	10,000	
Fund balance reserved for supplies inventory		7,000
Unreserved fund balance		21,000
Budgetary fund balance reserved for encumbrances		10,000
Budgetary fund balance		21,500
Estimated revenues—property taxes	125,000	
Estimated revenues—sales taxes	73,000	
Estimated revenues—charges for services	14,000	
Estimated revenues—fines and forfeits	8,500	
Estimated revenues—federal grants	10,000	
Estimated transfer in from Enterprise Fund	30,000	
Appropriations—salaries		107,000
Appropriations—contractual services		27,000
Appropriations—materials and supplies		15,000
Appropriations—capital equipment		70,000
Appropriations—transfer out to Debt Service Fund		20,000
Revenues—property taxes		117,500
Revenues—sales taxes		73,600
Revenues—charges for services		12,400
Revenues—fines and forfeits		8,900
Revenues—federal grants		10,000
Transfer in from Enterprise Fund		35,000
Expenditures—salaries	105,200	
Expenditures—contractual services	15,000	
Expenditures—materials and supplies	15,300	
Expenditures—capital equipment	69,100	
Transfer out to Debt Service Fund	20,000	
	$634,575	$634,575

Required: 1. Prepare closing entries for fiscal 2009.
2. Prepare a postclosing trial balance for fiscal 2009.
3. Prepare a balance sheet for fiscal 2009.
4. Prepare a statement of revenues, expenditures, and changes in fund balance for fiscal 2009.
5. Prepare a budgetary comparison schedule for fiscal 2009. Show outstanding encumbrances as expenditures, in order to provide a more meaningful comparison, and prepare a note to this effect on the statement (see Table 5-12). Assume that the originally approved budget and the final budget are identical.

P5-13 (CPA Examination question on activities of a General Fund)
The General Fund trial balance of the City of Avocado Heights at December 31, 2008, was as follows:

	Debits	Credits
Cash	$62,000	
Taxes receivable—delinquent	46,000	
Estimated uncollectible taxes—delinquent		$ 8,000
Stores inventory—special events	18,000	
Vouchers payable		28,000
Fund balance reserved for stores inventory		18,000
Fund balance reserved for encumbrances		12,000
Unreserved, undesignated fund balance		60,000
	$126,000	$126,000

Collectible delinquent taxes are expected to be collected within 60 days after the end of the year. Avocado Heights uses the purchases method to account for stores inventory. The following data pertain to 2009 General Fund operations:

1. Budget adopted:

Revenues and Other Financing Sources		
Taxes	$220,000	
Fines, forfeits, and penalties	80,000	
Miscellaneous revenues	100,000	
Share of bond issue proceeds	200,000	$600,000
Expenditures and Other Financing Uses		
Program operations	$300,000	
General administration	120,000	
Stores—program operations	60,000	
Capital outlay	80,000	
Periodic transfer to special revenue fund	20,000	580,000
Budgeted Increase in Fund Balance		$ 20,000

2. Taxes were assessed at an amount that would result in revenues of $220,800, after deduction of 4 percent of the tax levy as uncollectible.
3. Orders placed:

Program operations	$176,000
General administration	80,000
Capital outlay	60,000
	$316,000

4. The city council designated $20,000 of the unreserved, undesignated fund balance for possible future appropriation for capital outlays.
5. Cash collections and transfer:

Delinquent taxes	$ 38,000
Current taxes	226,000
Refund of overpayment of invoice for purchase of equipment	4,000
Fines, forfeits, and penalties	88,000
Miscellaneous revenues	90,000
Share of bond issue proceeds	200,000
Transfer of remaining fund balance of a discontinued fund	18,000
	$664,000

6. Vouchers received against encumbrances:

	Estimated	Actual
Program operations	$156,000	$166,000
General administration	84,000	80,000
Capital outlay	62,000	62,000
	$302,000	$308,000

7. Vouchers processed on items not requiring encumbrances:

Program operations	$188,000
General administration	38,000
Capital outlays	18,000
Transfer to special revenue fund	20,000
	$264,000

8. Albert, a taxpayer, overpaid his 2009 taxes by $2,000. He applied for a $2,000 credit against his 2010 taxes. The city council granted his request.
9. Vouchers paid amounted to $580,000.
10. Stores inventory on December 31, 2009, amounted to $12,000.

Required: Prepare journal entries to record the effects of the foregoing data as well as closing entries. Omit explanations.

(AICPA adapted)

Continuous Problem

(Complete Accounting Cycle of General Fund)
The city council of Leisure City approved the following budget for fiscal 2009
for that city's General Fund:

Estimated Revenues

Property taxes	$5,504,000	
Interest and penalties	38,000	
Sales taxes	900,000	
Fines and penalties	70,000	
Lottery receipts	225,000	
License fees	10,000	$6,747,000

Appropriations and Transfers

Salaries	$3,500,000	
Travel	31,500	
Equipment	600,000	
Contractual services	120,000	
Supplies and materials	40,000	
Liability insurance	16,500	
Advertising	600	
Legal services	10,000	
Audit fees	10,000	
Transfer to Debt Service Fund	900,000	
Transfer to Venus Park Fund	60,000	5,288,600
Budgeted Increase in Fund Balance		$1,458,400

The city's accounting policies include the following:

1. All purchases of supplies and materials and equipment are encumbered.
2. Expenditures for salaries, travel, services, and transfers to other funds do not require encumbrances.
3. Expenditures for salaries include fringe benefits paid by the city.
4. Outstanding encumbrances lapse at the end of each fiscal year. Outstanding purchase orders that will be honored the following year, however, are reported on its financial statements.
5. At the end of each fiscal year, all outstanding property tax receivables are reclassified as delinquent.
6. Leisure City uses the purchases method to record the purchase and use of supplies and materials. An inventory taken at the end of fiscal 2008 revealed that supplies and materials costing $30,000 were still on hand.

Encumbrances outstanding at the end of fiscal 2008 amounted to $25,000 and were for construction equipment ordered by the Streets and Parkways Department.

The postclosing trial balance of the General Fund of Leisure City, as of December 31, 2008, follows.

	Debits	Credits
Cash	$300,000	
Investments	500,000	
Property taxes receivable—delinquent	50,000	
Supplies and materials on hand	30,000	
Vouchers payable		$ 20,000
Fund balance reserved for encumbrances		25,000
Fund balance reserved for supplies and materials on hand		30,000
Unreserved fund balance		805,000
	$880,000	$880,000

During fiscal 2009, the following transactions occurred:

1. Fiscal 2008 encumbrances for construction equipment were restored.
2. Tax bills amounting to $5,504,000 were sent to fiscal 2009 property tax-payers. The entire amount billed is expected to be collected.
3. Property taxes outstanding at the end of fiscal 2008 were paid in full, along with a late payment penalty of $800.
4. Collections on fiscal 2009 property taxes during the year amounted to $5,200,000.
5. A property tax rebate of $20,000 was given to a property owner because of this company's effort to increase employment during the year. The city had previously made no provision for tax rebates. Assume that the property owner already paid its fiscal 2009 property taxes.
6. The equipment ordered in fiscal 2008 arrived, along with an invoice for $25,000. The invoice was paid immediately.
7. All outstanding fiscal 2008 vouchers were paid.
8. Travel costs of city personnel amounted to $31,000. (Charge contractual services.)
9. Supplies and materials expected to cost $40,000 were ordered.
10. Expenditures for contractual services amounted to $115,000. All were paid in cash upon completion of the services.
11. A transfer of $60,000 was made to the Venus Park Fund. Of this amount, $50,000 was paid in cash. The remainder will be paid in fiscal 2010.
12. Interest on investments amounting to $37,000, was received during the year.
13. Salaries for the year were $2,900,000. This amount includes $300,000 withheld from the employees' checks for their share of contributions to the Pension Fund. Another $300,000 was paid by the city as its share of the contribution to the Pension Fund. (Hint: Treat the city's contribution as an additional salaries expenditure.) The amount due to the Pension Trust Fund was paid several days after the city workers were paid.
14. A computer network was ordered for the use of the Public Safety and Administration Departments. It was expected to cost $544,000.
15. A transfer of $900,000 was made, in cash, to the Debt Service Fund.
16. By late November, the computer system had been installed and the vendor presented the city with a bill for $545,000. The bill was paid immediately.

17. Construction equipment expected to cost $31,000 was ordered.

18. Some of the construction equipment arrived, along with an invoice for $17,360, which was paid immediately. The city had expected the equipment to cost $19,000.

19. One-half of the supplies and materials ordered in part (9) arrived, along with an invoice for $22,000. The invoice was paid immediately.

20. Other fiscal 2009 revenues were:

Fines and penalties	$ 69,240
Lottery receipts	230,000
License fees	10,000

Sales taxes amounting to $850,000 were collected during the year. The city's accountant estimates that another $49,500 will be collected in January 2010 and, therefore, is "available."

21. The remainder of the construction equipment ordered in part (17) arrived, along with an invoice of $12,000. The invoice will be paid in fiscal 2010.

22. One-fourth of the materials and supplies arrived, along with an invoice for $8,000. The invoice was paid immediately.

23. During the year, the following amounts were paid, in cash, for nondepartmental expenditures:

Liability insurance	$16,285
Advertising	554
Legal services	9,500
Audit fees	9,600

24. Property taxes amounting to $304,000 not collected by the end of the year were reclassified as delinquent. The city expects to collect these taxes in fiscal 2010.

Required: 1. Prepare budgetary, operating, and closing entries for fiscal 2009 for the General Fund. Assume that outstanding purchase orders will be honored the following year and that supplies inventory at the end of fiscal 2009 amounts to $18,000.

2. Prepare preclosing and postclosing trial balances for fiscal 2009.

3. Prepare a balance sheet and a statement of revenues, expenditures, and changes in fund balance for fiscal 2009.

4. Prepare a budgetary comparison schedule for fiscal 2009.

6

THE GOVERNMENTAL FUND ACCOUNTING CYCLE

Capital Projects Funds, Debt Service Funds, and Special Assessments

Chapter Outline

After completing this chapter, you should be able to:

■ Explain why and how Capital Projects Funds are used in governmental accounting.
■ Prepare the journal entries normally made within Capital Projects Funds.
■ Prepare fund financial statements for Capital Projects Funds.
■ Explain why and how Debt Service Funds are used in governmental accounting.
■ Prepare the journal entries normally made within Debt Service Funds.
■ Prepare fund financial statements for Debt Service Funds.
■ Prepare journal entries pertaining to leased assets.
■ Understand the concept of special assessments.
■ Prepare the journal entries normally made for transactions associated with special assessments.

C apital Projects Funds and Debt Service Funds are straightforward applications of the "fund" concept in practice in that both types of funds account for resources that legally can be spent only for specific purposes. The need for these fund types arises primarily from large-scale public works projects and the manner in which they are financed. Typically, governments finance large capital acquisitions or construction projects, such as buildings and parks, with the proceeds from the sale of general obligation bonds. The related debt covenants often include two important requirements: First, that the bond proceeds be expended only for the purpose for which the bonds were sold, that is, the construction and/or purchase of a particular capital asset. Second, that the borrowing government set aside financial resources for the express purpose of "servicing"—making interest and principal payments on—the debt.

These debt covenant requirements make it prudent for a government to establish a Capital Projects Fund to account for the *construction* of the capital asset—but not the asset itself—and a Debt Service Fund to account for payments of interest and bond principal as those payments come due. Additionally, governmental GAAP *require* that a government use a Capital Projects Fund if the project is financed in whole or in part by general obligation proceeds.[1] Further, under governmental GAAP, "debt service funds are required if they are legally mandated and/or if financial resources are being accumulated for principal and interest payments maturing in future years."[2]

---

[1] GASB Cod. Sec. 1300.106.
[2] GASB Cod. Sec. 1500.113.

In the simplest case, if a government undertakes a single capital project, the Capital Projects Fund will be established and terminated over the life of the construction project, perhaps 2–3 years at most. The Debt Service Fund, on the other hand, will have a "life" equivalent to the duration of the financing bond issue; for example, 20, 25, or 30 years.[3]

In practice, there is little consistency among governments with respect to the number of Capital Projects Funds and Debt Service Funds they maintain, mostly as the result of local law. Some governments use the same Capital Projects Fund to account for a series of specific projects over several years if convenience dictates and legal requirements allow. Other governments establish a separate Capital Project Fund for each major project and abolish them when the related projects are completed. Indeed, the authoritative guidance is somewhat vague in the pertinent requirements for these fund types. On one hand, governmental GAAP[4] require that governments use the minimum number of funds practicable, suggesting that individual projects should be accounted for in a single Capital Projects Fund whenever possible. However, careful attention must be paid to any bond indenture provisions or restrictions placed on the use of certain types of resources. In many instances, such restrictions will prevent accounting for multiple projects in the same fund. The same facts and arguments apply to Debt Service Funds.[5]

MEASUREMENT FOCUS AND BASIS OF ACCOUNTING

As with all governmental-type funds, the measurement focus of Capital Projects Funds and Debt Service Funds is current financial resources, which means that these funds account for only the accumulation of financial resources and the expenditure of those resources. As a result, long-lived assets are not accounted for in Capital Projects Funds or Debt Service Funds, nor is any long-term debt accounted for within these funds. The current financial resources criterion focuses on assets currently available and the claims due and payable against those assets.

The basis of accounting for Capital Projects Funds and Debt Service Funds is the same as for the other governmental-type funds—modified accrual. Therefore, the recognition principles discussed previously in this text apply to these fund types. In general, revenues are recorded when they are measurable and available, and expenditures are recorded when the related liability is incurred. (An important exception to the liability recognition principle under modified accrual accounting involves the treatment of interest on long-term debt. We discuss this exception later in this chapter.)

This chapter first discusses and illustrates the Capital Projects Fund accounting and financial reporting for the transactions that normally occur over the life cycle of a large-scale public works construction project. The chapter then focuses on accounting and reporting for the operations of a Debt Service Fund. Finally, the chapter introduces the concept of *special assessments* and discusses their relationship to Capital Projects Funds and Debt Service Funds.

---

[3]Financing large capital projects with bond proceeds is traditional in American local government. On the assumption that a capital asset has a physical life of, say, 30 years, financing the assets with a 30-year bond issue means that the cost of the assets will be borne by approximately the generations of citizens (taxpayers) who will benefit from using the asset.

[4]GASB Cod. Sec. 1100.104.

[5]Some writers differentiate between the demands of *accounting* versus *financial reporting* in this regard. They suggest that a single Capital Projects Fund or Debt Service Fund may be sufficient in many cases for the purpose of financial reporting in compliance with GAAP provided that information pertaining to individual capital projects or bond issues is maintained internally within a government's accounting system.

CAPITAL PROJECTS FUNDS

Overview

Acquisition or construction of major capital facilities, other than those financed by proprietary and trust funds, is accounted for in Capital Projects Funds. Examples of capital projects include the construction of a new city hall, a new civic auditorium, or a bridge. The resources used to finance Capital Projects Funds usually come from general obligation debt, transfers from other funds, intergovernmental revenues, or private donations.

Acquisition of a capital asset of a relatively minor nature, such as a piece of furniture or an automobile, usually is financed through the General Fund or a Special Revenue Fund. For example, the purchase of a new police car or a desk for the mayor's office is recorded as an expenditure in the fund that made the acquisition (see Chapter 5).

Capital Budgets

Capital projects normally are controlled by capital budgets. A typical capital budget is illustrated in Table 6-1. Notice that a description of each project is given in addition to the amount requested and the source of funding. In the illustration, the city has been given a plantation house, which it intends to restore and turn into a museum. In addition, the city is planning to build a fire station, repair several bridges, and work on a stadium (a 3-year project).

Many governments supplement their current-year capital budgets with long-run capital programs. A long-run capital program presents information on the capital improvements desired over a multiyear period of time (e.g., 5 years). It lists the projects planned, the estimated cost of each project, and the proposed source or sources of financing for each project. Generally it is prepared on a "continuous" basis, with a future year added, the past year dropped, and the other years "fine tuned."

Although some people may regard long-run capital programs as "wish lists" and some projects may never materialize, long-run capital programs are good organizing, planning, and communicating tools. They enable users to see at a glance what is needed, what is wanted, and what the government can afford. Such information is particularly valuable to legislators who must balance the needs of one organization against the needs of others to allocate limited resources.

TABLE 6-1   Capital Budget

Date: September 15, 2008		*Prepared by* __BER__
Project Description	*Budget Request*	*Source of Funding*
Restore Ellett plantation house		
Purchase furniture	$ 200,000	Federal and state grants
Fire station—First and Magazine		
Streets Remodel	300,000	Bond proceeds
Repair bridges		
Short Bayou and Cutoff Bayou	700,000	Bond proceeds and federal grant
"Doc" Williams Stadium renovation	300,000	Tax revenues
Total	$1,500,000	

Summary of Fund Activities

The nature and order of events involving capital projects may vary according to local ordinances and procedures, the relative size of the project, and the type of financing involved; however, this section illustrates the typical sequence of project activities. After a project is approved, financing arrangements are made and contracts are let as applicable.

To obtain financing for projects, governmental units usually issue general obligation bonds and solicit federal and/or state grants. Bond and grant proceeds are not always spent immediately upon receipt. In such cases, the Capital Projects Fund will account for some investment activity. As the construction work progresses, investments are liquidated and payments are made to the contractor until the project is completed and finally accepted. At this time, any financial resources remaining in the fund are transferred to another fund or returned to grantors, as applicable.

Control of Fund Activities

The operations of a Capital Projects Fund are generally controlled through provisions of bond indentures, provisions of grant agreements, and so forth. Therefore, formal budgetary integration into the accounts, as used in the General Fund and Special Revenue Funds, is not always necessary. For consistency within this text, though, we will assume that a budget is recorded and used for control purposes. Such accounting procedures are especially helpful if a single fund is being used to account for more than one project.

Encumbrance accounting is ordinarily used for these funds because of the extent of involvement with contracts and purchase orders and because of the need to control the related expenditures. Thus, in our example of a construction project, a regular encumbrance entry is made upon signing the contract. Expenditures on the contract are treated in the manner previously illustrated for encumbered purchase orders.

Accounting for Fund Activities
Operating Entries

For illustrative purposes, assume that the City of Angusville decides to build a sports complex at a cost of $18 million and includes the project in its 2008 capital budget. Financing for the project consists of a general obligation bond issue for $10 million and an $8 million expenditure-driven grant from the state. The state grant proceeds are revenue to the Capital Projects Fund and the proceeds from the bond issue are classified as an other financing source. Accordingly, the following entry is made to record the budget:

Estimated revenues	8,000,000	
Estimated other financing sources	10,000,000	
Appropriations		18,000,000
To record the budget.		

If the bonds are sold at par (face) value, the following entry is made:

Cash	10,000,000	
Other financing source—long-term debt issued		10,000,000
To record the issuance of bonds.		

Because Capital Projects Funds follow a current financial resources measurement focus, bonded-debt principal is not recorded as a liability of a Capital Projects Fund.

If grant proceeds are received from the state before project costs are incurred, receipt of the cash is recorded as follows:

Cash	8,000,000	
Deferred revenues—construction grant		8,000,000
To record receipt of state grant.		

As the proceeds of the state grant are used to finance qualifying construction expenditures, revenue is recognized and the deferred revenue account is reduced.

The government will retain an architect to prepare plans for the project and to serve as project adviser. In this instance, assume the architectural firm's fee is $400,000. When the contract with the architect is signed, an encumbrance entry is made, as follows:

Encumbrances—capital project	400,000	
Budgetary fund balance reserved for encumbrances		400,000
To record encumbrance of architect's fee.		

(For purposes of simplicity, a single encumbrance control account will be used in the remainder of this chapter.)

The contract with the architect requires the city to pay 90 percent of the fee when the plans are completed; the remainder of the fee will be paid upon completion of the project. The following entries are made when the plans for the sports complex are accepted:

Budgetary fund balance reserved for encumbrances	360,000	
Encumbrances—capital project		360,000
To reverse encumbrance prior to recording expenditure.		
Expenditures—architect's fees	360,000	
Vouchers payable		360,000
To record the liability for architect's fees.		
Vouchers payable	360,000	
Cash		360,000
To record payment of vouchers payable.		

After evaluating bids for the project submitted by various contractors, the city accepts the bid of PPK Construction Company of $17.6 million. Upon signing the contract, the following entry is made:

Encumbrances—capital project	17,600,000	
Budgetary fund balance reserved for encumbrances		17,600,000
To record encumbrance of construction contract.		

Only part of the cash on hand is needed immediately, so the city invests $9 million in short-term securities:

Investments	9,000,000	
Cash		9,000,000
To record investment of idle cash.		

As the project advances, the contractor sends a progress billing report to the city, requesting payment of $5.5 million on the project. The payment is approved, less a 10 percent *retained percentage*. Retaining (holding back) a certain amount from each payment to a contractor provides incentive for the contractor to complete the job satisfactorily or a means to pay another contractor to complete the project, should that become necessary. (The retained percentage procedure, also called "retainage," is standard practice in the construction industry.) The following entries are made for the billing:

Budgetary fund balance reserved for encumbrances	5,500,000	
Encumbrances—capital project		5,500,000
To reverse part of the encumbrance		
for the construction contract.		

Expenditures—construction costs	5,500,000	
Retained percentage on construction contracts		550,000
Construction contracts payable		4,950,000
To record construction expenditure and related liabilities.		

Note the use of the Retained percentage on construction contracts account. Because the retainage is owed to the contractor, it is reported as a liability on the balance sheet of the Capital Projects Fund. The following entry is made to record payment of the construction voucher:

Construction contracts payable	4,950,000	
Cash		4,950,000
To record payment of amount currently due to contractor.		

Assuming the state agreed that the grant monies would be used before the bond proceeds, recording the $5,500,000 construction expenditure drives the recognition of construction grant revenue, so the following entry is needed:

Deferred revenues—construction grant	5,500,000	
Revenues—construction grant		5,500,000
To record revenues from state construction grant.		

Interest earned—but not yet received—on the investments to this point is $300,000. Assume that the local laws permit Capital Projects Funds to use any interest earned through the investment of idle funds to help finance the project.[6] The entry to record this interest is

Interest receivable on investments	300,000	
Revenues—investments		300,000
To record interest earned on investments.		

Notice that during the year, all costs incurred in the construction of the sports complex are charged (debited) to expenditures. At the end of the year, the Expenditures—construction costs account will be closed into Unreserved fund balance. As a result, the asset's cost is not capitalized on the books of the Capital Projects Fund. This approach is consistent with the financial resources measurement focus used for governmental-type funds. As mentioned in Chapter 5, these types of assets are reported in the government-wide financial statements. Financial reporting of these assets is explained in more detail at the end of this chapter and in Chapters 9 and 10.

---

[6]In some jurisdictions, interest earned on Capital Projects Funds investments must be used for debt service rather than being available to finance capital construction.

At this time, in excess of $3 million remains in the Cash account. Prudent management requires that $3 million be invested in short-term securities. The entry to record the investment is

Investments	3,000,000	
Cash		3,000,000
To record investment of excess cash.		

Investments held by governments generally are reported at fair market value.[7] Changes in the market value of most governmental investments are reported in the operating statement, along with interest and dividends received. Investments that are not reported at market value are those purchased with a maturity date of 1 year or less; for example, commercial paper and U.S. Treasury obligations. These investments are reported at amortized cost. It is possible that the carrying value of the investments would need to be adjusted to fair value at the end of the fiscal year. However, because this project is short term, the investments are likely to be short term; for instance, certificates of deposit or Treasury notes. As a result, the only entry needed in this year pertaining to investments is for interest as recorded in an earlier journal entry.

At this point, all entries for the year have been recorded, so a trial balance can be prepared (see Table 6-2).

TABLE 6-2   Trial Balance—Capital Projects Fund

The City of Angusville
Capital Projects Fund
Sports Complex Fund
Preclosing Trial Balance
December 31, 2008

	Debits	Credits
Cash	$ 690,000	
Investments	12,000,000	
Interest receivable	300,000	
Retained percentage on construction contracts		$ 550,000
Deferred revenue—construction grant		2,500,000
Revenues—construction grant		5,500,000
Revenues—investment interest		300,000
Other financing source—long-term debt issued		10,000,000
Expenditures—architect's fees	360,000	
Expenditures—construction costs	5,500,000	
Estimated revenues	8,000,000	
Estimated other financing sources	10,000,000	
Appropriations		18,000,000
Encumbrances—capital project	12,140,000	
Budgetary fund balance reserved for encumbrances		12,140,000
	$48,990,000	$48,990,000

---

[7]GASB Cod. I50.

Closing Entries, First Year

At the end of the accounting period, December 31, 2008, the following entries are necessary to close the books:

Appropriations	18,000,000	
Estimated revenues		8,000,000
Estimated other financing sources		10,000,000
To close the budgetary accounts.		
Revenues—state construction grant	5,500,000	
Revenues—investments	300,000	
Other financing source—long-term debt issued	10,000,000	
Expenditures—architect's fees		360,000
Expenditures—construction costs		5,500,000
Unreserved fund balance		9,940,000
To close the operating accounts.		
Budgetary fund balance reserved for encumbrances	12,140,000	
Encumbrances—capital project		12,140,000
To close encumbrance accounts.		
Unreserved fund balance	12,140,000	
Fund balance reserved for encumbrances		12,140,000
To establish the fund balance reserved for encumbrances.		

Financial Statements Illustration

Individual financial statements prepared for Capital Projects Funds include an operating statement and a balance sheet. The fiscal 2008 statements for the Sports Complex Fund are illustrated in Tables 6-3 and 6-4. The overall reporting process is discussed in Chapters 9 and 10.

The details regarding the composition of fund balance—such as reserves for encumbrances and so forth—are reported on the balance sheet. In this example, Unreserved fund balance has a debit balance of $2,200,000 ($9,940,000 − $12,140,000) and Fund balance reserved for encumbrances has a credit balance of $12,140,000. The apparent "deficit" in Unreserved fund balance occurs because only part of the total project revenues were recognized in fiscal 2008 (the remainder will be recognized in 2009), but the final closing entry (above) had the effect of removing from Unreserved fund balance the amount encumbered for all the remaining project costs.

Completing the Project: The Following Year

Although most governmental units use the fiscal year as their accounting period, authorization and control of capital projects are related to the projects' entire lives. In our illustration, therefore, at the beginning of 2009, it is necessary to record the unexpended portion of the original appropriation, $12,140,000. This amount is the originally approved total ($18,000,000) less the expenditures in 2008 ($5,860,000). In addition, the city must budget for the estimated project revenues—the unrecognized portion of the state grant ($2,500,000) and the earnings on the investments (estimated to be

TABLE 6-3   Statement of Revenues, Expenditures, and Changes in Fund Balance

The City of Angusville
Capital Projects Fund
Sports Complex Fund
Statement of Revenues, Expenditures, and
Changes in Fund Balance
For the Year Ended December 31, 2008

Revenues	
Construction grant	$ 5,500,000
Investments	300,000
Total revenues	$ 5,800,000
Expenditures	
Construction costs	$ 5,500,000
Architect's fees	360,000
Total expenditures	5,860,000
Excess of expenditures over revenues	60,000
Other Financing Sources	
Other financing source—long-term debt issued	10,000,000
Net change in fund balance	9,940,000
Fund balance at beginning of year	-0-
Fund balance at end of year	$ 9,940,000

TABLE 6-4   Balance Sheet—Capital Projects Fund

The City of Angusville
Capital Projects Fund
Sports Complex Fund
Balance Sheet
December 31, 2008

Assets	
Cash	$ 690,000
Investments	12,000,000
Interest receivable	300,000
Total assets	$12,990,000
Liabilities	
• Retained percentage on construction contracts	$ 550,000
Deferred revenue—construction grant	2,500,000
Total liabilities	3,050,000
Fund Balance	
Reserved for encumbrances	12,140,000
Unreserved	(2,200,000)
Total fund balance	9,940,000
Total liabilities and fund balance	$12,990,000

$150,000). The city also needs to reestablish the budgetary accounts for encumbrances ($12,140,000) at the beginning of 2009. The entries to record these items are as follows:

Fund balance reserved for encumbrances	12,140,000	
Unreserved fund balance		12,140,000
To reclassify fund balance reserved for		
encumbrances to unreserved fund balance.		
Encumbrances—capital project	12,140,000	
Budgetary fund balance reserved for encumbrances		12,140,000
To establish the encumbrances account.		
Estimated revenues	2,650,000	
Budgetary fund balance	9,490,000	
Appropriations		12,140,000
To record the remainder of the budget for		
the sports complex project.		

When the project is completed, the contractor will submit a final bill for the amount due, $12,100,000 (assume, for simplicity, that only one billing is made in 2009), and the architect will submit a final bill for $40,000. Because the project has not yet been inspected and accepted, the city will withhold the 10 percent retained percentage from the payment to the contractor. The entries to record these events are the following:

Budgetary fund balance reserved for encumbrances	12,140,000	
Encumbrances—capital project		12,140,000
To remove the encumbrances for the remaining		
cost of the contracts.		
Expenditures—architect's fees	40,000	
Vouchers payable		40,000
To record the balance due to the architect.		
Expenditures—construction costs	12,100,000	
Retained percentage on construction contracts		1,210,000
Construction contracts payable		10,890,000
To record the balance due to the contractor.		

To pay these liabilities, the city will liquidate all the investments held by the Capital Projects Fund and recognize the related income. The entry to record these amounts, assuming $12,430,000 is received, is as follows:

Cash	12,430,000	
Interest receivable on investments		300,000
Revenues—investment interest		130,000
Investments		12,000,000
To record liquidation of investments and related revenues.		
Construction contracts payable	10,890,000	
Vouchers payable	40,000	
Cash		10,930,000
To record payment of vouchers to contractor and architect.		

At this point, the balance of the Retained percentage on construction contracts account is $1,760,000. Assume that upon final inspection, the project manager finds some defects that need to be remedied before the project can be accepted. The construction company already has removed its equipment and employees, so it authorizes the city to have the repairs made by a local contractor. If these repairs cost $450,000, the following entry will be made:

Retained percentage on construction contracts	450,000	
Cash		450,000
To record payments to contractor to repair building defects.		

All of the expenditures related to the sports complex have been incurred, so the city recognizes the remainder of the state grant as revenue as follows:

Deferred revenue—construction grant	2,500,000	
Revenues—construction grant		2,500,000
To record revenue from state construction grant.		

After the building has been accepted, the contractor will be paid the remaining amount under the contract, $1,310,000 ($1,760,000 − $450,000). This payment will be recorded as follows:

Retained percentage on construction contracts	1,310,000	
Cash		1,310,000
To record the final payment to the contractor for sports complex construction.		

Closing Entries, Second Year

Upon completion and acceptance of the project, the Sports Complex Fund will be abolished. This process first involves reversing the budgetary entry and closing the operating accounts in standard fashion. The necessary entries are as follows:

Appropriations	12,140,000	
Estimated revenues		2,650,000
Budgetary fund balance		9,490,000
To close the budgetary accounts for 2009.		

Revenues—investment interest	130,000	
Revenues—construction grant	2,500,000	
Unreserved fund balance	9,510,000	
Expenditures—architect's fees		40,000
Expenditures—construction costs		12,100,000
To close the operating accounts for 2009.		

After the preceding entries are posted, the sports complex Capital Projects Fund has two "residual" account balances: Cash, $430,000, and Unreserved fund balance, $430,000, representing the earnings on the investments. Disposition of these resources will depend on the provisions of the state grant and the bond issue. For illustrative purposes, assume these amounts must be used for eventual retirement of the bonds sold to finance the project (a typical provision in practice). This requires the following entries in the Capital Projects Fund:

Transfer out to Debt Service Fund	430,000	
Cash		430,000
To record transfer to the Debt Service Fund.		
Unreserved fund balance	430,000	
Transfer out to Debt Service Fund		430,000
To close the transfer account.		

At this point, all the Capital Project Fund's balance sheet accounts have zero balances; the 2009 operating statement will reconcile the 2009 beginning fund balance to the ending balance of zero. The Debt Service Fund will record its "side" of the interfund transfer as follows:

Cash	430,000	
Transfer in from Capital Projects Fund		430,000
To record transfer from the Capital Projects Fund.		

Issuance of Bonds at a Premium or Discount

The bonds issued for the construction of the sports complex were sold at face value. Often government bonds are sold at a price above or below face value because of the prevailing interest rates. When the bond price is different from par, the entries made in the fund that receives the bond proceeds must properly account for the issue price.

As an example, assume that the bonds issued by the City of Angusville had been sold for $11 million. Because the face value of these bonds is $10 million, the city must account for the extra $1 million. The treatment of the premium is dependent on the bond indenture. In some instances, a premium may be used for the purpose for which the bonds were issued. In other instances, a premium must be used to retire the debt. If we assume that this premium may be used for construction of the sports complex, the following entry is made in the Capital Projects Fund when the bonds are issued:

Cash	11,000,000	
Other financing source — long-term debt issued		10,000,000
Other financing source — bond issue premium		1,000,000
To record the issuance of bonds.		

If the premium must be used to retire the bonds, the following entry is made in the Capital Projects fund:

Transfer out to Debt Service Fund	1,000,000	
Cash		1,000,000
To record transfer of bond premium to		
Debt Service Fund.		

This entry is made in the Debt Service Fund:

Cash	1,000,000	
Transfer in from Capital Projects Fund		1,000,000
To record transfer of bond premium from		
Capital Projects Fund.		

This sequence of journal entries maintains the total proceeds upon issuance in the fund that received them and leaves an audit trail for the transfer. If bonds are issued for less than face value, the total proceeds are recorded in the Capital Projects Fund, as indicated previously, except that Bond issue discount should be debited for the amount of the discount. This lower bond price may cause a problem, however, if the bonds do not provide enough resources to complete the project. At this point, the project manager must either scale down the project or seek additional resources.

Issuance of Bonds Between Interest Payment Dates

If bonds are issued between interest payment dates, the interest accrued to the date of sale must be paid to the issuing government by the buyer. Because this amount will be used to pay interest on the next interest date, it is recorded directly in the Debt Service Fund. It is not recorded in the Capital Projects Fund.

Arbitrage

As we have seen, Capital Projects Fund activities often involve short-term investment of idle cash. Making such investments is sound practice; however, government officials need to exercise care to avoid running afoul of *arbitrage* regulations. In simple terms, *arbitrage* refers to borrowing money at a certain interest rate while investing the money at a higher interest rate.

The Internal Revenue Code (the Code) has strict rules regarding tax-exempt interest paid by a governmental unit and investment interest earned. These rules provide that interest earned on the investment of tax-exempt debt proceeds cannot be greater than interest paid. If the interest earned is higher, then the government is subject to the arbitrage provisions of the Code. Excess interest earned by a government must be paid to the federal government or the government will be subject to either a 50 percent excise tax or revocation of the tax-exempt status of its debt. Revocation of the tax-exempt status of its debt would not harm the governmental unit immediately, but it would play an important role in the cost of future debt issues.

The arbitrage provisions of the Code are complex, and a complete discussion is beyond the scope of this text. Because of complex laws regulating the types of securities in which a governmental unit may invest and the arbitrage regulations, governmental units usually seek the aid of their accountants and attorneys whenever tax-exempt debt proceeds are invested.

GOVERNMENTAL ACCOUNTING IN PRACTICE
The City of Columbus, Ohio

The City of Columbus, Ohio, maintains 37 Capital Projects Funds. The purpose of each fund is to account for resources received and used for construction and development of specific projects. The balance sheet and statement of revenues, expenditures, and changes in fund balance presented in Tables 6-5 and 6-6 illustrate the Federal State Highway Engineering Fund. Columbus identifies its funds based on the primary sources of funding. Included in this fund are highway projects funded by grant revenue and other funding sources.

Notice that this fund contains the types of assets and liabilities described in this chapter as common to Capital Projects

TABLE 6-5   Balance Sheet—Capital Projects Fund—City of Columbus, Ohio

City of Columbus, Ohio
Capital Projects Fund
Federal State Highway Engineering Fund
Balance Sheet
December 31, 20X8

Assets	
Cash and cash equivalents with treasurer	$1,454,002
Due from other governments	97,368
Total assets	$1,551,370
Liabilities	
Accounts payable	$ 29,924
Due to other funds	4,440
Deferred revenue and other	1,517,006
Total liabilities	1,551,370
Fund Balance	
Reserved for encumbrances	4,458,759
Unreserved, undesignated	(4,458,759)
Total fund balance	-0-
Total liabilities and fund balance	$1,551,370

Source: Adapted from a recent annual report of the City of Columbus, Ohio.

TABLE 6-6   Statement of Revenues, Expenditures, and Changes in Fund Balance—
Capital Projects Fund—City of Columbus, Ohio

City of Columbus, Ohio
Capital Projects Fund
Federal State Highway Engineering Fund
Statement of Revenues, Expenditures, and Changes in Fund Balance
For the Year Ended December 31, 20X8

Revenues	
Grants and subsidies	$899,863
Expenditures	
Capital outlay	899,863
Excess of revenues over expenditures	-0-
Beginning fund balance	-0-
Ending fund balance	$ -0-

Source: Adapted from a recent annual report of the City of Columbus, Ohio.

Funds. Other Capital Projects Funds used by the City of Columbus show similar assets and liabilities, although none have all of the items included on the balance sheet of the Federal State Highway Engineering Fund. Also notice that the net fund balance of the Federal State Highway Engineering Fund is zero.

DEBT SERVICE FUNDS

Overview

Almost every government issues *general obligation* debt, typically to finance capital projects, as we have seen. General obligation debt also may be sold for other purposes, such as financing operating deficits. By definition, general obligation debt (usually bonds) is secured by the "full faith and credit" of the government; that is, repayment of principal and payment of interest on the debt is supported by a pledge of the entity's property tax collections and other tax revenues. The payment of principal and interest on a debt is referred to as *servicing* the debt. Thus, Debt Service Funds are used to accumulate resources that will be used to pay principal and interest on general obligation long-term debt. General obligation debt does not include debt that will be serviced from resources accumulated in Enterprise Funds or Internal Service Funds.[8]

In many instances debt that becomes due in installments, such as serial bonds, can be serviced directly by the General Fund. However, if a legal requirement dictates a separate Debt Service Fund, such a fund must be established. In addition, a separate Debt Service Fund must be established if the governmental unit is accumulating resources currently for the future servicing of debt, such as term bonds. Although this section will concentrate on bonds, it is important to remember that any form of long-term obligation, such as installment purchases or notes, may require the establishment of a Debt Service Fund.

Summary of Fund Activities

In practice, the sequence of events recorded in Debt Service Funds will vary according to the specific requirements of the bond indenture or the ordinance authorizing the bond issue. The following general summary of activity reflects the types of events that normally occur in Debt Service Fund operations. First, assets are received by the fund. They are recorded as revenues or transfers from other funds—usually the General Fund—depending on their nature. During the time between receipt of the resources and payment of principal and interest, the government will invest the assets to increase the resources available for debt service. The investing activities also are recorded in the Debt Service Fund. Finally, as the principal and interest come due, they are paid from Debt Service Fund assets.

Control of Fund Activities

The operations of Debt Service Funds generally are controlled through the provisions of bond indentures and budgetary authorizations. Many governmental units do not record a formal budget for these funds. For purposes of uniformity, however, we will assume that a budget is recorded and used for control purposes.

Encumbrance accounting is seldom applied in Debt Service Funds because of the absence of purchase orders, contracts, and so forth. The expenditures of these funds consist primarily of payments of bond principal and interest and fiscal agent's fees. Because these types of expenditures are made according to the terms prescribed in the bond indenture, encumbrance accounting in Debt Service Funds serves no meaningful control purpose.

---

[8]Although it is possible to have general obligation debt that will be serviced by an Enterprise Fund, a discussion of such debt is beyond the scope of this section. It is also possible, but not likely, that Permanent Funds could contain long-term debt that is serviced in that fund. This discussion, too, is beyond the scope of this section.

Accounting for Fund Activities
Operating Entries

Recall that the City of Angusville issued $10 million of serial bonds on March 1, 2008, for the construction of the sports complex we illustrated in the discussion of Capital Projects Funds. The bond indenture provides for semiannual interest payments of 5 percent on March 1 and September 1 (the annual interest rate is 10 percent on the outstanding debt), starting September 1, 2008, with $1 million of principal to be repaid on March 1, 2010, and every year thereafter until the bonds mature on March 1, 2019 (10 payments later). Further assume that the city desires to spread the taxpayers' burden of servicing the debt evenly throughout the life of the bonds. To meet this goal, the voters approved a special addition to the local property tax for servicing the bonds. This tax is estimated to provide $1.25 million of revenue in 2008. In addition, city management decides that the General Fund will transfer $250,000 to the Debt Service Fund on July 1, 2008. (Entries involved in the actual issuance of the bonds are illustrated in the preceding section on Capital Projects Funds.)

The entry to record the Debt Service Fund budget for the fiscal year beginning January 1, 2008, is as follows:

Estimated revenues	1,250,000	
Estimated other financing sources	250,000	
Appropriations		505,000
Budgetary fund balance		995,000
To record the budget.		

The "Estimated other financing sources" account is the budgetary account used to record the anticipated transfer from the General Fund.

Appropriations for the year include one interest payment that will be made on September 1, 2008, $500,000, and the *fiscal agent's* fee of $5,000. The fiscal agent will keep records of the sale of the bonds and will make semiannual interest payments and payments of principal as they come due. Usually, a fiscal agent is a local bank or other financial institution. Notice that only one interest payment will be made in 2008; therefore, only that amount is included in the current year's annual budget.

Recording the tax levy requires the following entry:

Property taxes receivable—current	1,256,000	
Allowance for uncollectible property		
taxes—current		6,000
Revenues—property taxes		1,250,000
To record the tax levy.		

The preceding entry assumes that $6,000 of the taxes will be uncollectible. Therefore, the governmental unit will have to bill $1,256,000 to collect the needed $1,250,000.

Collection of $1,150,000 of the taxes results in the same entries as those illustrated for the General Fund and the Special Revenue Funds.

Cash	1,150,000	
Property taxes receivable—current		1,150,000
To record collection of current taxes.		

If $2,500 of uncollectible taxes are written off, the following entry is made:

Allowance for uncollectible property taxes—current	2,500	
Property taxes receivable-current		2,500
To write off uncollectible accounts.		

To generate resources in addition to those contributed by the taxpayers and the General Fund, the tax receipts are invested in marketable securities. If $1 million is invested, the following entry is made:

Investments	1,000,000	
Cash		1,000,000
To record the investment of excess cash.		

When a portion of the investments ($450,000) mature, the following entry is made:

Cash	470,000	
Investments		450,000
Revenues—interest earned on investments		20,000
To record investments liquidated and related income.		

The interest due to the city's bondholders on September 1, 2008, is recorded as follows:

Expenditures—interest	500,000	
Matured interest payable		500,000
To record matured interest.		

When cash is disbursed to the fiscal agent for the September 1 interest payment, the following entry is made:

Matured interest payable	500,000	
Cash		500,000
To record the payment of cash to the fiscal agent.		

The transfer of $250,000 from the General Fund is recorded in the General Fund as follows:

Transfer out to Debt Service Fund	250,000	
Cash		250,000
To record transfer out to Debt Service Fund.		

The corresponding entry in the Debt Service Fund is this:

Cash	250,000	
Transfer in from General Fund		250,000
To record transfer in from General Fund.		

When the fiscal agent submits a bill for $5,000 to the fund for servicing the debt, the following entry is made:

Expenditures—fiscal agent fees	5,000	
Cash		5,000
To record fiscal agent fees.		

One of the most notable aspects of the modified accrual basis of accounting pertains to interest on long-term debt. Under modified accrual accounting, interest is recorded as an expenditure in the period in which it becomes legally due (matures) rather than being accrued based on the passage of time as is the case in full accrual accounting. The reason for this practice is that most governments' budgetary appropriations provide only for bond principal and interest *due* during the fiscal year. If interest payments are accrued or principal payments are recorded before due, it is possible that a debit balance (a deficit) will occur in fund balance. The reason an accrual is not recorded is that the liability is not yet due to be paid, which means the resources are not required to be available. An accrual for interest will be made when the fund financial statements are converted to government-wide statements, as discussed in Chapter 10.

In those instances when resources are available for Debt Service Fund payments and those payments will be made within the first month of the next period, governmental units have the option, under GAAP, of recording the liability and the associated expenditure at the end of the year before the payments are due.

In contrast to the treatment of bond interest payable just discussed, an end-of-year entry is needed to record interest earned but not received on the investments:

Interest receivable on investments	55,000	
Revenues—interest earned on investments		55,000
To record the interest earned on investments.		

Recall that investments held by governments generally are reported at fair market value. If the remaining $550,000 of marketable securities previously acquired, and still held at December 31, 2008, had a market value of $575,000, the following journal entry would be made to record the increase in value:

Investments	25,000	
Revenues—net increase in fair market value of investments		25,000
To record the increase in the fair market value of investments.		

A preclosing trial balance for Angusville's Debt Service Fund at the end of the year is shown in Table 6-7.

Closing Entries

At the end of the accounting period, December 31, 2008, in our example, the following entries will be necessary to close the books and reclassify Unreserved fund balance to Fund balance reserved for debt service:

Appropriations	505,000	
Budgetary fund balance	995,000	
Estimated revenues		1,250,000
Estimated other financing sources		250,000
To close the budgetary accounts for 2008.		

Revenues—property taxes	1,250,000	
Revenues—interest earned on investments	75,000	
Revenues—net increase in fair market value of investments	25,000	
Transfer in from General Fund	250,000	
Expenditures—interest		500,000
Expenditures—fiscal agent fees		5,000
Unreserved fund balance		1,095,000
To close the operating accounts for 2008.		

Unreserved fund balance	1,095,000	
Fund balance reserved for debt service		1,095,000
To reclassify fund balance from unreserved to reserved at fiscal year end.		

TABLE 6-7 Trial Balance—Debt Service Fund

The City of Angusville
Debt Service Fund
Sports Complex Bond Fund
Preclosing Trial Balance
December 31, 2008

	Debits	Credits
Cash	$ 365,000	
Property taxes receivable—current	103,500	
Allowance for uncollectible property taxes—current		$ 3,500
Investments	575,000	
Interest receivable	55,000	
Revenues—property taxes		1,250,000
Revenues—interest earned on investments		75,000
Revenues—net increase in fair market value of investments		25,000
Transfer in from General Fund		250,000
Expenditures—interest	500,000	
Expenditures—fiscal agent fees	5,000	
Estimated revenues	1,250,000	
Estimated other financing sources	250,000	
Appropriations		505,000
Budgetary fund balance		995,000
	$3,103,500	$3,103,500

Entry Necessary for Interest Payment in Subsequent Year

As already mentioned, interest on long-term debt generally is not accrued at the end of the year under the modified accrual basis of accounting. Thus, when the March interest payment is made in 2009, the following entries are necessary:

Expenditures—interest	500,000	
Matured interest payable		500,000
To record matured interest.		
Matured interest payable	500,000	
Cash		500,000
To record disbursement of cash to fiscal agent for bond interest payable.		

The remainder of the entries for the payment of the interest over the life of the debt are the same as those previously illustrated for the September 1 payment, except, of course, that interest amounts will decrease as the outstanding principal balance decreases.

Selected Entries for Payment of Principal

When all or a portion of the principal of the bond issue is due to be paid, the liability must be recorded in the Debt Service Fund. The following entries are made for this purpose (assume we are recording the first principal payment in 2010):

Expenditures—bond principal	1,000,000	
Matured serial bonds payable		1,000,000
To record matured bond principal.		

| Matured serial bonds payable | 1,000,000 | |
| Cash | | 1,000,000 |

To record disbursement of cash to fiscal agent
for matured principal.

Financial Statements Illustration

The fund financial statements for the Debt Service Funds are a balance sheet and an operating statement. These are illustrated for 2008 in Tables 6-8 and 6-9. The overall reporting process is discussed in Chapters 9 and 10.

TABLE 6-8 Statement of Revenues, Expenditures, and Changes in Fund Balance

The City of Angusville
Debt Service Fund
Sports Complex Bond Fund
Statement of Revenues, Expenditures,
and Changes in Fund Balance
For the Year Ended December 31, 2008

Revenues	
Property taxes	$1,250,000
Interest earned on investments	75,000
Net increase in fair market value of investments	25,000
Total revenues	$1,350,000
Expenditures	
Interest	$ 500,000
Fiscal agent fees	5,000
Total expenditures	505,000
Excess of revenues over expenditures	845,000
Other Financing Sources	
Transfer in	250,000
Net change in fund balance	1,095,000
Fund balance at beginning of year	-0-
Fund balance at end of year	$1,095,000

TABLE 6-9 Balance Sheet—Debt Service Fund

The City of Angusville
Debt Service Fund
Sports Complex Bond Fund
Balance Sheet
December 31, 2008

Assets	
Cash	$ 365,000
Property taxes receivable—current (net of allowance for uncollectibles of $3,500)	100,000
Interest receivable	55,000
Investments	575,000
Total assets	$1,095,000
Fund Balance	
Fund balance—reserved for debt service	$1,095,000

GOVERNMENTAL ACCOUNTING IN PRACTICE
The City of Columbus, Ohio

The City of Columbus maintains five Debt Service Funds:

1. General Bond Retirement Fund. This fund is required by the State of Ohio statutes and is used to account for all general obligation debt, except for Enterprise Fund general obligation debt of the city. As mentioned earlier in this chapter, this option provides an acceptable alternative to a separate fund for each bond issue if it does not violate any provisions of the bond indentures.

2. Special Income Tax Fund. This fund is used to account for 25 percent of income tax collections set aside for debt service and related expenses.

3. Recreation Debt Service Fund. This fund is used to account for revenues

set aside to pay for debt service on bonds issued for the acquisition of and improvements to city golf courses and other recreation facilities.

4. Tax Increment Financing Fund. This fund contains resources intended for the payment of principal and interest on long-term debt that was issued to pay for certain public improvements, primarily infrastructure.

5. Capitol South Debt Service Tax Fund. This fund is used to account for resources that will be used to service general obligation long-term debt that was previously accounted for in a Special Revenue Fund.

Tables 6-10 and 6-11 contain a balance sheet and operating statement for the

TABLE 6-10 Balance Sheet—Debt Service Fund—City of Columbus, Ohio

City of Columbus, Ohio
Debt Service Fund
General Bond Retirement Fund
Balance Sheet
December 31, 20X8

Assets

Cash and cash equivalents	
Cash and investments with treasurer	$ 3,958
Investments	3,271,158
Receivables (net of allowances for uncollectibles)	694,624
Total assets	$3,969,740
Liabilities	
Accounts payable	$ 1,773
Due to other funds	448,753
Deferred revenue and other	524,380
Matured bonds and interest payable	1,532,126
Total liabilities	2,507,032
Fund Balance	
Unreserved, undesignated	1,462,708
Total liabilities and fund balance	$3,969,740

Source: Adapted from a recent annual report of the City of Columbus, Ohio.

**TABLE 6-11   Statement of Revenues, Expenditures, and Changes in Fund Balance—
Debt Service Fund—City of Columbus, Ohio**

City of Columbus, Ohio
Debt Service Fund
General Bond Retirement Fund
Statement of Revenues, Expenditures, and Changes in Fund Balance
Year Ended December 31, 20X8

Revenues	
Income taxes	$89,777,690
Investment earnings	136,155
Special assessments	161,423
Miscellaneous	35,145
Total revenues	90,110,413
Expenditures	
Current	
General government	$ 245,627
Debt Service	
Principal retirement and payment of obligation under capital lease	59,991,053
Interest and fiscal charges	33,399,088
Total expenditures	93,635,768
Excess of expenditures over revenues	(3,525,355)
Other Financing Sources	
Transfers in	3,406,072
Net change in fund balance	(119,283)
Fund balance at beginning of year	1,581,991
Fund balance at end of year	$ 1,462,708

Source: Adapted from a recent annual report of the City of Columbus, Ohio.

General Bond Retirement Fund for the City of Columbus.

Notice that in Table 6-11 some of the expenditures from the General Bond Retirement Debt Service Fund were used for general government expenditures. The majority of the expenditures, however, were for servicing the debt.

LEASED ASSETS

Governmental units often lease assets rather than purchase them. Because governmental-type funds report only spendable resources, a lease presents problems beyond those found in commercial accounting. The illustration presented in this section is not intended to be all-inclusive with respect to leased assets. Complications like residual values and bargain purchase options are omitted in favor of a straightforward general lease model.

As in commercial accounting, governmental units enter into operating leases and capital leases in their everyday operations. A lease is classified as an operating lease if the lessee does not acquire any property rights through the contract. These leases are generally short term and are recorded by a debit to an expenditure account and a credit to Cash when the rental payments are made.

A lease is classified as a capital lease for the lessee if the lessee acquires property rights through the contract, the lease is noncancelable, and it meets at least one of the following tests:

1. The lessee owns the property at the conclusion of the lease, through either a transfer of title or a bargain purchase option.
2. The life of the lease is 75 percent or more of the expected economic life of the asset.
3. The present value of the minimum lease payments is 90 percent or more of the fair market value of the leased asset.

Items 2 and 3 are not considered if the lease term is in the last 25 percent of the economic life of the asset. If a government enters into a capital lease as a lessee, the government must record a capital expenditure and an other financing source. The reasoning for such an entry is this: In business-type accounting, a capital lease is reported as if the entity had financed the acquisition of a capital asset through long-term borrowing. Therefore, to adapt business-type capital lease accounting to governmental-type funds, at the inception of a capital lease, an entry is made *as if* the governmental-type fund had borrowed to acquire a capital asset—by recording a capital expenditure and an other financing source.[9]

To illustrate, assume the City of Angusville leases a new computer having a fair market value of $862,426 and an economic life of 5 years. Assume further that the relevant interest rate is 8 percent. Based on this information, the government (lessee) must record the present value of the minimum lease payments as an expenditure. If these payments are $200,000 per year, payable on January 1 of each year, the present value of the rental payments is $862,426 ($200,000 × 4.31213) or ($200,000 × [1 + 3.31213]). If the computer is to be used by a department in the General Fund, the following entry is required:

Expenditures—capital outlay	862,426	
Other financing sources—capital leases		862,426
To record a capital lease.		

Notice that the initial recording of the lease has no effect on the fund balance of the General Fund. The expenditure is offset by the other financing source.

Because the capital lease is recorded initially at the present value of the lease payments, each lease payment technically consists of both an interest component and a principal payment component. However, because the first lease payment of $200,000 is due at the time the lease is signed, that payment has no interest component. The second payment on the lease obligation occurs 1 year after the lease is signed, so a portion of that $200,000 lease expenditure represents interest. Thus,

---

[9]Notice that this entry "nets out" the receipt and disbursement of cash that would take place if money actually were first borrowed, then expended. In such a case, a governmental-type fund would record (1) a debit to cash offset by a credit to an other financing source and (2) a debit to capital expenditures offset by a credit to cash.

when the initial lease payment is made, at the inception of the lease, the following entry is made in the General Fund:

Expenditures—capital lease principal	200,000	
Vouchers payable		200,000
To record lease payment due.		

When the second lease payment is due, one year later, the following entry is made (the interest calculation is shown, also).

Expenditures—capital lease principal	147,006	
Expenditures—interest on capital leases	52,994	
Vouchers payable		200,000

Interest calculation:	
Initial debt	$862,426
Less: first payment	200,000
Book value of obligation during first year	$662,426
Interest rate	× .08
Interest portion of the second payment	$ 52,994

Governmental leases usually contain a fiscal funding clause. A fiscal funding clause is a provision in the lease that permits the government to cancel the lease if resources are not appropriated to make lease payments. If the possibility of actual cancellation is remote, a fiscal funding clause does not affect the noncancellable test. In other words, the lease is still capitalized.

SPECIAL ASSESSMENT PROJECTS

Description of Project Activities

Special assessments are a means of financing services or capital improvements that benefit one group of citizens more than the general public. Taxpayers who receive the benefits of these activities are assessed for their share of the cost. Examples of these activities include projects such as special police protection, paving of city streets, and building parking structures. The GASB requires that special assessment activities be reported as any other service or capital improvement-type project.

Control of and Accounting for Project Activities

Service Assessments

Service assessments generally include activities such as special police protection, storm sewer cleaning, and snowplowing. If these activities are financed by user charges in the form of special assessments, the reporting should be done in the General Fund, a Special Revenue Fund, or an Enterprise Fund, whichever best reflects the nature of the transactions.

Control over these activities is accomplished in the same manner as any other activity included in the particular fund type. In the governmental-type funds, control is accomplished through state and local laws and budgetary authorizations for the activities. When these funds are used, immediate control is achieved through a comparison of budget and actual data for revenues, expenditures, and other financing sources. Encumbrance accounting generally is used when the General Fund or a Special Revenue Fund accounts for a special assessment project. When an Enterprise Fund is used, a flexible budget is the central control feature. In general, a flexible budget is prepared based upon the level of activity of the fund, and this budget is compared with the actual results of the period. Revenues and expenditures (expenses) are recognized according to the basis of accounting and measurement focus rules that are applicable to the particular fund type being used. Examples of this type of accounting and reporting can be found in Chapters 4 and 5 for the General Fund and Special Revenue Funds and Chapter 7 for Enterprise Funds.

To illustrate the use of the General Fund to account for service assessment activities, assume that the City of Angusville levies a special assessment on the property holders in the central business district (CBD) to provide for special police protection. Assume further that these activities will be accounted for in the Police Department budget within the General Fund. The entries to levy the assessment and collection of part of the receivables are as follows (amounts assumed):

Special assessment receivables—current	200,000	
Revenues—special assessments		200,000
To record levy of assessments for special police protection in the CBD.		
Cash	190,000	
Special assessment receivables—current		190,000
To record collection of assessments for special police protection in the CBD.		

If any of the receivables are not expected to be collected, a provision for uncollectible receivables should be established. If these receivables are not collected within a specific period, they usually become delinquent and eventually are classified as a lien against the property in question. In these instances, the accounting would be the same as that illustrated in Chapter 5 for property taxes. Any expenditures associated with these activities are recorded in the fund involved. Unless the ordinance establishing the assessment requires a separate accounting, these activities should not be segregated from the other activities of the police department.

Capital Improvements Assessments

Capital improvements assessments involve construction projects, such as street improvements and sidewalks, and usually are undertaken in response to a petition from a group of property owners within a localized area. Typically, when such projects are undertaken, the government sells *special assessment bonds* to pay the construction costs; special assessments then are collected over a period of years to service the special assessment debt. If the government is obligated in some manner for the special assessment bonds, the reporting is done in two funds. The construction phase of the project is accounted for in a Capital Projects Fund, and the debt service phase of the project is accounted for in a Debt Service Fund. A governmental unit is "obligated in some manner" for the special assessment debt "if (a) it is legally obligated to assume all or part of the debt in the event of default or (b) the government may take certain action to assume secondary liability for all or part of the debt, and the government takes, or has given indication that it will take, those actions."[10]

Accounting for capital improvements assessments in which the government is "obligated in some manner" is exactly like that previously illustrated in this chapter for capital projects. If you need to brush up on those procedures, review that material before continuing.

In those (uncommon) instances in which the governmental unit is not obligated in any manner for special assessment debt, the construction phase is still accounted for in a Capital Projects Fund. The debt service phase of the project is reported in an Agency Fund "to reflect the fact that the government's duties are limited to acting as an agent for the assessed property owners and the bondholders."[11] In addition, the proceeds from the issuance of the special assessment bonds is reported as "Contribution from property owners" rather than "Bond proceeds" in the Capital Projects Fund.

When special assessments are collected over a period of years, it is necessary to compute the annual amount of revenue to be recognized in the Debt Service Fund. Applying the current financial resources concept results in recognition of revenue when the special assessment installments become current assets. Thus, if an assessment of $1 million is levied, of which $100,000 is current, the following entries are appropriate in the Debt Service Fund:

Special assessments receivable—current	100,000	
Special assessments receivable—deferred	900,000	
Revenues—special assessments		100,000
Deferred revenues		900,000
To record the levy of special assessments.		

Collections of the assessments are recorded in the normal manner for receivables. When the second installment receivable from property owners becomes a current asset, a proportionate amount of revenue is recognized (amounts assumed):

Special assessments receivable—current	100,000	
Special assessments receivable—deferred		100,000
To record the current status of the second installment of the receivable.		
Deferred revenues	100,000	
Revenues—special assessments		100,000
To record the revenue from current special assessments.		

Financial Statements

Special assessment activities are reported in the manner described in this and previous chapters, depending on the type of activity involved and the extent to which the governmental unit is obligated for any debt. As a result, you should review the accounting and reporting requirements for the General Fund, Special Revenue Funds, Debt Service Funds, and Capital Projects Funds.

---

[10]GASB Cod. Sec. S40.115.
[11]GASB Cod. Sec. S40.119.

CONCLUDING COMMENT

Recall that under governmental GAAP, neither capital assets nor long-term debt are reported in fund-level financial statements. Depending on the size of the government, however, capital assets are required to be reported in the government-wide financial statements. In any event, all governments should keep detailed records of their capital assets and periodically verify their physical existence with these records.

Capital asset adjustments needed for preparing government-wide financial statements generally can be made by analyzing capital asset expenditures and sales during the year. However, not all transactions affecting capital assets flow through the financial accounting records; for example, assets may be written off because of expiration of useful life or theft. To improve internal controls over capital assets and to facilitate preparation of the government-wide financial statements, we suggest that governments establish a memorandum set of records. These records can be called the Capital Investment Account Group (CIAG). Chapter 10 contains a description of the workings of the CIAG.

Review Questions

Q6-1 Explain the relationship between Debt Service Funds and Capital Projects Funds.

Q6-2 Are acquisitions of capital assets always accounted for through Capital Projects Funds? Explain.

Q6-3 Under what circumstances are Capital Projects Funds used?

Q6-4 How are Capital Projects Funds controlled?

Q6-5 Why is encumbrance accounting generally used for Capital Projects Funds?

Q6-6 Are closing entries necessary in the accounting records for a capital project that is not completed in the first year?

Q6-7 Are fixed assets recorded in Capital Projects Funds? Why or why not?

Q6-8 Under what circumstances are Debt Service Funds used?

Q6-9 How are the activities of Debt Service Funds controlled?

Q6-10 Are budgets typically recorded in Debt Service Funds?

Q6-11 When is interest recorded as an expenditure in Debt Service Funds?

Q6-12 When is general long-term debt principal recorded in Debt Service Funds?

Q6-13 What information can a city oversight body obtain from a Debt Service Fund?

Q6-14 On what bases are investments valued on governmental balance sheets?

Q6-15 Bonds that finance capital projects sometimes are issued at a premium or a discount. How might a bond premium be accounted for? A bond discount?

Q6-16 What is *arbitrage* and what is its significance in government financial management?

Q6-17 What is the purpose of *special assessments*? How are special assessments accounted for?

Cases

C6-1 Julius I. Tornado is the chief operating officer of Green Valley. One day last week he came to your office to discuss the terms of a new bond issue the city plans to sell. The proceeds from these bonds will be used to construct a new city hall and courthouse building. The total estimated cost of the project is $100 million. Tornado believes that as chief finance officer, you should have some input into the terms included in the bond indenture. The bonds will be redeemed in a lump sum at the end of 25 years. The city is barely balancing its budget now, so Tornado is concerned that there will not be enough resources available to pay the interest for the next 25 years and redeem the principal when it comes due. What recommendations do you have for Tornado?

C6-2 Janet Figg, the chief financial officer for Pine City, is involved in the planning process for an arena. The city is trying to attract a professional basketball team and to do so, it must have a first-class arena available. If you were Figg, what suggestions would you bring to the first committee meeting regarding financing and construction of the arena?

Ethics Cases

EC6-1 Assume you are the accounting supervisor for the City of Secret Valley, and you discover a violation the city made regarding its bond indentures. The city has four bond issues outstanding, and the bond indenture for each requires a separate accounting. In error, a new entry-level accounting clerk did not set up separate debt service funds for each bond issue. It is the end of the current year, and you are responsible for preparing the annual report. In desperation, you go to your superior, Janet Well, the chief financial officer of the city, and ask her for guidance. She suggests that you not worry about such a petty thing—"No one reads these reports anyway." What would you do?

EC6-2 Reginald Canary, the mayor of the City of Bloomerville, is trying to locate available resources in the governmental-type funds to help "bail out" the General Fund. The General Fund expenditures currently exceed budgetary amounts by $10 million, with 2 months remaining in the fiscal year. Canary feels some unused resources in a Capital Projects Fund or a Debt Service Fund could be transferred to the General Fund to alleviate the impending budget deficit. Each of these funds has a fund balance of at least $50 million. If Canary cannot locate the needed resources, he will have to borrow money using tax anticipation notes based on an emergency tax levy. This prospect is a major problem for him because the current year is an election year. Is Canary's plan ethical? If you were the chief financial officer of Bloomerville, how would you respond to Canary? How could such a situation be prevented?

Exercises

E6-1 (Fill in the blanks—general terminology)

1. Encumbrance accounting usually (is or is not) _____ used in Capital Projects Funds.
2. The entry to record the budget of a Capital Projects Fund would include a (debit or credit) _____ to Appropriations.
3. A contractor recently completed a bridge for the City of Paige. After the contractor removed his workers and equipment, several deficiencies were noticed. Another contractor was hired to repair these deficiencies. The cost of the repairs should be charged to _____ .

4. Long-term bonds issued by a Capital Projects Fund (are or are not) _____ reported as a liability of that fund.

5. During the year, a city acquired furniture for the mayor's office, land for a parking garage, and a fire truck. The furniture was financed from general city revenues; the land and the cost of the parking garage were financed primarily from bond proceeds; and the fire truck was financed from general tax revenues. Which of these projects would require the use of a Capital Projects Fund?

E6-2   (Use of Capital Projects Funds)
The City of New Falls is planning to acquire furniture and fixtures for the mayor's office and the council chambers. One of the council members, Council Member Dunn, sent you a memo asking whether a Capital Projects Fund is needed to record the acquisition of the furniture. Write a memo in response to Council Member Dunn.

E6-3   (Multiple choice)

1. The resources used to finance Capital Projects Funds may come from which of the following sources?
   a. Private donations
   b. General obligation debt
   c. Intergovernmental revenues
   d. All of the above

2. The issuance of bonds to provide resources to construct a new courthouse should be recorded in a Capital Projects Fund by crediting which of the following accounts?
   a. Bonds payable
   b. Revenues—bonds
   c. Fund balance
   d. Other financing source—long-term debt issued

3. What entry must be made at the beginning of the new period when encumbrance accounting is used for a construction project that continues beyond the end of an accounting period?
   a. A credit to Revenues
   b. A debit to Cash
   c. A debit to Expenditures
   d. A debit to Encumbrances

4. What is done with resources that remain in a Capital Projects Fund after the project is completed?
   a. Always transferred to a Debt Service Fund
   b. Always returned to the provider(s) of the resources
   c. Disbursed according to the directives of the resource provider
   d. Always transferred to the General Fund

5. What journal entry is made in the Capital Projects Fund when a contract is signed and encumbrance accounting is used?
   a. Encumbrances   xxxx
      Budgetary fund balance reserved for encumbrances   xxxx

    b. Vouchers payable   xxxx

        Reserve for encumbrances   xxxx

    c. Expenditures—construction costs   xxxx

        Vouchers payable   xxxx

    d. Reserve for encumbrances   xxxx

        Fund balance   xxxx

6. The principal amount of bonds issued to finance the cost of a new city hall would be recorded as a liability in which of the following funds?
   a. General Fund
   b. Special Revenue Fund
   c. Capital Projects Fund
   d. Debt Service Fund
   e. None of the above

7. Why is encumbrance accounting usually used in Capital Projects Funds?
   a. Long-term debt is not recorded in these funds.
   b. The budget must be recorded in these funds.
   c. It helps the government control the expenditures.
   d. The modified accrual basis of accounting is used.

8. The City of New Easton constructed a convention center. After completion of the project, the convention center should be recorded as an asset in which of the following funds?
   a. General Fund
   b. Capital Projects Fund
   c. Debt Service Fund
   d. Both b and c
   e. None of the above

E6-4   (Use of a Capital Projects Fund)

Explain why a separate fund generally is used to account for the construction and acquisition of major general fixed assets.

E6-5   (Closing journal entries)

The following are selected accounts from the trial balance of the Walker Tunnel Fund, a Capital Projects Fund, as of June 30, 2008 (the end of the fiscal year):

Appropriations	$4,711,000
Fund balance	78,000
Cash	245,000
Encumbrances	1,345,000
Revenues—grants	3,000,000
Estimated revenues	2,020,000
Expenditures—construction costs	3,000,000
Investments	75,000
Revenue—investments	19,000

Required: 1. Prepare the closing entries for June 30, 2008.

               2. Assuming no revenues are budgeted for fiscal 2009, prepare the opening entries necessary for July 1, 2008.

E6-6 (Fill in the blanks—general terminology)

1. Payment of principal and interest on debt is referred to as _____ .
2. A periodic transfer of resources from the General Fund to a Debt Service Fund is reported as a(n) _____ on the operating statement of both funds.
3. Payment of principal is reported as a(n) _____ on the _____ of a Debt Service Fund.
4. A financial institution that makes principal and interest payments in the name of a governmental unit is called a(n) _____ .
5. A debit balance in Fund balance is called a(n) _____ .

E6-7 (Use of a Debt Service Fund)
The City of Crestview has only one Debt Service Fund for all of its bond issues. Is the city in compliance with GAAP for governmental units? Explain.

E6-8 (Multiple choice)

1. Several years ago a city established a sinking fund to retire an issue of general obligation bonds. This year the city made a $50,000 contribution to the sinking fund from general revenues and realized $15,000 in revenue from securities in the sinking fund. The bonds due this year were retired. These transactions require accounting recognition in which of the following funds?
   a. General Fund
   b. Debt Service Fund
   c. Debt Service Fund and General Fund
   d. Capital Projects Fund, Debt Service Fund, and General Fund
   e. None of the above

   (AICPA adapted)

2. To provide for the retirement of general obligation bonds, a city invests a portion of its general revenue receipts in marketable securities. This investment activity should be accounted for in which of the following funds?
   a. Trust Fund
   b. Enterprise Fund
   c. Special Assessment Fund
   d. Special Revenue Fund
   e. None of the above

   (AICPA adapted)

3. In preparing the General Fund budget of Brockton City for the forthcoming fiscal year, the city council appropriated a sum greater than expected revenues. What will be the result of the council's action?
   a. A cash overdraft during the fiscal year
   b. An increase in encumbrances by the end of the fiscal year
   c. A debit to Budgetary Fund balance
   d. A necessity for compensatory offsetting action
   e. None of the above

   (AICPA adapted)

4. Which of the following funds is used to account for the operations of a public library receiving the majority of its support from property taxes levied for that purpose?
   a. General Fund
   b. Special Revenue Fund
   c. Enterprise Fund
   d. Internal Service Fund
   e. None of the above

   (AICPA adapted)

5. A special tax was levied by Downtown City to retire and pay interest on general obligation bonds that were issued to finance the construction of a new city hall. Where are the receipts from the tax recorded?
   a. Capital Projects Fund
   b. Special Revenue Fund
   c. Debt Service Fund
   d. General Fund
   e. None of the above
6. Which of the following funds uses modified accrual accounting?
   a. All governmental-type funds
   b. General Fund and Special Revenue Funds only
   c. Only the General Fund
   d. Only Debt Service Funds
   e. None of the above
7. To what does the term current financial resources measurement focus refer?
   a. The use of the modified accrual basis of accounting
   b. The measurement of resources available for spending
   c. The use of the full accrual basis of accounting
   d. The timing of the recognition of revenues and expenditures
   e. None of the above

E6-9   (Discussion of control in the General Fund and in Debt Service Funds)
Compare and contrast the methods used to control expenditures in the General Fund and in Debt Service Funds. Be sure to explain the reasons for any differences.

E6-10   (Journal entries in a Debt Service Fund)
Green Valley issued $20 million of general obligation bonds to construct a multipurpose arena. These bonds will be serviced by a tax on the revenue from events held in the arena and will mature in 2013. During 2008, Green Valley budgeted $2,500,000 of tax revenues and $2 million for interest on the bonds in its Debt Service Fund.

Required: Prepare the journal entries necessary to record (a) the budget and (b) the expenditure when the interest comes due for payment.

E6-11   (Leases)
Plymouthville leased equipment with a fair market value of $905,863. The life of the noncancelable lease is 10 years and the economic life of the property is

10 years. Using an 8 percent interest rate, the present value of the minimum lease payments is $905,863. The first payment of $125,000 is due January 1 of the current year. Each additional payment is due on the first of January in the next 9 years. What is the amount of the asset to be recorded in Plymouthville's Capital Projects Fund? If no asset will be recorded, explain why.

Problems

P6-1　(Journal entries and financial statements—Capital Projects Fund)
The following transactions occurred during 2008:

1. The City of Watersville approved the construction of an enclosed concert arena for a total cost of $75 million to attract professional events. On the same day, a contract with a 6 percent retainage clause was signed with B. P. Construction Company for the arena. The arena will be financed by a $75 million general obligation bond issue. Investment revenue of $4 million was also included in the budget. (Assume that the budget is recorded in the accounts and encumbrance accounting is used.)
2. Watersville received $76 million from the sale of bonds, which included a premium of $1 million over the $75 million face value. The $1 million premium was transferred immediately to the appropriate Debt Service Fund.
3. The city invested $74.9 million in securities.
4. The contract signed with B. P. stipulated that the contract price included the architect fees. On this date, the architects were paid their fee of $25,000 by Watersville. (Assume that a vouchers payable account was not used.)
5. The contractor submitted a progress billing of $3 million; the billing (less a 6 percent retainage) was approved.
6. Investments that cost $3 million were redeemed for $3 million plus $50,000 interest.
7. B. P. was paid the amount due in transaction 5 above.
8. Income totaling $3.7 million was received on the investments.
9. B. P. submitted another progress billing of $8 million. The billing, less the retainage, was approved.
10. Additional investments were redeemed to make the payment to B. P. The investments originally cost $7.8 million. The proceeds of $8.1 million included investment income of $300,000.
11. The contractor was paid the amount due in transaction 9.
12. Investment income of $60,000 was accrued.
13. Investment income of $10,000 was received in cash.

Required:　1. Prepare the journal entries necessary to record these transactions in the Capital Projects Fund. Assume that the city operates on a calendar year.
2. Prepare a trial balance for the Capital Projects Fund at December 31, 2008, before closing.
3. Prepare any necessary closing entries at December 31, 2008.

4. Prepare a statement of revenues, expenditures, and changes in fund balance for 2008, and a balance sheet as of December 31, 2008.

5. Prepare the journal entries necessary to record the remainder of the budget and to reestablish the budgetary accounts for encumbrances at January 1, 2009.

P6-2 (Journal entries, financial statements, and closing entries for a Capital Projects Fund)

The following transactions occurred during the fiscal year July 1, 2008, to June 30, 2009:

1. The City of Red Ridge approved the construction of a city hall complex for a total cost of $120 million. A few days later, a contract with a 5 percent retainage clause was signed with Walker Construction for the complex. The buildings will be financed by a federal grant of $25 million and a general obligation bond issue of $100 million. During the current year, investment revenue of $4 million is budgeted. (Assume the budget is recorded in the accounts and encumbrance accounting is used.)

2. The bonds were issued for $90 million (the face amount of the bonds was $100 million). The difference between the actual cost of the project and the bond proceeds and the grant was expected to be generated by investing the excess cash during the construction period.

3. The city collected the grant from the government.

4. The city invested $90 million.

5. The contract signed with Walker stipulated that the contract price included architect fees. On this date, the architects were paid their fee of $45,000 by Red Ridge. (Assume a vouchers payable account is used.)

6. Walker submitted a progress billing for $25 million. The billing, less 5 percent retainage, was approved. Assume that the city will use resources from the federal grant to make this payment.

7. Investments that cost $5 million were redeemed for a total of $5,020,000.

8. Investment income totaling $3,500,000 was received in cash.

9. The contractor was paid the amount billed in part 6, less a 5 percent retainage.

10. The contractor submitted another progress billing for $25 million. The billing, less retainage, was approved.

11. Investments totaling $14,600,000 were redeemed, together with additional investment income of $1,400,000.

12. The contractor was paid the amount billed in part 10, less a 5 percent retainage.

13. Investment income of $250,000 was accrued.

14. Bond interest totaling $10 million was paid.

Required: 1. Prepare the journal entries necessary to record these transactions in a Capital Projects Fund for the City of Red Ridge. Assume the city operates on a fiscal year July 1 to June 30.

2. Prepare a trial balance for the fund at June 30, 2009, before closing.

3. Prepare any necessary closing entries at June 30, 2009.
4. Prepare a statement of revenues, expenditures, and changes in fund balance for the year ended June 30, 2009, and a balance sheet as of June 30, 2009.
5. Prepare the journal entry (entries) necessary to record the remainder of the budget and to reestablish the budgetary accounts for encumbrances as of July 1, 2009. Assume investment revenues of $2 million are expected in the 2009 fiscal year.

P6-3 (Journal entries regarding a bond issue and accounting for a premium) Archambault Township authorized a bond issue for a parking garage. The estimated cost was $4 million. The garage would be financed through a $2.5 million bond issue and a $1.5 million contribution from the General Fund. The General Fund made its contribution and the bonds were sold for $2,700,000, which includes a $200,000 premium over the face amount of the bonds.

Required: 1. Prepare journal entries to record the budget for the parking garage, the payment and receipt of the General Fund's contribution, and the issuance of the bonds, assuming the premium remained in the Capital Projects Fund. Identify the fund(s) used to record the transactions.
2. Identify alternate methods of disposing of the bond premium.

P6-4 (Journal entries for several funds and financial statements for a Capital Projects Fund)

Following is a trial balance for the Raccoon Falls Boat Marina Capital Projects Fund and the transactions that relate to the 2008–2009 fiscal year:

Raccoon Falls
Boat Marina Capital Projects Fund
Trial Balance
July 1, 2008

	Debits	Credits
Cash	$ 30,000	
Investments	500,000	
Retained percentage on construction contracts		$ 10,000
Fund balance reserved for encumbrances		500,000
Unreserved fund balance		20,000
	$530,000	$530,000

1. The budget for the marina project provided for a remaining appropriation of $500,000. Record the budget and reestablish the budgetary accounts for encumbrances. Assume $30,000 of investment income (dividends and interest) is budgeted.
2. The contractor, Ace Construction, submitted a progress billing on the marina for $300,000. The billing, less retained percentage of 10 percent, was approved.
3. Investments were redeemed for $320,000. This amount included $20,000 of investment income.

4. Ace Construction was paid the amount billed, less a 10 percent retainage.
5. Investment income of $15,000 was received in cash.
6. The final billing was received from Ace Construction for $200,000. The billing, less the retainage, was approved.
7. All remaining investments were redeemed for $205,000. This amount included $5,000 of investment income.
8. Ace Construction was paid the amount billed, less a 10 percent retainage.
9. During final inspection of the project, pending official acceptance, several construction defects were noted by the city engineer. Because Ace Construction had already relocated its workers and equipment, the city was authorized to have the repairs made by a local contractor at a cost not to exceed $40,000. The actual cost of the repairs totaled $32,000. The remainder of the retainage was sent to Ace Construction.
10. After the repairs, the project was formally approved and the accounting records were closed. The remaining cash was transferred to the Debt Service Fund.

Required: 1. Prepare all the journal entries necessary to record these transactions and close the Capital Projects Fund. In addition, identify the fund(s) used. A vouchers payable account is not used.
2. Prepare a statement of revenues, expenditures, and changes in fund balance for the Boat Marina Capital Projects Fund for the 2008–2009 fiscal year.

P6-5   (Budgetary journal entries for a capital project and the related bond issue) Parkdale Township plans to build an auditorium. The plans were drawn by an architect for $100,000. The township accepted a bid from Boom-Up Contractors for $8 million for the entire project. The project should take 2 years to build. It will not be started until October 1, 2008, so the projected completion date is September 30, 2010. The township's accounting supervisor plans to establish a Debt Service Fund for the bonds that will be issued to finance the project. These bonds will be serviced from tax revenues. During 2008, $100,000 of revenue is expected to be available. The bonds will pay interest on April 1 and October 1 of each year, beginning in 2009.

Required: Prepare the journal entries necessary to record the preceding budgetary information in the appropriate funds for 2008.

P6-6   (Journal entries, financial statements, and closing entries for a Debt Service Fund) The following are a trial balance and several transactions that relate to Lewisville's Concert Hall Bond Fund:

Lewisville
Debt Service Fund
Concert Hall Bond Fund
Trial Balance
July 1, 2008

Cash	$ 60,000	
Investments	40,000	
Unreserved fund balance		$100,000
	$100,000	$100,000

The following transactions took place between July 1, 2008, and June 30, 2009:

1. The city council of Lewisville adopted the budget for the Concert Hall Bond Fund for the fiscal year. The estimated revenues totaled $100,000, the estimated other financing sources totaled $50,000, and the appropriations totaled $125,000.
2. The General Fund transferred $50,000 to the fund.
3. To provide additional resources to service the bond issue, a tax was levied upon the citizens. The total levy was $100,000, of which $95,000 was expected to be collected. Assume the allowance method is used.
4. Taxes of $60,000 were collected.
5. Revenue received in cash from the investments totaled $1,000.
6. Taxes of $30,000 were collected.
7. The liability of $37,500 for interest was recorded, and that amount of cash was transferred to the fiscal agent.
8. A fee of $500 was paid to the fiscal agent.
9. Investment revenue totaling $1,000 was received in cash.
10. The liabilities for interest in the amount of $37,500 and principal in the amount of $50,000 were recorded and cash for the total amount was transferred to the fiscal agent.
11. Investment revenue of $500 was accrued.

Required: 1. Prepare all the journal entries necessary to record the preceding transactions on the books of the Concert Hall Bond Fund.
2. Prepare a trial balance for the Concert Hall Bond Fund as of June 30, 2009.
3. Prepare a statement of revenues, expenditures, and changes in fund balance and a balance sheet for the Concert Hall Bond Fund.
4. Prepare closing entries for the Concert Hall Bond Fund.

P6-7   (Journal entries, financial statements, and closing entries for a Debt Service Fund)

Following is a trial balance and the transactions that relate to the City of Vermillion Heights's Debt Service Fund:

City of Vermillion Heights
Bridge Bonds Debt Service Fund
Trial Balance
December 31, 2008

	Debit	Credit
Cash	$60,000	
Investments	30,000	
Unreserved fund balance		$90,000
	$90,000	$90,000

1. The city council of Vermillion Heights adopted the budget for the Debt Service Fund for 2009. The estimated revenues totaled $1 million, the estimated other financing sources totaled $500,000, and the appropriations totaled $202,000.

2. The $500,000 transfer from the General Fund was accrued.
3. To provide additional resources to service the bond issue, a tax was levied upon the citizens. The total levy was $1 million, of which $975,000 was expected to be collected. (Use the allowance method.)
4. Taxes of $780,000 were collected.
5. Receivables of $5,000 were written off.
6. Income received in cash from investments totaled $5,000.
7. Taxes of $150,000 were collected.
8. The liability of $50,000 for interest was recorded, and that amount of cash was transferred to the fiscal agent.
9. Investment income of $3,000 was received in cash.
10. The liabilities for interest in the amount of $50,000 and principal in the amount of $100,000 were recorded, and cash for the total amount was transferred to the fiscal agent.
11. The fiscal agent's fee, $1,000, was accrued (credit Vouchers payable).
12. Investment revenue of $1,500 was accrued.
13. The transfer accrued in item 2 was collected.
14. Investments totaling $1 million were purchased.

Required:
1. Prepare all the journal entries necessary to record these transactions on the books of the Debt Service Fund.
2. Prepare a trial balance for the Debt Service Fund as of December 31, 2009.
3. Prepare a statement of revenues, expenditures, and changes in fund balance for 2009 and a balance sheet as of December 31, 2009, for the Debt Service Fund.
4. Prepare closing entries for the Debt Service Fund.

P6-8 (Journal entries for several funds)

Following are several transactions that relate to Baseline Township for the fiscal year 2008 (assume a voucher system is not used):

1. The general operating budget was approved. It included estimated revenues of $1,200,000, estimated other financing sources of $300,000, appropriations of $1,150,000, and estimated other financing uses of $100,000.
2. The police department paid its salaries of $50,000.
3. The General Fund made a transfer to a Debt Service Fund of $100,000.
4. The office furniture previously ordered for $45,000 was received and the bill was paid. Old furniture that cost $23,000 was sold for $500. The proceeds could be used in any manner by the city.
5. The fire chief ordered $1,000 of supplies.
6. General obligation long-term debt principal matured, and the final interest payment became due. These amounts were $75,000 and $7,500, respectively. (Assume a Debt Service Fund and a fiscal agent are used.)
7. The appropriate amount of cash was sent to the fiscal agent to process the debt service payments described in part 6.
8. The supplies ordered in part 5 arrived along with an invoice for $1,025. The excess amount was approved and a check was sent to the supplier.

9. The property tax for the year was levied by the General Fund. The total amount of the tax was $500,000. City officials estimated that 99 percent would be collected.
10. Collections of property taxes during the year totaled $490,000.
11. The remaining property taxes were classified as delinquent after $2,000 was written off as uncollectible.
12. The General Fund received a $1,000 transfer from an Enterprise Fund (record only the General Fund portion).

Required: Prepare all the journal entries necessary to record these transactions in the appropriate governmental-type fund(s) and identify the fund(s) used.

P6-9 (Journal entries for several funds and a trial balance for a Debt Service Fund) Following are several transactions that relate to the Village of Desert Haven in 2008.

1. The general operating budget was approved. It included estimated revenues of $500,000, appropriations of $400,000, and estimated other financing uses of $90,000.
2. Encumbrances of $50,000 were recorded in the General Fund.
3. The budget for the Parks Special Revenue Fund was approved. It included estimated revenues of $60,000 and appropriations of $59,000.
4. The General Fund made its annual transfer of $100,000 to a Debt Service Fund.
5. The Debt Service Fund recorded the liability for principal and interest, $20,000 and $40,000, respectively.
6. The Debt Service Fund invested $10,000 of Debt Service Fund cash in securities.
7. The salaries of the general governmental administrative staff were paid: $15,000. Assume that salaries were not encumbered.
8. The fiscal agent who manages the investment activities of the Debt Service Fund was paid a fee of $1,000.
9. The tax used to service the bond issue was levied. The total levy was $30,000, of which $29,000 is expected to be collected.
10. A cash expenditure for office supplies for the mayor's office was made: $900. The encumbered amount was $1,000.
11. Debt Service Fund cash of $60,000 was paid to the fiscal agent to pay interest and principal. (See transaction 5.)

Required: 1. Prepare all the journal entries necessary to record these transactions. In addition, identify the fund(s) in which each entry is recorded.
2. Prepare a trial balance for the Debt Service Fund as of December 31, 2008.

P6-10 (Journal entries for several funds)
Prepare journal entries for each of the following transactions. In addition, identify the fund in which each entry would be recorded.

1. The General Fund made its annual contribution of $1,500,000 to the fund that will pay $1 million principal and $500,000 interest on outstanding general obligation debt.
2. The city paid $1 million of principal and $500,000 of interest on outstanding general obligation bonds from resources previously accumulated.
3. A Debt Service Fund previously retired the total principal and the interest in full on an outstanding bond issue. Currently the fund carries a balance of $300,000. These resources can be spent by the General Fund in any way the city manager deems is appropriate.
4. The Police Department paid $300,000 for equipment. This equipment was ordered 3 months prior to delivery at an estimated cost of $295,000 (assume a voucher system is used and the excess expenditure is approved).
5. The fiscal agent for the city was paid its annual $10,000 fee from resources accumulated in the only Debt Service Fund used by the city.

P6-11 (Journal entries for several funds)

The following transactions were incurred by East Minster Township.

1. The township paid cash for four police cars. Each car cost $18,000. They were originally ordered at $20,000 each.
2. The township issued bonds for the purpose of constructing playgrounds in the city. The bonds had a face value of $20 million and were sold for $19,900,000.
3. The mayor of the township signed a contract with the Dumas Office Furniture Company to buy furniture for his office. The total cost of the furniture was $8,900. The furniture will be delivered next month.
4. Two additional police officers were hired to help patrol the new playgrounds.
5. The fire department sold several pieces of used equipment. They originally cost the township $20,000. The fire chief negotiated a selling price of $3,000 for the equipment.
6. The township made its annual payment of principal and interest on its outstanding debt. A total of $5 million was paid: $1 million of principal and $4 million of interest.
7. The township levied a property tax to service the outstanding debt. The total amount of the tax was $4 million, of which $3,900,000 was expected to be collected. (Assume the use of a separate fund.)
8. The city hall construction project started in the prior year was completed this year. This year $1,500,000 of costs were incurred. In the prior year a total of $7,500,000 was incurred. Financing for the project came from a bond issue that was sold at the time the project was started.
9. The township's board of supervisors approved a budget amendment for the General Fund. An extra $300,000 appropriation was included in the budget for the current year.
10. The township made payments on outstanding leases totaling $300,000. This amount included $175,000 for interest. The leases are accounted for in the General Fund and encumbrance accounting is used.

Required: Record these transactions in journal form. Also indicate the fund in which each transaction is recorded.

P6-12 (Leased assets)

On January 1, 2008, the chief operating officer of New Belgium signed a non-cancelable lease for street equipment. The lease was for 10 years, the economic life of the property. The fair market value of the equipment (and present value of the minimum rentals) is $75,152. The township's incremental borrowing rate is 7 percent. The $10,000 annual lease payment is due on the first day of the year.

Required: Prepare all journal entries necessary to record the lease transaction for 2008 and the payment made in 2009.

P6-13 (Journal entries for several funds)

The following transactions took place during 2009:

1. The city sold some of its street repair equipment. The equipment originally cost $50,000, but it was sold for $500.
2. A $2 million bond issue was sold at par. The bonds were general obligation debt issued to finance the cost of an addition to the local court system building.
3. Nondedicated property taxes totaling $100,000 were collected.
4. Construction of a bridge across the Mississippi River was completed at a total cost of $8 million. The bridge had been under construction since 2008. Costs incurred in previous years totaled $7 million. With respect to the Capital Projects Fund, prepare only the closing entry for the expenditure.
5. A Debt Service Fund paid the interest on outstanding debt: $800,000.
6. A Debt Service Fund retired bonds with a face value of $3 million.
7. The General Fund made its annual transfer of $6 million to a Debt Service Fund.
8. Old office equipment in the mayor's office was discarded. The original cost of the equipment was $900.
9. A contract was signed with Legal, Inc., to construct an addition to the court building. The amount of the contract was $5 million.
10. The construction costs paid during the year on the court addition were $500,000. With respect to the Capital Projects Fund, record only the closing entry for the expenditure.
11. The Fire Department acquired a fire engine. The vehicle was ordered earlier in the year. The order was encumbered for $140,000. The actual cost was $138,000.

Required: Record these transactions in journal form. Also indicate the fund in which each transaction is recorded.

P6-14 (Leased assets)

The Police Department of High Falls signed a noncancelable lease for computer equipment. The lease was for 5 years, the economic life of the property. The fair market value of the equipment (and present value of the minimum rentals) is $21,198 and the city's incremental borrowing rate is 9 percent. The annual rentals are $5,000 and are due on the first day of the year, beginning January 1, 2008.

Required: Assuming the equipment is delivered when the lease is signed, prepare all journal entries necessary to record the lease transaction for 2008 and the payment made in 2009.

P6-15 (Journal entries and correcting entries for several funds)

Following is a selection of improperly recorded transactions that occurred during 2008 and a description of how each transaction was recorded by a township. Prepare the necessary entries to correct these mistakes. Also identify the fund(s) involved. Closing entries are not required. If no entry is required, indicate "None." The books for the current year, 2008, have not been closed.

1. The governing board adopted a budget for the General Fund for 2008 that included estimated revenues of $900,000, estimated other financing sources of $200,000, appropriations of $800,000, and estimated other financing uses of $150,000. The budget was not recorded in the books.

2. The levee board purchased a fire truck in February. The bookkeeper made the following entry in the General Fund:

Fire truck	125,000	
Vouchers payable		125,000

The voucher was paid, but the payment was not recorded.

3. A property tax levy was made in March. The total levy was $500,000. Approximately 3 percent was expected to be uncollectible. By the end of the year $390,000 had been collected and the remainder was delinquent. The only entries made during the year were for the collections as a debit to Cash and credit to Revenues—property taxes.

4. Bonds were retired in June. The township accumulated $505,000 in a Debt Service Fund by the end of 2008. Part of these resources ($500,000) were used to retire the bonds. The remainder were available to be used by the township in any way it desired. The only entries recorded during the year were as follows (these entries were recorded in the General Fund, using Debt Service Fund resources):

Bonds payable	500,000	
Vouchers payable		500,000
Vouchers payable	500,000	
Cash		500,000

5. Some surplus equipment was sold in September for $20,000 (with no restrictions on the use of these resources). The equipment was originally purchased for $245,000 several years ago. The following entry was made in the General Fund:

Cash	20,000	
Loss on sale of equipment	225,000	
Equipment		245,000

6. The General Fund made its annual contribution to a Debt Service Fund. These resources will be used to pay interest. The only entry made was in the General Fund:

Bonds payable	100,000	
Cash		100,000

7. The interest paid during 2008 on the debt mentioned in part 6 was recorded in the General Fund as follows:

Interest expense	100,000	
Cash		100,000

P6-16 (Use of Special Assessments to Finance a Capital Project)

Property owners in Quail Hollow (a neighborhood of Choice City) petitioned the city council to improve drainage in their neighborhood after a series of heavy summer thunderstorms did considerable flood damage. The council responded by approving a construction project with an estimated cost of $1 million. Aero-Nocturnal Contractors was retained to design and build the project. Contract terms call for a 5 percent retainage of amounts billed pending formal acceptance of the project by the city.

The city will contribute $200,000 toward the project's cost; the balance will be paid from assessments against properties within Quail Hollow. Construction costs will be financed by issuing $800,000 worth of 5-year, 6 percent bonds, guaranteed by the City. Bond principal will be repaid in *semiannual* installments, along with accrued interest, each December 31 and June 30, commencing December 31, 2008. The resources to pay the bond principal and interest will come from interest-bearing special assessments on Quail Hollow properties to be levied after the project is complete. Any financial assets remaining after construction is completed will be applied toward servicing the bonds.

Choice City will establish a Capital Projects Fund to account for construction of the drainage improvement project and a Debt Service Fund to account for receipt of special assessments from property owners and principal and interest payments to bondholders. The city will not employ budgetary accounting for either fund. The city's fiscal year ends December 31.

Required: Prepare the journal entries required in the appropriate funds for the following events and transactions (explanations may be omitted). Closing entries are not required.

1. January 2, 2008: The bonds were issued at par.
2. January 23, 2008: The city's share of project costs was transferred from the General Fund to the Capital Projects Fund.
3. April 20, 2008: The project was completed at a total cost of $990,000 and liability for construction costs was recorded, pending final approval by the city engineer.
4. May 6, 2008: The amount immediately due the contractor was paid.
5. July 1, 2008: The special assessment of $800,000 was levied. One fifth of the total levy plus 6 percent interest on the unpaid balance is payable by the property owners *annually* commencing December 31, 2008. (*Hint:* At this point, record only the principal portion of the assessment, not the interest).
6. July 7, 2008: The city engineer inspected the project and found it completely satisfactory. Accordingly, the engineer authorized payment of the remaining amount due to Aero-Nocturnal Contractors.

7. The remaining assets in the Capital Projects Fund were transferred to the Debt Service Fund.
8. As of December 31, special assessments currently due, and accrued interest thereon, was collected in full from property owners.
9. December 31, 2008: The amounts due on the bonds were paid.
10. January 2, 2009: The current portion of special assessments receivable and revenues pertaining to 2009 were recognized.

Continuous Problem

Leisure City's 2008 capital budget included $50 million for a new courthouse. Financing for the project will come from a 10 percent $25 million bond issue and a $25 million federal construction grant. The bonds pay interest semiannually on September 1 and March 1. The bonds are to be serviced from an annual $1 million transfer from the General Fund and a 3 percent hotel-motel tax. The following is a listing of the events that took place during 2008.

1. Budgets were adopted for the Capital Projects Fund and the Debt Service Fund as follows:

Capital Projects Fund
Estimated revenues—federal construction grant	$25,000,000
Estimated other financing sources—bond issue	25,000,000
Estimated revenues—investment revenues	3,000,000
Appropriations—construction costs	50,000,000

Debt Service Fund
Estimated revenues—hotel-motel tax	2,000,000
Estimated other financing sources—transfer from General Fund	900,000
Appropriations—bond servicing	1,250,000

2. The bonds were sold for $26 million. The entire proceeds were recorded in the Capital Projects Fund and the premium was transferred to the Debt Service Fund immediately.
3. Leisure City received the $25 million cash proceeds from the federal grant.
4. $20 million was invested in interest-bearing securities.
5. A contract was signed with Thomas Brothers for the construction of the courthouse totaling $50 million.
6. The General Fund transferred $900,000 to the fund that will service the bonds.
7. The fund that will service the bonds collected $1,300,000 of hotel-motel taxes.
8. Thomas Brothers submitted a bill to Leisure City for work done to date. The total amount of the bill was $3 million. The construction contract provided for a 5 percent retained percentage. The bill, less the retainage, was approved.
9. Investments in the Capital Projects Fund matured. The principal was $5 million. In addition, $250,000 of interest income was collected.
10. The progress billing in part 8 was paid.

11. An additional $750,000 of hotel-motel taxes were collected.
12. Interest on the construction debt was paid; $1,250,000 was paid to the fiscal agent, who will distribute the money to the bondholders.
13. Thomas Brothers submitted another progress billing. The amount of the bill was $5 million. The bill, less the retainage, was approved.
14. Interest was accrued on the investments in the Capital Projects Fund in the amount of $580,000.
15. Based on the provisions of the federal grant, grant revenues are to be recognized in 50 percent proportion to construction expenditures incurred each year.

Required: 1. Prepare the journal entries necessary to record the preceding transactions and identify the fund(s) used.
2. Prepare a trial balance at December 31, 2008, for the Capital Projects Fund and the Debt Service Fund, before closing.
3. Prepare any necessary closing entries for the Capital Projects Fund and the Debt Service Fund.
4. Prepare a statement of revenues, expenditures, and changes in fund balance for the Capital Projects Fund and the Debt Service Fund for 2008.
5. Prepare a balance sheet as of December 31, 2008, for the Capital Projects Fund and the Debt Service Fund.

CHAPTER

7

THE GOVERNMENTAL FUND ACCOUNTING CYCLE

Proprietary-Type Funds

Chapter Outline

After completing this chapter, you should be able to:

- Understand the similarities between Internal Service Funds and Enterprise Funds.
- Explain why and how Internal Service Funds are used in governmental accounting.
- Prepare the journal entries normally recorded in Internal Service Funds.
- Prepare fund financial statements for Internal Service Funds.
- Explain why and how Enterprise Funds are used in governmental accounting.
- Prepare the journal entries normally recorded in Enterprise Funds.
- Prepare fund financial statements for Enterprise Funds.

This chapter discusses fund-level financial accounting and reporting for proprietary funds; that is, Internal Service Funds and Enterprise Funds. Government-wide financial reporting of these funds is discussed in Chapters 9 and 10.

OVERVIEW

One definition of the word *proprietary* used as an adjective is "privately owned and operated for profit."[1] It is a short step, then, to say that proprietary means "businesslike." Proprietary funds in state and local government are used to account for certain government activities in essentially a private-sector, business, fashion (although, of course, such activities are not privately owned). There are two types of proprietary funds: Internal Service Funds and Enterprise Funds. The essential difference between the two fund types is the customer base. The customers of Internal Service Fund activities are various departments within the same government (and, occasionally, other nearby governments), while the customers of Enterprise Funds are primarily individual citizens but can include government departments as well.

Proprietary funds account for activities involved in providing goods and/or services to paying customers *on an exchange basis*. Thus, the operating cycle of a proprietary fund is similar to that of a business organization: During the fiscal period, the fund acquires assets such as supplies, property, and equipment. Goods or services are provided to paying customers, so revenues from user charges are recorded. The cost of assets used is recorded along with other operating and nonoperating expenses. Revenues earned are matched with expenses incurred and the resulting profit or loss increases or decreases net assets.

Some Internal Service Funds price goods and services above cost to provide financing for expansion or to cover anticipated inflation when equipment must be replaced. In contrast, in some governments the goods and services provided by Internal Service Funds and Enterprise Funds are "underpriced" and subsidized by General Fund revenues as a matter of policy. By computing the activity's full cost of operations and comparing these costs with the revenues earned, the extent of the subsidy needed can be determined.

Because of the need to measure full costs, proprietary funds employ the total economic resources measurement focus. Accordingly, fixed assets (and depreciation

---

[1] *Random House Webster's College Dictionary,* p. 1083. New York: Random House, 1991.

thereof) are accounted for within proprietary funds, as is any long-term debt serviced exclusively by proprietary fund revenues. Also, proprietary funds use the full accrual basis of accounting so that revenues are recorded when they are earned (without regard to "measurable and available" considerations) and expenses are recorded in the period in which they are incurred. Also, because the purpose of this type of fund is to provide information for a businesslike evaluation of its operations, it is essential that each activity be accounted for by a separate fund.

What Determines Whether a Proprietary Fund Is an Enterprise Fund or an Internal Service Fund?

As we have mentioned, the deciding factor in whether a proprietary fund is classified as an Enterprise Fund or an Internal Service Fund is the customer base. In this regard, the GASB states that "Internal service funds should be used only if the reporting government is the predominant participant [customer] in the activity. Otherwise, the activity should be reported as an enterprise fund."[2] Thus, the GASB Codification discusses proprietary fund accounting primarily in terms of Enterprise Funds. According to the GASB, Enterprise Funds *may* be used to report any activity for which a fee is charged to external users for goods or services. Activities *are required* to be accounted for as Enterprise Funds if any one of the following criteria is met:

a.   The activity is financed with debt that is secured solely by a pledge of the net revenues from fees and charges of the activity [debt of this kind usually is in the form of *revenue bonds*]. . . .

b.   Laws or regulations require that the activity's costs of providing services including capital costs (such as depreciation or debt service) be recovered with fees and charges, rather than with taxes or similar revenues.

c.   The pricing policies of the activity establish fees and charges designed to recover its costs, including capital costs (such as depreciation or debt service).[3]

Governments should apply each of these criteria in the context of the activity's principal revenue sources. Further, when applying these criteria, a governmental unit is not required to use an Enterprise Fund if an insignificant activity (activities) is (are) funded by user charges.

GASB *Statement No. 20,* "Accounting and Financial Reporting for Proprietary Funds and Other Governmental Entities That Use Proprietary Fund Accounting," defines the applicability of business-type pronouncements for governmental entities. Proprietary activities should apply all applicable GASB pronouncements as well as FASB *Statements and Interpretations*, Accounting Principles Board *Opinions*, and Committee on Accounting Procedure *Accounting Research Bulletins* issued on or before November 30, 1989, *unless* those non-GASB pronouncements conflict with or contradict GASB pronouncements. Proprietary activities may also apply *all* FASB Statements and Interpretations issued after November 30, 1989, except for those that conflict with or contradict GASB pronouncements.[4] In any

[2]GASB Cod. Sec. 1300.110.
[3]GASB Cod. Sec. 1300.109.
[4]GASB Cod. Sec. P80.102.

event, they may *not* apply FASB standards whose provisions are limited to or address issues that concern primarily not-for-profit organizations, such as those discussed in Chapter 12. (The purpose of the all-or-none requirement is to prevent governments from selectively applying FASB Statements and Interpretations issued after November 30, 1989.)

The financial statements for individual proprietary funds are a statement of revenues, expenses, and changes in fund net assets; a balance sheet (or statement of net assets); and a statement of cash flows. Proprietary fund balance sheets should be prepared using a classified format. Under this format, assets and liabilities are grouped into current and noncurrent classifications similar to those used on commercial balance sheets.

The general format for the statement of revenues, expenses, and changes in fund net assets is presented as follows:

Operating revenues (detailed)
   Total operating revenues
Operating expenses (detailed)
   Total operating expenses
   Operating income (loss)
Nonoperating revenues and expenses (detailed)
   Income before other revenues, expenses, gains, losses, and transfers
Capital contributions and transfers (detailed)
   Increase (decrease) in net assets
Net assets—beginning of period
Net assets—end of period[5]

On a statement of net assets, the GASB requires that the net assets section be reported in three components: (1) net assets invested in capital assets, net of related debt; (2) restricted net assets; and (3) unrestricted net assets.

SPECIFIC ASPECTS OF INTERNAL SERVICE FUNDS

Summary of Fund Activities

Governments establish Internal Service Funds to account for the operations of providing goods or services in-house to departments in circumstances where it can be done at a lower cost, or perhaps more conveniently, than if the same goods or services were obtained externally. Internal Service Funds typically are used to account for activities such as central data-processing services, motor pools, risk management, and inventory and supply (central stores) functions. In this chapter we focus our discussion on the activities of a central motor pool. The operations of this type of service are typical for governmental units and are illustrative of the general operations of Internal Service Funds.

The first step is to acquire capital from the General Fund or some other fund. This money is used to acquire automobiles, trucks, and so forth. As the vehicles are used,

---

[5]GASB Cod. Sec. 2200.167.

each department is billed based on the miles driven. Revenue from the billings is used to pay the operating costs of the vehicles and, possibly, for their replacement.

Control of Fund Activities

The operations of Internal Service Funds are controlled indirectly by the operating budgets of the funds using the goods or services and directly by means of flexible budgets. Because other funds must pay for the goods or services supplied, the approval of their budgets acts as an indirect control device for Internal Service Funds.

A flexible budget is a budget in which most of the budgeted expenses are related to the level of operations. Thus, in our example of a central motor pool, the allowable gasoline and oil costs will vary directly with the number of miles the vehicles are driven. Governmental-type funds, by contrast, operate under a fixed budget. Thus, if a department is appropriated $4,000 for supplies for the year, for example, that amount cannot be exceeded — regardless of the level of operations. In effect, the use of a fixed budget actually sets a limit on the level of operations of governmental-type funds.

The difference in budgeting practices between governmental-type funds and Internal Service Funds results because the revenue generated by the latter increases as the level of operations increases. Because of a general cause-and-effect relationship between the level of operations and revenues earned and expenses incurred, a flexible budget allows higher levels of expenses at higher levels of operating activity. As previously explained, no such relationship usually exists between revenues and expenditures of governmental-type funds. For example, a police department usually must request an additional budget allocation if it uses all of its appropriation; such an allocation does not result automatically.

Typically we do not find the budget recorded in the accounts of Internal Service Funds, nor do we usually find the use of encumbrance accounting for these funds. Without an absolute spending limit, the use of encumbrance accounting serves no purpose. A few state or local governments are subject to laws that require the use of encumbrances for Internal Service Funds, but here we will assume that encumbrance accounting is not used.

Accounting for Fund Activities

Operating Entries

Let us illustrate the operations of an Internal Service Fund with the example of a central motor pool. Assume that to start up the fund, the General Fund makes a transfer of $500,000 to the Motor Pool Fund. The entries to record this transfer are presented below. In the General Fund:

Transfer out to Motor Pool Fund	500,000	
Cash		500,000
To record transfer of initial capital to		
Internal Service Fund.		

In the Internal Service Fund:

Cash	500,000	
Transfer in from General Fund—capital contribution		500,000
To record transfer of initial capital from		
General Fund.		

If the Internal Service Fund acquires a fleet of vehicles for $400,000, the following entry is made:

Automobiles	300,000	
Trucks	100,000	
Cash		400,000
To record the acquisition of vehicles.		

Billings of $57,000 to various General Fund departments for use of the vehicles are recorded as follows:

Entry in the Internal Service Fund:

Due from General Fund	57,000	
Revenues—vehicle charges		57,000
To record charges to departments for use of vehicles.		

Entry on the books of a department that received $8,000 worth of services:

Expenditures—vehicle usage	8,000	
Due to Motor Pool Fund		8,000
To record the use of vehicles during the period.		

Collections of $45,000 from the user departments accounted for within the General Fund are recorded in the Internal Service Fund as follows:

Cash	45,000	
Due from General Fund		45,000
To record payments received from departments using vehicles.		

The corresponding disbursement entry in a using fund (amount assumed) would be:

Due to Motor Pool Fund	8,000	
Cash		8,000
To record payment to Motor Pool Fund.		

During the year, gasoline, oil, and maintenance expenses totaling $14,000 are incurred, of which $10,000 are paid in cash. These expenses are recorded in the Internal Service Fund as follows:

Gasoline and oil expense	9,500	
Maintenance expense	4,500	
Cash		10,000
Accounts payable		4,000
To record the gasoline and oil and maintenance expenses for the period.		

Payment of salaries of $10,000, ignoring withholdings, is recorded as follows:

Salaries expense	10,000	
Cash		10,000
To record salaries expense.		

If the motor pool rents warehouse space from the government for $2,000 per year, the entry to record the rental will be this:

Rent expense	2,000	
Cash		2,000
To record the rent for the year.		

The General Fund will record the receipt of the rent as follows:

Cash	2,000	
Revenues—rental of warehouse space		2,000
To record the receipt of the rent from the motor pool.		

As previously indicated, depreciation is an expense that is recognized in Internal Service Funds. Assuming the amounts given, the entry to record depreciation for the year is

Depreciation expense—automobiles	20,000	
Depreciation expense—trucks	10,000	
Accumulated depreciation—automobiles		20,000
Accumulated depreciation—trucks		10,000
To record depreciation for the year.		

Although additional entries can be made, the preceding summary journal entries are sufficient to illustrate the activities of Internal Service Funds and the recording of the related revenues and expenses. A trial balance for the Motor Pool Fund at the end of the year is shown in Table 7-1.

Closing Entry

The closing process for Internal Service Funds is similar to the one used for commercial enterprises. Each of the revenue, expense, and other temporary accounts is closed

TABLE 7-1   Trial Balance—Internal Service Fund

City of Angusville
Internal Service Fund
Motor Pool Fund
Trial Balance
December 31, 2008

	Debits	Credits
Cash	$123,000	
Due from General Fund	12,000	
Automobiles	300,000	
Accumulated depreciation—automobiles		$ 20,000
Trucks	100,000	
Accumulated depreciation—trucks		10,000
Accounts payable		4,000
Transfer in from General Fund—capital contribution		500,000
Revenues—vehicle charges		57,000
Gasoline and oil expense	9,500	
Maintenance expense	4,500	
Salaries expense	10,000	
Rent expense	2,000	
Depreciation expense—automobiles	20,000	
Depreciation expense—trucks	10,000	
	$591,000	$591,000

and the change in assets recorded in the Net assets account. The following entry relates to the previous illustration:

Revenues—vehicle charges	57,000	
Transfer in from General Fund—capital contribution	500,000	
Gasoline and oil expense		9,500
Maintenance expense		4,500
Salaries expense		10,000
Rent expense		2,000
Depreciation expense—automobiles		20,000
Depreciation expense—trucks		10,000
Net assets		501,000

To close the revenue, expense, and transfer accounts for the period.

Financial Statements Illustration

As indicated in the Overview section of this chapter, the individual financial statements for Internal Service Funds are a statement of revenues, expenses, and changes in fund net assets; a balance sheet or statement of net assets; and a statement of cash flows. The general format for the statement of revenues, expenses, and changes in fund net assets was introduced in the Overview section of the chapter. It is applied here in Table 7-2. The financial reporting format for the assets and liabilities may be

---

TABLE 7-2   Statement of Revenues, Expenses, and Changes in Fund Net Assets—Internal Service Fund

City of Angusville
Internal Service Fund
Motor Pool Fund
Statement of Revenues, Expenses, and Changes in Fund Net Assets
For the Year Ended December 31, 2008

Operating revenues:		
Vehicle charges		$ 57,000
Operating expenses:		
Gas and oil expense	$ 9,500	
Maintenance expense	4,500	
Salaries expense	10,000	
Rent expense	2,000	
Depreciation expense—automobiles	20,000	
Depreciation expense—trucks	10,000	
Total operating expenses		56,000
Operating income		1,000
Capital contribution from General Fund		500,000
Change in net assets		501,000
Net assets at beginning of year		-0-
Net assets at end of year		$501,000

TABLE 7-3   Statement of Net Assets—Internal Service Fund

City of Angusville
Internal Service Fund
Motor Pool Fund
Statement of Net Assets
December 31, 2008

Assets		
Current assets:		
Cash	$123,000	
Due from General Fund	12,000	
Total current assets		$135,000
Noncurrent assets:		
Automobiles (net of accumulated depreciation of $20,000)	280,000	
Trucks (net of accumulated depreciation of $10,000)	90,000	
Total noncurrent assets		370,000
Total assets		$505,000
Liabilities		
Current liabilities:		
Accounts payable		4,000
Net Assets		
Invested in capital assets, net of related debt	370,000	
Unrestricted net assets	131,000	
Total net assets		$501,000

presented in either a conventional *balance sheet* format (assets equal liabilities plus net assets) or in a *statement of net assets* format (assets less liabilities equal net assets). The latter is illustrated in Table 7-3. The cash flow statement is illustrated at Table 7-4.

Recall that on a statement of net assets, the GASB requires that the net assets section be reported in three components: (1) net assets invested in capital assets, net of related debt; (2) restricted net assets; and (3) unrestricted net assets. One way to derive the balances of the three net asset classifications is to close all nominal accounts to a Net assets account and then analyze that account to determine its components for financial reporting purposes. Notice that in the statement of net assets for the Motor Pool Fund (Table 7-3), only components 1 and 3 are reported, because the fund has no restricted net assets. Restricted assets result from contractual and other restrictions placed on the use of the assets by outside parties or by law. Restricted assets are discussed in greater detail in the next section of this chapter.

For the Motor Pool Fund, the net assets invested in capital assets, net of related debt, is equal to $370,000 − $0, or $370,000. Nothing is deducted from the net capital (noncurrent) assets because the Fund has no related debt. The remainder of the net assets, $131,000 ($501,000 − $370,000), is reported as unrestricted.

TABLE 7-4   Statement of Cash Flows—Internal Service Fund

City of Angusville
Internal Service Fund
Motor Pool Fund
Statement of Cash Flows
For the Year Ended December 31, 2008

Cash Flows from Operating Activities

Receipts from customers	$ 45,000	
Payments to suppliers	(10,000)	
Payments to employees	(10,000)	
Payments for rent	(2,000)	
Cash flows from operations		$ 23,000

Cash Flows from Capital and Related Financing Activities

Purchase of capital assets	$(400,000)	
Capital contributed by municipality	500,000	
Cash flows from capital and related financing activities		100,000
Net increase in cash		123,000
Cash balance at beginning of year		-0-
Cash balance at end of year		$123,000

Reconciliation of operating income to net cash provided
by operating activities:

Operating income	$ 1,000	
Adjustments to reconcile operating income to net cash provided by operating activities:		
Depreciation expense	30,000	
Changes in assets and liabilities:		
Due from General Fund	(12,000)	
Accounts payable	4,000	
Net cash provided by operations		$ 23,000

A detailed discussion of the cash flow statement is beyond the scope of this text. An example appears at Table 7-4, however, to complete the illustration of financial statements for Internal Service Funds. More information is provided about this statement in the next section of this chapter.

The combined totals for all Internal Service Funds should be reported in a separate column on the face of the proprietary fund financial statements to the right of the total Enterprise Funds column.[6] This aggregate information is supported by a combining statement for Internal Service Funds in the annual report.

---

[6]GASB Cod. Sec. 2200.162.

GOVERNMENTAL ACCOUNTING IN PRACTICE
The City of Columbus, Ohio

The City of Columbus, Ohio, uses Internal Service Funds to account for employee benefits, a central purchasing function, telecommunications, land acquisition, information services, and fleet management. For illustrative purposes, we will use the land acquisition fund. The financial statements for this fund are presented in Tables 7-5, 7-6, and 7-7. Notice that the statement of net assets contains only two subclassifications of net assets, like our example.

TABLE 7-5 Statement of Revenues, Expenses, and Changes in Fund Net Assets—Internal Service Fund—City of Columbus, Ohio

City of Columbus, Ohio
Internal Service Fund
Land Acquisition Fund
Statement of Revenues, Expenses, and Changes in Fund Net Assets
For the Year Ended December 31, 20X8
(amounts in thousands)

Operating revenues:		
Charges for services		$477
Operating expenses:		
Personal services	$486	
Materials and supplies	6	
Contractual services	32	
Depreciation	16	
Total operating expenses		540
Operating loss (change in net assets)		$ (63)
Net assets at beginning of year		439
Net assets at end of year		$376

Source: Adapted from a recent annual report of the City of Columbus, Ohio.

TABLE 7-6 Statement of Net Assets—Internal Service Fund—City of Columbus, Ohio

City of Columbus, Ohio
Internal Service Fund
Land Acquisition Fund
Statement of Net Assets
December 31, 20X8
(amounts in thousands)

Assets		
Current assets:		
Cash and investments with treasurer	$361	
Due from other funds	31	
Total current assets		$392

(continued)

City of Columbus, Ohio
Internal Service Fund
Land Acquisition Fund
Statement of Net Assets
December 31, 20X8 *(amounts in thousands)*

Noncurrent assets:		
Capital assets:		
Property, plant, and equipment, at cost	96	
Less accumulated depreciation	(82)	
Net property, plant, and equipment		14
Total assets		$406
Liabilities		
Current liabilities:		
Accounts payable	5	
Accrued wages and benefits	18	
Accrued vacation and sick leave	7	
Total current liabilities		30
Net Assets		
Invested in capital assets, net of related debt		14
Unrestricted		362
Total net assets		$376

Source: Adapted from a recent annual report of the City of Columbus, Ohio.

City of Columbus, Ohio
Internal Service Fund
Land Acquisition Fund
Statement of Cash Flows
December 31, 20X8 *(amounts in thousands)*

Operating Activities	
Quasi-external operating receipts	$488
Cash paid to employees	(500)
Cash paid to suppliers	(35)
Net cash used by operating activities	(47)
Decrease in cash and cash equivalents	(47)
Cash and cash equivalents at beginning of year	408
Cash and cash equivalents at end of year	$361
Reconciliation of operating loss to net cash used by operating activities	
Operating loss	$(63)
Depreciation	16
Decrease (increase) in operating assets and increase (decrease) in operating liabilities:	
Due from other governments	17
Due from other funds	(7)
Accounts payable	3
Accrued wages and benefits	(15)
Accrued vacation and sick leave	2
Net cash used by operating activities	$(47)

Source: Adapted from a recent annual report of the City of Columbus, Ohio.

SPECIFIC ASPECTS OF ENTERPRISE FUNDS

Summary of Fund Activities

Enterprise Funds are used when a governmental unit provides goods or services to customers who, to a significant extent, are not part of the government. Utility operations—providing electric, water, and sewer service—are activities that normally require use of Enterprise Funds. Also, Enterprise Funds are used for the operations of ports, airports, public swimming pools, and golf courses.[7]

Additionally, many governments have created business-type entities, called *public benefit corporations* or *public authorities,* that use proprietary fund accounting. We deal with these latter entities in our discussion of the governmental reporting entity in Chapter 9.

Control of Fund Activities

The operations of an Enterprise Fund are controlled by many means. Because the functions of this type of activity are to supply goods or services to a general market, the consumer exercises some control. Whether a consumer decides to purchase a particular good or service is true "marketplace control." However, because many Enterprise Funds are public utilities, they possess monopoly operating rights. In many cases, therefore, no competitive goods or services are available to provide market-based charges for services. Control is achieved through approval of rates and charges by legislative bodies or by governing boards that determine the rates the utility can charge. Legislative bodies and governing boards use operating data extensively to determine reasonable service charges, sometimes with the assistance of outside consultants. In these cases, accounting data are invaluable for measuring the results of operations.

Flexible budgets are used for the measurement and control of operations in Enterprise Funds in the same manner as in Internal Service Funds. They provide an additional element of control. The use of flexible budgets precludes recording the budget in the accounts, so the direct spending control found in the General Fund is not present in Enterprise Funds. In addition, because of the absence of absolute spending control, encumbrance accounting generally is not used for Enterprise Funds.

Accounting for Fund Activities
Operating Entries

For illustrative purposes, assume the City of Angusville owns and operates the French Market Corporation. This organization operates a large open market like those used by the early colonists and is a tourist attraction. Individuals and

---

[7]Some Enterprise Funds routinely serve other government departments of the government in addition to third-party customers, but the revenues obtained from governmental customers are only a small portion of the Enterprise Fund's total revenues. Prime examples are utility operations that supply water and electricity to a government's buildings and facilities as well as to the citizenry.

TABLE 7-8	Trial Balance—Enterprise Fund

City of Angusville
Enterprise Fund
French Market Corporation Fund
Postclosing Trial Balance
December 31, 2007

	Debits	Credits
Cash	$ 25,000	
Accounts receivable	15,000	
Supplies	2,000	
Cash—restricted for debt service	150,000	
Land	500,000	
Equipment	200,000	
Accumulated depreciation—equipment		$ 90,000
Buildings	1,500,000	
Accumulated depreciation—buildings		600,000
Accounts payable		20,000
Revenue bonds payable		500,000
Net assets		1,182,000
	$2,392,000	$2,392,000

businesses rent space in the market from the city and sell anything from fresh fruits and vegetables to clothing and jewelry. A fiscal 2008 beginning trial balance for the fund is presented in Table 7-8.

The Cash—restricted for debt service account represents the amounts the corporation is required to set aside each year according to a bond indenture. This amount will be held in escrow until the bonds are retired and all interest is paid. Notice that the total of the net assets is $1,182,000. This total consists of the following elements:

1. Net assets invested in capital assets (net of related debt) in the amount of $1,010,000. This total includes land ($500,000), equipment ($200,000), and buildings ($1,500,000), less the accumulated depreciation ($90,000 + $600,000), less the related debt of $500,000.
2. Net assets that are restricted in the amount of $150,000. This total equals the restricted assets ($150,000) less the liabilities payable with restricted assets ($0). The *difference* between restricted assets and liabilities reported as payable from restricted assets is reported as Net assets—restricted.
3. Net assets—unrestricted of $22,000. This total represents the net assets not included in the first two categories.

Notice that we accumulated these amounts in one account: Net assets. At the end of each year all nominal accounts are closed into the Net assets account and then, for reporting purposes, the total is segregated into the three elements previously described.

If billings to the retailers during 2008 totaled $500,000, and $5,000 of that amount is for space provided to the city, the following entry should be made:

Accounts receivable	495,000	
Due from General Fund	5,000	
Revenue from rentals		500,000
To record rental revenue for the year.		

Collections during the year total $490,000, of which $5,000 is from the General Fund. They are recorded as follows:

Cash	490,000	
Accounts receivable		485,000
Due from General Fund		5,000
To record collections from customers.		

The appropriate entries in the books of the General Fund for these two events are

Expenditures—rentals	5,000	
Due to French Market Corporation Fund		5,000
To record cost of rentals of 2008.		
Due to French Market Corporation Fund	5,000	
Cash		5,000
To record payment made to French Market Corporation Fund.		

French Market Corporation operating expenses before depreciation are $400,000 for 2008. Of this amount, $50,000 is paid in cash and the remainder is on credit. The entry to record this information is

Personal services expense	280,000	
Utilities expense	50,000	
Repairs and maintenance expense	40,000	
Other expenses	30,000	
Cash		50,000
Accounts payable		350,000
To record operating expenses for 2008.		

Because the city is accumulating the full cost of operating the market, depreciation must be recorded. Assuming the appropriate amounts are as indicated in the entry, the following is recorded:

Depreciation expense—equipment	15,000	
Depreciation expense—buildings	50,000	
Accumulated depreciation—equipment		15,000
Accumulated depreciation—buildings		50,000
To record depreciation for 2008.		

Payments to creditors total $350,000 during the year. These payments are recorded as follows:

Accounts payable	350,000	
Cash		350,000
To record payments on accounts payable.		

The French Market Corporation's long-term debt is in the form of Revenue bonds payable. Revenue bonds are debt securities that are secured exclusively by the revenues generated by the fund (in contrast to general obligation bonds, which are secured by the "full faith and credit"—the general taxing power—of the government). The entry to record interest of $40,000 for the current year on the long-term debt is:

Interest expense	40,000	
Cash		40,000
To record bond interest paid for the year.		

In this illustration, we assume the bond interest is all paid in cash; that is, $20,000 is payable on June 30 and December 31 of each year. If the interest is not due at the end of the year, a proportionate amount is accrued as an expense, just as with commercial accounting.

In this illustration, $50,000 of revenue bonds are paid this year and another $50,000 will be paid next year; moreover, the $50,000 due next year is classified as a current liability (as shown in Table 7-11). The entry in the Enterprise Fund to record the 2008 payment of principal is:

Revenue bonds payable	50,000	
Cash		50,000
To record payment of principal of revenue bonds due in 2008.		

Assume that during the year the French Market management institutes a policy of requiring a $500 deposit from each customer renting space in the market. This policy is designed to reduce the losses suffered in prior years due to customers not paying their bills. The cash collected is considered a restricted asset because it must be refunded to the market's customers when their rental agreements with the market expire. The offsetting liability is Customers' deposits. If $20,000 is collected, the entry appears as follows:

Cash—restricted for customer deposits	20,000	
Customer deposits payable		20,000
To record amounts received for customers' deposits.		

Also assume that in addition to requiring deposits, management establishes a provision for uncollectible accounts. The provision for 2008 is $5,000, which is recorded as follows:

Uncollectible accounts expense	5,000	
Allowance for uncollectible accounts		5,000
To record the estimated uncollectible accounts at December 31, 2008.		

The Allowance for uncollectible accounts account is a contra asset and as such is reported as a deduction from Accounts receivable on the balance sheet. The Uncollectible accounts expense is reported on the operating statement. Notice the treatment afforded uncollectible accounts expense for proprietary-type funds as opposed to that used for governmental-type funds. Recall that in governmental-type funds, the provision for uncollectible accounts is treated as a direct reduction from revenue rather than as an expenditure.

During the year the fund used $1,000 of supplies. The entry to record this usage is

Supplies expense	1,000	
Supplies		1,000
To record supplies used during 2008.		

TABLE 7-9   Trial Balance—Enterprise Fund

City of Angusville
Enterprise Fund
French Market Corporation Fund
Preclosing Trial Balance
December 31, 2008

	Debits	Credits
Cash	$ 25,000	
Accounts receivable	25,000	
Allowance for uncollectible accounts		$ 5,000
Supplies	1,000	
Cash—restricted for customer deposits	20,000	
Cash—restricted for debt service	150,000	
Land	500,000	
Equipment	200,000	
Accumulated depreciation—equipment		105,000
Buildings	1,500,000	
Accumulated depreciation—buildings		650,000
Accounts payable		20,000
Customer deposits		20,000
Revenue bonds payable		450,000
Net assets		1,182,000
Revenue from rentals		500,000
Personal services expense	280,000	
Utilities expense	50,000	
Repairs and maintenance expense	40,000	
Other expense	30,000	
Depreciation expense—equipment	15,000	
Depreciation expense—building	50,000	
Interest expense	40,000	
Uncollectible accounts expense	5,000	
Supplies expense	1,000	
	$2,932,000	$2,932,000

The preceding summary journal entries reflect the typical activities of Enterprise Funds and the resulting revenues generated and expenses incurred.

The preclosing trial balance for the French Market Corporation Fund at December 31, 2008, is presented in Table 7-9.

Closing Entry

The closing process for Enterprise Funds involves transferring the balances of the revenues, expenses, and other temporary accounts to the Net assets account. The entry, using the data given in the example, is:

Revenues from rentals	500,000	
Net assets	11,000	
Personal services expense		280,000
Utilities expense		50,000
Repairs and maintenance expense		40,000
Other expenses		30,000
Depreciation expense—building		50,000
Depreciation expense—equipment		15,000
Interest expense		40,000
Uncollectible accounts expense		5,000
Supplies expense		1,000

To close the revenue and expense accounts for the period.

Notice the debit to Net assets, which results from the use of one net assets account in the accounting records. The total in the Net assets account is segregated into its three components for financial reporting purposes as discussed in the next section.

Financial Statements Illustration

Individual financial statements for Enterprise Funds are the same as those for Internal Service Funds; that is, a statement of revenues, expenses, and changes in net assets, a balance sheet or statement of net assets, and a statement of cash flows. These statements for the French Market Corporation Enterprise Fund are illustrated for 2008 in Tables 7-10, 7-11, and 7-12.

TABLE 7-10   Statement of Revenues, Expenses, and Changes in Fund Net Assets—Enterprise Fund

City of Angusville
Enterprise Fund
French Market Corporation Fund
Statement of Revenues, Expenses, and Changes in Fund Net Assets
For the Year Ended December 31, 2008

Operating revenues:		
Charges for services		$ 500,000
Operating expenses:		
Personal services expense	$280,000	
Utilities expense	50,000	
Repairs and maintenance expense	40,000	
Depreciation expense	65,000	
Uncollectible accounts expense	5,000	
Supplies expense	1,000	
Other expenses	30,000	
Total operating expenses		471,000
Operating income		29,000
Nonoperating expenses:		
Interest expense		(40,000)
Decrease in net assets		(11,000)
Total net assets at beginning of year		1,182,000
Total net assets at end of year		$1,171,000

TABLE 7-11   Statement of Net Assets—Enterprise Fund

City of Angusville
Enterprise Fund
French Market Corporation Fund
Statement of Net Assets
December 31, 2008

Assets

Current assets:

Cash	$25,000	
Accounts receivable (net of estimated uncollectible accounts of $5,000)	20,000	
Supplies	1,000	
Total current assets		$ 46,000

Noncurrent assets:

Cash—restricted for debt service	150,000
Cash—restricted for customer deposits	20,000
Total restricted assets	170,000

Capital assets:

Land	500,000	
Buildings (net of accumulated depreciation of $650,000)	850,000	
Equipment (net of accumulated depreciation of $105,000)	95,000	
Total capital assets		1,445,000
Total assets		1,661,000

Liabilities

Current liabilities:

Accounts payable	20,000
Current portion of revenue bonds payable	50,000
Total current liabilities	70,000

Noncurrent liabilities:

Customer deposits	20,000
Revenue bonds payable	400,000
Total noncurrent liabilities	420,000
Total liabilities	490,000

Net Assets

Invested in capital assets net of related debt	995,000
Restricted for debt service	150,000
Unrestricted	26,000
Total net assets	$1,171,000

Refer to the statement of net assets in Table 7-11. The total balance of net assets is $1,171,000. This total consists of the following components:

1. Net assets invested in capital assets, net of related debt, $995,000. This amount is equal to the sum of the carrying values of the land, the buildings, and the equipment ($500,000 + $850,000 + $95,000), less the debt (revenue bonds payable) of $450,000.

TABLE 7-12　Statement of Cash Flows—Enterprise Fund

City of Angusville
Enterprise Fund
French Market Corporation Fund
Statement of Cash Flows
For the Year Ended December 31, 2008

Cash Flows from Operating Activities		
Receipts from customers	$490,000	
Customer deposits	20,000	
Payments to suppliers	(120,000)	
Payments to employees	(280,000)	
Cash flows from operations		$110,000
Cash Flows from Capital and Related Financing Activities		
Payments for debt service		(90,000)
Net increase in cash		20,000
Unrestricted cash and restricted cash balance at beginning of year		175,000
Unrestricted cash and restricted cash balance at end of year		$195,000
Reconciliation of operating income to net cash provided by operating activities:		
Operating income	$ 29,000	
Adjustments to reconcile operating income to net cash provided by operating activities:		
Depreciation expense	65,000	
Changes in assets and liabilities:		
Supplies	1,000	
Customers' deposits	20,000	
Accounts receivable (net)	(5,000)	
Net cash provided by operations		$110,000

2. Net assets that are restricted, $150,000. This amount represents the assets restricted for payment of revenue bonds. The $20,000 cash restricted for customer deposits is not included here because it is offset by the $20,000 liability reported for customers' deposits.

3. Net assets—unrestricted $26,000. This total represents the net assets that have no restrictions on their use, or the net assets not included in the previous two categories ($1,171,000 − 995,000 − 150,000).

GOVERNMENTAL ACCOUNTING IN PRACTICE
The City of Columbus, Ohio

The City of Columbus, Ohio, uses three Enterprise Funds: Water, Sewer, and Electricity. The use of each fund is explained by its title. Table 7-13 contains the statement of revenues, expenses, and changes in net assets for the Electricity Fund.

The statement of net assets used by the city is similar to that used by a business organization. Notice that the total of the net assets invested in capital assets, net of related debt, is $6,221 [($1,739 + $71,108) − ($1,830 + $64,796)]. The restricted net assets total $6,737 [$7,034 − ($288 + $9)]. Notice also that the City of Columbus specifically identifies the assets and liabilities that are restricted. One account is used in the text illustrations for simplicity. The traditional way of reporting these items is illustrated in Table 7-14.

The direct format is used for the statement of cash flows by the City of Columbus. As mentioned earlier in our discussion of Internal Service Funds, the direct approach should be used. For reporting purposes, as shown in the statement of cash flows in Table 7-15, cash receipts and disbursements are classified into four categories: operating activities, noncapital financing activities, capital and related financing activities, and investing activities. Notice that Columbus did not have any noncapital financing activities.

TABLE 7-13   Statement of Revenues, Expenses, and Changes in Fund Net Assets—Enterprise Fund—City of Columbus, Ohio

City of Columbus, Ohio
Enterprise Fund
Electricity Fund
Statement of Revenues, Expenses, and Changes in Fund Net Assets
For the Year Ended December 31, 20X8
(amounts expressed in thousands)

Operating revenues:		
Charges for services	$51,677	
Other	883	
Total operating revenue		$52,560
Operating expenses:		
Personal services	7,430	
Materials and supplies	200	
Contractual services	5,398	
Purchased power	33,217	
Depreciation	4,412	
Other	101	
Total operating expenses		50,758
Operating income		1,802
Nonoperating revenue (expenses)		
Investment income	421	
Interest expense	(3,138)	
Other, net	(92)	
Total nonoperating expenses		(2,809)
Loss before transfers		(1,007)
Transfers in		2,000
Change in net assets		993
Net assets at beginning of year		13,027
Net assets at end of year		$14,020

Source: Adapted from a recent annual report of the City of Columbus, Ohio.

TABLE 7-14   Statement of Net Assets—Enterprise Fund—City of Columbus, Ohio

City of Columbus, Ohio
Enterprise Fund
Electricity Fund
Statement of Net Assets
December 31, 20X8
(amounts expressed in thousands)

Assets		
Current assets:		
Cash and investments with treasurer	$ 342	
Receivables (net of allowance for uncollectibles)	5,352	
Due from other funds	321	
Inventory	922	
Total current assets		$6,937
Noncurrent assets:		
Restricted assets:		
Cash and cash equivalents with treasurer and other		7,034
Capital assets:		
Land and construction in progress	1,739	
Other capital assets, net of accumulated depreciation	71,108	
Net capital assets		72,847
Total assets		$86,818
Liabilities		
Current liabilities:		
Accounts payable	2,752	
Customer deposits	321	
Due to other:		
Governments	334	
Funds	227	
Others	73	
Total current liabilities		3,707
Noncurrent liabilities:		
Payable from restricted assets:		
Accounts payable	288	
Due to others	9	
Deferred revenue and other	664	
Accrued interest payable	658	
Accrued wages and benefits	218	
Accrued vacation and sick leave	628	
Notes payable	1,830	
Bonds and loans payable	64,796	
Total noncurrent liabilities		69,091
Total liabilities		72,798
Net Assets		
Invested in capital assets, net of related debt		6,221
Restricted for construction		6,737
Unrestricted		1,062
Total net assets		$14,020

Source: Adapted from a recent annual report of the City of Columbus, Ohio.

TABLE 7-15 Statement of Cash Flows—Enterprise Fund—City of Columbus, Ohio

City of Columbus, Ohio
Enterprise Fund
Electricity Fund
Statement of Cash Flows
December 31, 20X8
(amounts expressed in thousands)

Operating activities:		
Cash received from customers	$ 52,084	
Cash paid to employees	(7,563)	
Cash paid to suppliers	(37,813)	
Other receipts	842	
Other payments	(317)	
Net cash provided by operating activities		$ 7,233
Capital and related financing activities:		
Proceeds from sale of land	42	
Purchases of property, plant, and equipment	(5,114)	
Proceeds from issuance of bonds, loans, and notes	36,624	
Principal payments on bonds and loans	(52,799)	
Interest paid on bonds, loans, and notes	(1,900)	
Transfers in	2,000	
Net cash used in capital and related financing activities		(21,147)
Investing activities:		
Proceeds from maturity of investment securities	4,509	
Interest received on investments	827	
Net cash provided by investing activities		5,336
Decrease in cash and cash equivalents		(8,578)
Cash and cash equivalents at beginning of year (including restricted accounts)		15,954
Cash and cash equivalents at end of year (including restricted accounts)		$ 7,376
Reconciliation of operating income to net cash provided by operations:		
Operating income		$ 1,802
Adjustments to reconcile operating income to net cash provided by operating activities:		
Depreciation		4,412
Amortization, net		(109)
Decrease (increase) in operating assets and increase (decrease) in operating liabilities:		
Receivables		365
Due from other governments		148
Due from other funds		3
Inventory		(7)
Accounts payable		889
Customer deposits		(3)
Due to other funds		51

(continued)

| TABLE 7-15   Statement of Cash Flows—Enterprise Fund—City of Columbus, Ohio *(continued)* |

City of Columbus, Ohio
Enterprise Fund
Electricity Fund
Statement of Cash Flows
December 31, 20X8
(amounts expressed in thousands)

Deferred revenue	(185)
Accrued wages and benefits	(121)
Accrued vacation and sick leave	(12)
Net cash provided by operating activities	$ 7,233
Supplemental information:	
Change in fair value of investments	$ 36

Source: Adapted from a recent annual report of the City of Columbus, Ohio.

Use of Special Assessments

As we discussed in Chapter 6, special assessments are a means of financing services or capital improvements that benefit one group of citizens more than the general public. Taxpayers who receive the benefits of these activities are assessed for their share of the cost. Examples of special assessment activities include projects such as special police protection, paving streets, and building parking structures.

If a governmental unit wishes to charge a full-cost price for the services to determine the "true" subsidy provided to the citizens, an Enterprise Fund should be used to account for the service. Because the total economic resources measurement focus is used, this approach includes a calculation of a charge for depreciation, as applicable.

Use of an Enterprise Fund for service activities that are financed with special assessments results in entries similar to those previously presented in this chapter. The only major change is that the term *special assessment* is generally used to describe the receivable for the charge.

Review Questions

Q7-1   What is the cause-and-effect relationship between the revenues and expenses of a proprietary fund?

Q7-2   Why are the revenues and expenditures of governmental-type funds "independent" of each other?

Q7-3   When should an Internal Service Fund be used?

Q7-4   What is a flexible budget?

Q7-5   How does the fund balance (net assets) section of a balance sheet of a proprietary fund differ from that of a governmental-type fund?

Q7-6   Why is depreciation recorded as an expense in proprietary funds, but not as an expenditure in governmental-type funds?

Q7-7   What is the difference between an Enterprise Fund and an Internal Service Fund?

Q7-8 Does the accounting guidance issued by the Financial Accounting Standards Board apply to proprietary funds? Explain.

Q7-9 Contrast the accounting treatment for uncollectible accounts used in proprietary funds with that used by governmental-type funds.

Q7-10 What are revenue bonds? How do they differ from general obligation bonds?

Cases

C7-1 The City of Iota recently incorporated and, therefore, became a separate legal entity in Bosco County. As the first chief administrative officer, you have the task of determining how to account for three activities in which the government is involved.

    The first activity is a hotel-motel tax that is dedicated to providing resources for building a sports arena. The mayor, Phinius T. Bower, feels that these activities should be accounted for in a Capital Projects Fund. He remembers from his college days at Old War-Horse U. that Capital Projects Funds are used for construction of major fixed assets. After examining the situation, you find that the city has arranged temporary financing from the Only National Bank in Cut-Off. Permanent financing will be achieved through a bond issue when the project is completed.

    The second activity is a printing office. This office has extensive up-to-date facilities and prepares documents for the city. In addition, to help finance the cost of the equipment and operating costs, the city does private printing and copying for various companies and citizens. Mayor Bower suggests that you use a Special Revenue Fund for these activities because the revenues from the outside will be used for a specific purpose.

    The third activity is a central purchasing function. In order to ensure that the city obtains the best possible price for its supplies and equipment, all purchases must be made through the Purchasing Department. Mayor Bower feels that the city could also use its Purchasing Department for control purposes. He says that when he attended a meeting of mayors in Gulfberg last year, one of the speakers discussed controlling purchases through a centralized purchasing function.

    Write a report to the mayor that offers your suggestions for these items.

C7-2 You recently agreed to make a presentation to an accounting class at your alma mater. Your topic will be governmental financial reporting. Carefully review the financial statements for the Internal Service Funds (Tables 7-5 through 7-7), and contrast them with the statements prepared for the Capital Projects Funds (Tables 7-10 through 7-12). Identify similarities and differences between thsese statements as the basis for your presentation.

C7-3 Mary Ann LaPlace, the president of the city council of West Sunview, asked you to assist the council in setting the pricing policy for its only Internal Service Fund. The fund is the Motor Pool Fund, and its operations are similar to those described in the illustration in this chapter. Write a report to President LaPlace and outline the options the city has with respect to pricing the use of the vehicles in the Motor Pool Fund. After you complete your report, write a recommendation for one of your choices and justify it.

Ethics Case

EC7-1 Iber Township is in need of resources to finance its operations for the remainder of 2008. Poor internal control procedures under the previous administration created a serious funding problem for the new administration. Walter Buckhouse, the new mayor, feels that if he can get through the current year, he can develop a new budget and control future expenditures to create a surplus. After reviewing the township's financial statements, Buckhouse believes that the only possible source of money is borrowing from restricted assets in an Enterprise Fund. As the chief financial officer, you listen as Buckhouse discusses his plan with you. His main argument is his certainty that future surpluses from the township's operating budget will allow him to replace the borrowed funds in 3 to 5 years. How would you respond to the mayor?

Exercises

E7-1 (Interpreting the operating statement for an Internal Service Fund)
Angusville maintains a policy that its Internal Service Funds operate on a break-even basis; that is, revenues must equal expenses. Did the Motor Pool Fund illustrated in this chapter operate at a break-even level during 2008? Explain.

E7-2 (Journal entries for an Internal Service Fund)
The following transactions were incurred in establishing a central purchasing fund (an Internal Service Fund):

1. The General Fund made a permanent transfer of $100,000 to establish the fund.
2. The Purchasing Fund billed revenues of $200,000.
3. The Purchasing Fund incurred expenses of $300,000. *Hint:* Credit Cash for $250,000 and Accumulated depreciation for $50,000.
4. The General Fund subsidized the operations of the Purchasing Fund by transferring an additional $100,000 to the fund.

Required: Record the preceding entries and identify the fund(s) used.

E7-3 (Relationship of a fixed asset to depreciation)
Considering that the Motor Pool Fund illustrated in this chapter records the acquisition of an automobile by debiting an asset account, does the cost of that automobile ever enter into the determination of income? Explain.

E7-4 (Fill in the blanks)

1. An Internal Service Fund is used when goods and/or services are provided to _____ .
2. A budget that is based on the level of activity attained in a fund is called a _____ .
3. The _____ basis of accounting is used in Internal Service Funds.

4. A permanent transfer of equity to an Internal Service Fund is credited to _____ in the Internal Service Fund's balance sheet.

5. When an Internal Service Fund acquires a truck, the account that is debited is _____ .

E7-5   (True or false)

Indicate whether the following statements are true or false. For any false statement, indicate why it is false.

1. A direct cause-and-effect relationship exists between the revenues and expenses of an Internal Service Fund.

2. Internal Service Funds are used to account for activities that involve providing services and/or products to the general public.

3. Internal Service Funds use the modified accrual basis of accounting.

4. All capital contributions received by an Internal Service Fund are credited directly to the Net assets account.

5. A fixed budget is used to control an Internal Service Fund.

6. The budget is not usually recorded for an Internal Service Fund.

7. Fixed assets used in an Internal Service Fund are not reported in the fund-level statements.

8. Depreciation expense is not recorded in an Internal Service Fund that uses fixed assets.

9. A net change in fund balance is calculated for Internal Service Funds.

10. Internal Service Funds do not have restricted net assets accounts.

E7-6   (True or false)

Indicate whether the following statements are true or false. For any false statement, indicate why it is false.

1. Enterprise Funds are not used to account for the construction of major highways financed from tax revenues.

2. User charges must be assessed if an Enterprise Fund is to be used for accounting purposes.

3. Flexible budgets are used to control Enterprise Fund operations.

4. Depreciation is recorded in an Enterprise Fund.

5. Estimated bad debts are charged to an expense account in an Enterprise Fund.

6. Restricted assets are separately reported on an Enterprise Fund balance sheet.

E7-7   (Billings and collections between an Enterprise Fund and the General Fund)
A city used an Enterprise Fund to provide services to the General Fund and its citizens. A total of $50,000 was billed to the General Fund and collected 30 days later. Prepare the journal entries necessary to record this information and label the fund(s) used.

E7-8   (Closing entries for an Enterprise Fund)
The Municipal Park Fund for Possum Valley Township had the following pre-closing trial balance:

Possum Valley Township
Enterprise Fund
Municipal Park Fund
Preclosing Trial Balance
June 30, 2008

	Debits	Credits
Cash	$ 1,500	
Membership dues receivable	10,200	
Land	7,600	
Equipment	2,000	
Accumulated depreciation—equipment		$ 400
Accounts payable		500
Revenues from fees		14,000
Salaries expense	4,500	
Depreciation expense—equipment	300	
Utilities expense	400	
Miscellaneous expense	700	
Net assets	—	12,300
	$27,200	$27,200

Required: 1. Prepare the closing entry necessary at June 30, 2008.
2. Compute the components of net assets as they should be reported as of June 30, 2008.

E7-9 (Comparison of accounting for long-term debt and acquisition of fixed assets, using governmental-type funds and proprietary-type funds)

The Village of d'East acquired a computer for $300,000. The computer was financed through a bond issue. Prepare the journal entries necessary to record these events assuming the computer was acquired using (1) the General Fund and (2) an Enterprise Fund. Also label the fund(s) used.

E7-10 (Setting prices for an Internal Service Fund)

The City of York uses an Internal Service Fund to account for its motor pool activities. Based on the following information, calculate the price per trip that the Internal Service Fund needs to charge users of the motor pool during calendar year 2009 in order to break even:

Automobiles:
   The motor pool uses two sedans, each costing $25,000 and each estimated to have a five-year life when they were acquired in 2007.

Driver salaries:
   The motor pool has a driver-administrator, who earns $45,000 a year, and a driver who earns $35,000. The city uses a rate (to cover pensions and other payroll fringe benefits) of 30 percent for planning purposes.

Insurance:
   In 2009, the city purchased a 3-year automobile accident policy at a cost of $3,000.

Fuel and maintenance costs:
   Based on experience, the driver-administrator estimates that total fuel and maintenance costs for the year will be $5,000.

Billing units:

To simplify record-keeping, the Fund charges a fixed price per trip. York's budget office estimates that 800 trips will be taken in 2009.

E7-11 (Journal entries for an Internal Service Fund)

The City of York motor pool Internal Service Fund had the following transactions and events during January 2009. Using the data in exercise E7-10 where applicable, as well as the solution to the exercise, prepare journal entries to record the transactions.

1. Paid salaries for the month in cash (1/12 of $80,000)
2. Paid $600 cash for fuel and maintenance expenses.
3. Recorded depreciation expense for the month.
4. Recorded insurance expense for the month.
5. Accrued fringe benefits expense for the month.
6. Billed for motor vehicle services, as follows: General Fund, 70 trips; Water Enterprise Fund, 5 trips.

Problems

P7-1 (Journal entries and financial statements for an Internal Service Fund)

The following entries and financial statements relate to the City of Kachina Village. (Assume a voucher system is used.)

1. The General Fund made a $2 million transfer of cash to establish the Data Processing Fund (an Internal Service Fund). This fund will provide data-processing services to all governmental units for a fee.
2. The fund paid $1.9 million for a Tops computer.
3. Supplies costing $1,500 were purchased on credit.
4. Bills totaling $750,000 were sent to the various city departments.
5. Repairs to the computer were made at a cost of $2,400. A voucher was prepared for that amount.
6. Collections from the departments for services were $729,000.
7. Salaries of $200,000 were paid to the employees.
8. Vouchers totaling $2,900 were paid.
9. As of the end of the period, $300 of supplies had not been used.
10. Depreciation on the computer was $250,000.
11. The city charged the computer center $2,000 for the rental of office space and $500 for the rental of office equipment for the year. This amount was not paid at the end of the year.
12. Miscellaneous expenses not paid by the end of the year totaled $700. These amounts were owed to businesses outside the governmental unit.

Required: 1. Prepare the journal entries necessary to record the preceding information in the Data Processing Fund.
  2. Prepare a statement of revenues, expenses, and changes in net assets for the Data Processing Fund for 2008 and a statement of net assets as of December 31, 2008.

P7-2   (Journal entries for several funds)
The following transactions were incurred by the City of Mountain View. Record the journal entry (entries) necessary for each and identify the fund(s) used. If no entry is required, write "None" next to the transaction number.

1. The mayor hired a chief financial officer.
2. The Police Department ordered 10 cruisers at a cost of $14,000 each.
3. The Central Computer Fund billed the General Fund for $2,000 of services.
4. The Central Computer Fund acquired a computer at a cost of $450,000. The old computer was sold for $50,000; it originally cost $245,000 and had a book value of $45,000 at the time of the sale.
5. The fund used to account for the construction of a bridge over the Mississippi River received a progress billing from the contractor for $500,000. The bill, less an 8 percent retainage, was paid.
6. Interest of $100,000 and principal of $1,000,000 were paid on general obligation bonds. The bond indenture required a separate accounting for these types of transactions.
7. The police cruisers ordered in part 2 arrived. The total invoice cost was $139,000. This amount was paid to the dealer.
8. The city collected $200,000 of gasoline taxes. These taxes must be used to repair streets. A separate accounting is required.
9. The mayor was paid a salary of $5,000.
10. The General Fund budget was amended. The appropriation for supplies was increased $45,000.

P7-3   (Journal entries for several funds and statements for an Internal Service Fund)
The following transactions relate to City of Aaronsville for the fiscal year ended June 30, 2008:

1. The city established a Central Supplies Fund for the purpose of handling the acquisition and disbursement of supplies for the entire governmental unit. The General Fund made an initial capital contribution of $75,000 to the fund.
2. The Police Department ordered equipment at a total cost of $34,000.
3. The Central Supplies Fund purchased supplies for $29,000. This amount will be paid later.
4. The Debt Service Fund paid $120,000 of interest not previously recorded.
5. Central Supplies Fund billings to departments totaled $31,000. These supplies cost $25,000. Record the cost of the supplies as an expense: Cost of sales.
6. A Capital Projects Fund paid a contractor $100,000 for a previously submitted progress billing of $110,000. The difference between the billing and the amount paid is the retained percentage. The billing was properly recorded when received by the fund.
7. The Central Supplies Fund acquired office equipment for $2,000. A 90-day note was signed for that amount.
8. Collections from the departments by the Central Supplies Fund totaled $27,500.

9. Collections of current special assessments for debt service totaled $50,000.
10. Salaries paid to Central Supplies Fund employees were $22,500.
11. The Police Department equipment ordered in part 2 was delivered at a cost of $35,000. The invoice price will be paid later. Assume the excess was approved.
12. Depreciation on the office equipment of the Central Supplies Fund was $400.
13. Old office furniture used by the governmental unit was scrapped, with no cash received. The furniture originally cost $2,800.
14. The Central Supplies Fund paid $25,000 to various creditors outside the governmental unit.
15. Interest expense of $50 on the note payable was accrued by the Central Supplies Fund.

Required: 1. Prepare all the journal entries necessary to record the preceding transactions and identify the fund(s) used.
2. Prepare a statement of revenues, expenses, and changes in net assets for the Central Supplies Fund for fiscal 2007–2008 and a statement of net assets as of June 30, 2008.

P7-4   (Journal entries and financial statements for an Enterprise Fund)
The following transactions relate to the City of Ravensborough's Municipal Airport Fund for the fiscal year ended June 30, 2008:

1. The General Fund made a permanent contribution of $2 million for working capital to start a municipal airport. The city used part of that money, together with the proceeds from a $25 million revenue bond issue, to purchase an airport from a private company. The fair values of the assets and liabilities were as follows:

Accounts receivable	$ 8,000
Land	19,000,000
Buildings	5,000,000
Equipment	1,800,000
Accounts payable	(12,000)

The city purchased the airport for the fair market value of its net assets.
2. Airlines were billed $3,900,000 for rental rights to use ticket counters and landing and maintenance space. Of this amount, $3,890,000 is expected to be collectible.
3. Supplies totaling $4,500 were purchased on credit.
4. Collections from airlines totaled $3,850,000.
5. Salaries of $200,000 were paid to airport personnel employed by the city.
6. Utility bills totaling $100,000 were paid.
7. A notice was received from the Last District Bankruptcy Court. Air Lussa was declared bankrupt. The airport collected only $1,000 on its bill of $3,000.
8. The airport obtained $3 million of additional permanent contributions from the city to help finance improvements at the airport.

9. Interest of $1,825,000 was paid to the bondholders.

10. Supplies used during the year totaled $3,600.

11. The General Fund made an advance to the airport of $1,500,000. Airport management plans to repay the advance in full in 2011.

12. A contract was signed with The Construction Company for the new facilities for a total price of $5 million.

13. The Municipal Airport Fund invested $2 million in certificates of deposit.

14. The Municipal Airport Fund received $315,000 upon redeeming $300,000 of the certificates of deposit mentioned in part 13.

15. The airport purchased additional equipment for $300,000 cash.

16. Interest expense of $350,000 was accrued at the end of the year.

17. Other accrued expenses totaled $55,000.

18. Depreciation was recorded as follows:

Buildings	$500,000
Equipment	180,000

19. Paid $12,500 of Accounts payable.

20. Received $150,000 of interest revenue.

21. Excess cash of $4,500,000 was invested in certificates of deposit.

Required: 1. Prepare the journal entries necessary to record the preceding transactions in the Municipal Airport Fund.

2. Prepare a trial balance at June 30, 2008.

3. Prepare a statement of revenues, expenses, and changes in net assets for the 2007–2008 fiscal year and a statement of net assets as of June 30, 2008.

P7-5   (Computation of proprietary fund net assets)
Given below is the December 31, 2009, preclosing trial balance for the City of Argos Golf Course Enterprise Fund.

Required: Compute

1. Total net assets
2. Net assets invested in capital assets, net of related debt
3. Restricted net assets
4. Unrestricted net assets as of December 31, 2009

City of Argos
Golf Course Enterprise Fund
Preclosing Trial Balance
December 31, 2009

	Debits	Credits
Cash	$ 15,045	
Accounts receivable	37,000	
Estimated uncollectible accounts		$ 5,000
Cash—restricted for debt service	150,000	
Cash—restricted for customer deposits	23,000	
Land	900,000	
Equipment	325,000	

Accumulated depreciation—equipment		105,000
Buildings	1,500,000	
Accumulated depreciation—buildings		650,000
Accounts payable		20,000
Customers' deposits payable		23,000
Interest payable on customer deposits		835
Revenue bonds payable		1,000,000
Accrued interest payable—revenue bonds		6,500
Net assets		940,740
Revenue from rentals		800,000
Personal services expense	380,000	
Utilities expense	63,000	
Repairs and maintenance expense	47,000	
Depreciation expense—equipment	15,000	
Depreciation expense—building	50,000	
Interest expense	40,030	
Uncollectible accounts expense	5,000	
Supplies expense	1,000	
	$3,551,075	$3,551,075

P7-6 (Journal entries for several funds)

1. The city council of Bellview approved its General Fund budget for the year July 1, 2007–June 30, 2008. The budget contained the following: revenues, $3,500,000; transfers from other funds, $200,000; transfers to other funds, $500,000; and expenditures, $4,000,000. The city had a fund balance of $2,300,000 at the beginning of the year.

2. During the year, interest of $400,000 and principal of $2,000,000 were paid from resources accumulated for that purpose.

3. T. J. Construction submitted a progress billing for work done on a new city hall. The bill was for $800,000. This billing was for work done to the end of the year. Bonds were used to finance this project. The contract contained a 10 percent retainage clause.

4. The Airport Fund submitted a bill to the city and to Mid-West Airlines for $200,000 each. The bill was for landing fees for aircraft owned by the two entities.

5. The city sold surplus equipment. The equipment originally cost $45,000. Only $500 was received from the sale. There are no restrictions placed on the use of the $500.

6. The Airport Fund paid the bill received from T. J., less the 10 percent retainage.

7. Bellview paid the bill received from the Airport Fund.

8. Books R Us won a suit against the city. Bellview had attempted to revoke the store's license so that it could sell the land used by Books to a theater group. The court gave Books an award of $400,000. This amount will be paid from general tax revenues. An encumbrance was not set up.

9. A bridge over the East River was completed at a total cost of $5,000,000. In previous years, costs of $4,500,000 were recorded. The bridge was paid

for from bond proceeds. After paying all bills, including the retainage percentage, $200,000 remained in the construction fund. The bond indenture requires that this amount be transferred into the fund that will service the bonds.

10. The Electric Utility Fund paid $1,200,000 to contractors for various construction jobs currently in progress. This amount was not previously recorded. Assume encumbrance accounting is not used.

Required: Prepare the journal entries to record the preceding events and transactions. Identify each fund used.

P7-7 (Explanation of basis of accounting and fixed assets for different funds)
The accounting system of the municipality of Kemp is organized and operated on a fund basis. Among the types of funds used are a General Fund, a Special Revenue Fund, and an Enterprise Fund.

1. Explain the basic differences in revenue recognition between the accrual basis of accounting and the modified accrual basis of accounting, as it relates to governmental accounting.

2. What basis of accounting should be used in fund-level accounting for each of the following funds and why?

- General Fund
- Special Revenue Funds
- Enterprise Funds

3. How should fixed assets and long-term liabilities related to the General Fund and to the Enterprise Fund be accounted for in the funds?

(AICPA adapted)

P7-8 (Budget for an Internal Service Fund)
The City of Eagle Rock uses an Internal Service Fund to provide printing services to its various departments. It bills departments on the basis of an estimated rate per page of printed material, computed on the accrual basis of accounting. From the following information, compute the total cost that will be used to develop the cost per page. Assume that the equipment in item 6 was contributed by the city and that the pricing objective was to recoup the cost of equipment in the rate charged over the life of the equipment.

1. Inventory of paper on hand at beginning of year: $10,000.

2. Estimated paper purchases during the year: $60,000.

3. Estimated amount of paper to be consumed during the year: $55,000.

4. Estimated salaries to be paid during the year: $255,000.

5. Estimated salaries earned during the year, including both what was paid and what was owed at year end: $265,000.

6. Cost of equipment on hand at beginning of the year (estimated life was 10 years): $1,000,000.

P7-9 (Continuation of P7-8)
Assume the information presented in P7-8, except that the city did not contribute the equipment. Instead, the manager of the Internal Service Fund arranged to buy the equipment, paying for it over a period of 5 years. The

terms of the acquisition required annual payments of $200,000 at the end of each year, with interest of 8 percent on the unpaid balance. The first payment was made, and it is in the second year of operations. Assume also that the fund has just enough cash on hand to finance its working capital needs, such as inventory requirements. Using these assumptions, would you make a different calculation of the total cost to be recouped in the billing rate? If so, explain why you would make a different calculation and how it would change.

P7-10   (Journal Entries and Financial Statements for an Enterprise Fund)
The City of Paradise Falls is located in an attractive Sunbelt area of the country. It is experiencing a retiree population boom with an attendant increase in the demand for recreation facilities. Accordingly, the city plans to develop its first golf course during 2009 and account for it as the Golf Enterprise Fund (GEF). The course will be built on a parcel of land to be purchased from a private party. The planned out-of-pocket costs for the new course and their financing are as follows:

Spending:

Acquisition of land from private party	$ 500,000
Installation of sod, sprinklers, landscaping, and fencing	1,000,000
Construction of clubhouse	3,000,000
	$4,500,000

Financing:

Contribution from the General Fund	$1,500,000
Term revenue bonds, 8 percent, interest payable semiannually	3,000,000
	$4,500,000

The city plans to sell the bonds on February 1, 2009. Because the bonds are a term issue, bond principal matures in full February 1, 2019. Interest is payable each August 1 and February 1 beginning August 1, 2009. The bond covenant requires that assets equal to one-tenth of bond principal be transferred to a restricted account within the GEF on December 31 of each year. Paradise Falls observes a calendar fiscal year.

    Jewell Design and Construction, Inc., has been awarded the contract to develop the course due to Jewell's reputation for high-quality, on-time work. Construction will commence February 15, 2009, and be completed no later than May 31, in order that the course can open for business during June. The terms of the contract stipulate that progress billings from Jewell will be paid within 30 days of receipt, with 5 percent retainage held back pending final completion and official acceptance of the project. The city engineer will inspect the contractor's work and approve progress payments.

    Accounting for the GEF will be done by the city's existing accounting department (a General Fund department), which will bill the GEF for services rendered at the end of the year. To help the GEF get on its feet financially, no interfund payables will be settled in cash during 2009.

Required: a. Prepare the journal entries (including closing entries) necessary to record the following events and transactions related to the construction and operation of the golf course for the year ending December 31, 2009, in the Golf Enterprise Fund. The corresponding entries that would be made in other funds are not required.

b. Prepare the Statement of Net Assets and the Statement of Revenues, Expenses, and Changes in Net Assets for the Golf Enterprise Fund as of, and for the fiscal year ending, December 31, 2009.

Events and Transactions During 2009:

1. January 3, 2009: Paradise Falls formally established the GEF; the fund's first transaction was the receipt, in cash, of the capital contribution from the General Fund.
2. January 24: The city acquired the adjacent parcel of land from the private owner for the planned $500,000.
3. February 1: The revenue bonds were sold at par.
4. February 15: Development of the golf course itself and construction of the clubhouse commenced.
5. March 31: The first progress billing from Jewell, $1,800,000, was approved and vouchered in accordance with the terms of the contract. (Due to the short duration of the construction period, no construction in progress accounts will be used.) $400,000 of the amount billed represents the cost of sod, sprinklers, landscaping, and fencing (which the city classifies as "improvements other than buildings"). The balance applies to the cost of the clubhouse ("buildings").
6. April 25: The amount currently due Jewell was paid.
7. April 30: The second progress billing from Jewell, $1,500,000, was approved and vouchered; $600,000 applies to sod, sprinklers, landscaping, and fencing (which is now fully installed).
8. May 19: The amount currently due Jewell was paid.
9. May 23: Jewell's third and final progress billing, $700,000 (all of which represents clubhouse construction costs), was approved and vouchered.
10. The amount currently due Jewell was paid.
11. June 1: The new golf course was formally accepted by the city (without need for "touchup" work), and all remaining amounts due to Jewell were vouchered for payment.
12. June 1: Golf course maintenance equipment costing $300,000 was acquired via a 5-year 10 percent capital lease. The lease required no down payment. Lease payments are due quarterly, beginning September 1. The amortization table for the lease for the first six payments is as follows:

Due Date	Payment	Interest	Principal Reduction	Carrying Value
				$300,000
Sept. 1, 2009	$19,244	$7,500	$11,744	288,256
Dec. 1, 2009	19,244	7,206	12,038	276,218
Mar. 1, 2010	19,244	6,905	12,339	263,879
June 1, 2010	19,244	6,597	12,647	251,232
Sept. 1, 2010	19,244	6,281	12,963	238,269
Dec. 1, 2010	19,244	5,957	13,287	224,982

13. June 2: Pro shop inventory, $12,000, was acquired; the purchase was vouchered for payment.
14. June 4: The course opened for business. Green fees (charges for services) aggregated $209,000 for June. Pro shop sales amounted to $5,000. The golf course will not accept credit cards or other forms of credit (e.g., open accounts) until 2010.
15. June 30: Expenses for June were as follows:

Maintenance and pro shop labor (paid in cash)	48,000
Maintenance supplies (from the Parks Department—a Special Revenue Fund)	4,000
Water (supplied by the Paradise Falls water utility—an Enterprise Fund)	80,000
Pro shop cost of goods sold	2,200

(Charge all expenses to "Operating expenses—cost of sales and services.")

16. August 1: The first debt service payment on the revenue bonds was made.
17. September 1: The first payment on the lease was made.
18. December 1: The second lease payment was paid.
19. December 31: Green fee revenues for the second half of 2009 totaled $370,000; pro shop sales for the same period were $21,200.
20. December 31: Second-half 2009 expenses were:

Maintenance and pro shop labor (paid in cash)	$ 70,000
Maintenance supplies (from the Parks Department—a Special Revenue Fund)	4,000
Water (supplied by the Paradise Falls water utility—an Enterprise Fund)	80,000
Pro shop cost of goods sold	2,900
Accounting and administrative services provided by the city's accounting department (General Fund)	9,000
Total expenses	$165,900

21. December 31: Interest was accrued on the revenue bonds and the capital lease liability (make separate entries).
22. December 31: The GEF recorded depreciation for 2009 using the half-year convention. The building's useful life is estimated at 20 years (salvage value, $200,000) and will be depreciated straight line. Improvements other than buildings will be depreciated, straight line, over 10 years, with no salvage value. Equipment will be depreciated, straight line, over 5 years, with no salvage value.
23. The current portion of the capital lease liability was reclassified to a current liability to aid in balance sheet preparation.
24. December 31: The restricted asset account—"Cash restricted for bond principal retirement"—was established pursuant to the requirements of the bond covenant.

Continuous Problem

(Journal entries for several funds and a statement of revenues, expenses, and changes in net assets for an Internal Service Fund and an Enterprise Fund)

Leisure City has one Internal Service Fund, a central purchasing fund, and one Enterprise Fund, an electric utility fund. During 2008 the following events occurred:

1. Police Department salaries of $30,000 were paid.
2. The General Fund collected $100,000 of taxes previously levied against property holders in the city.
3. The Electric Fund mailed bills of $400,000 to the residents.
4. The Central Purchasing Fund ordered supplies for its inventory totaling $15,000.
5. Two years ago, the city began to construct several housing units. Currently the Iberville Street units are under construction. The contractor submitted a progress billing for $300,000. The total contract price was $1 million. Encumbrance accounting is used. Record the progress billing. Bonds were used to finance this project. The contract provides for a 5 percent retainage.
6. Salaries paid to Electric Fund and Central Purchasing Fund employees totaled $130,000 and $10,000, respectively.
7. Collections of electric bills were $385,000.
8. The Electric Fund issued $150,000 of 2-year notes.
9. The Central Purchasing Fund acquired various pieces of office equipment for cash, $55,000.
10. The Central Purchasing Fund billed the Electric Fund $20,000; the cost of the supplies was $19,000.
11. To provide funds for the construction of new housing units on Fifth Street, $1,500,000 of general obligation bonds were issued.
12. Other operating expenses of the Electric Fund were $150,000. Of this amount, $130,000 was paid in cash.
13. Homeowners were billed $12,000 for electric service.
14. Depreciation on Central Purchasing Fund equipment totaled $5,500.
15. The Central Purchasing Fund invested $25,000 in interest-bearing notes.
16. Depreciation on plant and equipment for the Electric Fund was $50,000.
17. Supplies ordered by the Internal Service Fund in part 4 were received. The actual cost was $14,000.
18. Interest accrued on Central Purchasing Fund investments totaled $250.

Required: 1. Prepare all the journal entries necessary to record these transactions; identify the fund(s) involved.
2. Prepare a statement of revenues, expenses, and changes in net assets for the Electric Fund and the Central Purchasing Fund for 2008. (Assume that the beginning net assets in the Electric Fund and the Central Purchasing Fund were $31,400 and $15,000, respectively.)

CHAPTER

8

THE GOVERNMENTAL FUND ACCOUNTING CYCLE

Fiduciary Funds

Chapter Outline

After completing this chapter, you should be able to:

- Distinguish between employer government pension accounting and Pension Trust Fund accounting.
- Understand the basic types of pension plans.
- Understand the role of actuaries in pension accounting.
- Understand how pension contributions and pension costs are calculated.
- Explain why and how Pension Trust Funds are used in governmental accounting.
- Prepare the journal entries normally used in Pension Trust Funds.
- Prepare financial statements for Pension Trust Funds.
- Explain why and how Investment Trust Funds are used in governmental accounting.
- Prepare the journal entries normally used in Investment Trust Funds.
- Prepare financial statements for Investment Trust Funds.
- Explain why and how Private Purpose Trust Funds are used in governmental accounting.
- Prepare the journal entries normally used in Private Purpose Trust Funds.
- Prepare financial statements for Private Purpose Trust Funds.
- Explain why and how Agency Funds are used in governmental accounting.
- Prepare the journal entries normally used in Agency Funds.
- Prepare a financial statement for Agency Funds.

One definition of the word *fiduciary* is "a person to whom property or power is entrusted for the benefit of another."[1] In government, fiduciary funds are used to account for assets held in a trustee or agency capacity for entities outside the government. The assets of fiduciary funds, therefore, cannot be used to finance the

---

[1]*Random House Webster's College Dictionary*, p. 495. New York: Random House, 1991.

government's own programs. The four types of funds included in this fund category are Employee Pension Trust Funds, Investment Trust Funds, Private Purpose Trust Funds, and Agency Funds. The first three fund types involve establishing a formal (and usually long-lived) trust relationship between the government and the party(ies) at interest. Agency funds, in contrast, are used in situations in which a government takes only custodial responsibility of resources belonging to others, usually for a comparatively short time.

We will discuss the various accounting and financial reporting aspects of these funds in this chapter. An informed discussion of Pension Trust Funds, however, requires understanding of how governments account for and report the contributions they make to pension plans. Thus, we preface our illustration of Pension Trust Funds with a discussion of the basics of employer pension accounting and reporting.

OVERVIEW OF EMPLOYER GOVERNMENT PENSION ACCOUNTING

Most governments provide retirement benefits for their employees by making periodic payments (contributions) to pension plans. The employees receiving pension coverage can be defined as narrowly as the employees of a particular department of a governmental unit, or as broadly as the employees of an entire state. The expenditures (or expenses) associated with employers' contributions to the pension plans generally are recorded in the particular funds from which the employees are paid.[2] The authoritative guidance for employer government pension accounting is found in GASB *Statement No. 27,* "Accounting for Pensions by State and Local Governmental Employers."

It is important to understand that Pension Trust Funds are maintained only by governments that *sponsor* a pension plan. That is, while every government that provides pension benefits to its employees makes pension contributions, governments that do not sponsor pension plans make their contributions to external pension plans that may have dozens or hundreds of participating member governments. The authoritative guidance for pension trust fund accounting and reporting is found in GASB *Statement No. 25,* "Financial Reporting for Defined Benefit Pension Plans and Note Disclosures for Defined Contribution Plans."

Types of Pension Plans

Pension plans can be grouped in two major categories: defined contribution plans and defined benefit plans. Defined contribution plans are retirement plans that do not guarantee specific benefits. Instead, the employee's retirement benefits are determined when he or she retires, based on the amount accumulated in the plan. In most instances, the government and the employees contribute to both types of plans, but any combination of relative contributions is possible.

Because benefits are not guaranteed under a defined contribution plan, the government's obligation to a plan member depends only on the amount contributed to the member's account, earnings on investments of those contributions, and forfeitures of contributions made for other members that may be allocated to the member's

---

[2]Many governments offering pension benefits to their employees require their employees to contribute to their pension plans through payroll deductions. Employee pension contributions are accounted for in the same fashion as any other payroll deduction. For simplicity, we focus only on employers' pension contributions in this discussion.

account.[3] Contributions made by the government are expenses or expenditures of the period and, if the amount required is paid to the plan, the governmental unit has no further obligation. Disclosures required for defined contribution plans are minimal.

Defined benefit plans are retirement plans that guarantee the specific dollar amounts of benefits when employees retire. These benefits are usually determined by a formula. A relatively common formula is one that gives employees a specific percentage credit (e.g., 2 percent) of their average salary over some period, such as the employee's 3 highest-paid years. This credit would be computed as follows: Assume an employee works for 25 years and her highest 3 consecutive years' salaries are $45,000, $47,000, and $49,000—an average of $47,000. Using the formula, she would be entitled to retirement benefits of $23,500 ($47,000 × 25 × .02) per year. Defined benefit plans are common in local government, so we focus on them here.

The Role of Actuaries

The calculations necessary to administer defined benefit pension plans are quite complex because they require a number of economic and demographic assumptions, such as investment returns, projected salary increases, mortality rates, and terminations before employees obtain vested pension rights. *Actuaries* normally are called on to make these calculations. Actuaries are professionals with particular expertise in computing the costs of long-term business risks. The financial evaluations of risk provided by actuaries are essential to the successful operations of insurance companies and pension plans. As such, governments normally rely on the advice of actuaries in making pension-related decisions. Actuaries develop their recommendations, plan by plan, by performing *actuarial valuations*, usually annually or biennially. (Actuarial measures of assets and liabilities are not necessarily equivalent to accounting measures of assets and liabilities.)

Technical Differences in the Structure of Pension Plans

In practice, a pension plan will have one of the following structures: sole-employer, agent multi-employer, or cost sharing. According to the GASB, "sole and agent employers are individually responsible for the accumulation of sufficient plan net assets to pay the actuarial accrued liabilities for benefits to their employees as they come due."[4] Thus, the required pension contribution rates for such employers are unique in each case. In contrast, in cost-sharing plans, "the actuarial accrued liabilities of the various employers are shared, and the plan net assets are pooled and are available to pay the shared actuarial accrued liabilities as they come due."[5] As a result, the contribution rate as a percentage of payroll is the same for all employers participating in the plan.

The significance of these distinctions to our discussion is that *annual pension cost* is measured differently for sole-employer governments and governments participating in agent multi-employer plans than it is for governments participating in cost-sharing plans. Moreover, governments participating in cost-sharing plans legally are

---

[3]GASB Cod. Sec. Pe5.533.

[4]GASB 2006–2007 Comprehensive Implementation Guide, Chapter 5—Pensions—Employer and Plan Accounting and Reporting, answer to question 5.2.5.

[5]Ibid.

obligated to make their annual contributions in full as specified by the plan administrator; sole-employer governments and governments participating in agent multi-employer plans have flexibility to contribute less in a given year than the actuarially recommended amount—a practice that can cause the pension plan to be severely underfunded.

Employer Accounting for Defined Benefit Pension Contributions

As mentioned, every government that offers pension benefits to its employees makes pension contributions, but pension trust funds are used only by governments that sponsor a pension plan. Governments that do not sponsor a pension plan participate in external plans administered for several—or many—governments. Table 8-1 provides an overview of the operations of external pension plans and internal pension plans. Notice that, regardless of whether the pension plan is external or internal to an employer government, that government generally records its contributions to the pension plan as expenditures/expenses in the same funds in which it records other payroll-related expenditures/expenses (for example, the General Fund, a water utility Enterprise Fund).

Notice, also, that an employer government is required always to make pension-related disclosures in its annual financial report. The nature and extent of these disclosures depends on the nature of the pension plan. Finally, notice that, when a government participates in an external pension plan only, financial statements for the pension plan are issued by the plan and not the participating government. In contrast, when an employer government also sponsors a pension plan, that government maintains a Pension Trust Fund to account for the receipt, investment, and disbursement of pension contributions and will prepare annual financial statements for the fund.

Computing the Pension Contribution

One of the most fundamental pension-related decisions a government faces each year is how much money it should contribute to the pension plan. Fortunately, a pension plan's actuarial valuation provides the "right" answer—even though the actuary makes many assumptions and considers a variety of options—whether the plan is external to the government or sponsored by the government. That is, if a government contributes the entire amount recommended by the actuary for the year, that government will meet its current obligation to provide pension benefits to its employees.

In practice, however, governments sometimes make annual pension contributions in amounts less than those recommended by actuaries. In such cases, the entire amount of the required contribution will be recorded in proprietary funds as pension expense and an accrued liability will be recorded for the excess of expense over cash contributed. In governmental-type funds, though, consistent with the current financial resources measurement focus, the amount of expenditure recognized will be equal to the amount contributed to the plan or expected to be liquidated with expendable available financial resources.

Regardless of the fund type involved, a government's failure to contribute the annual required amount to a pension plan gives rise to a "net pension obligation" (NPO), which must be disclosed in the notes to the financial statements and reported as a liability in the *government-wide* statement of net assets. Additionally, as we will see in the next section, the existence of an NPO has a direct influence on required pension contributions in subsequent years.

TABLE 8-1   Defined Benefit Pension Plan Arrangements—External versus Government-Sponsored

Pension Plan Is External to the Employer Government

| **Funds of Employer Government** | | The funds of the employer government that record payroll expenditures/expenses also make contributions to the external pension plan on behalf of covered employees. | 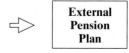 | **External Pension Plan** |

The various funds account for pension contributions as payroll-related expenditures/expenses.

The employer government makes pension-plan disclosures in the notes to the financial statements.

The pension plan issues financial statements and makes extensive disclosures.

Pension Plan Is Sponsored by the Employer Government

Funds of Employer Government

⇩

Pension Trust Fund

The funds of the employer government account for pension contributions as payroll-related expenditures/expenses, not interfund transfers.

The employer government makes additional pension-related disclosures in the notes to the financial statements.

The pension trust fund receives the pension contributions from the various employer funds and accounts for them as "Additions—contributions from employer."

The pension trust fund prepares fund-level financial statements that are included in the employer government's annual financial report.

Additional arrangements found in practice include the following and combinations thereof:

■ The government sponsors a pension plan for a specific employee group, such as uniformed public safety employees, and participates in an external pension plan for the remainder of the workforce eligible for pension coverage.

■ The government sponsors a pension plan in which other governments participate.

Annual Pension Cost (APC)

Annual pension cost is an important concept because it represents the economic cost to a government of providing pension coverage for its employees in a given year. Indeed, employer governments should report pension expense for the year equal to their annual pension cost in the government-wide financial statements.[6] We discuss government-wide financial reporting in depth in Chapters 9 and 10.

Sole-Employer and Agent Multi-Employer Plans

For governments either sponsoring a sole-employer pension plan or participating in an agent multi-employer plan, *annual pension cost* in the simplest case is equal to its *annual required contribution* (ARC), as determined by the actuarial valuation. The ARC has two components, normal cost and amortization of the unfunded actuarially accrued liability, and is calculated using one of several acceptable actuarial funding methods. The normal cost is generally the present value of the pension benefit earned by each employee for the year. The unfunded actuarial accrued liability results from a variety of factors, such as previous underfunding and benefit increases attributable to earlier years of service that have not yet been fully funded. The ARC will change with each actuarial valuation because of turnover in the government's workforce, revisions to actuarial assumptions, and other factors.

As mentioned in the preceding section, if, in any prior year, the government has contributed less than the ARC for that year, it will have a net pension obligation (NPO). In such a case, the annual pension cost will include three elements: (1) the ARC, (2) interest on the NPO, and (3) an adjustment to the ARC. If the NPO is positive (a net liability), interest is added to the calculation and the adjustment to the ARC is deducted. If the NPO is negative (a net asset), interest is deducted from the calculation and the ARC adjustment is added. A more detailed discussion of how the APC is calculated is beyond the scope of this text.

Cost-Sharing Plans

The annual pension cost to a government participating in a cost-sharing pension plan is much more straightforwardly calculated. The cost is equal to the contractually required contribution as determined by the plan administrator (based on an actuarial valuation).

Pension-Related Note Disclosures

GASB *Statement No. 27* requires extensive note disclosure by governments that provide pension benefits to their employees. Disclosures required of all employer governments include:

- A detailed description of the pension plan, including the types of benefits it provides, and whether the pension plan issues a financial report.
- The authority under which obligations to contribute to the plan are established, the required contribution rates of active plan members, and the required contribution rates of employers.[7]

---

[6]GASB Cod. Sec. P20.115. (Note, however, that the limitations of modified accrual accounting could result in reporting a smaller pension expenditure in fund financial statements should the government contribute less than the ARC, as described in the next paragraph.)

[7]GASB Cod. Sec. P20.117.

Additional disclosures required of employer governments participating in sole-employer or agent multi-employer plans include:

- Annual pension cost and the dollar amount of contributions made for the current year. If the employer has an NPO, the employer also should disclose the components of annual pension cost (ARC, interest on the NPO, and adjustment to the ARC), the increase or decrease in the NPO, and the NPO at the end of the year.
- Annual pension cost, percentage of annual pension cost contributed that year, and NPO at the end of the year—for the current year and each of the two preceding years.
- Date of the actuarial valuation and identification of the actuarial methods and significant assumptions used to determine the ARC for the current year.[8]

FIDUCIARY-TYPE FUNDS: PENSION TRUST FUNDS

Pension trust fund activities are controlled by pension agreements and local and state laws. These laws cover the operations of retirement systems in general and individual pension plans in particular. They vary in scope, ranging from laws that limit the types of investments that can be made with fund assets to laws that require specified periods of service before employees can qualify for pension benefits.

The financial statements of Pension Trust Funds include a statement of plan net assets and a statement of changes in plan net assets. The financial statements are prepared using the economic resources measurement focus and the full accrual basis of accounting, with the exception that plan liabilities for benefits and refunds should be recognized when due and payable in accordance with the terms of the plan. This exception does not mean that the liabilities as reported are only current liabilities. It is possible for a plan to report some noncurrent liabilities such as a mortgage loan or a capital lease. Pension trust funds account for their investments at fair value. Notice that a statement of cash flows is not prepared.

Operating Entries

For illustrative purposes, assume that the City of Angusville has had a Pension Trust Fund in operation for several years. The Pension Trust Fund trial balance as of December 31, 2008, is presented in Table 8-2.

The following transactions took place during 2008. Investment income of $500,000 is received in cash. This amount includes income accrued at the beginning of the year: $55,000. This investment income is recorded as follows:

Cash	500,000	
Interest receivable		55,000
Additions—interest on investments		445,000
To record the receipt of interest from investments.		

---

[8]GASB Cod. Sec. P20.118.

TABLE 8-2   Trial Balance—Pension Trust Fund

City of Angusville
Pension Trust Fund
Public Employees' Retirement System
Trial Balance
December 31, 2008

	Debits	Credits
Cash	$ 15,000	
Interest receivable	55,000	
Investments—U.S. government securities	2,000,000	
Investments—corporate stocks	3,067,000	
Building	500,000	
Accumulated depreciation—building		$ 100,000
Equipment	50,000	
Accumulated depreciation—equipment		10,000
Accounts payable		65,000
Net assets held in trust for pension benefits		5,512,000
	$5,687,000	$5,687,000

When retirement benefits of $230,000 are paid, a "deduction" is recorded:

Deductions—retirement benefits	230,000	
Cash		230,000
To record retirement benfits.		

Some Pension Trust Funds have their own administrative staffs. In other instances the operating costs of a Pension Trust Fund are borne by the General Fund, and no operating costs appear on the financial statements of the Pension Trust Fund. In our illustration, however, we assume that General Fund employees administer the Pension Trust Fund and that the Pension Trust Fund reimburses the General Fund for its share of the accounting and investment management costs. If accounting costs are $12,000 and investment management costs amount to $8,000, the following entries are made in the Pension Trust Fund and General Fund, respectively:

Deductions—administrative costs	12,000	
Deductions—investment management costs	8,000	
Due to General Fund		20,000
To record operating costs for the current year.		
Due from Pension Trust Fund	20,000	
Expenditures—administrative costs		12,000
Expenditures—investment management costs		8,000
To record reimbursement of operating costs from Pension Trust Fund.		

Investment income of $50,000 earned but not received at the end of the year is recorded as follows:

Interest receivable	50,000	
Additions—interest on investments		50,000
To record interest earned but not received.		

Dividends received during the year from investments are recorded as follows:

Cash	10,000	
Additions—dividends		
To record dividends received during the year.		10,000

Assume that sales of investments in corporate stocks result in a gain of $10,000 and the amount collected from these sales is $50,000.

Cash	50,000	
Investments—corporate stocks		40,000
Additions—net appreciation in fair value of		
investments		10,000
To record the sale of investments.		

Assuming the value of the investment portfolio increased by $25,000, the following entry is made to write up the carrying amount of fund investments:

Investments—corporate stocks	25,000	
Additions—net appreciation in fair value of		
investments		25,000
To record increase in fair value of investments.		

Notice that the realized gains and the unrealized gains are reported in a single account called Additions—net appreciation in fair value of investments. If losses were involved, the net amount would be reported. The realized gains and losses may be separately disclosed in the notes to the financial statements, subject to certain restrictions imposed by the GASB. For financial reporting purposes, investments must be grouped by type.

During the year, the fund incurred maintenance costs on its building totaling $5,000 and purchased computer equipment at a cost of $30,000. Depreciation on all of the equipment owned by the Pension Trust Fund is $1,000, plus $10,000 for the building. These expenses are recorded as follows:

Deductions—building maintenance costs	5,000	
Cash		5,000
To record building maintenance costs.		

Equipment	30,000	
Cash		30,000
To record purchase of equipment.		

Deductions—depreciation on equipment	1,000	
Deductions—depreciation on building	10,000	
Accumulated depreciation—equipment		1,000
Accumulated depreciation—building		10,000
To record depreciation for the year.		

During the year additional administrative costs of $15,000 are incurred. These are recorded as follows:

Deductions—administrative costs	15,000	
Accounts payable		15,000
To record accrued administrative expenses.		

Payments on accounts payable during the year are recorded as follows:

Accounts payable	75,000	
Cash		75,000
To record payments on accounts payable.		

The retirement plan illustrated requires equal contributions by the employees and the government. When the amount of each contribution is determined, $200,000 in this case, the following entry is made:

Due from General Fund	400,000	
Additions—pension contributions—		
plan members		200,000
Additions—pension contributions—		
employer		200,000
To record amount due from the General Fund		
for pension contributions.		

In this illustration, we assume that the General Fund is the only fund that is financing pension expenditures. If any other funds become involved, a separate receivable is established for each fund. Collections from the General Fund of $400,000 are recorded as follows:

Cash	400,000	
Due from General Fund		400,000
To record payment received from the General Fund.		

The entries on the books of the General Fund are (amounts assumed):

Expenditures—personal services	997,000	
Due to U.S. government		120,000
Due to Pension Trust Fund		200,000
Cash		677,000
To record payroll and the liability for the		
employees' share of pension contributions.		
Expenditures—retirement benefits	200,000	
Due to Pension Trust Fund		200,000
To record employer's pension contribution.		
Due to Pension Trust Fund	400,000	
Cash		400,000
To record payment to Pension Trust Fund.		

If cash of $600,000 is invested in corporate stocks, the entry to record this investment on the books of the Pension Trust Fund is as follows:

Investments—corporate stocks	600,000	
Cash		600,000
To record investment.		

The preceding summary entries are sufficient to illustrate the activities typically accounted for by a Pension Trust Fund. The preclosing trial balance for the fund as of the end of the fiscal year is shown in Table 8-3.

TABLE 8-3   Preclosing Trial Balance—Pension Trust Fund

City of Angusville
Pension Trust Fund
Public Employees' Retirement System
Preclosing Trial Balance
December 31, 2008

	Debits	Credits
Cash	$ 35,000	
Interest receivable	50,000	
Investments—U.S. government securities	2,000,000	
Investments—corporate stocks	3,652,000	
Building	500,000	
Accumulated depreciation—building		$ 110,000
Equipment	80,000	
Accumulated depreciation—equipment		11,000
Due to General Fund		20,000
Accounts payable		5,000
Net assets held in trust for pension benefits		5,512,000
Additions—interest on investments		495,000
Additions—net appreciation in fair value of investments		35,000
Additions—dividends		10,000
Additions—pension contributions—employer		200,000
Additions—pension contributions—plan members		200,000
Deductions—retirement annuities	230,000	
Deductions—administrative costs	27,000	
Deductions—investment management costs	8,000	
Deductions—building maintenance	5,000	
Deductions—depreciation on equipment	1,000	
Deductions—depreciation on building	10,000	
	$6,598,000	$6,598,000

Closing Entry

At the end of the accounting period the books must be closed and financial statements prepared. The following closing entry is generally used for Pension Trust Funds:

Additions—interest on investments	495,000	
Additions—net appreciation in fair market value of investments	35,000	
Additions—dividends		10,000
Additions—pension contributions—employer	200,000	
Additions—pension contributions—plan members	200,000	
Deductions—retirement annuities		230,000
Deductions—administrative costs		27,000
Deductions—investment management costs		8,000
Deductions—building maintenance		5,000
Deductions—depreciation on equipment		1,000
Deductions—depreciation on building		10,000
Net assets held in trust for pension benefits		659,000
To close the nominal accounts for 2008.		

TABLE 8-4   Statement of Changes in Fiduciary Fund Net Assets—Pension Trust Fund

City of Angusville
Pension Trust Fund
Public Employees' Retirement System
Statement of Changes in Fiduciary Fund Net Assets
For the Year Ending December 31, 2008

Additions		
Contributions		
Employer	$200,000	
Plan members	200,000	
Total contributions		$400,000
Investment income		
Interest income	495,000	
Net appreciation in fair value of investments	35,000	
Dividends	10,000	
	540,000	
Less investment expense	(8,000)	
Net investment income		532,000
Total additions		932,000
Deductions		
Benefits	230,000	
Administrative costs	27,000	
Building maintenance	5,000	
Depreciation on equipment	1,000	
Depreciation on buildings	10,000	
Total deductions		273,000
Change in net assets		659,000
Net assets held in trust for pension benefits—beginning of year		5,512,000
Net assets held in trust for pension benefits—end of year		$6,171,000

Financial Statements Illustration

The individual financial statements for Pension Trust Funds are a statement of changes in fiduciary net assets and a statement of fiduciary net assets. These statements are illustrated in Tables 8-4 and 8-5. The GASB also requires two supplementary schedules for defined benefit pension plans. These two schedules are (1) a schedule of funding progress (see Table 8-6) and (2) a schedule of employer contributions (see Table 8-7).

The schedule of funding progress helps financial statement users determine whether the financial status of the pension trust fund is improving over time. This schedule reports the trend in the funded ratio (actuarial value of assets [AVA] divided by actuarial accrued liability [AAL]). The schedule also shows the trend in the unfunded actuarial accrued liability (UAAL) as a percentage of covered payroll. (The UAAL is simply the difference between the AAL and the AVA.) As a general rule, the financial status of the pension fund is improving if the first ratio increases over time and if the second ratio decreases.

TABLE 8-5   Statement of Fiduciary Fund Net Assets—Pension Trust Fund

City of Angusville
Pension Trust Fund
Public Employees' Retirement System
Statement of Fiduciary Fund Net Assets
December 31, 2008

Assets		
Cash	$ 35,000	
Interest receivable	50,000	
Investments, at fair value	5,652,000	
Building (less accumulated depreciation, $110,000)	390,000	
Equipment (less accumulated depreciation, $11,000)	69,000	
Total assets		$6,196,000
Liabilities		
Due to General Fund	20,000	
Accounts payable	5,000	
Total liabilities		25,000
Net assets held in trust for pension benefits		$6,171,000

TABLE 8-6   Schedule of Funding Progress

City of Angusville
Pension Trust Fund
Public Employees' Retirement System
Schedule of Funding Progress
December 31, 2003–2008
(amounts in thousands)

Actuarial Valuation Date	Actuarial Value of Assets	Actuarial Accrued Liability (AAL)— Entry Age	Unfunded AAL (UAAL)	Funded Ratio	Covered Payroll	UAAL as a Percentage of Covered Payroll
12/31/03	$5,000	$5,750	$750	87.0%	$ 998	75.2%
12/31/04	5,100	5,800	700	87.9	997	70.2
12/31/05	5,350	6,100	750	87.7	995	75.4
12/31/06	5,700	6,300	600	90.5	998	60.1
12/31/07	6,000	6,400	400	93.8	1,000	40.0
12/31/08	6,200	6,500	300	95.4	997	30.1

Notice that in developing these ratios, actuarial, not accounting, information is used. Actuaries generally "smooth" changes in market values of investments over periods of 3–5 years. The AAL is generally a by-product of the method used by the actuary to compute the funding requirement for a particular pension plan. It provides a rough measure of the present value of the pension benefit earned to date by retired and active members of the plan. A key element in calculating the AAL is the investment

TABLE 8-7   Schedule of Employer Contributions

City of Angusville
Pension Trust Fund
Public Employees' Retirement System
Schedule of Employer Contributions
December 31, 2008

Year Ended	Annual Required Contribution	Percentage Contributed
2003	$197,000	100.0%
2004	193,000	100.0
2005	197,500	100.0
2006	202,000	100.0
2007	197,000	100.0
2008	200,000	100.0

earnings assumption (discount rate)—the plan's estimated long-term investment yield. Thus, the higher the investment earnings assumption used by the actuary, the lower the AAL. Also, the AAL is not a uniform measure of the earned pension benefit, because the AAL would be different for different actuarial funding methods. Thus, the trend in funded ratio is useful for measuring the status of the trust fund itself, but is less useful for comparing the funded status of one plan against another.

The 6-year schedule of employer contributions shows how the amounts contributed to the pension system compare each year with the annual required contributions (ARC), calculated in accordance with the requirements discussed on page 285. The percentages might differ from 100 percent if the ARC differs from the actuary's recommendations or if the employers do not contribute the ARC.

The notes to the financial statements for defined benefit plans must include (1) a description of the plan, (2) a summary of significant accounting policies, (3) information about contributions and reserves, and (4) identification of concentrations of investments in certain organizations.

Financial Reporting for Defined Contribution Plans

Under defined contribution plans, the governmental unit does not commit itself to paying specified benefits but merely to making payments from the amount accumulated for the employee or distributing the total amount to the employee for his/her investment. The governmental unit does not have a specified liability, so financial reporting for these plans is much simpler. For these types of plans, the GASB requires notes disclosing the following: (1) a description of the plan, (2) a summary of significant accounting policies, and (3) identification of concentrations of investments in certain organizations.

Other Postemployment Benefits (OPEB)

The GASB recently issued two standards that specifically address issues related to other postemployment benefits, such as health care benefits that some governments offer their retirees. The perspectives of these new standards are similar to the perspective that the GASB employed for pensions. GASB *Statement No. 45,* "Accounting and Financial Reporting by Employers for Postemployment Benefits Other Than Pensions," deals with accounting for other postemployment benefits by employer governments. GASB *Statement No. 43*, "Financial Reporting for Postemployment Benefit Plans Other Than Pension Plans,"addresses other postemployment benefits accounting and reporting from the standpoint of entities that administer such benefits. Moreover, the requirements of GASB *Statements Nos. 45* and *43* are similar in substance to their counterpart pension standards, *Statements Nos. 27* and *25*.

It is important to point out, however, that there is a major difference in how pension benefits and OPEB benefits are financed. Most employers finance pension benefits during the working lives of their employees (resulting in the accumulation of significant amounts of assets in pension trust funds), but they generally *do not* finance OPEB benefits that way. Instead, most employers finance OPEB benefits on a cash basis—after their employees retire.

Unfortunately, the means of financing OPEB benefits has a major effect on the fund financial statements. For proprietary-type funds, as stated on page 283, the annual expense, calculated on the accrual basis of accounting, is shown in the employer's operating statement and the unpaid expense is reported as a liability. For governmental-type funds, however, the amount reported as the OPEB expenditure is "the amount contributed to the plan or expected to be liquidated with expendable available financial resources." Hence, the amount reported in governmental-type funds may be the (modified accrual basis) amount paid on behalf of retired employees after they retire, rather than the (accrual basis) OPEB benefit earned by current working employees. Further, at transition to the OPEB standard (effective between 2007 and 2009, depending on the size of the government), employers may report the accumulated OPEB obligation either gradually or all at once.

To illustrate, New York City implemented GASB *Statement No. 45* early. Its 2006 General Fund financial statements report OPEB expenditures of $2.2 billion—$1.2 billion payments on behalf of already retired employees and a $1.0 billion contribution to a trust fund to start financing its accumulated OPEB obligation. The OPEB expense applicable to current employees in 2006, however, was $3.1 billion, not including interest on the unfunded obligation. Notes to the financial statements show that the present value of the city's OPEB obligation was $53.5 billion in 2006. In short, for most governmental employers, the reader must look to the accrual-basis government-wide statements (see Chapter 10) and to the note disclosures for more complete data on OPEB expenses/expenditures and liabilities.

GOVERNMENTAL ACCOUNTING IN PRACTICE
The City of Baton Rouge and Parish of East Baton Rouge Employees' Retirement System

The City of Baton Rouge and the Parish of East Baton Rouge, Louisiana, accounts for its employees' retirement system (the System) using GASB *Statement No. 25*. Tables 8-8 through 8-11 illustrate the financial statements and supporting schedules described in this chapter for the System. Notice that the System identifies the major classes of investments on its statement of plan net assets. These investments have a broad base, from U.S. government obligations to real estate. Strict rules govern what types of investments are permissible. These rules are described in the notes to the statements and include, among other provisions, a prohibition against the use of certain types of investments and a limit on the size of an investment that can be held in any individual organization. The Pending trades and Pending trades payable reported on the statement of plan net assets represent the receivable (payable) related to trades made by the System. Purchases and sales of investments are recorded on a "trade date" basis. Because the final accounting is determined on the "settlement date," usually three business days later, an asset or liability account results.

The statement of changes in plan net assets format presented in Table 8-8 is exactly like that presented in the text. In addition, Tables 8-10 and 8-11 present the supplementary schedules as required by GASB *Statement No. 25*.

TABLE 8-8 Statement of Changes in Fiduciary Net Assets—Pension Trust Fund—City of Baton Rouge and Parish of East Baton Rouge

City of Baton Rouge and
Parish of East Baton Rouge
Employees' Retirement System
Statement of Changes in Fiduciary Fund Net Assets
For the Years Ended December 31, 20X9 and 20X8

	20X9 Combined Total	20X8 Combined Total
Additions:		
Contributions:		
Employee	$ 8,672,779	$ 9,273,287
Employer	11,634,531	13,648,350
Severance contributions from employees	344,953	—
Total contributions	20,652,263	22,921,637
Investment income:		
Net appreciation in fair value of investments	(25,849,218)	9,459,899
Interest	9,140,808	9,458,887
Dividends	2,287,755	2,378,005
Total investment income	(14,420,655)	21,296,791
Less investment expenses	1,184,537	1,375,172
Net investment income	(15,605,192)	19,921,619
Total additions	5,047,071	42,843,256
Deductions:		
Benefit payments	44,051,754	44,803,115
Refunds and withdrawals	2,000,368	1,760,184
Administrative expenses	1,091,294	1,198,053
Total deductions	47,143,416	47,761,352
Net decrease	(42,096,345)	(4,918,096)
Net assets held in trust for pension benefits:		
Beginning of year	839,965,938	844,884,034
End of year	$797,869,593	$839,965,938

Source: Adapted from a recent annual report of the City of Baton Rouge and Parish of East Baton Rouge, Louisiana, Employees' Retirement System.

TABLE 8-9   Statement of Fiduciary Net Assets—Pension Trust Fund—City of Baton Rouge and Parish of East Baton Rouge

City of Baton Rouge and
Parish of East Baton Rouge
Employees' Retirement System
Statement of Fiduciary Fund Net Assets
Years Ended December 31, 20X9 and 20X8

	20X9 Combined Total	20X8 Combined Total
Assets		
Cash	$ 630,708	$ 64,311
Receivables:		
Employer contributions	917,728	820,592
Employee contributions	756,131	626,240
Interest and dividends	1,747,430	1,813,625
Pending trades	10,321,898	1,366,052
Other	2,386,865	344,844
Total receivables	16,130,052	4,971,353
Investments (at fair value):		
U.S. government obligations	68,259,778	56,853,146
Bonds—domestic	61,986,427	71,439,334
Bonds—Index Fund	152,447,365	146,107,737
Equity securities—domestic	399,981,638	437,734,515
Equity securities—international	84,014,529	106,147,731
Cash equivalents	28,200,000	18,111,000
Total investments	794,889,737	836,393,463
Land and buildings at cost, net of accumulated depreciation of $616,652 and $587,632, respectively	814,168	837,077
Total assets	812,464,665	842,266,204
Liabilities		
Accrued expenses and benefits	617,416	650,818
Pending trades payable	13,977,656	1,649,448
Total liabilities	14,595,072	2,300,266
Net assets held in trust for pension benefits	$797,869,593	$839,965,938

Source: Adapted from a recent annual report of the City of Baton Rouge and Parish of East Baton Rouge, Louisiana, Employees' Retirement System.

TABLE 8-10   Schedule of Funding Progress—Pension Trust Fund—City of Baton Rouge and Parish of East Baton Rouge

City of Baton Rouge and
Parish of East Baton Rouge
Employees' Retirement System
Required Supplementary Information Under GASB Statement No. 25
Schedule of Funding Progress

Actuarial Valuation Date	Actuarial Value of Assets (a)	Actuarial Accrued Liability (AAL) (b)	Unfunded AAL (b − a)	Funded Ratio (a/b)	Annual Covered Payroll (c)	UAAL as a Percentage of Covered Payroll [(b − a)/c]
12/31/X2	$480,505,268	$657,162,178	$176,656,910	73.1%	$100,596,231	175.6%
12/31/X3	551,301,959	718,277,070	166,975,111	76.8%	104,601,384	159.6%
12/31/X4	587,193,233	773,936,127	186,742,894	75.9%	109,658,886	170.3%
12/31/X5	635,463,896	811,977,242	176,513,346	78.3%	114,102,750	154.7%
12/31/X6	740,257,038	875,075,687	134,818,649	84.6%	118,742,991	113.5%
12/31/X7*	741,562,144	809,012,654	67,450,510	91.7%	96,744,086	69.7%
12/31/X8	786,941,507	855,994,379	69,052,872	91.9%	99,510,155	69.4%
12/31/X9**	813,977,773	902,821,264	88,843,491	90.2%	102,793,456	86.4%

* These results are adjusted to reflect the impact of the February 26, 20X7, police transfers out to MPERS and the actuarial assumption changes adopted by the Retirement Board.
** These results reflect the impact of the change in Asset Valuation Method described in the Summary of Actuarial Assumptions and Methods.

Source: Adapted from a recent annual report of the City of Baton Rouge and Parish of East Baton Rouge, Louisiana, Employees' Retirement System.

TABLE 8-11   Schedule of Employer Contributions—Pension Trust Fund—City of Baton Rouge and Parish of East Baton Rouge

City of Baton Rouge and
Parish of East Baton Rouge
Employees' Retirement System
Required Supplementary Information Under GASB Statement No. 25, Continued
Schedule of Employer Contributions
CPERS Trust

Year Ended	Annual Required Contribution	Percentage Contributed
12/31/X3	$17,845,851	80.0%
12/31/X4	17,773,028	91.3%
12/31/X5	19,510,792	94.3%
12/31/X6	17,967,514	112.0%
12/31/X7*	15,658,856	129.9%
12/31/X8	11,240,695	120.9%
12/31/X9	13,708,997	84.0%

*These results are adjusted to reflect the impact of the February 26, 20X7, police transfers out to MPERS and the actuarial assumption changes adopted by the Retirement Board.
Note: Only 7 years of data are available.

Source: Adapted from a recent annual report of the City of Baton Rouge and Parish of East Baton Rouge, Louisiana, Employees' Retirement System.

FIDUCIARY-TYPE FUNDS: INVESTMENT TRUST FUNDS

Fund Overview

Some governments maintain external investment pools, an arrangement that combines the monies of more than one legally separate entity and invests them on behalf of the participants to achieve economies of scale. By definition, an external investment pool can account for monies of the sponsoring government, but one or more of the participants must be a legally separate government that is not part of the same reporting entity as the sponsoring government.

External investment pools are created, for example, when state laws authorize a state treasurer to hold and invest temporarily idle cash deposited by local governments with the state treasurer, or when state laws require legally separate local school districts to deposit temporarily idle cash with a county treasurer for investment. In such instances, a fiduciary relationship develops between the entity that manages the external investment pool and the participating governments.

Although the resources of external investment pools are commingled, the portion of the investment pool that belongs to the sponsoring government should be reported in an appropriate fund of the sponsoring government. The portion of the resources belonging to the other participants should be reported in a fiduciary-type fund called an Investment Trust Fund.

Summary of Fund Activities

Investment Trust Funds receive resources from the participating governments. These resources are then invested in securities. Income from these securities is accounted for using the economic resources measurement focus and the full accrual basis of accounting. Gains and losses incurred in trading securities and adjusting them to fair value are recorded during the period along with any expenses incurred. Once the income is determined for the period, it is allocated to each participant depending on the trust agreement, usually based on the amount invested.

Control of Fund Activities

Investment Trust Funds are controlled primarily by the trust agreement. A trust agreement is a legal document that specifies what type of investments can be made, how the income will be measured and distributed, and how much the sponsoring government can charge for managing the fund. A key element that should be specifically identified is how much income can be distributed. In most instances a net figure is used (Investment income − Investment losses − Expenses). The trust agreement should be specific regarding how much, if any, of the investment net income must be retained as a protection against possible future losses.

Accounting for Fund Activities
Operating Entries

To illustrate an Investment Trust Fund, assume that two small cities (Tinyville and Microville) each deposit $50,000 in the City of Angusville external investment pool. Although Angusville could participate in the fund, for illustrative purposes we assume it does not. Instead, Tinyville and Microville are seeking to use the fund management skills of Angusville's finance staff. The entry to record the receipt of the money on the books of Angusville's Investment Trust Fund is:

Cash	100,000	
Additions—contributions from Tinyville		50,000
Additions—contributions from Microville		50,000
To record the receipt of deposits made by Tinyville and Microville.		

The entry on the books of each of the participating governments is:

Equity in Angusville's investment pool	50,000	
Cash		50,000
To record investment of cash in a pool managed by the City of Angusville.		

Investments of pool cash should be separated into various categories (e.g., U.S. government obligations, municipal obligations, etc.). If $40,000 is invested in U.S. government securities and $55,000 in corporate securities, the following entry is needed on the books of the investment pool:

Investments—U.S. government securities	40,000	
Investments—corporate securities	55,000	
Cash		95,000
To record investment of pool cash.		

Notice that no entry is made on either the books of Tinyville or Microville at this time.

During the year, the fund earns $5,000 of interest, of which $4,000 is received in cash. The entry to record this interest income on the books of the investment pool is:

Cash	4,000	
Interest receivable	1,000	
Additions—interest		5,000
To record interest earned and received during 2008.		

Securities are reported at fair value in investment trust funds. If the value of corporate investments increased by $3,000 during the year, the following entry is needed on the investment pool books:

Investments—corporate securities	3,000	
Additions—net increase in fair value of investments		3,000
To record the increase in the fair value of investments for 2008.		

Administrative expenses incurred by the fund during 2008 totaled $800. Assuming these expenses are paid in cash, they are recorded on the books of the investment pool as follows:

Deductions—administrative expenses	800	
Cash		800
To record administrative expenses for 2008.		

During 2008 corporate securities totaling $6,000 were sold for $7,000. These transactions are recorded on the books of the investment pool as follows:

Cash	7,000	
Investments—corporate securities		6,000
Additions—net increase in fair value of		
investments		1,000
To record sale of investments.		

Notice that no entry for the preceding four events is made on either the books of Tinyville or Microville at this time. They are recorded only in the investment pool on Angusville's books. If $1,600 is distributed each to Tinyville and Microville, the following entry is made on Angusville's books:

Deductions—distributions to pool participants	3,200	
Cash		3,200
To record the distribution of part of the fund's		
resources to its participants.		

Each of the pool's participants would record the receipt of cash as follows:

Cash	1,600	
Revenues—net increase in value of investments		1,600
To record a partial distribution of cash from		
Angusville's external investment pool.		

Although other entries could be illustrated, the preceding entries are typical of an investment trust fund.

Closing Entry

The closing entry on the books of the Investment Trust Fund is as follows:

Additions—contributions from Tinyville	50,000	
Additions—contributions from Microville	50,000	
Additions—interest	5,000	
Additions—net increase in fair value of	4,000	
investments		
Deductions—administrative expenses		800
Deductions—distributions to pool participants		3,200
Net assets		105,000
To close the operating accounts of the external		
investment pool.		

In this illustration all items of revenue, expense, gain, or loss are divided based on the share of investments each participant had at the beginning of the year. Because both are equal, each of the cities would record the following:

Equity in Angusville's investment pool	2,500	
Revenues—net increase in value of		
investments		2,500
To record a city's share of pooled investment		
changes during 2008.		

A trial balance for Angusville's Investment Trust Fund is presented in Table 8-12.

TABLE 8-12   Trial Balance—Investment Trust Fund

City of Angusville
Trial Balance
Investment Trust Fund
December 31, 2008

	Debits	Credits
Cash	$ 12,000	
Interest receivable	1,000	
Investments—U.S. government securities	40,000	
Investments—corporate securities	52,000	
Additions—contributions from Tinyville		$ 50,000
Additions—contributions from Microville		50,000
Additions—interest		5,000
Additions—net increase in fair value of investments		4,000
Deductions—administrative expenses	800	
Deductions—distribution to pool participants	3,200	
	$109,000	$109,000

Financial Statements Illustration

The financial statements normally prepared for Investment Trust Funds are a statement of changes in fiduciary net assets and a statement of fiduciary net assets. These statements are illustrated in Tables 8-13 and 8-14. Notice that no cash flow statement is prepared.

TABLE 8-13   Statement of Changes in Fiduciary Net Assets—Investment Trust Fund

City of Angusville
Fiduciary Fund
Statement of Changes in Fiduciary Net Assets
Investment Trust Fund
For the Year Ending December 31, 2008

Additions		
Contributions from participating governments		$100,000
Investment earnings:		
Interest	$5,000	
Increase in fair value of investments	4,000	
Less investment expense	(800)	
Net investment earnings		8,200
Total additions		108,200
Deductions		
Distributions to fund participants		(3,200)
Change in net assets		105,000
Net assets—beginning of the year		0
Net assets—end of the year		$105,000

TABLE 8-14   Statement of Fiduciary Net Assets—Investment Trust Fund

City of Angusville
Fiduciary Fund
Statement of Fiduciary Net Assets
Investment Trust Fund
December 31, 2008

Assets	
Cash	$ 12,000
Interest receivable	1,000
Investments	92,000
Total assets	$105,000
Net assets	
Net assets held in trust	$105,000

GOVERNMENTAL ACCOUNTING IN PRACTICE
The State of Wisconsin Local Government Pooled Investment Fund

The State of Wisconsin maintains a Local Government Pooled Investment Fund similar to that used by the City of Angusville. The statement of changes in fiduciary net assets is presented in Table 8-15, and the statement of fiduciary net assets is presented in Table 8-16. The State of Wisconsin follows the same accounting and measurement focus procedures as Angusville.

TABLE 8-15   Statement of Changes in Fiduciary Net Assets—Investment Trust Fund

State of Wisconsin
Statement of Changes in Fiduciary Net Assets
Local Government Pooled Investment Fund
For the Fiscal Year Ended June 30, 20X8

Additions		
Deposits		$11,113,321
Investment income of investment trust funds	$ 182,250	
Less: Investment expense	(1,705)	
Net investment income		180,545
Total additions		11,293,866
Deductions		
Distributions	10,040,381	
Administrative expenses	166	
Total deductions		10,040,547
Net increase in net assets		1,253,319
Net assets—Beginning of year		2,563,920
Net assets—End of year		$ 3,817,239

Source: Adapted from a recent annual report of the State of Wisconsin.

TABLE 8-16 Statement of Fiduciary Net Assets—Investment Trust Fund

State of Wisconsin
Statement of Fiduciary Net Assets
Local Government Pooled Investment Fund
June 30, 20X8

Assets	
Cash and cash equivalents	$3,817,266
Liabilities and Net Assets	
Due to other funds	27
Net assets held in trust for pooled participants	$3,817,239

Source: Adapted from a recent annual report of the State of Wisconsin.

FIDUCIARY-TYPE FUNDS: PRIVATE PURPOSE TRUST FUNDS

Fund Overview

Private Purpose Trust Funds are used to account for resources held by a government, in a trustee capacity, that must be maintained intact and whose beneficiaries must be "outside" of the government. These beneficiaries may be other governments, individuals, or private organizations. A typical fund of this type is one used by state governments to report escheat property.[9] These funds follow the economic resources measurement focus and the full accrual basis of accounting.

Summary of Fund Activities

The activities of Private Purpose Trust Funds are similar to those of Investment Trust Funds. They entail the receipt of resources from direct contributions made by private individuals or organizations. These resources are invested and the income and/or principal is disbursed from the trust fund according to the trust agreement. Formal budgets and budgetary accounting are seldom employed in Private Purpose Trust Funds.

Accounting for Fund Activities

Operating Entries

Activities accounted for in Private Purpose Trust Funds generally are similar to those detailed in Chapter 5 for Permanent Funds and Special Revenue Funds. However, as noted previously, Private Purpose Trust Funds employ the full accrual basis of accounting and the economic resources measurement focus. All the operating activities related to the purposes for which the trust was established are recorded within the Private Purpose Trust Fund.

As an example of the accounting procedures for Private Purpose Trust Funds, assume a prominent citizen of Angusville establishes an educational trust fund for children of police and fire department employees killed in the performance of their duties. The trust agreement provides for an initial contribution of $2 million. This amount is to

---

[9]GASB Cod. Sec. 1300.113.

be invested, and income generated by the investments is to be spent on college scholarships for the children of qualified employees.

The entries to record receipt of the gift and the original investment of the monies are as follows:

Cash	2,000,000	
Additions—donations		2,000,000
To record the receipt of donations during 2008.		

Investments—municipal bonds	500,000	
Investments—U.S. government securities	1,500,000	
Cash		2,000,000
To record investments made during 2008.		

If the earnings on the investments amount to $60,000, the following entry would be recorded:

Cash	60,000	
Additions—investment earnings		60,000
To record investment earnings during 2008.		

During the year, scholarships totaling $55,000 are awarded, and recorded with the following entry:

Deductions—scholarships	55,000	
Cash		55,000
To record scholarships for 2008.		

During 2008, operating costs of $1,000 are incurred, of which $600 is paid in cash. The entry to record these costs follows:

Deductions-operating costs	1,000	
Accounts payable		400
Cash		600
To record operating costs for 2008.		

Investments in municipal bonds totaling $200,000 are redeemed for $225,000 and the total proceeds are immediately reinvested in the same type of securities. The entries to record these events follow:

Cash	225,000	
Investments—municipal bonds		200,000
Additions—net appreciation in fair value		
of investments		25,000
To record redemption of investments.		

Investments—municipal bonds	225,000	
Cash		225,000
To record additional investments made in 2008.		

Additional income earned on investments, but not received by year end, is recorded as follows:

Investment income receivable	10,000	
Additions—investment earnings		10,000
To record accrual of investment earnings at		
the end of 2008.		

If the fair value of the municipal bonds held by the fund increased in value by $15,000 by the end of 2008, the following entry is made:

Investments—municipal bonds	15,000	
Additions—net appreciation in fair value		
of investments		15,000
To record the increase in fair value of investments		
at the end of 2008.		

Closing Entry

At the end of the year, the following entry is made to close the books:

Additions—donations	2,000,000	
Additions—investment earnings	70,000	
Additions—net appreciation in fair value		
of investments	40,000	
Deductions—scholarships		55,000
Deductions—operating costs		1,000
Net assets		2,054,000
To close the books for 2008.		

Financial Statements Illustration

The financial statements for a Private Purpose Trust Fund are a statement of changes in fiduciary net assets and a statement of fiduciary net assets. These statements are illustrated for the City of Angusville in Tables 8-17 and 8-18.

TABLE 8-17   Statement of Changes in Fiduciary Net Assets—Private Purpose Trust Fund

City of Angusville
Private Purpose Trust Fund
Scholarship Fund
Statement of Changes in Fiduciary Net Assets
For the Year Ended December 31, 2008

Additions		
Contributions		
Donations		$2,000,000
Investment earnings:		
Net increase in fair value of investments	$ 40,000	
Income from investments	70,000	
Total investment earnings	110,000	
Less investment expense	(1,000)	
Net investment earnings		109,000
Total additions		2,109,000
Deductions		
Scholarships		55,000
Change in net assets		2,054,000
Net assets—beginning of year		0
Net assets—end of year		$2,054,000

TABLE 8-18	Statement of Fiduciary Net Assets—Private Purpose Trust Fund

City of Angusville
Private Purpose Trust Fund
Scholarship Fund
Statement of Fiduciary Net Assets
December 31, 2008

Assets		
Cash	$ 4,400	
Investment income receivable	10,000	
Investments—U.S. Government securities	1,500,000	
Investments—municipal bonds	540,000	
Total assets		$2,054,400
Liabilities		
Accounts payable		400
Net assets in trust for scholarships		$2,054,000

GOVERNMENTAL ACCOUNTING IN PRACTICE
The State of Michigan Private Purpose Trust Fund

The State of Michigan maintains five Private Purpose Trust Funds: (1) Escheats Fund; (2) Gifts, Bequests, and Deposits Investment Fund; (3) Hospital Patients' Trust Fund; (4) Michigan Education Savings Program; and (5) Workers' Disability Compensation Trust Fund. The Michigan Education Savings Program Fund is illustrated here. This fund is a college tuition savings plan, designed to collect and invest deposits made by contributors, for purposes of financing tuition on behalf of future students. Investment earnings held in trust by the fund are federal and state tax-deferred until the student is ready to attend college. The federal government and the state both offer tax deductions for contributions made each year. Tables 8-19 and 8-20 show statements for this fund. Note in Table 8-20 that the numbers do not add up because of rounding.

TABLE 8-19	Statement of Changes in Fiduciary Net Assets—Private Purpose Trust Fund—State of Michigan

State of Michigan
Statement of Changes in Fiduciary Net Assets
Private Purpose Trust Fund
Michigan Education Savings Program
Fiscal Year Ended September 30, 20X8
(amounts in thousands)

Additions		
Contributions from participants		$62,849
Investment income:		
Net depreciation in fair value of investments	$(6,704)	
Interest, dividends, and other	843	

(continued)

TABLE 8-19   Statement of Changes in Fiduciary Net Assets—Private Purpose Trust Fund—State of Michigan (*continued*)

State of Michigan
Statement of Changes in Fiduciary Net Assets
Private Purpose Trust Fund
Michigan Education Savings Program
Fiscal Year Ended September 30, 20X8
(amounts in thousands)

Less investment expense:		
Investment activity expense	(119)	
Net investment loss		(5,980)
Miscellaneous income		1
Total additions		56,869
Deductions		
Benefits paid to participants		888
Refunds and transfers to other systems		1
Total deductions		889
Net increase		55,980
Net assets held in trust for others—beginning of fiscal year		—
Net assets held in trust for others—end of fiscal year		$55,980

Source: Adapted from a recent annual report of the State of Michigan.

TABLE 8-20   Statement of Fiduciary Net Assets—Private Purpose Trust Fund—State of Michigan

State of Michigan
Statement of Fiduciary Net Assets
Private Purpose Trust Fund
Michigan Education Savings Program
September 30, 20X8
(amounts in thousands)

Assets		
Cash		$ 355
Investments at fair value:		
Mutual funds	$51,314	
Pooled investment funds	4,437	
Total investments		55,751
Other current assets		339
Total assets		56,444
Liabilities		
Accounts payable and other liabilities		464
Net Assets		
Net assets held in trust for others		$55,980

Source: Adapted from a recent annual report of the State of Michigan.

FIDUCIARY-TYPE FUNDS: AGENCY FUNDS

Fund Overview

An Agency Fund is a fiduciary-type fund used when a governmental unit is the custodian of resources that belong to some other organization. Agency Funds typically involve only the receipt, temporary investment, and remittance of fiduciary resources to individuals, private organizations, or other governments.[10] Because an Agency Fund does not have title to or control over these resources, there is no fund balance for this type of fund. Instead, all the resources held are balanced against the liabilities to be paid from those resources. Therefore, the Agency Fund accounting equation is Assets = Liabilities. Likewise, operating statements are not prepared for Agency Funds.

One of the most common uses of an Agency Fund is as a clearing mechanism to record the collection of property taxes by one government on behalf of several taxing authorities. For example, a county may collect the property taxes due to the county, one or more cities within the county, and, say, a flood control district located within the county. A county Agency Fund would account for the receipt of the tax proceeds and their subsequent disbursement to other county funds and the other governments.

Agency Funds sometimes are used to record FICA and other payroll deductions before these amounts are sent to the appropriate recipients, as well as to account for assets held in escrow and deposits from contractors doing business with the government. A key factor in determining whether an Agency Fund should be used is whether the governmental unit disburses the assets according to a previously agreed-upon formula, legal requirement, or instruction by the "owner." In short, Agency Funds should be used when the government has no discretionary use of the assets over which it has temporary custody and no trust agreement is established.

Accounting for Fund Activities

Operating Entries

For illustrative purposes, assume the City of Angusville uses a Property Tax Collection Fund and that the city collects all property taxes and distributes two-thirds of the collections to other governments (the local school board and a levee district) and one-third to the General Fund of the city. Also assume that the school board and the levee district are not part of the Angusville government. The levy of the tax is recorded by each governmental unit. To keep the example manageable, however, we will illustrate only the General Fund and the Agency Fund for Angusville. Entries similar to those for the General Fund are made by the other governmental units. The appropriate entry on the General Fund books is as follows, assuming the amounts as given:

Property taxes receivable—current	5,000,000	
Estimated uncollectible property taxes—current		1,000
Revenues—property taxes		4,999,000
To record levy of property taxes for 2008.		

---

[10]GASB Cod. Sec. 1300.114.

must equal liabilities. Therefore, there is no fund balance (net assets). Notice that the statement of net assets includes only amounts held for other governments. The amounts within the Agency Fund accounts that pertain to other funds of the governmental unit are not reported by the agency fund. Rather, these amounts are reported as assets and liabilities in the appropriate funds.[11] In this instance they are reported in the General Fund for the City of Angusville.

GOVERNMENTAL ACCOUNTING IN PRACTICE
The City of Columbus, Ohio, Agency Fund

The City of Columbus, Ohio, has 17 individual agency funds. They range from a Payroll Deposit Fund to a Police Property Room Deposit Fund. The city reports a statement of fiduciary net assets (see Table 8-23). In addition, the city provides a schedule of changes in assets and liabilities for each fund. This schedule is prepared based on the total assets and the total liabilities of each fund. No separate identification of the causes of the changes is made, except for the general categories of "additions" and "deductions."

TABLE 8-23   Statement of Fiduciary Net Assets—City of Columbus, Ohio

City of Columbus, Ohio
Statement of Fiduciary Net Assets
Agency Funds
December 31, 20X8
(amounts in thousands)

Assets	
Cash and cash equivalents:	
Cash and investments with treasurer	$38,523
Cash and investments with trustee	20
Investments	31
Receivables (net of allowances for uncollectibles)	20
Total assets	$38,594
Liabilities	
Due to:	
Other governments	$27,156
Other	11,438
Total liabilities	$38,594

Source: Adapted from a recent annual report of the City of Columbus, Ohio.

---

[11]GASB Cod. Sec. 2200.176.

Review Questions

Q8-1   Does a government that offers pension benefits to its employees necessarily maintain a Pension Trust Fund? Explain.

Q8-2   Distinguish between a defined benefit pension plan and a defined contribution pension plan.

Q8-3   What is an actuary? What is the actuary's role in pension administration?

Q8-4   Distinguish between a pension contribution and pension cost.

Q8-5   How are the operations of a Pension Trust Fund controlled?

Q8-6   What financial statements are prepared for Pension Trust Funds?

Q8-7   Identify and explain the schedules that are prepared for Pension Trust Funds.

Q8-8   What are other postemployment benefits?

Q8-9   Can the governmental unit sponsoring an external investment pool participate in it?

Q8-10 What financial statements are prepared for an Investment Trust Fund?

Q8-11 How are investments in an Investment Trust Fund valued? How are changes in value treated?

Q8-12 When are Private Purpose Trust Funds used?

Q8-13 How are Private Purpose Trust Funds controlled?

Q8-14 What financial statements are used for Private Purpose Trust Funds?

Q8-15 Define an agency relationship.

Q8-16 Is an operating statement prepared for an Agency Fund? Why or why not?

Q8-17 Does an Agency Fund have a fund balance? Why or why not?

Cases

C8-1   J. S. Moneybaggs wants to include a provision in her will that will assure her that her life's work of caring for small children will continue after her death. She is concerned that any resources given to the city might be used for some other purpose. Moneybaggs hires you as her financial consultant. How will you advise her?

C8-2   A new employee of the City of Kashime was working with the accounting records of several of its funds. This employee, John Fergie, wanted to set up a Permanent Fund for the principal of some donations to the library and use a Special Revenue Fund to account for the earnings of the investment and their use. Another employee argued that a Private Purpose Trust Fund should be used for both principal and income. Do you agree with either of these individuals, or do you have a better suggestion?

C8-3   The City of Macroville hires you as a consultant to help establish a procedure to simplify its property tax collection processing and make the process more efficient. Currently the city and six special districts receive money from a property tax. Each district and the city has its own billing, recording, and collection functions. In addition, the taxpayers are upset about paying seven tax bills. At a recent town hall–type meeting, several citizens demanded that the city do something to simplify the process. As a consultant, how would you advise the city?

Ethics Cases

EC8-1 Aaronsborough's city manager, Thomas Smith, is facing a financial dilemma. The General Fund will not have enough revenues to cover the current year's expenditures. After an all-night session, he reduced the expenditures by only 5 percent, which is not enough to balance the budget. His wife, Jane Smith, mentioned to him that whenever they did not have enough money to meet their bills for a particular month, she merely borrowed money from the bank. At that time, Smith decided to borrow from the Pension Trust Fund. His intention was to repay the loan as soon as possible. Will the loan solve his problem? Explain. Is an ethical problem raised here? Explain.

EC8-2 Assume the same facts as stated in EC8-1, except that the Pension Trust Fund is operated by a five-member board of directors. Before the end of the current fiscal year, three of the board members' terms expire. If Smith appoints three new board members who are sympathetic to his plan, do you see a potential ethical problem?

Exercises

E8-1 (Fiduciary Funds in practice)
Obtain a recent Comprehensive Annual Financial Report for a county or a municipality. Identify any fiduciary funds included in the report. Does the government have any Pension Trust Funds? If not, does the government contribute to an external pension plan?

E8-2 (Journal entries for a Pension Trust Fund)
The Pension Trust Fund maintained by the City of Linden had the following transactions during 2008. Record each transaction in the Pension Trust Fund. Ignore any other funds that may be involved in a transaction.

1. Contributions of $600,000 were received from General Fund employees and the General Fund contributed its share of $100,000.
2. The fund paid $500 for investment management fees.
3. Investments held by the fund increased in value by $3,500.
4. Depreciation on fund assets totaled $800.
5. Retirement benefits of $7,700 were paid to retirees.
6. Interest of $2,500 and dividends of $1,400 were received from investments.

E8-3 (Terminology)
Define the following terms as they apply to pension plans and postretirement benefit plans:

1. Defined benefit plan
2. Defined contribution plan
3. Postemployment benefits
4. Net assets held in trust for pension benefits
5. Unfunded actuarial accrued liability
6. Net pension obligation

E8-4 (Journal entries for an Investment Trust Fund)
Prepare the journal entries to record the following transactions in an Investment Trust Fund.

1. Turtle Creek and Pineview contributed $60,000 and $40,000, respectively, to an investment trust fund operated by Seggen County during 2008.
2. Investments totaling $75,000 were purchased.
3. Income from the investments during the year totaled $8,000.
4. The fund paid $1,500 to the county for investment management fees.

5. The investments increased in value by $3,000.
6. Income of $10,000 is paid to the two cities based on the relative amount of their initial investment.

E8-5 (Financial statements for an Investment Trust Fund)

Based on the information in E8-4, prepare a statement of changes in fiduciary fund net assets and a statement of fiduciary fund net assets.

E8-6 (Discussion)

Why would one entity permit another entity to invest its resources?

E8-7 (Journal entries for a Private Purpose Trust Fund)

Record the following journal entries in the Children's Book Fund, a Private Purpose Trust Fund that supplies books for children in privately owned battered women's shelters.

1. A citizen donated $500,000 to a Private Purpose Trust Fund. The trust specified that this money was to be used to acquire children's books for battered women's shelters.
2. The fund invested $420,000 in certificates of deposit.
3. Books costing $45,000 were acquired.
4. Income of $20,000 was received in cash from the investments.
5. The accounts were closed for the year.

E8-8 (Multiple choice)

1. Which of the following funds can be used to account for the spendable income from a Private Purpose Trust Fund?
   a. Agency Fund
   b. General Fund
   c. Capital Projects Fund
   d. Pension Trust Fund
   e. None of the above
2. To what provisions must the use of assets accumulated in a trust fund conform?
   a. State and local laws
   b. The trust agreement
   c. Both a and b
   d. The modified accrual basis of accounting
   e. None of the above
3. A citizen donated $1 million to a city upon her death. Her will provided that these resources be maintained in a trust and spent to provide free tickets to local baseball games for schoolchildren. In which fund is accounting for these activities done?
   a. General Fund
   b. Special Revenue Fund
   c. Investment Trust Fund
   d. Private Purpose Trust Fund
   e. Both c and d

E8-9 (Fill in the blanks)

1. Private Purpose Trust Funds are controlled through _____ and _____.

    2. Private Purpose Trust Funds follow the _____ measurement focus and the _____ basis of accounting.

    3. Amounts originally contributed to a Private Purpose Trust Fund are recorded as _____.

    4. The following financial statements are prepared for a Private Purpose Trust Fund: _____ and _____.

    5. The operations of a Private Purpose Trust Fund are usually (more or less) _____ complex than those of the General Fund.

    6. The most important document, with respect to a Private Purpose Trust Fund, is the _____.

E8-10 (Compare and contrast an Investment Trust Fund with a Private Purpose Trust Fund) Identify the major similarities and differences between an Investment Trust Fund and a Private Purpose Trust Fund. Be sure to specify when each is used.

E8-11 (Discussion of alternatives for use of trusts) You were recently approached by an individual who wants to set up a trust for the education of children of deceased schoolteachers. That person asked you to explain the best method of achieving this goal. Prepare a written statement regarding your response.

E8-12 (Multiple choice)

    1. The principal amount of a gift held in a trust that cannot be spent should be accounted for in which of the following funds?
      a. General Fund
      b. Special Revenue Fund
      c. Capital Projects Fund
      d. Private Purpose Trust Fund

    2. In what way can the amounts in an Investment Trust Fund be invested?
      a. Any way the government that operates the fund wishes
      b. Only in corporate stocks and bonds
      c. Only as provided in the trust agreement
      d. Only in governmental bonds

    3. To what type of account are contributions to a Pension Trust Fund usually credited?
      a. A revenue account
      b. An expenditure account
      c. An additions account
      d. A net assets account

    4. How are proceeds on the sale of an investment in excess of its book value handled in a Private Purpose Trust Fund?
      a. May be credited to the asset account
      b. May be debited or credited to the asset account
      c. Must be credited to an additions account
      d. May be debited to the assets or an additions account

    5. Financial statements for a Pension Trust Fund
      a. Are included in a government's annual financial report.
      b. Are categorized as governmental fund financial statements.
      c. Are included in the General Fund for financial reporting purposes.
      d. Are included in a Special Revenue Fund for financial reporting purposes.

E8-13 (Fill in the blanks)

1. Agency Funds are classified as _____ type funds.
2. An Agency Fund is used when the governmental unit is the _____ of resources that belong to some other organization.
3. Agency Funds (do or do not) _____ have title to the resources in the fund.
4. The financial statement for an Agency Fund is _____.
5. Revenues generated by the activities recorded in an Agency Fund are usually recorded in the _____ Fund.
6. Agency Funds (are or are not) _____ used only as tax collection funds.

E8-14 (Multiple choice)

1. The fee for the collection of property taxes by an Agency Fund will result in revenue in which of the following funds?
   a. General Fund and Agency Fund
   b. Agency Fund
   c. Capital Projects Fund
   d. Special Revenue Fund and Agency Fund
   e. None of the above
2. Blaken Township established an Agency Fund to account for the collection and distribution of a general sales tax. The tax is collected for the General Fund, an independent school district, and several independent drainage districts. The school district and the drainage districts are entities that are separate from the city. During the year, $500,000 was collected in sales taxes. Entries to record the collection and distribution of the resources for the city should be made in the books for which of the following funds?
   a. General Fund
   b. Agency Fund
   c. General Fund and Agency Fund
   d. Special Revenue Fund and Agency Fund
   e. None of the above
3. Collection of resources that must be distributed to other funds should be recorded in an Agency Fund as a debit to Cash and a credit to which account?
   a. Revenues
   b. Expenditures
   c. Other financing sources
   d. Other financing uses
   e. None of the above
4. Which of the following funds does not have a fund balance account or net assets account?
   a. General Fund
   b. Special Revenue Fund
   c. Capital Projects Fund
   d. Permanent Fund
   e. Agency Fund

5. For which of the following activities might an Agency Fund be used?
    a. Revenue generated from a property tax levy
    b. Expenditures of the General Fund
    c. Debt service for Enterprise Fund debt
    d. Debt service of general obligation bonds used to finance an addition to city hall
    e. None of the above

6. According to GAAP for Pension Trust Funds, which of the following is true?
    a. Revenues must be transferred to a Permanent Fund.
    b. Payments of resources are recorded as deductions. ·
    c. There is no concept of fund balance or net assets. `
    d. All disbursements must be made to the General Fund.
    e. None of the above

E8-15 (Journal entries for an Agency Fund)
Prepare the following journal entries in the Bid Deposits Fund, an Agency Fund. This fund is used to record all deposits made by contractors doing work for the city. Any earnings on these resources are required to be paid to the depositing companies.

1. Deposits totaling $750,000 were received.
2. The amount received in part 1 was invested in certificates of deposit.
3. Income from the investments totaling $70,000 was received.
4. Deposits of $93,750 were returned to contractors upon successful completion of the projects on which they were working. In addition, these contractors received $8,750 of earnings on their deposits (their share of the earnings of the fund for the year). (*Hint:* Do not forget to liquidate some of the investments.)
5. The books were closed for the year.

Problems

P8-1 (Journal entries and statements for a Pension Trust Fund)
The City of Green Meadows has had an employee pension fund for several years. The following is a trial balance for the fund at December 31, 2008, and several transactions that occurred during 2009:

City of Green Meadows
Pension Trust Fund
Employees' Retirement Fund
Trial Balance
December 31, 2008

	Debits	Credits
Cash	$ 52,500	
Investment income receivable	210,000	
Investments—corporate stocks	20,000,000	
Investments—U.S. government securities	30,575,000	
Accrued expenses		$ 12,000
Net assets held in trust for pension benefits		50,825,500
	$50,837,500	$50,837,500

1. Contributions from the General Fund totaled $750,000; included in this amount was $258,750 from the employees and $491,250 from the city.
2. Investments in corporate stocks costing $500,000 were purchased.
3. The fund collected interest accrued at December 31, 2008. Investment income for 2009 totaled $4,800,000, of which $4,290,000 was collected in cash. Investment income earned in 2009 included dividends of $850,000 and the remainder was interest.
4. Employee retirement benefits of $3,500,000 were paid.
5. Additional U.S. government securities totaling $1,100,000 were acquired.
6. Costs of operating the plan were $175,000; of this amount $150,000 was paid in cash and the remainder was accrued. The accrued expenses at the beginning of the year were also paid. These expenses are administrative in nature.
7. U.S. government securities that had a book value of $500,000 were redeemed for $600,000.
8. The market value of the corporate stocks at the end of the year increased by $1,000,000.

Required: 1. Prepare the journal entries necessary to record these transactions.
2. Prepare a statement of changes in fiduciary net assets for the fund for 2009.
3. Prepare a statement of fiduciary net assets as of December 31, 2009.

P8-2   (Preparation of a statement of fiduciary net assets for a Pension Trust Fund) The following information is available for Russellville at June 30, 2009:

Additions—interest	$250,000
Member contributions	340,000
Loss on sale of investments	30,000
Cash	180,000
Accrued expenses	56,000
Interest receivable	20,000
Accounts payable	33,000
Due to other funds	54,000
Investments	10,000,000
Deductions—operating costs	42,000
Retirement annuities paid	987,000

Required: Prepare a statement of fiduciary net assets for Russellville's Pension Trust Fund as of June 30, 2009.

P8-3   (Journal entries and financial statements for an Investment Trust Fund) Pinnacle County operates an Investment Trust Fund for cities located in the county. The following entries are associated with the fund during 2008:

1. The cities of Clarksville and Kingsville contributed assets, $75,000 and $50,000, respectively.
2. The entire amount received in part 1 was invested: $65,000 in certificates of deposit (CDs) and $60,000 in Treasury notes.

3. Interest income of $37,500 was received.
4. CDs totaling $40,000 and Treasury notes totaling $30,000 matured. Interest income of $1,000 was also received.
5. The money received in part 4 was reinvested in CDs.
6. Additional interest income was received: $17,500.
7. The General Fund charged the Investment Trust Fund $500 for administrative expenses. This amount was paid in cash.
8. Income of $50,000 was distributed to the participating cities according to the trust agreement (Clarksville 60 percent, Kingsville 40 percent).

Required: 1. Prepare journal entries to record the 2008 transactions in the Investment Trust Fund.
2. Prepare a statement of changes in fiduciary net assets for the fund for 2008.
3. Prepare a statement of fiduciary net assets for the fund as of December 31, 2008.

P8-4 (Journal entries and financial statements for an Investment Trust Fund) The City of Titanville established an Investment Trust Fund for Bay Town and Valley City. The cities contributed $200,000 and $100,000, respectively, to the fund. During 2008 the following transactions took place:

1. Bay Town contributed certificates of deposit (CDs) valued at $200,000, and Valley City contributed $100,000 to the fund.
2. The cash contributed by Valley City was invested in U.S. government securities.
3. The CDs matured. The principal was $70,000. Interest on the CDs was $3,000.
4. The principal amount received in part 3 was reinvested in municipal bonds.
5. The fund incurred internal administrative expenses totaling $700, of which $500 was paid in cash.
6. The General Fund charged the Investment Trust Fund $500 for managing the investments. This amount was paid in cash.
7. The trust fund income of $1,800 ($3,000 − $700 − $500) was distributed as provided in the trust agreement: two-thirds to Bay Town and one-third to Valley City.

Required: 1. Prepare journal entries to record the 2008 transactions in the Investment Trust Fund.

P8-5 (Journal entries and financial statements for a Private Purpose Trust Fund) Seaview Township received a $1 million gift from J. R. Chancellor to sponsor an annual community picnic. All reasonable costs associated with sponsoring the picnic are to paid from the gift. To guarantee proper use of the money, Chancellor made the donation in the form of a Private Purpose Trust. The following events took place during 2008:

1. The township received the gift.
2. The city paid $10,000 to an advertising agency to publicize the picnic.
3. The cost of permits for the picnic totaled $500.

4. The Seaview Cafe agreed to cater the entire picnic for $75,000, payable in advance.

5. Various performers were engaged to provide entertainment during the picnic at a total cost of $12,500. Cash was paid in advance.

6. The picnic was held and was a great success. The weather cooperated and picnic attendance met all expectations.

7. The Police Department spent $15,000 for extra police to control the traffic and crowds at the picnic. The trust reimbursed the department for these costs in cash.

8. The Sanitation Department incurred $35,000 of costs in cleaning up after the picnic. The trust agreed to reimburse the department (in the General Fund) for these costs. No cash has yet been paid.

9. The remaining cash, except for $10,000, was invested in certificates of deposit. According to the trust agreement, this money would be invested and used to provide for the 2009 picnic.

Required: 1. Record these entries in the Chancellor Community Picnic Fund.
2. Prepare a statement of changes in fiduciary net assets for 2008 and a statement of fiduciary net assets as of December 31, 2008, for the fund.

P8-6 (Journal entries and financial statements for a Private Purpose Trust Fund)

1. The City of Rocky Basin received a $2 million gift from a prominent citizen. The terms of the gift require the city to maintain the principal intact; investment income is to be used to provide college scholarships for deserving graduates of Rocky Basin High School.

2. The city invested the entire gift in certificates of deposit (CDs).

3. Investment income of $100,000 was received in cash.

4. The $100,000 from part 3 was reinvested in short-term CDs.

5. The short-term CDs matured, yielding interest income of $1,000.

6. Investment income of $112,000 was received in cash.

7. Scholarships totaling $65,000 were paid to eligible students.

8. Interest income of $2,300 was accrued at the end of 2008.

9. The General Fund charged the Scholarship Fund $3,000: $2,000 for managing the investments and $1,000 for administering the fund. The amounts were unpaid at fiscal year-end.

Required: 1. Prepare the journal entries necessary to record these events on the books of the College Scholarship Fund.
2. Prepare a statement of changes in fiduciary fund net assets for 2009 for the College Scholarship Fund.
3. Prepare a statement of fiduciary fund net assets for the College Scholarship Fund at December 31, 2009.
4. Prepare the 2009 closing entry (entries) for the College Scholarship Fund.

P8-7 (Journal entries for three Agency Funds and a trial balance for each fund) Assume that the Town of Boonsville maintains an Agency Fund for its employees' insurance withholdings, another for its employees' income tax withholdings, and a third for its employees' pension contributions. The following are selected transactions, incurred during 2009, related to these funds:

1. The town recorded its monthly payroll. Salaries totaled $350,000. The withholdings were as follows: $70,000 for employees' income taxes, $30,000 for employees' insurance, and $15,000 for employees' pension contributions. The General Fund paid the appropriate amount to each Agency Fund.
2. The Employees' Insurance Deposits Fund made a payment of $25,000 to the various insurance companies providing insurance coverage to the employees.
3. The town recorded its monthly payroll. Salaries totaled $375,000. The withholdings were as follows: $75,000 for employees' income taxes, $20,000 for employees' insurance, and $18,000 for employees' pension contributions. The General Fund paid the appropriate amount to each Agency Fund.
4. The town recorded its monthly payroll. Salaries totaled $350,000. The withholdings were as follows: $70,000 for employees' income taxes, $30,000 for employees' insurance, and $15,000 for employees' pension contributions. The General Fund paid the appropriate amounts to the appropriate Agency Fund.
5. The appropriate Agency Funds made a payment of $215,000 to the U.S. government and $48,000 to the Pension Trust Fund.
6. The town recorded its monthly payroll. Salaries totaled $375,000. The withholdings were as follows: $75,000 for employees' income taxes, $20,000 for employees' insurance, and $18,000 for employees' pension contributions. The General Fund paid the appropriate amounts to the appropriate Agency Fund.

Required: Prepare the journal entries necessary to record these events on the books of the Employees' Insurance Agency Fund, Employees' Income Tax Agency Fund, and the Employees' Pension Agency Fund and prepare a trial balance for each fund.

P8-8   (Pension fund schedule of funding progress)
The following data come from the report prepared by the actuary for York City's retirement system at December 31, 2009:

Investments (at actuarial value)	$2,921,000
Actuarial accrued liability	$5,586,000
Annual covered payroll	$1,128,000

The actuary's report also notes that the investment earnings assumption used in calculating the actuarial accrued liability was 8 percent, compared with 7.5 percent used in the preceding year.

Required: 1. Compute the following ratios: (a) funded ratio and (b) unfunded actuarial accrued liability as a percentage of covered payroll.
2. Discuss the significance of the change in the investment earnings assumption in the calculation of the actuarial accrued liability.

3. Based solely on the information in this problem, discuss whether the system is reasonably funded. What additional data do you need to help reach a conclusion?

Continuous Problems

Pension Trust Fund

Leisure City maintains a Pension Trust Fund for its employees. The following is a trial balance for the fund at December 31, 2008, and several transactions that occurred during 2009:

Leisure City
Pension Trust Fund
Employees' Retirement Fund
Trial Balance
December 31, 2008

	Debits	Credits
Cash	$ 78,750	
Investment income receivable	315,000	
Investments—U.S. government securities	25,287,500	
Investments—corporate stocks	50,575,000	
Accrued expenses		$ 18,000
Net assets held in trust for pension benefits		76,238,250
	$76,256,250	$76,256,250

The following transactions took place during 2009:

1. The fund contributions from the General Fund totaled $1,000,000; included in this amount was $500,000 from the employees and $500,000 from the city.
2. Investments in certificates of deposit (CDs) costing $600,000 and U.S. government securities costing $400,000 were purchased.
3. Collected interest accrued at December 31, 2008. Interest income for 2009 totaled $7,000,000, of which $6,000,000 was collected in cash.
4. Employee retirement benefits of $6,100,000 were paid.
5. Additional U.S. government securities of $200,000 were acquired.
6. Costs of operating the plan were $180,000; of this amount $100,000 was paid in cash and the remainder was accrued. The accrued expenses at the beginning of the year were also paid. These expenses are administrative in nature.
7. CDs with a book value of $500,000 were redeemed for $510,000.
8. The fair value of the corporate stocks increased by $50,000 by the end of 2008.

Required: 1. Prepare the journal entries necessary to record these transactions.
2. Prepare a statement of changes in fiduciary net assets for the fund for 2009.
3. Prepare a statement of fiduciary net assets as of December 31, 2009.

Investment Trust Fund

Leisure City established an Investment Trust Fund to manage the investments of the cities of Zeus and Comusville. The cities contributed $500,000 each to the fund. During 2009 the following transactions took place:

1. Leisure City received the contributions from Zeus and Comusville.
2. The cash was immediately invested in U.S. government securities.
3. Some of the investments matured. The principal was $300,000. Interest on the securities was $5,000.
4. The principal amount received in part 3 was reinvested in municipal bonds.
5. The fund incurred internal administrative expenses totaling $1,000, of which $700 were paid in cash.
6. The Investment Trust Fund paid $900 to an investment adviser for managing the investments. This amount was paid in cash.
7. Accrued interest income at the end of the year totaled $30,000.
8. Cash in the amount of $1,800 was distributed as provided in the trust agreement: one-half to the City of Zeus and one-half to Comusville.

Required:
1. Prepare the journal entries to record the preceding events.
2. Prepare a statement of changes in fiduciary net assets for 2009.
3. Prepare a statement of fiduciary net assets at December 31, 2009.

Agency Fund

Leisure City recently hosted a state fair. The city collected a special 1 percent sales tax levied by the county on all sales made at the fair; the proceeds of the tax and all investment income were to be used to provide resources to the county to build new roads. The tax was collected by Leisure City and disbursed to the county as provided in the agreement between the two. The dates of the fair spanned two fiscal periods. The following trial balance is available at the end of 2008:

Leisure City
Fiduciary Fund
Agency Fund
State Fair Sales Tax Fund
Trial Balance
December 31, 2008

	Debits	Credits
Cash	$ 3,500	
Investments—certificates of deposit	46,600	
Due to other governmental funds		$50,100
	$50,100	$50,100

The following transactions took place during 2009:

1. Investments costing $15,000 were redeemed for a total of $18,000; the difference was investment revenue.
2. The Agency Fund collected $150,000 of sales taxes.
3. The Agency Fund distributed $1,000 to the county.

4. The Agency Fund collected $800 in interest on investments.

5. An additional $13,500 was paid to the county.

6. The Agency Fund paid $35,000 to the county.

7. The remaining investments were redeemed by the Agency Fund for $36,000.

8. The remaining assets in the Agency Fund were transferred to the county.

Required: 1. Prepare the entries necessary for the Agency Fund during 2009.

2. Prepare the statement of fiduciary net assets for the Agency Fund at the end of 2009, if necessary.

9

REPORTING PRINCIPLES AND PREPARATION OF FUND FINANCIAL STATEMENTS

Chapter Outline

After completing this chapter, you should be able to:

- Describe the objectives of governmental financial reporting.
- Explain how governmental accountants define the "reporting entity."
- Describe how financial data for component units are incorporated in the financial statements of a reporting entity.
- Identify the major sections of a Comprehensive Annual Financial Report (CAFR).
- Identify and describe the seven fund financial statements.
- Describe the content of Management's Discussion and Analysis.
- Discuss the measurement focus and basis of accounting used in the fund financial statements.
- Explain the relationship between fund financial statements and combining statements.
- Describe the content of budgetary comparison schedules.
- Explain how notes are used for financial statement reporting.
- Describe the content of the statistical section of the CAFR.

To meet the reporting objectives outlined in its *Concepts Statement No. 1,* "Objectives of Financial Reporting," the Governmental Accounting Standards Board (GASB) concluded that state and local governments should prepare two sets of financial statements for external users. One set, called *fund financial statements,* reports on individual "major" funds, with a total column for all nonmajor funds. The fund financial statements are based on the accounting principles used within the funds, discussed in Chapters 4 through 8. The other set, called *government-wide financial statements,* reports on the government as a whole. The applicable financial reporting standards were established in GASB *Statement No. 34,* "Basic Financial Statements—and Management's Discussion and Analysis—for State and Local Governments" (June 1999).

This chapter covers the general principles of financial reporting for state and local governments, as well as the details of the fund financial statements. Chapter 10 covers the government-wide financial statements, the adjustments needed to the fund financial statements to produce the government-wide statements, and certain other provisions of GASB *Statement No. 34.*

We illustrate financial reporting in both chapters by using financial statements and other data from the Comprehensive Annual Financial Report (CAFR) prepared by the Village of Grafton, Wisconsin, for the calendar year 2005. The Village of Grafton (estimated 2005 population of 11,310) was one of the first municipalities in the nation to implement GASB *Statement No. 34.* Grafton has been awarded the Certificate of Achievement for Excellence in Financial Reporting by the Government Finance Officers Association of the United States and Canada for many years.

FINANCIAL REPORTING OBJECTIVES (GASB *CONCEPTS STATEMENT NO. 1*)

To get some insight into governmental financial reporting, it is helpful to understand the GASB's perspective on the objectives of financial reporting. GASB *Concepts Statement No. 1* (May 1987) suggests that state and local governmental financial reporting should meet the needs of three major groups of external users:

- The citizenry—those to whom the government is primarily accountable
- Legislative and oversight bodies—those who directly represent the citizens
- Lenders and creditors—those who provide resources to the government through the capital markets

The GASB considered the financial reporting needs of intergovernmental resource providers and other users of external financial reporting to be encompassed by the needs of the three primary external user groups.

The GASB issued *Concepts Statement No. 1* after undertaking a user needs study. Based on the study, the GASB concluded that governmental financial reporting should provide information to assist users in assessing the accountability of public officials and in making economic, social, and political decisions. Accountability was considered to be the paramount objective from which all other objectives must flow. Specifically:

a. Financial reporting should assist in fulfilling government's duty to be publicly accountable and should enable users to assess that accountability by:
   (1) providing information to determine whether current-year revenues were sufficient to pay for current-year services
   (2) demonstrating whether resources were obtained and used in accordance with the entity's legally adopted budget, and demonstrating compliance with other finance-related legal or contractual requirements
   (3) providing information to assist users in assessing the service efforts and accomplishments of the governmental entity
b. Financial reporting should assist users in evaluating the operating results of the governmental entity for the year by:
   (1) providing information about sources and uses of financial resources
   (2) providing information about how it financed its activities and met its cash requirements

(3) providing information necessary to determine whether its financial position improved or deteriorated as a result of the year's operations

c. Financial reporting should assist users in assessing the level of services that can be provided by the governmental entity and its ability to meet its obligations as they become due by:

(1) providing information about its financial position and condition

(2) providing information about its physical and other nonfinancial resources having useful lives that extend beyond the current year, including information that can be used to assess the service potential of those resources

(3) disclosing legal or contractual restrictions on resources and the risk of potential loss of resources[1]

INTRODUCTION TO THE FINANCIAL REPORTING MODEL (GASB *STATEMENT NO. 34*)

Before the GASB issued *Statement No. 34,* governmental financial reporting focused on the fund *types* discussed in Chapters 4 through 8. Financial statements had separate columns for the General Fund, aggregated Special Revenue Funds, aggregated Capital Projects Funds, and so on. Because the measurement focus and basis of accounting used for governmental-type funds differed from that used for proprietary type funds, separate operating statements were prepared for each fund category. Some critics advocated presentation of financial statements that gave the reader an overview of the financial results and financial position of the government as a whole. Others were concerned that the operating statement for governmental-type funds, based on the current financial resources measurement focus and modified accrual basis of accounting, could mislead the reader, particularly when reporting on operating results.

Lengthy debate preceded the issuance of GASB *Statement No. 34.* The effort to achieve the objectives laid out in *Concepts Statement No. 1* resulted in a compromise that, in essence, retained the previous fund-oriented reporting requirement (albeit in somewhat different form) but added a new highly aggregated top layer of financial statements. To provide the top layer—the government-wide set of statements— GASB *Statement No. 34* requires governments to convert the financial data for the governmental-type funds to the economic resources measurement focus and the accrual basis of accounting.

The government-wide layer of statements is intended to help statement users:

- Assess a government's finances in its entirety
- Determine whether its overall financial position improved or deteriorated
- Evaluate whether its current-year revenues were sufficient to pay for current-year services
- Ascertain the way it financed its programs; that is, through user fees, other program revenues, or general tax revenues[2]

---

[1]GASB Cod. App. B, para. 77–79.

[2]GASB *Statement No. 34,* "Basic Financial Statements—and Management's Discussion and Analysis—for State and Local Governments," Preface.

In addition to the change in measurement focus and basis of accounting for governmental funds, the government-wide financial statements have several other distinguishing features:

- To avoid potential confusion caused by reporting resources for which the government has a fiduciary responsibility but which it cannot legally use to finance its own activities, fiduciary-type funds are omitted from the government-wide statements.
- To provide a broader overview of the government as a whole, certain legally separate entities for which the government has financial accountability are included in the government-wide statements. We will discuss these entities in the next section.
- To provide another perspective on governmental costs and revenues, the government-wide operating statement is formatted in a different manner from the fund operating statement.

Does the financial reporting model introduced by GASB *Statement No. 34* achieve all the objectives set forth in GASB *Concepts Statement No. 1?* Many observers believe that, although the requirement to report on the accrual basis of accounting for governmental-type funds is helpful, much more needs to be done to achieve objective a.3—"providing information to assist users in assessing the service efforts and accomplishments of the governmental entity." To accomplish this objective, governments need to measure and report on the outputs (physical quantities of services provided) and outcomes (results achieved because of the services provided) of their programs. As of this writing, the GASB has issued a concepts statement (GASB *Concepts Statement No. 2*—Service Efforts and Accomplishments Reporting) and done extensive research on this subject, but does not currently require such reporting.

THE FINANCIAL REPORTING ENTITY (GASB *STATEMENT NO. 14*)

Before discussing the financial reporting requirements of GASB *Statement No. 34,* we need to cover *the reporting entity,* a subject that we mentioned briefly in Chapter 2. Recall that, in Chapter 2, we stated that there are two dimensions to the entity concept in government. In Chapters 3 through 8, we focused on one aspect of the entity concept: funds—accounting subdivisions *within* a governmental entity. But there is another aspect to the entity concept in government—one that is similar to the entity concept in private sector business enterprise.

When the term *reporting entity* is used in the private sector, it refers to the boundaries of a particular financial reporting unit; that is, it identifies *whose* assets, liabilities, revenues, expenses, and equities are embraced within the entity's financial statements. A private sector business enterprise may exercise control over legally separate organizations by owning a controlling share of their voting stock. Excluding the financial activities of these entities from the financial statements of the parent enterprise would cause the parent's statements to be incomplete and even misleading. The same type of reporting entity issue also occurs in the public sector, because governments often create and control (or are otherwise financially accountable for) a number of legally separate entities.

To illustrate: A government may provide sanitation and hospital services or supply water to its residents through the legally constituted government, using the General Fund or perhaps an Enterprise Fund to account for the services. On the other hand, it may decide to provide some of these services by creating legally separate corporations. In fact, governments provide many business-type services, such as electric and water supply, mass transit, parking lots, and toll roads or toll bridges, through specially created, legally separate corporations. Often, these entities are authorized to sell debt to construct facilities and to operate the facilities after they are built. Governments even create legally separate entities to perform financing activities for the government itself, sometimes to circumvent constitutional limits on the government's ability to borrow. These entities (referred to as public authorities or public benefit corporations) are generally created by statute, but they may be created through a state's not-for-profit corporation laws. In any event, depending on the circumstances, not reporting the financial activities of these enterprises within the financial statements of the larger government could cause the larger government's statements to be incomplete and possibly misleading.

Defining the Financial Reporting Entity

The GASB developed reporting entity standards for state and local governments in GASB *Statement No. 14,* "The Financial Reporting Entity." The main governmental unit—the unit whose financial statements include the financial activities of the legally separate entities—is called the *primary government.* The other governmental units whose financial activities are included in the primary government's financial statements are called *component units.*

All state governments and general-purpose local governments, such as counties, cities, towns, and villages, are primary governments. A special-purpose government (such as a local school board or a hospital district) is also defined as a primary government, provided it has a separately elected governing body, is legally separate (for example, it is created as a body corporate and politic), *and* is fiscally independent of other state and local governments. To be considered fiscally independent, as defined by the GASB, the organization must be authorized to take three specific actions without the approval of another government: (1) determine its budget, (2) levy taxes or set user charges, and (3) issue bonded debt.[3]

Component units are legally separate organizations for which the elected officials of a primary government are *financially accountable.* A primary government is financially accountable for a legally separate organization if:

1. The primary government can appoint a voting majority of the organization's governing body; *and*
2. a. The primary government is able to impose its will on that organization; *or*
   b. There is a potential for the organization to provide specific financial benefits to, or to impose specific financial burdens on, the primary government.[4]

A primary government has the ability to impose its will on an organization if it can significantly influence its day-to-day operations, including its programs, its activities, or

---

[3]GASB Cod. Sec. 2100.112 and 2100.115.
[4]GASB Cod. Sec. 2100.120a.

the level of services it provides. For example, a mayor can impose his or her will on an organization if he or she has the ability to remove members of the organization's governing board at will, or to modify or approve its budgets or the fees it charges for services.

A primary government has a financial benefit or burden relationship with an organization if (1) the primary government is legally entitled to or can otherwise access the organization's resources; (2) is legally obligated or has otherwise assumed the obligation to finance the deficits of, or provide financial support to, the organization; or (3) the primary government is obligated in some manner for the organization's debt.[5]

Notice that two conditions must be met for a legally separate organization to be deemed a component unit of a primary government: (1) appointment of a voting majority of the component unit's governing board, and (2) either ability to impose will or benefit/burden. The following examples illustrate circumstances under which the second element is met:

- A state lottery and off-track betting corporation, where the benefit/burden criterion is met because the law provides that the corporation's net revenues must be remitted to the state
- A city toll bridge authority, where the "imposition of will" criterion is met because the law provides that the city council must approve toll rates, or because the law allows the mayor to remove any board member at will
- A county building construction authority, where the benefit/burden criterion is met because the law provides that the county will guarantee payment of principal and interest on the debt issued by the authority

A primary government's financial reporting entity also includes organizations that, if omitted, would cause the primary government's financial statements to be misleading or incomplete. New York City's financial statements, for example, included the financial activities of a state-created financing agency whose governing board consisted primarily of state officials or state-appointed officials. The agency was created during the city's fiscal crisis for the sole purpose of refinancing a portion of the city's debt. Interest and principal on the agency's debt, which replaced the city's debt, is paid with city sales taxes diverted by law to the state agency.

GOVERNMENTAL FINANCIAL REPORTING IN PRACTICE
When Is an Entity a Component Unit?

Here is an example of the thought process behind the decision as to whether an entity is a component unit of a primary government. The Oneida-Herkimer Solid Waste Management Authority was created in 1988 as a public benefit corporation under New York State law to provide solid waste management services for two counties, Oneida and Herkimer. The "reporting entity" footnote in Oneida County's financial statements for the year ended December 31, 2003, explains that the Authority is part

---

[5]GASB standards take a broad view of when a primary government is "obligated in some manner" for the debt of a legally separate entity. The standards provide that the obligation may be either expressed or implied by certain indications that make assumption of the debt probable (GASB Cod. Sec. 2100.132.).

of the Oneida County reporting entity because it meets the two "financial accountability" criteria established by the GASB:

a. **Oneida County appoints a voting majority of the authority's governing body.** The authority has a 10-member governing board, appointed as follows: 4 by the Oneida County executive and confirmed by the County legislature, 3 by the Oneida County legislature, and 3 by Herkimer County. (Appointing 7 of the 10 members gives Oneida a voting majority of the authority's governing body.)

b. **There is a potential for the authority to impose specific financial burdens on the county.** According to the note, "[Oneida] County officials do not exercise oversight responsibility for the Authority's operations." But "the County is obligated to finance deficits, if necessary, and the County is a joint guarantor with Herkimer County on the revenue bonds [sold by the Authority]." (The obligation to finance deficits and the guaranty of payment of the Authority's debt imposes a potential financial burden on Oneida.)

Note that the Authority is not a component unit of Herkimer County because Herkimer does not appoint a majority of the authority's governing board. Herkimer County would, however, disclose in a note to its financial statements its financial exposure resulting from the arrangement with Oneida and the authority.

Reporting Component Units in the Reporting Entity's Financial Statements

After all the organizations to be included in the reporting entity are identified, a decision needs to be made as to *how* these organizations should be included in the financial statements. The two methods for inclusion are blending and discrete presentation. *Blending* is the process of treating the funds used by the component unit as if they were the funds of the primary government. *Discrete presentation* of a component unit involves reporting the component unit's funds in a separate column in the reporting entity's government-wide financial statements.

Blending is used when the component unit, although legally separate from the primary government, is so intertwined with the primary government that it is substantively the same as the primary government. This occurs when the primary government's governing body is represented on the component unit's governing body to such an extent that it can completely control the component unit. It also occurs when the goods or services provided by the component unit are all or almost all for the primary government itself.[6]

Blending should be used, for example, when a specially created, legally separate financing agency issues debt solely to finance construction for the primary government, and pays off the debt with rental payments received from the primary government. The financing agency, a component unit, is, in substance, a Debt Service Fund of the primary government and should be treated that way for financial reporting purposes.

---

[6]GASB Cod. Sec. 2600.113.

Discrete presentation is more common than blending. The typical discretely presented organization is one that provides services to the general public, similar to an enterprise fund. It may, for example, operate a toll road, a toll bridge, a lottery, an electric utility, or a public hospital.

In accordance with the reporting requirements of GASB *Statement No. 34,* the financial information of blended component units is reported in both the fund financial statements and the government-wide financial statements. As a general rule, financial information of discretely presented component units is reported only in the government-wide statements, as discussed in Chapter 10.

Notes to the reporting entity's financial statements should contain an identification of the component units, the criteria for including them in the financial statements, and how they are reported.

GOVERNMENTAL FINANCIAL REPORTING IN PRACTICE
When Are Component Units Blended?

Although most component units are reported discretely, the financial statements of financing-type agencies are often blended with the Capital Projects Funds and Debt Service Funds of the primary government. The notes to New York City's financial statements for the year ended June 30, 2006, for example, refer to several component units that "although legally separate, all provide services exclusively to the City and are thus reported as if they were part of the primary government." Here are some excerpts from the notes regarding the New York City Transitional Finance Authority (TFA).

TFA, a corporate governmental agency constituting a public benefit corporation and instrumentality of the State of New York, was created in 1997 to assist the City in funding its capital program....

In addition to State legislative authorization to issue Future Tax Secured bonds for capital purposes, TFA is authorized to have outstanding Recovery Bonds to fund the City's costs related to and arising from events on September 11, 2001 at the World Trade Center....

Debt service requirements and operating expenses are funded by allocations from the State's collection of personal income taxes (imposed by the City and collected by the State).... Net collections of personal income taxes not required by TFA are paid to the City by TFA...."

The notes make it clear that the TFA, though legally separate from New York City, in essence is a capital construction financing arm of the city. When it borrows to finance capital construction projects, it functions as a Capital Projects Fund of the city. When it receives personal income taxes (that would otherwise go to the city) so it can redeem the debt, the TFA functions as a Debt Service Fund of the city. New York City's fund financial statements report TFA's financial activities as two governmental-type funds—as if the activities were undertaken by the city itself.

OVERVIEW OF THE COMPREHENSIVE ANNUAL FINANCIAL REPORT

In previous chapters we discussed the process of accumulating financial information for governmental units. This information is communicated to users of financial information through a *Comprehensive Annual Financial Report (CAFR)*. A CAFR should be prepared and published by all governmental entities as a matter of public record. Based on the GASB *Statement No. 34* requirements, the major components of a CAFR are as follows:

I. Introductory Section
II. Financial Section
    A. Auditor's Report
    B. Management's Discussion and Analysis (MD&A)
    C. Basic Financial Statements
        1. Government-Wide Financial Statements
        2. Fund Financial Statements
        3. Notes to the Financial Statements
    D. Required Supplementary Information (other than MD&A)
    E. Combining Statements and Individual Fund Statements and Schedules
III. Statistical Section

Preparing the CAFR is basically an aggregation process. Using the individual fund and component unit financial statements as building blocks, you first prepare the combining statements (level II.E). (Combining statements aggregate the elements of individual fund statements into totals that are carried forward to higher-level statements.) Then, the fund financial statements (level II.C.2) are prepared. The fund financial statements are then adjusted to prepare the government-wide financial statements (level II.C.1). The notes are often prepared as the financial statements are developed. After the financial statements are completed, the MD&A can be prepared, based on the financial statements and other financial, economic, and demographic data.

The components of the CAFR are discussed briefly in the next few pages. They are covered in greater detail and illustrated in the rest of this chapter and in Chapter 10.

Introductory Section

The CAFR begins with an introductory section that includes a table of contents and a transmittal letter containing comments that the management of the government unit feels are important to the reader. Care should be taken to avoid duplication of content between the introductory section and the MD&A. After the introductory section comes the financial section.

Financial Section

Auditor's Report

The financial section of the CAFR starts with the auditor's report, which contains the auditor's opinion on the entity's financial statements. After describing the scope of their audit, the auditors state whether, in their opinion, the basic financial statements present fairly, in all material respects, the financial position and results of operations of the entity, in conformity with generally accepted accounting principles. The auditors also indicate the extent to which they examined the other data contained in the CAFR, and the nature of their opinion on the other data.

Management's Discussion and Analysis

MD&A introduces the basic financial statements and provides an objective analysis of the government's financial operations and financial position, based on facts known to management as of the date of the auditor's report. MD&A should be easily readable and help the reader understand the fiscal policies, the economic factors, and other matters that affect the data reported in the financial statements.

Basic Financial Statements

The basic financial statements consist of the following:

1. Government-Wide Financial Statements
   a. Statement of net assets
   b. Statement of activities
2. Fund Financial Statements
   a. Governmental funds
      (1) Balance sheet
      (2) Statement of revenues, expenditures, and changes in fund balances
   b. Proprietary Funds
      (1) Statement of net assets (or balance sheet)
      (2) Statement of revenues, expenses, and changes in fund net assets or fund equity
      (3) Cash flows statement
   c. Fiduciary Funds
      (1) Statement of fiduciary net assets
      (2) Statement of changes in fiduciary net assets

Notes to the financial statements provide information that is essential for fair presentation of the financial statements but not shown on the face of the statements. Notes are therefore an integral part of the statements themselves.

Required Supplementary Information Other Than MD&A

Required supplementary information includes schedules, statistical data, and other information identified by the GASB as essential for financial reporting and that should be presented with, but not as part of, the basic financial statements. For example, in addition to MD&A, the GASB requires that governmental units report a comparison of the budget with actual results for certain funds, as well as certain data on pensions.

Combining Statements, Individual Fund Statements, and Schedules

Combining financial statements are needed if the primary government has more than one nonmajor fund or the reporting entity has more than one nonmajor component unit. Because the focus of the fund financial statements is on *major* funds (defined later), financial information for the total nonmajor funds is presented in a single column of the fund statements. Combining financial statements for nonmajor funds and component units provide details on each of those funds. Although they are presented in the CAFR, combining statements are not classified as basic financial statements.

Schedules included in the CAFR provide useful details not otherwise included in the basic financial statements. Schedules might, for example, be prepared to present additional details regarding sources of revenues and object of expenditure data for each department. Schedules could also be used to pull together into a more useful format data that might be spread throughout the various financial statements.

Statistical Section

The *statistical section* of the CAFR provides financial report users with trend data helpful in assessing the government's financial and economic condition. The statistical section covers such matters as the government's capacity to raise revenues and the extent of the government's long-term debt burden. The GASB does not require a statistical section to be prepared as part of the basic financial statements or as required supplementary information; rather, the statistical section is prepared by governments that choose to issue a CAFR.

MINIMUM EXTERNAL FINANCIAL REPORTING REQUIREMENTS

CAFRs are often lengthy documents—Grafton's 2005 CAFR, for example, is 154 pages long. For external financial reporting purposes, a government may wish to issue *general purpose financial reports* separately from the CAFR. For example, when official statements are prepared for bond offerings, financial statements are needed, but not in the detail provided in a CAFR. Also, some governments, especially smaller ones, question whether the benefits of issuing a CAFR justify the expense needed to prepare it.

To accommodate the need for financial reporting without the detail that goes into a CAFR, the GASB has established *minimum requirements* for general purpose external financial statements. The minimum requirements consist of the MD&A, the basic financial statements, and required supplementary financial information other than MD&A (levels II.B, II.C, and II.D of the CAFR). Exhibit 9-1 illustrates these minimum requirements and how they relate to each other.[7]

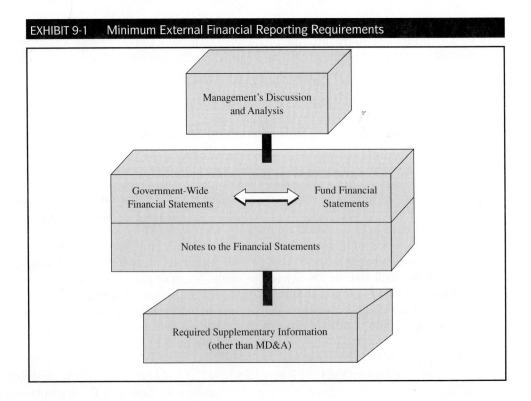

EXHIBIT 9-1   Minimum External Financial Reporting Requirements

---

[7]GASB Cod. Sec. 2200.103.

PREPARING MANAGEMENT'S DISCUSSION AND ANALYSIS

GASB *Statement No. 34* requires that the basic financial statements be preceded by an objective analytical commentary called Management's Discussion and Analysis (MD&A). MD&A details for the reader of the statements an analysis of the government's financial activities and financial position, based on facts, decisions, and conditions known to management as of the date of the auditor's report. It should focus on the primary government, compare the current year with the previous year, and discuss both the positive and negative aspects of that comparison. MD&A should cover the following aspects:

- *Brief discussion of the basic financial statements.* It includes a discussion of how the government-wide and fund financial statements relate to each other, and why the results reported in the two sets of statements either reinforce each other or provide additional information.
- *Condensed financial information from the government-wide statements comparing the current year and the prior year.* Condensed financial information (such as current assets and long-term assets, current liabilities and long-term liabilities, total revenues, total expenses, excess of revenues over expenses before special items, extraordinary items, and transfers) supports the analysis of financial position and results of operations, discussed in the next point.
- *Analysis of the government's overall financial position and results of operations.* The objective of this analysis is to help users assess whether the government's financial position improved or deteriorated as a result of the year's operations. It covers both governmental and business-type activities as reported in the government-wide financial statements. Most important, the analysis covers the reasons for significant change from the previous year, such as changes in tax rates and numbers of government employees. Major economic factors affecting operating results (such as changes in tax bases and employment rates) should also be discussed.

GOVERNMENTAL FINANCIAL REPORTING IN PRACTICE
Explaining How Economics and Demographics Affect Tax Revenues

New York City's fiscal year 2005 tax revenues increased sharply—by 11.3 percent—over 2004. Here's how the city explained some of the causes for this increase in the MD&A section of its 2005 CAFR:

- An increase in the real estate tax resulting from the continuing increase in billable assessed value
- An increase in the sales tax resulting from the boom in construction-based taxable sales related to new housing construction, and the sale of durable goods related to the unprecedented level of real estate transactions

- An increase in personal income tax collections resulting from the payout of almost $20 billion in Wall Street bonuses
- An increase in business income taxes resulting from the strong growth in payments from corporate, bank, and unincorporated business taxpayers, as Wall Street profits continued strong in fiscal year 2005
- Large increases in real estate transaction taxes . . . as homeowners moved to lock in historically low interest rates and as investor interest in Manhattan commercial real estate continued as a result of low vacancy rates and high rents

SOURCE: CAFR, the City of New York, New York, June 30, 2005, MD&A, p. 8.

- *Analysis of balances and transactions of individual funds.* This analysis covers reasons for significant changes in fund balances or fund net assets. It also addresses restrictions and other limitations on the availability of fund resources for future use.
- *Analysis of budgetary variations.* A discussion of significant variances between the original budget, the final budget, and actual results on a budgetary basis for the General Fund is important. Currently known reasons for variations that might significantly affect future services or liquidity are also mentioned.
- *Capital asset and long-term debt activity.* The analysis covers significant transactions and events affecting capital assets and long-term debt (such as capital expenditure commitments, credit rating changes, and debt limitations) that might affect the financing of planned facilities or services.
- *Infrastructure assets.* For governments using the modified approach to reporting infrastructure assets (covered in Chapter 10), the discussion includes significant changes in the condition assessment of the assets from previous assessments, how the current condition assessment compares with the desired condition level established by the government, and significant differences between estimated and actual amounts spent during the year to maintain the assets.
- *Future impacts.* A description of facts, decisions, or conditions currently known to management that are expected to significantly affect the financial position or results of operations of the government needs to be included.

Exhibit 9-2 contains excerpts from the MD&A prepared by the Village of Grafton, Wisconsin, for its calendar year 2005 annual financial report. These excerpts explain (a) why a large portion of the combined fund balance is not available for discretionary spending, (b) why the village was able to avoid using part of the fund balance of the General Fund to finance 2005 operations even though it had originally planned to do so, and (c) how the available fund balance relates to Grafton's financial planning policies.

PREPARING FUND FINANCIAL STATEMENTS: GENERAL

Focus on Major Funds

The focus of the fund financial statements is on the primary government's major funds. GASB *Statement No. 34* defines a major fund as:

a. The General Fund; and
b. A governmental or enterprise fund (including a blended component unit) whose total assets, liabilities, revenues, or expenditures/expenses are at least 10 percent of the corresponding element for all funds of that category or type (that is, total governmental or total enterprise funds), and the same element that met the 10 percent criterion is also at least 5 percent of the corresponding element total for all governmental and enterprise funds combined; and
c. Any other governmental or enterprise fund that governmental officials believe is particularly important (for example, because of public interest) to financial statement users.[8]

---

[8]GASB Cod. Sec. 2200.150.

EXHIBIT 9-2   Management's Discussion and Analysis

Village of Grafton, Wisconsin
Management's Discussion and Analysis (Excerpts)
December 31, 2005

Financial Analysis of the Government's Funds
"As of December 31, 2005, the Village of Grafton's governmental funds reported combined ending balances of $14,549,797, an increase of $5,992,734 in comparison with the prior year. Approximately 31 percent or $4,535,749 constitutes unreserved fund balance, which is available for spending at the government's discretion. The remainder of the fund balance is reserved to indicate that it is not available for new spending because it has already been committed (1) to pay debt service ($1,638,026), (2) to pay for capital projects ($6,682,502) . . . , (3) for long-term receivables from participants of the Village of Grafton's economic development revolving loan fund ($762,172), (4) to generate income to pay for the perpetual care of the municipal cemetery ($63,840), (5) for advances to other funds ($790,912), and (6) for prepaid insurance premiums, delinquent taxes, and noncurrent receivables ($76,596).

"The fund balance of the General Fund increased by $11,773 in fiscal year 2005. The 2005 annual program budget for the Village of Grafton's General Fund identified the appropriation of $327,938 in fund balance to reduce the impact of taxes levied and to balance the budget. However, actual [expenditures] and other uses were less than budgeted [expenditures] and other uses by approximately 1.7 percent or $114,744, and actual revenues and other sources exceeded budgeted revenues and other sources in the general fund by $224,937 or approximately 3.4 percent."

Economic Factors and Next Year's Budgets and Rates
". . . $280,709 of the unreserved fund balance in the General Fund was appropriated for spending in the 2006 budget. It is intended that the use of available fund balance will lessen the required tax levy yet meet the Village of Grafton's guidelines to maintain a minimum unreserved fund balance of 20 percent of General Fund expenditures."

SOURCE: CAFR, Village of Grafton, Wisconsin, Year 2005, MD&A, pp. 23 and 27.

Funds that do not meet this definition are "nonmajor" funds. Each major fund is presented in a separate column of the fund financial statements. Nonmajor funds are aggregated and displayed in a single column. Combining statements for the nonmajor funds may be presented as supplementary information to the basic statements, but are ordinarily shown in the combining statements part (level 2.E.) of the CAFR.

Major fund reporting requirements do not apply to Internal Service Funds. Instead, the combined totals for all Internal Service Funds should be presented in a single column to the right of the total Enterprise Funds column. A combining statement should be prepared to report the details of the individual Internal Service Funds.

Measurement Focus and Basis of Accounting

Financial statements for governmental funds should be presented using the *current financial resources measurement focus* and the *modified accrual basis of accounting,* as described in Chapters 2, 4, 5, and 6. This approach means, among other things, that general capital assets acquired with governmental fund resources are not reported as assets in the financial statements prepared for governmental funds. It also means that general long-term liabilities, such as the unmatured principal of bonds or other forms of long-term indebtedness are not reported as liabilities in the governmental fund financial statements. (These assets and liabilities are, however, reported in the government-wide financial statements.)

Financial statements for proprietary funds should be presented using the *economic resources measurement focus* and the *accrual basis of accounting,* as discussed in Chapter 7. Financial statements of fiduciary funds generally should be reported using the *economic resources measurement focus* and the *accrual basis of accounting.* The exception regarding fiduciary funds pertains to certain liabilities of defined benefit plans and postemployment health care plans, discussed in Chapter 8.

Special and Extraordinary Items

To aid the report user in assessing a governmental entity's financial condition, GASB *Statement No. 34* requires that special and extraordinary items be displayed in a separate caption on operating statements. *Extraordinary items* are defined as transactions that are *both* unusual in nature *and* infrequent in occurrence. *Special items* are significant transactions or other events within the control of management that are *either* unusual in nature *or* infrequent in occurrence. Assume, for example, that a government encountering fiscal stress decides to balance its budget in form, though not in substance, with a "one-shot" financial resource resulting from the sale and leaseback of capital assets through one of its public authorities. That type of transaction probably would meet the definition of "special," although it might not rise to the level of being "extraordinary."

PREPARING FUND FINANCIAL STATEMENTS FOR GOVERNMENTAL FUNDS

Balance Sheet

The governmental funds balance sheet in the fund financial statements should report information about the current financial resources of each major governmental fund and for the total of the nonmajor funds. Resources and claims against the resources should be presented in balance sheet format (Assets = Liabilities + Fund Balance). Governmental fund balances should be segregated between reserved and unreserved amounts.

Table 9-1 contains the governmental funds balance sheet for the Village of Grafton, Wisconsin, as of December 31, 2005. Table 9-2 shows the combining balance sheet for Grafton's nonmajor governmental funds. (Even though the combining statement is not a basic statement, as previously mentioned, it is presented here to illustrate its relationship to the basic statement.)

Grafton actually has 5 governmental funds that meet the GASB's criteria for classification as major, although we have shown only 3 (General, Debt Service, and Capital Projects) to simplify the presentation in Table 9-1. Grafton also has 15 nonmajor funds, covering all 5 governmental-type funds, but again we showed only a few to simplify the presentation of the combining balance sheet in Table 9-2. The amounts reported in the column captioned "other governmental funds" (Table 9-1) are the sums of the amounts for the 15 nonmajor funds combined (Table 9-2).

TABLE 9-1 Governmental Funds Balance Sheet

Village of Grafton
Balance Sheet
Governmental Funds
December 31, 2005

	General	Debt Service	Capital Projects		Nonmajor Governmental Funds	Total Governmental Funds
Assets:						
Cash and Investments	$1,597,015	$ 383,070	$1,011,715		$2,950,183	$14,476,718
Receivables (Net):						
Taxes	4,531,504	995,082	260,395		507,986	6,617,499
Delinquent Personal Property Taxes	13,673					13,673
Accounts	169,026	14,032	5,475		—	196,977
Special Assessments	—		149,687		50,352	200,039
Loans	—				282,841	282,841
Due from Other Funds	90,221				—	90,221
Advances to Other Funds	—		790,912		—	790,912
Prepaid Items	62,923				4,515	286,492
Total Assets	**$6,464,362**	**$1,392,184**	**$2,218,184**		**$3,795,877**	**$22,955,372**
Liabilities and Fund Balances:						
Liabilities:						
Accounts Payable	$ 154,680	$ 21	$ 2,496		$ 29,665	$ 346,567
Accrued Liabilities	139,358				14,545	153,903
Deposits	59,460				138,867	198,327
Due to Other Funds	2,193				—	92,414
Due to Plan Participants	3,625				—	3,625
Advances from Other Funds					—	70,912
Unearned Revenues	4,531,504	995,082	255,000		507,986	6,619,788
Deferred Special Assessments	—		149,687		50,352	200,039
Total Liabilities	**4,890,820**	**995,103**	**407,183**		**741,415**	**8,405,575**
Fund Balances:						
Reserved	76,596	397,081	790,912		1,035,748	10,014,048
Unreserved, Reported In:						
General Fund	1,496,946					1,496,946
Special Revenue Funds					1,390,296	1,390,296
Capital Project Funds	—		1,020,089		628,418	1,648,507
Total Fund Balances	**1,573,542**	**397,081**	**1,811,001**		**3,054,462**	**14,549,797**
Total Liabilities and Fund Balances	**$6,464,362**	**$1,392,184**	**$2,218,184**		**$3,795,877**	

Reconciliation
Amounts reported for governmental activities in the statement of net assets are different because:
Capital assets used in governmental funds are not financial resources and therefore are not reported in the funds. 34,713,307
Other long-term assets are not available to pay for current-period expenditures and therefore are deferred in the funds. 583,521
Some liabilities, including long-term debt, are not due and payable in the current period and therefore are not reported in the funds. (25,506,378)
$24,340,247

See Accompanying Notes
Source: Comprehensive Annual Financial Report, Year 2005, Village of Grafton, Wisconsin.
Note: Two major funds are not shown here to simplify presentation.

TABLE 9-2 Nonmajor Governmental Funds Combining Balance Sheet

Village of Grafton
Combining Balance Sheet
Nonmajor Governmental Funds
December 31, 2005

	Special Revenue Funds		Capital Projects Fund	Permanent Fund	Total Nonmajor Funds
	Park and Open Space	Revolving Loan	Equipment	Cemetery Perpetual Care	
Assets:					
Cash and Investments	$71,194	$480,083	$ 50,216	$63,840	$2,950,183
Taxes Receivable	20,000	—	255,000	—	507,986
Special Assessments	—	—	—	—	50,352
Loans Receivable	—	282,841	—	—	282,841
Prepaid Items	—	—	—	—	4,515
Total Assets	$91,194	$762,924	$305,216	$63,840	$3,795,877
Liabilities and Fund Balances:					
Liabilities:					
Accounts Payable	$ 1,758	$ 752	$ 455	$ —	$ 29,665
Accrued Liabilities	—	—	—	—	14,545
Deposits	—	—	—	—	138,867
Deferred Special Assessments	—	—	—	—	50,352
Unearned Revenues	20,000	—	255,000	—	507,986
Total Liabilities	21,758	752	255,455	—	741,415
Fund Balances:					
Reserved:					
Culture and Recreation	50,000	—	—	—	503,419
Community Development	—	282,841	—	63,840	346,681
Retirement of Long-Term Debt	—	—	—	—	185,648
Unreserved	19,436	479,331	49,761	—	2,018,714
Total Fund Balances	69,436	762,172	49,761	63,840	3,054,462
Total Liabilities and Fund Balances	$91,194	$762,924	$305,216	$63,840	$3,795,877

Source: Comprehensive Annual Financial Report, Year 2005, Village of Grafton, Wisconsin

Note: The actual statement has columns for 15 funds, only 4 of which are shown here, to simplify presentation.

Notice the amounts reported next to the captions for taxes receivable and un-earned revenues. Most governments use the caption "deferred revenues" rather than unearned revenues. Grafton reports significant unearned revenues because it levies property taxes and mails the bills in advance of the year for which the taxes are levied. The general rule for property taxes is that a receivable is recognized when an enforce-able legal claim arises, and revenue is recognized in the period *for which the taxes are levied, subject to the "available" criterion.*

Notice also that the caption "total fund balances" (in the lower part of the balance sheet) is reconciled to "net assets of governmental activities." The latter is the net asset amount shown in the governmental activities column of the government-wide state-ment of net assets, which will be discussed in Chapter 10. Also, notice the nature of the reconciling items, including the fact that the governmental fund balance sheets report neither capital assets (because they are not financial resources) nor long-term debt (because the debt is not due and payable in the current period).

Statement of Revenues, Expenditures, and Changes in Fund Balances

The statement of revenues, expenditures, and changes in fund balances included in the fund financial statements shows information about inflows, outflows, and balances of resources, based on the current financial resources measurement focus and the modi-fied accrual basis of accounting. This statement contains a separate column for each major fund and for the total of the nonmajor governmental funds. This statement is sequenced as follows:

> Revenues (by type)
> − Expenditures (by program or function)
> _____
> = Excess (deficiency) of revenues over expenditures
> ± Other financing sources and uses (such as proceeds
>   of debt and transfers)
> ± Special and extraordinary items
> _____
> = Net change in fund balances
> + Fund balances at beginning of period
> _____
> = Fund balances at end of period[9]

Table 9-3 contains the Village of Grafton's governmental funds statement of rev-enues, expenditures, and changes in fund balances for the year ended December 31, 2005. Table 9-4 shows Grafton's combining statement of revenues, expenditures, and changes in fund balances for the nonmajor governmental funds. Notice that the totals in Table 9-4 agree with the totals for the "other governmental funds" column in Table 9-3. (Once again, we left out some of the funds to simplify the presentation.)

Notice the significant amount of activity reported below the caption "excess (defi-ciency) of revenues over (under) expenditures." The major activities concern the sale of long-term debt and interfund transfers:

- Grafton sold $9,615,000 of long-term debt during 2005, primarily for two Tax In-cremental Financing District (TID) funds, the two major funds not shown here. TIDs are generally created for the purpose of making public improvements and

_____
[9]GASB Cod. Sec. 2200.156.

Village of Grafton
Statement of Revenues, Expenditures, and Changes in Fund Balances
Governmental Funds
For the Year Ended December 31, 2005

	General	Debt Service	Capital Projects	Other Governmental Funds	Total Governmental Funds
Revenues:					
Taxes	$4,641,176	$ 959,693	$ 247,066	$ 520,673	$ 6,550,849
Intergovernmental	1,285,395	117,109	50,619	19,890	1,528,927
Licenses and Permits	346,166	—	—	—	346,166
Fines, Forfeitures, and Penalties	123,888	—	—	—	123,888
Public Charges for Services	224,821	—	58,166	154,001	436,988
Intergovernmental Charges for Services	41,822	—	—	145,030	186,852
Impact Fees	—	—	—	114,332	114,332
Investment Income	85,569	36,213	41,577	122,600	400,206
Miscellaneous	25,353	—	97,650	56,173	216,438
Total Revenues	6,774,190	1,113,015	495,078	1,132,699	9,904,646
Expenditures:					
Current:					
General Government	740,403	—	82,629	—	823,032
Public Safety	3,261,589	—	—	—	3,261,589
Public Works	1,906,633	—	—	—	1,906,633
Community Enrichment Services	363,459	—	—	683,086	1,046,545
Conservation and Development	137,982	—	—	109,591	2,462,302
Capital Outlay	—	—	792,460	863,124	2,003,905
Debt Service:					
Principal Retirement	—	1,309,479	—	—	1,309,479
Interest and Fiscal Charges	—	685,221	—	—	685,221
Debt Issuance Costs	—	26,850	3,297	4,044	84,781
Total Expenditures	6,410,066	2,021,550	878,386	1,659,845	13,583,487
Excess (Deficiency) of Revenues Over (Under) Expenditures	364,124	(908,535)	(383,308)	(527,146)	(3,678,841)
Other Financing Sources (Uses):					
Long-Term Debt Issued	—	—	285,000	500,000	9,615,000
Premium of Issuance	—	—	1,315	2,308	56,575
Transfers In	48,959	842,648	55,000	401,310	1,347,917
Transfers Out	(401,310)	—	(112,937)	(469,561)	(1,347,917)
Total Other Financing Sources (Uses)	(352,351)	842,648	228,378	434,057	9,671,575
Net Change In Fund Balances	11,773	(65,887)	(154,930)	(93,089)	5,992,734
Fund Balances—Beginning	1,561,769	462,968	1,965,931	3,147,551	8,557,063
Fund Balances—Ending	$1,573,542	$ 397,081	$ 1,811,001	$3,054,462	$14,549,797

See Accompanying Notes
Source: Comprehensive Annual Financial Report, Year 2005, Grafton, Wisconsin
Note: Two major funds are not shown here, to simplify presentation.

Village of Grafton
Combining Statement of Revenues, Expenditures, and Changes in Fund Balances
Nonmajor Governmental Funds
For the Year Ended December 31, 2005

	Special Revenue Funds		Capital Projects Fund	Permanent Fund	Total Nonmajor Funds
	Park and Open Space	Revolving Loan	Equipment	Cemetery Perpetual Care	
Revenues:					
Taxes	$ —	$ —	$244,845	$ —	$ 520,673
Intergovernmental	—	—	—	—	19,890
Public Charges for Services	—	—	—	—	154,001
Intergovernmental Charges for Services	—	—	—	—	145,030
Impact Fees	—	—	—	—	114,332
Investment Income	1,917	24,608	3,574	1,892	122,600
Miscellaneous	30,050	—	12,636	4,950	56,173
Total Revenues	31,967	24,608	261,055	6,842	1,132,699
Expenditures:					
Current:					
Community Enrichment Services	16,696	—	—	—	683,086
Conservation and Development	—	38,049	—	—	109,591
Capital Outlay	—	—	241,686	—	863,124
Total Expenditures	16,696	38,049	241,686	—	1,655,801
Excess of Revenues Over (Under) Expenditures	15,271	(13,441)	19,369	6,842	(523,102)
Other Financing Sources (Uses):					
Debt Proceeds	—	—	—	—	500,000
Transfers In	—	—	—	—	401,310
Bond Premium	—	—	—	—	2,308
Debt Issue Costs	—	—	—	—	(4,044)
Transfers Out	(55,000)	—	—	(1,892)	(469,561)
Total Other Financing Sources (Uses)	(55,000)	—	—	(1,892)	430,013
Net Change In Fund Balances	(39,729)	(13,441)	19,369	4,950	(93,089)
Fund Balances—Beginning	109,165	775,613	30,392	58,890	3,147,551
Fund Balances (Deficit)—Ending	$69,436	$762,172	$ 49,761	$ 63,840	$3,054,462

Source: Comprehensive Annual Financial Report, Year 2005, Grafton, Wisconsin.

Note: The actual statement has columns for 15 funds, only 4 of which are shown here, to simplify presentation.

345

stimulating economic development, often in downtown or "urban renewal" areas. Debt service on the bonds is financed from property taxes resulting from the increase in property values within the district affected by the improvements.

- Grafton also had $1,347,917 of interfund transfers. Details of interfund transfers should be explained in the notes to aid in analyzing the financial statements. According to the note in Grafton's statements, most of the transfers went to the Debt Service Fund, primarily from the TIDs. The largest transfer out of the General Fund went to the Library Fund (not shown here) to cover operating expenditures.

As previously stated, GASB standards permit a government to designate any fund as "major" if it believes the fund is important to users of financial statements. However, the government must designate a fund as major if it meets certain criteria. For example, the Debt Service Fund is major based on the expenditure criterion. Notice that Debt Service Fund expenditures (see Table 9-3) were $2,021,550 in 2005. This amount is more than 10 percent of total governmental fund expenditures ($13,583,487, shown in Table 9-3) and more than 5 percent of total expenditures/expenses for governmental and enterprise funds combined ($13,583,487 + $2,517,275, shown in Table 9-6, = $16,100,762).

Just as the fund and the government-wide balance sheets are reconciled with each other, so are the two operating statements reconciled. This reconciliation is discussed and illustrated in Chapter 10.

PREPARING FUND FINANCIAL STATEMENTS FOR PROPRIETARY FUNDS

Statement of Net Assets (or Balance Sheet)

Fund financial statements for proprietary funds should be presented using the economic resources measurement focus and the accrual basis of accounting. As a result, proprietary fund statements of net assets normally show both capital assets and long-term debt. This statement may be prepared either in the statement of net assets format (Assets − Liabilities = Net Assets) or in the balance sheet format (Assets = Liabilities + Net Assets).

The assets and liabilities should be presented in *classified* format, to distinguish between those that are current and those that are noncurrent. Current assets are assets that are expected to be converted to cash or consumed in operations within 1 year, and current liabilities are liabilities that are due to be paid within 1 year.

Regardless of whether the statement is prepared in net assets or balance sheet format, the net assets should be classified in three components: (1) invested in capital assets, net of related debt, (2) restricted, and (3) unrestricted. The component *invested in capital assets, net of related debt* represents the capital assets of the proprietary funds, minus accumulated depreciation and outstanding balances of bonds, notes, or other borrowings attributable to acquiring, constructing, or improving those assets.

Net assets are reported as *restricted* when constraints are imposed on the use of the assets either externally (by creditors, grantors, or laws or regulations of other governments) or by the entity's constitution or enabling legislation. For example, restrictions may be imposed by (a) debt covenant or by (b) higher-level government's requirement that resources be spent only for a particular capital project.

Table 9-5 contains the proprietary funds statement of net assets for the Village of Grafton at December 31, 2005. Grafton has a single proprietary fund, the Water and

TABLE 9-5   Proprietary Funds Statement of Net Assets

Village of Grafton
Statement of Net Assets
Proprietary Fund-Water and Wastewater Utility
December 31, 2005

Current Assets:	
Cash and Investments	$ 4,193,025
Customer Accounts Receivable	437,313
Other Accounts Receivable	49,926
Due from Municipality	2,193
Prepaid Insurance	11,112
Inventories	1,910
Total Current Assets	4,695,479
Noncurrent Assets:	
Restricted Assets:	
Replacement Fund	818,772
Capital Assets:	
Water	
Plant in Service	14,092,435
Accumulated Depreciation	(3,173,522)
Wastewater	
Plant in Service	19,293,583
Accumulated Depreciation	(6,780,515)
Construction Work in Progress	10,312
Other Assets:	
Unamortized Debt Discount	6,011
Total Noncurrent Assets	24,267,076
Total Assets	28,962,555
Current Liabilities:	
Current Portion of General Obligation Debt	353,262
Accounts Payable	282,211
Accrued Payroll Expense	28,926
Accrued Interest	34,861
Unearned Revenues	56,464
Total Current Liabilities	755,724
Noncurrent Liabilities:	
General Obligation Debt	2,362,319
Accrued Compensated Absences	36,279
Security Deposits	4,800
Total Noncurrent Liabilities	2,403,398
Total Liabilities	3,159,122
Net Assets:	
Invested in Capital Assets, Net of Related Debt	20,726,712
Restricted for Replacement Fund	818,772
Unrestricted	4,257,949
TOTAL NET ASSETS	$25,803,433

See Accompanying Notes
Source: Comprehensive Annual Financial Report, Year 2005, Grafton, Wisconsin.

Wastewater Utility Fund. If the village had more than one proprietary fund, this statement would need to show financial information for each major fund and a total for nonmajor funds.

Notice that Table 9-5 is presented in classified format, with current assets and liabilities separated from noncurrent ones. Therefore, the amount of long-term debt due in 1 year is classified as current. Notice also that the net assets section of the statement is classified as invested in capital assets, net of related debt; restricted; and unrestricted. The amount shown as invested in capital assets, net of related debt ($20,726,712) is calculated as follows: net capital assets ($14,092,435 − $3,173,522 + $19,293,583 − $6,780,515 + $10,312 = $23,442,293) minus related general obligation debt ($353,262 current portion + $2,362,319 noncurrent = $2,715,581). The amount shown as restricted ($818,772) is equal to the amount reported as Restricted assets—replacement fund.

Statement of Revenues, Expenses, and Changes in Fund Net Assets

The proprietary funds operating statement is called the statement of revenues, expenses, and changes in fund net assets. This statement should be prepared in a format that distinguishes between operating and nonoperating revenues and expenses, and provides separate captions for *operating income* and *income before other revenues, expenses, gains, losses, and transfers,* as shown below.

> Operating revenues (show details and total)
> − Operating expenses (show details and total)
> = Operating income (loss)
> ± Nonoperating revenues and expenses (show details)
> = Income before other revenues, expenses, gains, losses, and transfers
> ± Capital contributions, additions to endowments, special items, extraordinary items, and transfers
> = Change in net assets
> + Net assets at beginning of period
> = Net assets at end of period[10]

For an illustration, see Table 9-6 for the proprietary funds statement of revenues, expenses, and changes in fund net assets for the Village of Grafton for the year ended December 31, 2005.

Statement of Cash Flows

GASB *Statement No. 34* also requires preparation of a statement of cash flows for proprietary activities, using the direct method of presenting cash flows from operating activities.

Table 9-7 presents the proprietary funds statement of cash flows for the Village of Grafton for the year ended December 31, 2005. Extensive discussion of this statement is outside the scope of this text. Note, however, that this statement supplements the accrual-basis statement of revenues, expenses, and changes in fund net assets by giving the reader a more complete understanding of the nature of the fund's financial activities. For example, the statement of cash flows shows how much the fund spent to

---

[10]GASB Cod. Sec. 2200.167 (adapted).

TABLE 9-6   Proprietary Funds Statement of Revenues, Expenses, and Changes in Fund Net Assets

Village of Grafton
Statement of Revenues, Expenses, and Changes in Fund Net Assets
Proprietary Fund—Water and Wastewater Utility
For the Year Ended December 31, 2005

Operating Revenues	$ 2,743,564
Operating Expenses:	
Operation and Maintenance	1,545,994
Depreciation	738,768
Taxes	232,513
Total Operating Expenses	2,517,275
Operating Income	226,289
Nonoperating Revenues (Expenses):	
Investment Income	45,004
Interest Expense	(76,403)
Amortization Expense	(553)
Total Nonoperating Expenses	(31,952)
Income Before Capital Contributions	194,337
Capital Contributions	75,788
Change in Net Assets	270,125
Total Net Assets—Beginning	25,533,308
Total Net Assets—Ending	$25,803,433

See Accompanying Notes
Source: Comprehensive Annual Financial Report, Year 2005, Grafton, Wisconsin.

acquire capital assets and how much it spent to pay debt principal, neither of which are evident from the accrual-basis financial statements. It also demonstrates that, because depreciation did not require a cash outlay, the net cash flows from operating activities ($1,129,182) and proceeds from the sale of long-term debt ($822,892) helped provide cash to acquire capital assets.

PREPARING FUND FINANCIAL STATEMENTS FOR FIDUCIARY FUNDS

GASB *Statement No. 34* requires two fiduciary fund financial statements, a statement of fiduciary net assets and a statement of changes in fiduciary net assets. These statements should provide information about all fiduciary funds of the primary government, as well as component units that are fiduciary in nature. The statements should have separate columns for each fund type, that is, Pension and Other Employee Benefit Trust Funds, Investment Trust Funds, Private Purpose Trust Funds, and Agency Funds.

The requirement for showing individual major funds does not extend to the fiduciary fund basic financial statements. Financial statements for individual pension and postemployment health care plans, however, must be presented in the notes to the financial statements if separate GAAP financial statements have not been issued, but if such statements have been issued, the notes need only contain information about how to obtain these statements.

TABLE 9-7   Proprietary Funds Statement of Cash Flows

Village of Grafton
Statement of Cash Flows
Proprietary Fund—Water and Wastewater Utility
For the Year Ended December 31, 2005

Cash Flows From Operating Activities:	
Cash Received from Customers	$ 2,743,329
Cash Paid to Other Funds for Services	(221,317)
Cash Paid to Suppliers for Goods and Services	(1,437,573)
Cash Paid to Employees for Services	44,743
Net Cash Flows from Operating Activities	1,129,182
Cash Flows From Noncapital Financing Activities:	
Tax Equivalent Paid to Municipality	(207,807)
Cash Flows From Investing Activities:	
Investment Income Received	45,004
Cash Flows From Capital and Related Financing Activities:	
Acquisition and Construction of Capital Assets	(1,038,575)
Proceeds from Long-Term Debt	822,892
Interest Paid	58,042
Capital Contributions Received	75,788
Net Cash Flows from Capital and Related Financing Activities	(81,853)
Net Increase In Cash and Cash Equivalents	884,526
Cash and Cash Equivalents—Beginning	4,127,271
Cash and Cash Equivalents—Ending	$ 5,011,797
Reconciliation of Cash and Cash Equivalents to the	
Statement of Net Assets—Proprietary Fund:	
Unrestricted Cash and Investments	$ 4,193,025
Restricted Cash and Investments	818,772
Cash and Cash Equivalents Per Statement of Cash Flows	$ 5,011,797
Cash Flows From Operating Activities:	
Operating Income	$ 226,289
Adjustments to Reconcile Operating Income to Net	
Cash Flows from Operating Activities	
Noncash Items Included in Income-Depreciation	738,768
Change in Noncash Components of Working Capital	
Accounts Receivable	28,574
Other Accounts Receivable	(28,143)
Prepaid Insurance	381
Inventories	4,805
Accounts Payable	116,624
Due to Other Funds	76,705
Accrued Sick Leave	(1,418)
Other Liabilities	(30,544)
Accrued Revenues	(2,859)
Net Cash Flows From Operating Activities	$ 1,129,182

See Accompanying Notes

Source: Comprehensive Annual Financial Report, Year 2005, Grafton, Wisconsin.

TABLE 9-8 Fiduciary Funds Statement of Fiduciary Net Assets

Village of Grafton
Fiduciary Funds (Agency Tax Collection Fund)
Statement of Fiduciary Net Assets
December 31, 2005

Assets	
Cash and investments	$ 11,218,854
Taxes receivable	1,629,838
Total Assets	$12,848,692
Liabilities	
Due to other taxing units	$ 12,848,692
Total Liabilities	$ 12,848,692

Source: Comprehensive Annual Financial Report, Year 2005, Village of Grafton, Wisconsin. (Adapted)

The statement of fiduciary net assets should have information about the assets, liabilities, and net assets for each fund type. The statement of changes in fiduciary net assets reports additions to, deductions from, and net increase (or decrease) for the year in net assets. The reporting requirements for Pension Funds are described in Chapter 8.

The Village of Grafton has a single fiduciary fund—a Tax Collection Agency Fund. As discussed in Chapter 8, Agency Funds are custodian accounts that collect and disburse resources. They have only assets and liabilities, and no net assets. Therefore, the only financial statement that needs to be prepared for Agency Funds is the statement of fiduciary net assets. Table 9-8 presents the Village of Grafton's statement of fiduciary net assets at December 31, 2005.

PREPARING BUDGETARY COMPARISON SCHEDULES

In addition to the basic fund financial statements, state and local governments are required to present fund-level budgetary comparison schedules for the General Fund and for each major Special Revenue Fund with a legally adopted annual budget. These schedules should be presented as required supplementary information (RSI). (Governments may choose, however, to present them as basic financial statements, rather than as RSI.)

Budgetary comparison schedules compare the original appropriated budget, the final appropriated budget, and the actual inflows, outflows, and balances for the year, stated on the government's *budgetary* basis of accounting. GASB *Statement No. 34* defines the original budget as the first appropriated budget. This budget includes any modifications, such as transfers, allocations, and other legally authorized legislative and executive changes made before the start of the fiscal year. The final budget includes all subsequent legally authorized legislative and executive changes applicable to the fiscal year.

Before GASB *Statement No. 34* became effective, budgetary comparison schedules showed only the final budget. Adding a requirement for presenting the original budget gives the reader a more complete picture of the factors causing actual results to vary from the budget, and how management adapted to change. For example, if economic factors caused a reduction in tax collections, the budgetary comparison statement provides a clue about the actions taken to keep expenditures in line with the reduced revenues.

In presenting the budgetary comparison schedules, governments may choose to use either the format, terminology, and classifications used in the budget document or the same format used in the statement of revenues, expenditures, and changes in fund balances. In either event, the entity should reconcile the actual data on the budgetary basis of accounting, as shown in the budgetary comparison schedules, with the data presented in the fund financial statements of revenues, expenditures, and changes in fund balances.

The general fund budgetary comparison schedule for the Village of Grafton for the year ended December 31, 2005, is shown in Table 9-9. Notice that the amounts shown in

TABLE 9-9　Budgetary Comparison Statement

Village of Grafton
Budgetary Comparison Statement
General Fund
For the Year Ended December 31, 2005

	Budgeted Amounts		Actual Amounts	Variance with Final Budget Positive (Negative)
	Original	Final		
Revenues:				
Taxes	$4,630,913	$4,630,913	$4,641,176	$ 10,263
Intergovernmental	1,287,821	1,287,821	1,285,395	(2,426)
Licenses and Permits	287,215	287,215	346,166	58,951
Fines, Forfeitures and Penalties	81,500	81,500	123,888	42,388
Public Charges for Services	216,625	216,625	224,821	8,196
Intergovernmental Charges for Services	41,963	41,963	41,822	(141)
Investment Income	32,000	32,000	85,569	53,569
Miscellaneous	19,625	19,625	25,353	5,728
Total Revenues	6,597,662	6,597,662	6,774,190	176,528
Expenditures:				
General Government	741,687	748,947	740,382	8,565
Public Safety	3,306,293	3,333,136	3,261,589	71,547
Public Works	1,856,299	1,917,587	1,906,633	10,954
Community Enrichment Services	330,837	356,198	363,459	(7,261)
Conservation and Development	158,194	161,830	137,982	23,848
Nondepartmental	124,409	21	21	—
Total Expenditures	6,517,719	6,517,719	6,410,066	107,653
Excess of Revenues Over Expenditures	79,943	79,943	364,124	284,181
Other Financing Sources (Uses):				
Transfers In	550	550	48,959	48,409
Transfers Out	(408,431)	(408,431)	(401,310)	7,121
Total Other Financing Sources (Uses)	(407,881)	(407,881)	(352,351)	55,530
Net Change In Fund Balances	(327,938)	(327,938)	11,773	339,711
Fund Balance—Beginning	1,440,805	1,440,805	1,561,769	120,964
Fund Balance—Ending	$1,112,867	$1,112,867	$1,573,542	$460,675

See Accompanying Notes
Source: Comprehensive Annual Financial Report, Year 2005, Village of Grafton, Wisconsin.

the "actual" columns are the same in Tables 9-3 and 9-9. This is because Grafton's budgetary basis of accounting is effectively the same as that used in the fund financial statement for the General Fund—modified accrual. If the amounts shown in the "actual" columns differed, however, Grafton would be required to show a reconciliation of the amounts. As discussed in Chapter 5, a common reconciling item results from the fact that encumbrances often are reported as outflows in the budgetary comparison schedule, but not in the statement of revenues, expenditures, and changes in fund balances.

PREPARING NOTES TO THE FINANCIAL STATEMENTS

At the bottom of each financial statement is the notation "See Accompanying Notes." *Notes to the financial statements* contain information essential to a user's understanding of the financial position and changes in financial position of the reporting unit, but that either does not meet the criteria for recognition in a financial statement or provides more detail than can appropriately be included in the body of a financial statement.[11] The focus of the notes should be on the primary government, but certain information should also be included on the major component units. Notes tend to be lengthy and may run 30 to 40 pages. The discussion that follows covers some, but by no means all, of the disclosure requirements.

The notes generally start with a summary of the primary government's significant accounting policies. Significant accounting policies include the following:

- A description of the government-wide financial statements
- The component units of the financial reporting entity, the criteria for including them in the reporting entity, and their relationships with the primary government
- A description of the activities accounted for in certain columns (that is, major funds, Internal Service Funds, and fiduciary-type funds) presented in the basic financial statements (for example, the transportation fund accounts for constructing, maintaining, and policing state highways)
- The measurement focus and basis of accounting used in the government-wide statements, and the revenue recognition policies (such as length of time used to define "available") in the fund financial statements
- The policy for capitalizing assets and estimating their useful lives
- The policy for defining operating and nonoperating revenues of proprietary funds

GOVERNMENTAL FINANICAL REPORTING IN PRACTICE
Disclosing Risks Associated with Bank Deposits and Investments

During the 1980s, several governments suffered losses when they invested in a type of financial instrument called repurchase agreements. These instruments have characteristics similar to bank deposits, because they involve giving cash to another party who promises to return the cash (with interest) and who pledges collateral for the promise. When the governments didn't hold the collateral and the

---

[11]GASB *Statement No. 38,* "Certain Financial Statement Note Disclosures," para. 34.

securities dealers handling the investments collapsed, the governments were left holding empty promises. This caused the GASB to require certain note disclosures on deposits and investments.

One of the required disclosures concerns *custodial credit risk*—the risk that "in the event of failure of a depository financial institution, a government will not be able to recover deposits or will not be able to recover collateral securities that are in the possession of an outside party." GASB standards say that bank deposits are exposed to custodial risk if they are not covered by depository insurance (the Federal Deposit Insurance Corporation insures bank deposits up to $100,000) or if they are not collateralized with securities that are held *in the name of the depositor government.*

The GASB requires governments to disclose the extent to which their bank deposits at the financial statement date are (a) uncollateralized, (b) collateralized with securities held by the pledging financial institution, or (c) collateralized with securities held by the pledging financial institution's trust department or agent but not in the depositor government's name. For example, the notes to New York City's June 30, 2006, financial statements said that the carrying amount of the unrestricted cash and cash equivalents was $10.097 billion and the bank balances were $2.204 billion. Of the unrestricted bank balances, $8 million was exposed to custodial credit risk because they were uninsured or uncollateralized. The note also said the banks used by the city are well capitalized and that independent bank rating agencies are used to assess their financial soundness.

Governments are also required to make note disclosure of material violations of finance-related legal and contractual provisions, as well as the actions taken to address the violations. A government might, for example, violate a statute that prohibits incurring a deficit in a particular fund, or it might violate the debt service coverage requirements of a bond covenant. In these cases, the government would need to disclose not only the violation, but also the nature of the action (such as an increase in user charges) taken to overcome the violation.

A note requirement of particular concern to analysts of a government's financial condition concerns short-term and long-term debt. A schedule of short-term debt shows beginning balances, increases, decreases, and ending balances, as well as the purposes for which the debt was issued. For long-term debt and obligations under capital and noncancelable operating leases, governments need to disclose details of debt requirements to maturity, including principal and interest requirements, stated separately, for each of the 5 subsequent fiscal years, and in 5-year increments thereafter. (The significance of this requirement is discussed in Chapter 14.)

Some governments have significant dollar amounts of interfund transfers and year-end interfund balances. The nature of interfund transactions and balances is generally not apparent from data shown on the face of the financial statements. Many transfers are routine in nature; for example, to move revenues from a collecting fund to another fund (such as a Debt Service Fund) required by statute to expend them. Other transfers, however, are not routine and may be indicators of fiscal stress. Required disclosures therefore include such matters as (1) interfund balances that are not expected to be repaid within 1 year from the date of the financial statements, and

(2) interfund transfers that are not consistent with the activities of the fund that makes the transfer.[12]

Exhibt 9–3 contains excerpts from several notes to the Village of Grafton's financial statements. The discussion of "Unearned Revenue" is from Grafton's Summary of Significant Accounting Policies. The excerpt from Note 6 shows sources and purposes

---

Exhibit 9-3   Notes to Financial Statements

Village of Grafton, Wisconsin
Notes to Financial Statements
December 31, 2005

NOTE 1—SUMMARY OF SIGNIFICANT ACCOUNTING POLICIES (Continued):

UNEARNED REVENUE

The Village reports unearned revenues on its balance sheet. Unearned revenues arise when a potential revenue does not meet both the "measurable" and "available" criteria for recognition in the current period. Unearned revenues also arise when resources are received before the Village has a legal claim to them, as when grant monies are received prior to the incurrence of qualifying expenditures. In subsequent periods, when both revenue recognition criteria are met, or when the Village has a legal claim to the resources, the liability for unearned revenue is removed from the balance sheet and revenue is recognized.

NOTE 6—INTERFUND TRANSFERS (Continued):

Fund Transferred To	Fund Transferred From	Amount	Purpose
Debt Service Fund	Environmental Fund	$ 1,800	Share of Debt Service Requirements
Debt Service Fund	Tax Incremental District No. 2	193,487	Share of Debt Service Requirements
Debt Service Fund	Capital Improvement Fund	112,937	Share of Debt Service Requirements
Debt Service Fund	Park & Recreation Facilities	46,658	Share of Debt Service Requirements
Debt Service Fund	Library Fund	4,543	Share of Debt Service Requirements
Debt Service Fund	Impact Fee Fund	119,114	Share of Debt Service Requirements
Debt Service Fund	Tax Incremental District No. 3	364,109	Share of Debt Service Requirements
Debt Service Subtotal		842,648	
Capital Improvement Fund	Park and Open Spaces	55,000	Transfer of Impact Fee Revenues
Library	General Fund	355,764	Annual Operating Subsidy
Recreation	General Fund	3,960	Annual Operating Subsidy
Aquatics Fund	General Fund	41,407	Annual Operating Subsidy
Cable Television Fund	General Fund	179	Annual Operating Subsidy
Other Governmental Funds Subtotal		401,310	
Total		$1,347,917	

---

[12]GASB *Statement No. 38,* para. 14 and 15.

NOTE 10—LONG-TERM OBLIGATIONS (Continued):
Debt service requirements to maturity are as follows:

Years	Governmental-Type Long-Term Debt		Business Type Long-Term Debt	
	Principal	Interest	Principal	Interest
2006	$ 1,471,842	$1,126,272	$ 352,279	$ 81,363
2007	1,603,599	968,987	355,089	72,630
2008	1,794,648	908,101	369,961	62,553
2009	1,854,977	841,771	386,326	51,876
2010	2,936,202	769,707	320,430	40,676
2011–2015	5,491,252	2,739,362	423,816	122,774
2016–2020	5,065,996	1,627,665	239,004	74,012
2021–2025	4,456,856	475,982	268,676	18,528
Total	$24,675,372	$9,457,847	$2,715,581	$524,412

Source: Comprehensive Annual Financial Report, Year 2005, Grafton, Wisconsin.

of the interfund transfers. Notice that the detail of the amount reported as transferred to the Debt Service Fund equals the amount reported as Transfers In to the Debt Service Fund in Table 9-3 ($842,648). The excerpt from Note 10—Long-Term Obligations is useful in financial analysis, which we cover in Chapter 14.

PREPARING THE STATISTICAL SECTION

Preparation of the *statistical section* of the CAFR is guided by GASB *Statement No. 44*, "Economic Condition Reporting: The Statistical Section" (May 2004). The trend data (generally for 10 years) contained in the statistical section provide users with financial, economic, and demographic data helpful in placing the financial statements, notes, and required supplementary information in a broader context. It thus gives the analyst a starting point for assessing the government's financial condition.

The statistical section of the CAFR has the following five categories of data, generally presented in the form of tables:

- *Financial trends*—to help assess how the government's financial position has changed over time
- *Revenue capacity*—to help assess the factors affecting a government's ability to generate revenues from its most significant own source of revenues, generally property taxes
- *Debt capacity*—to help assess debt burden and its legal and financial capacity to borrow long-term
- *Demographic and economic information*—to help understand the socioeconomic environment within which the government operates
- *Operating data*—to help understand how the reported financial information relates to the services the government performs

The information content of the various tables that should be provided by general governments in the statistical section of the CAFR is shown below. Except as indicated, each table should present data for the year covered by the financial statements and the preceding 9 years.

Financial Trends
- Net assets by component (invested in capital assets, net of related debt; restricted; and unrestricted)
- Changes in net assets, showing expenses by function and revenues by source
- Fund balances (reserved and unreserved) for the general fund and other governmental funds
- Changes in fund balances, showing revenues by source and expenditures by function, for governmental funds

Revenue Capacity
- Taxable assessed value and estimated actual value of taxable property
- Direct and overlapping property tax rates
- Principal property tax payers (for current year and 9 years ago)
- Property tax levies and collections

Debt Capacity
- Total outstanding debt, showing amount of each type of debt, ratio of total debt to personal income, and per capita debt
- Total general obligation bond outstanding debt, showing ratio of debt to estimated actual value of taxable property and per capita debt
- Direct and overlapping outstanding governmental activities debt (for current year only)
- Legal debt margin
- Debt service coverage for long-term debt backed by pledged revenues

Demographic and Economic Information
- Demographic and economic statistics, such as population, personal income, per capita personal income, median age, education level (years of schooling), and unemployment rate
- Principal employers, showing number of employees and percentage of total employment (for current year and 9 years ago)

Operating Data
- Full-time equivalent number of government employees, by function/program
- Operating statistics by function/program—primarily workload-type data, such as number of arrests (police) and tons of refuse collected (sanitation)
- Capital asset and infrastructure statistics by function/program—such as number of stations (police) and number of refuse collection trucks (sanitation)

Illustrations of statistical tables are presented in Tables 9-10 and 9-11. Table 9-10 shows the 10-year trend in Grafton's revenues, by revenue source. Notice that the total revenues shown for 2005 are the same as the revenues reported in Grafton's statement of revenues, expenditures, and changes in fund balances (Table 9-3). The analyst might use Table 9-10 to determine, for example, the annual rate of increase in property tax revenues; he or she might then ascertain what portion of the increase was caused by an increase in tax rates versus growth of property values. Table 9-11 shows the growth in Grafton's long-term debt burden, expressed in debt per capita and as a percentage of full property value. Grafton's debt burden might then be compared with the debt burden of similar governments. We cover financial condition analysis in more detail in Chapter 14.

TABLE 9-10 Statistical Tables—General Governmental Revenues by Source

Village of Grafton, Wisconsin
General Governmental Revenues By Source
Last Ten Fiscal Years

Fiscal Year	Taxes		Intergovernmental		Licenses and Permits		Fines, Forfeitures and Penalties		Public Charges for Services	
1996	$4,068,573	53.7%	$1,568,901	20.7%	$249,739	3.3%	$95,773	1.3%	$218,013	2.9%
1997	3,691,704	54.2%	1,449,832	21.3%	285,951	4.2%	106,169	1.6%	250,058	3.7%
1998	4,007,070	49.0%	1,513,110	18.5%	328,697	4.0%	101,811	1.2%	235,171	2.9%
1999	4,288,079	46.4%	1,466,071	15.8%	427,171	4.6%	111,082	1.2%	265,797	2.9%
2000	4,419,878	51.4%	1,865,753	21.7%	364,728	4.2%	108,557	1.3%	239,927	2.8%
2001	4,970,737	55.2%	1,623,329	18.0%	382,643	4.3%	90,413	1.0%	230,237	2.6%
2002	5,474,432	60.7%	1,557,256	17.3%	360,404	4.0%	93,744	1.0%	230,241	2.6%
2003	5,852,747	64.6%	1,681,403	18.5%	362,380	4.0%	84,654	0.9%	300,834	3.3%
2004	6,323,210	63.9%	1,457,049	14.7%	368,947	3.7%	79,309	0.8%	386,337	3.9%
2005	6,550,849	66.1%	1,528,927	15.4%	346,166	3.5%	123,888	1.3%	436,988	4.4%

Fiscal Year	Intergovernmental Charges for Services		Special Assessments		Investment Income		Miscellaneous Revenues		Total Revenues
1996	$107,015	1.4%	$479,999	6.3%	$305,193	4.0%	$482,830	6.4%	$7,576,036
1997	112,105	1.6%	436,209	6.4%	386,879	5.7%	93,587	1.4%	6,812,494
1998	121,922	1.5%	742,170	9.1%	535,404	6.6%	590,303	7.2%	8,175,658
1999	134,946	1.4%	1,330,932	14.4%	432,038	4.7%	793,339	8.6%	9,249,455
2000	129,965	1.5%	599,098	7.0%	558,006	6.5%	312,995	3.6%	8,598,907
2001	140,252	1.6%	823,847	9.2%	456,810	5.1%	279,038	3.1%	8,997,306
2002	147,050	1.6%	747,657	8.3%	278,981	3.1%	127,395	1.4%	9,017,160
2003	190,731	2.1%	294,827	3.3%	202,401	2.2%	96,934	1.1%	9,066,911
2004	184,993	1.9%	552,327	5.6%	165,645	1.7%	374,053	3.8%	9,891,870
2005	186,852	1.9%	114,332	1.2%	400,206	4.0%	216,438	2.2%	9,904,646

Includes General, Special Revenue, Debt Service, and Capital Projects Funds. GASB No. 34 was implemented in 2000. Therefore, general governmental revenues for the year 2000 and later include funds presented as trust funds in previous years. In addition, taxes paid by the enterprise fund are treated as transfers.

Source: Comprehensive Annual Financial Report, Year 2005, Grafton, Wisconsin.

TABLE 9-11   Statistical Tables—Long-Term Debt Trends

Village of Grafton, Wisconsin
Ratio of Net General Obligation Debt to Equalized Value
Last Ten Fiscal Years

As of December 31	Total G.O. Debt Outstanding	Less: Funds Available for Debt Service	Net Debt Outstanding	Equalized Value	Statutory Debt Capacity (5% of Equalized Value)
1996	$8,650,109	$ 48,823	$ 8,601,286	$492,688,500	$24,634,425
1997	12,607,945	81,699	12,526,246	543,110,400	27,155,520
1998	11,691,203	186,647	11,504,556	583,558,000	29,177,900
1999	11,486,660	289,166	11,197,494	621,228,600	31,061,430
2000	13,155,000	447,167	12,707,833	682,825,600	34,141,280
2001	13,705,000	284,426	13,420,574	747,854,900	37,392,745
2002	15,590,001	288,095	15,301,906	812,421,400	40,621,070
2003	16,612,546	228,451	16,384,095	865,725,500	43,286,275
2004	18,278,478	194,715	18,083,763	916,618,600	45,830,930
2005	27,340,421	397,080	26,943,341	994,070,400	49,703,520

As of December 31	Ratio of Net Debt to Debt Capacity	Population	Net Debt Per Capita	Net Debt Per $1,000 of Equalized Value
1996	34.92%	9,720	$ 885	$17.46
1997	46.13%	9,861	1,270	23.06
1998	39,43%	10,080	1,141	19.71
1999	36.05%	10,236	1,094	18.02
2000	37.22%	10,467	1,214	18.61
2001	35.89%	10,668	1,258	17.95
2002	37.67%	10,878	1,407	18.83
2003	37.85%	11,098	1,476	18.93
2004	39.46%	11,160	1,620	19.73
2005	54.21%	11,310	2,382	27.10

Source: Comprehensive Annual Financial Report, Year 2005, Grafton, Wisconsin.

AUDITOR'S REPORT

The independent audit lends credibility to the financial statements prepared by an entity's management. Exhibit 9-4 is an excerpt from the independent auditor's report issued by the firm of Kerber, Rose & Associates, S.C., on the financial statements of the Village of Grafton, Wisconsin, for the year ended December 31, 2005. The third paragraph of the auditor's report states that the financial statements "present fairly, in all material respects . . . the financial position . . . and the changes in financial position . . . in conformity with accounting principles generally accepted." This type of opinion is often called a "clean opinion."

EXHIBIT 9-4   Independent Auditor's Report

Independent Auditor's Report

To the Village Board
Village of Grafton
Grafton, Wisconsin

We have audited the accompanying financial statements of the governmental activities, the business-type activities, each major fund, and the aggregate remaining fund information of the Village of Grafton, Wisconsin, as of and for the year ended December 31, 2005, which collectively comprise the Village's basic financial statements, as listed in the table of contents. These financial statements are the responsibility of the Village's management. Our responsibility is to express opinions on these financial statements based on our audit.

We conducted our audit in accordance with auditing standards generally accepted in the United States of America. Those standards require that we plan and perform the audit to obtain reasonable assurance about whether the financial statements are free of material misstatement. An audit includes examining, on a test basis, evidence supporting the amounts and disclosures in the financial statements. An audit also includes assessing the accounting principles used and significant estimates made by management, as well as evaluating the overall financial statement presentation. We believe that our audit provides a reasonable basis for our opinions.

In our opinion, the financial statements referred to above present fairly, in all material respects, the respective financial position of the governmental activities, the business-type activities, each major fund, and the aggregate remaining fund information of the Village of Grafton, Wisconsin, as of December 31, 2005, and the respective changes in financial position and cash flows, where applicable, thereof and the respective budgetary comparisons for the general fund for the year then ended in conformity with accounting principles generally accepted in the United States of America.

The management's discussion and analysis on pages 15 through 27 is not a required part of the financial statements but is supplementary information required by accounting principles generally accepted in the United States of America. We have applied certain limited procedures, which consisted principally of inquiries of management regarding the methods of measurement and presentation of the required supplementary information. However, we did not audit the information and express no opinion on it.

Source: Excerpt from the report issued by Kerber, Rose & Associates, S.C., included in the Comprehensive Annual Financial Report, Year 2005, Grafton, Wisconsin.

Review Questions

Q9-1   Which groups are the major external users of governmental financial reports?

Q9-2   How can financial reporting assist in fulfilling government's duty to be publicly accountable and assist users in assessing that accountability?

Q9-3   Define the term *reporting entity*.

Q9-4   Under what circumstances is a primary government considered to be financially accountable for a legally separate organization?

Q9-5   When reporting component units in a governmental organization's financial statements, what is the difference between blending and discrete presentation?

Q9-6   What are the major sections of a comprehensive annual financial report?

Q9-7 What are the minimum requirements established by the GASB for general purpose external financial reports?

Q9-8 List the nine statements that comprise the basic financial statements.

Q9-9 What is the purpose of Management's Discussion and Analysis?

Q9-10 What is the difference between fund financial statements and government-wide financial statements?

Q9-11 Define the term *major fund* in fund financial statements.

Q9-12 What measurement focus and basis of accounting should be used in reporting each of the three fund categories in fund financial statements?

Q9-13 What is a *special item* in financial reporting?

Q9-14 Describe the format of the governmental funds statement of revenues, expenditures, and changes in fund balances.

Q9-15 What are the three components of net assets in the proprietary funds statement of net assets?

Q9-16 What kind of information is compared in a budgetary comparison schedule?

Q9-17 Describe and illustrate the kind of information that should be reported in notes to the financial statements.

Q9-18 Describe and illustrate the kind of information that should be reported in the statistical section of the CAFR.

Cases

C9-1 The Building Authority was created by the city and organized as a separate legal entity. The authority is governed by a five-person board appointed for 6-year terms by the mayor, subject to city council approval. The authority uses the proceeds of its tax-exempt bonds to finance the construction or acquisition of general capital assets for the city only. The bonds are secured by the lease agreement with the city and will be retired through lease payments from the city. Is the Building Authority a component unit of the city? If so, how should the city report the financial activities of the Building Authority?

(GASB *Statement 14,* para. 134)

C9-2 The Municipal Electric Utility (MEU) was created as a separate legal entity in accordance with state law to own, manage, and operate an electric utilities system in the city. The MEU's governing body consists of five members. It is a self-perpetuating board composed of four citizens (customers) and the mayor of the city serving ex officio. The four citizen board members provide representation from each of the MEU's main service areas. When a board vacancy occurs, the remaining board members must nominate the successor. The MEU board chooses the nominee from a list of candidates proposed by an independent citizens' committee. The MEU's board may reject these candidates for any reason and request additional candidates. The MEU's nomination is then subject to confirmation by the city council. The council's confirmation procedure is essentially a formality. After confirmation, the council cannot remove a member for any reason.

The MEU uses various services provided by departments of the city, including insurance, legal, motor pool, and computer services. The MEU is billed for these services on a proportionate cost basis with other user departments and agencies. The MEU provides customer service and related functions to the city's water department. The estimated cost of providing these services is paid by the water department. The MEU also provides electric service to the city and its agencies and bills the city for those services using established rate schedules. The MEU selects and employs its executives, controls the hiring of its employees, and is responsible for rate setting and its overall fiscal management. The city is not legally or morally obligated for the MEU's debt. The MEU receives no appropriations from the city. In compliance with its charter, the MEU is required to make a payment in lieu of taxes annually to the General Fund, calculated according to a formula based on kilowatt-hour sales for the preceding 12-month period. Is the MEU a component unit of the city? If so, how should the city report the financial activities of the MEU?

(GASB *Statement 14,* para. 141)

C9-3   The State Turnpike Commission (STC) was established by the state to construct, operate, and maintain the state turnpike system. The STC was created as an instrumentality of the state as a separate legal entity with powers to issue revenue bonds payable from tolls and other revenues. The governing body of the STC consists of eight members appointed by the governor for fixed 10-year terms and three state officials serving ex officio—the elected state treasurer, the elected state controller, and the appointed superintendent of highways.

The STC is financially self-sufficient, and the state cannot access its assets or surpluses and is not obligated to subsidize deficits of the STC. The STC sets its own rates and approves its own budget. The bond agreement states that the debt of the STC is not an obligation of the state. However, state statutes authorize the state's budget director to include in the budget submitted to the legislature an amount sufficient to make the principal and interest payments on the STC bonds in the event STC revenues are insufficient to meet debt service requirements. Is the STC a component unit of the state? If so, how should the state report the financial activities of the STC?

(GASB *Statement 14,* para. 142)

C9-4   The Board of Education (BOE) is a separately elected body that administers the public school system in the city. The BOE is not organized as a separate legal entity and does not have the power to levy taxes or issue bonds. Its budget is subject to approval by the city council to the extent that, under state law, the BOE has the discretionary authority to expend the amount appropriated to it by the city. The BOE requests a single amount to fund its operations; the city council can reject the BOE's requested budget.

How should the city report the financial activities of the BOE?

(GASB *Statement 14,* para. 144)

Ethics Case

EC9-1 Several years ago the citizens of Jefferson Heights approved a ¼ percent increase in the sales tax dedicated to law enforcement. The legislation provided that a Special Revenue Fund be established to account for the collection and disbursement of the tax resources. In addition, the legislation specifically included a provision that prohibited any other use of these funds. John Morris, the chief financial officer of Jefferson Heights, discovered that the General Fund does not have enough resources to meet the final payroll of the fiscal year. Morris presented a proposal to the mayor, Jane Dufrend, that the Special Revenue Fund loan resources to the General Fund until the General Fund can repay the loan. The county attorney, Jerry Carson, gave Morris and Dufrend a legal opinion that indicated that such a loan was against the wording and the spirit of the Special Revenue Fund and the city's charter. Morris told Dufrend that no one could tell because he could combine the resources of all of the smaller Special Revenue Funds in the financial statements and the loan would not show up as being specifically related to this fund. How would you advise Dufrend? Explain.

Exercises

E9-1   (Organization of the CAFR)
You are asked to explain the organization of the Comprehensive Annual Financial Report, as specified in GASB *Statement No. 34.* Outline your talk.

E9-2   (Analysis of the MD&A section of a CAFR)
Obtain a CAFR from a governmental unit and read Management's Discussion and Analysis. Describe three significant comments made by management.

E9-3   (Analysis of the notes to the financial statements in a CAFR)
Obtain a CAFR from a governmental unit and read the statement of significant accounting policies in the notes to the financial statements. Write a brief report summarizing those policies.

E9-4   (Analysis of the notes to the financial statements in a CAFR)
Obtain a CAFR from a governmental unit and read the notes other than the statement of significant accounting policies. Write a brief report summarizing three of the notes.

E9-5   (Analysis of a budgetary comparison statement in a CAFR)
Obtain a CAFR from a governmental unit and read the budgetary comparison statement. Also, read what management says in its MD&A, if anything, about the results of its budgetary activities for the year. What conclusions can you reach from reading the budgetary comparison statement? How do management's comments in the MD&A improve your understanding of the budgetary comparison statement?

E9-6   (Multiple choice)

1. In governmental financial reporting, what is blending?
    a. A method of preparing the notes to the CAFR
    b. The process of including the financial data of a component unit with the financial data of the primary government
    c. The process of reporting the financial data of a component unit as a separate column in the reporting entity's financial statements
    d. The process of combining intergovernmental revenues with the revenues of the reporting government

2. From the following, select the two conditions that, taken together, will cause an entity to be reported as a component unit of a primary government:
    a. The primary government's director of finance serves as a member of the entity's governing body.

b. The primary government's chief executive can appoint a voting majority of the entity's governing body.

c. The primary government is required by law to finance the entity's deficits.

d. The primary government is required by law to purchase its electricity from the entity, which also supplies electricity to the residents of the community.

e. The primary government is authorized by law to bill the entity the cost of police and fire protection.

3. What items are compared in a budgetary comparison schedule for the General Fund?

a. Last year's final budget; current year's final budget; current year's actual inflows and outflows on budgetary basis of accounting

b. For the current year: final budget; actual inflows and outflows on budgetary basis of accounting; actual inflows and outflows on modified accrual basis of accounting

c. For the current year: original budget; final budget; actual inflows and outflows on budgetary basis of accounting

d. Last year's actual inflows and outflows on budgetary basis of accounting; current year's final budget; current year's actual inflows and outflows on budgetary basis of accounting

4. Which of these items should be reported as "other financing uses" in a governmental funds statement of revenues, expenditures, and changes in fund balances?

a. Transfers out

b. Repayment of long-term debt principal

c. Capital outlays

d. Interest on long-term debt

5. Which of these items is normally reported as an "operating expense" in a proprietary funds statement of revenues, expenses, and changes in fund net assets?

a. Interest expense on long-term debt

b. Transfers out

c. Repayment of long-term debt principal

d. Depreciation expense

6. What are the *minimum* requirements established by the GASB for general purpose external financial reports?

a. A CAFR

b. Fund financial statements and government-wide financial statements

c. Basic financial statements and notes to the financial statements

d. MD&A, basic financial statements, and required supplementary information other than MD&A

7. In fund financial statements, for which funds is depreciation reported?

a. Only for governmental-type funds

b. Only for proprietary-type funds

c. For both governmental-type and proprietary-type funds

d. For neither governmental-type nor proprietary-type funds

8. In fund financial statements, which of the following funds are reported using the economic resources measurement focus?
   a. General Fund
   b. Debt Service Funds and Capital Projects Funds
   c. All funds that meet the definition of *major*
   d. Enterprise Funds

E9-7 (Fill in the blanks)

1. The annual financial report of a governmental unit is called a _____.
2. Government-wide financial statements include a statement of _____ and a statement of _____.
3. Fund financial statements for fiduciary funds generally include a statement of _____ and a statement of _____.
4. Budgetary comparison schedules should always have at least three columns for _____, _____, and _____.
5. In fund financial statements, governmental funds should be presented using the _____ measurement focus and the _____ basis of accounting.

E9-8 (True or false)
State whether each of these statements is true or false. For any false statement, indicate why it is false.

1. In fund financial statements, the General Fund should always be reported as a major fund.
2. In fund financial statements, Enterprise Funds are reported using the economic resources measurement focus and the modified accrual basis of accounting.
3. When an auditor states that an entity's financial statements present fairly its financial position and results of operations, it is reasonable to assume that the entity's financial condition is healthy.
4. Notes to the financial statements are a form of required supplementary information.
5. Nonmajor funds may be combined and presented in a single column in the fund financial statements.

Problems

P9-1 (Multiple choice — theory)

1. In fund financial statements, for which of the following funds are financial statements prepared using the current financial resources measurement focus and the modified accrual basis of accounting?
   a. Both Enterprise Funds and Special Revenue Funds
   b. Both the General Fund and Debt Service Funds
   c. Both Capital Projects Funds and Pension Trust Funds
   d. Both Permanent Funds and Private Purpose Trust Funds
2. In fund financial statements, for which of the following funds are you most likely to see the category Long-term bonds payable?
   a. General Fund
   b. Capital Projects Fund

   c. Enterprise Fund
   d. Debt Service Fund
3. Which basis of accounting is used in preparing the budgetary comparison
   statement?
   a. The budgetary basis
   b. The accrual basis
   c. The modified accrual basis
   d. The cash receipts and disbursements basis
4. In fund financial statements, where are the revenues and expenditures
   (expenses) of governmental-type and proprietary-type funds reported?
   a. On different financial statements
   b. On the same financial statement
   c. Not on any financial statement
   d. On the same financial statement where fiduciary funds are
       reported
5. Fund financial statements have columns for which of the following?
   a. Major funds only
   b. All funds
   c. Each major fund plus a column for nonmajor funds combined
   d. Only the combined total of all funds
6. Which of the following best expresses the accounting equation for Agency
   Funds?
   a. Assets = Liabilities
   b. Assets = Liabilities + Net Assets
   c. Assets − Liabilities = Net Assets
   d. Assets = Net Assets
7. Which of the following is part of the *minimum requirements* established
   by the GASB for general-purpose external financial reports?
   a. An introductory section
   b. Management's Discussion and Analysis
   c. A statistical section
   d. A schedule of cash receipts and disbursements for all funds
8. The process of *blending* is accomplished by reporting a component unit's
   funds in which manner?
   a. In the notes to the primary government's financial statements
   b. In a separate column to the left of the primary government's funds
   c. As if they were always fiduciary funds of the primary government
   d. As if they were the funds of the primary government
9. Which of the following situations would be defined as a *special item?*
   a. The amount of a revenue or an expenditure item increased by at least
       10 percent over the previous year
   b. A significant transaction within the control of management is either
       unusual in nature or infrequent in occurrence
   c. A significant event outside the control of management causes the
       expenses or expenditures of a fund to exceed its revenues
   d. A vibrant economy causes an entity's tax revenues to rise by an extra-
       ordinary amount over the budgetary estimate

10. When preparing a fund statement of revenues, expenditures, and changes in fund balances for the Capital Projects Fund, how should proceeds of debt be reported?
    a. As a revenue
    b. As a transfer
    c. As an other financing source
    d. As bonds payable

11. In fund financial statements, where are the categories Capital assets, less accumulated depreciation, and Long-term bonds payable likely to appear?
    a. The General Fund, but not an Enterprise Fund
    b. An Enterprise Fund, but not a Capital Projects Fund
    c. Both an Enterprise Fund and a Capital Projects Fund
    d. An Enterprise Fund and a Capital Projects Fund or a Debt Service Fund

P9-2   (Preparation of a governmental funds balance sheet)
The following information is available for the governmental funds of Tom's Village:

Account	General	Debt Service	Special Revenue Funds	
			Fund A	Fund B
Cash	$10,000	$5,000	$600	$1,000
Taxes receivable	5,000			
Due from other funds		2,000		
Accounts payable	9,000		200	400
Due to other funds	2,000			
Reserved for encumbrances	1,000			
Reserved for debt service		7,000		
Unreserved fund balance	3,000		400	600

Required: Prepare the governmental funds balance sheet for Tom's Village. The Tom's Village officials do not consider either Special Revenue Fund as particularly important to financial statement users.

P9-3   (Multiple choice: miniproblems)
The following information relates to questions 1, 2, and 3. A village levied property taxes in the amount of $800,000 for calendar year 2008. By year end, the village had collected $775,000. It expected to collect $15,000 more in January and February of 2009 and the remaining $10,000 after February but before September 2009. Answer the following questions regarding the fund financial statements for the General Fund at December 31, 2008, and for the calendar year 2008.

1. What amount of property tax revenues should be recognized for calendar year 2008?
    a. $775,000
    b. $785,000
    c. $790,000
    d. $800,000

2. What amount of property taxes receivable should be reported at December 31, 2008?
   a. $0
   b. $10,000
   c. $15,000
   d. $25,000

3. What amount of deferred property tax revenues should be reported at December 31, 2008?
   a. $0
   b. $10,000
   c. $15,000
   d. $25,000

4. A city operates on a calendar-year basis. On April 1, 2008, the city issues general obligation bonds in the amount of $1,000,000 to build a new city hall. The debt is to be paid off at the rate of $100,000 a year, with interest of 6 percent per annum on the outstanding debt, starting April 1, 2009. Although it maintains a Debt Service Fund, it has not transferred any resources to that fund to pay any interest or principal on the debt. When it prepares its governmental fund financial statements as of December 31, 2008, how much should the city report as Debt Service Fund expenditures?
   a. $0
   b. $45,000
   c. $60,000
   d. $120,000

5. Assume the same set of facts as in problem 4, except that the debt had been issued by the Water Enterprise Fund to extend water mains. When it prepares its proprietary fund financial statements, how much should the city report as interest expense?
   a. $0
   b. $45,000
   c. $60,000
   d. $120,000

6. A city operates on a calendar-year basis. On October 1, 2008, it sold general obligation bonds in the amount of $1 million. The debt was to be paid off in 5 years, starting April 1, 2009, in equal semiannual installments of $100,000, with interest at the rate of 5 percent per annum on the outstanding debt. How much should the city report as interest expenditures in its Debt Service Fund for the calendar year 2009?
   a. $45,000
   b. $47,500
   c. $50,000
   d. $100,000

7. Thomas Village operates on a calendar-year basis. On January 1, 2009, it had outstanding property taxes receivable of $40,000 and deferred property tax revenue of $10,000. On January 1, 2009, it levied property taxes of $1,000,000 to cover its 2009 activities. During 2009, it collected the entire

$40,000 of receivables that were outstanding as of January 1, as well as $975,000 against the 2009 levy. With regard to the uncollected 2009 taxes, the village expected to collect $20,000 during the first 60 days of 2010 and the remaining $5,000 during the rest of 2010. How much should Thomas Village recognize as property tax revenues in its General Fund for calendar year 2009?

a. $995,000
b. $1,000,000
c. $1,005,000
d. $1,015,000

P9-4   (Net asset classification)

Nuevo York County maintains the Metro Bus Enterprise Fund to account for the activities of its municipal bus service. The following information is reported in the assets and liabilities sections of the proprietary funds statement of net assets.

Cash and investments	$ 250,000
Buses and bus garage	2,500,000
Accumulated depreciation, buses and garage	1,100,000
Accounts payable	62,000
Current amount of long-term bonds payable	250,000
Long-term bonds payable — noncurrent amount	1,000,000
Other long-term liabilities	50,000

Required: Compute the amount Nuevo York County should report as Invested in capital assets, net of related debt in the proprietary funds statement of net assets. Assume the long-term debt was issued to finance acquisition of the buses.

P9-5   (Preparation of proprietary funds statement of revenues, expenses, and changes in fund net assets)

The City of Breukelen maintains a rapid transit system, which is accounted for in a proprietary fund called Breukelen RTS. The following excerpt from the trial balance shows all the information needed to prepare an operating statement.

Revenues from fares	$3,150,000
Train operating expenses	2,430,000
Track and train maintenance expenses	565,000
Depreciation	325,000
Investment income	50,000
Interest expense on long-term debt	320,000
Cash subsidy from the City of Breukelen	500,000
Net assets, January 1, 2009	7,430,000

Required: Prepare a statement of revenues, expenses, and changes in fund net assets for the Breukelen RTS for the year ended December 31, 2009, using the appropriate format.

Summary Problems

Summary Problem 1. (Fund accounting and preparation of financial statements)
Part A. (Identification of funds)
Coco City established funds to account for the following activities:

1. To account for its day-to-day operating activities
2. To acquire or construct major capital assets
3. To accumulate resources to service long-term debt
4. To operate a municipal swimming pool

Required: State the names of the funds that Coco City will use for each of these activities.

Part B. (Budgetary accounting for the General Fund)

1. Coco City opened the year beginning January 1, 2009, with cash of $40,000, vouchers payable of $35,000, and unreserved fund balance of $5,000.
2. The Coco City Council adopted the following budget for the General Fund at the beginning of the year:

Revenues—property taxes	$400,000
Revenues—sales taxes	70,000
Revenues—parks admission fees	10,000
Appropriations:	
Police salaries	300,000
Police supplies	40,000
Parks salaries	80,000
Transfer to Debt Service Fund	45,000

3. Two purchase orders, one for $35,000 and one for $4,000, were placed against the appropriation for police supplies.
4. Because the unit price was lower than anticipated, an invoice for $33,000 was received and approved for supplies that had been ordered for $35,000.
5. The invoice for $33,000 was paid.

Required: Record the opening account balances; prepare journal entries to record transactions 2–5; post the journal entries to T-accounts; post the Police supplies budgetary transactions to an appropriations ledger.

Part C. (Other General Fund transactions)

1. Property taxes were levied in the amount of $404,000 in order to provide revenues of $400,000. Tax bills were sent to the property owners.
2. The account of a taxpayer who owed $3,000 was written off as uncollectible.
3. Property taxes of $370,000 were collected in cash.
4. At year end, all uncollected taxes were declared delinquent. The Coco City finance director concluded that all the property taxes would be

collected, so there was no need for any allowance for uncollectible taxes. She estimated that $21,000 of the delinquent taxes would be collected in January and February of 2010 and that the rest of the taxes would be collected later in the year.

5. The state collects sales taxes on behalf of all cities in the state. During the year, Coco City received $68,000 in sales taxes from the state. The state also advised Coco that it would remit an additional $6,000 in sales taxes by January 20.

6. Coco City collected parks admissions fees of $18,000 during the year.

7. The unpaid vouchers of $35,000 at the beginning of the year were paid.

8. Salaries in the amount of $360,000 ($290,000 for the Police Department and $70,000 for the Parks Department) were paid.

9. The payroll for the period ended December 31, 2009 ($8,000 for the Police Department and $5,000 for the Parks Department), which was included in the year 2009 budget, will be paid on January 5, 2010.

10. A Police Department sedan accidentally sideswiped a citizen's vehicle in November 2009. Coco City's corporation counsel estimated that the city would ultimately settle the citizen's claim for about $4,000. It usually takes about 18 months to settle cases of this kind.

Required: Prepare journal entries, as appropriate, to record these transactions, and post the journal entries to T-accounts.

Part D. (Capital Projects Fund and Debt Service Fund transactions)

1. To provide financing for a new police station, Coco City sold bonds on April 1, 2009, in the amount of $500,000. Bond principal is payable over a 10-year period in 20 equal semiannual installments of $25,000, with interest of 6 percent per annum on the unpaid balance. The first payment is due on October 1, 2009.

2. Coco City purchased a prefabricated police station and paid $500,000 for it on delivery. The building, ready for occupancy on July 1, 2009, was expected to have a useful life of 25 years.

3. The General Fund transferred $45,000 to the Debt Service Fund in anticipation of the first installment of debt service.

4. The first installment of debt service became due and payable on October 1, 2009.

5. The first installment of debt service was paid.

Required: Prepare journal entries for all funds, as appropriate, to record these transactions, and post the journal entries to T-accounts for each fund.

Part E. (Enterprise Fund transactions)

1. Coco City operates a municipal swimming pool. It started the year with cash of $5,000; net capital assets of $510,000 (the swimming pool cost $600,000 and the accumulated depreciation was $90,000); and outstanding bonds of $480,000 (the original debt of $600,000 was being paid off over 15 years in equal annual installments of $40,000 at December 31 of each year, with interest of 5 percent per annum on the outstanding balance).

2. Coco received swimming pool admissions fees of $70,000.
3. Salaries totaling $8,000 were paid to a lifeguard and a clerk.
4. Coco paid the annual debt service requirement on the swimming pool bonds.
5. Coco recorded depreciation on the swimming pool. The cost of the pool is amortized over 20 years.

Required: Record the opening balances in T-accounts, prepare journal entries to record the transactions, and post the journal entries to T-accounts.

Part F. (Preparation of fund financial statements)
Required: Prepare preclosing trial balances for all funds. Prepare the following fund financial statements:

1. Governmental funds balance sheet
2. Governmental funds statement of revenues, expenditures, and changes in fund balances
3. Proprietary funds statement of net assets
4. Proprietary funds statement of revenues, expenses, and changes in fund net assets

Part G. (Preparation of journal entries for government-wide financial statements and preparation of government-wide financial statements)
See Summary Problem at the end of Chapter 10 for remainder of this problem, to be done after reading Chapter 10.

Summary Problem 2. (Fund accounting and preparation of fund financial statements)

Part A. (Identification of funds)
Croton Village maintains separate funds to account for the following activities:

1. To account for its day-to-day operating activities
2. To account for its library activities
3. To acquire or construct capital assets
4. To accumulate resources to service long-term debt

Required: State the names of the funds that Croton Village uses for each activity.

Part B. (1) (General Fund budgetary journal entries)
Croton Village started its calendar year 2009 with the following General Fund balances. (All numbers are in thousands of dollars, so, for example, $700 means $700,000.)

	Debits	Credits
Cash	$1,800	
Property taxes receivable	800	
Salaries payable		$ 700
Deferred property tax revenues		300
Unreserved fund balance		1,600
Totals	$2,600	$2,600

1. The Croton council adopted the following General Fund budget for 2009:

Revenues—property taxes	$9,000
Revenues—sales taxes	5,000
Revenues—intergovernmental	1,000
Revenues—recreation fees	600
Appropriations:	
Public safety salaries	7,000
Public safety supplies	500
Public works salaries	5,000
Parks salaries	2,000
Transfer to Library Fund	400
Transfer to Debt Service Fund	1,200

2. Croton's Public Safety Department placed two purchase orders against its supplies appropriation, one for $300 for firearms and one for $150 for uniforms.
3. The firearms were received, with an invoice for $330. The purchase order allowed the supplier to ship 10 percent more than the amount ordered, so the invoice was approved.
4. The invoice for firearms was paid.

Required: Record the opening account balances in T-accounts. Prepare journal entries to record transactions 1–4. Post the journal entries to general ledger T-accounts and to an appropriations ledger.

Part B. (2) (Journal entries for General Fund financial transactions)

1. Of the $800 property taxes receivable at January 1, $780 was collected in cash. The remaining $20 was written off as uncollectible. Deferred property taxes at the beginning of the year were recognized as revenue.
2. Accrued salaries from the previous year ($700) were paid.
3. Property taxes in the amount of $9,030 were levied in order to provide revenues of $9,000. Tax bills were sent to the property owners. An allowance for uncollectible taxes was established
4. During the year, property taxes of $8,100 were collected in cash.
5. The state collects sales taxes on behalf of its local governments. During the year, Croton received sales taxes of $4,600 from the state.
6. The Parks Department collected $700 in recreation fees during the year.
7. Croton paid salaries of $13,000, charging the salary appropriations as follows:

Public safety	$6,500
Public works	4,700
Parks	1,800

8. The state provides financial assistance to its local governments for certain public safety programs. The $6,500 public safety salaries paid in transaction 7 include $1,000 of salaries on these programs. Croton therefore billed the state for $1,000.
9. Croton received $950 from the state against the billings made in transaction 8.

10. Unpaid salaries at year end (to be paid during the first week of 2010) were as follows:

Public safety	$300
Public works	250
Parks	100

11. At year end, the uncollected property taxes were declared delinquent. Croton's director of finance estimated that $500 of the uncollected taxes would be collected in January and February of 2010 and $400 would be collected during the rest of 2010. He decided to leave the allowance for uncollectible taxes on the books.

12. In January 2010, the state advised Croton that it held $500 in sales taxes on its behalf and that it would send the sales taxes to Croton by February 10.

13. Croton allows its employees to accumulate unused vacation days and to receive cash for up to 30 days' unused vacation leave at retirement. Police officers who retired at the end of 2009 will be paid $10 for unused vacation pay on January 6, 2010. Croton requires such payments to be charged to the department's salary appropriation.

Required: Prepare journal entries, as appropriate, to record these transactions, and post the journal entries to T-accounts.

Part C. (Journal entries for Special Revenue Fund transactions)

The Library Special Revenue Fund commenced calendar year 2009 with a cash balance of $5 and zero liabilities.

1. The General Fund transferred $400 cash to the Library Special Revenue Fund to enable the library to finance its activities for the year.

2. The library received $20 from fines, donations, and various fundraising events. Croton's accounting policy requires crediting these revenues to miscellaneous revenues.

3. The library paid $350 for salaries and $40 to acquire books and periodicals. Charge the expenditures to Culture—salaries and Culture—supplies, respectively.

Required: Record the opening account balances in T-accounts. Prepare appropriate journal entries to record the transactions and post the journal entries to T-accounts.

Part D. (Journal entries for Capital Projects Fund transactions)

At the start of 2009, Croton's Capital Projects Fund had no assets or liabilities.

1. Croton undertook construction of a new police station, designed to house both the Croton police and the county sheriff and to serve as a detention center. To finance construction, Croton received a cash grant of $1,000 from the county and sold $2,000 of 20-year general obligation bonds. The bonds, sold April 1, 2009, were to be redeemed in equal semiannual installments of principal, with interest payable at the rate of 5 percent per annum, starting October 1, 2009.

2. Croton awarded two contracts, one for architectural and construction supervision services ($300) and one for construction ($2,700).

3. Both contracts were completed in a timely manner during 2009 and the architect and the contractor were paid in full.

Required: Prepare appropriate journal entries to record the transactions and post the journal entries to T-accounts.

Part E. (Journal entries for Debt Service Fund transactions)

At the start of 2009, Croton's Debt Service Fund had no assets or liabilities.

1. The General Fund transferred $1,200 cash to the Debt Service Fund.
2. The first installment of principal and interest on the bonds sold in transaction 1 of Part D came due for payment.
3. Principal and interest due for payment (see transaction 2, above) was paid.
4. Debt service on bonds sold by Croton in previous years came due and was paid. Principal and interest payments on those bonds were $600 and $470, respectively.

Required: Prepare appropriate journal entries to record the transactions and post the journal entries to T-accounts.

Part F. (Preparation of fund financial statements)

Required: Prepare preclosing trial balances for all funds. Prepare a governmental funds balance sheet and a governmental funds statement of revenues, expenditures, and changes in fund balances. Consider all funds as major funds for this exercise.

Summary Problem 3. (Adjusting and correcting journal entries)

You were hired to examine the financial statements of the City of York for the year ended December 31, 2009. York uses only a General Fund to record all its transactions. The following General Fund trial balance had been prepared as of December 31, 2009.

City of York
General Fund
Trial Balance
December 31, 2009

	Debits	Credits
Cash	$ 20,800	
Short-term investments	180,000	
Accounts receivable	11,500	
Taxes receivable—current	30,000	
Tax anticipation notes payable		$ 58,000
Appropriations		927,000
Expenditures	795,200	
Estimated revenues	927,000	
Revenues		750,000
General city property	98,500	
General obligation bonds payable	52,000	
Unreserved fund balance		380,000
	$2,115,000	$2,115,000

You discovered that the inexperienced bookkeeper made errors on some transactions and merely guessed at the correct accounting treatment of other transactions. This is what you found:

1. Outstanding purchase orders at December 31, 2009, totaling $22,000, had not been recorded. The city's accounting policies require use of encumbrance accounting.

2. On December 31, 2009, the state department of tax and finance advised the city that it had collected $58,500 of sales tax revenues on behalf of the city and that a check would be sent to the city by January 20, 2010. No entry was made for this information.

3. York collects property taxes on behalf of the county in which it is located. The entire amount received in November 2009 ($15,000) was recorded as York's revenues and not sent to the county.

4. Analysis of the taxes receivable—current account shows the following:
   a. The entire $30,000 of receivables is delinquent.
   b. Based on the history of delinquent taxes, it is anticipated that $12,000 of the receivable amount will not be received until April or May and that $3,000 will ultimately need to be written off as uncollectible.

5. Analysis of the account General obligation bonds payable shows that the debit balance of $52,000 arose from a journal entry made on December 30, 2009, to record a payment of debt service ($40,000 bond principal and $12,000 interest).

6. Analysis of the account General city property shows that the $98,500 debit balance is the result of two journal entries:
   a. Sale of used truck for $6,400.
   b. Purchase of new firefighting equipment for $104,900.

7. During the year, a resident donated land to the city for use as an industrial park. The city estimated that the land had a value of $125,000. The bookkeeper decided not to make any journal entry in the General Fund.

8. Two lawsuits were brought against the city as a result of damages caused by its trucks during trash collection. One case was settled in late December and York will pay $2,000 damages in January 2010. The city attorney believes the city will probably lose the other case as well and may need to pay out $6,000 to settle it. However, the case is complex and is not likely to be resolved for another 15 months. The bookkeeper didn't think any entry was needed because no cash was paid.

Required: Prepare journal entries, as necessary, to correct the City of York's records. Record all adjustments to the revenue and expenditure accounts as simply "revenues" or "expenditures" without showing details. Make the adjusting journal entries in the General Fund only. If some other fund would normally be used to record the transaction, however, state which one would be used.

Summary Problem 4. (Journal entries for several funds and financial statements for a Capital Projects Fund)

The City of Peak's Kill had the following transactions during the calendar year 2009. The transactions relate to financing and constructing a new city hall. Peak's Kill uses budgetary accounting in its Capital Projects Fund.

1. Peak's Kill adopted a budget for the Capital Projects Fund on January 1, based on the following assumptions:

   Bonds would be issued for $10 million.
   Interest earned on investment of idle cash would be $300,000.
   Contracts would be awarded for $10 million.

2. On April 1, Peak's Kill issued $10 million of 5 percent general obligation bonds to build a new city hall. Principal and interest payments are made each June 30 and December 31 for 20 years, starting December 31, 2009. Principal is amortized in equal semiannual payments of $250,000. The bonds were sold for $10,100,000. The premium of $100,000 was transferred to the Debt Service Fund, to be used to defray the first payment of principal and interest.

3. On May 1, Peak's Kill contracted with Howard Architects for $500,000 to design the building and supervise construction.

4. On July 1, the Capital Projects Fund invested $7,500,000 in a certificate of deposit.

5. On September 1, Peak's Kill entered into a contract with Eddie Construction to build the city hall for $9,300,000.

6. On December 10, Eddie Construction billed Peak's Kill $2 million for work done through November 30. Peak's Kill paid the bill, after approval by Howard Architects, less 10 percent retainage pending completion of construction.

7. On December 30, the General Fund transferred to the Debt Service Fund an amount sufficient to pay the December 31 installment of principal and interest on the bonds, after considering the $100,000 cash already in the Debt Service Fund.

8. On December 30, the city received a bill from Howard Architects for $175,000. The bill was approved and scheduled for payment on January 10, 2010.

9. On December 31, the Debt Service Fund paid the first installment of principal and interest on the bonds issued to construct city hall.

10. On December 31, in anticipation of preparing financial statements, the accountant accrued interest at the rate of 4 percent per annum on the certificate of deposit.

Required: 1. Prepare journal entries to record the transactions and identify the fund(s) used.
2. Prepare a balance sheet for the City of Peak's Kill Capital Projects Fund as of December 31, 2009.
3. Prepare a statement of revenues, expenditures, and changes in fund balance for the City of Peak's Kill Capital Projects Fund for the year ended December 31, 2009.

Summary Problem 5. (Journal entries for several funds)
Following are several transactions that relate to Weaverstown for 2009.

1. The general operating budget was approved as follows:

Appropriations	$5,200,000
Estimated revenues	5,000,000
Estimated other financing sources	300,000

2. Plans for a new criminal courts building were approved. General obligation bonds with a face value of $7 million were issued for $7,200,000. Local laws stipulate that any premium must be transferred to the appropriate Debt Service Fund. In addition, a federal grant of $8 million was received.

encumbrance

3. The Fire Department ordered a new sedan for the fire chief at a cost of $25,000. The old sedan was sold for $750.
4. The city received $400,000 from the state. This amount was the city's share of the state gasoline tax. This money can be spent only to repair streets, and a separate accounting is required by the state.
5. General obligation bonds of $300,000 were retired by a Debt Service Fund. At this time, interest of $150,000 was also paid to the bondholders.
6. The 2009 property tax was levied by the city. The total amount was $3,000,000, of which $2,990,000 was expected to be collected.
7. Salaries of governmental employees were paid, totaling $800,000. Of this amount, $65,000 was withheld and included in an account called Due to federal government as income tax payments. In addition, the city made a contribution of $100,000 to the city-operated pension system. Assume that all employees were paid through the General Fund.
8. The Central Supplies Fund, an Internal Service Fund, billed the General Fund $15,000 and the Gas Service Fund, an Enterprise Fund, $8,000 for supplies. Assume that the General Fund previously had encumbered $15,500 for supplies.
9. The Gas Service Fund billed the General Fund for $2,500, the Central Supplies Fund for $1,000, and the remainder of its customers for $2,500,000.
10. The General Fund made its annual contribution of $200,000 to the Debt Service Fund.
11. The contract for the new court building was signed with Excell Construction Company for $14,500,000. It contained a 10 percent retainage clause.
12. The sedan ordered in part 3 arrived. The total cost was $24,000. The city paid the bill upon delivery.
13. Excell Construction Company sent a progress billing for $1,500,000.
14. Property taxes of $2,800,000 were collected and $5,000 was written off as uncollectible. The remainder became delinquent.
15. Equity securities, carried in the city's pension fund at $3,200,000, had a fair value of $3,050,000 at year end.
16. A property tax bill from 2008 for $200 was written off as uncollectible. At this time the receivable was in a delinquent state.

Required: Prepare the journal entries necessary to record these transactions and indicate the fund(s) used.

10

GOVERNMENT-WIDE FINANCIAL STATEMENTS

Chapter Outline

After completing this chapter, you should be able to:

- List four basic principles for preparing the government-wide financial statements.
- Describe the conceptual differences between the fund financial statements and the government-wide financial statements.
- Describe the format of the government-wide statement of net assets and statement of activities.
- Discuss how interfund balances and transfers and Internal Service Fund activities are handled in government-wide statements.
- Describe and prepare the major adjustments needed to convert fund financial statements to government-wide financial statements.
- Prepare the government-wide financial statements.
- Describe and explain the content of the reconciliations between fund financial statements and government-wide statements.
- Discuss the "modified approach" for reporting infrastructure assets.

In addition to the fund financial statements described in Chapter 9, GASB *Statement No. 34* requires preparation of two government-wide financial statements: a statement of net assets and a statement of activities. Government-wide financial statements are prepared using the following basic principles:

a. Information is reported about the overall government, without showing individual funds or fund types.
b. Assets, liabilities, revenues, and expenses are reported using the economic resources measurement focus and the accrual basis of accounting for all activities, regardless of the types of funds used to account for them.
c. Financial statements are formatted to distinguish between the primary government and its discretely presented component units; also, for the primary government, the formatting distinguishes between governmental and business-type activities.
d. Information about fiduciary activities is excluded from the statements.[1]

The fund financial statements provide the starting point for preparing the government-wide statements. Because of the way the fund financial statements are prepared, complying with principles a, c, and d presents no major difficulties. Some effort is required,

---

[1]GASB Cod. Sec. 2200.110

however, to convert the governmental-type fund financial data to the economic resources measurement focus and accrual basis of accounting, as required by principle b. The major purpose of this chapter is to show how to make this conversion. We also discuss the standards for reporting on capital assets, including infrastructure assets, as well as methods for maintaining control over capital assets and long-term liabilities. First, we discuss the format of the government-wide financial statements.

FORMAT OF GOVERNMENT-WIDE FINANCIAL STATEMENTS

Focus of Government-Wide Financial Statements

Government-wide financial statements report on the governmental entity as a whole, rather than on individual funds. Within the governmental entity, the focus is on the primary government. Further, the government-wide statements distinguish between two types of activities: governmental (those that obtain resources primarily from taxes and intergovernmental grants) and business-type (those that obtain resources primarily from user charges to third parties). This is what happens to the financial data for the funds and the component units when you prepare the government-wide financial statements:

- *Governmental-type funds:* The financial data for governmental-type funds is converted to the economic resources measurement focus and accrual basis of accounting and consolidated to produce the governmental activities portions of the statements.
- *Proprietary-type funds:* The financial data for enterprise funds is consolidated to produce the business-type activities sections. Revenues of the internal service funds are offset against expenditures of the activities that bought the services and the net assets of the internal service funds are allocated as appropriate to those activities.
- *Fiduciary-type funds:* Fiduciary funds cannot be used to support a government's programs, so they are not included in the government-wide statements.
- *Component units:* The financial data for the discretely presented component units are aggregated and shown separately in the government-wide statements.

The Statement of Net Assets

The *statement of net assets* generally has four columns of financial data: one for governmental activities, one for business-type activities, another for the total of those columns, and one for discretely presented component units. The column for discretely presented component units is presented to the right of the total column. The statement would, of course, have fewer columns if the entity had no business-type activities or component units.

The statement of net assets shows all financial and capital resources. The statement may be formatted either in the form of Assets − Liabilities = Net Assets or in the traditional balance sheet form of Assets = Liabilities + Net Assets. Either way, the difference between assets and liabilities should be shown as *net assets,* not fund balance or equity.

Table 10-1 presents the government-wide statement of net assets for the Village of Grafton, Wisconsin, at December 31, 2005. Grafton has no component units, so its

TABLE 10-1 Government-Wide Statement of Net Assets

Village of Grafton
Statement of Net Assets
As of December 31, 2005

	Governmental Activities	Business-Type Activities	Total
Assets:			
Cash and Investments	$14,476,718	$ 4,193,025	$18,669,743
Receivables (Net)			
Taxes	6,617,499	—	6,617,499
Accounts	196,977	437,313	634,290
Loans	282,841	—	282,841
Other	213,712	49,926	263,638
Pledges	190,371	—	190,371
Interfund Balances	(2,193)	2,193	—
Prepaid Items and Inventories	286,492	13,022	299,514
Other Assets	193,111	6,011	199,122
Restricted Cash and Investments	—	818,772	818,772
Capital Assets:			
Capital Assets not being depreciated	12,305,092	448,472	12,753,564
Other Capital Assets, net of depreciation	22,408,215	22,993,821	45,402,036
Total Assets	57,168,835	28,962,555	86,131,390
Liabilities:			
Accounts Payable and Accrued Expenses	851,554	345,998	1,197,552
Unearned Revenues	6,619,788	56,464	6,676,252
Security Deposits	—	4,800	4,800
Long-Term Obligations:			
Due Within One Year	1,506,118	353,262	1,859,380
Due in More Than One Year	23,851,128	2,398,598	26,249,726
Total Liabilities	32,828,588	3,159,122	35,987,710
Net Assets:			
Invested in Capital Assets, net of related debt	17,751,646	20,726,712	38,478,358
Restricted for:			
Loan Programs	282,841	—	282,841
Park and Recreational Impact Fees	453,419	—	453,419
Park and Open Spaces	50,000	—	50,000
Debt Service	397,081	—	397,081
Library and Fire Impact Fees	185,648	—	185,648
Permanent Fund	63,840	—	63,840
Equipment Replacement	—	818,772	818,772
Unrestricted	5,155,772	4,257,949	9,413,721
Total Net Assets	$24,340,247	$25,803,433	$50,143,680

See Accompanying Notes

Source: Comprehensive Annual Financial Report, Year 2005, Village of Grafton, Wisconsin.

statement of net assets has just three columns. Notice that this statement is presented in the form of Assets − Liabilities = Net Assets.

Reporting on Liquidity

GASB standards encourage reporting on the relative liquidity of the assets and liabilities. This may be done either by presenting assets and liabilities in order of liquidity or by preparing the statement of net assets in classified form. For assets, relative liquidity means nearness in time to conversion to cash; for liabilities, it means nearness in time to payment. *Classified statements* of net assets distinguish between current and noncurrent, with the term *current* defined the way it is defined in reporting on business-type activities. Current assets include cash and assets that the entity expects to convert to cash or to be consumed in operations within 1 year. Current liabilities are those that are due to be paid within 1 year, including the portion of long-term bonds payable due to be paid in the year following the date of the statement of net assets.

Classification of Net Assets

The difference between assets and liabilities—the net assets—should be separated into three components: (1) invested in capital assets, net of related debt, (2) restricted, and (3) unrestricted. The net asset component *invested in capital assets, net of related debt* represents the entity's capital assets, minus accumulated depreciation and outstanding balances of bonds, notes, or other borrowings attributable to acquiring, constructing, or improving those assets. The calculation of this net asset component will be illustrated later in the chapter.

Net assets are reported as *restricted* when constraints are imposed on the use of assets, either externally (by creditors, grantors, or laws or regulations of other governments) or by the entity's charter or in enabling legislation. For example, restrictions may be imposed by debt covenants or by higher-level governments when they provide resources with the explicit requirement that the resources be used only for a specific purpose, such as a particular capital project or a particular operating function.

The amount reported as *unrestricted net assets* in the governmental activities column of the government-wide statement of net assets can differ significantly from the total unreserved fund balances reported in the governmental funds balance sheet. Possible causes of the difference include the use of different bases of accounting in the two statements and outstanding debt issued to finance prior-year operating deficits.

Return to Table 10-1 and notice that Grafton's assets and liabilities are shown in order of relative liquidity. Capital assets are shown as the last item in the assets section. Long-term obligations are separated between those due within 1 year and those due in more than 1 year. A note to Grafton's finanicial statements shows that long-term obligations are primarily bonds payable, but they also include compensated absences and landfill post-closure liabilities.

The Statement of Activities

The entity's government-wide operations are reported in a *statement of activities,* presented in a format that shows the extent to which each function is "self-financing" (through fees and intergovernmental grants) and the extent to which it draws on the government's taxes and other general revenues. That is, this statement presents the gross expenses and the net expenses (or net revenues) of each function or program in arriving at the government-wide change in net assets for the year.

To prepare this report, gross expenses are first listed in columnar form in the upper left part of the financial statement. Revenues directly related to each function or program (called *program revenues*) are listed in columns to the immediate right of gross expenses. The differences between gross expenses and program revenues are the net expenses or revenues for each function or program; these differences are presented in a column to the right of the program revenues columns. Then, in this same column, taxes, other general revenues (such as investment earnings and grants not restricted to specific purposes), and special items (such as gains on the sale of capital assets) are displayed in the lower part of the statement to arrive at the change in net assets for the year.

Table 10-2 presents the government-wide statement of activities for the Village of Grafton, Wisconsin, for the year ended December 31, 2005. Notice that expenses and related program revenues are displayed in the upper half of the financial statement, with governmental activities separated from business-type activities. Taxes, other general revenues, and special items are shown in the lower part of the statement.

If Grafton had component units, captions for each function/program would be shown on the left side of the page after business-type activities, and a component units column would be included after the total column on the right side of the page.

Reporting Expenses

Governmental units report expenses by function or program (such as public safety and culture and recreation), except for expenses that meet the definition of special or extraordinary, which need to be shown separately, as discussed in Chapter 9. At a minimum, the statement of activities should show the direct functional expenses—those that are clearly identifiable to a particular function. Although not required to do so, governmental units may allocate certain indirect expenses (such as general government and support services) among the functions.

Depreciation expense for capital assets that can be specifically identified with a function (for example, a police station or a firehouse) should be included with the direct expenses of the function. Depreciation expense for general infrastructure assets (such as water mains) may be reported either as a direct expense of the function (such as public works) that acquires and maintains the assets or as a separate line item in the statement of activities. Interest on general long-term debt generally should be shown separately.

Notice that Grafton's statement of activities (Table 10-2) shows the same five functions in its governmental activities that it reports in its governmental funds statement of revenues, expenditures, and changes in fund balances (Table 9-3 on page 344). In reporting on business-type activities in its statement of activities, it separated the Proprietary Fund operating statement (Table 9-6 on page 349) into two functions, water and wastewater.

Reporting Net Functional Expenses

The statement of activities must be displayed in a manner that shows the net expense or revenue for each function or program. For this reason, the statement of activities uses columns for three types of "program revenues" associated directly with each function. They are charges for services, program-specific operating grants and contributions, and program-specific capital grants and contributions.

TABLE 10-2 Government-Wide Statement of Activities

Village of Grafton
Statement of Activities
For the Year Ended December 31, 2005

Functions/Programs	Expenses	Program Revenues			Net (Expenses) Revenues and Changes in Net Assets		
		Charges for Services	Operating Grants and Contributions	Capital Grants and Contributions	Governmental Activities	Business-Type Activities	Totals
Governmental Activities:							
General Government	$ 849,959	$ 175,375	$ —	$ —	$ (674,584)	$ —	$ (674,584)
Public Safety	3,545,072	608,130	34,717	—	(2,902,225)	—	(2,902,225)
Public Works	2,990,123	59,696	602,823	50,619	(2,276,985)	—	(2,276,985)
Community Enrichment Services	1,491,828	184,045	159,853	53,401	(1,147,930)	—	(1,147,930)
Conservation and Development	2,730,714	26,989	—	—	(2,650,324)	—	(2,650,324)
Interest and Fiscal Charges	797,016	—	—	—	(797,016)	—	(797,016)
Total Governmental Activities	12,404,712	1,054,235	797,393	104,020	(10,449,064)	—	(10,449,064)
Business-Type Activities:							
Water	1,178,433	1,321,531	—	21,272	—	164,370	164,370
Wastewater	1,415,798	1,422,033	—	54,516	—	60,751	60,751
Total Business-Type Activities	2,594,231	2,743,564	—	75,788	—	225,121	225,121
TOTAL	$14,998,943	$3,797,799	$797,393	$179,808	(10,449,064)	225,121	(10,223,943)

General Revenues:

Taxes:

Property Taxes, Levied for General Purposes					4,620,712	—	4,620,712
Property Taxes, Levied for Debt Service					890,000	—	890,000
Property Taxes, Levied for Capital Assets Including TIF					949,980	—	949,980
Other Taxes					20,464	—	20,464
Intergovernmental Revenues Not Restricted to Specific Programs					655,435	—	655,435
Investment Income					400,206	45,004	445,210
Miscellaneous					297,869	—	297,869
Impact Fees					114,332	—	114,332
Total General Revenues					7,948,998	45,004	7,994,002
Changes in Net Assets					(2,500,066)	270,125	(2,229,941)
Net Assets — Beginning of Year					26,840,313	25,533,308	52,373,621
Net Assets — End of Year					$ 24,340,247	$25,803,433	$50,143,680

See Accompanying Notes

Source: Comprehensive Annual Financial Report, Year 2005, Village of Grafton, Wisconsin.

Charges for services are revenues based on exchange or exchange-like transactions. They include fees for specific services (such as garbage collection, water use, or parks admissions fees), licenses and permits (such as liquor licenses and building permits), and other amounts charged to service recipients. Charges for services also include fines and forfeitures (such as parking fines and fines arising out of inspections) because they are revenues generated by specific programs. Although charges for services tend to defray only a small part of the expenses of governmental activities, they often exceed the expenses of business-type activities.

Program-specific operating grants and contributions arise out of revenues received from other governments, organizations, or individuals that are restricted for use in a particular program. Grants and contributions reported in this column are those received for operating purposes or either operating or capital purposes at the receiving government's discretion. Program-specific operating grants and contributions include the typical program-oriented state aid programs such as aid for education and health care purposes.

Program-specific capital grants and contributions are reported in a separate column. In analyzing financial statements, amounts in this column need to be considered carefully because significant revenues from capital grants and contributions can distort amounts reported as net expenses or revenues. For example, the full amount of the revenue from a capital grant may be recognized in a single year, but program expenses may show only the year's depreciation on the asset acquired with the grant.

Examine the upper part of Grafton's statement of activities (Table 10-2). Notice the amounts in the three columns headed Program Revenues, as well as the amounts shown in the Net (Expenses) Revenues and Changes in Net Assets columns. Notice that the amounts in the governmental activities column are generally net expenses and the amounts in the business-type activities columns are generally net revenues. The aggregate of the net expenses in the governmental activities column ($10,449,064) is the amount that is financed by taxes, other general revenues, and net assets available at the beginning of the year, all of which are shown in the lower part of the statement.

Interfund and Internal Service Fund Balances and Activity

As discussed in previous chapters, fund accounting often results in transfers among, charges to, and balances due to and from the various funds. As a general rule, these types of internal activities and balances—reported in the fund financial statements—are eliminated when preparing the government-wide statement of net assets and statement of activities. Unless the eliminations are made, totals for the entity as a whole will be inflated. How are these eliminations made?

Interfund Receivables and Payables

Amounts due between individual governmental funds, as reported in the governmental funds balance sheet, are eliminated against each other and not carried forward to the governmental activities column of the government-wide statement of net assets. The same should be done for amounts due between individual proprietary funds. In contrast, amounts due between the two fund categories (that is, governmental and proprietary) are carried forward to the respective columns for governmental and business-type activities in the statement of net assets, and reported as *internal balances*. The internal balances are eliminated against each other within the statement of net assets.

To see how to make these adjustments, turn to Grafton's governmental funds balance sheet (Table 9-1 on page 341) and statement of net assets (Table 10-1). In Table 9-1, Due from other funds shows $90,221 in the Total Governmental Funds column, and Due to other funds shows $92,414. Amounts due to and due from the various governmental-type funds ($90,221) are offset against each other. The difference ($2,193), which is the net amount due to proprietary funds, is reported as a negative amount next to the caption Interfund balances in the Governmental Activities column of the statement of net assets (Table 10-1). Grafton's proprietary funds statement of net assets (Table 9-5) shows an amount of $2,193, captioned Due from municipality. This amount is reported next to the caption Interfund balances in the Business-Type Activities column of the statement of net assets (Table 10-1). The debits and credits of $2,193 offset each other so that the total column of Table 10-1 shows zero.

Interfund Transfers

In the statement of activities, the same treatment just described for interfund receivables and payables should be given to interfund transfers and charges. Trace the elimination of the interfund activity by referring to Table 9-3 of the Grafton illustration. Notice that both transfers in and transfers out were $1,347,917 in Table 9-3; this occurred because all the transfers were among governmental-type funds. For government-wide reporting, these transfers cancel each other and, because there were no transfers between governmental-type and proprietary-type funds, no interfund transfers are shown in Table 10-2. If transfers had occurred between governmental-type and proprietary-type funds, they would have been eliminated against each other in Table 10-2.

The fact that interfund transfers are eliminated in the statement of activities does not mean that they should be ignored when analyzing governmental financial statements. Some transfers may be considered as routine transfers from a resource-collecting fund to a fund authorized by law to incur expenditures or expenses. Other interfund transfers, however, may indicate that a particular activity is experiencing financial difficulties and requires continuing subsidies.

Internal Service Fund Balances and Activity

For government-wide financial reporting, the assets and liabilities of Internal Service Funds (ISFs) are aggregated with those of the activities that are the primary consumers of ISF services. (ISFs generally provide services primarily to departments accounted for in the General Fund, so ISF assets and liabilities are aggregated most often with those of governmental activities.) Also, to avoid artificially inflating the activity reported in the government-wide statements, an elimination is needed for ISF activity. This is because (a) ISF operating statements show both revenues (from sales to other funds) and expenses and (b) funds that buy services from ISFs report expenditures or expenses as a result of the billings. Further, ISFs often generate "artificial" profits or losses as a result of their billing practices.

To understand the nature of the adjustments, assume the following set of facts: An ISF buys, stores, and sells supplies to two departments accounted for in the General Fund and reported in the public safety and recreation functions. During the year, the ISF billed public safety departments for $60,000 and recreation departments for $40,000. The ISF had expenses of $95,000, so it had "net profit" of $5,000, equivalent to 5 percent of its revenues. As a result of the year's activities, the ISF's net assets increased by $5,000, so its year-end net assets were cash of $3,000 and supplies inventory of $12,000.

The following journal entry, when posted to the eliminations column of a work sheet containing colums for the General Fund and the ISF, would eliminate the interfund activity and the interfund profit:

Revenues (ISF)	100,000	
Expenses (ISF)		95,000
Public safety expenditures		3,000
Recreation expenditures		2,000

Notice that the credits to public safety and recreation expenditures represent 5 percent of the amounts purchased from the ISF—the interfund profit. Also, note that the assets of the ISF would be picked up automatically by extension of asset balances in the ISF column to a governmental activities column.[2]

PREPARING GOVERNMENT-WIDE FINANCIAL STATEMENTS

Overview

GASB *Statement No. 34* requires using the economic resources measurement focus and accrual basis of accounting for *all* activities, including the governmental activities, in the government-wide financial statements. Because the fund financial statements for governmental-type funds are based on the current financial resources measurement focus and modified accrual basis of accounting, the data used to prepare the fund financial statements must be adjusted. The nature of the adjustments depends on the nature of an entity's activities, but the following adjustments are almost always needed:

- Capital assets, including infrastructure assets, are reported as assets and depreciated, subject to certain permitted modifications for infrastructure assets.
- Proceeds from issuing long-term debt are reported as liabilities, and payments of debt principal are reported as reductions of liabilities.
- Revenues are recognized on the accrual basis of accounting, so the "measurable and available" rule for recognizing tax revenues in the governmental-type funds is discarded.
- Expenses are recognized when incurred, so long-term liabilities resulting from current transactions and events are reported.

In addition, adjustments are generally needed if an entity sells capital assets, issues debt at a premium or discount, or maintains internal service funds.

Proprietary fund financial statements are prepared using the economic resources measurement focus and accrual basis of accounting, so no measurement focus and basis of accounting adjustments are needed when enterprise funds are incorporated in the government-wide financial statements. Notice, for example, that the net assets reported in Grafton's enterprise fund ($25,803,433 in Table 9-5) and the change in net assets ($270,125 in Table 9-6) are the same as the corresponding amounts reported in the business-type activities part of the government-wide statements in Tables 10-1 and 10-2.

---

[2]The same result could be accomplished with journal entries affecting only the governmental activities. The ISF balances could be assumed by governmental activities by debiting cash for $3,000 and supplies inventory for $12,000 and crediting net assets for $15,000. The interfund profit could be eliminated from governmental activities expenses by debiting net assets for $5,000 and crediting public safety and recreation expenditures for $3,000 and $2,000, respectively.

Process for Preparing Government-Wide Statements

The simplest way to prepare the government-wide financial statements—the method we use to illustrate the process later in the chapter—is to use a six-column work sheet to record the adjustments. (Later in the chapter we will show how keeping a separate set of accounts for capital assets can facilitate making some of the adjustments.) Using a work sheet requires three sets of debit and credit columns:

- Starting balances (an aggregation of the preclosing trial balances of the governmental-type funds)
- Adjustments needed to convert the measurement focus and basis of accounting of the governmental-type funds from current financial and modified accrual to economic resources and accrual
- Adjusted preclosing trial balances

When you use a work sheet, the adjustments generally take the following forms:

- Entering beginning-of-year balances of accounts that affect the government-wide statements, such as capital assets and bonds payable
- Making adjustments for transactions and events that occurred during the year and that affect the accounts differently when the economic resources measurement focus and accrual basis of accounting are used rather than the current financial resources measurement focus and modified accrual basis of accounting
- Eliminating transfers and interfund balances among governmental-type funds

There is no need for concern with terminology in the work sheet because terms like "expenditures" can be converted to "expenses" and "fund balances" can be converted to "net assets" when you prepare the government-wide statements.

Discussion of Adjustments for Government-Wide Statements

This section describes and illustrates some of the adjustments needed for preparing the government-wide financial statements, using the fund preclosing trial balances as a starting point. It also covers revenue and expense recognition standards under the accrual basis of accounting. The comprehensive illustration later in the chapter provides additional adjustments needed for preparing the government-wide financial statements.

Acquiring and Depreciating Capital Assets

As you know, when capital assets are acquired with governmental fund resources, they are recorded in the funds as capital outlay expenditures, rather than as assets. Further, capital assets are not depreciated in the funds. Therefore, to report using the economic resources measurement focus and accrual basis of accounting, adjustments are needed to decrease capital outlay expenditures, record capital acquisitions as assets, and record depreciation expense. In all likelihood, the entity will have reported capital assets at the beginning of the year. Therefore, beginning-of-year balances of capital assets and related depreciation also need to be entered in the work sheet.

To illustrate, assume a city had $1 million of capital assets (equipment) at the start of its calendar year 2009 and that accumulated depreciation on those assets was $400,000. During 2009, the city had $200,000 of capital outlay expenditures. Depreciation on old and new assets during 2009 was $110,000. Regarding these transactions and events, the only data reported in the fund financial statements were the expenditures for acquiring the new equipment. Preparing the government-wide statements requires recording the opening balances, adjusting the accounting for equipment acquired during the year, and recording depreciation expense for the year. This is accomplished by making the following adjusting entries.

Capital assets—equipment	1,000,000	
Accumulated depreciation—equipment		400,000
Net assets		600,000
To record account balances at January 1, 2009.		
Capital assets—equipment	200,000	
Expenditures—capital outlay		200,000
To reduce 2009 expenditures and record capital assets.		
Depreciation expense—equipment	110,000	
Accumulated depreciation—equipment		110,000
To record depreciation expense for 2009.		

Notice that recording net capital assets at the start of the year requires a credit to net assets. This is because reporting capital acquisitions as assets rather than as expenditures causes governmental "equity" (net assets) to be greater than that reported under the current financial resources measurement focus. (Similarly, as the next section shows, reporting proceeds from the sale of bonds as liabilities reduces governmental "equity.")

Selling and Redeeming Long-Term Debt

Fund level reporting on governmental-type funds requires that you report the proceeds of long-term debt as financing sources, not as liabilities; and that you report redemptions of long-term debt as expenditures, not as reductions of liabilities. The economic resources measurement focus used in government-wide financial reporting requires adjustments to report long-term debt as liabilities. The adjustments needed to record beginning-of-year outstanding long-term debt, sale of new long-term debt, and redemption of outstanding long-term debt are similar to the adjustments described regarding capital assets—except that the effect on net assets is just the opposite.

Assume, for example, that the city in the previous illustration had outstanding long-term debt of $500,000 at the start of the year. During the year, it sold $200,000 of debt to acquire capital assets and redeemed $100,000 of debt that was outstanding at the beginning of the year. The following adjustments are needed to prepare the government-wide financial statements from the fund preclosing trial balances.

Net assets	500,000	
Bonds payable		500,000
To record account balances at January 1, 2009.		
Other financing sources—proceeds from bond issue	200,000	
Bonds payable		200,000
To reduce financing source and record liability.		
Bonds payable	100,000	
Expenditures—bond principal		100,000
To reduce expenditures and record repayment of liability.		

Accruing Revenues

When reporting on governmental-type funds, taxes are recognized as revenues in the accounting period that they become measurable and available. For government-wide financial reporting, the GASB adopted specific accrual-basis rules for taxes and other nonexchange revenues in GASB *Statement No. 33*. The rules and resulting adjustments needed to prepare government-wide financial statements are summarized as follows:

Derived Tax Revenues (Sales Taxes, Income Taxes).   As discussed in Chapter 5, *derived* tax revenues are taxes resulting from assessments imposed by a government on external exchange transactions. They include the general sales tax, sales taxes on specific commodities, personal income taxes, and corporate income taxes.

For government-wide financial reporting, derived tax revenues are recognized (net of estimated refunds and estimated uncollectible amounts) when the assets are recognized—generally, on occurrence of the exchange transaction on which the tax is imposed. With regard to sales taxes, the practical effect of the standard is to require revenue recognition at the time of the taxable sale, *even though the government may not receive the cash until the following year.*[3]

To illustrate, suppose a state collects sales taxes on behalf of a city whose fiscal year ends December 31, 2009. The state's practice is to remit the taxes to the city between 90 and 120 days after the end of the quarter for which it has collected the taxes. When preparing its 2009 fund financial statements, the city would report sales taxes receivable for the quarter ended December 31, 2009, but would defer recognition of the revenues, because they are not "available." For its 2009 government-wide financial statements, however, the city would recognize sales tax revenues for the quarter ended December 31, 2009, even though it will not receive the taxes until April 2010.

Imposed Nonexchange Revenues (Real Property Taxes, Fines).   Imposed nonexchange revenues are taxes and other assessments levied without an underlying external exchange, such as real property taxes and fines. For government-wide financial reporting, real property tax revenues are recognized (net of estimated refunds and estimated uncollectible amounts) in the period for which the taxes are levied, even if the enforceable legal claim arises or the due date for payment occurs in a different period.[4] The accrual-basis standard makes no reference to the term *measurable and available*. Therefore, for government-wide reporting, if a city levies real property taxes on January 1, 2009, for the calendar year 2009, property tax revenues are recognized in 2009 for the amount levied (net of estimated refunds and uncollectible amounts), even though some of the taxes may not be collected for many months beyond the 60-day availability criterion discussed in Chapter 5.

Adjustments for Preparing Government-Wide Statements.   Modified accrual accounting for tax revenues makes it likely that deferred revenues will be reported at year end for tax revenues applicable to a particular year that have not yet met the "measurable and available" criteria for revenue recognition. Therefore, two adjustments are needed when the government-wide statements are prepared: (1) to take account of the beginning-of-year deferral and (2) to remove the current year's deferral. (You need to be

---

[3]GASB Cod. Sec. N50.113
[4]GASB Cod. Sec. N50.115

careful when making the first adjustment because the deferral was reversed in the funds when the receivable was collected during the year.)

To illustrate: Assume a city started calendar year 2009 with deferred property taxes of $10,000. The entire $10,000 was collected in 2009. Property taxes of $800,000 were levied for 2009. Although the city expected to collect the entire $800,000, it actually collected only $760,000 in 2009; it expected to collect $25,000 more by February 28, 2010, and the remaining $15,000 in the latter part of 2010.

Based on the foregoing data, the city reported $15,000 of deferred property tax revenues in its fund financial statements for 2009. The city also reported $795,000 of property tax revenues in 2009—$10,000 from reversing the prior year's deferral, plus $785,000 that met the measurable and available criteria for the 2009 tax levy. Based on the accrual accounting criteria, however, $800,000 of property tax revenues—the entire 2009 property tax levy—should be recognized in the government-wide statements. Therefore, the end product of the adjustments must be to increase property tax revenues by $5,000 and to remove the $15,000 of deferred property tax revenues. To accomplish that result, you need to make the following adjustments to the data reported in the fund financial statements.

Revenues—property taxes	10,000	
Net assets		10,000
To reverse revenues applicable to 2008, but recognized in the fund statements during 2009.		
Deferred property tax revenues	15,000	
Revenues—property taxes		15,000
To recognize additional revenues from 2009 property tax levy by removing the deferral.		

Government-Mandated Nonexchange Transactions (Intergovernmental Aid). Higher-level governments often provide resources to lower-level governments to be used for specific purposes set forth in the higher-level government's enabling legislation. In addition to purpose restrictions, the provider government may establish other eligibility requirements, such as time and expenditure-incurrence requirements. The GASB standard requires that the receiving government recognize receivables and revenues (net of uncollectible amounts) when all eligibility requirements, including time requirements, are met.[5] For example, a state law may provide that the state reimburse counties 50 percent of all allowable costs incurred on a specific health program, subject to maximum amounts specified in annual contracts between the state health department and the counties. In these so-called expenditure-driven grants, counties recognize receivables and revenues as they incur allowable costs—the point when they meet the eligibility requirements—up to the maximum amount specified in the contract.

In these situations, financial reporting in the fund and the government-wide financial statements are likely to be the same. If, for some reason, revenue recognition was deferred in the fund financial statements because it wasn't considered "available," an adjustment similar to that made for deferred taxes would be needed for the government-wide statements.

---

[5]GASB Cod. Sec. N50.118

Accruing Expenses

As discussed in Chapters 5 and 6, the modified accrual basis of accounting provides for several significant departures from accrual accounting when recognizing expenditures. You need to adjust for these accrual accounting departures to report governmental activity expenses in the government-wide financial statements.

"Stub Period" Interest on General Obligation Long-Term Debt.   As discussed in Chapter 6, under modified accrual accounting, interest on general obligation long-term debt and capital leases is, as a general rule, recognized only to the extent the interest matures and is payable. Interest for the "stub period"—the period between the last interest payment in one fiscal year and the fiscal year end—is generally not accrued. Therefore, one of the common adjustments needed when preparing the accrual-basis government-wide financial statements concerns the stub period interest.

To understand the calculation of the adjustment, assume a city that operates on a calendar-year basis sold long-term debt of $200,000 on October 1, 2008. The debt matures at the rate of $50,000 a year, starting September 30, 2009. Interest is payable each September 30 at the rate of 4 percent per annum on the outstanding balance. What adjustment is needed for interest when the city prepares its government-wide financial statements at December 31, 2009?

Answer: The city had no matured interest during 2008, so it recorded no interest in its 2008 fund financial statements. But, for its 2008 government-wide statements, the city reported an expense and a liability of $2,000 for the stub period interest ($2,000 × 4% × ¼ year). For its 2009 fund statements, the city reported interest expenditures of $8,000 ($200,000 × 4% × 1 year) because that was the amount of matured interest during the year. So, for its 2009 government-wide statements, the interest expense should be $7,500, consisting of these two components:

- Interest for 9 months (previously paid) on $200,000 @ 4 percent, or $6,000
- Unpaid accrued interest for 3 months on $150,000 @ 4 percent, or $1,500

Therefore, the $8,000 interest expenditure reported in the 2009 fund statements must be reduced by $500. You do that by first recording the beginning-of-year interest liability and then adjusting it to the appropriate end-of-year liability, as follows:

Net assets	2,000	
Accrued interest payable		2,000
To record interest liability at January 1, 2009.		
Accrued interest payable	500	
Expenditures—interest on bonds		500
To adjust expenditure and liability to the		
accrual basis of accounting.		

When reporting the interest in the government-wide financial statements, you should describe it as *expense* rather *expenditure,* because the journal entries adjusted the amount from the modified accrual expenditure to the full accrual expense needed for government-wide financial reporting.

Expenses Incurred, But Not Currently Due and Payable.   As discussed in Chapter 5, when the modified accrual basis of accounting is used, certain specific expenditures are recognized as fund liabilities only to the extent the liabilities are "normally expected to be liquidated with expendable available resources." In effect, these items—which include compensated absences, judgments and claims, and landfill closure and postclosure costs—are not recognized as expenditures until they come due for payment. Under accrual accounting, however, expenses are recognized when the liabilities are incurred, regardless of when the cash outflows occur. For example, compensated absences are recognized as employees earn the right to the benefits. When preparing government-wide financial statements, it is likely that additional expenses will need to be accrued and additional liabilities (probably noncurrent) will need to be recognized. The adjustment

---

TABLE 10-3   Reconciliation of Fund and Government-Wide Operating Statements

Village of Grafton
Reconciliation of the Statement of Revenues, Expenditures and Changes in Fund Balances
of Governmental Funds to the Statement of Activities
For the Year Ended December 31, 2005

Net Change in Fund Balances—Total Governmental Funds	$ 5,992,734
Amounts reported for governmental activities in the statement of activities are different because:	
Governmental funds report capital outlays as expenditures. However, in the statement of net assets the cost of these assets is capitalized and depreciated over their estimated useful lives and reported as depreciation expense in the statement of activities. This is the amount by which Village depreciation ($1,026,885) exceeds capital outlays plus capital contributions ($831,245) in the current period.	(195,640)
Debt proceeds provide current financial resources to governmental funds, but issuing debt increases long-term liabilities in the statement of net assets. Repayment of debt principal is an expenditure in the governmental funds, but the repayment reduces long-term liabilities in the statement of net assets. This is the amount by which debt proceeds ($9,615,000) exceeded debt payments ($1,309,479) and payments on the noncurrent landfill post-closure liability ($30,000).	(8,275,521)
Revenues in the statement of activities that do not provide current financial resources are not reported as revenues in the funds. This is the amount by which the change in the deferred revenue for special assessments ($6,001) exceeded the change in pledges receivable ($19,422).	(13,421)
The gain on disposal of capital assets does not increase the current financial resources and therefore is not reported as a revenue in the governmental funds.	30,000
Some expenses reported in the statement of activities do not require the use of current financial resources and therefore are not reported as expenditures in the governmental funds. This is the amount by which interest expense ($57,014) exceeded the change in compensated absences ($11,337)	(45,677)
Governmental funds report debt discount/premium and issuance costs as expenditures/revenues. However, in the statement of net assets these are reported as deferred charges. These are allocated over the period the debt is outstanding in the statement of activities and are reported as amortization expense. This is the amount by which debt discount and issuance costs of the current year ($84,781), exceeded the premium ($56,575) and amortization expense ($20,747).	7,459
Change in Net Assets of Governmental Activities— Statement of Activities	$(2,500,066)

See Accompanying Notes
Source: Comprehensive Annual Financial Report, Year 2005, Village of Grafton, Wisconsin.

is similar to that described above for compensated absences; that is, first, record the beginning-of-year liability and then, adjust it to the appropriate end-of-year liability.

Required Reconciliations of Fund and Government-Wide Statements

GASB *Statement No. 34* requires that the fund financial statements be reconciled in summary form with the government-wide financial statements, to help users assess the relationship between the two sets of statements. These reconciliations explain the specific differences resulting from using different measurement focuses and bases of accounting in the two sets of statements. Two reconciliations are needed, one for the two financial position statements and one for the two operating statements. They may be presented either at the bottom of the fund financial statements or in an accompanying schedule.

The Village of Grafton used its governmental funds balance sheet (see Table 9-1 on page 341) to reconcile the total of its fund balances ($14,549,797) to the net assets of governmental activities reported in its government-wide statement of net assets ($24,340,247). Notice that the major reconciling items relate to the reporting of capital assets and long-term debt in the government-wide statement but not in the funds statement.

Table 10-3 presents Grafton's reconciliation of the governmental funds statement of revenues, expenditures, and changes in fund balances to the government-wide statement of activities. This statement shows in summary form why the "bottom lines" of the two operating statements differ. Notice again that the most significant differences relate to the treatment of debt proceeds and capital asset outlays.[6] The other differences are relatively small, but they could be much larger in a particular situation.

GOVERNMENTAL FINANCIAL REPORTING IN PRACTICE
New York City Takes a Big Accounting Bang!

As discussed in Chapter 8, GASB *Statement No. 45* (June 2004) requires employers to report the expense of postemployment health care and other benefits in the period the employees work, rather than when the benefits are paid. For many governmental employers, transition to the new accounting standard resulted in the need to take account of a large "actuarial accrued liability" for postemployment health care benefits attributable to retired employees and to the past service of active employees.

The standard allowed employers to record this liability gradually (over 30 years) or all at once. New York City opted to record the entire actuarial accrued liability at once. Result: a huge accounting bang—$53.5 billion! That number appears in the city's reconciliation of its fund and government-wide operating statements for the fiscal year ended June 30, 2006. The fund balances of its governmental-type funds (shown in the fund statement) declined by $736 million, but the decision to record the $53.5 billion transition liability for postemployment health care benefits all at once caused the net assets of its governmental activities (which appears in the government-wide statement) to decline by a total of $53.7 billion.

---

[6]It is probable that actual capital outlays shown in this reconciliation are larger than the amount shown in Table 10-3 because construction-in-progress expenditures were not reported as assets in the government-wide statement of net assets. We were advised by Grafton officials that procedures were being developed to change accounting procedures for construction-in-progress.

CREATING GOVERNMENT-WIDE FINANCIAL STATEMENTS FROM FUND FINANCIAL DATA: COMPREHENSIVE ILLUSTRATION

This section illustrates the preparation of government-wide financial statements by making adjustments to the fund financial statements on a work sheet. The major objective of this illustration is to show the types of adjustments needed to convert data originally reported in statements using the current financial resources measurement focus and modified accrual basis of accounting to statements using the economic resources measurement focus and accrual basis of accounting. Therefore, the illustration is limited to a series of basic transactions in three governmental-type funds: a General Fund, a Debt Service Fund, and a Capital Projects Fund.

Opening Balances, Transactions, and Events

Assume, for simplicity, that Eunee City's General Fund has just two programs, Public Safety and Parks. To further simplify the illustration, all numbers are expressed in thousands of dollars and budgetary accounting is not shown.

At January 1, 2009, there were zero account balances both in the Debt Service Fund and the Capital Projects Fund. The General Fund had the following balances:

Cash	$25	
Property taxes receivable—delinquent	35	
Deferred property tax revenues		$10
Unreserved fund balance		50
Totals	$60	$60

Eunee City's government-wide financial statements for the year ended December 31, 2008, reported that the city had (a) capital assets of $400 and accumulated depreciation on the assets of $280; (b) outstanding long-term general obligation bonds of $60; (c) accrued interest of $2 on the long-term bonds; and (d) an accrual of $4 for long-term compensated absences.

The following transactions and events occurred during the calendar year 2009.

1. On January 1, the city levied property taxes of $710, all of which were expected to be collected.
2. During the year, the city collected $35 of delinquent property taxes outstanding on January 1, 2009. (This amount included $10 for which revenue had been deferred because the city did not expect to collect it until May, 2009.)
3. During the year, the city collected $660 of the $710 levied for property taxes. At year end, the remaining $50 was declared delinquent. The city expected to collect $32 of it in the first 60 days of 2010 and the other $18 during the rest of 2010.
4. The city paid $610 cash for salaries and supplies, charging $470 to Public Safety and $140 to Parks.
5. The Parks Department collected fees of $20 for parking in the city's parks.
6. At the beginning of the year, the city sold the police chief's old sedan for $1. The sedan had originally cost $20 and had accumulated depreciation of $16.
7. The General Fund transferred $65 to the Debt Service Fund to provide resources for payment of debt service.

8. On April 1, 2009, the city paid off its outstanding general obligation debt of $60, together with interest of $4 for the period October 1, 2008, to April 1, 2009.

9. On April 1, 2009, the city sold $400 of general obligation debt, to be used solely to acquire capital assets. It will repay the debt in 10 equal annual installments of principal, starting April 1, 2010, together with interest at the rate of 5 percent per annum on the unpaid principal.

10. On July 1, 2009, the city used $300 of bond proceeds to acquire capital assets. The capital assets have a useful life of 20 years.

11. At year end, the city estimated that the long-term accrual for compensated absences had increased to $5. All compensated absences apply to Public Safety.

12. Depreciation for the year on the city's capital assets was $30. The entire depreciation amount applies to Public Safety.

Journal Entries to Record Transactions in Funds

Journal entries to record the foregoing transactions in the three governmental-type funds are as follows.

Entry in General Fund	1. Property taxes receivable—current	710	
	Revenues—property taxes		710
	To record property tax levy.		
Entries in General Fund	2. Cash	35	
	Property taxes receivable—delinquent		35
	To record collection of property taxes.		
	Deferred property tax revenues	10	
	Revenues—property taxes		10
	To recognize revenues previously deferred.		
Entries in General Fund	3. Cash	660	
	Property taxes receivable—current		660
	To record collection of 2009 property taxes.		
	Property taxes receivable—delinquent	50	
	Property taxes receivable—current		50
	To record delinquent tax receivables.		
	Revenues—property taxes	18	
	Deferred tax revenues		18
	To record property taxes not available.		
Entry in General Fund	4. Expenditures—public safety	470	
	Expenditures—parks	140	
	Cash		610
	To record expenditures paid in cash.		
Entry in General Fund	5. Cash	20	
	Revenues—parking fees		20
	To record parking fee revenues.		
Entry in General Fund	6. Cash	1	
	Other financing sources—sale of assets		1
	To record sale of used sedan.		

| Entry in
General
Fund | 7. | Transfer out to Debt Service Fund
    Cash
    To record transfer out. | 65 | 65 |

| Entry in
Debt Service
Fund | | Cash
    Transfer in from General Fund
    To record transfer in. | 65 | 65 |

| Entries in
Debt Service
Fund | 8. | Expenditues—bond principal
Expenditures—bond interest
    Matured bond principal payable
    Matured bond interest payable
    To record liability for matured debt service. | 60
4 | 60
4 |

| | | Matured bond principal payable
Matured bond interest payable
    Cash
    To record payment of debt service. | 60
4 | 64 |

| Entry in
Capital
Projects Fund | 9. | Cash
    Proceeds of bonds
    To record proceeds of bonds | 400 | 400 |

| Entry in
Capital
Projects Fund | 10. | Expenditures—capital outlay
    Cash
    To record acquisition of capital assets | 300 | 300 |

11. No entry required in funds.

12. No entry required in funds.

Preclosing Trial Balances and Fund Financial Statements

Preclosing trial balances, based on the foregoing journal entries, are shown in Table 10-4. Eunee City's governmental funds balance sheet at December 31, 2009, is shown in Table 10-5, and its governmental funds statement of revenues, expenditures, and changes in fund balances for the year ended December 31, 2009, is shown in Table 10-6. Trace the items shown in the trial balance to the two financial statements.

Adjustments for Preparing Government-Wide Statements

To prepare the government-wide financial statements, we will start by making adjusting entries and posting them to a six-column work sheet. The adjusting entries take account of (a) the opening balances in the accounts needed to produce the government-wide statements, (b) the transactions and events during the year that affected those accounts, and (c) the elimination of interfund transfers. For illustrative purposes, we present the adjustments in five groups: capital asset adjustments, long-term debt adjustments, revenue adjustments, expense adjustments, and interfund transfer eliminations. Each adjustment is keyed to the data provided in the section headed "Opening Balances, Transactions, and Events." Trace the journal entries to the data provided in that section.

TABLE 10-4 Preclosing Trial Balances

Eunee City
Preclosing Trial Balance
General Fund
December 31, 2009

	Debits	Credits
Cash	$ 66	
Property taxes receivable—delinquent	50	
Deferred tax revenue		$ 18
Unreserved fund balance		50
Revenues—property taxes		702
Revenues—parking fees		20
Other financing sources—sales of assets		1
Expenditures—public safety	470	
Expenditures—parks	140	
Transfer out to Debt Service Fund	65	
Totals	$791	$791

Debt Service Fund

	Debits	Credits
Cash	$ 1	
Expenditures—bond principal	60	
Expenditures—bond interest	4	
Transfer in from General Fund		$ 65
Totals	$ 65	$ 65

Capital Projects Fund

	Debits	Credits
Cash	$100	
Expenditures—capital outlay	300	
Proceeds of bonds		$400
Totals	$400	$400

TABLE 10-5 Fund Financial Statement—Balance Sheet

Eunee City
Balance Sheet
Governmental Funds
December 31, 2009

	General	Debt Service	Capital Projects	Total
Assets				
Cash	$ 66	$1	$100	$167
Property taxes receivable—delinquent	50			50
Total assets	$116	$1	$100	$217
Liabilities				
Deferred tax revenue	$ 18	$	$	$ 18
Total liabilities	18	—	—	18
Fund Balances				
Reserved for debt service		1		1
Unreserved	98	—	100	198
Total fund balances	98	1	100	199
Total liabilities and fund balances	$116	$1	$100	$217

TABLE 10-6 Fund Financial Statement—Statement of Revenues, Expenditures, and Changes in Fund Balances

Eunee City
Statement of Revenues, Expenditures, and Changes in Fund Balances
Governmental Funds
December 31, 2009

	General	Debt Service	Capital Projects	Total
Revenues				
Property taxes	$702			$702
Parking fees	20			20
Total revenues	722			722
Expenditures				
Current:				
Public safety	470			470
Parks	140			140
Debt service:				
Principal		$ 60		60
Interest		4		4
Capital outlay			$300	300
Total expenditures	610	64	300	974
Excess (deficiency) of revenues over expenditures	112	(64)	(300)	(252)
Other Financing Sources (Uses)				
Proceeds of bonds			400	400
Sales of assets	1			1
Transfers in		65		65
Transfers out	(65)			(65)
Total other financing sources (uses)	(64)	65	400	401
Net change in fund balances	48	1	100	149
Fund balances—beginning	50	0	0	50
Fund balances—ending	$ 98	$ 1	$100	$199

Capital Asset Adjustments:

a. Capital assets　　　　　　　　　　　　　　　　　400
　　　Accumulated depreciation—capital assets　　　　　　　　　　280
　　　Net assets　　　　　　　　　　　　　　　　　　　　　　120
　　To record beginning-of-year account balances.
　　　(Opening Balances data)

b. Accumulated depreciation—capital assets　　　　　16
　　Other financing sources—sale of assets　　　　　　1
　　Loss on sale of assets　　　　　　　　　　　　　　3
　　　Capital assets　　　　　　　　　　　　　　　　　　　　　20
　　To adjust for loss on sale of assets under economic
　　　resources measurement focus. (Transaction 6)

Comment on adjustment b: Governments dispose of capital assets relatively often, sometimes realizing significant amounts of financial resources. Under the financial resources measurement focus, the sale of capital assets results either in a financing source or a special item. When capital assets are reported under the economic resources measurement focus, the assets need to be reduced when sold or otherwise disposed of. Eunee City sold an asset during the year so an adjusting entry is needed to account for the sale under the economic resources measurement focus. Although the sale resulted in a financing source of $1 under the current financial resources measurement focus, there was a $3 loss under the economic resources measurement focus.

c. Capital assets	300	
Expenditures—capital outlay		300
To reduce 2009 expenditures and record capital assets. (Transaction 10)		
d. Depreciation expense—public safety	30	
Accumulated depreciation		30
To record depreciation for 2009. (Transaction 12)		

Long-Term Debt Adjustments

e. Net assets	60	
Bonds payable		60
To record beginning-of-year account balances. (Opening Balances data)		
f. Bonds payable	60	
Expenditures—bond principal		60
To reduce expenditures and record repayment of liability. (Transaction 8)		
g. Proceeds of bonds	400	
Bonds payable		400
To reduce financing source and record liability. (Transaction 9)		

Revenue Adjustments

h. Revenues—property taxes	10	
Net assets		10
To reverse revenues applicable to 2008, but recognized in fund statements in 2009. (Transaction 2)		
i. Deferred tax revenues	18	
Revenues—property taxes		18
To recognize 2009 property tax revenues on accrual basis of accounting. (Transaction 3)		

Comment on adjustments h and i: As shown in Table 10-6, Eunee recognized $702 of property tax revenues in the 2009 fund financial statements. (The entire 2009 property tax levy of $710 was expected to be collected, but $18 of that amount was deferred; on the other hand, an additional $10 from the 2008 tax levy was recognized in 2009.) On the accrual-basis government-wide statements, however, property tax revenues of $710 are recognized (eliminating the deferral) because the "availability" criterion does not apply. Adjustments h and i increase revenues by a net amount of $8 and remove the deferral.

Expense Adjustments

j. Net assets	2	
Accrued interest payable		2
To record beginning-of-year balance.		
(Opening Balances data)		
k. Interest expense	13	
Accrued interest payable		13
To record increase in interest liability on accrual		
basis of accounting (Transaction 9)		

Comment on adjustments j and k: As a result of transaction 8, Eunee City recognized interest expenditures of $4 in the fund statements. Under the accrual basis of accounting, Eunee would have recognized only $2 in 2009, because there was an accrued liability of $2 at December 31, 2008. Therefore, the expenditures shown in the work sheet are overstated by $2 for government-wide reporting purposes. But Eunee sold new debt in 2009 (transaction 9) and, under the modified accrual basis of accounting, made no accrual for the unpaid interest of $15 on that debt ($400 × 5% × 9 months). The government-wide financial statements at December 31, 2009, need to show the full liability of $15. However, because we recorded the opening liability of $2 in adjustment j, we need to record only the $13 *increase* in adjustment k. The effect of adjustment k on the government-wide statements is that total interest expense will be $17—$4 previously reported as expenditures plus the $13 adjustment.

l. Net assets	4	
Accrued compensated absences		4
To record beginning-of-year balance.		
(Opening balances data)		
m. Compensated absences expense	1	
Accrued compensated absences		1
To record increase in long-term compensated		
absences liability (Transaction 11)		

Interfund Eliminations

n. Transfer in from General Fund	65	
Transfer out to Debt Service Fund		65
To eliminate transfers among governmental funds.		
(Transaction 7)		

Preparing Government-Wide Financial Statements and Reconciliations

The work sheet (Table 10-7) has two columns for the combined balances of the preclosing governmental fund trial balances (based on Table 10-4), two for the adjusting entries, and two for the adjusted trial balance. Trace the adjusting entries to the work sheet, using the letter symbols to the left of each adjusting entry. The work sheet can now be used to prepare the government-wide financial statements (Tables 10-8 and 10-9). The reconciliations between the fund financial statements and the government-wide

TABLE 10-7 Work Sheet for Preparing Government-Wide Financial Stat

	Aggregated Balances Fund Statements		Adjustments				Adjus	
	Debit	**Credit**		**Debit**		**Credit**	**Debit**	
Cash	167						167	
Property taxes receivable	50						50	
Deferred tax revenues		18 i		18				
Unreserved fund balance		50						50
Revenues:								
Property taxes		702 h		10 i		18		710
Parking fees		20						20
Expenditures:								
Public safety	470						470	
Parks	140						140	
Bond principal	60				f	60		
Bond interest	4		k	13			17	
Capital outlay	300				c	300		
Other financing items:								
Sales of assets		1 b		1				
Proceeds of bonds		400 g		400				
Transfers in		65 n		65				
Transfers out	65				n	65		
	1,256	1,256						
Capital assets			a	400	b	20		
			c	300			680	
Accumulated depreciation			b	16	a	280		
					d	30		294
Accrued interest payable					j	2		
					k	13		15
Bonds payable			f	60	e	60		
					g	400		400
Accrued comp. absences					l	4		
					m	1		5
Net assets			e	60	a	120		
			j	2	h	10		
			l	4				64
Loss on sale of assets			b	3			3	
Depreciation expense			d	30			30	
Comp. absences expense			m	1			1	
				1,383		1,383	1,558	1,558

statements can be prepared by referring to the two sets of financial statements and the adjusting entries. The reconciliations are presented in Table 10-10. Trace the government-wide financial statements back to the "adjusted balances" columns of the work sheet. Also, trace the amounts appearing in the reconciliation back to the two sets of financial statements and the adjusting entries.

TABLE 10-8   Government-Wide Statement of Net Assets

Eunee City
Statement of Net Assets
December 31, 2009
($ in 000)

	Governmental Activities
Assets	
Cash	$167
Property taxes receivable—delinquent	50
Capital assets, net of $294 accumulated depreciation	386
Total assets	$603
Liabilities	
Accrued interest payable	15
Bonds payable:	
Due within 1 year	40
Due in more than 1 year	360
Other long-term liabilities	5
Total liabilities	420
Net Assets	
Invested in capital assets, net of related debt	86
Restricted for:	
Capital projects (see note)	
Debt service	1
Unrestricted	96
Net assets	$183

Note: Cash and bonds payable include $100 of proceeds from bonds that are restricted for spending on capital projects.

TABLE 10-9   Government-Wide Statement of Activities

Eunee City
Statement of Activities
For the Year Ended December 31, 2009
($ in 000)

	Expenses	Charges for Services	Net (Expense) Revenue
Programs			
Public safety	$504		$(504)
Parks	140	$ 20	(120)
Interest on long-term debt	17		(17)
Total governmental activities	$661	$ 20	(641)
General revenues—property taxes			710
Change in net assets			69
Net assets, beginning			114
Net assets, ending			$ 183

TABLE 10-10 Financial Statement Reconciliations

A. Reconciliation of Funds Balance Sheet to Government-Wide Statement of Net Assets ($ in 000)

Total fund balances (Table 10-5)	$ 199
Amounts reported in the statement of net assets are different because:	
Capital assets used in governmental activities are not financial resources and therefore are not reported in the funds.	386
A portion of the revenues is not available to pay for current-period expenditures and therefore is deferred in the funds.	18
Bonds payable are not due and payable in the current period and therefore are not reported in the funds	(400)
Interest on long-term debt and other liabilities are not due and payable in the current period and therefore are not reported in the funds.	(20)
Net assets of governmental activities (Table 10-8)	$ 183

B. Reconciliation of Funds Statement of Revenues, Expenditures, and Changes in Fund Balances to Government-Wide Statement of Activities ($ in 000)

Net change in fund balances (Table 10-6)	$ 149
Governmental funds report capital assets as expenditures. In the statement of activities, the costs of capital assets are allocated over their useful lives as depreciation. The amount by which capital outlays in the current period ($300) exceeded depreciation ($30) is	270
Bond proceeds provide current financial resources (and debt repayments are expenditures) in governmental funds. Issuing debt increases liabilities (and repaying debt decreases them) in the statement of net assets. The amount by which bond proceeds ($400) exceeded repayments ($60) is	(340)
Revenues in the statement of activities that do not provide current resources are not reported as revenues in the funds. The increase in deferred revenues is	8
Expenses reported in the statement of activities that did not require use of current financial resources and therefore not reported as expenditures in the funds were	(14)
The disposal of assets resulted in reporting a $3 loss in the statement of activities. The sale resulted in reporting a $1 other financing source in the funds, causing a difference of	(4)
Change in net assets (Table 10-9)	$ 69

Notice the following items in the government-wide financial statements.

- Long-term bonds payable are presented in two amounts in the government-wide statement of net assets, due within 1 year and due in more than 1 year. The amount due in 1 year ($40) is based on the data in Transaction 9.
- The amount reported in the statement of net assets as invested in capital assets, net of related debt is $86 (capital assets net of accumulated depreciation [$386] less *related* debt [$300]). The total amount of bonds payable is $400, but only $300 is *related* to the capital assets, because the remaining $100 of bonds payable has not yet been invested in capital assets. Also, because the $100 is reported as bonds payable, it cannot be shown as an amount restricted for capital projects. To avoid misleading inferences from the face of the statement of net assets, this restriction on the use of assets should be disclosed in a note to the statements.

- The amount shown in the statement of activities as net assets at the beginning of the year ($114) consists of the unreserved fund balance at the beginning of the year ($50) plus the net amount of the adjustments to net assets ($64).
- The amount shown in the statement of activities for public safety expenses ($504) consists of the public safety expenditures reported in the fund statements ($470) plus other items applicable to the public safety function (depreciation expense — $30; compensated absences expense — $1; loss on sale of assets — $3).

CAPITAL ASSETS, INCLUDING INFRASTRUCTURE ASSETS

GASB *Statement No. 34* prescribes standards for reporting on capital assets and provides for special treatment of certain infrastructure assets. The basic rules regarding capital assets are:

- Capital assets of proprietary funds are reported in both the government-wide and fund financial statements.
- Capital assets of fiduciary funds are reported only in the statement of fiduciary net assets.
- All other capital assets are general capital assets; general capital assets are not reported as assets in governmental funds but are reported in the governmental activities column of the government-wide statement of net assets.[7]

Capital assets are reported at historical cost. Capital assets costs include ancillary charges needed to place the asset into its intended location and condition for use, such as freight and transportation costs and site preparation costs. The assets are depreciated over their estimated useful lives, unless they are inexhaustible (such as land) or are infrastructure assets that are reported using the *modified approach*, as described in the next section.

Reporting on Infrastructure Assets

Infrastructure assets are defined as

> ... long-lived capital assets that normally are stationary in nature and normally can be preserved for a significantly greater number of years than most capital assets. Examples of infrastructure assets include roads, bridges, tunnels, drainage systems, water and sewer systems, dams, and lighting systems. Buildings, except those that are an ancillary part of a network of infrastructure assets, should not be considered infrastructure assets.[8]

All governments, regardless of their size, are required to capitalize their infrastructure assets. (Governments with total annual revenues of less than $10 million were not required to capitalize infrastructure assets in existence before implementation of GASB *Statement No. 34*.) Further, once they are capitalized, infrastructure assets must be depreciated over their estimated useful lives, unless the government adopts the *modified approach*.

The modified approach was developed in response to concerns about the usefulness of depreciation based on historical costs for assets likely to have long lives if

---

[7]GASB Cod. Sec. 1400 Statement of Principle.
[8]GASB Cod. Sec. 1400.103.

appropriately maintained, such as roads and water distribution systems. Under the modified approach, infrastructure assets need not be depreciated, provided the government has an asset management system and documents that the assets are being preserved at or above a condition level that it establishes and discloses.

To meet the requirement for having an asset management system, a government would need to do the following:

- Have an up-to-date inventory of the infrastructure assets.
- Make periodic assessments of the physical condition of the assets and summarize the results using a measurement scale.
- Estimate each year the annual amount needed to maintain and preserve the assets at the condition level that it establishes and discloses.[9]

Governments would also need to document that:

- Complete condition assessments are made at least every 3 years.
- The results of the three most recent condition assessments give reasonable assurance that the assets are indeed being preserved approximately at or above the established condition levels.[10]

If these sets of requirements are met and the infrastructure assets are not depreciated, all expenditures made for the assets (except for additions and improvements) are treated as expenses in the year they are incurred. Additions or improvements (which increase the capacity or efficiency of the assets, rather than preserve their useful lives) are capitalized.

Documentation regarding the management and preservation of infrastructure assets needs to be provided in the financial report as required supplementary information (RSI). To illustrate, a government might rate the condition of its roads on a scale of 1 to 7, based on various distress factors found in the pavement surfaces. To make the ratings, it might use pavement distress measurement techniques, such as special machines and visual inspections compared with pictures that describe various degrees of distress. It might consider a rating of 5 as good and 7 as perfect. Its policy might be that sufficient repair and maintenance will be scheduled each year so that at least 90 percent of the road miles will be rated 5 or better. It could demonstrate in RSI that it is complying with its condition assessment standards by showing:

- For the three most recent condition assessments, the percentage of lane-miles of streets and roads that is rated 5 or better, and the percentage that is rated 4 or less.
- For the last five reporting periods, the estimated dollar requirement to maintain and preserve the streets and roads at the established condition level (at least 90 perecent of road miles are rated 5 or better), and the amounts actually expensed in each period.

Capital Asset Accounting

Governments need to maintain financial control over their capital asset inventories to ensure accountability for the assets and to provide data for the government-wide financial statements. At a minimum, the accounting system needs to be structured so

---

[9]GASB Cod. Sec. 1400.105.

[10]GASB Cod. Sec. 1400.106.

that postings to the capital outlay expenditure account are accompanied with postings to the detail capital asset inventory records. Two factors, however, can create some complications: (a) accounting for the sale of capital assets for government-wide accounting is different from accounting within governmental-type funds, and (b) government-wide accounting calls for reporting the amount invested in capital assets, net of *related* debt.

One way to accomplish financial control and to deal with the complications is to maintain a Capital Investment Account Group (CIAG). Maintaining a CIAG requires journal entries for transactions that affect the amount reported as invested in capital assets, net of related debt. This net asset subdivision is affected when the governmental unit acquires, depreciates, or disposes of capital assets and when it issues debt to acquire capital assets or repays the debt.

The CIAG has these balance sheet accounts: capital assets, accumulated depreciation, available for investment in capital assets, bonds payable, and invested in capital assets, net of related debt. It also has accounts for increasing and decreasing invested in capital assets, net of related debt.

To illustrate the journal entries used to maintain a CIAG, go back to the transactions provided in the comprehensive illustration regarding Eunee City. Based on the opening balances provided in that illustration, Eunee's CIAG accounts would be: capital assets—$400; accumulated depreciation—$280; bonds payable—$60; and invested in capital assets, net of related debt—$60. The entries to record the CIAG-related transactions in the CIAG are shown below, keyed to the transaction numbers. They are generally similar to the adjustments needed to prepare the government-wide financial statements from the balances in the fund accounts, except that they are designed also to keep track of the amount invested in capital assets, net of related debt.

6.	Accumulated depreciation—capital assets	16	
	Decreases—realized on sale of capital asset	1	
	Decreases—loss on sale of asset	3	
	Capital assets		20
	To record disposal of capital asset.		
8.	Bonds payable	60	
	Increases—repayment of debt		60
	To record increase in net assets invested in capital assets.		
9.	Available for investment in capital assets	400	
	Bonds payable		400
	To record issuance of long-term debt.		
10.	Capital assets	300	
	Increases—capital outlay expenditures		300
	To record increase in net assets invested in capital assets.		
	Decreases—debt used to acquire capital assets	300	
	Available for investment in capital assets		300
	To record decrease in net assets invested in capital assets.		
12.	Decreases—depreciation expense	30	
	Accumulated depreciation—capital assets		30
	To record decrease in net assets invested in capital assets.		

The increase and decrease accounts, which net to an increase of $26, are closed to Invested in capital assets, net of related debt. That amount, together with the opening balance of $60, leaves a net balance of $86, the amount shown in the statement of net assets in Table 10-8.

The CIAG, though not essential for accounting purposes, improves internal control over the entity's capital assets and facilitates preparation of the government-wide financial statements. It is possible to construct other forms of memorandum accounts to aid in preparing the government-wide statements.

Review Questions

Q10-1   What are the four basic principles for preparing government-wide statements?

Q10-2   Describe the column headings generally used in the government-wide statement of net assets.

Q10-3   Describe the three components of net assets in the government-wide statement of net assets.

Q10-4   What is the purpose of a *classified* statement of net assets?

Q10-5   What three categories of revenues are deducted from expenses to compute the net expenses or revenues for each function or program shown in the government-wide statement of activities?

Q10-6   How are interfund activities and balances reported in government-wide financial statements?

Q10-7   How is Internal Service Fund activity reported in government-wide statements?

Q10-8   When should sales tax revenues and property tax revenues be recognized for governmental activities in the government-wide statement of activities?

Q10-9   Describe the difference between expenditure recognition and measurement in the governmental funds financial statements and expense recognition for governmental activities in government-wide financial statements.

Q10-10 Describe the difference in reporting capital assets and long-term debt in the governmental funds financial statements and reporting those elements for governmental activities in government-wide financial statements.

Q10-11 Describe three items that require reconciliation between fund financial statements and government-wide financial statements.

Q10-12 Define and give illustrations of infrastructure assets.

Q10-13 Discuss under what circumstances a governmental unit may choose not to depreciate infrastructure assets.

Ethics Case

EC10-1 Mayor Meier served for many years as the chief executive officer of a city. During that time he used his red pencil liberally when reviewing the draft of the introductory section of the CAFR, prepared by finance director Ted Gee. For example, when Ted made reference to large amounts of accumulating leave and unsettled claims that might affect future General Fund expenditures, Meier struck it out. When Ted discussed the implications of the city's recent issuance of large amounts of general obligation debt, with debt service payments scheduled to begin 10 years after the bonds were issued, Meier crossed it out. When Ted mentioned in the introductory section that the city had been neglecting to maintain its capital assets, Meier struck that out also. Ted never even bothered to mention that the city's credit rating had been gradually reduced during Meier's tenure, knowing that the mayor would surely delete it.

Last year, the city implemented the requirements of GASB *Statement No. 34.* Ted Gee read its requirements carefully. He made the necessary accruals when he prepared the government-wide financial statements. He also concluded that many of the comments he had made in previous years' drafts of the introductory section (which Meier had crossed out) and other comments that he didn't make (because he knew Meier would cross them out) should be made in Management's Discussion and Analysis (MD&A). Ted made all the comments he felt were needed to comply with the MD&A requirements of GASB *Statement No. 34,* and gave his draft of the MD&A to the mayor. The mayor applied his red pencil in the usual manner and dumped the draft on Ted's desk. What should Ted do?

Exercises

E10-1 (Analysis of financial statements)
Obtain a CAFR from a governmental unit. Examine the governmental fund financial statements, the governmental activities sections of the government-wide financial statements, and the reconciliations between the two sets of statements. Trace the items comprising the reconciliations back to the financial statements as best you can. Write a brief report explaining the nature of each item of the reconciliation.

E10-2 (Analysis of the MD&A)
Obtain a CAFR from a governmental unit. Review all financial statements carefully. Read the MD&A. Consider the comments made in the MD&A in light of the financial statements. Write a brief report assessing the quality of the MD&A based on the data in the financial statements.

E10-3 (Multiple choice)

1. In government-wide financial statements, for which activities is depreciation reported?
   a. Only for governmental activities
   b. Only for business-type activities
   c. For both governmental and business-type activities
   d. For neither governmental nor business-type activities

2. In government-wide financial statements, for which activities is the economic resources measurement focus and accrual basis of accounting used?
   a. Only for governmental activities
   b. Only for business-type activities
   c. For both governmental and business-type activities
   d. For neither governmental nor business-type activities

3. In which set of financial statements are fiduciary-type funds reported?
   a. Only in the fund financial statements
   b. Only in the government-wide financial statements

c. In both fund and government-wide financial statements
d. In neither fund nor government-wide financial statements

4. The General Fund makes a transfer to the Debt Service Fund. How should the transfer be reported in the financial statements?
   a. The transfers in and out should be reported in both the fund operating statement and the government-wide operating statement.
   b. The transfers in and out should be reported in neither the fund operating statement nor the government-wide operating statement.
   c. The transfers in and out should be reported in the fund operating statement, but not in the government-wide operating statement.
   d. The transfers in and out should be reported in the government-wide operating statement, but not in the fund operating statement.

5. In government-wide financial statements, how are the net assets of Internal Service Funds generally treated?
   a. They are ignored.
   b. They are aggregated with business-type activities.
   c. They are aggregated with fiduciary-type activities.
   d. They are aggregated with governmental activities.

6. A city issues $100,000 of 10-year general obligation bonds on April 1, 2009. It is required to redeem debt principal of $10,000 on April 1 of each year, starting April 1, 2010, with interest of 4 percent per annum on the unpaid principal. How much interest expenditure or expense should the city recognize in its operating statements for the calendar year 2009?

	Fund Statement	*Government-Wide Statement*
a.	$3,000	$ 0
b.	3,000	3,000
c.	0	3,000
d.	0	0

7. A village issues $3,000,000 of general obligation bonds to build a new firehouse. How should the debt be reported?
   a. As a liability in the government-wide statement of net assets
   b. As a liability in the fund balance sheet
   c. As proceeds of debt in the government-wide statement of activities
   d. As a liability in both the fund balance sheet and the government-wide statement of net assets

8. A village levies property taxes in the amount of $1,260,000 for the fiscal year ended June 30, 2009. It collects $1,200,000 during the year. Regarding the $60,000 of delinquent receivables, it expects to collect $25,000 in July and August of 2009 and another $20,000 after August but before March of 2010. It expects to write off $15,000 as uncollectible. How much should the village recognize as property tax revenue in its government-wide statement of activities for the fiscal year ended June 30, 2009?
   a. $1,260,000
   b. $1,245,000
   c. $1,225,000
   d. $1,200,000

E10-4   (True or false) For any false statement, indicate why it is false.

1. In government-wide financial statements, information about fiduciary funds should be presented in a discrete column to the right of the business-type activities.
2. In government-wide financial statements, expenses for each program should be presented in such a way that charges for services directly related to the programs are shown to reduce the gross expenses of the programs.
3. In government-wide financial statements, interest on long-term general obligation debt should be recognized in the period that the interest is due and payable.
4. In government-wide financial statements, real property tax revenues are recognized (net of estimated refunds and estimated uncollectible amounts) in the period for which the taxes are levied.
5. The economic resources measurement focus and accrual basis of accounting are used in reporting on enterprise funds in both the fund statements and the government-wide statements.
6. The existence of Internal Service Funds does not affect amounts reported as expenses in the governmental activities column of government-wide financial statements, as compared with the expenditures reported in the fund statements.
7. Fiduciary funds are reported in fund financial statements but are not reported in government-wide financial statements.
8. Only the major proprietary funds are reported in government-wide financial statements.

E10-5   (Capital asset adjustments for government-wide financial statements)
Oliver City reported capital assets of $1,250,000 and accumulated depreciation of $630,000 in the governmental activities column of its government-wide statement of net assets for the year ended December 31, 2008. The total governmental funds column in Oliver's calendar year 2009 statement of revenues, expenditures, and changes in fund balances showed that Oliver's capital outlay expenditures were $120,000. Oliver City's director of finance estimated that total depreciation for 2009 was $85,000. Based on this information, prepare adjusting entries needed to develop Oliver's 2009 government-wide financial statements.

E10-6   (Sale of assets adjustments for government-wide financial statements)
Simon County realized $2,500 in cash when it auctioned off three automobiles previously used by its inspectors. It deposited the proceeds in its General Fund. According to its capital asset records, Simon had originally purchased these automobiles for $70,000. Accumulated depreciation on the automobiles as of the date of the auction was $66,000. Prepare the adjusting entry needed to develop Simon's 2009 government-wide financial statements based on this information.

E10-7   (Long-term debt adjustments for government-wide financial statements)
Sai-Tu Village reported outstanding long-term bonds payable of $4,200,000 in the governmental activities column of its government-wide statement of net

assets for the year ended December 31, 2009. During 2010, Sai-Tu Village sold $500,000 of new general obligation bonds and redeemed $300,000 of bonds outstanding at the beginning of the year. Based on this information, prepare adjusting entries needed to develop Sai-Tu's government-wide financial statements for the year ended December 31, 2010.

E10-8 (Expense adjustments for government-wide financial statements)
At January 1, 2009, the start of its fiscal year, Punkeytown had no outstanding claims. During 2009 the town hired several inexperienced truck drivers who accidentally sideswiped some privately owned vehicles while driving the town's sanitation trucks. (Trash collection is financed through the General Fund.) The town settled one claim in December 2009 for $2,000 and expected to pay it in early January 2010. The other accidents were more serious and the town acknowledged liability. The town's counsel thought he could settle the claims for $24,000, but he expected negotiations to drag on for 18 months before reaching agreement. Based on this information, prepare the adjusting entry (if needed) to develop Punkytown's 2009 government-wide financial statements.

E10-9 (Interest expense adjustments for government-wide financial statements)
Thomas County pays all the debt service on its long-term general obligation bonds on April 1 and October 1 of each year. Accrued interest on these bonds for the stub period October 1–December 31, 2008, was $75,000. During its fiscal year ended December 31, 2009, Thomas paid $350,000 interest on its long-term general obligation bonds. Accrued interest for the stub period October 1–December 31, 2009, was $88,000. Based on this information, prepare adjusting entries needed to develop Thomas County's 2009 government-wide financial statements.

E10-10 (Property tax adjustments for government-wide financial statements)
Oscar City levied real property taxes in the amount of $975,000 to finance its General Fund budget for calendar year 2009. During the year, Oscar collected $950,000 against this levy. It also wrote off $2,000 as uncollectible. With regard to the remaining $23,000, Oscar expected to collect $16,000 during the first two months of calendar year 2010 and $7,000 between March and August of 2010. In addition to the $950,000 cash that Oscar collected against the 2009 tax levy, Oscar also collected $14,000 against the 2008 tax levy; of this amount, $4,500 had been recorded as deferred property tax revenues in Oscar's governmental funds balance sheet at December 31, 2008. Based on this information, prepare adjusting entries needed to develop Oscar City's 2009 government-wide financial statements.

E10-11 (Reporting Internal Service Fund financial information)
The Village of Delmar is preparing its government-wide statement of activities for the year ended December 31, 2009. Analysis of the data accumulated thus far shows the following expenses for each of its programs:

Program	Salaries	Supplies	ISF Billings	Total Expenses
General	$ 250,000	$ 45,000	$ 20,000	$ 315,000
Police	675,000	75,000	35,000	785,000
Fire	380,000	40,000	30,000	450,000
Parks	200,000	35,000	15,000	250,000
Totals	$1,505,000	$195,000	$100,000	$1,800,000

The Internal Service Fund (ISF) billings are from the village's Motor Pool ISF. The Internal Service Fund column of the proprietary funds statement of revenues, expenses, and changes in fund net assets, prepared by the Village of Delmar, shows the following:

Charges for services	$100,000
Operating expenses:	
Personal services	70,000
Repairs and maintenance	5,000
Depreciation	15,000
Total operating expenses	90,000
Operating income	10,000
Total net assets—beginning	45,000
Total net assets—ending	$55,000

Required: Calculate the amounts that the Village of Delmar should report as expenses for each of its programs in its government-wide statement of activities for the year ended December 31, 2009.

Problems

P10-1 (Accounting for and reporting on capital assets acquired using governmental funds)

Marilyn County operates on a calendar-year basis. It uses a Capital Projects Fund to account for major capital projects and a Debt Service Fund to accumulate resources to pay principal and interest on general obligation debt. It does not use encumbrance accounting in the Capital Projects Fund. The following transactions occur:

1. On January 1, 2009, Marilyn County issues general obligation bonds in the amount of $900,000 to build a community center. The debt will be paid off in 30 equal semiannual installments of $30,000 over a 15-year period commencing October 1, 2009, with interest of 6 percent per annum on the outstanding debt.
2. The village realizes that the community center will cost more than it originally anticipated. On May 1, the village transfers $20,000 from its General Fund to its Capital Projects Fund to help meet project costs.
3. Construction is completed on July 1, 2009, and the community center is ready for occupancy. The village pays the contractor a total of $920,000 on July 1. The county anticipates that the community center will have a useful life of 20 years.
4. On September 30, 2009, the General Fund transfers an amount to the Debt Service Fund that is sufficient to pay the first debt service installment, which is due October 1.
5. The village pays the debt service due on October 1.

Required: 1. Prepare journal entries to record the foregoing transactions in the Capital Projects Fund, the General Fund, and the Debt Service Fund.

2. Prepare adjustments needed to develop the governmental activities column of the government-wide financial statements.
3. Calculate the amount that Marilyn County will report in its December 31, 2009, government-wide statement of net assets as Invested in capital assets, net of related debt. Also, assuming all debt service installments are paid when due in 2010, calculate the amount invested in capital assets, net of related debt at December 31, 2010.

P10-2 (Preparation of statement of activities)

The following information is taken from Hamilton Township's December 31, 2009, trial balance after all adjustments had been made for preparation of the government-wide financial statements. Hamilton Township has governmental activities, but no business-type activities.

Revenues—property taxes	$3,250,000
Revenues—sales taxes	2,175,000
State operating aid—police program	410,000
State operating aid—town road maintenance	250,000
State capital aid—town road maintenance	50,000
Fees—sanitation	75,000
Fees—programs for youth and seniors	65,000
Fees—parks admissions	85,000
Revenue from disposal of donated property	425,000
General government expenses	625,000
Police program expenses	2,615,000
Road maintenance program expenses	975,000
Sanitation program expenses	1,410,000
Parks and recreation programs expenses	525,000
Youth and senior programs expenses	325,000
Net assets—beginning of year	3,125,000

Required: Prepare, using the appropriate format, a statement of activities for the Town of Hamilton for the year ended December 31, 2009.

P10-3 (Property tax revenue transactions and measurement in financial statements)

A village levies property taxes in March of each year to help finance the General Fund expenditures for the calendar year. Property owners are required to pay the taxes in equal installments in April and October. Taxes remaining uncollected are declared delinquent at the end of the year. The facts regarding property taxes levied and collected for calendar years 2008 and 2009 are as follows:

2008: The village levied property taxes of $700,000, anticipating the entire amount to be collected. It actually collected $650,000 during the year. When the village prepared its financial statements, it assumed all the delinquent taxes would be collected during 2009: $37,000 in the first 60 days and the remaining $13,000 later in 2009.

2009: The village levied property taxes of $730,000, again expecting the entire amount to be collected. It actually collected $690,000 in the year of the levy. When it prepared its 2009 financial statements, the village assumed all delinquent 2009 taxes would be collected during 2010: $25,000 in the first 60 days and the remaining $15,000 later in 2010. Regarding the $50,000 of delinquent 2008 taxes, it collected $38,000 in the first 60 days of 2009, $7,000 during the rest of 2009, and wrote off the remaining $5,000 as uncollectible.

Required: Prepare journal entries as follows:

1. Record the year 2008 transactions in the General Fund, including the year-end adjustment needed to prepare the fund financial statements.
2. Make the adjustment needed to prepare the governmental activities column of the 2008 government-wide statements.
3. Record the year 2009 transactions in the General Fund, including the year-end adjustment needed to prepare the fund financial statements.
4. Make the adjustment needed to prepare the governmental activities column of the 2009 government-wide statements.

Also, calculate the amount of property tax revenues that the village should recognize in its fund financial statements and in its government-wide financial statements for both 2008 and 2009.

P10-4 (Conversion to government-wide financial statements)

Harlan City, a small city with revenues less than $10 million a year, is planning to issue its first set of government-wide financial statements for the year ended December 31, 2008. To prepare for the transition, the city comptroller wants to have a government-wide statement of net assets as of January 1, 2008, the beginning of the year. The available information includes extracts from the governmental funds portion of the balance sheet prepared as of December 31, 2007, together with other data necessary to construct a government-wide statement of net assets for governmental activities, using the economic resources measurement focus and accrual basis of accounting.

The balance sheet for the combined governmental funds as of December 31, 2007, is as follows:

Assets	
Cash	$175,000
Property taxes receivable	85,000
Total assets	$260,000
Liabilities	
Accounts payable	$ 43,000
Accrued salaries and other expenses	14,000
Deferred property tax revenues	18,000
Total liabilities	75,000
Fund Balances	
Unreserved	185,000
Total fund balances	185,000
Total liabilities and fund balances	$260,000

The following additional information is available as of December 31, 2007:

Capital assets: Harlan's capital asset records show that the total cost of the assets in use as of December 31, 2007, is $8,400,000. Estimated accumulated depreciation on the assets is $4,600,000.

Bonds payable: Harlan has outstanding bonds payable at December 31, 2007, of $2,600,000. Of this amount, principal due to be paid during the calendar year

2008 is $150,000. Analysis of the outstanding bonds shows that all of the debt had been sold to finance the acquisition of capital assets.

Interest on long-term debt: In its fund statements, Harlan recognizes interest on bonds payable when it is due and payable. It does not accrue interest for year-end "stub periods" that will be paid early in the following year. Stub period interest at December 31, 2007, was $20,000.

Property taxes: Harlan expects that all of its property taxes receivable will be collected in 2008. Property tax revenues of $18,000 were deferred because Harlan did not expect to collect them during the first 60 days of 2008.

Other expenses: Employees may accumulate vacation pay, subject to certain limits, that they may receive in cash on retirement. Accrued expenses of $14,000 include $2,000 of accrued vacation pay that the city will pay early in 2008 to retired employees. Other employees have accumulated vacation pay of $42,000 that Harlan expects to pay when they retire in future years. No accrual has been made for this amount.

Required: 1. Prepare a six-column work sheet similar to that shown in Table 10-7, showing the balances in the fund accounts, the adjusting entries needed to prepare a government-wide statement of net assets as of January 1, 2008, and the adjusted balances. Make the adjustments needed to prepare a government-wide statement of net assets, and support the adjustments with journal entries. (Hint: Reclassify the fund balance to net assets. Because no statement of activities is required, the adjustments to report the additional assets and liabilities will directly affect net assets.)

2. Prepare a statement of net assets as of January 1, 2008, in classified format. Show the net assets either as invested in capital assets, net of related debt, or as unrestricted.

3. Prepare a reconciliation of the funds balance sheet to the government-wide statement of net assets.

Summary Problems

Summary Problem 1. (Preparation of government-wide financial statements)
This problem is a continuation of Summary Problem 1 at the end of Chapter 9. It is Part G of the problem.

Required: 1. Prepare journal entries needed to convert the governmental funds financial statements to the governmental activities column of the government-wide financial statements. Post the journal entries to a six-column work sheet similar to that shown on page 403 of this chapter.

2. Prepare Coco City's financial statements: the government-wide statement of net assets and the government-wide statement of activities.

Summary Problem 2. (Preparation of government-wide financial statements)
This problem is a continuation of Summary Problem 2 (Croton Village) at the end of Chapter 9. The following additional information is furnished to complete this part of the problem.

Item a. The village has no activities other than governmental activities. The village's government-wide statement of net assets for the year ended

December 31, 2008, showed general capital assets of $14,000 and related accumulated depreciation of $6,400.

Item b. Depreciation expense on all the village's general capital assets for 2009 (including assets acquired in 2009) was $700, all of which was applicable to the public safety program.

Item c. The village's government-wide statement of net assets for the year ended December 31, 2008, showed bonds payable of $5,500. All the debt had been issued to finance capital assets. (Analysis of village debt service requirements showed that $700 of the total bonds payable at December 31, 2009, should be reported as current because it was due to be paid during 2010.)

Item d. The village's government-wide statement of net assets for the year ended December 31, 2008, showed accrued interest payable of $120 on its outstanding long-term debt. Analysis of village debt service requirements showed accrued interest payable of $135 on all outstanding long-term debt at December 31, 2009, including the debt sold by the village during 2009.

Required: 1. Prepare journal entries needed to convert the governmental funds financial statements to the governmental activities columns of the government-wide financial statements. Post the journal entries to a six-column work sheet similar to that shown on page 403 of this chapter.

2. Prepare Croton Village's government-wide financial statements: (a) a statement of net assets and (b) a statement of activities.

3. Prepare Croton Village's financial statement reconciliations: (a) the funds balance sheet to the government-wide statement of net assets, and (b) the funds statement of revenues, expenditures, and changes in fund balances to the government-wide statement of activities.

11

FEDERAL GOVERNMENT ACCOUNTING AND REPORTING

Chapter Outline

After completing this chapter, you should be able to:

- Discuss the federal budgetary process.
- Discuss the similarities and differences between federal government accounting and state and local government accounting.
- Describe the function of "earmarked" funds used by the federal government.
- Explain the function of the Federal Accounting Standards Advisory Board and discuss several of its accounting standards.
- Briefly describe the federal government's consolidated financial statements.
- Prepare budgetary and proprietary accounting journal entries to record basic transactions of a federal agency.
- Describe and prepare simple financial statements of a federal agency.

The secretary of the Treasury, the director of the Office of Management and Budget (OMB), and the comptroller general of the United States created the Federal Accounting Standards Advisory Board in 1990. The board's work provided the accounting standards that formed the basis, in 1997, for the very first set of audited consolidated financial statements issued by the federal government. The consolidated statement of operations and changes in net position for the fiscal year ended September 30, 2006, shows consolidated revenue of more than $2.4 trillion, consolidated net costs of $2.9 trillion, and a resulting net operating deficit of some $450 billion!

Needless to say, the operating activities of the federal government are complex. Although most of the captions in its financial statements will look familiar to you, you cannot grasp the information content of the statements—particularly the data concerning Social Security, Medicare, and other social insurance programs—without studying carefully the notes and supplementary information that accompany the statements.

Like the accounting systems of state and local governments, budgetary accounts are integrated with financial accounts in the federal government. In fact, federal agencies literally use a two-track accounting system—one with budgetary accounts and one with financial (called proprietary) accounts. The proprietary accounts are generally kept on the accrual accounting basis. Before discussing accounting and financial reporting within the federal agencies, however, we will briefly review the federal budgetary and accounting processes, and present some excerpts from the consolidated federal financial statements.

THE FEDERAL BUDGETARY PROCESS

The federal budgetary process begins about 18 months before the beginning of a fiscal year (October 1). At this time overall policy issues are identified, budget projections are made, and preliminary program plans are presented to the president. The president reviews this information, along with data on projected revenues and economic conditions. On the basis of this review, the president establishes general budgetary and fiscal policy guidelines.

Using presidential guidelines, agencies prepare their budgetary requests. These requests are reviewed in detail by the departments of which the agencies are a part (e.g., the U.S. Forest Service is a part of the Department of Agriculture) and by the OMB.[1] After differences between the OMB, the departments, and the agencies are resolved, revised agency budgets are presented to the president, who reviews them in light of the latest economic data and revenue estimates. Last-minute revisions are made, and the agency budgets are combined and presented to the Congress. The budgetary document represents the president's recommendations for new and existing programs, as well as projections of receipts and expenditures.

Formal congressional review of the budget begins shortly after the president transmits it to the Congress, about 8 or 9 months before the fiscal year begins. The Congress considers the president's budget proposals and may change funding levels of individual programs, add or eliminate programs, and add or eliminate taxes and other sources of

---

[1]The OMB is an agency within the Executive Office of the President, which has responsibility for the overall financial management of the federal government. It is ultimately responsible for preparing the executive budget and for apportioning resources to the various departments and agencies.

receipts. Before passing *appropriations* for specific programs, however, the Congress passes a budget resolution that sets levels for budgetary receipts and for budgetary authority and outlays, in total and by functional category.

Requests for appropriations and for changes in revenue laws are first considered in the House of Representatives. The House Ways and Means Committee reviews proposed revenue measures, and the House Appropriations Committee studies requests for appropriations. These committees then make their report to the entire House of Representatives, which acts on the revenue and appropriations bills. After the bills are approved, they are sent to the Senate, where the process is repeated. If the two houses of Congress cannot agree on the various fiscal measures, a conference committee (consisting of members of both houses) resolves the issues and submits a report to both houses for approval.

After approval by the Congress, the various revenue and appropriations measures are transmitted to the president in the form of enrolled bills. The president then approves or vetoes these bills. If appropriations bills are not passed by the beginning of the fiscal year, the Congress passes a *continuing resolution*. This resolution provides the authority for affected agencies to continue spending until a specified date, or until their regular appropriations are approved. When the appropriations bill is signed by the president, *appropriations warrants* are sent to the various agencies by the Treasury. Each agency then revises its budget in accordance with the appropriations bill and, within 30 days, submits a request for apportionment to the OMB.

Congressional appropriations are not based directly on expenditures. Rather, each agency is given *budget authority,* which is the authority to obligate the government to ultimately make disbursements for expenditures, repayment of loans, and the like.[2] A congressional appropriation is really nothing more than a spending authority or limit for that fiscal year. It does not mean that cash is immediately available for spending. Availability of cash depends on many factors, such as inflows of tax revenues and the level of surplus funds from prior years.

Most appropriations are for 1 year only. If they are not spent or obligated by the end of the fiscal year, they expire. In some cases, however, the Congress makes multiyear or indefinite appropriations. Examples of this latter type of appropriation include those used to fund Social Security and to service public debt. The remainder of this chapter will be devoted to 1-year appropriations.

When the OMB receives a request for *apportionment* from an agency, it apportions a part of the agency's appropriation to the department of which the agency is a part, based on a time period (usually quarterly) or activity. The purpose of the apportionment system is to help prevent agencies from obligating or spending more than their appropriations, to enable the Treasury to better match revenues and disbursements (cash management), and to monitor expenditure levels.

When a department receives its apportionment from the OMB, the department head (or his or her representative) *allots* all or a part of the amount of the apportionment intended for each agency under the department's control. Each agency can obligate (and spend) only the allotted portion of its appropriation.

---

[2]Budget authority may take several forms, the most common of which is appropriations. Budget authority may also take the form of borrowing authority, contract authority (which generally requires a subsequent appropriation), and authority to spend from offsetting collections.

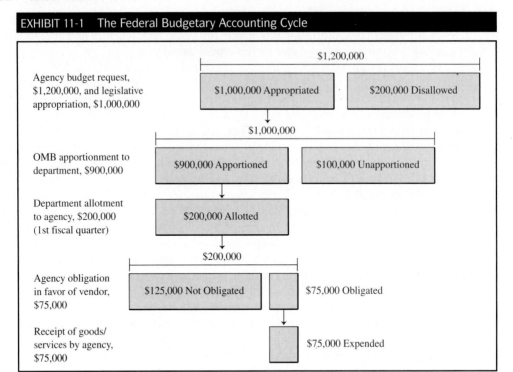

EXHIBIT 11-1   The Federal Budgetary Accounting Cycle

When an agency receives its allotment, it is free to spend up to that amount of money, within budgetary guidelines. Agency personnel, however, cannot spend more than the amount appropriated for (and allotted to) that agency without violating the *Anti-Deficiency Act* (31 U.S.C. 1517 of the Revised Statutes). The main purposes of this act are to prevent the incurring of obligations, and making of disbursements, in excess of appropriations and to fix responsibility within each agency for the incurrence of obligations and expenditures. Agency personnel who violate this law are subject to both civil and criminal penalties.

Before an agency makes a disbursement, it generally "obligates" the resources. An obligation, which is recorded as an "undelivered order," is similar to an encumbrance. It represents resources earmarked for a specific purpose. When the goods are received, the undelivered orders become "expended authority." Instead of making direct payment, however, the agency sends a *disbursement schedule* to the Treasury. The Treasury then sends a check to the vendor. The payments of obligations become "outlays." This process, which results primarily in budgetary accounting entries, is illustrated in Exhibit 11-1.

FEDERAL ACCOUNTING—BACKGROUND

Comparison with State and Local Government Accounting

There are both similarities and differences between federal accounting and state and local governmental accounting. The introduction to state and local government financial reporting of government-wide reporting on the full accrual basis of accounting, however, reduced the number of differences. Some differences relate to the degree to which one or the other has adopted a particular practice. Other differences relate to the size and scope of the U.S. government. The following is a comparison of some of the accounting and financial reporting practices.

1. ***Integration of budgetary accounting.*** Both the federal government and state and local governments integrate budgetary accounting into their financial accounting systems. Federal use of budgetary accounting, however, is more pervasive than state and local government use. As discussed subsequently, the federal government uses a two-track accounting system, one for budgetary transactions and the other for financial accounting transactions.

2. ***Use of funds and basis of accounting within the funds.*** Both the federal government and state and local governments use funds, many of which are similar in nature. In its financial accounting system, however, the federal government uses a greater degree of accrual accounting within the funds than do state and local governments. Because of certain practical limitations, the federal government recognizes tax revenues on what might best be characterized as a "modified cash" basis. Expenses, however, are generally recognized on the full accrual basis. For example, inventories are recognized when consumed and fixed assets generally are capitalized and depreciated. State and local governments use the modified accrual basis of accounting within some funds and the full accrual basis in others.

3. ***Financial reporting practices.*** In the federal government, separate accounting records are maintained and financial statements are issued for each agency and/or fund. In most cases, the agency statements cover a portion of a particular fund (e.g., the General Fund), not the entire fund. The U.S. government also issues consolidated financial statements. Further, federal government reporting is based on a single set of integrated financial reports. State and local government reporting, on the other hand, covers all agencies of the government, rather than just a single department. Although individual departments of state and local governments sometimes prepare departmental financial statements, they are usually for internal use only. Finally, state and local governments have a dual set of reports, one based on government-wide data using the full accrual basis of accounting and another based on fund-level data using the modified accrual basis for some funds and the full accrual basis for others.

4. ***Treatment of fund balances.*** Residual balances of funds used by state and local governmental units (assets minus liabilities, or "net assets") are shown in the fund balance accounts of those funds. They represent, among other things, the amount available for expenditures. In federal accounting, activities of many agencies can be recorded in a "common" fund. Because each agency is an accounting entity, it is necessary to use terms to identify the portion of each common fund that represents that agency's net assets. Terms used for this purpose are *net position, unexpended appropriations,* and *cumulative results of operations.*

5. ***Treatment of cash.*** State and local governmental units have direct relationships with banks. But individual federal agencies do not generally deal directly with banks. Rather, the Treasury acts as their banker. At the beginning of a fiscal year, each agency is provided with an account with the Treasury for each appropriation. The size of this account is equal to the agency's appropriation

plus any amounts left over from previous periods that have not expired. To make a disbursement, the agency sends a disbursement schedule to the Treasury. The Treasury writes a check for the amount of the schedule. The account used by federal agencies to record their claims against the Treasury is "Fund balance with U.S. Treasury." When agencies receive resources from the Treasury, this account is debited. When the disbursements ordered by the agencies are made by the Treasury, this account is credited.

Types of Funds Used

The consolidated statement of operations and changes in net position, illustrated in the next section, separates the funds used by the federal government into two broad types— nonearmarked and earmarked. Earmarked funds generally include special funds, trust funds, and public enterprise revolving funds. These funds are financed by specifically identified revenues, which may be supplemented by other sources. Statutes require the revenues to be used for designated activities, benefits, or purposes. Earmarked funds are accounted for separately from the federal government's general revenues.

Cash receipts collected from the public for an earmarked fund are deposited in the U.S Treasury, which uses the cash for general governmental purposes. Most of the assets of the earmarked funds are invested in U.S. Treasury securities. These securities need to be redeemed if a fund's disbursements exceed its receipts. Redeeming the securities will increase the government's financing needs and therefore require more borrowing from the public, higher taxes, less spending, or a combination of the three.[3]

1. *The General Fund.* This fund, a nonearmarked fund, comprises the greater part of the federal budget. It accounts for receipts (primarily individual and corporation income taxes, other taxes, and the proceeds of general borrowing) that are not earmarked for a specific purpose. It also accounts for most of the expenditures of the federal departments, such as the Department of Defense and the Department of Health and Human Services. General Fund expenditures are recorded in appropriation accounts maintained by the individual departments and agencies.

2. *Special Funds.* These funds are used to account for resources from specific sources earmarked by law for special purposes and for spending in accordance with specific legal provisions. They are similar to state and local government Special Revenue Funds.

3. *Trust Funds.* Trust funds account for receipts and expenditures of resources used to carry out specific purposes and programs in accordance with the terms of a statute that designates the fund as a trust fund. Many significant governmental activities are financed through trust funds, such as Social Security (through the Federal Old Age and Survivors Insurance and Federal Disability Insurance Trust Funds) and Medicare Part A (the Federal Hospital Insurance Trust Fund). The federal budget meaning of the term *trust* differs from the private sector fiduciary notion. The federal government owns the assets of most trust funds, and there is no substantive difference between a trust fund and a special fund.

---

[3]*2006 Financial Report of the United States Government,* Notes to the Financial Statements, Note 20, Earmarked Funds.

4. ***Public Enterprise Revolving Funds.*** These funds are used for programs authorized by law to conduct business-type activities, primarily with the public. Outlays from the funds generate collections that are credited directly to the funds and are available for expenditure without further congressional action. They are thus similar to state and local government enterprise funds.

The journal entries covered later in this chapter relate to general fund activities. We will also comment on the status of the Social Security trust funds.

Federal Accounting Standards

In October 1990 the secretary of the Treasury, the director of the OMB, and the comptroller general established the Federal Accounting Standards Advisory Board (FASAB), whose purpose is to consider and recommend accounting principles for the federal government.

The FASAB, which currently has 10 members, considers financial and budgetary information needs of the public, executive agencies, congressional oversight groups, and others who use federal financial information. The FASAB proposes accounting standards after appropriate due process, which includes publication of "exposure drafts" of proposed standards and, sometimes, public hearings. After considering the comments received in response to the due process, the FASAB submits proposed standards to the three sponsors for review. If neither the director of the OMB nor the comptroller general object, the standard is published by the FASAB and becomes GAAP for federal financial reporting entities.

The FASAB completed a basic set of accounting and financial reporting standards, which provided the basis for issuing audited consolidated federal government financial statements in 1997. As of this writing, the FASAB has issued several concepts statements and more than 30 Statements of Federal Financial Accounting Standards (SFFAS). Comments on some of the standards follow.

1. ***Inventory and related property.*** Inventory appearing in federal financial statements consists primarily of inventory purchased for resale (mostly within the same department), operating materials and supplies held for use or repair, and stockpile materials. SFFAS No. 3 requires that inventory held for sale and materials and supplies consumed in the normal course of operations be valued at historical cost or any other valuation method that approximates historical cost. It also permits using latest acquisition cost to value inventories, provided it is adjusted for unrealized holding gains and losses. The Defense Department, which holds more than 80 percent of the government's inventory, has been using latest acquisition cost and is transitioning to moving average cost.

2. ***Property, plant, and equipment (PP&E).*** SFFAS No. 6, as amended, establishes three categories of PP&E: general PP&E, heritage assets, and stewardship land. General PP&E includes items that have useful lives of 2 years or more and that are used (a) to produce goods or services to support an entity's mission, (b) in business-type activities, or (c) in activities where costs can be compared with other entities. General PP&E is recorded at acquisition cost and depreciated over the estimated useful lives of the assets using the straight line method. The Defense Department holds more than two-thirds of the net PP&E reported in the consolidated federal balance sheet.

Heritage assets include government-owned assets that have historical or natural significance, or cultural, educational, or artistic importance, such as the Mount Rushmore National Memorial, the Washington Monument, and the Declaration of Independence. The cost of these assets is often not determinable or relevant to their significance. Stewardship land is land the government does not expect to use to meet its obligations. Most of it is part of the 1.8 billion acres of public domain land acquired between 1781 and 1867; currently, stewardship land represents 28 percent of the U.S. landmass. The existence of both heritage assets and stewardship land is disclosed in notes, but their costs are not reported in the balance sheet.

SFFAS No. 6 also requires estimating and recognizing expenses and liabilities for environmental cleanup costs. Cleanup costs are costs incurred in removing, containing, and disposing of hazardous waste. They include the cost of decontaminating and decommissioning nuclear submarines, and disposal or containment of hazardous and radioactive waste from the production of nuclear weapons and toxic chemical sites. Estimating these costs is extremely complex, and the financial statement user must read the notes to grasp the limitations of the amount reported for "environmental and disposal liabilities" in the consolidated balance sheet.

The standards also require disclosure of deferred maintenance, which is maintenance that was not performed when it should have been and was, therefore, delayed to a future period. Deferred maintenance may be estimated by several methods including condition assessment surveys, which are periodic inspections that assess the condition of capital assets and estimate the costs to restore the assets to acceptable operating condition.

3. *Accounting for federal liabilities.* Although many transactions and events that create federal liabilities are similar to those encountered by state and local government and business enterprises, some are unique to the federal government. As a general rule, federal liabilities arising from exchange transactions (in which each party to the transaction sacrifices value and receives value in return) are accounted for on the accrual basis of accounting. The federal reporting entity recognizes a liability when it receives goods or services in return for a promise to pay in the future.

The federal government also engages, however, in many nonexchange transactions, in which it promises to provide benefits pursuant to law or grant without directly receiving value in return. An example is payments to health care providers for services under the Medicaid program. In those cases, the federal reporting entity recognizes a liability for any unpaid amounts as of the reporting date. The liability includes an estimate for services rendered by providers but not yet reported to the federal entity.

4. *Accounting for social insurance programs.* Perhaps the most controversial issue dealt with by the FASAB concerned Social Security and similar social insurance programs. Some believed that a liability for Social Security ought to be reported only for amounts due but unpaid as of the reporting date. They argued that Social Security was enacted as a compulsory intergenerational transfer program and that the government has the ability to cancel or significantly reduce program benefits. Others believed a liability should be reported (similar to a pension

plan) for the unfunded present value of amounts due in the future to current Social Security beneficiaries, as well as for amounts earned by active future beneficiaries. They argued that the Social Security program has elements of exchange transactions, and the commitments, expectations, and political climate affecting the program make future payment so highly probable as to meet the liability definition.

The issue was resolved with the publication of SFFAS No. 17, *Accounting for Social Insurance,* in 1999. SFFAS No. 17 requires that liabilities for social insurance programs be recognized only for benefits that are *due and payable at the end of the reporting period*— basically, the amount due for the month of September. The standard, as amended, also requires that data be provided to facilitate assessment of long-term program sustainability, including the ability of the nation to raise resources from future program participants to pay for benefits promised to present participants. Required reporting and disclosures include projections of future cash inflows and outflows; projections of ratios of number of contributors to number of beneficiaries; actuarial present values of future contributions from or for, and expenditures to or on behalf of, current participants who have attained retirement age and for participants who have not attained retirement age; and a discussion of the significant assumptions used in making projections.

The issue, however, remains controversial. At the time of this writing, the FASAB was seeking comments on a proposal that would report an expense and a balance sheet liability for social insurance programs when participants "substantially meet eligibility requirements during their working lives in covered employment." This proposal would, in effect, report a balance sheet liability for those already receiving benefits and for those who have attained fully insured status but have not yet reached retirement age. Liabilities reported in the consolidated federal balance sheet would increase significantly if that view prevails. (See *What Is the Status of Social Security?* later in this chapter.)

CONSOLIDATED U.S. GOVERNMENT FINANCIAL STATEMENTS

The financial statements prepared by the U.S. government consist of a statement of net cost, a statement of operations and changes in net position, a reconciliation of net operating cost and unified budget deficit, a statement of changes in cash balance from unified budget and other activities, a balance sheet, and a statement of social insurance. The statements are accompanied with extensive notes and supplemental data. We reproduced several of the statements issued for the fiscal year ended September 30, 2006, to provide a framework for the ensuing discussion of accounting within the government's departments and agencies, but we deleted some of the content to simplify the presentation.

The complete financial report, including management's discussion and analysis, the comptroller general's disclaimer of opinion, and the statements, notes and other disclosures, is available at the U.S. Government Accountability Office Web site, www.gao.gov. That Web site is the source of these statements. As you read the statements, keep the following in mind:

- The financial statements are prepared in accordance with generally accepted accounting principles promulgated by the FASAB. Expenses are generally

TABLE 11-1   U.S. Government Statement of Net Cost

United States Government
Statement of Net Cost
For the Year Ended September 30, 2006
(in billions of dollars)

	Gross Cost	Earned Revenue	Net Cost
Department of Defense	$ 658.0	$ 24.1	$ 633.9
Department of Health and Human Services	678.8	51.4	627.4
Social Security Administration	593.1	0.3	592.8
Interest on Treasury Securities held by the public	221.5	—	221.5
Department of Veterans Affairs	117.3	3.5	113.8
Department of Agriculture	109.0	11.4	97.6
Department of Education	97.3	4.7	92.6
Department of the Treasury	85.5	4.1	81.4
Department of Transportation	66.6	0.6	66.0
Department of Energy	70.9	5.1	65.8
Department of Homeland Security	63.4	6.8	56.6
U.S. Postal Service	58.9	71.6	(12.7)
Other agencies (see Note)	307.4	42.8	264.6
Total	$3,127.7	$226.4	$2,901.3

Note: The authors of the text combined entities whose gross costs were less than $50 billion.

recognized when incurred, except for the costs of social insurance programs, which are recognized only for amounts currently due and payable. Taxes and other nonexchange revenues are recognized when collected, adjusted by the change in measurable and legally collectible amounts receivable.

- The statement of net costs (Table 11-1) shows the full costs (including allocated payroll fringe benefit costs) of all departments, net of revenues from providing goods and services to the public at a price.
- The statement of operations and changes in net position (Table 11-2) is the consolidated operating statement, and shows all revenues and expenses. Activities financed by nonearmarked funds are separated from those financed by earmarked funds, which include the Social Security and Medicare trust funds.
- Receipts and outlays in the president's budget are measured primarily on the cash basis of accounting. Hence, the reconciliation of the accrual-based net operating cost and the unified budget deficit (Table 11-3) helps you understand the cash-basis nature of the budget—about which you hear so much in the media.
- Note that the net deficit reported in the balance sheet (Table 11-4) is almost $9 trillion. If you read the notes and the supplemental data, particularly the material on Social Security, Medicare, and other social insurance programs, you may conclude the deficit is even greater.

TABLE 11-2   U.S. Government Statement of Operations and Changes in Net Position

United States Government
Statement of Operations and Changes in Net Position
For the Year Ended September 30, 2006
(in billions of dollars)

	Nonearmarked Funds	Earmarked Funds	Consolidated
Revenue:			
Individual income tax, tax withholdings	$ 1,045.7	$ 800.4	$ 1,846.1
Corporation income taxes	350.0	—	350.0
Unemployment taxes	—	41.4	41.4
Excise taxes	24.5	49.6	74.1
Estate and gift taxes	27.4	—	27.4
Other (details not shown here)	84.6	17.2	101.8
Intragovernmental interest	—	185.3	Note
Consolidated revenue	1,532.2	1,093.9	2,440.8
Net cost:			
Net cost	1,635.1	1,266.2	2,901.3
Intragovernmental interest	185.3	—	Note
Consolidated net cost	1,820.4	1,266.2	2,901.3
Intragovernmental transfers	(344.3)	344.3	—
Other — unmatched transactions, balances	11.0	—	11.0
Net operating (cost)/revenue	$ (621.5)	$ 172.0	$ (449.5)
Net position, beginning of period	$(8,714.1)	$ 247.2	$(8,466.9)
Net operating (cost)/revenue	(621.5)	172.0	(449.5)
Net position, end of period	$(9,335.6)	$ 419.2	$(8,916.4)

Note: Intragovernmental interest of $185.3 billion was eliminated in consolidation. The authors changed the format of this statement slightly to simplify it.

TABLE 11-3   U.S. Government Reconciliation of Net Operating Cost and Unified Budget

United States Government
Reconciliation of Net Operating Cost and Unified Budget
For the Year Ended September 30, 2006
(in billions of dollars)

Net operating cost	$(449.5)
Components of net operating cost not part of budget deficit:	
Increase in liability for military employee benefits	74.7
Increase in liability for veterans compensation	31.2
Increase in liability for civilian employee benefits	81.3
Increase in environmental liabilities	45.4
Depreciation expense	82.9
Other (see Note)	2.5
Components of the budget deficit not part of net operating cost:	
Acquisition of capital assets	(103.7)
Other (see Note)	(11.7)
All other reconciling items	(0.8)
Unified budget deficit	$(247.7)

Note: The actual statement is much more detailed. The authors showed the major items reported in the reconciliation and summarized the others in the "Other" captions.

TABLE 11-4 U.S. Government Balance Sheet

United States Government
Balance Sheet
As of September 30, 2006
(in billions of dollars)

Assets:	
Cash and other monetary assets	$ 97.9
Accounts and taxes receivable	68.8
Loans receivable	220.8
Inventories and related property, net	281.3
Property, plant, and equipment, net	688.5
Securities and investments	83.8
Other assets	55.4
Total assets	$ 1,496.5
Stewardship property, plant, and equipment	
Stewardship land and heritage assets	
Liabilities:	
Accounts payable	$ 58.4
Federal debt securities held by the public and accrued interest	4,867.5
Federal employee and veteran benefits payable	4,679.0
Environmental and disposal liabilities	305.2
Benefits due and payable	129.3
Insurance program liabilities	72.8
Loan guarantee liabilities	66.4
Other liabilities	234.3
Total liabilities	10,412.9
Contingencies and commitments	
Net position:	
Earmarked funds	419.2
Nonearmarked funds	(9,335.6)
Total net position	(8,916.4)
Total liabilities and net position	$ 1,496.5

Note: Captions shown without numbers are described in the notes to the financial statements.

ACCOUNTING WITHIN THE FEDERAL AGENCIES

Accounting systems within the federal agencies help agency managers to meet their budgetary and financial reporting responsibilities to the OMB and also to:

1. Control expenditure levels and ensure the agency doesn't obligate more than the amounts available.
2. Account for the full costs of services provided, using the accrual basis of accounting, to assist them in accomplishing program objectives.
3. Fulfill their stewardship responsibilities for the resources entrusted to them.

TABLE 11-5   Summary of Key Entries Prepared by Federal Agencies

Who Acts?	What Action?	Budgetary Entry	Proprietary Entry
Congress	Appropriates	Other appropriations realized Unapportioned authority—available	Fund balance with Treasury Unexpended appropriations
OMB	Apportions	Unapportioned authority—available Apportionment	None
Department	Allots	Apportionment Allotments—realized resources	None
Agency	Commits	Allotments—realized resources Commitments	None
Agency	Obligates	Commitments Undelivered orders	None
Agency	Receives services	Undelivered orders Expended authority	Operating/program expenses Accounts payable Unexpended appropriations Appropriations used
Agency	Receives goods or equipment	Undelivered orders Expended authority	Assets Accounts payable Unexpended appropriations Appropriations used
Agency	Requests payment for goods or equipment	None	Accounts payable Disbursements in transit
Agency	Uses goods	None	Operating/program expenses Assets
Agency	Records depreciation	None	Operating/program expenses Accumulated depreciation

Because the accounting procedures for budgetary control purposes differ from the accounting procedures needed to help meet program objectives, federal agencies use a *two-track accounting system*. One track is a self-balancing set of *budgetary accounts*, to help ensure budgetary control and compliance. The other is a self-balancing set of proprietary accounts, to help in financial and program management.

As shown in Table 11-5 and the detailed journal entries, some transactions and events affect only the budgetary accounts, some affect only the proprietary accounts, and some affect both. The budgetary entries are more extensive than in state and local government accounting. The proprietary entries produce results more closely akin to state and local government accrual-basis government-wide financial statements than fund-level statements prepared for governmental-type funds.

Illustrative Transactions

To illustrate the transactions of a federal agency, assume the Federal Oversight Agency was created in September 2008, just before the fiscal year beginning October 1, 2008. In

September, the agency bought furniture for $40,000. Hence, its balance sheet at the start of the new fiscal year showed an asset captioned General property, plant, and equipment and a net position item called Cumulative results of operations, each for $40,000.

Opening Entries

The accounting cycle of a federal agency begins at the start of the fiscal year when the Congress makes (and the president approves) an appropriation. If the appropriation is $150,000, entries on the books of the agency are as follows:

Budgetary entry	Other appropriations realized	150,000	
	Unapportioned authority—available		150,000
	To record receipt of appropriation authority.		

Proprietary entry	Fund balance with Treasury	150,000	
	Unexpended appropriations		150,000
	To record receipt of appropriation warrant.		

The first entry establishes initial accountability by the agency for its appropriation. The debit to Other appropriations realized distinguishes the agency's basic operating appropriation from other special purpose appropriations it might have received. The second entry records the establishment of a "line of credit" with the Treasury. The account Fund balance with Treasury is the equivalent of a cash account, and Unexpended appropriations represents the increase in the equity of the agency.

After Congress makes the appropriation, the OMB apportions it to the department of which the agency is a part. As was mentioned earlier, the OMB is an agency within the Executive Office of the President and has broad financial management powers. Among its responsibilities are the apportionment of appropriations among departments and the establishment of "reserves" in anticipation of cost savings, contingencies, and so on. Thus, the fact that an agency is appropriated a given amount of resources by Congress does not always mean that the agency will have that amount to spend.

If all of the agency's appropriation is apportioned by the OMB to the department of which the agency is a part, the entry on the books of the agency is:

Budgetary entry	Unapportioned authority—available	150,000	
	Apportionment		150,000
	To record apportionment of resources by OMB.		

Proprietary entry None

The amount of its apportionment that an agency can actually use is up to departmental management, which will allot a part of, or the entire, apportionment to the agency. Allotments are usually made each quarter. However, for simplicity, we will assume that the agency in this illustration receives its entire allotment at the beginning of the fiscal year. If departmental management allots $148,000 to the agency, the entry on the books of the agency is:

Budgetary entry	Apportionment	148,000	
	Allotments—realized resources		148,000
	To record allotment of resources to finance operations.		

Proprietary entry None

The account Allotments—realized resources is particularly important. The balance of this account represents the amount of resources available for the agency to carry out its operations. If the agency has not expended or obligated its apportionment and its allotments by the end of the fiscal year, it must return these resources to the Treasury. All of the preceding entries are made as of October 1, the first day of the fiscal year. This record is made even if the appropriation bill has not been enacted by that date.

Operating Entries

When an agency receives notice of its allotment, it can begin (or continue) its fiscal operations. To enhance planning and fund control, many agencies use what is known as "commitment accounting." *Commitments* reserve budgetary authority from an allotment for the estimated amount of orders to be placed. They do not legally encumber the allotment. Rather, they formally disclose purchase requests before actual orders are placed. If requests are made by agency personnel to spend $100,000 of the agency's allotment on supplies and $12,000 on outside services, the entry to record the commitments is:

Budgetary entry	Allotments—realized resources	112,000	
	Commitments		112,000
	To record purchase requests placed for supplies and services.		

Proprietary entry   None

When a purchase order is issued, an *obligation* is created. Obligations are the federal equivalent of encumbrances used by state and local governmental units. They charge the allotment with the most recent estimate of the cost of items ordered and release any related prior commitments. If the agency places formal purchase orders for supplies whose cost is expected to be $95,000, the entry is:

Budgetary entry	Commitments	95,000	
	Undelivered orders		95,000
	To obligate funds for supplies ordered but not delivered.		

Proprietary entry   None

The debit in the budgetary entry represents the reduction of outstanding commitments. The credit represents the actual obligation and is similar to the Reserve for encumbrances account used by state and local governmental units.

When goods arrive or services are performed, the following entries are made. The budgetary entry removes the obligation. It also records the amount of the appropriation expended at this time. Assume that the actual cost of supplies ordered amounts to $94,000.

Budgetary entry	Undelivered orders	95,000	
	Expended authority		94,000
	Allotments—realized resources		1,000
	To record expenditure of portion of allotment.		

Notice that because the actual cost of the supplies is less than the amount estimated, the difference is returned to Allotments—realized resources, from where it was first taken.

Proprietary entries	Inventory of supplies	94,000	
	Accounts payable		94,000
	To record receipt of supplies.		

	Unexpended appropriations	94,000	
	Appropriations used		94,000
	To record financing source of supplies.		

The first proprietary entry records the receipt of supplies and the resulting liability. It is similar to the entry that would be made by a commercial organization. The second proprietary entry records the reduction in unexpended appropriations as a result of the acquisition of supplies.

In addition, when goods arrive or services are performed, a *disbursement schedule* is sent to the Treasury ordering it to pay the vendors. This does not reduce the agency's balance with the Treasury until checks are actually issued. As a result, the processing of payables is recorded in two steps. When the disbursement schedule is sent to the Treasury, the entry, assuming that the preceding purchase of supplies is the only transaction on the schedule, is:

Budgetary entry	None		
Proprietary entry	Accounts payable	94,000	
	Disbursements in transit		94,000
	To record request to Treasury for check(s).		

When the agency is notified by the Treasury that the check(s) requested was issued, the entry on the agency's books is:

Budgetary entry	None		
Proprietary entry	Disbursements in transit	94,000	
	Fund balance with Treasury		94,000
	To record issuance of check by the Treasury.		

If supplies costing $50,000 are used by the agency, their cost is recorded as an expense. No budgetary entry is necessary because the expending of the appropriation has already been recorded.

Budgetary entry	None		
Proprietary entry	Operating/program expenses—supplies	50,000	
	Inventory of supplies		50,000
	To record supplies used.		

Purchases of services are treated in the same manner as purchases of supplies except that, because they are used immediately upon receipt, an entry is needed to record the use of the appropriation. Entries recording the commitment and obligation are similar to those shown for the purchase of supplies; when services (expected to cost $12,000) are received, the entries are:

Budgetary entry	Undelivered orders	12,000	
	Expended authority		12,000
	To record expenditure of portion of allotment.		

Proprietary entries	Operating/program expenses—contractual services	12,000	
	Accounts payable		12,000
	To record receipt of contractual services.		
	Unexpended appropriations	12,000	
	Appropriations used		12,000
	To record financing source of outside services.		

If a disbursement schedule is sent to the Treasury listing this expense, the entry is:

Budgetary entry	None		
Proprietary entry	Accounts payable	12,000	
	Disbursements in transit		12,000
	To record request to Treasury for check.		

Items such as salaries, rent, and utilities are also recorded as expenses, just as they are in commercial organizations. However, entries recording the sources of financing and the expenditure of budgetary authority are also required. In many cases (as in this example) these items have not been previously obligated. Assume that the agency incurs the following costs:

Rent	$ 6,000
Utilities	2,000
Miscellaneous	1,500
Salaries and benefits	22,000
Total	$31,500

The salaries will be paid immediately, and liabilities will be set up for the other costs. The entries to record these costs are:

Budgetary entry	Allotments—realized resources	31,500	
	Expended authority		31,500
	To record expenditure of portion of allotment.		

Proprietary entries	Operating/program expenses—rent	6,000	
	Operating/program expenses—utilities	2,000	
	Operating/program expenses—miscellaneous	1,500	
	Operating/program expenses—salaries and benefits	22,000	
	Accounts payable		9,500
	Fund balance with Treasury		22,000
	To record certain operating expenses.		
	Unexpended appropriations	31,500	
	Appropriations used		31,500
	To record financing source of operating expenses.		

Recall that this agency started the fiscal year with General property, plant, and equipment of $40,000. The agency had received an appropriation to acquire the assets and had made both budgetary and proprietary entries to record the transaction, similar to the entries shown previously to record the purchase of supplies. Now it needs to record depreciation of the asset. Because depreciation is not chargeable against an appropriation, a budgetary entry is not needed. A proprietary entry is needed, however, to record the depreciation expense. If depreciation of $8,000 is recorded, the entries are:

Budgetary entry	None		
Proprietary entry	Operating/program expenses—depreciation	8,000	
	Accumulated depreciation		8,000
	To record depreciation on fixed assets.		

If year-end entries are made to record accrued, but unpaid, salaries and benefits of $3,500, the entries are:

Budgetary entry	Allotments—realized resources	3,500	
	Expended authority		3,500
	To record expenditure of portion of allotment.		
Proprietary entries	Operating/program expenses—salaries and benefits	3,500	
	Accrued funded payroll		3,500
	To record accrual of year-end payroll.		
	Unexpended appropriations	3,500	
	Appropriations used		3,500
	To record financing source of operating expenses.		

Closing Entries

At the end of the year, most appropriations lapse unless they are classified as multiyear or no-year (permanent). To "lapse" means that any resources not spent or formally obligated by this time must be returned to the Treasury. These amounts cannot be carried forward to finance operations of the following year. Resources formally obligated by the end of the year, however, may be carried forward to meet given obligations. If these resources are not expended within 5 years, they must be returned to the Treasury.

After the transactions of the year are recorded and appropriate adjusting entries are prepared, budgetary entries are made to close accounts representing expired budget authority and Expended authority. Proprietary entries are made to close expense accounts and Appropriations used.

Budgetary entries	Apportionment	2,000	
	Allotments—realized resources	2,000	
	Commitments	5,000	
	Other appropriations realized		9,000
	To close Apportionment, Allotment, and Commitment accounts and to record expiration of budgetary authority.		
	Expended authority	141,000	
	Other appropriations realized		141,000
	To close Expended authority account.		
Proprietary entries	Appropriations used	141,000	
	Operating/program expenses—supplies		50,000
	Operating/program expenses—contractual services		12,000
	Operating/program expenses—salaries and benefits		25,500
	Operating/program expenses—rent		6,000
	Operating/program expenses—utilities		2,000
	Operating/program expenses—miscellaneous		1,500
	Operating/program expenses—depreciation		8,000
	Cumulative results of operations		36,000
	To close proprietary accounts.		

Notice that the differences between Appropriations used and the expense accounts is closed to Cumulative results of operations, an equity account.

FEDERAL AGENCY FINANCIAL REPORTING REQUIREMENTS

Federal agencies must report in accordance with standards established by the FASAB, as implemented by the OMB. At the time this text was written, the OMB's reporting requirements were set forth in OMB Circular No. A-136, subject: Financial Reporting Requirements—Revised (July 24, 2006). The OMB Circular requires all federal agencies to prepare an annual *Performance and Accountability Report,* covering both financial and program performance, as well as quarterly interim financial statements. These reports are in addition to reports routinely submitted to the OMB for monitoring budget execution.

The financial section of the *Performance and Accountability Report* has a balance sheet, a statement of net cost, a statement of changes in net position, a statement of budgetary resources, and a statement of financing. When applicable, federal agencies also prepare statements of custodial activity and social insurance. Because the financial statements shown here are based only on the transactions in the preceding section, they have much less detail than the typical statements for a federal agency. You can see the full OMB Circular No. A-136 at the OMB Web site, www. whitehouse.gov/omb.

To prepare financial statements based on the previously illustrated transactions of the Federal Oversight Agency, we start with a preclosing trial balance (Table 11-6). The preclosing trial balance includes the opening balances in the General property, plant, and equipment and Cumulative results of operations accounts. The financial statements are shown in Table 11-7 through 11-11.

Notice that the net position ($85,000) shown on the *balance sheet* (Table 11-7) is the difference between proprietary account assets and liabilities. Net position generally consists of the entity's unexpended appropriations and cumulative results of operations. Cumulative results of operations represents amounts accumulated by the entity over the years from its financing sources, less expenses and losses. Cumulative results of operations in this illustration ($76,000) equals the inventory of supplies and the net General property, plant, and equipment account, because they required previous financing sources but have not yet become expenses.

The *statement of net costs* (Table 11-8) shows the costs of programs that are supported with taxes. Costs are presented on the accrual basis of accounting, so, for example, the illustration shows the amount of supplies used ($50,000) rather than the amount purchased ($94,000). If the entity earned revenues (e.g., through fees charged for services), they would be deducted in determining net cost of operations.

The statement of net costs presented here shows objects of account because those accounts were used in the illustrative journal entries. In practice, however, this financial statement would be presented on a program basis in a matrix format, showing program costs incurred by each suborganization in the department. This statement supports the department's performance measurement statistics, showing how net costs relate to program outputs and outcomes.

The *statement of changes in net position* (Table 11-9) summarizes the factors that caused increases or decreases in the components of net position (cumulative results of

TABLE 11-6   Preclosing Trial Balance

Federal Oversight Agency
Preclosing Trial Balance
September 30, 2009

Budgetary Accounts

Other appropriations realized	$150,000	
Unapportioned authority—available		$ —
Apportionment		2,000
Allotments—realized resources		2,000
Commitments		5,000
Undelivered orders		—
Expended authority		141,000
Totals	$150,000	$150,000

Proprietary Accounts

Fund balance with Treasury	$ 34,000	
Inventory of supplies	44,000	
General property, plant and equipment	40,000	
Accumulated depreciation		$ 8,000
Disbursements in transit		12,000
Accounts payable		9,500
Accrued funded payroll		3,500
Unexpended appropriations		9,000
Cumulative results of operations		40,000
Appropriations used		141,000
Operating/program expenses—salaries and benefits	25,500	
Operating/program expenses—contractual services	12,000	
Operating/program expenses—supplies	50,000	
Operating/program expenses—rent	6,000	
Operating/program expenses—utilities	2,000	
Operating/program expenses—depreciation	8,000	
Operating/program expenses—miscellaneous	1,500	
Totals	$223,000	$223,000

TABLE 11-7   Balance Sheet of Federal Agency

Federal Oversight Agency
Balance Sheet
September 30, 2009

Assets		
Fund balance with Treasury		$ 34,000
Inventory of supplies		44,000
General property, plant, and equipment	$40,000	
Less: Accumulated depreciation	(8,000)	32,000
Total assets		$110,000

TABLE 11-7   Balance Sheet of Federal Agency *(continued)*

Federal Oversight Agency
Balance Sheet
September 30, 2009

Liabilities and Net Position

Liabilities:

Disbursements in transit	12,000	
Accounts payable	9,500	
Accrued funded payroll	3,500	
Total liabilities		$ 25,000

Net Position:

Unexpended appropriations	9,000	
Cumulative results of operations	76,000	
Total net position		85,000
Total liabilities and net position		$110,000

TABLE 11-8   Statement of Net Costs of Federal Agency

Federal Oversight Agency
Statement of Net Costs
For Fiscal Year Ended September 30, 2009

Program costs:

Salaries and benefits	$ 25,500
Contractual services	12,000
Supplies	50,000
Rent	6,000
Utilities	2,000
Depreciation	8,000
Miscellaneous	1,500
Net cost of operations	$105,000

TABLE 11-9   Statement of Changes in Net Position

Federal Oversight Agency
Statement of Changes in Net Position
For the Year Ended September 30, 2009

Cumulative results of operations, beginning balance		$40,000
Budgetary financing sources:		
Appropriations used	$141,000	
Other financing sources	—	
Net cost of operations	105,000	
Net change		36,000
Cumulative results of operations, ending balance		76,000
Unexpended appropriations:		
Beginning balance		—
Appropriations received	$150,000	
Appropriations used	141,000	
Total unexpended appropriations		9,000
Net position, end of period		$85,000

TABLE 11-10   Statement of Budgetary Resources

Federal Oversight Agency
Statement of Budgetary Resources
For the Year Ended September 30, 2009

Budgetary Resources:	
Appropriation	$150,000
Other (not illustrated)	—
Total budgetary resources	$150,000
Status of Budgetary Resources:	
Obligations incurred	$141,000
Unobligated balance	—
Unobligated balance not available	9,000
Total status of budgetary resources	$150,000
Change in Obligated Balance:	
Unpaid obligations, beginning of period	—
Obligations incurred	$141,000
Less gross outlays	116,000
Unpaid obligated balance, end of period	$ 25,000
Net (and Gross) Outlays	$116,000

TABLE 11-11   Statement of Financing

Federal Oversight Agency
Statement of Financing
For the Year Ended September 30, 2009

Resources used to finance activities:	
Obligations incurred	$141,000
Other (not illustrated)	—
Total resources used to finance activities	141,000
Resources used to finance items not part of the net cost of operations:	
Change in budgetary resources obligated for goods, services, and benefits ordered, but not yet provided (not illustrated)	—
Resources that finance the acquisition of assets	(94,000)
Total resources used to finance items not part of net cost of operations	(94,000)
Total resources used to finance the net cost of operations	47,000
Components of the net cost of operations that will not require or generate resources in the current period:	
Components requiring or generating resources in future periods (not illustrated)	—
Components not requiring or generating resources:	
Depreciation and amortization	8,000
Supplies consumed	50,000
Total components of net cost of operations that will not require or generate resources in current period	58,000
Net cost of operations	$105,000

operations and unexpended appropriations) for the year. In this illustration, the agency's net position increased from $40,000 to $85,000. The major cause of the increase was a $36,000 increase in cumulative results of operations. This increase occurred because the agency used $141,000 of budgetary resources, but its net cost of operations was only $105,000. The statement of financing (Table 11-11) details the causes of the net change in cumulative results of operations—primarily a buildup in the inventory of supplies.

The *statement of budgetary resources* (Table 11-10) has four parts: budgetary resources; status of budgetary resources; change in obligated balance; and outlays.

- The budgetary resources part of the statement, derived from the left side of the budgetary part of the trial balance in Table 11-6, shows the appropriations and other forms of budget authority made available to the agency.
- The status part of the statement comes from the right side of the budgetary part of the trial balance. Obligations incurred includes expended authority ($141,000) plus undelivered orders ($0). Unobligated balances not available ($9,000) are the balances in the other three accounts on the right side of the trial balance: Apportionment, Allotments—realized resources, and Commitments. They are not available for future obligation by the agency because they expire at year end.
- The change in obligated balance is determined by deducting gross outlays from the total of unpaid obligations at the beginning of the period and the obligations incurred during the period.
- Outlays are payments by the U.S. Treasury to liquidate obligations. The outlay of $116,000 in this illustration is the difference between $141,000 of obligations incurred and $25,000 of liabilities on the balance sheet. It is also the difference between the opening proprietary entry of $150,000 in Fund balance with Treasury and the $34,000 closing balance of that account.

The *statement of financing* (Table 11-11) reconciles budgetary resources consumed in financing the entity's activities with the net cost of operations. In this illustration, the entity consumed $141,000 of budgetary resources, but its net cost of operations was only $105,000. The difference could be explained by several factors comprising the difference between budget-based obligation accounting and accrual-based proprietary accounting:

- The entity could have used budget resources for assets ordered but not received (not illustrated), or assets received but not consumed in this period's operations (such as capital assets or supplies acquired for inventory).
- It could have incurred costs in this period that will require budgetary resources in a subsequent period, such as accrued vacation costs or environmental liabilities.
- It could have incurred costs in this period by using assets acquired with budgetary resources from an earlier period, such as depreciation. (Note that we also showed $50,000 supplies consumed in this section because we reported the full amount of supplies acquired, $94,000, in an earlier section of this statement.)

FEDERAL FINANCIAL REPORTING IN PRACTICE
What Is the Status of Social Security?

To learn about the status of Social Security, go to the notes and the supplemental information provided with the federal government's financial statements and the Social Security Administration's (SSA) Performance and Accountability Report. You can read them at www.gao.gov and www.ssa.gov.

SSA administers the Social Security program through two trust funds, the Federal Old Age and Survivors Insurance Trust Fund and the Federal Disability Insurance Trust Fund. For the year ended September 30, 2006, the two Social Security Trust Funds combined received Social Security taxes of $620 billion and were credited with interest revenue of $100 billion. They made benefit payments of about $540 billion. After other items, the net position of the two funds increased by more than $180 billion, to $1.955 trillion. Each year, the cash resulting from the excess of revenues over benefit payments is used by the U.S. Treasury to help finance the annual deficits in the nonearmarked portion of the budget. Hence, the major asset of the two trust funds takes the form of IOUs—investments in U.S. Treasury securities.

Here's a thumbnail sketch of the financial data of the combined Social Security trust funds (in billions of dollars), based on data in the notes to the federal government's 2006 financial statements.

These statements tell you about the current Social Security tax revenue inflows, benefit payment expenses, and net assets. But they don't tell you much about the status of the Social Security program. To understand its status, you need to know about how Social Security is financed, understand the demographics of Social Security, and read the notes and supplementary data accompanying the financial statements.

First, let's discuss Social Security financing. Federal Social Security is not financed like most state and local government pension plans. Most pension plans are "advance-funded" during the working lifetimes of the employees, but Social Security is financed essentially on a "pay-as-you-go" basis. The Social Security taxes that you pay during your working life are used primarily to pay the benefits of those already retired.

According to SSA, the nearly $2 trillion of assets held by the Social Security funds will cover about 41 months' Social Security benefit payments. By contrast, the net assets of better-funded state and local government pension systems are sufficient to cover more than 15 years of pension benefit payments. Further, if $2 trillion sounds like a lot of assets, the Statement of Social Insurance (one of the financial statements prepared by the

Balance Sheet			Change in Net Position	
Assets:			Beginning net position	$1,771
Investments in U.S.			Investment revenue	100
Treasury securities	$1,995		Tax revenue	620
Other assets	30		Other changes	7
Total assets	$2,025		Program expenses	
			(mostly benefit payments)	(543)
Total liabilities	$ 70		Ending net position	$1,955
Net position	1,955			
Total liabilities and net position	$2,025			

federal government) shows that the present value of future payments to Social Security participants over the age of 62—most of whom are already drawing benefits—was $5.9 trillion at September 30, 2006. That number does not include people who are otherwise eligible for benefits but have not yet reached the age of 62.

Now for the demographics—and the impact of the so-called baby boom generation, born in the years 1946–1964. As the baby boom generation becomes eligible for receiving Social Security payments, the number of beneficiaries will increase faster than the number of workers who pay the taxes that provide the benefits. In 1960, for every 100 workers, there were about 20 Social Security beneficiaries. In 2006, 100 workers covered about 30 beneficiaries. SSA projects that, by 2030, 100 workers will cover only 46 beneficiaries—and the ratio will gradually worsen after that.

What are the financial implications of those demographics? The FASAB requires that financial reports contain extensive supplementary data about the financial status of Social Security and other social insurance programs. Here are some things you can learn by reading the data. As you read, keep in mind that long-term financial projections of Social Security inflows and outflows depend on estimates of economic and demographic factors such as long-term birthrates, mortality rates, immigration rates, and inflation rates—all of which can vary greatly from the best estimates.

- Starting in about 2009, as the baby boom generation reaches retirement age, Social Security benefit payments will increase rapidly. SSA estimates that benefit payments will exceed Social Security tax revenues in about 2017. Instead of a positive cash flow, the trust funds will experience cash flow deficits.
- When benefit payments start to exceed tax revenues, SSA will draw down the trust fund assets—meaning the U.S. Treasury needs to redeem the IOUs it gave the trust fund for borrowing its cash. To do that, the federal government must raise taxes, borrow from the public, or cut other expenditures. (So the Social Security problem also creates broader budgeting and financing problems!)
- SSA estimates that the trust fund assets will be fully exhausted by 2040. At that point, SSA estimates that Social Security tax revenue inflows will be sufficient to pay only about 74 percent of the scheduled benefits.

Whether that makes you optimistic or pessimistic depends on whether you think the cup is half full or half empty.

Review Questions

Q11-1   The terms *appropriation, apportionment,* and *allotment* are used in the federal budget process. Describe what they are and which unit of the government makes them.

Q11-2   The Congress appropriates $2 million to fund the fiscal year 2009 activities of a bureau within a department. Can the bureau director immediately place a purchase order to buy supplies? If not, why not?

Q11-3   The term *obligation* is commonly used in federal government accounting. What is an obligation and what is its equivalent in state and local government accounting?

Q11-4   What is the meaning of the term *expended authority*? How does it differ from an *outlay*?

Q11-5 What are *earmarked funds*? Which funds are characterized as earmarked?

Q11-6 Compare the use of accrual accounting in federal accounting and financial reporting with the use of accrual accounting and financial reporting in state and local government.

Q11-7 How is depreciation handled in federal accounting and financial reporting? How does it differ from the treatment of depreciation in state and local government accounting and financial reporting?

Q11-8 Describe the purpose of the Federal Accounting Standards Advisory Board and how it functions.

Q11-9 Briefly describe the federal accounting standards regarding inventory and related property; property, plant, and equipment; and liabilities.

Q11-10 Describe five financial statements prepared by federal agencies.

Q11-11 Describe the purpose of the statement of financing. Discuss and illustrate the major components of that statement.

Q11-12 How does the financing of Social Security differ from the financing of most state and local government pension plans?

Cases

C11-1 Financial reporting of Social Security has been a controversial subject in the federal government. Current federal accounting standards require that liabilities be reported only for Social Security payments that are currently due and payable, but that no liability be reported for the unfunded actuarial present value of amounts due to retirees or their beneficiaries or the unfunded actuarial present value of benefits earned by other participants in the Social Security system. However, the standard does require various disclosures regarding the financial status of Social Security. Give arguments for and against the current financial reporting standard and state your opinion about the soundness of the standard.

C11-2 A federal agency receives a separate appropriation for supplies. A large number of purchase orders, marked "Rush," are processed in August. Because several clerks are on vacation, however, they are not recorded as obligations. The supplies are received in early September, before the end of the fiscal year. After matching the invoices with the receiving reports, the accountant finds the agency has insufficient funds to process many of the payments. On further inquiry, the accountant locates the batch of unrecorded purchase orders. He also finds that the supplies were used immediately upon receipt. He explains the problem to his immediate supervisor, who says, "Forget it. Just charge the bills to next year's appropriation." Explain the nature of the accountant's dilemma and discuss what you think he should do.

C11-3 Recently your manager expressed concern about a lack of planning and control in the placement of purchase orders by your agency. He felt that orders were placed on a first-come, first-served basis and when the allotment was used up there would be no money for the agency to continue operations vital to its mission. At an Association of Government Accountants meeting, a friend of yours employed by the National Finance Center mentioned that his agency uses commitment accounting to enhance planning and fund control. You become curious and call him for more information. Write a brief report explaining what commitment accounting is, what it does, how it works, and any negative factors that should be taken into consideration before implementing it.

Exercises

E11-1 (Multiple choice)

1. What funds are used by federal agencies to account for receipts of resources from specific sources, earmarked by law for special purposes?
    a. Special Revenue Funds
    b. Special Funds
    c. Revolving Funds
    d. Deposit Funds
2. Who sets federal accounting standards?
    a. The Congress
    b. The Financial Accounting Standards Board (FASB)
    c. The Federal Accounting Standards Advisory Board (FASAB)
    d. The Governmental Accounting Standards Board (GASB)
3. What does an unliquidated obligation represent?
    a. Resources that cannot be spent for any purpose
    b. Resources that have already been disbursed
    c. Resources that must be returned to the Treasury
    d. Resources earmarked for a specific purpose
4. Who makes apportionments of appropriations to an agency?
    a. The Congress
    b. The Office of Management and Budget (OMB)
    c. The agency
    d. The department of which the agency is a part
5. What is the function of commitments?
    a. To legally encumber an allotment
    b. To formally disclose purchase requests before actual orders are placed
    c. To represent the authority to spend money for a particular project
    d. To represent legally enforceable promises to specific vendors
6. What account is used to show that an agency has requested payment by the Treasury to a certain vendor(s)?
    a. Fund balance with Treasury
    b. Accounts payable
    c. Disbursements in transit
    d. Processed invoices
7. To prepare the "Status of budgetary resources" section of the Statement of Budgetary Resources, you would use the balances in which of the following accounts?
    a. Expended authority, undelivered orders, and commitments
    b. Cumulative results of operations, undelivered orders, and disbursements in transit
    c. Fund balance with treasury, expended authority, and undelivered orders
    d. Fund balance with treasury, undelivered orders, and commitments

8. In the Statement of Financing, which of these factors helps explain the difference between the budgetary resources used to finance activities and net cost of operations?
a. Fund balance with Treasury
b. Beginning balance in cumulative results of operations
c. Resources used to finance the acquisition of capital assets
d. Allotments

E11-2 (Matching)
Match the items in the following right column with those in the left column.

____ **1.** An act of Congress that gives a department and/or agency authority to obligate the federal government to make disbursements for goods and services	a. Outlays b. Obligation c. Disbursement schedule
____ **2.** Document sent to the Treasury ordering it to pay vendors and employees	d. GASB e. Appropriation
____ **3.** Sets standards for federal government accounting	f. Revolving fund g. Apportionment
____ **4.** Type of fund used to account for commercial-type operations of federal agencies	h. FASAB i. Allotment
____ **5.** Action by which the OMB distributes amounts available for obligation to agencies	j. Trust fund k. Deferral l. Commitment
____ **6.** Payments of obligations	
____ **7.** Reserves budgetary authority from an allotment for the estimated amount of orders to be placed	
____ **8.** Federal equivalent of encumbrances used by state and local governmental units	
____ **9.** Type of fund that finances Social Security payments	

E11-3 (Use of the budgetary accounts)
In federal accounting the most frequently used budgetary accounts are the following:

Other appropriations realized
Unapportioned authority—available
Apportionment
Allotments—realized resources
Commitments
Undelivered orders
Expended authority

Required: Determine which of these account titles best describes each of the following situations:

____ **1.** Spending authority allotted but not yet committed
____ **2.** Resources obligated but not yet expended
____ **3.** Spending authority apportioned, but not yet allotted, to an agency
____ **4.** The portion of an agency's appropriation that has been used

    5. Spending authority appropriated, but not yet apportioned, by the OMB

    6. Spending authority reserved for the estimated amount of orders to be placed

E11-4 (Federal accounting cycle)

The Geological Resources Agency is an agency within the Department of Resources. The following transactions took place in October, the first month of FY 2009.

1. The agency was notified that its appropriation was $2,500,000.
2. The OMB apportioned $600,000 to the Department of Resources for the first quarter of the fiscal year.
3. The Department of Resources' CEO allotted $200,000 to the agency for its October operations.
4. Purchase orders placed during the month for materials and supplies were $150,000. (The agency does not use commitment accounting.) The materials and supplies arrived during the month, along with an invoice for $148,000.
5. Materials costing $100,000 and supplies costing $20,000 were used during the month. In addition, salaries amounting to $48,000 were paid on the last day of the month.
6. A disbursement schedule was sent to the Treasury ordering payment for the materials and supplies.

Required: Make appropriate journal entries to record these transactions.

E11-5 (Accounting for the acquisition and use of equipment)

The Bureau of Port Inspection of the Department of National Security began operations on October 1. The following transactions relate to the bureau's acquisition of equipment.

1. The bureau received an appropriation of $2,000,000.
2. The OMB apportioned the entire amount of the appropriation.
3. The secretary of the Department allotted $500,000 of the apportionment for the bureau's October operations.
4. The bureau's planning unit requested that the purchasing department award a contract estimated at $180,000 for special equipment capable of scanning inside shipping containers.
5. The bureau's purchasing department awarded a contract for $200,000 for the special scanning equipment. The purchasing department advised the planning unit that the additional cost over the estimate was caused by the special specifications.
6. The bureau received the equipment ordered in transaction 5, with an invoice for $200,000. The equipment was expected to have a 10-year life.
7. The bureau sent a disbursement schedule to the Treasury, requesting payment of the $200,000 invoice.
8. The Treasury notified the bureau that the invoice for $200,000 had been paid.
9. The bureau recorded six months' depreciation ($10,000) on the equipment.

Required: Prepare journal entries to record these transactions

E11-6 (Journal entries—emphasis on budgetary entries and statements)

The Central Think Tank (CTT) receives a separate appropriation from the Congress for the acquisition of advanced intelligence gathering components. The following is a summary of transactions affecting the CTT's intelligence gathering component appropriation for the year ended September 30, 2009.

1. The CTT received an appropriation of $400,000.
2. The OMB apportioned to the agency the entire amount that the Congress appropriated.
3. To keep control over its rate of expenditures, the agency used an allotment system. During the year, the entire apportionment was allotted.
4. Commitments placed during the year for intelligence gathering components totaled $390,000.
5. Purchase orders issued against the commitments totaled $375,000.
6. Of the intelligence gathering components ordered, $360,000 worth was delivered this year; the remaining $15,000 worth will be delivered next year. The delivered components were accepted and placed in inventory.
7. During the year, intelligence gathering components of $140,000 were consumed in operations.
8. The CTT sent a disbursement schedule to the Treasury requesting payment of the invoice for $360,000 received from the vendor in transaction 6. The Treasury later notified the CTT that the invoice had been paid.

Required: 1. Prepare journal entries to record these transactions. State which entries are budgetary and which are proprietary.
2. Prepare a statement of budgetary resources. Assume that all resources not obligated by year end are not available for future spending.

E11-7 (Journal entries—relationship of statements of net costs and financing)

The Central Think Tank (CTT) receives a separate appropriation from the Congress for the purpose of testing advanced intelligence gathering components. The appropriation covers salaries, supplies, equipment, and rent and utilities. Assume that entries to record appropriations, apportionments, allotments, and obligations have been made. The following transactions affect the agency's net costs for the year ended September 30, 2009.

1. Salaries amounting to $425,000 were paid.
2. Salaries of $15,000 were unpaid at year end and had to be accrued.
3. Rent and utilities bills amounting to $65,000 were received and payables set up.
4. Supplies of $35,000, acquired in previous years and placed in inventory, were consumed in testing the intelligence gathering components.
5. Depreciation on testing equipment acquired in previous years was $75,000.

Required: 1. Prepare journal entries to record these transactions and events. State which journal entries are budgetary and which are proprietary.

2. Prepare a statement of net costs for the year.
3. Prepare a statement of financing for the year. (Assume obligations incurred equals the expended authority in this problem.)

Problems

P11-1 (Accounting cycle for 1 month)

The Federal Commission on Governmental Performance was formed on October 1, 2008. This agency does not use commitment accounting. Among the transactions that took place that year were the following:

1. An appropriation of $6,500,000 was passed by the Congress and approved by the president. The resources are to be used for operating purposes.
2. The OMB notified the Department of Administration, of which the agency is a part, of the following apportionment:

    First quarter $2,000,000

3. The Department of Administration allotted $700,000 to the Commission for its operations in October.
4. Purchase orders were placed in October for the following:

Materials	$150,000
Rent	50,000
Supplies	40,000

5. The payroll for October amounted to $400,000. It was paid on October 31.
6. Invoices approved by the agency for payment were as follows:

XYZ Widget Co.—materials	$120,000
Scrooge Realty Co.—October rent	50,000
L & K Supply—supplies	10,000

    The Treasury informed the Commission that all invoices were paid in full. Supplies and rent are expensed upon approval for payment. Materials are inventoried when purchased and expensed when used.
7. Materials costing $85,000 were used during October.

Required: 1. Prepare appropriate journal entries for the transactions of October 2008.
2. Prepare appropriate monthly closing entries. (*Hint:* Do not close out the budgetary accounts.)
3. Prepare the following month-end statements:
   a. Balance sheet
   b. Statement of net costs
   c. Statement of changes in net position
   d. Statement of financing
   e. Statement of budgetary resources (*Note:* Consider amounts not yet allotted as balances not available.)

P11-2 (Accounting cycle for 1 month)

The Star Exploration Agency, a unit of the Space Department, was established by the Congress to begin operations at the beginning of FY 2009. Following are the agency's transactions during October, its first month of operations:

October 1   The Congress passed and the president approved a $1,000,000 appropriation for this agency.

October 1   Of the amount appropriated, $950,000 was apportioned by the OMB.

October 1   The Space Department allotted the agency $100,000 to carry out its October operations.

October 1   Purchase requests were made for materials and supplies, estimated to cost $88,000.

October 4   Purchase orders were placed for materials and supplies, estimated to cost $85,000.

October 10 Materials and supplies previously ordered were received, together with invoices for $88,000 ($70,000 for materials and $18,000 for supplies). The agency accepted the items despite the higher price. All the items were considered as program expenses because they would be consumed within 1 year.

October 14 A disbursement schedule was sent to the Treasury, requesting that it pay invoices amounting to $60,000.

October 31 The Treasury informed the agency that it had paid invoices amounting to $55,000. It also told the agency it had issued checks in the amount of $10,000 for October salaries.

Required: 1. Prepare journal entries to record the events of October.
2. Post the journal entries.
3. Prepare a preclosing trial balance.
4. Prepare appropriate closing entries. (*Hint:* Do not close out the budgetary accounts.)
5. Prepare a postclosing trial balance for the proprietary accounts.
6. Prepare the following month-end statements:
   a. Balance sheet
   b. Statement of net costs
   c. Statement of changes in net position
   d. Statement of budgetary resources (*Note:* Consider amounts not yet allotted as balances not available.)

P11-3 (Financial statements after initial month of operations)

The Bureau of Astrology, a unit of the Space Department, was established October 1, 2008. Its purpose is to provide astrological services to the general public. It is financed by an appropriation from the Congress. Following are the transactions of the agency during October 2008.

October 1   The agency received a certified copy of an appropriation warrant from the Department of the Treasury for $900,000.

October 1   Of the amount available for apportionment, $850,000 was apportioned by the OMB.

October 1   Of the amount apportioned, $120,000 was allotted to the agency by the Space Department to finance its October operations.

October 1   Purchase requests were made for materials and equipment, estimated to cost $48,000.

October 3   Purchase orders were placed for materials, estimated to cost $30,000, and for equipment, estimated to cost $15,000.

October 15 All the equipment ordered October 3 was received with an invoice for $14,800.

October 16 Some of the materials ordered October 3 were received with an invoice for $22,000. The cost estimate used to record the obligation on October 3 was $22,500. The materials were recorded as inventory. A disbursement schedule for this invoice was sent to the Treasury.

October 27 The Treasury paid the $22,000 invoice for the materials.

October 31 Materials costing $18,000 were used by the agency during October.

October 31 Salaries for October totaled $50,000. The agency's FICA contributions were $2,000.

October 31 Depreciation of $1,200 was recorded by the agency.

Required: 1. Record these transactions in general journal form.
2. Post the journal entries to the general ledger and compute the account balances.
3. Prepare a preclosing trial balance.
4. Prepare month-end closing entries. (*Hint:* Because it is month-end, you need not close the budgetary accounts.)
5. Prepare a postclosing trial balance.
6. Prepare the following financial statements:
   a. Balance sheet
   b. Statement of net costs
   c. Statement of changes in net position
   d. Statement of financing
   e. Statement of budgetary resources (*Note:* Consider amounts not yet allotted as balances not available.)

Chapter Outline

After completing this chapter, you should be able to:

- Describe the characteristics that distinguish not-for-profit organizations (NFPOs) from for-profit organizations and from governmental entities.
- Identify the types of organizations classified as voluntary health and welfare organizations (VHWOs) and as other not-for-profit organizations (ONPOs).
- Name and discuss the financial statements prepared by NFPOs.
- Discuss the characteristics of the three classifications of net assets reported on the statement of financial position.
- Describe the nature of donor-imposed restrictions and how they are reported.
- Discuss the journal entries needed when resources are released from restrictions.
- Discuss the nature of and the difference in accounting for unconditional and conditional promises to give.
- Discuss accounting for contributed services.
- Discuss accounting for collections of works of art, rare books, and similar assets.
- Discuss how investments are measured for financial reporting purposes.
- Prepare journal entries to record the activities of VHWOs and ONPOs.
- Describe the major types of funds used by NFPOs.

CHARACTERISTICS OF NOT-FOR-PROFIT ORGANIZATIONS

Not-for-profit organizations (NFPOs) deliver many types of services, particularly in such fields as health care, social services, and higher education, that are also performed by for-profit enterprises and governmental agencies. How can you tell when a particular activity is being performed by an NFPO, a for-profit enterprise, or a governmental agency?

The Financial Accounting Standards Board (FASB) states that the characteristics that distinguish NFPOs from for-profit business enterprises are that NFPOs (1) receive contributions of significant amounts of resources from resource providers who do not expect to receive proportionate monetary benefits in return; (2) operate for purposes other than to provide goods or services at a profit; and (3) lack defined ownership interests that can be sold, transferred, or redeemed.[1] NFPOs possess these characteristics in varying degrees. As we shall see, the need for demonstrating accountability to donors and the lack of ownership interests has influenced the development of accounting and financial reporting standards for NFPOs.

---

[1]FASB *Concepts Statement No. 4,* "Objectives of Financial Reporting by Nonbusiness Organizations," (Norwalk, CT: FASB, 1980), para. 6.

The distinction between NFPOs and governmental entities is sometimes fuzzy, because governments have increasingly provided social services and other functions by contracting with NFPOs. Entities such as states, cities, counties, and towns (including public corporations and "bodies corporate and politic") are clearly governmental. However, an entity created by charter under state corporation or not-for-profit corporation laws may perform activities so closely related to what governments do that it may not be clear what kind of entity it is. As distinguished from NFPOs, governmental entities have one or more of these characteristics: (1) their officers are either popularly elected or a controlling majority of their governing boards are appointed or approved by entities that are clearly governmental; (2) they may have the power to tax; (3) they may have the power to issue tax-exempt debt; or (4) they can be dissolved unilaterally by a government and their net assets assumed by it without compensation.[2]

Examples of Not-for-Profit Organizations

The four broad NFPO categories are voluntary health and welfare organizations (VHWOs), health care organizations, colleges and universities, and other not-for-profit organizations (ONPOs). The accounting and financial reporting principles covered in this chapter apply to all four NFPO categories, but the illustrations relate primarily to VHWOs and ONPOs. Not-for-profit colleges and universities are discussed in an appendix to this chapter. Health care entities, as well as discussions of accounting and financial reporting matters unique to them, are covered in Chapter 13.

VHWOs are entities formed for the purpose of providing voluntary services for various segments of society, in the fields of health, welfare, and other social services. They obtain resources primarily from voluntary contributions from the general public. They may also receive grants and contracts from governmental agencies to provide specific social services. Because they are organized for the benefit of the public, they are exempt from many taxes. Well-known examples of VHWOs are the American Cancer Society, the Boy Scouts of America, the National Urban League, and the Young Women's Christian Association of the U.S.A. A VHWO may provide such services as family counseling, recreation and work for youth, and meals for the needy and the elderly, often at no charge or low charge to the service recipients.

The category ONPOs includes other types of NFPOs that are not VHWOs, colleges and universities, or health care entities. Some of them provide services similar to those provided by VHWOs, and charge user fees. Many of them, however, are organized to provide benefits to their members, and hence derive their revenues primarily from membership dues and fees. Examples of ONPOs include the following:

- Cemetery organizations
- Civic and community organizations
- Labor unions
- Nongovernmental libraries and museums
- Performing arts organizations
- Political parties
- Private foundations
- Private not-for-profit elementary and secondary schools

---

[2]*AICPA Audit and Accounting Guide—Health Care Organizations* (New York: AICPA, 2006), para.1.02.c.

- Professional associations and trade associations
- Religious organizations
- Research and scientific organizations
- Social and country clubs

Major Sources of Accounting and Financial Reporting Guidance

Statements and Interpretations issued by the FASB provide the primary source of accounting and financial reporting guidance for NFPOs. Many FASB pronouncements apply equally to for-profit entities and NFPOs, but several cover only transactions unique to NFPOs and financial reporting for NFPOs. They include FASB *Statement No. 116*, "Accounting for Contributions Received and Contributions Made," and FASB *Statement No. 117*, "Financial Statements of Not-for-Profit Organizations." We concentrate on those Statements in this chapter. Another significant source of accounting and financial reporting guidance for NFPOs is the *Not-for-Profit Organizations Audit and Accounting Guide*, which is published by the American Institute of Certified Public Accountants and is updated periodically to conform to FASB requirements.

FINANCIAL REPORTING

Overview

NFPOs account for revenues, expenses, assets, and liabilities on the full accrual basis of accounting. They have traditionally used fund accouting to maintain accountability for restrictions placed by donors and others on the use of resources. Before the FASB issued *Statement No. 117* in 1993, NFPOs also prepared financial statements by fund type. Although many NFPOs continue to use funds for internal accounting purposes, FASB *Statement No. 117* changed the focus of their financial reporting. The FASB requires that NFPO financial reporting focus on the organization as a whole, rather than on fund type.

The FASB states that the primary purpose of NFPO financial statements is to provide information that meets the common interests of donors, members, creditors, and other resource providers. To meet these needs, all NFPOs must prepare (1) a statement of financial position, (2) a statement of activities, and (3) a statement of cash flows. In addition, VHWOs are required to provide information in a separate financial statement about expenses by natural classification. (Reporting by natural classifiction breaks down the broad functional catergories shown in the statement of activities into components such as salaries, supplies, and depreciation.)

Reporting by Net Asset Classification

Donor-imposed restrictions affect the purposes for which NFPOs may spend the donated resources, when they may spend them, and even whether they may spend them. Therefore, the FASB requires that the net assets shown in NFPO statements of financial position and inflows and outflows of resources shown in NFPO statements of activities be reported as either unrestricted, temporarily restricted, or permanently restricted, depending on the existence and nature of donor-imposed restrictions.

Sometimes, restrictions on using resources arise out of circumstances other than those imposed by donors, such as those resulting from the requirements of contracts and bond agreements. However, only donor-imposed restrictions are classified as temporarily or permanently restricted. Information about the amounts and nature of different types of temporarily or permanently donor-imposed restrictions must be reported on the face of the statement of financial position or in notes to the financial statements.

Permanently restricted net assets are ones resulting

(a) from contributions and other inflows of assets whose use by the organization is limited by donor-imposed stipulations that neither expire by passage of time nor can be fulfilled or otherwise removed by actions of the organization,

(b) from other enhancements and diminishments subject to the same kinds of stipulations, and

(c) from reclassifications from (or to) other classes of net assets as a consequence of donor-imposed stipulations.[3]

Temporarily restricted net assets are ones resulting

(a) from contributions and other inflows of assets whose use by the organization is limited by donor-imposed stipulations that either expire by passage of time or can be removed by actions of the organization pursuant to those stipulations,

(b) from other asset enhancements and diminishments subject to the same kinds of stipulations, and

(c) from reclassifications to (or from) other classes of net assets as a consequence of donor-imposed stipulations, their expiration by passage of time, or their fulfillment and removal by actions of the organization pursuant to those stipulations.[4]

Unrestricted net assets are ones that are neither permanently nor temporarily restricted. The only limits on their use are ones resulting from the nature of the organization and the environment in which it operates and contractual agreements with creditors, suppliers, and others entered into in the ordinary course of business. Information about such limits should be disclosed in the notes to the financial statements. Because they are not donor imposed, however, those limitations do not meet the FASB's definition of restrictions.

Statement of Financial Position

A statement of financial position provides important financial information about the assets, liabilities, and net assets of the organization and their relationship to each other. This information, when used with information on other financial statements and related disclosures, helps donors, members, and other interested parties assess the organization's ability to continue operations and its liquidity, financial flexibility, ability to meet obligations, and future financing needs.[5] To help accomplish these purposes, assets are presented in order of liquidity, and liabilities are presented in order of anticipated liquidation. Showing the amount and nature of donor-imposed restrictions on the statement of net assets helps the reader assess the NFPO's financial flexibility.

---

[3]FASB *Statement No. 117,* "Financial Statements of Not-for-Profit Organizations" (Norwalk, CT: FASB), 1993, para. 168.
[4]Ibid.
[5]Ibid, para. 9.

FASB *Statement No. 117* does not specify or preclude any one format of financial statement, so long as it shows the amounts and flows of unrestricted, temporarily restricted, and permanently restricted resources. Following is a skeletal outline of the broad elements of a statement of financial position.

Assets (presented generally in order of nearness to cash)	XXX
Total assets	XXX
Liabilities and net assets:	
Liabilities (presented generally in order of nearness to liquidation)	XXX
Total liabilities	XXX
Net assets:	
Unrestricted	XXX
Temporarily restricted	XXX
Permanently restricted	XXX
Total net assets	XXX
Total liabilities and net assets	XXX

Statement of Activities

A statement of activities provides information about "the effects of transactions and other events and circumstances that change the amount and nature of net assets" and "how the organization's resources are used in providing various programs or services."[6] The changes in the three asset classifications can be presented in multicolumn format or in single-column "pancake" style. The multicolumn format is generally preferred because it lets the reader observe, at a glance, the effects of revenues, gains, other support, expenses, and losses on each category of net assets. It also lets the reader observe, at a glance, the effect on net assets of changes in levels of restrictions. Following is a skeletal outline of the elements of a statement of activities, prepared in a multicolumn format:

	Unrestricted	Temporarily Restricted	Permanently Restricted	Total
Revenues, gains, and other support:				
(Details by source)	XXX	XXX	XXX	XXX
Net assets released from restrictions	XXX	(XXX)		
Total	XXX	XXX	XXX	XXX
Expenses and losses:				
Program (details by program)	XXX			XXX
Management and general	XXX			XXX
Fund raising	XXX			XXX
Total expenses	XXX			XXX
Losses	XXX	XXX	XXX	XXX
Total expenses and losses	XXX	XXX	XXX	XXX
Change in net assets	XXX	XXX	XXX	XXX
Net assets at beginning of year	XXX	XXX	XXX	XXX
Net assets at end of year	XXX	XXX	XXX	XXX

---

[6]Ibid., para. 17.

Notice that revenues, gains, and other support in the statement of activities are reported as increases in either unrestricted or restricted assets, depending on whether the use of assets is limited by donor-imposed restrictions. However, in accordance with FASB *Statement No. 117,* all expenses must be reported as decreases in unrestricted net assets, even if they were financed with restricted resources. This is accomplished by means of journal entries that reduce restricted assets and increase unrestricted assets, as resources are released from restrictions through their satisfaction, such as incurring program expenses or the expiration of time restrictions. Notice the reduction reported for temporarily restricted net assets next to the caption "Net assets released from restrictions" and the corresponding increase in unrestricted net assets.

Notice also that the first caption in the outline is Revenues, Gains, and Other Support. What is the difference between revenue and gains? Revenues are inflows from selling goods and providing services that constitute the organization's ongoing major or central operations, such as fees for providing child care services, college and university tuition, and services to hospital patients. Gains are inflows from peripheral or incidental transactions, such as profits from selling securities or operating a parking lot in conjunction with an NFPO's major activities. It is possible that an activity considered by one organization to produce "revenues" will be considered by another organization to produce "gains." In fact, donor contributions received by NFPOs may be called revenues or gains, depending on whether they are actively sought and frequently received. The term *support* describes broadly the nature of the resources received by many NFPOs and is used throughout the FASB's literature on NFPOs.

Expenses incurred by NFPOs must be reported on the statement of activities or in the notes to the financial statements "by their functional classification such as major classes of program services and supporting activities."[7] When functional classifications are used, individual types of expenses (such as salaries and supplies) within a function or program are aggregated and reported by function or program. Functional classifications are required because they enable the reader to determine the cost of various programs offered by the organization. The organization's programs should also be described in the notes to the financial statements.

For financial reporting purposes, a *program* is considered to be an activity that is directly related to the purpose(s) for which the organization was established. Although most organizations are involved in several programs, it is possible that an organization may have only one such activity.

Expenses identified as *management and general* are those associated with the overall direction and management of the organization, in addition to those associated with record keeping, the annual report, and so forth. *Fund-raising* and other supporting services are associated with the solicitation of money, materials, and the like, for which the individual or organization making the contribution receives no direct economic benefit. They include such items as printing, personnel, the cost of maintaining a mailing list, and the cost of any gifts that are sent to prospective contributors.

The distinction between program, management and general, and fund-raising expenses is useful to those interested in knowing the percentage of total expenses that an NFPO devotes to program activities. Form 990 "Return of Organization Exempt from Income Tax," used both by the Internal Revenue Service and by state agencies responsible

---

[7]Ibid., para. 26.

for oversight of charitable organizations, also requires program service, management and general, and fund-raising expenses to be reported on separate lines.

Statement of Functional Expenses

All VHWOs are required to prepare both a statement of activities and a statement of functional expenses. The statement of functional expenses, which provides another perspective on the way resources are spent, is presented in matrix format. For each program or function, this statement identifies the expenses by natural or object classification (e.g., salaries, supplies, travel, depreciation expense, and occupancy expense). Although they are not required to prepare a statement of functional expenses, many ONPOs choose to do so because the statement is useful to managers and others.

NOT-FOR-PROFIT ACCOUNTABILITY STANDARDS

The BBB (Better Business Bureau) Wise Giving Alliance has established standards to assist donors in making giving decisions and to foster public confidence in charitable organizations. The standards cover governing, financial, and disclosure practices. Some of the standards relate to matters discussed in this chapter. For example, the standards provide that a charitable organization should:

- Spend at least 65% of its total expenses on program activities.
- Spend no more than 35% of related contributions on fund-raising. Related contributions include donations, legacies, and other gifts received as a result of fund-raising efforts.

- Avoid accumulating funds that could be used for current program activities. To meet this standard, the charity's unrestricted net assets available for use should not be more than three times the size of the past year's expenses or three times the size of the current year's budget, whichever is higher.
- Include in the financial statements a breakdown of expenses (e.g., salaries, travel, postage, etc.) that shows what portion of these expenses was allocated to program, fund-raising, and administrative activities.

SOURCE: Web site at www.give.org/standards/newcbbbstds.asp

Statement of Cash Flows

A statement of cash flows provides the financial statement user with information on cash receipts and cash payments of the organization during the same period as the statement of activities. The statement is organized so that the effect of operating, investing, and financing activities on cash flows is clearly shown.

Illustration of NFPO Financial Statements

County Food Harvest, an NFPO, rescues and distributes surplus and donated food to social service agencies, soup kitchens, homeless shelters, and other agencies that provide free meals to the hungry and homeless throughout a county. Food donors include retailers, whole-salers, bakeries, and other entities. County Food Harvest's financial statements for the year ended June 30, 2008, (amounts in thousands of dollars) are shown to illustrate the financial statements previously discussed.

Notice the classification of net assets among unrestricted ($3,035), temporarily restricted ($2,992), and permanently restricted ($835) in Table 12-1. Details of the nature and amounts of the restrictions could be presented either on the face of the statement of financial position or in the notes. In this instance, the notes show the following:

Temporarily restricted net assets are available for the following purposes:	
Acquisition of warehouse and office facility	$2,140
Food distribution program, on expiration of time restrictions	300
Food distribution program, on expiration of purpose restrictions	552
Total	$2,992

Permanently restricted net assets are restricted to investment in perpetuity, with the investment return available to support the food distribution program.

Notice also the caption "assets restricted to investment in land, buildings, and equipment" (Table 12-1), showing that those assets are not available for operations.

TABLE 12-1   Statement of Financial Position—NFPO

County Food Harvest
Statement of Financial Position
June 30, 2008
(Amounts in Thousands)

Assets:	
Cash and cash equivalents	$2,094
Contributions receivable	654
Grants receivable	310
Food inventory	452
Other current assets	215
Equipment, net of $215 depreciation	640
Assets restricted to investment in land, buildings, and equipment	2,140
Long-term investments	835
Total assets	$7,340
Liabilities and Net Assets:	
Liabilities:	
Accounts payable and accrued expenses	$ 478
Total liabilities	478
Net assets:	
Unrestricted	3,035
Temporarily restricted	2,992
Permanently restricted	835
Total net assets	6,862
Total liabilities and net assets	$7,340

TABLE 12-2   Statement of Activities

County Food Harvest
Statement of Activities
Year Ended June 30, 2008
(Amounts in Thousands)

	Unrestricted	Temporarily Restricted	Permanently Restricted	Total
Revenues, Gains, and Other Support:				
Contributions—food	$ 9,752			$ 9,752
Contributions—support	5,854	$2,084		7,938
Contributions—services	420			420
Revenues—government grants	612			612
Special events	820			820
Investment income	75	90		165
Net unrealized and realized gains on long-term investments		28	$ 35	63
Net assets released from restriction due to satisfaction of:				
Program restrictions	312	(312)		
Time restrictions	156	(156)		
Total revenues, gains, and other support	18,001	1,734	$ 35	19,770
Expenses:				
Food distribution program	14,804			14,804
Management and general	956			956
Fund-raising	1,714			1,714
Total expenses	17,474			17,474
Change in net assets	527	1,734	35	2,296
Net assets at beginning of year	2,508	1,258	800	4,566
Net assets at end of year	$ 3,035	$2,992	$835	$ 6,862

TABLE 12-3   Statement of Functional Expenses

County Food Harvest
Statement of Functional Expenses
Year Ended June 30, 2008
(Amounts in Thousands)

	Food Distribution	Management and General	Fund-Raising	Total
Salaries	$ 3,420	$380	$ 473	$ 4,273
Employee benefits	861	95	118	1,074
Food rescued	9,752			9,752
Food packing supplies	126			126
Rent and utilities	315	40	38	393
Communication	52	21	53	126
Professional fees	110	180	250	540
Advertising			678	678
Office expenses	73	210	74	357
Depreciation	95	30	30	155
Total expenses	$14,804	$956	$1,714	$17,474

TABLE 12-4 Cash Flow Statement	

County Food Harvest
Cash Flow Statement
Year Ended June 30, 2008
(Amounts in Thousands)

Cash flows from operating activities:	
Change in net assets	$ 2,296
Adjustments to reconcile change in net cash (used in) provided by operating activities:	
Depreciation and amortization	155
Increase in contributions receivable	(85)
Increase in grants receivable	(15)
Decrease in other current assets	10
Increase in accrued expenses and accounts payable	30
Net unrealized and realized gains on long-term investments	(63)
Net cash provided by operating activities	2,328
Cash flows from investing activities:	
Purchase of securities	(2,000)
Net cash (used in) investing activities	(2,000)
Net increase in cash and cash equivalents	328
Cash and cash equivalents at beginning of year	1,766
Cash and cash equivalents at end of year	$ 2,094

CONTRIBUTIONS OTHER THAN SERVICES AND COLLECTIONS

General Rule

A contribution is an unconditional transfer of cash or other assets from one entity to another; the entity making the contribution does not directly receive value in exchange.[8] NFPOs may receive contributions in the form of cash, investments, supplies and materials, rights to use facilities, pledges of cash, personal services, works of art, and so on. NFPOs may also receive contributions with "strings attached"; that is, with restrictions on the purposes for which the donations may be used or when they may be used. The general rule for reporting the receipt of contributions other than services and collections is that they must be:

(a) reported as revenues or gains in the period received,
(b) reported as assets, decreases of liabilities, or expenses, depending on the form the benefits take,
(c) measured at the fair value of the contribution received, and
(d) reported as either restricted support or unrestricted support.[9]

Unrestricted Contributions

Contributions may be received with or without donor-imposed restrictions. Unrestricted contributions should be reported on the statement of activities as unrestricted

---

[8]FASB *Statement No. 116*, "Accounting for Contributions Received and Contributions Made," para. 5.
[9]Ibid., para. 8.

revenues or gains (unrestricted support), which increase unrestricted net assets. Expenses incurred from unrestricted net assets are reported as decreases in those assets.

To illustrate the application of the general rule to unrestricted contributions, assume an NFPO operates a clinic that provides services to substance abusers. It received the following donations that may be used for any purpose: (a) $25,000 of cash, (b) 100 shares of stock having a fair market value of $40 a share at the time of the donation, and (c) medical supplies (from a pharmaceutical company) having a fair value of $10,000. When it receives medical supplies, the NFPO initially records them in inventory. The NFPO would make the following journal entry in the period the resources are received.

Cash	25,000	
Investments	4,000	
Inventory—medical supplies	10,000	
Unrestricted support—contributions		29,000
Unrestricted support—supplies		10,000
To record unrestricted contributions.		

If a donor provides free use of a building that normally leases for $15 per square foot, the NFPO would recognize the fair value of the contribution ($15 per square foot) as a revenue and as an expense. Likewise, if a utility provides free electricity, the NFPO would also recognize the fair value of the electricity as a revenue and as an expense.

HOW DO YOU PLACE A VALUE ON DONATED FOOD?

The requirement to record donated non-cash assets, such as supplies and materials, at fair value sometimes can be a daunting task. Food banks, for example, receive millions of pounds of donated perishable and packaged food (and even prepared food) from restaurants, bakeries, retailers, and manufacturers to help feed the needy and the homeless. Fortunately, accounting standards allow for using estimates in financial reporting. Here's how two food banks valued donated food:

- City Harvest, Inc., collected and distributed about 12.6 million pounds of perishable and packaged food in fiscal year 2001. For financial reporting purposes, City Harvest valued the food at 69.1 cents a pound. It made this calculation based on the United States Department of Agriculture's (USDA) "thrifty food plan" average weight of food needed by an individual to meet basic daily needs. City Harvest placed no value on 873,000 pounds of prepared food because "donated prepared food does not have a determinable market value."

- FOOD—People Allied to Combat Hunger, Inc., used several methods to value donated food in 2005. It valued food received from the USDA at average wholesale values provided by the USDA. It valued food received from other sources at an average wholesale value of $1.49 a pound, based on studies made by America's Second Harvest—The Nation's Food Bank Network.

SOURCES: City Harvest, Inc. (New York, NY), Notes to financial statements, June 30, 2001; and FOOD—People Allied to Combat Hunger, Inc. (Millwood, NY), Notes to financial statements, June 30, 2005.

Contributions with Donor-Imposed Restrictions

A donor-imposed restriction limits the use of the contributed resources beyond the broad limits resulting from the nature of the organization and the purposes for which it was organized. Contributions received with donor-imposed restrictions must be reported as *restricted* support. These contributions will increase either temporarily restricted or permanently restricted net assets. As an option, if the NFPO receives donor-restricted contributions whose restrictions are met in the same reporting period the contributions are received, the contribution may be reported as unrestricted support, provided the entity reports similar types of contributions that way consistently from one period to another.

For example, a contributor may stipulate that a cash donation be used only to perform a specific research project or to construct a building. These *purpose-type* restrictions are classified as temporary restrictions, because they may be satisfied by the NFPO's performance of the research or construction of the building. Another donor may require that his or her cash contribution be maintained permanently, with the income from investing the cash to be used to perform a specific research project. The permanent restriction can never be removed by action of the entity, but the income is classified as temporarily restricted until it is used to perform the specified research.

Rather than purpose-type restrictions, a donor may impose a *time* restriction on the use of resources. For example, a donor may make a $30,000 cash contribution to an NFPO, stipulating that the contribution may be used for any pupose the trustees choose, but only at the rate of $10,000 a year, starting at the beginning of the next year. This, too, should be classified as a temporarily restricted contribution.

To illustrate accounting for receipt of contributions with donor-imposed restrictions, assume the NFPO in the preceding section received three additional cash donations: (a) $5,000 from a donor who said it must be used only for research into a new method for treating substance abusers; (b) $7,000 from a donor who said it may be used for any purpose the trustees choose, but not until the following year; and (c) $25,000 from a donor who said the gift must be maintained in perpetuity, with the income from it to be used for any purpose the trustees choose. The NFPO would make this journal entry:

Cash	37,000	
Temporarily restricted support—contributions		5,000
Temporarily restricted support—contributions		7,000
Permanently restricted support—contributions		25,000
To record temporarily and permanently restricted		
gifts.		

Accounting for Reclassifications

An NFPO must recognize the expiration of a donor-restricted contribution in the period the restriction expires. Expiration occurs when the stipulated purpose for which the contribution was made has been fulfilled, when the stipulated time period has elapsed, or both. FASB *Statement No. 117* requires, however, that all expenses be reported in the statement of activities as decreases in unrestricted net assets, even though the original contribution that financed the expense was reported as an increase in restricted net assets. Restricted net assets are reclassified as unrestricted net assets by means of journal entries.

Reclassifications have an effect similar to interfund transfers in governmental accounting. They increase net assets of one net asset class and correspondingly reduce net assets of another. As shown in the skeletal statement of activities, reclassification transactions are reported as Revenues, gains, and other support under the caption Net assets released from restrictions. The journal entry to record these transactions should be prepared in sufficient detail to enable reporting the cause of the reclassification, such as satisfaction of program restrictions or expiration of time restrictions.

To illustrate, let's return to the illustration in the preceding section, "Contributions with Donor-Imposed Restrictions." As the NFPO spends the $5,000 to do research on the project for which the donor made the contribution (donation a), the gift is being used as intended and the purpose restriction is being satisfied. As the spending occurs, the resources are released from the temporary restriction and become unrestricted; at the same time, the expense is reported as a reduction of unrestricted net assets. When the new year arrives, the time restriction imposed by the donor who contributed $7,000 (donation b) has been satisfied, and the gift becmes available for spending. The NFPO would make the following journal entries to record the expiration of the restrictions:

Expenses—special research programs	5,000	
Cash		5,000
To record payment for research expenses.		
Temporarily restricted asset reclassifications out—satisfaction of purpose restrictions	5,000	
Unrestricted asset reclassifications in—satisfaction of purpose restrictions		5,000
To record satisfaction of purpose restrictions.		
Temporarily restricted asset reclassifications out—satisfaction of time restrictions	7,000	
Unrestricted asset reclassifications in—satisfaction of time restrictions		7,000
To record satisfaction of time restriction.		

Financial reporting of the reclassification transactions is shown in the statement of activities illustrated in Table 12-2 on page 461. The debit to Reclassifications out is reported as a negative amount under Net assets released from restrictions, in the temporarily restricted column. The credit to Reclassifications in is reported as a positive amount—alongside the negative amount—under Net assets released from restrictions in the unrestricted column. Thus, the reclassifications cancel each other.

From an organization-wide perspective, the contribution revenue is recognized at the time of the donation and the expense is recognized when incurred. These transactions could occur in different accounting periods. However, when viewed from the perspective of changes in unrestricted net assets, the inflow (reported by means of the reclassification) and the outflow (the expense) occur in the same accounting period.

Unconditional Promises to Give

A *promise to give,* sometimes called a pledge or a charitable subscription, is a written or oral agreement to contribute cash or other assets to another entity. The FASB concluded that *unconditional promises to give* — those that depend only on the passage of time or demand by the receiver of the promise — meet the definition of assets because promise makers generally feel bound to honor them. Therefore, unconditional promises to give should be recognized in the financial statements as receivables and as revenues or gains when the promises are received.

To report receivables at net realizeable value, an allowance for uncollectible promises should be established, based on the NFPO's experience with collecting pledges and current economic circumstances. Instead of recording "bad debts expense" for estimated uncollectible pledges, NFPOs generally record contribution revenues net of the allowance for uncollectible promises, similar to the way governments record property tax revenues.

A promise to give cash contains an inherent time restriction, because it is not available for spending until the NFPO receives the cash. Thus, as a practical matter, whether promises to give are recorded initially as unrestricted or temporarily restricted depends on the accounting period in which the cash is likely to be received. FASB standards say that "receipts of unconditional promises to give with payments due in future periods shall be reported as restricted support [generally, temporarily restricted] unless explicit donor stipulations or circumstances surrounding the receipt of a promise make clear that the donor intended it to be used to support activities of the current period."[10]

Consistent with the requirement for measuring donations at fair value, the FASB requires that promises to give cash in the future (that is, more than one year after the balance sheet date) be discounted to present value. The discount rate is generally the NFPO's average earning rate on investments or average borrowing rate. As time passes, the discount is accreted and recorded as contribution revenue. When reporting promises to give, the following must be disclosed:

(a) Amounts of promises receivable within one year, from one to five years, and in more than five years, and
(b) The allowance for uncollectible pledges.[11]

To illustrate, assume the NFPO in our illustration received unconditional promises to give totaling $50,000, and expected to receive the gifts in the current period. Based on experience, the NFPO expects to collect 90 percent of the promised cash. It also received a promise from an individual to give $10,000 cash in two payments: $5,000 in the

---

[10]Ibid., para. 15.
[11]Ibid., para. 20, 21, and 24.

next year and $5,000 in the year following. It expects that person to fulfill the promise. The NFPO would make the following journal entries:

Contributions receivable	50,000	
Allowance for uncollectible contributions		5,000
Unrestricted support — contributions		45,000
To record receipt of promises to give cash this year, less provision for estimated uncollectible promises.		
Contributions receivable	10,000	
Temporarily restricted support — contributions		9,800
Discount on contributions receivable		200
To record receipt of promises to give cash next year and the year following, discounted to present value.		

Conditional Promises to Give

Conditional promises to give are promises that bind the donor on the occurrence of a specified "future and uncertain" event. Examples of conditional promises to give are: (a) a donor promises to give $15,000 cash to an NFPO, but only if the NFPO raises an equal amount from other contributors by a specific date; and (b) a donor promises to contribute $20,000 as soon as the NFPO establishes a day care center and starts admitting children. A bequest is also a conditional promise — a future and uncertain event — because the person making the will may change his or her mind prior to death.

Conditional promises to give are not recognized as receivables and as revenues (or gains) until the conditions on which they depend are substantially met. At that point, the conditional promise becomes unconditional and should be recognized as a receivable and a revenue. When an NFPO receives conditional promises to give, it must disclose the total amount promised and describe each group of promises having similar characteristics, such as amounts of promises conditioned on completing a building and raising matching gifts by a specified date.

If a donor were to actually transfer assets to an NFPO simultaneously with a conditional promise, the NFPO could not recognize revenues. Instead, the receipt of the assets would be accounted for as a refundable advance (deferred revenue) until the conditions were substantially met.

Notice how the accounting treatment of *conditions* differs from that regarding *restrictions*. Conditions may involve significant uncertainty, including events outside the organization's control. Recognizing assets before the uncertainty is sufficiently resolved may cause the information to be unreliable. Therefore, judgment must be exercised in determining when a condition is "substantially met." For example, suppose a donor promises on April 1, 2008, to give an NFPO $50,000, payable March 31, 2009, provided the entity raises a total of $50,000 from other donors by March 15, 2009. By December 31, 2008, when it closes its books, the NFPO has raised only $20,000 from other donors and the contribution rate has been declining. Has the condition been "substantially met" as of December 31, 2008? Probably not.

If a promise is received with ambiguous donor stipulations, the promise should be presumed to be conditional until the ambiguities are resolved. On the other hand, if a donor attaches a condition to a promise and the possibility that the condition will not be met is remote, the promise should be considered to be unconditional. (An example of the latter is an administrative requirement to file a routine annual report.)

Now, let's continue with the NFPO in our illustration. Suppose it received a matching grant from T. Elias on January 1, 2009. He promised to contribute up to $25,000, dollar for dollar, for each dollar obtained from other donors through December 31. 2009. The NFPO received $8,000 cash on January 31, 2009, from other donors. This is a conditional promise to give, and the conditions are met each time a dollar is collected from other donors. Therefore, the NFPO would make no entry on January 1, when it received the conditional promise, but would make the following journal entry on January 31, 2009:

Cash	8,000	
Contributions receivable	8,000	
Unrestricted support—contributions		16,000

To record receipt of $8,000 cash from various donors and related promise by T. Elias to match those donations.

CONTRIBUTED SERVICES

The rule on accounting for contributed services is more limited than the general rule for contributions. An NFPO must record the fair value of contributed services, provided the services received (1) create or enhance nonfinancial assets or (2) require specialized skills, *and* are provided by individuals who possess those skills, *and* would typically need to be purchased if the services were not donated. Services requiring "specialized skills" are those provided by "accountants, architects, carpenters, doctors, electricians, lawyers, nurses, plumbers, teachers, and other professionals and craftsmen."[12] When these criteria are met, a contribution revenue and an offsetting expense should be recorded for the fair value of the donated services.

The rule regarding contributed services is intended to be restrictive, so that contributed services that do not meet the enumerated criteria may not be recognized. For example, assume a lawyer donates 5 hours to a performing arts center. She spends 3 hours preparing contracts with artists and 2 hours selling tickets at the box office. The fair value of the time she spends drawing up contracts should be recognized as a contribution and as an expense. The 2 hours she spends selling tickets should not be recognized, however, because the work—even even though needed by the center—does does not require specialized skills.

An NFPO that receives contributed services must describe, in notes to its financial statements, the nature and extent of services received, programs or activities for which they were used, and the amount recognized as revenues. If practicable, the fair value of contributed services received but not recognized should also be disclosed. For example, a note to the financial statements of a performing arts center might say: "Donated service revenues and program expenses include the fair value of professional services contributed by performing artists. During the year, performing artists contributed services valued at $60,000 for the free summer concert series. Local residents donated about 200 hours serving as ushers, but those services do not meet the requirement for recognition in the financial statements."

To illustrate accounting for contributed services, assume a psychiatrist donated 25 hours to the NFPO in our continuing example. She spent 20 hours counseling drug

---

[12]Ibid., para. 9.

abuser patients and 5 hours serving food to them at lunchtime. The NFPO would have purchased both types of services had the psychiatrist not donated her time. She normally gets $150 an hour when counseling her patients. The NFPO would make the following journal entry:

Expenses—counseling services	3,000	
Unrestricted support—services		3,000
To record donation of professional services. (No entry is made for serving meals, because it requires no specialized skills.)		

CONTRIBUTIONS TO COLLECTIONS

A museum in dire financial straits receives a gift of a painting, having a fair value of $1 million, that it plans to display. The museum's trustees think it would be misleading to report the contribution as revenue and as an asset. They fear that potential donors, noting the revenue, might conclude that the museum does not need financial support for day-to-day operating expenses. Must the museum recognize the contribution as revenue and an asset?

The FASB resolved this controversial issue by giving NFPOs the option of not recognizing donated works of art, historical artifacts, rare books, and similar assets as revenues or gains and assets, provided the donated items are added to collections and the collections meet all of the following conditions:

(a) Are held for public exhibition, education, or research in furtherance of public service rather than financial gain,

(b) Are protected, kept unencumbered, cared for, and preserved, and

(c) Are subject to an organizational policy that requires the proceeds from sales of collection items to be used to acquire other items for collections.[13]

Thus, NFPOs, such as museums, art galleries, and similar entities that have collections meeting all three of these conditions, have a choice when new items are added. If they choose to capitalize their collections, they must recognize new items as revenues or gains. If they choose not to capitalize their collections, their revenues or gains cannot be recognized. Furthermore, they must follow a consistent policy. They cannot capitalize selected collections or items within a collection.

On the other hand, NFPOs must recognize contributions of works of art, historical treasures, and similar items that are not part of a collection as revenues or gains and assets when received. For example, suppose an NFPO holds a collection of art that meets all three criteria for triggering the choice either to capitalize or not capitalize the collection. The NFPO chooses not to capitalize. However, it receives a donation of a work of art that it intends to sell rather than add to its collection. In that situation, the NFPO must recognize the fair value of the donation as revenues or gains and assets when the work of art is received.

---

[13]Ibid., para. 11.

If an NFPO does not capitalize its collections, it must report the following information on the face of its statement of activities, separately from revenues, expenses, gains, and losses:

(b) Proceeds from sale of collection items as an increase in the appropriate class of net assets

(c) Proceeds from insurance recoveries of lost or destroyed collection items as an increase in the appropriate class of net assets.[14]

In addition, an NFPO that does not capitalize its collections must make various disclosures in the notes to the statements. It must describe its collections, "including their relative significance, and its accounting and stewardship policies for collections."[15] If items in the collection are deaccessed (removed from the collection) during the period, the NFPO must describe the items deaccessed during the period or disclose their fair value. In addition, these disclosures must be referred to in a line item shown on the face of the statement of financial position.

OTHER ACCOUNTING MATTERS

Investments: Valuation, Income, Gains, and Losses

As a general rule, investments held by NFPOs in equity securities that have readily determinable fair values, and all investments in debt securities, must be reported at fair value (market price) in the statement of financial position. Thus, although investments are initially recorded at cost (if purchased by the NFPO) and at fair value (if received by the NFPO as a contribution), the carrying amount of the investments will usually need to be adjusted so fair values are reported in the financial statements.

Because investments must be reported at fair value, unrealized gains and losses resulting from changes in market price need to be recognized in the statement of activities. If unrealized gains and losses were recognized in previous reporting periods on investments sold in the current period, the amount of gain or loss reported in the current period should exclude the amount previously reported in the statement of activities.

One way to account for investment gains and losses is to use a single account, called "Net unrealized and realized investment gains and losses," to report all investment gains and losses, whether realized or not. To illustrate, let's return to the illustration in the section, "Unrestricted Contributions," wherein the NFPO received 100 shares of a stock having a fair value of $40 a share. The investment was recorded at $4,000 when it was received. Assume the investment was worth $43 a share when the NFPO prepared its financial statements on December 31, 2008, and was subsequently sold for $42 a share on March 15, 2009. The NFPO would make the following journal entries:

Entry at December 31, 2008:

Investments	300	
Net unrealized and realized investment gains and losses		300
To record unrealized gain on investments.		

---

[14]Ibid., para. 26.
[15]Ibid., para. 27.

Entry at March 15, 2009 (time of sale):

Cash	4,200	
Net unrealized and realized investment gains and losses	100	
Investments		4,300
To record sale of investment and loss in investment value.		

The effect of these entries is to report a net gain of $200, resulting from a gain of $300 in 2008 and a loss of $100 in 2009. In an economic (opportunity cost) sense, there was indeed a gain of $300 in 2008, followed by a loss of $100 in 2009. For financial reporting purposes, however, some prefer to separate the realized gains and losses from unrealized gains and losses. This is done by maintaining the Investment account at the original carrying value and using an Investment valuation account to record changes in unrealized gains and losses. Although the net effect of the accounting is the same, it allows the financial reporting to be structured differently. Using the same illustration, the journal entries to accomplish this result would be as follows:

Entry at December 31, 2008:

Investment valuation account	300	
Change in net unrealized investment gains and losses		300
To record change in unrealized investment gains and losses.		

Entries at March 15, 2009 (time of sale):

Change in unrealized investment gains and losses	300	
Investment valuation account		
To reverse unrealized investment gain.		300
Cash	4,200	
Realized gains and losses on investments		200
Investments		4,000
To record realized gain on sale of investment.		

Investment income, such as interest and dividends, should be recognized as the income is earned. Such income should be reported on the statement of activities as increases in unrestricted net assets, unless use of the income is limited by donor-imposed restrictions. For example, a donor may stipulate that investment income from a permanently restricted contribution be used to support a particular program. In that case, the investment income would be reported as an increase in temporarily restricted net assets. As the income is used in support of the program, a reclassification from temporarily restricted to unrestricted net assets would be necessary.

Exchange Transaction Revenues

Many NFPOs obtain revenues from exchange transactions. As distinguished from contributions, an exchange is a transaction wherein each participant both receives and sacrifices value, as in the case of a purchase of services. NFPOs provide many types of social and health-related services by contracting with state and local governments. NFPOs may also provide day care for children, the elderly, or the infirm, charging fees for their services.

NFPOs account for exchange revenues and receivables in a manner similar to for-profit entities. Revenues from exchange transactions should be recognized using accrual accounting principles. Related estimated bad debts should be recognized as an expense, and accounts receivable should be reported net of an allowance for uncollectible amounts.

When an NFPO provides services to a government agency under a cost-reimbursement type contract, revenues should be recognized as costs are incurred. If the NFPO receives advance payments under the contract, it would report the advance as deferred revenue. Assume, for example, that the NFPO in our continuing illustration provides treatment planning, counseling, urine testing, and other services to parolees who have been substance abusers. The contract provides that the government agency will make monthly advance payments to the NFPO and that the NFPO will bill the agency at the end of the month for costs incurred, offsetting the advance against the costs. If the government agency provides an advance payment of $10,000 and the NFPO incurs costs of $12,000, it should record the advance and the related revenue as follows:

Cash	10,000	
Deferred contract revenue		10,000
To record advance payment on contract.		
Deferred contract revenue	10,000	
Accounts receivable	2,000	
Revenues from services		12,000
To record service revenues on government contract,		
and billing for costs incurred in excess of advance.		

Subscription and Membership Income

Subscription and membership dues are the primary means of support for the operating activities of many ONPOs. Membership dues are recognized as revenue in the period or periods during which they are used to provide services to the organization's members. Membership dues collected in advance of the service period are initially recorded as deferred revenue and then recognized as revenue during the period in which members receive services.

Nonrefundable initiation fees are generally reported as revenues in the period or periods in which the organization is entitled to receive them. Initiation fees are generally reported as unrestricted revenue. If, however, there is a clear understanding with the membership that the fees will be used to acquire or improve capital assets, they are reported as temporarily restricted.

Depreciation Expense

As a general rule, NFPOs must allocate the cost of their long-lived tangible assets, whether acquired in exchange transactions or through donation, over the estimated lives of the assets. Like other expenses, depreciation expense is reported as a decrease in unrestricted net assets. If the capital asset is temporarily restricted, because of donor-imposed restrictions on its use, reclassifications from temporarily restricted to unrestricted must be recorded. Disclosures regarding long-lived assets and depreciation methods are also required.

Separate rules, however, apply to works of art, historical treasures, and collections. The circumstances under which NFPOs are permitted not to capitalize these assets were discussed previously. But suppose NFPOs elect to capitalize works of art, historical treasures, and collections. If they capitalize them, must they depreciate them? The answer is "not necessarily." Consistent with practice regarding land used as a building site, depreciation need not be recognized on individual works of art or historical treasures "whose economic benefit or service potential is used up so slowly that their estimated useful lives are extraordinarily long."[16] A work of art or historical treasure is deemed to have this characteristic only if verifiable evidence indicates that the NFPO has the technological and financial capacity to preserve the asset.

Fund-Raising Expenses

NFPOs may undertake significant fund-raising activities to induce potential donors to contribute resources. Costs that relate solely to fund-raising are reported separately as fund-raising expenses. Sometimes, however, an NFPO may incur costs relating both to fund-raising and one of its programs. Joint costs may be incurred, for example, when an NFPO distributes a brochure containing information about the entity's programs as well as an appeal for funds.

When an NFPO incurs costs on a brochure (or similar activity) that has elements of both fund-raising and program, the appropriate accounting for the costs depends on three criteria—the brochure's *purpose,* the *audience* it is intended to reach, and its *contents.* As a general rule, if the purpose, audience, and content criteria are met, the joint costs should be allocated between the fund-raising and program functions. If *any* of the three criteria is not met, however, all costs of the joint activity should be reported as fund-raising.

The purpose and content criteria of the rule are met if the solicitation for support also calls on the audience to take specific action that will help accomplish the organization's mission. For example, if an organization's mission is to improve individuals' physical health, sending a brochure that urges the audience to stop smoking and that suggests specific methods that may be used to stop smoking is an activity that helps accomplish the mission.

The presumption is that the audience criterion is not met if the audience includes prior donors or was selected based on the likelihood of their contributing to the organization. This presumption can be overcome, however, if the audience was also selected for other reasons, such as a need to take the specific action called for in the brochure.

To illustrate, assume that one mission of the NFPO in our continuing illustration is to prevent teenage drug abuse. The NFPO mails a brochure to the parents of all high school students, describing methods for counseling children about drug abuse and showing how parents can detect signs of drug abuse. The mailing also appeals for contributions. In this illustration the nature of the action requested and the audience contacted are such that the three criteria are met. The audience was not limited to persons likely to contribute. The audience was called on to take actions related to the purposes of the NFPO, and the brochure described specific actions to be taken. Therefore, the cost of preparing and mailing the brochure should be allocated between fund-raising and program expenses, using appropriate cost accounting techniques.[17] If the cost of preparing and mailing the brochure was $8,000 and the NFPO estimates 75 percent of

---

[16]FASB *Statement No. 93,* "Recognition of Depreciation by Not-for-Profit Organizations," para 6.

[17]For extensive discussion of this subject, see *AICPA Audit and Accounting Guide—Not-for-Profit Organizations* (New York: AICPA, 2006), Sec. 13.41–13.55 and Appendix A, Sec. 37–64. The 2001 edition of the *Guide* also contains numerous illustrations of the application of the basic principles.

the costs should be allocated to program and 25 percent to fund-raising, it would make the following journal entry:

Program expenses—drug abuse prevention	6,000	
Fund-raising expenses	2,000	
Cash		8,000

To record payment of expenses related to drug abuse prevention brochure.

TELEMARKETING AS A SOURCE OF DONATIONS

The New York State attorney general estimated that Americans donated over $240 billion to charitable organizations in 2005. In a report titled *Pennies for Charity,* however, the attorney general noted that 440 charitable entities registered to solicit contributions in New York retained only 37.2 percent of the funds raised by telemarkers on their behalf in 2004. The rest "was paid to the fund raisers for fees and/ or used to cover the costs of conducting the campaign." The percentage retained by the charitable organizations was an improvement over the 4 previous years, when it ranged from 31 to 33 percent.

According the report, there are wide differences among individual campaigns in the ratio of funds received by the charity to the gross amount raised by the telemarketer. In 30 telemarketing campaigns, the charity received from 70 to 100 percent of the amount raised. But, in almost 250 campaigns, the charity received less than 30 percent of the amount raised, and in 23 of those campaigns, there was an apparent loss to the charity. The report noted that losses can occur if the fund-raising contract does not guarantee the charity a specific dollar amount or percentage of the gross receipts or does not hold the charity harmless when expenses or fees exceed the gross amount contributed by donors.

SOURCE: *Pennies for Charity,* New York State Department of Law, Charities Bureau, December 2005, at www.oag.state.ny.us/charities/charities.html

---

FUND ACCOUNTING IN NFPOs

Although not required to do so for financial reporting purposes, many NFPOs use fund accounting for internal record-keeping purposes. The way in which funds are used differs to some extent among the various types of NFPOs. Fund accounting can cause additional record-keeping complexities for several reasons:

- Using funds may cause the need to record resource transfers from one fund to another. At the same time, to comply with financial reporting requirements, there is also a need to record net asset reclassifications within the funds.
- The notion of "restricted" has traditionally been broader in the funds than it is in the current requirement for financial reporting. Therefore, when funds

are used in the accounting process, the NFPO may need to separate fund balances into more than one net asset classification when preparing financial statements.

NFPOs generally use the following types of funds:

1. *Unrestricted Current Fund—UCF* (also called Unrestricted Operating Fund, General Fund, or Current Unrestricted Fund). UCFs are used to account for resources over which governing boards have discretionary control. Therefore, the resources of the UCF are available not only for general operating purposes, but also for transfer to other funds. UCF resources come primarily from unrestricted donor contributions; exchange-type transactions with members, clients, students, customers and others; and investment income.

Governing boards may designate portions of the UCF resources for specific purposes, such as capital asset acquisition or research activities. When this happens, the resources either remain in the UCF or are transferred to some other fund, such as a Plant Fund. For financial reporting purposes, however, designations of resources made by the governing board are classified as unrestricted because they are not donor restricted. Depending on fund accounting policies adopted by the NFPO, capital assets may be accounted for in the UCF or in a separate Plant Fund.

2. *Restricted Current Funds—RCFs* (also called Restricted Operating, Specific-Purpose, or Current Restricted Funds). For financial reporting purposes, temporarily restricted net assets are those whose restrictions are donor imposed. When funds are used, however, RCFs may include not only contributions from donors that are restricted for specific operating purposes, but also resources received on contracts whose use is limited by external parties other than donors. Therefore, for financial reporting purposes, if the NFPO uses fund accounting, the fund balances need to be separated between net assets restricted by donors (classified as temporarily restricted) and net assets restricted as to use by contract or other limitation (classified as unrestricted).

3. *Endowment Funds—EFs*. Several types of endowments may be included in EFs. For financial reporting purposes, however, how they are classified depends on the nature of the endowment:

- Permanent or pure endowments are those wherein the donor specifies that the principal be invested and maintained in perpetuity and only the income earned may be used for operations. These endowments are classified as permanently restricted for financial reporting purposes.
- Term endowments are those wherein the resources originally contributed become available for use in operations after a specific time period or the occurrence of a specified event. They are classified as temporarily restricted net assets until the term expires or the specified event occurs.
- Quasi-endowment funds, often used by colleges and universities, are funds set aside by the governing board for lengthy but unspecified periods of time. Because they are not donor-restricted, they are classified as unrestricted.

4. *Plant Funds* (or Land, Building, and Equipment Funds or Plant Replacement and Expansion Funds). These funds take a variety of forms. Some contain only financial resources, to be used for plant acquisition. Some account not only for financial resources, but also for land, buildings, and equipment currently used in operations, together with associated depreciation and long-term debt. Colleges and universities sometimes divide their plant funds into four subfund account groups: Unexpended Plant Funds, Funds for Renewal and Replacement, Funds for Retirement of Indebtedness, and Net Investment in Plant. Depending on the nature of restrictions imposed by donors on the use of Plant Fund resources, the net assets may need to be separated among unrestricted, temporarily restricted, or permanently restricted for financial reporting purposes.

Some NFPOs also use other types of funds, such as Loan Funds, Annuity Funds, and Agency Funds. Colleges and universities, for example, commonly use Loan Funds to account for loans made to students. Loan Fund resources are classified as unrestricted if unrestricted resources were designated by governing boards for use as Loan Funds. Or, they may be classified as temporarily or permanently restricted depending on the nature of donor-imposed restrictions.

Interfund Transfers

Using fund accounting may result not only in reclassification transactions, but also interfund transfers. For example, an interfund transfer occurs when a governing board transfers resources from the UCF to a Plant Fund for capital acquisition purposes. To record the transfer, the fund that transfers resources debits a Transfer to . . . account and the fund that receives the resources credits a Transfer from . . . account.

Colleges and universities classify interfund transactions as either nonmandatory or mandatory. *Nonmandatory transfers* are those made at the discretion of the governing board for such purposes as additions to Loan Funds, Plant Funds, or Quasi-Endowment Funds. *Mandatory transfers* are those arising out of binding legal agreements, such as requirements to set aside amounts for debt service or to match gifts or grants.

ILLUSTRATION USING FUNDS

This section illustrates NFPO accounting and financial reporting when fund accounting is used. For purposes of this illustration, revenues and gains within each fund are classified as unrestricted, temporarily restricted, or permanently restricted to facilitate reporting by net asset classification.

Assume that Kezar Cares, a VHWO that offers counseling services to abused persons of all ages, was formed at the beginning of 2009. It received contributions from various sources and performed counseling services under a government contract. Kezar classifies expenses by object of account (salaries and other) within four major functions (counseling program, education program, administration, and fundraising).

Kezar uses fund accounting because it believes fund accounting is useful for internal accounting purposes. It prepares financial statements, however, in accordance with generally accepted accounting principles. Kezar uses a UCF, an RCF, an EF, and a Plant Fund (PF). Donor gifts with time or purpose restrictions are recorded in the RCF. Resources received and expenses incurred under the government contract are also recorded in the RCF, even though the net assets are not donor restricted, because Kezar believes it will improve controls over contract costs. To simplify its accounting, Kezar accounts for its capital assets in the UCF and uses the PF to account only for financial resources that will be used to acquire capital assets.

Kezar had the following transactions in 2009. For each transaction, the fund in which the transaction is recorded is shown in **bold type** to the left of the journal entry and the net asset classification, where applicable, is shown in **bold type** within the journal entry.

1. At the beginning of the year, Kezar received unrestricted promises of cash donations in the amount of $130,000. Kezar expected to collect $115,000 of that amount in 2009, and estimated that $15,000 would not be collected.

UCF	Contributions receivable	130,000	
	Allowance for uncollectible		
	contributions		15,000
	Unrestricted support—contributions		115,000
	To record unrestricted promises to give		
	cash.		

2. Kezar collected $118,000 of the unrestricted promises to donate cash and wrote off $12,000 as uncollectible. It reversed the remaining $3,000 allowance for uncollectible receivables. (Notice that the effect of the reversal is to increase unrestricted support.)

UCF	Cash	118,000	
	Allowance for uncollectible contributions	15,000	
	Contributions receivable		130,000
	Unrestricted support—contributions		3,000
	To record collection of pledges and write-off		
	of uncollectible contributions.		

3. Kezar received two donations that contained restrictions imposed by the donors: (a) cash in the amount of $20,000 that could be used only for research into counseling methodology, and (b) investments that had a fair value of $100,000. The donor making the contribution stipulated that the investment corpus had to be maintained in perpetuity, but the investment income could be used for any purpose the Kezar trustees designated.

RCF	Cash	20,000	
	Temporarily restricted support—		
	contributions		20,000
	To record temporarily restricted		
	contribution.		
EF	Investments	100,000	
	Permanently restricted support—		
	contributions		100,000
	To record permanently restricted		
	contribution.		

4. Kezar received the following donated services:

- A psychologist donated 20 hours of her time to Kezar's counseling program. Kezar would have paid $4,000 for these services if they had not been donated.
- A lawyer donated 10 hours to review a contract Kezar was negotiating with a government. He would normally have charged Kezar $2,000 for the services.

UCF	Expenses—counseling services (other)	4,000	
	Expenses—administration (other)	2,000	
	Unrestricted support—donated services		6,000
	To record receipt of donated services.		

5. Kezar held a book sale as part of its fund-raising program. It raised $12,000 cash, but it paid $2,000 of that amount for various expenses. Several high school students donated 16 hours of their time, selling refreshments and books at the event. Kezar would have paid them $5 an hour for these services had they not been donated.

UCF	Cash	10,000	
	Expenses—fund-raising (other)	2,000	
	Unrestricted gains—special events		12,000
	To record net gain from fund-raising event.		

[*Note:* The revenue from this event was recorded as a gain because it was considered as a peripheral or incidental transaction. The refreshment and book-selling services were not recognized as expenses and revenues because they did not require specialized skills.]

6. Kezar paid salaries of $14,000 and other expenses of $2,000 in performing research into counseling methodology, using the restricted gift in transaction 3.

RCF	**Temporarily restricted** net asset reclassifications out—satisfaction of program restrictions	16,000	
	Cash		16,000
	To record payment of research expenses and reclassification of temporarily restricted net assets due to satisfaction of restrictions.		

UCF	Expenses—counseling (salaries)	14,000	
	Expenses—counseling (other)	2,000	
	Unrestricted net asset reclassifications in— satisfaction of program restrictions		16,000
	To record reclassification to unrestricted net assets due to satisfaction of restrictions and payment of expenses.		

[*Note:* Expenses are recorded in the UCF because temporarily restricted net assets have been reclassified as unrestricted. The journal entries are organized somewhat differently from those shown on page 465 because of the use of fund accounting.]

7. Income of $4,000 was earned and received on the investments in the endowment fund.

UCF	Cash	4,000	
	Unrestricted revenue — investment income		4,000
	To record income, usable for any purpose, on endowment investments.		

8. Kezar's contract with a government agency for counseling services provides for quarterly advance payments. At the end of each quarter, Kezar is required to submit a statement of actual costs incurred. Based on the statement, Kezar is entitled to receive the difference between the advance and its actual costs. In accordance with these arrangements, Kezar received an advance payment of $27,000 on October 1 and incurred actual costs of $30,000 ($26,000 salaries and $4,000 other costs) between October 1 and December 31, 2009.

RCF	Cash	27,000	
	Deferred revenues		27,000
	To record advance payment received on contract.		

RCF	Expenses — counseling (salaries)	26,000	
	Expenses — counseling (other)	4,000	
	Cash		30,000
	To record expenses incurred on contract.		

RCF	Deferred revenues	27,000	
	Accounts receivable	3,000	
	Unrestricted revenue — contract		30,000
	To record revenues earned on contract.		

9. Kezar incurred the following expenses in undertaking its unrestricted programs. All the expenses were paid in cash, except for $4,000, which was accrued.

Function	Salaries	Other
Counseling	$30,000	$ 5,000
Education	20,000	
Administration	9,000	
Fund-raising	5,000	2,000
Total	$64,000	$ 7,000

UCF	Expenses — counseling (salaries)	30,000	
	Expenses — counseling (other)	5,000	
	Expenses — education (salaries)	20,000	
	Expenses — administration (salaries)	9,000	
	Expenses — fund-raising (salaries)	5,000	
	Expenses — fund-raising (other)	2,000	
	Cash		67,000
	Accrued expenses		4,000
	To record payment of expenses and accrual of unpaid expenses.		

10. Before preparing financial statements, Kezar ascertained that the investments held in its endowment fund had a fair value of $102,000.

EF	Investments	2,000	
	Permanently restricted net unrealized and realized investment gains/losses		2,000
	To record increase in fair value of investments.		

11. Kezar's trustees decided that Kezar Cares should construct a building rather than continue to rent space. Kezar approached several philanthropists to raise funds. Sara Dawn said she would contribute up to $50,000 to match other contributions as received, dollar for dollar. Larry Johns said he would contribute $25,000, provided Kezar raised a total of $100,000 from all other donors. As a result of its fund-raising program, Kezar raised $12,000 from other donors. Kezar then sent a letter to Ms. Dawn, advising her of the receipt of the $12,000.

PF	Cash	12,000	
	Temporarily restricted support—contributions		12,000
	To record receipt of contributions for building.		

PF	Contributions receivable	12,000	
	Temporarily restricted support— contributions		12,000
	To record promise to give from Sara Dawn.		

[*Note:* Sara Dawn's promise of $50,000 and Larry Johns' promise of $25,000 are conditional promises to give, which cannot be recognized as revenue until the conditions regarding the promises have been substantially met. In this situation, Ms. Dawn's condition is met each time other donors make cash contributions. Therefore, $12,000 should be recognized as contributions receivable and revenue based on her promise. Mr. Johns' promise, however, cannot be recognized because his condition has not been substantially met.]

12. Kezar received a gift of $5,000 cash. The donor stipulated that the gift may be used for any activities the trustees direct, except that it must be used to finance 2010 activities.

RCF	Cash	5,000	
	Temporarily restricted support—contributions		5,000
	To record receipt of gift for 2010 activities.		

[*Note:* At the beginning of 2010, the time restriction on this gift will expire and journal entries will be made to reclassify the net assets from temporarily restricted to unrestricted, because of satisfaction of time restrictions. The cash will also be transferred to the UCF. For fund accounting purposes, Kezar could record the receipt of cash initially in the UCF, but would still need to classify the net assets as temporarily restricted and reclassify the net assets as unrestricted at the beginning of 2010.]

Fund Trial Balances

Based on the foregoing journal entries, preclosing trial balances for each fund are shown in Tables 12-5, 12-6, 12-7, and 12-8, respectively.

TABLE 12-5   Trial Balance—UCF

Kezar Cares
Unrestricted Current Fund
Preclosing Trial Balance
December 31, 2009

Cash	$ 65,000	
Accrued expenses		$ 4,000
Unrestricted support—contributions		118,000
Unrestricted support—donated services		6,000
Unrestricted revenue—investment income		4,000
Unrestricted gains—special events		12,000
Unrestricted net asset reclassification in—		
satisfaction of program restrictions		16,000
Expenses—counseling (salaries)	44,000	
Expenses—counseling (other)	11,000	
Expenses—education (salaries)	20,000	
Expenses—administration (salaries)	9,000	
Expenses—administration (other)	2,000	
Expenses—fund-raising (salaries)	5,000	
Expenses—fund-raising (other)	4,000	
Totals	$160,000	$160,000

TABLE 12-6   Trial Balance—RCF

Kezar Cares
Restricted Current Fund
Preclosing Trial Balance
December 31, 2009

Cash	$ 6,000	
Accounts receivable	3,000	
Temporarily restricted support—contributions		$25,000
Unrestricted revenue—contract		30,000
Temporarily restricted net asset reclassifications		
out—satisfaction of program restrictions	16,000	
Expenses—counseling (salaries)	26,000	
Expenses—counseling (other)	4,000	
Totals	$55,000	$55,000

TABLE 12-7   Trial Balance—EF

Kezar Cares
Endowment Fund
Preclosing Trial Balance
December 31, 2009

Investments	$102,000	
Permanently restricted support—contributions		$100,000
Permanently restricted net unrealized and realized		
investment gains and losses		2,000
Totals	$102,000	$102,000

TABLE 12-8   Trial Balance—Plant Fund

Kezar Cares
Plant Fund
Preclosing Trial Balance
December 31, 2009

Cash	$12,000	
Contributions receivable	12,000	
Temporarily restricted support—contributions		$24,000
Totals	$24,000	$24,000

Preparing Financial Statements from Fund Trial Balances

The required financial statements can be prepared directly from the fund trial balances with the help of a multicolumn spreadsheet. Kezar's statement of activities, statement of financial position, and statement of functional expenses are shown in Tables 12-9, 12-10 and 12-11, respectively. Trace the information from the fund trial balances to the financial statements, noticing the following matters in particular:

1. All expenses are reported in the unrestricted column of the statement of activities, even though some expenses are recorded in the RCF.

TABLE 12-9   Statement of Financial Position

Kezar Cares
Statement of Financial Position
December 31, 2009

Assets:	
Cash	$ 83,000
Accounts receivable	3,000
Contributions receivable, restricted for building acquisition	12,000
Investments, restricted for endowment	102,000
Total assets	$200,000
Liabilities and net assets:	
Liabilities:	
Accrued expenses	$ 4,000
Net assets:	
Unrestricted	61,000
Temporarily restricted:	
For next year's general activities	5,000
For counseling research	4,000
For building acquisition	24,000
Permanently restricted	102,000
Total net assets	196,000
Total liabilities and net assets	$200,000

TABLE 12-10   Statement of Activities

Kezar Cares
Statement of Activities
Year Ended December 31, 2009

	Unrestricted	Temp. Restricted	Perm. Restricted	Total
Revenues, Gains, Other Support				
Contributions	$118,000	$49,000	$100,000	$267,000
Donated services	6,000			6,000
Contract revenue	30,000			30,000
Special events	12,000			12,000
Investment income	4,000			4,000
Unrealized and realized investment gains			2,000	2,000
Net assets released from restrictions—satisfaction of program restrictions	16,000	(16,000)		
Total revenues, gains, other support	186,000	33,000	102,000	321,000
Expenses				
Counseling	85,000			85,000
Education	20,000			20,000
Administration	11,000			11,000
Fund-raising	9,000			9,000
Total expenses	125,000			125,000
Change in net assets	61,000	33,000	102,000	196,000
Net assets, beginning of year	—	—	—	—
Net assets, end of year	$ 61,000	$33,000	$102,000	$196,000

TABLE 12-11   Statement of Functional Expenses

Kezar Cares
Statement of Functional Expenses
Year Ended December 31, 2009

Function	Total	Salaries	Other
Counseling	$ 85,000	$ 70,000	$15,000
Education	20,000	20,000	
Administration	11,000	9,000	2,000
Fund-raising	9,000	5,000	4,000
Total	$125,000	$104,000	$21,000

2. Required reporting by net asset classification is facilitated by (a) designating the appropriate net asset classification for revenues as the transactions are recorded and (b) recording net asset reclassifications within each fund as they occur.

3. Restrictions on the use of resources are reported on the face of the statement of financial position. (Financial reporting standards provide that such restrictions may be reported either on the face of the statements or in the notes to the statements.)

Review Questions

Q12-1   What characteristics distinguish NFPOs from for-profit organizations? What characteristics distinguish government organizations from NFPOs?

Q12-2   What body has the final authority for determining the accounting procedures for NFPOs?

Q12-3   Identify several organizations that would be classified as VHWOs. Identify several types of organizations that would be classified as ONPOs.

Q12-4   What financial statements must be prepared by all VHWOs and ONPOs? What additional financial statements must be prepared by VHWOs?

Q12-5   Identify and briefly describe the three classifications of net assets on the financial statements of NFPOs.

Q12-6   Illustrate the kinds of restrictions that donors may impose on the use of resources they contribute to NFPOs.

Q12-7   Discuss the differences between a donor-imposed restriction and a conditional promise to give. How is each reported in the financial statements?

Q12-8   How are pledges that are expected to be uncollectible reported in the financial statements of NFPOs?

Q12-9   Describe the circumstances under which contributed services must be recognized as revenues and expenses in the financial statements.

Q12-10 Under what circumstances must an NFPO recognize a contributed work of art as revenue? Under what circumstances does the organization have an option not to recognize it as revenue?

Q12-11 When is a reclassification made and what is its purpose?

Q12-12 Identify and briefly describe the major funds used by NFPOs.

Exercises

E12-1   (Identifying the appropriate net asset classification)
For each of the following transactions, identify the net asset classification (unrestricted, temporarily restricted, permanently restricted) that is affected in the NFPO's financial statements for the year ended December 31, 2008. (More than one net asset class may be affected in some transactions.)

1. Donor A gave an NFPO a $50,000 cash gift in June 2008. Donor A told the NFPO the gift could not be used until 2009.

2. Donor B gave an NFPO a $25,000 cash gift in July 2008, telling the NFPO the gift could be used at any time for any purpose consistent with its objectives.

3. In response to an NFPO's fund-raising campaign for a new building, a large number of individuals promised to make cash contributions totaling $2 million in 2008. The NFPO believes it will actually collect 80 percent of the promised cash.

4. Donor C gave an NFPO several investments having a fair value of $3 million in 2008. Donor C stipulated that the NFPO must hold the gift in perpetuity, but that it could use the income from the gift for any purpose the trustees considered appropriate. (Consider only the gift, not the income from the gift.)

5. An NFPO paid an architect $50,000 in 2008 to make preliminary designs for a new building, using the funds raised in transaction 3.

E12-2 (Recording journal entries for NFPOs)

Prepare journal entries to record the transactions in E12-1.

E12-3 (Identifying the appropriate net asset classification)

For each of the following transactions, identify the net asset classification (un-restricted, temporarily restricted, permanently restricted) that is affected in the NFPO's financial statements for the year ended December 31, 2009. (More than one net asset class may be affected in some transactions.)

1. Donor A had given the NFPO a cash gift of $50,000 in June 2008, telling the NFPO the gift could not be used until 2009. (Identify the net asset classification(s) in the journal entry made at the start of 2009.)

2. Howard Gorman, a professional contractor, volunteered his services to ARTS, an NFPO. He spent 12 hours designing and building sets for an ARTS performance and 8 hours manning ARTS's ticket booth. The NFPO normally pays $50 an hour for set design and construction and $5 an hour for selling tickets

3. Donor B sent a letter to an NFPO, saying she would donate $20,000 cash to the NFPO, provided the NFPO raised an equal amount of cash from other donors.

4. Donor C gave an NFPO a $50,000 cash gift, stipulating that the gift could be used only to undertake a specific research project.

5. By December 31, 2009, the fair value of investments held in perpetuity by an NFPO increased by $30,000.

E12-4 (Recording journal entries for NFPOs)

Prepare journal entries to record the transactions in E12-3.

E12-5 (Investment transactions and events)

An NFPO had the following transactions and events:

1. On October 12, 2008, an NFPO received a donation of Microsoft stock that had a fair value of $75,000 at the time of the donation. The donor told the NFPO that the stock may be sold and used only to finance a particular research project.

2. On December 31, 2008, when the NFPO closed its books, the stock had a fair value of $73,500.

3. On February 15, 2009, the NFPO sold the stock for $77,000.

4. On March 15, 2009, the NFPO spent the entire $77,000 on the research project for which the donor made the gift.

Required: Prepare journal entries to record these transactions and events, based on the assumption that the NFPO uses a single account to record all un-realized and realized investment gains and losses. Then, prepare journal entries for events 2 and 3, based on the assumption that the NFPO separates unreal-ized from realized investment gains and losses.

E12-6 (True or False)

State whether each of these sentences is true or false:

1. FASB standards require that NFPO financial statements report on activi-ties by major fund.

2. If an NFPO reports temporarily restricted resources, it is likely the restric-tions could have been placed either by donors or by the NFPO's board of directors.

3. When an NFPO spends temporarily restricted resources on the project for which a donor made the contribution, the expenses must be reported in the unrestricted column of the statement of activities.
4. Members of an NFPO donated their time to construct a garage for the NFPO's automobile. The NFPO would have paid $8,000 for the labor had it not been donated. The garage will last 20 years. The NFPO should report the contributed labor as an asset and as contribution revenue.
5. Cash donated specifically for constructing a building that will have an estimated life of 40 years should be reported as permanently restricted.
6. Depending on the circumstances, a not-for-profit museum has the option to either record or not record an asset when it receives a donation of a valuable art work.
7. From the perspective of NFPO accounting, there is no difference between a donor-imposed restriction and a donor-imposed condition.
8. An NFPO held a fund-raising campaign at year end. It received pledges of $45,000, but it did not receive any cash until the following year. The NFPO should not report any revenue in the year it conducted its fund-raising campaign, but it should report the amount of the pledges in a note to the financial statements.

E12-7 (Multiple choice)

1. How should expenses be reported in an NFPO's statement of activities?
   a. As decreases in the net asset classification where the revenues were reported
   b. As decreases of permanently restricted net assets
   c. As decreases of temporarily restricted net assets
   d. As decreases of unrestricted net assets
2. Which of the following is a general rule established by the Financial Accounting Standards Board regarding contributions received in the form of investments by an NFPO?
   a. They must be recorded either in a restricted fund or in an unrestricted fund.
   b. They must be reported either as restricted support or unrestricted support.
   c. They must be recorded at the amount paid by the donor for the investment.
   d. They must be reported in an endowment fund.
3. Which of the following financial statements is required for VHWOs but not for ONPOs?
   a. Statement of financial position
   b. Statement of activities
   c. Statement of functional expenses
   d. Statement of cash flows
4. If a donor provides that interest earned on an endowment must be used to finance a particular program, how should the interest revenue be classified?
   a. As unrestricted
   b. As temporarily restricted
   c. As permanently restricted
   d. As quasi-endowment income

5. How should land and buildings owned by a VHWO be classified in its financial statements?
   a. As unrestricted.
   b. As temporarily restricted.
   c. As permanently restricted.
   d. They need not be reported.

6. Which of the following net asset classifications may have one or more items of donor support?
   a. Unrestricted net assets
   b. Temporarily restricted net assets
   c. Permanently restricted net assets
   d. All of the above

7. The Prevent Cancer Organization incurred several expenses during 2008. Which of the following would not be classified as program support?
   a. Instruction for cancer prevention to the general public
   b. Pamphlets mailed to the general public regarding the "danger signals of cancer"
   c. Postage for announcements of the 2008 Kickoff Dinner
   d. Salaries of personnel who perform cancer research

8. As a result of its annual fund-raising program, an NFPO receives pledges in the amount of $300,000 during December 2008, the last month of its reporting period. Based on its previous history regarding pledges, the NFPO believes that about $250,000 will be collected in the first 60 days of 2009, some will trickle in during the rest of 2009, and 10 percent will not be collected at all. How much should the NFPO report as net contributions receivable on its 2008 financial statements?
   a. $0
   b. $250,000
   c. $270,000
   d. $300,000

9. Mae Wood, a certified public accountant, donated 60 hours of her time to Food Kitchen, an NFPO that serves food to needy people. She spent 20 hours auditing Food Kitchen's books and 40 hours serving food to the needy. Ms. Wood normally earns $200 an hour as a CPA, and Food Kitchen normally pays $5 an hour to students when it can't find volunteers to serve the needy. How much should Food Kitchen report as contribution revenue for Ms. Wood's services?
   a. $0
   b. $200
   c. $4,000
   d. $4,200

E12-8 (Statement of activities for a country club)
The following information was taken from the records of the Land's End Country Club. All account balances are as of the end of the accounting year, June 30, 2009.

Dues	631,000
Locker room rentals to members	20,000
Expenses associated with the golf course	255,000
Expenses associated with the tennis courts	105,000
Initiation fees	78,000
Administration expenses	65,000
Fees: Golf course	87,000
Swimming pool	44,000
Tennis courts	12,000
Expenses associated with the swimming pool	31,000
Assessments against members restricted for capital improvements	200,000
Net assets—6/30/08 (unrestricted)	97,000

Required: Prepare a statement of activities for the Land's End Country Club.

E12-9 (Journal entries for an NFPO)

The Good Health Society, a VHWO, was founded in 2008. This organization conducts two types of programs: education and testing. It maintains three funds: Unrestricted Current, Restricted Current, and Buildings and Equipment. During 2008, the following events took place:

1. Pledges amounting to $200,000 were received. Of this amount, $50,000 was restricted for a special education research program. All of the restricted pledges and $140,000 of the unrestricted pledges are expected to be collected.
2. Les Miller made a $1,000 cash contribution to be used as the directors of the society see fit. However, Mr. Miller stipulated that it not be used until 2009.
3. The restricted pledges were all collected. With respect to the unrestricted pledges, $120,000 was collected and $5,000 was written off.
4. The society received a $10,000 allocation from the United Fund. Of this amount, $2,000 was deducted for fund-raising costs.
5. The society invested $10,000 of unrestricted funds in government securities. Earnings on these resources amounted to $500 in 2008.
6. During the year, $40,000 of restricted funds was spent on the special research program.
7. A grant of $50,000 was made to the society by the Allen Company. The grant was to be used to purchase equipment.
8. Equipment was purchased for 50,000, using resources donated by the Allen Company. (Assume all capital assets are accounted for in the UCF.)
9. The following services were donated to the society, all of which should be recorded:
   a. Free accounting work by an accounting firm—$500
   b. Free tests by a national testing laboratory—$1,000
   c. The services, at no cost, of several teachers from a junior college, who conducted physical fitness and wellness programs—$2,000
10. Salaries, wages, and other operating expenses for 2008 amounted to $135,000. They were paid with unrestricted monies and were allocated as follows:

Administration	$20,000
Education	90,000
Testing	15,000
Fund-raising	10,000

11. Depreciation amounted to $10,000 on the equipment. It was allocated as follows:

Education	$3,000
Testing	7,000

12. Revenues from membership dues amounted to $18,000 in 2008.

Required: Prepare journal entries for the preceding transactions by fund, identifying increases and decreases by net asset classification as appropriate.

E12-10 (Journal entries using classifications of net assets)

The Mon Elisa Museum of Fine Arts is an NFPO that derives most of its resources from wealthy patrons. Mon Elisa has recently changed its accounting system to eliminate the use of separate funds. All journal entries are made so as to indicate which of the three net asset classifications are affected. The following transactions and events occurred during 2008.

1. Cash of $40,000 was received from donors, who stated that it may be used for any purpose desired by the museum.

2. A donor gave the museum $10,000, stipulating that the money may be used only to acquire fine examples of Weller Dickensware pottery.

3. Elias Gotbucks sent Mon Elisa a letter, stating he would donate $15,000 to the museum to purchase examples of Sara Dawn's quilt work, provided the museum conducted a special campaign that raised at least $25,000 to buy additional examples.

4. The museum spent $4,000 to acquire a fine Weller Dickensware vase. (Assume that Mon Elisa capitalizes its art collections.)

5. Mon Elisa contacted wealthy patrons to raise funds to buy Sara Dawn's quilt work. It obtained $30,000 in pledges, all likely to be collected. Mon Elisa then wrote to Elias Gotbucks, advising him it had raised $30,000.

6. Attorney Ted Floot donated his services to the museum. He spent 4 hours on museum legal matters and 3 hours as a salesperson in the museum shop. Mr. Floot bills $250 an hour when he works as an attorney.

7. A wealthy patron donated "The Portrait of Samantha," which had a fair value of $6,000, to the museum. The museum accepted the gift with the understanding that it would be sold at auction and the proceeds used for any purpose the museum wished.

Required: Prepare journal entries for these transactions and events and identify the affected classification of net assets.

Problems

P12-1 (Journal entries for contributions to a VHWO)

Food Services, Inc. (FSI), a VHWO, provides meals for the needy in its own facility. It also distributes food to other facilities that serve the needy and serves food at a senior citizens center under contract with the County Department of the Aging. FSI maintains a warehouse to store donated food and has cooking and serving facilities. It does not use fund accounting. Prepare journal entries to record the following transactions and events during calendar year 2008.

1. On January 10, 2008, in response to its annual fund-raising drive to finance its day-to-day operations, FSI received $152,000 of cash donations and $400,000 of promises to donate cash. Based on experience, FSI expected to collect 80 percent of the promises to donate cash, all of which was to be used to finance its activities during 2008.

2. During the year, FSI received cash of $310,000 from the promises to give (see transaction 1) and wrote off the remaining receivables as uncollectible.

3. FSI determined that it needed to add storage facilities at an estimated cost of $300,000 to meet its expanding operations. Dr. Ted Golfit, noted research engineer, advised FSI that he would contribute $150,000, provided FSI raised an equal amount from other sources.

4. Attorneys A. and E. Gorman provided free legal services to FSI during the year. FSI would have purchased the services for $10,000 if they had not been donated.

5. FSI raised $165,000 cash as a result of its fund-raising campaign to add to its storage facilities (see transaction 3). FSI contacted Dr. Golfit, who gave FSI a check for $150,000.

6. FSI constructed additional storage facilities at a cost of $318,000. It paid for the facility by using $315,000 it had raised for that purpose (see transaction 5) and by using $3,000 of its unrestricted available cash.

7. FSI's contract with the County Department of the Aging called for the county to make quarterly advance payments to FSI based on an estimate. The contract also provided for FSI to report to the county after the end of each quarter, showing actual costs to provide food to the senior citizens during the quarter, and billing for any difference between actual costs and the estimate. On January 5, 2008, FSI received a $20,000 advance payment from the county.

8. Between January and March 2008, FSI spent $23,000 cash providing services on its contract with the county (see transaction 7). On April 4, 2008, FSI sent an invoice to the county, showing it had spent $23,000 on the program, deducting the $20,000 advance, and requesting an additional $3,000.

9. During 2008, FSI received donations of 1.2 million pounds of food from supermarkets, bakeries, and food wholesalers. FSI valued the food at $1.50 per pound, based on a study undertaken by a national NFPO. All donated food is initially recorded in inventory.

10. Local residents donated 1,000 hours of their time serving food at FSI's facility. If the residents had not donated their time, FSI would have paid $5.50 an hour for the services.

P12-2 (Journal entries for a VHWO, using funds)

Eye Institute (EI) uses a UCF, an RCF, and a PF to account for its activities. The RCF is used to record contributions for specific research projects and for contributions with time restrictions. The PF is used only to accumulate financial resources, including donations restricted to capital acquisition and resources transferred from the UCF for capital acquisition purposes. As soon as PF financial resources are expended to acquire capital assets, the assets are transferred to the UCF. All expenses incurred using RCF resources are reclassified to the UCF to facilitate financial reporting by net asset classification. Prepare journal entries to record the following calendar year 2008 transactions.

1. EI received the following contributions:
   a. Cash of $2.7 million, to be used for any purpose the trustees chose.
   b. Pledges of $300,000, to be used to finance activities during 2008. Based on experience, EI estimated it would collect 90 percent of the pledged amounts.
   c. Pledges of $650,000, which were restricted by donors to use on Research Program B. EI believed it would collect all those pledges.
2. The United Fund gave EI a cash allocation of $1.5 million, but withheld $100,000 for EI's share of fund-raising costs.
3. EI had the following expenses from its unrestricted resources, all paid in cash. (Record the expenses to show both major function and object of account.)

	Program A	Management	Fund Raising
Salaries, benefits	$400,000	$ 85,000	$60,000
Supplies and travel	40,000	10,000	30,000
Occupancy expense	120,000	6,000	5,000
Total	$560,000	$101,000	$95,000

4. EI trustees received a cash donation of $200,000, the donor stipulating that the gift must be used solely for the purpose of acquiring land and a building. The trustees also transferred $300,000 from its UCF to the PF, for future capital acquisition purposes.
5. EI acquired land and a building, using resources in its PF for that purpose. The land was valued at $75,000 and the building was valued at $350,000. All of the donor's cash (see transaction 4) was used in acquiring these assets.
6. EI collected $600,000 cash on the pledges received in transaction 1.c. It used $430,000 of the cash to pay salaries and benefits on Research Program B.

P12-3 (Journal entries for an NFPO)

Oliver's Place is a not-for-profit entity that cares for dogs until they are adopted. It uses a UCF, an RCF, and an EF. It charges expenses to the care of animals program, special programs, and administrative expenses. Following are some of its transactions for 2008:

1. During the year, it received unrestricted pledges of $100,000. It estimated that 95 percent of the pledges would be collected in cash.
2. Oliver's Place received the following gifts from various donors:
   a. Donor A made a gift of common stock that had a fair market value of $20,000. Donor A stated that the gift may be used for any purpose.
   b. Donor B made a cash gift of $5,000, stipulating that it may be used only for a new program to take calm dogs to visit elderly people.
   c. Donor C made a gift of common stock that had a fair market value of $50,000. Donor C stipulated that the gift, and any gains on the sale of the stock, shall be maintained in perpetuity, and that the dividends received on the investment may be used for any purpose.

3. Volunteers contributed their time to Oliver's Place, as follows:
   a. Dr. D, a veterinarian, spent 10 days caring for medical needs of the dogs. Those services would normally cost Oliver's Place $10,000.
   b. Dr. E, a kidney surgeon, spent 12 days feeding the dogs, keeping them occupied, and placing them for adoption. He earns $2,000 a day as a surgeon.
4. Oliver's Place received dividends of $400 on the common stock donated by Donor A and $600 on the common stock donated by Donor C.
5. At year end, the stock donated by Donor A had a fair value of $22,000 and the stock donated by Donor C had a fair value of $47,000.
6. During the year, Oliver's Place collected $80,000 in cash on the pledges made in transaction 1.
7. Oliver's Place spent $3,000 on the special program designed to take calm dogs to visit elderly people.
8. Oliver's Place paid the following expenses:

Care of animals	$40,000
Administrative expenses	30,000

9. Cash gifts of $12,000 were received from various donors who stipulated that the resources must be used in 2009.

Required: Prepare the journal entries needed to record these transactions; also, indicate the fund used for each entry. (You can check the accuracy of your work by preparing a trial balance and comparing it with the trial balances in P12-4.)

P12-4 (Preparation of financial statements for an NFPO)
Following are the preclosing fund trial balances as of December 31, 2008, for Oliver's Place, an NFPO. (The trial balances are based on the transactions contained in P12-3.)

Oliver's Place
Preclosing Trial Balances
December 31, 2008
Unrestricted Current Fund

	Debit	Credit
Cash	$ 11,000	
Contributions receivable	20,000	
Investments	22,000	
Allowance for uncollectible contributions		$ 5,000
Unrestricted support—contributions		115,000
Unrestricted support—donated services		10,000
Unrestricted revenue—investment income		1,000
Unrestricted gains—unrealized investment gains		2,000
Unrestricted asset reclassifications in—satisfaction of program restrictions		3,000
Care of animals expense	50,000	
Special programs expense	3,000	
Administrative expenses	30,000	
	$136,000	$136,000

Restricted Current Fund

	Debit	Credit
Cash	$14,000	
Temporarily restricted support—contributions		$17,000
Temporarily restricted asset reclassifications out— satisfaction of program restrictions	3,000	
	$17,000	$17,000

Endowment Fund

	Debit	Credit
Investments	$47,000	
Permanently restricted support—contributions		$50,000
Permanently restricted losses—unrealized investment losses	3,000	
	$50,000	$50,000

Required: 1. Prepare a statement of activities for the year ended December 31, 2008.

2. Prepare a statement of financial position as of December 31, 2008.

P12-5 (Journal entries for a VHWO)

Youth Services Agency (YSA) is a VHWO that provides counseling and recreation programs for youthful offenders. YSA's programs are financed through a contract with the county in which it is located and through contributions from local citizens. Its contract with the county provides for reimbursement of allowable costs based on monthly billings to the county. YSA does not use fund accounting, but it does identify all revenues by net asset class. The following transactions occurred during 2008:

1. YSA received pledges of gifts in the amount of $20,000, to be used as the YSA trustees consider appropriate. Based on experience, YSA's CEO believed that 90 percent of the pledges would be collected.
2. YSA collected $17,000 cash on the pledges received in transaction 1. It also wrote off $1,500 of the pledges as uncollectible.
3. YSA received a gift of 50 shares of General Electric stock that had a fair value of $1,300 at the time of the gift. The donor sent the CEO a letter with the gift, saying that proceeds of the stock should be used only to purchase athletic equipment for the basketball team.
4. YSA realized $1,400 in cash from the sale of the stock received in transaction 3.
5. YSA paid $800 cash for athletic equipment, using the proceeds received in transaction 4. The expense was charged to Recreation programs.
6. YSA spent $12,000 cash on the following:

Counseling programs	$ 8,000
Recreation programs	3,000
Administration expense	1,000
Total	$12,000

7. YSA billed the county $6,500 for costs incurred under its contract.

Required: Prepare journal entries to record these transactions. Identify all revenues within the journal entries as unrestricted, temporarily restricted, or permanently restricted.

P12-6 (Preparation of financial statements for a VHWO)

Following are the preclosing trial balances of Marilyn Township Senior Citizens Center at December 31, 2008.

	Unrestricted		Temporarily Restricted	
	Debit	Credit	Debit	Credit
Cash	$ 3,000		$1,600	
Pledges receivable	1,000		500	
Allowance for uncollectible pledges		$ 300		
Investments	3,200			
Accrued interest receivable	100			
Net assets, January 1, 2008		6,700		$2,000
Contributions		1,000		500
Membership dues		1,500		
Program service fees		3,000		
Grant from county		2,500		
Grant from state		2,500		
Unrealized and realized gains on investments		200		
Investment income		100		
Luncheon program expenses	7,200			
Recreation program expenses	3,400			
Administration expenses	300			
Temporarily restricted asset reclassifications out—satisfaction of program restrictions			400	
Unrestricted asset reclassifications in—satisfaction of program restrictions		400		
	$18,200	$18,200	$2,500	$2,500

Required: Prepare a statement of financial position and a statement of activities at and for the year ended December 31, 2008.

P12-7 (Discussion problems for specific not-for-profit transactions)

For each of the following transactions, discuss the issues and state the appropriate accounting solution:

1. The Society to Eliminate Hunger spent $8,000 to prepare and mail a two-page brochure to potential contributors. The brochure contained general information about the society, described its accomplishments, pointed out that a contribution of $25 would provide 25 dinners, and urged recipients to contribute. The trustees want the accountant to charge the cost of preparing and mailing the brochures to the Distribution of Food Program.

The executive director thinks the expenses should be charged to fund-raising expenses.

2. Professional lawyers and accountants volunteered to perform all the legal and audit services required by Youth Services, an NFPO. The trustees of the NFPO take great pride in their low overhead rate. They tell the accountant: "We didn't pay for these services, so there's really no point in recording any expenses for them."

3. Sam Rich made annual contributions of $100,000 for the past 3 years to Cardinal House, a not-for-profit drug treatment center. On December 20, 2008, Cardinal House received a letter from Sam, promising to contribute $500,000 if the organization would change the name of the entity to Rich House. The trustees debated the name change until it was time to issue the annual financial report but could not decide whether to make the change. They told the accountant: "We'd really like to report Sam's pledge as a receivable, because it will cause other donors to contribute. Besides, Sam has been a major supporter in the past and will probably contribute even if we don't change the name. We think we ought to recognize Sam's offer of $500,000 as a revenue and a receivable."

4. A wealthy individual donated a valuable work of art to a museum. The museum intends to keep the work, protect it from harm and deterioration, and hang it in a location so all can see it. The accountant sees no need either to recognize the asset or to depreciate it. However, one of the newer trustees, the chief executive of a large business entity, said, "In our company, we depreciate everything. And we know that, ultimately, everything turns to dust. So, why don't we recognize the work of art as an asset and depreciate it?"

5. On March 1, 2008, Dr. Rebecca offered to contribute $15,000, which was 50 percent of the estimated cost of a special program to be undertaken by the Shelley Center, an NFPO. Dr. Rebecca stated, however, that she would make the contribution only if the Center would raise the rest of the needed funds from other donors during the next 12 months. By December 31, 2008, the Center had raised $6,000 of the additional amount needed. The Center expected to mount a special campaign to obtain the other $9,000 and thought it would be successful. Should the Center recognize Dr. Rebecca's promise as a revenue for the year ended December 31, 2008?

P12-8 (Journal entries for a not-for-profit college)

Manny Saxe College is a small, not-for-profit college known for its excellence in teaching accounting. The college uses fund accounting and has an Unrestricted Current Fund, a Restricted Current Fund, a Plant Fund, and an Endowment Fund. It charges its expenses to Instruction and research, Student services, Plant operations, and Auxiliary enterprises. It had the following transactions and events during 2008:

1. Revenues from student tuition and fees were $2.5 million, all of which were collected.

2. Revenues from auxiliary enterprises were $400,000 in cash.

3. Salaries and wages, all of which were paid, were $1.8 million, chargeable as follows:

Instruction and research	$1,200,000
Student services	200,000
Plant operations	250,000
Auxiliary enterprises	150,000

4. Materials and supplies costing $800,000 were purchased on account and placed in inventory during the year.
5. Materials and supplies used during the year were $700,000, chargeable as follows:

Instruction and research	$300,000
Student services	50,000
Plant operations	150,000
Auxiliary enterprises	200,000

6. A cash transfer of $100,000 was made from the Unrestricted Current Fund to the Plant Fund to start the design work on a new student services building.
7. The college received a cash gift of $20,000 from K. Schermann to finance a 3-year research project on governmental service efforts and accomplishments reporting.
8. The college paid B. Chaney $7,000 to do research on the project in transaction 7.
9. P. Defliese donated $1 million in equity securities to the college, stipulating that the corpus and all gains and losses on the sale of the securities remain intact in perpetuity. He also stipulated that income on the investments be used solely to finance a chair in governmental accounting.
10. At year end, the securities donated by Mr. Defliese in transaction 9 had a fair value of $1,030,000. Income earned on the investments during the year was $45,000.
11. Antonio Harmer sent a letter to the college at the end of the year, promising to contribute $25,000 to equip the new student services building if the college raised an equal amount from other contributors. The college planned to write to the alumni to seek additional funds.

Required: Prepare the journal entries necessary to record these transactions, identifying the net asset classification as appropriate. Show which fund is used to record each transaction.

Appendix 12A

NOT-FOR-PROFIT COLLEGES AND UNIVERSITIES

Not-for-profit colleges and universities are required to follow the same accounting standards used by other not-for-profit organizations, as discussed in this chapter. They also prepare financial statements using the unrestricted, temporarily restricted, and permanently restricted net asset classifications. Those that use fund accounting also use the fund types previously discussed.

The major functional expense categories used by colleges and universities in financial reporting are instruction, research, public service, academic support, student services, auxiliary enterprises, and institutional support. Instruction, research, and public service are considered to be the primary programs, while academic support, student services, and auxiliary enterprises support the primary programs. Auxiliary enterprises include the operation of bookstores, residence halls, dining services, and intercollegiate athletics. Institutional support includes management and general and fund-raising expenses. Costs of operating and maintaining the physical plant, including depreciation, are generally allocated to the other functions.

Financial Statements of Not-for-Profit Colleges and Universities

Not-for-profit colleges and universities, like other not-for-profit organizations, are required to prepare a statement of financial position, a statement of activities, and a cash flow statement. Tables 12A-1 and 12A-2 illustrate not-for-profit college and university statements of financial position and statements of activities, using the fiscal year 2006 financial statements of Fordham University. Located in the City of New York,

Fordham University serves about 8,500 undergraduate students and 7,100 graduate and professional students.

Notice that Fordham University prepares its statement of activities in "pancake" format, separating the changes in unrestricted net assets from the changes in temporarily restricted and permanently restricted net assets. The FASB permits this type of display as an alternative to a columnar format. The $7,265,764 of "Net assets released from restrictions," reported among the operating revenues for fiscal year 2006, is the same as the decrease shown for that caption in the temporarily restricted net asset section.

Notice also that Fordham University's statement of activities for unrestricted net assets distinguishes between "net operating revenue" and "nonoperating activities." Generally, captions such as "net operating revenue" and "excess of operating revenues over expenses" are used to provide the reader with a measure of operating results from basic operations. The FASB explored the use of such intermediate captions in deliberations leading to FASB *Statement No. 117*, but it decided not to prescribe specific operating measures, choosing instead to let them evolve for the various types of not-for-profit organizations.

Notes to the Financial Statements

Notes are an integral part of financial statements and you need to read them carefully to understand the information content of the statements. Space limitations preclude presentation of all the notes to Fordham University's statements. Several of them are discussed here, however, to further illustrate

497

TABLE 12A-1   Statement of Financial Position—Not-for-Profit University

Fordham University
Statements of Financial Position
As of June 30, 2006 and 2005

	2006	2005
Assets		
Cash and cash equivalents	$ 724,148	$ 359,643
Accounts and grants receivable		
Students	14,029,568	12,515,956
Government	4,601,818	4,893,131
Other	10,887,490	2,609,398
Contributions receivable (see text)	33,903,772	34,651,744
Prepaid expenses and other assets	9,614,270	3,218,652
Investments	402,998,599	351,508,091
Student loans receivable	14,015,311	13,538,713
Deposits with bond trustees	5,194,298	26,234,095
Bond issuance costs	4,607,792	4,516,510
Investment in plant assets, net	448,080,111	398,676,666
Total assets	$948,657,177	$852,722,599
Liabilities and net assets		
Liabilities		
Accounts payable and accrued expenses	$ 53,656,755	$ 41,207,357
Loans payable	—	—
Deferred revenues and deposits	17,685,220	16,896,551
Amounts held for others	2,351,852	2,723,917
U.S. Government refundable advances	4,980,424	4,843,930
Postretirement benefits other than pensions	33,261,000	25,826,000
Long-term debt	203,797,895	200,574,689
Total liabilities	315,733,146	292,072,444
Commitments and contingent liabilities		
Net assets		
Unrestricted	335,406,950	297,230,111
Temporarily restricted	151,530,325	134,870,310
Permanently restricted	145,986,756	128,549,734
Total net assets	632,924,031	560,650,155
Total liabilities and net assets	$948,657,177	$852,722,599

Note: The notes accompanying these statements and the related note references made in the captions are not reproduced in this text. However, captions labeled "see text" are discussed in this appendix.

Source (for Tables 12A-1 and 12A-2): Fordham University 2006 Financial Statements.

TABLE 12A-2   Statement of Activities—Not-for-Profit University

Fordham University
Statements of Activities
For the Years Ended June 30, 2006 and 2005

	2006	*2005*
Operating revenues		
Tuition and fees, net	$ 259,221,878	$246,910,451
Government grants	18,920,926	15,678,158
Investment return (see text)	11,118,486	9,909,548
Contributions and private grants	21,092,203	17,265,843
Auxiliary enterprises, net	47,997,883	45,768,953
Other revenues	18,448,692	7,635,051
Net assets released from restrictions	7,265,764	7,056,011
Total operating revenues	384,065,832	350,224,015
Operating expenses		
Program services		
Instruction	140,221,832	130,072,271
Research	5,325,381	4,761,761
Public service	7,079,306	7,799,070
Academic support	51,817,372	48,048,323
Student services	42,806,231	41,896,676
Auxiliary enterprises	49,649,601	45,985,012
Total program services	296,899,723	278,563,113
Supporting services—institutional support	50,875,139	46,084,190
Total operating expenses	347,774,862	324,647,303
Net operating revenue	36,290,970	25,576,712
Nonoperating activities		
Investment return (see text)	10,343,270	8,439,375
Effect of refunding and defeasance of debt	(7,358,065)	—
Gain on interest rate swap	6,105,379	—
Marymount College closing expenses	(4,014,677)	—
Increase in net assets before cumulative effect of change in accounting principle	41,366,877	34,016,087
Cumulative effect of change in accounting principle	(3,190,038)	—
Increase in unrestricted net assets	38,176,839	34,016,087
Changes in temporarily restricted net assets		
Contributions and private grants	$ 9,777,103	$ 2,855,428
Investment return (see text)	15,296,239	11,386,331
Net assets released from restrictions	(7,265,764)	(7,056,011)
Change in provision on contributions receivable	(1,147,563)	(444,592)
Increase in temporarily restricted net assets	16,660,015	6,741,156
Changes in permanently restricted net assets		
Contributions	17,941,152	8,811,080
Investment return (see text)	597,954	337,790
Appreciation (depreciation) in value of perpetual trust	25,000	(365,000)
Change in provision on contributions receivable	(1,127,084)	(1,436,024)
Increase in permanently restricted net assets	17,437,022	7,347,846
Increase in net assets	72,273,876	48,105,089
Net assets at beginning of year	560,650,155	512,545,066
Net assets at end of year	$ 632,924,031	$560,650,155

Note: The notes accompanying these statements and the related note references made in the captions are not reproduced in this text. However, captions labeled "see text" are discussed in this appendix.

matters covered in this chapter or to comment on matters that are better discussed in the context of an actual situation.

Contributions Receivable

Contributions receivable, reported in the statement of financial position at June 30, 2006, consist of the following:

Amounts expected to be collected in:

Less than 1 year	$11,639,783
1 to 5 years	21,858,648
More than 5 years	1,922,628
Less allowance for uncollectible accounts	(8,712,443)
Less discount to present value	(2,384,338)
Subtotal	24,324,278
Funds held in perpetual trust	6,575,000
Charitable remainder trusts	3,004,494
Total	$33,903,772

Note that the allowance for estimated uncollectible contributions is significant in relation to the total contributions receivable. Also, note that the receivables have been discounted to present value. This adjustment is in accordance with FASB standards, which provide that unconditional promises to contribute cash that are expected to be collected more than 1 year after the balance sheet date should be discounted to their present value. Subsequent accretion of the interest element is reported as contribution revenue.

Colleges, universities, and other NFPOs may be beneficiaries of various types of trusts or other arrangements, generally called split-interest agreements. A revocable split-interest agreement is not recognized as revenue, but an irrevocable one is recognized as contribution revenue and as assets when the trust is executed.

- A perpetual trust is one in which the NFPO has an irrevocable right to receive the *income* from the trust assets in perpetuity, but not the assets held in trust. When the trust is established, the fair value of the asset—the present value of estimated future cash receipts from the trust—is reported as contributions receivable, and the related contribution revenue is classified as permanently restricted support. Subsequent distributions from the trust are recorded as unrestricted investment income in the year received.

- A charitable remainder trust is one in which a donor establishes and finances a trust. Specified distributions are made over the term of the trust to beneficiaries (say, a spouse or children), and the NFPO receives the assets remaining in the trust at its termination. The notes to Fordham's statements say: "At the dates these charitable remainder trusts are established or the University becomes aware of their existence, contribution revenue and receivables are recognized at the present value of the estimated future benefits to be received when the trust assets are distributed. The receivable is adjusted during the term of the trust for changes in the value of the assets. . . ."

Investments and Investment Income

Fordham's statement of financial position reports investments having a fair value of almost $403 million at June 30, 2006. Its statement of activities reports "investment return" in four captions: under operating revenues and under nonoperating activities in the section on unrestricted net assets and among the changes in both temporarily and permanently restricted net assets.

As Fordham explains in a note to the financial statements, dividends, interest, and net gains on investments are reported as increases in permanently restricted net assets if the terms of the gift require that they be added to the principal of permanently restricted net assets; and as increases in temporarily restricted net assets if the gift terms impose restrictions on the current use of the income. Otherwise, they are reported as increases in unrestricted net assets.

But why is some investment income reported in these statements as operating revenue and some as nonoperating? Some colleges and universities include all *realized* gains and losses as part of operating revenues and all *unrealized* gains and losses as nonoperating. Others manage their investments on a total return basis, focusing on the long-term overall return on investment, including both investment income and net appreciation. They use a trustee-authorized spending rate formula to determine how much of the income will be used for current operations. The trustees may also authorize additional spending from investment return. The balance is reported as nonoperating income.

A note to Fordham's financial statements indicates that the university manages its investment pool to achieve the maximum prudent long-term total return. Its policy is "to preserve the value of these investments in real terms (after inflation) and provide a predictable flow of funds to support operations." The investment return for the unrestricted net assets in fiscal year 2006 consisted of the following components:

Dividends and interest (net of expenses of $1,542,443)	$ 3,705,775
Net realized gain on sale of investments	23,464,996
Net (decrease) in unrealized appreciation on investments	(5,709,015)
Total return on investments	21,461,756
Investment return recognized in operating activities	11,118,486
Investment return greater than amounts recognized in operating activities [included in nonoperating activities]	$10,343,270

CHAPTER

13

ACCOUNTING FOR HEALTH CARE ORGANIZATIONS

Chapter Outline

After completing this chapter, you should be able to:

- Identify the sources of generally accepted accounting principles for health care organizations.
- Prepare journal entries related to hospital patient service revenue and patient receivables.
- Prepare journal entries used to record investment income and other revenues and gains.
- Describe the accounting principles regarding hospital medical malpractice claims.
- Prepare journal entries to account for transactions with restrictions.
- Describe how not-for profit hospitals calculate an indicator of financial performance.
- Identify and prepare financial statements for not-for-profit and governmental hospitals.

Health care is one of the most rapidly growing industries in the United States. According to the U.S. Bureau of Economic Analysis, the number of full-time equivalent employees in all industries increased 1.0 percent to 126.9 million between 2000 and 2005. During this brief period, although employment in manufacturing declined 17.1 percent to 14.0 million, employment in health care and social assistance jumped 15.9 percent to 13.6 million. Within health care and social assistance, the number employed by hospitals, nursing, and residential care facilities increased by 12.9 percent to 6.6 million.

Health care in the United States is characterized not only by rapidly rising employment among service providers, but also by increasing costs and the involvement of third parties (such as government, private insurance companies, and health maintenance organizations) in financing health care services. We read almost daily about threats to the financial health of Medicare, increased taxes related to increasing Medicaid costs, disputes between health maintenance organizations and service providers, and reductions in employer-provided health care benefits. Implementation of GASB

Statement No. 45, on financial reporting of postemployment health care benefits (discussed in Chapter 7), will focus additional attention on health care costs borne by state and local governments as employers.

Public programs that receive the most attention are Medicare and Medicaid. The Medicare program is financed primarily by the federal government. Medicaid is a public assistance–type program financed by the federal, state, and sometimes local governments.

Accounting and financial reporting are important tools in health care administration, not only in keeping track of costs, but also because third parties often base their payments to health care providers on allowable costs, some form of fixed-rate reimbursement, or a combination of both. Measurement and control of costs are critical, both to health care providers and to third-party payers.

HEALTH CARE SERVICE PROVIDERS

Health care services are provided in many types of settings and by entities having different ownership structures and operating orientations. Health care services may be provided, for example, in hospitals, surgery centers, clinics, laboratories, group medical practices, nursing homes (that differ in the intensity of the medical care they provide), home health agencies, and continuing care retirement communities. Health care organizations may be organized as not-for-profit, governmental, or private for-profit entities. Not-for-profit health care entities may be classified as having either a business orientation or a nonbusiness orientation. This chapter focuses on accounting and financial reporting by a major health care provider—hospitals—organized either as governmental or as not-for-profit with a business orientation.

The characteristics of governmental entities, as distinguished from not-for-profit entities, are discussed in Chapter 12. Some governmental hospitals are organized within departments of state or local governments. Others are organized as legally separate corporations, governed by boards appointed by government officials. Legally separate governmental corporations may have the power to tax and to issue tax-exempt debt directly, rather than through a state or local government agency.

Not-for-profit hospitals, like other not-for-profit entities, have no ownership interests and thus do not operate to maximize profits for owners. Not-for-profit health care entities with a business orientation are basically self-supporting as a result of fees they charge for their services, but they may also receive relatively small amounts of contributions. Non-business-oriented not-for-profit health care entities are considered so because they obtain most of their revenues from contributions, grants, and other support. Non–business-oriented not-for-profit health care entities are included in the voluntary health and welfare organizations (VHWOs) discussed in Chapter 12.

INTRODUCTION TO HOSPITAL ACCOUNTING AND FINANCIAL REPORTING

Sources of Generally Accepted Accounting Principles

The Financial Accounting Standards Board (FASB) establishes accounting standards for for-profit and not-for-profit entities. The Governmental Accounting Standards Board (GASB) establishes them for governmental entities. Although some differences exist in the standards established for not-for-profit versus government health care entities, the move for comparability among entities that perform similar functions has resulted in far more similarities than differences. The *AICPA Audit and Accounting Guide — Health Care Organizations,* which provides general accounting guidance for all health care entities except VHWOs, has been approved as a source of accounting principles by both the FASB and the GASB.[1]

In this chapter we discuss transactions simultaneously for not-for-profit and governmental entities, pointing out differences where they exist. Most of the differences occur in accounting for certain contributions and in financial reporting. Keep the following factors in mind as you read this chapter:

- Governmental hospitals are subject to the accounting and reporting requirements for governmental *proprietary funds,* discussed in Chapter 7. Not-for-profit hospitals are subject to the accounting and reporting requirements for *not-for-profit organizations,* discussed in Chapter 12.
- Governmental hospitals use the economic resources measurement focus and the full accrual basis of accounting, as discussed in Chapter 7. The GASB permits governmental entities that use proprietary fund accounting to apply FASB standards, except for those that conflict with or contradict GASB standards.[2] For example, the GASB does not permit proprietary funds to apply FASB standards whose provisions are limited to or are developed primarily for not-for-profit entities, such as FASB *Statement Nos. 116 and 117,* discussed in Chapter 12.[3] The implications of that requirement will become clear later in this chapter.
- Not-for-profit business-oriented health care entities also use full accrual accounting. Even though most of their revenues are obtained from fees and charges for services, they are subject to the accounting and financial reporting standards of FASB *Statement Nos. 116 and 117* because they are not-for-profit entities.

Financial Reporting Framework

Like all not-for-profit entities, not-for-profit hospitals are required to report net assets and changes in net assets by net asset classification — unrestricted, temporarily restricted, and permanently restricted. To more clearly present operating results, the *AICPA Audit and Accounting Guide — Health Care Organizations* recommends that hospitals and other health care entities prepare two operating statements. One, the statement of operations, reports on the basic day-to-day revenues and expenses by covering only changes in unrestricted net assets. The other, called the statement of changes in net assets, reports on changes in all three net asset classifications, and deals primarily with transactions and events other than day-to-day operating activities.

Later in the chapter, we present a more detailed discussion and illustrations of hospital financing reporting. The following skeletal outline of a not-for-profit hospital

---

[1]American Institute of Certified Public Accountants, *AICPA Audit and Accounting Guide — Health Care Organizations* (New York, AICPA, 2006). As discussed in Chapter 1, AICPA Audit and Accounting Guides made applicable by the FASB and the GASB are in the second level of the respective GAAP hierarchies.
[2]GASB Cod. (2006), Sec. P80.102 and 103.
[3]GASB Cod. (2006), Sec. P80.103.

operating statement provides a framework for the ensuing discussion of hospital accounting.

Unrestricted revenues, gains, and other support:	
Net patient service revenues	XXX
Premium revenue	XXX
Other revenue	XXX
Net assets released from restrictions, used for operations	<u>XXX</u>
Total revenues, gains and other support	<u>XXX</u>
Expenses:	
Details by function or natural classification	XXX
Provision for bad debts	<u>XXX</u>
Total expenses	<u>XXX</u>
Operating income	XXX
Other income (or expenses)	
Details, such as investment income	<u>XXX</u>
Excess of revenues over expenses	XXX
Change in net unrealized gains and losses on securities	
other than trading securities	XXX
Change in interest in net assets of NFP Hospital Foundation	XXX
Net assets released from restrictions, used to purchase capital assets	<u>XXX</u>
Increase in unrestricted net assets	<u>XXX</u>

Net assets of governmental hospitals are classified as either unrestricted or restricted, without distinction between temporarily and permanently restricted. Further, the operating statement of governmental hospitals is all inclusive, with resources received with restrictions shown separately from unrestricted resources. The operating statement, called a statement of revenues, expenses, and changes in net assets, is presented in the same format as other governmental enterprise activities (see Chapter 7). In this statement, operating expenses are deducted from operating revenues to show operating income. Nonoperating revenues (such as investment income) and expenses (such as interest expense) are then added or subtracted, to show income before capital contributions and transfers. The latter are then added or subtracted, to report the change in net assets.

Fund Accounting Framework

Many not-for-profit and governmental hospitals used fund accounting in the past for internal accounting and managerial control purposes and, though not required for external reporting purposes, may continue to do so. Hospital funds are categorized into two groups: the General Fund and Restricted Funds. Resources and liabilities included within a hospital's General Fund fall into four broad categories:

- *Operating resources* are assets and liabilities associated with the day-to-day hospital activities.
- *Assets limited as to use* are resources set aside internally by the hospital's governing board or in accordance with an agreement with an external party other than a donor or grantor.
- *Agency resources* are resources held by a hospital that belong to other persons such as doctors and patients.

- *Plant resources* are the property, plant, and equipment used by a hospital in its general operations, and any related liabilities.

Restricted funds are used to account for resources that must be used in compliance with the terms of agreements, like those related to donor gifts or grants. Restricted funds are used only when an external limitation is placed on the use of resources and the resources are not related to a bond agreement or third-party reimbursement. These are the most common types of restricted funds used by hospitals:

- *Specific Purpose Funds* are resources that are restricted by donors or grantors for specific operating purposes, such as a gift that must be used for cancer research.
- *Plant Replacement and Expansion Funds* are resources contributed by outsiders that can be used only to replace existing plant or expand existing plant. The assets acquired from those resources are recorded in the General Fund.
- *Endowment Funds* may be either Permanent or Term. A permanent endowment is one where the donor requires that the principal be maintained in perpetuity. A term endowment is one where the donor requires that the principal be maintained for a specific period or the donor imposes other restrictions. After the term restrictions have been satisfied, the principle can be unrestricted or restricted. Income from endowment funds may be unrestricted (and recorded in the General Fund) or restricted (and recorded in one of the other restricted funds).

The transactions described in this section deal with a hospital's basic operating activities. If fund accounting is used, these transactions are accounted for primarily in the General Fund. Because of the decreasing emphasis on funds in actual practice, our journal entries refer to the unrestricted net asset class, rather than the General Fund, when they apply to not-for-profit hospitals. We cover transactions with restrictions in a later section of this chapter.

PATIENT SERVICE REVENUES

Nature of Hospital Payment Systems

Hospitals obtain operating revenues primarily from patient services (based on charges for nursing and other professional services) and health care insurance premiums (based on agreements to provide care). Most of these revenues come from third-party payers, including both public sources such as Medicare and Medicaid and private insurers such as health maintenance organizations (HMOs) and Blue Cross.

Third-party payers have developed various payment systems, generally paying hospitals at amounts less than the hospital's established rates. Differences between a hospital's established rates and amounts set by or negotiated with third-party payers are referred to as contractual adjustments. Hospitals also provide services to uninsured patients, some of whom may receive discounts from established rates or who may not pay at all (charity cases). The different payment arrangements affect the way hospitals account for patient service revenues and receivables.

Hospital payment systems include prospectively determined rates per discharge; reimbursed costs; negotiated fee schedules; per diem payments; discounts from established charges; and capitation premiums paid per member, per month (PMPM). Some payment rates are established prospectively (i.e., in advance of service delivery) at fixed amounts. Others are based on interim billing amounts, subject to retrospective (i.e., after the accounting period ends) adjustment.

Medicare generally pays hospitals at prospectively determined rates, which vary according to a patient classification system based on clinical, diagnostic, and other factors. Under the diagnosis-related group (DRG) system, all potential diagnoses are classified into a number of medically meaningful groups, each of which has a different value. Each hospital in a specific geographic region receives the same amount for each DRG, depending on whether the hospital is classified as urban or rural. Thus an uncomplicated appendectomy results in the same basic reimbursement to all hospitals in a given urban or rural area. Other factors, such as whether the entity is a teaching hospital and the intensity of service rendered, are also considered in the payments a hospital will receive.

Third-party payers that pay hospitals retrospectively reimburse hospitals initially on the basis of interim payment rates. The interim payment rates are then adjusted retrospectively based on stipulated allowable costs after the hospitals submit required cost reports to the third-party payers. The rates reached on final settlement may differ significantly from the interim payment rates. Therefore, to ensure that revenues and net assets are reported on the accrual basis of accounting, reasonable estimates of the amounts receivable from or payable to the third-party payers need to be made in the period that the services are rendered.

Under *capitation agreements* with HMOs, hospitals generally receive agreed-upon premiums per member, per month, based on the number of participants in the HMO. In exchange, the hospitals agree to provide all medical services to the HMO's subscribers. The hospitals thus earn these revenues from *agreeing to provide* care and will receive the capitation payments regardless of the actual services they perform. The hospitals may also receive fees from the HMO for certain services.

Accounting for Net Patient Service Revenues

Revenues based on fees for services *actually provided* by hospitals are classified as *patient service revenues*. These revenues include those derived from Medicare and Medicaid beneficiaries. Revenues based on *agreements to provide* care (regardless of whether care is actually provided) are classified as premium revenues and include revenues from capitation arrangements with HMOs. If the amount is significant, patient service revenues are reported separately from premium revenues in the financial statements.

Hospitals record patient service revenues and receivables initially at their gross (established) rates, even if they do not expect to collect those amounts. As previously noted, several factors are likely to cause the amount realized from these services to be significantly less than the established rates. These factors include contractual rate adjustments with third-party payers, provision of charity care, discounts granted to various persons, bad debts, and retrospective adjustments.

For financial reporting purposes, patient service revenue is reported on the operating statement *net* of contractual rate adjustments, charity care, and similar items that the hospital does not expect to collect. Patient service revenue is not reduced, however, by a provision for uncollectible accounts (bad debts expense). Instead, bad debts expense is reported in the expenses section of the operating statement. (See the skeletal outline on page 506 for financial reporting of net patient service revenues and provision for bad debts.) Receivables resulting from health care services are reported on the balance sheet at the amount likely to be realized in cash. Therefore, gross receivables must be reduced by allowances needed to present the receivables at their *net realizable value.*

Gross Patient Service Revenues and Contractual Adjustments

To illustrate, assume that a hospital's regular charges (at established rates) for nursing and other professional services (including services provided to patients covered by Medicare and other third-party payers, self-pay patients, and charity patients) are $1,700,000. To record this information, the following entry is made:

Patient accounts receivable	1,700,000	
Patient service revenue		1,700,000
To record gross patient service revenue at		
established rates.		

Although we use one account for each type of revenue, remember that this *control account* is used in the same manner as a control account in general accounting. Subsidiary records are used to accumulate the revenues for the unit to which the patient was admitted or whose services were used—for example, general nursing services, surgery, pediatrics, and radiology.

As previously stated, payment rates may be established either prospectively or retrospectively. When established prospectively, the full contractual adjustment is known at billing time. When established retrospectively, the full adjustment may not be known until the following year. In that case, interim rates reflecting a tentative contractual adjustment may be used for billing purposes. Provision for further contractual adjustment (upward or downward), however, may be needed at year end to report revenues and receivables from third-party payers at net realizable amounts.

For example, assume that under a prospective billing arrangement with third-party payer X, the hospital has contractual adjustments of $80,000. Under a retrospective rate arrangement with third-party payer Y, it has contractual adjustments of $40,000 based on interim rates, pending later negotiation of final rates. The hospital would make the following entry at the time of the billings:

Provision for contractual adjustments	120,000	
Patient accounts receivable		120,000
To record adjustments to revenue and receivables, based		
on prospective billing contract with payer X and		
interim rates negotiated with payer Y.		

After reducing the patient accounts receivable by the provision for contractual adjustments, the outstanding receivables from third-party payers would include only the amount the hospital expects to collect from them.

Other types of adjustments to gross patient revenues are made for charity services and "discounts" granted to the clergy, volunteers, and employees. These adjustments also represent the amount of the established rates that the hospital will not collect. The only difference between these and the contractual adjustments lies in the reason they will not be collected. Assume, for example, that the previously recorded revenues include services of $50,000 to charity patients. As soon as the hospital classifies the patients as "charity patients," the following entry is made:

Provision for charity services	50,000	
Patient accounts receivable		50,000
To record adjustment to revenues and receivables because of charity care.		

If collections of receivables during the year total $1,400,000, they would be recorded as follows:

Cash	1,400,000	
Patient accounts receivable		1,400,000
To record collection of receivables.		

Provision for Uncollectible Receivables

Accounts receivable must be stated in the financial statements at their net realizable value. Therefore, patient accounts receivable need to be reviewed for likelihood of collectiblity. An estimate for uncollectible accounts receivable is reported as a bad debts expense. Recall from previous discussions that an allowance for uncollectible accounts is reported as a contra to accounts receivable because it is not known which specific accounts will turn out to be "bad debts." If hospital management estimates uncollectible amounts from self-pay patients to be $30,000, the following entry would be made:

Provision for bad debts (or bad debts expense)	30,000	
Allowance for uncollectible accounts		30,000
To record allowance for uncolectible accounts.		

If $20,000 of individual patient accounts become uncollectible, patient accounts receivable and the allowance for uncollectible accounts are reduced, as follows:

Allowance for uncollectible accounts	20,000	
Patient accounts receivable		20,000
To record write-off of accounts determined to be uncollectible.		

Estimated Third-Party Settlements

As previously stated, arrangements with some third-party payers may call for billing at interim rates, subject to retrospective adjustment based on a review of cost reports submitted by the hospital. To ensure that amounts reported as net patient service revenues, receivables, or payables in the financial statements are valid, estimates must be made of the settlement amounts for all billing arrangements that have not been settled as of the date of the financial statements. The adjustment, which takes the form of an additional contractual adjustment, must be made even if the final settlement amount has not been negotiated.

Regarding its retrospective rate arrangement with third-party payer Y, assume the hospital estimates at year end that it will need to refund $15,000 because its analysis of reimbursable costs shows that the interim rates negotiated with Y were too high. If Y had paid all amounts previously billed by the hospital, the following entry would be needed at year end:

Provision for contractual adjustments	15,000	
Estimated third-party payer settlements		15,000
To record provision for estimated refund to payer Y,		
pending negotiation of retrospective rate.		

Based on these journal entries, the amount reported on the hospital's operating statement as net patient service revenue would be $1,515,000 (gross billings of $1,700,000, less the $135,000 provision for contractual adjustments and the $50,000 provision for charity services). Net patient accounts receivable reported on the hospital's balance sheet would be $100,000 (gross outstanding receivables of $110,000, less $10,000 remaining in the contra account allowance for uncollectible accounts). The $15,000 estimated third-party payer settlements account would be reported as a liability. (Note that, in the previous journal entry, we assumed that third-party payer Y had paid all amounts previously billed by the hospital. If Y had not paid all amounts previously billed, the $15,000 estimated settlement would be reported as a reduction of the outstanding receivables in order to state the receivables at net realizable value.)

Accounting for Capitation Premiums

In addition to billing fees for services, the hospital also has capitation agreements with various HMOs, wherein it receives agreed-upon premiums per member, per month. If the hospital receives $400,000 of capitation fees at the beginning of the month, it would make the following entry:

Cash	400,000	
Premium revenue		400,000
To record capitation premium revenues.		

Assume that, at the end of the month, hospital records show that it provided services to participants in these HMOs amounting to $375,000 at its established billing rates. Although this information is valuable for internal management purposes, no entry is made in the financial accounting records.

For an example of the effect of these entries on financial reporting, see Patient accounts receivable and Estimated third-party payer settlements in Table 13-1 (page 512) and Net patient service revenue in Table 13-2 (page 513).

Notes to Financial Statements Regarding Patient Revenue Recognition

The nature of the third-party arrangements, revenue recognition practices, and charity care policies should be described in notes to the financial statements. The following is an illustration of a note regarding these arrangements that might be made in the summary of significant accounting policies.

Net Patient Service Revenue. The hospital has agreements with third-party payers, providing for payments at amounts different from its established rates. The agreements provide both for prospectively and retrospectively determined rates. Net patient service revenue is reported at estimated net realizable amounts from

TABLE 13-1 Balance Sheet—Not-for-Profit Hospital

Hudson Valley Hospital Center
Balance Sheets
December 31, 2005 and 2004

	2005	2004
Assets		
Current assets:		
Cash and cash equivalents	$ 9,544,764	$10,524,715
Investments	17,665,267	9,570,503
Patient accounts receivable, less allowance for uncollectible accounts of approximately $4,240,000 in 2005 and $4,880,000 in 2004	12,317,650	10,657,163
Other receivables	1,516,119	576,110
Supplies and prepaid expenses	1,744,525	1,669,344
Total current assets	42,788,325	32,997,835
Interest in Foundation of Hudson Valley Hospital Center	5,947,723	5,313,105
Assets whose use is limited—externally restricted	6,692,714	7,064,422
Long-term investments	1,674,619	669,163
Property, plant, and equipment, net	32,436,683	30,516,903
Other assets	1,785,804	1,231,723
Total assets	$91,325,868	$77,793,151
Liabilities and Net Assets		
Current liabilities:		
Current portion of long-term debt	$ 645,349	$ 639,238
Current portion of capital lease obligations	904,412	1,421,699
Accounts payable and accrued expenses	6,419,826	6,852,313
Accrued salaries and benefits	6,089,351	5,222,043
Estimated payable to third-party payers	1,761,172	694,000
Total current liabilities	15,820,110	14,829,293
Long-term debt	17,321,911	18,120,671
Capital lease obligations	1,839,810	1,722,328
Estimated payable to third-party payers, malpractice and other liabilities	14,883,123	12,857,742
Total liabilities	49,864,954	47,530,034
Net assets		
Unrestricted	34,245,544	24,280,849
Temporarily restricted	5,540,751	5,313,105
Permanently restricted	1,674,619	669,163
Total net assets	41,460,914	30,263,117
Total liabilities and net assets	$91,325,868	$77,793,151

Source: Hudson Valley Hospital Center financial statements, December 31, 2005 and 2004. Reprinted with permission. (Accompanying notes, which are an integral part of these statements, are not shown here.)

TABLE 13-2   Statement of Operations—Not-for-Profit Hospital

Hudson Valley Hospital Center
Statements of Operations
Years Ended December 31, 2005 and 2004

	2005	2004
Operating revenues		
Net patient service revenue	$89,517,295	$84,542,802
Other operating revenue	2,342,573	2,415,522
Total operating revenues	91,859,868	86,958,324
Operating expenses		
Salaries	37,531,888	34,763,509
Physician fees	1,918,099	2,001,851
Fringe benefits	7,580,312	6,995,657
Supplies and other expenses	27,366,422	28,610,259
Provision for bad debts	1,775,068	3,238,525
Interest	1,341,181	1,518,418
Depreciation and amortization	4,488,172	4,962,198
Total operating expenses	82,001,142	82,090,417
Operating gain	9,858,726	4,867,907
Investment income	806,560	554,012
Loss on transfer	(477,840)	—
Excess of revenues over expenses	10,187,446	5,421,919
Change in net unrealized gains and losses on investments	(75,897)	230,272
Net assets released from restrictions for capital expenditures	—	3,126,250
Increase in unrestricted net assets before cumulative effect of change	10,111,549	8,778,441
Cumulative effect of change in accounting principle	(146,854)	—
Increase in unrestricted net assets	$ 9,964,695	$ 8,778,441

Source: Hudson Valley Hospital Center financial statements, December 31, 2005 and 2004. Reprinted with permission. (Accompanying notes, which are an integral part of these statements, are not shown here.)

patients, third-party payers, and others for services rendered, including estimated retroactive adjustments under agreements with third-party payers. Estimated retroactive adjustments are accrued in the period services are provided and adjusted in future periods as final settlements are made.

Premium Revenue. The hospital has agreements with various health maintenance organizations to provide services to subscribing participants. In accordance with the agreements, the hospital receives monthly capitation payments based on the number of participants, regardless of the services the hospital actually performs.

Charity Care. The hospital provides care to patients either without charge or at less than its established rates. These patients must meet the criteria under the hospital's charity care policy. The value of these services is not reported as revenue because the hospital does not seek to collect amounts that qualify as charity care.

REPORTING ON CHARITY CARE

Hospitals generally provide additional details regarding charity care, including the dollar amount of charges foregone for services provided under their charity care policies, in separate notes to their financial statements. For example, this is how the Hudson Valley Hospital Center reported on charity care:

"The Hospital provides a significant amount of partially or totally uncompensated patient care to patients who are unable to compensate the Hospital for their treatment either through third-party coverage or their own resources.

Patients who meet certain criteria under the Hospital's charity care policy are provided care without charge or at amounts less than established rates. Because charity care amounts are not expected to be paid, they are not reported as revenue. The amount of charges foregone for total uncompensated care (includes uncompensated care reported as bad debt expense), based on established rates under the Hospital's policy for the years ended December 31, 2005 and 2004 was approximately $7,258,000 and $8,538,000, respectively."

SOURCE: Notes to financial statements, Hudson Valley Hospital Center, Cortlandt Manor, NY, December 31, 2005 and 2004.

INVESTMENT INCOME, OTHER REVENUES, GAINS

Investment Returns

Investment activities often provide a major source of revenue for hospitals. Not-for-profit hospitals account for investments in accordance with FASB *Statement No. 124,* "Accounting for Certain Investments Held by Not-for-Profit Organizations," discussed in Chapter 12. Governmental hospitals account for investments in accordance with GASB *Statement No. 31,* "Accounting and Financial Reporting for Certain Investments and for External Investment Pools," discussed in Chapter 8. Both standards require that, in general, hospitals report investments in equity and debt securities at fair value on the balance sheet. Reporting investments at fair value on the balance sheet means that investment returns in the operating statement include dividends and interest, realized gains and losses, and unrealized gains and losses.

As discussed later in this chapter, the AICPA Guide for Health Care Organizations recommends that not-for-profit hospitals display a measure of financial performance in their operating statements.[4] They also recommend that all realized gains and losses be included in the performance indicator, but that unrealized gains and losses on securities other than trading securities be excluded from that measure. (A security is classified as *other than trading* if it is acquired without the intent to sell it in the near term.) GASB accounting standards on investments, which are applicable to governmental hospitals, generally do not permit realized gains and losses to be displayed in

---

[4]*AICPA Audit and Accounting Guide—Health Care Organizations* (2006), para. 4.07. (Because the performance indicator relates only to changes in unrestricted net assets, the AICPA's suggested separation of realized from unrealized gains and losses does not extend to investments made with temporarily and permanently restricted resources.)

the financial statements separately from the net increase or decrease in the fair value of investments.[5]

Accomplishing the different methods of financial reporting requires differences in financial accounting. Combining realized and unrealized gains and losses in a single account is the simpler of the two methods. To illustrate, assume a governmental and a not-for-profit hospital each purchase a security for $100,000 on March 15, 2008. (The not-for-profit hospital considers it to be other than trading.) Both would make the following entry:

Investments	100,000	
Cash		100,000
To record purchase of investment.		

Both securities increase in value to $115,000 at December 31, 2008, the balance sheet dates, and both are sold in the year 2009 for $120,000. Both hospitals have an unrealized gain of $15,000 in 2008 and both have an additional gain of $5,000 in 2009. The $5,000 gain in 2009 can be separated into two components—a realized gain of $20,000 and a decrease in the unrealized gain of $15,000. The governmental hospital would carry the investment at fair value and report both the unrealized and the realized gain in a single account called "Net realized and unrealized gains and losses on investments." It would make the following entries to record the transactions:

Investments	15,000	
Revenues—net realized and unrealized gains and losses on investments		15,000
To record unrealized gain on investments in 2008.		

Cash	120,000	
Investments		115,000
Revenues—net realized and unrealized gains and losses on investments		5,000
To record gain on sale of investments in 2009.		

The governmental hospital would report investment revenue as nonoperating revenue in its operating statement.

The not-for-profit hospital would carry the investment at original cost and use an "investment valuation account" to record the adjustment to fair value. It would also use separate accounts for the unrealized gain and the realized gain. It would make the following journal entries.

Investment valuation account	15,000	
Unrestricted revenue—change in net unrealized gains and losses on investments		15,000
To record unrealized gain on investments in 2008.		

Cash	120,000	
Unrestricted revenue—realized gain on investments		20,000
Investments		100,000
Unrestricted revenue—change in net unrealized gains and losses on investments	15,000	
Investment valuation account		15,000
To record realized gain on investments and reverse unrealized gain in 2009.		

---

[5]GASB Cod. (2001), Sec. I50.111. (The GASB does, however, permit note disclosure of realized gains and losses.)

For financial reporting purposes, the not-for-profit hospital would add the $15,000 balance in the investment valuation account to the investments account in order to report investments at fair value at the end of 2008. It would report the $15,000 unrealized gain below Excess of revenues over expenses. In 2009, the realized gain of $20,000 would be included with other investment income and reported above Excess of revenues over expenses. The negative $15,000 net change in unrealized gains and losses would be reported below that caption. (Despite the different presentation methods, the net effect for both hospitals is to increase net assets by $15,000 in 2008 and by $5,000 in 2009.)

Other Revenues, Gains, and Operating Support

Hospitals may also derive revenues and gains from services and activities other than services to patients and investing. Other sources of revenue and gains include educational program fees (including tuition for schools), sales of medical and pharmaceutical supplies to doctors and others, parking fees, cafeteria sales, and gift shop sales. Contributions also provide a source of operating support for hospital activities. For analytical purposes, other forms of revenue, gains, and support are reported in captions separate from net patient service revenue and premium revenue.

Accountants sometimes make a fine distinction between revenues and gains. Revenues are inflows from delivering goods, providing services, or other activities that constitute the entity's ongoing major or central operations. Gains are increases in net assets from an entity's peripheral or incidental transactions. An activity peripheral to one entity might be a normal, ongoing activity of another. Depending on materiality of individual items, revenues and gains may be aggregated as Other revenues for reporting purposes.

Parking and Other Revenues or Gains

Revenues received from parking fees, the cafeteria, educational programs (such as nursing school tuition), and so forth are recorded as follows (amounts assumed):

Cash	245,000	
Other receivables	5,000	
Other revenues (or gains)		250,000
To record other revenues.		

Contributions of Cash and Supplies

Contributions to hospitals may take the form of unrestricted or restricted cash donations, supplies and commodities (such as medicines or materials) to cover the cost of charity services, and professional or nonprofessional services. Unrestricted contributions are recorded as other revenue or gains, measured at fair value. Restricted contributions are discussed later in this chapter.

Contributions received by not-for-profit hospitals are accounted for and reported in accordance with FASB *Statement Nos. 116 and 117,* as discussed in Chapter 12. Contributions received by governmental hospitals are accounted for and reported in accordance with GASB standards for voluntary nonexchange transactions, as described in GASB *Statement No. 33.* For example, a governmental hospital should recognize the fair value of donated commodities as revenue in the period when all eligibility requirements are met, which is usually in the period when the commodities are received.

To illustrate, assume a private organization makes an unrestricted cash donation of $100,000 and medicines having a fair value of $75,000 to both a not-for-profit hospital and a governmental hospital. Both hospitals would report both donations as revenues on receipt of the contributions. The not-for-profit hospital would report the contributions as increases in unrestricted net assets (other revenue), and the governmental hospital would report them as nonoperating income:

Cash	100,000	
Other revenue (or gains)—unrestricted support		100,000
To record receipt of unrestricted cash donation.		
Inventory—medicines and drugs	75,000	
Other revenue (or gains)—donated commodities		75,000
To record receipt of medicines at fair value.		

Contributed Services

Services donated to not-for-profit hospitals are accounted for based on the criteria set forth in FASB *Statement No. 116,* discussed in Chapter 12. For example, if doctors and nurses donated professional services having a fair value of $10,000 to a not-for-profit hospital, and the services would typically need to be purchased, the following entry is made:

Patient care expense	10,000	
Other revenue (or gains)—donated services		10,000
To record receipt of donated services.		

If donated services do not meet the criteria discussed in Chapter 12 (i.e., if they do not require specialized skills, are not provided by individuals who possess those skills, and would not need to be purchased), the hospital should not recognize the expenses and revenues. Thus, a not-for-profit hospital should not recognize the value of many donated services that do not require specialized skills, such as moving wheelchairs and selling at gift shops.

GASB *Statement No. 33* does not apply to donated services. In the absence of standards regarding donated services, governmental hospitals often do not record them. Others record them if the hospital controls the employment and duties of the donors and the services are of significant value.

EXPENSES

Operating Expenses

Expenses related to the general operation of a hospital consist of nursing and other professional services, general services, fiscal services, and administrative services. The *Health Care Organization Guide* states that expenses may be reported on the face of the financial statements either by natural classification (e.g., salaries and benefits, medical supplies and drugs, insurance) or by function (e.g., patient care expense, dietary services).[6] Not-for-profit entities that report by natural classification on the face of the financial statements are required also to show expenses by functional classification in the notes. In this chapter, we illustrate expenses by functional classification. The entry used to record some of these expenses is (amounts assumed):

Patient care expense	750,000	
Dietary services expense	50,000	
General services expense	200,000	
Administrative services expense	145,000	
Interest expense	155,000	
Cash		1,100,000
Accounts payable, salaries payable, and so on		200,000
To record certain operating expenses.		

---

[6]*AICPA Audit and Accounting Guide—Health Care Organizations* para. 10.29.

For simplicity, we combined the recording and payment of expenses in the preceding entry, and we combined several liability items. Because we are dealing with summary journal entries that cover an entire year, this aggregation will have no effect on the results of our illustrations.

During the year, the acquisition and use of inventory items is recorded as follows (amounts assumed):

Inventories	150,000	
Accounts payable		150,000
To record purchase of inventory.		

Patient care expense	70,000	
Dietary services expense	50,000	
Administrative services expense	20,000	
Inventories		140,000
To record use of inventory.		

Because full accrual accounting is used for hospitals, items of property, plant, and equipment are recorded as assets when acquired and are depreciated over their useful lives. The entry to record this expense is as follows (amounts assumed):

Depreciation expense	200,000	
Accumulated depreciation—plant and equipment		200,000
To record depreciation for the year.		

Medical Malpractice Claims

Settlements and judgments on medical malpractice claims constitute a potential major expense for hospitals. Whether expenses and liabilities need to be recognized on malpractice claims depends on whether risk has been transferred by the hospital to third-party insurance companies or to public entity risk pools.

FASB *Statement No. 5,* "Accounting for Contingencies," and GASB *Statement No. 10,* "Accounting and Financial Reporting for Risk Financing and Related Insurance Issues," provide guidance regarding medical malpractice claims. The basic rule is: If risk of loss has not been transferred to an external third party, expenses must be recognized and liabilities reported if it is probable that a loss has been incurred and the amount of the loss can be reasonably estimated.

The basic rule applies whether or not claims for incidents occurring before the balance sheet date are known. These claims are called incurred but not reported (IBNR) claims. An estimate must be made for losses on IBNR claims if it is probable that claims will be asserted and losses can be reasonably estimated. Historical experience of both the entity and the industry may be used in estimating the probability of IBNR claims.

Estimates of losses from malpractice claims may be based on a case-by-case review of all claims, or by applying historical experience regarding losses (e.g., the ratio of settlement amounts to claimed amounts) to outstanding claims, or both. For example, if an uninsured hospital has 10 medical malpractice claims aggregating $1,000,000 and historical experience shows that claims have been settled for an average of 30 percent of the amount claimed, the hospital should accrue an expense and a liability for $300,000.

What if one patient has filed a claim for $500,000 and negotiations between the attorneys, though not complete, indicate that the claim probably can be settled for an amount within the range of $150,000 and $300,000? For that situation, the basic rule is: If it is probable that a loss has occurred, but analysis shows that the amount of loss is within a range of amounts, the most likely amount within the range should be accrued as an expense. If no amount in the range is more likely than any other, the minimum amount in the range should be accrued, and the potential additional loss should be disclosed in the notes if a reasonable possibility exists for loss greater than the amount accrued. (As a practical matter, care should be taken in presenting this disclosure to preserve the ability to negotiate an appropriate settlement.)

For financial reporting purposes, amounts accrued that are expected to be paid within 1 year after the date of the financial statements should be reported as current liabilities and the rest of the accrual should be reported as noncurrent. Hospitals should also disclose their programs of malpractice insurance coverage and their basis for recording accruals.

REPORTING ON MEDICAL MALPRACTICE CLAIMS

Risks regarding medical malpractice claims are generally transferred to third-party insurers by means of claims-made policies. A claims-made policy covers losses from claims that have been asserted or filed against the policy-holder during the policy period, regardless of whether the events occurred during the current or any previous period in which the policy-holder was insured. It does not insure the policy-holder, however, for incidents not reported to the insurer. Therefore, the hospital needs to make an accrual in its financial statements for incurred but not reported claims (IBNR). To illustrate, this is how the Hudson Valley Hospital Center reported on medical malpractice claims:

> The Hospital maintains a commercial claims-made policy for its medical malpractice insurance. The policy does not represent a transfer of risk for claims and incidents incurred but not reported (IBNR) to the insurance carrier. Therefore, the Hospital has recorded an estimated malpractice liability related to IBNR of approximately $2.9 million and $2.6 million at December 31, 2005 and December 31, 2004, respectively.

SOURCE: Notes to financial statements, Hudson Valley Hospital Center, Cortlandt Manor, NY, December 31, 2005 and 2004.

OTHER TRANSACTIONS

Contributions Received by a Hospital's Foundation

As a means of obtaining contributions, a not-for-profit hospital may establish a separate but financially interrelated fund-raising foundation. A financial interrelationship exists if the hospital is able to influence the foundation's operating and financial decisions and has an ongoing economic interest in the foundation's net assets. A hospital has the ability to influence the foundation's operating and financial decisions if, for example, the foundation's charter limits its activities to those that are beneficial to the hospital or the hospital has considerable representation on the foundation's governing board.

Under those circumstances, the not-for-profit hospital would report in its financial statements its interest in the foundation's net assets and adjust that interest for its share of the change in the foundation's net assets. Assume, for example, that a hospital established a foundation on January 2 for the sole purpose of raising funds on behalf of the hospital. During the year, the foundation obtained contributions of $900,000. Of this amount, $100,000 was unrestricted and $800,000 was restricted by the donors to acquisition of new equipment. At the hospital's request, the foundation transferred cash of $280,000 to the hospital, consisting of $30,000 that was unrestricted and $250,000 that was restricted for equipment acquisition. The hospital used the restricted cash immediately to acquire equipment. The hospital would make the following journal entries.

Interest in Hospital Foundation	900,000	
Unrestricted gains—Change in interest in net assets of Hospital Foundation		100,000
Temporarily restricted gains—Change in interest in net assets of Hospital Foundation		800,000
To record change in interest in net assets of Hospital Foundation.		
Cash, restricted for capital acquisition	250,000	
Cash	30,000	
Interest in Hospital Foundation		280,000
To record receipt of cash from Hospital Foundation.		
Equipment	250,000	
Cash, restricted for capital acquisition		250,000
To record acquisition of equipment.		
Temporarily restricted net asset reclassifications out—satisfaction of equipment acquisition restrictions	250,000	
Unrestricted net asset reclassifications in—satisfaction of equipment acquisition restrictions		250,000
To record reclassification of net assets.		

For financial reporting purposes, Interest in Hospital Foundation is an asset account. Temporarily restricted gains—change in interest in net assets is reported as increases in temporarily restricted net assets in the statement of changes in net assets. And Unrestricted gains—change in interest in net assets is reported as increases both in the statement of operations and in the unrestricted net assets section of the statement of changes in net assets.

Transactions Creating Assets Limited as to Use

Not-for-profit hospital balance sheets often show resources as "assets limited as to use" or "assets whose use is limited." These are designations of unrestricted resources that have been set aside either as a result of a contractual agreement with an external party other than a donor or as a result of a an internal decision by a hospital's governing board. For example:

- To secure payment of debt service, a hospital that sells revenue bonds may be required by the bond agreement to maintain a deposit with a trustee equal to, say, one year's debt service. Or, a hospital may be required by a third-party payer to fund depreciation on certain capital assets.

- A hospital's governing board may decide to set aside funds for a specific project or function, such as a special training program or a capital acquisition. Although these resources have been set aside, the segregation has no legal consequence because the board can readily reverse its decision.

To illustrate how the resources are set aside, assume a not-for-profit hospital sells revenue bonds for $10 million. From the proceeds of the sale, $800,000 is forwarded to a trustee to hold in escrow until the hospital makes final payment of debt service on the bonds. The hospital would make the following journal entry:

Cash	9,200,000	
Cash with trustee	800,000	
Bonds payable		10,000,000
To record proceeds from sale of bonds and cash held in escrow by trustee.		

If the hospital's governing board formally sets aside $750,000 of existing investments to create a fund to modernize equipment, it would make the following entry:

Investments—board-designated for equipment	750,000	
Investments		750,000
To record board designation of resources for equipment modernization		

ACCOUNTING FOR TRANSACTIONS WITH RESTRICTIONS

Not all resources held by an entity may be spent by its governing board in accordance with the board's desires. A donor, for example, may stipulate that a gift be used only for a particular purpose. Or, an entity may enter into a transaction, such as a borrowing, and make a legally binding agreement that a portion of the proceeds will be held by a trustee in escrow for a specific purpose. Restrictions on how resources may be used need to be recorded in the internal accounting records to ensure management compliance. They also need to be reported in the financial statements so users are not misled regarding their availability for the entity's general purposes.

Before the FASB introduced new financial reporting requirements, many not-for-profit entities (including not-for-profit hospitals) used fund accounting for internal purposes to provide information concerning restrictions. Fund accounting is not necessary to comply with FASB financial reporting requirements. Nevertheless, because many hospitals find value in fund accounting and continue to use it, we discuss accounting for restricted resources with the use of funds in this section of the chapter. (Whether or not fund accounting is used, the content of the journal entries is the same; the only difference is in how the journal entries are organized.)

The discussion of transactions with restrictions is complicated by two factors:

- The notion of *restricted,* as used in not-for-profit fund accounting, is broader than the FASB definition of the term for financial reporting. Specific Purpose

Funds, for example, can include both unrestricted and temporarily restricted resources because they can include both gifts contributed by donors and grants made by resource providers other than donors.

- The GASB defines the term *restricted* differently from the FASB. The GASB does not distinguish between temporarily restricted and permanently restricted, and it does not limit restricted net assets to those subject to donor-imposed restrictions.

Because of these complications, we discuss accounting for transactions with restrictions by not-for-profit hospitals separately from governmental hospitals.

Not-for-Profit Hospital Accounting for Restrictions
General Rules
The general rules for not-for-profit hospital accounting within each of the funds are similar to those discussed in Chapter 12 for other not-for-profit organizations. They are as follows:

- All donor-restricted contributions are recorded as either temporarily or permanently restricted revenues or gains when received.
- When temporarily restricted resources are released from restriction, not-for-profit hospitals record a reclassification out of temporarily restricted resources and a reclassification in to unrestricted net assets.
- Expenses resulting from use of the reclassified resources are reported as decreases in unrestricted net assets.

Specific Purpose Funds
Specific purpose funds are used to account for resources that are restricted for specific operating purposes. Restrictions on their use are temporary, expiring either with the passage of time or by fulfillment of the purpose stipulated by the donor. Assume a not-for-profit hospital receives a $500,000 gift, to be used specifically for research into methods of counseling individuals who have become addicted to drugs. Later, the hospital incurs $25,000 in research program expenses. The entries to record those transactions and the funds used to record them are as follows:

Entries to accounts for Specific Purpose Funds	Cash	500,000	
	Temporarily restricted support—contributions		500,000
	To record contribution for research.		
	Temporarily restricted asset reclassifications out— net assets released from restriction used for operations	25,000	
	Cash		25,000
	To record payment of research program expenses and net assets released from restriction.		
Entry to accounts for General Fund	Research program expenses	25,000	
	Unrestricted asset reclassifications in—net assets released from restrictions used for operations		25,000
	To record research program expenses and net assets released from restriction.		

Plant Replacement and Expansion Funds

Plant replacement and expansion funds accumulate resources from donors or grantors that can be used only to replace or expand existing plant assets. Because hospital plant is reported in the General Fund, Plant Replacement and Expansion Funds contain only financial resources that will be used to acquire capital resources. To illustrate, assume that Rocky MacDuff donates $100,000 cash to a not-for-profit hospital and that the gift must be used to replace existing assets. Then, $80,000 of the contribution is used to acquire equipment, causing expiration of the temporary restriction. The entries to record these transactions are as follows:

Entries to	Cash	100,000	
accounts for	Temporarily restricted support—contributions		100,000
Plant	To record MacDuff gift for capital assets replacement.		
Replacement and	Temporarily restricted asset reclassifications out—		
Expansion Fund	net assets released from restriction for purchase		
	of equipment	80,000	
	Cash		80,000
	To record release of net assets from		
	restriction and payment for equipment.		
Entry to accounts	Equipment	80,000	
for General Fund	Unrestricted assets reclassifications in—net		
	assets released from restriction for purchase		
	of equipment		80,000
	To record purchase of equipment and release of		
	net assets from restriction.		

If fund resources are invested in marketable securities until the plant is acquired, the recording of income from the securities is determined by the restrictions, if any, placed on that income. If no restrictions are placed on the use of the investment income, it is recorded in the General Fund as unrestricted. Assume income from the securities in this illustration must be used for the same purpose as the gift itself, which is what usually occurs. If $2,000 of income accrues from investment of the MacDuff gift, the investment income is recorded in the Plant Replacement and Expansion Fund, as follows:

Interest receivable	2,000	
Temporarily restricted revenue—investment income		2,000
To record investment income from MacDuff gift.		

Endowment Funds

Endowment funds are used when a donor gives a hospital assets whose principal must be maintained intact. Income from the investment of the assets can be either restricted or unrestricted in use. Assume that Sam and Max Katz give a hospital marketable securities with a fair market value of $500,000. The principal of the fund must be maintained in perpetuity (and is, therefore, considered as a Permanent or Pure Endowment Fund). The income from the endowment is restricted to finance the cost of cancer research. Income of $30,000 is received during the year. The entries to record those transactions are as follows:

Entry to accounts	Marketable securities	500,000	
for Endowment	Permanently restricted support—contributions		500,000
Fund	To record receipt of Sam and Max Katz gift.		

Entry to accounts	Cash	30,000	
for Specific	Temporarily restricted revenue—investment income		30,000
Purpose Fund	To record investment income from Sam and Max		
	Katz fund to be used for cancer research.		

(*Note:* In the preceding entry, the investment income was recorded directly in the Specific Purpose Fund. Some prefer to record the revenue initially in the Endowment Fund and establish a "due to" the Specific Purpose Fund, to provide control over the investment income. When the resources of the Specific Purpose Fund are used to conduct research, the expenses are reported in the General Fund and the temporarily restricted net assets are released from restrictions. This journal record is made with reclassification entries, as shown in the journal entries on page 523.)

If the contribution specified that the income from the endowment could be used for any purpose desired by the hospital's management, the investment income would be reported in the General Fund with a credit to Unrestricted revenue—investment income.

Financial Reporting Effect

The foregoing illustrations assume the use of fund accounting for internal control purposes. For external financial reporting, however, not-for-profit hospitals must report on the entity as a whole (distinguishing among unrestricted, temporarily restricted, and permanently restricted resources) just like any other not-for-profit entity.

Donor-restricted contributions are reported in the Statement of Changes in Net Assets as increases in temporarily or permanently restricted net assets. Net assets released from restrictions are reported in that statement as decreases in temporarily restricted net assets. Net assets released from restrictions used for operations (reclassification in) and related program expenses are reported on the Statement of Operations (see skeletal outline on page 506) and in the Statement of Changes in Net Assets. Net assets released from restrictions used for purchase of property and equipment (reclassification in) are also reported on both statements, but below the line showing Excess of revenues over expenses (see skeletal outline).

Governmental Hospital Accounting for Restrictions

General Rules

For financial reporting purposes, the GASB defines the term *restricted* differently from the FASB. The GASB requires that net assets be reported as restricted when constraints are imposed either:

- Externally, by creditors (such as through debt covenants), grantors, contributors, or laws or regulations of other governments, or
- By law, through constitutional provisions or enabling legislation.[7] (Enabling legislation, as the term is used by the GASB, includes a legally enforceable requirement that resources be used only for the purposes stipulated in the legislation.)

Governmental hospitals engaged in business-type activities follow GASB standards for proprietary funds. Pursuant to GASB *Statement No. 34,* all proprietary fund revenues, including capital contributions and additions to permanent and term endow-

---

[7]GASB Cod. Sec. 1800.134.

ments, should be reported on the all-inclusive statement of revenues, expenses, and changes in net assets.[8]

Hospital transactions accounted for in restricted funds are often what the GASB defines as *voluntary nonexchange transactions.* They include certain governmental grants and entitlements as well as donations by nongovernmental entities, including individuals. Governmental hospitals receiving such grants and donations should recognize revenues when all applicable eligibility requirements, including time requirements, are met.[9]

GASB *Statement No. 33* distinguishes between time requirements and purpose restrictions. *Time requirements* specify the period when resources must be used or when use may begin. Time requirements affect revenue recognition. For example, if a hospital receives resources before it is eligible to use them, the grant or gift should be reported as deferred revenue. *Purpose restrictions* specify the purpose for which the resources are required to be used. They do not affect revenue recognition, but instead affect whether the net assets should be classified as restricted or unrestricted.

In addition to time requirements, other types of eligibility requirements affect the timing of revenue recognition. For example, a higher-level government may specify that the recipient of a hospital construction grant does not qualify for resources until allowable costs are incurred (as in the case of expenditure-driven grants). In those instances, revenues are recognized as allowable costs are incurred. Gifts received as endowments should be recognized as revenues upon receipt, provided all eligibility requirements are met.

When restricted fund resources are used for the intended purposes, expenses or assets should be recorded in the General Fund. The credit part of the entry to record these transactions in the General Fund should be labeled "Amounts released from restriction," which is narrower and hence more descriptive than the term *transfers.*

Illustration of Private Donation with Purpose Restriction

A corporation makes a donation to a governmental hospital, stipulating that the donation must be used solely for the purpose of training nurses. For this voluntary nonexchange transaction, the hospital should recognize the entire amount as revenue (reported as nonoperating revenues) when the gift is received. The resulting net assets should be reported as restricted until the purpose restriction (training nurses) is fulfilled. If $50,000 is donated and $20,000 of that amount is used, the following entries would be made to record the transaction.

Entries to accounts for Specific Purpose Funds	Cash	50,000	
	Restricted revenue (nonoperating)—contributions		50,000
	To record contribution for nurse training.		
	Amounts released from restriction to General Fund	20,000	
	Cash		20,000
	To record fulfillment of purpose restriction for nurse training.		

---

[8]GASB Cod. (2006), Sec. P80.119.

[9]GASB Cod. (2006), Sec. N50.104d.

Entry to accounts	Training expenses	20,000	
for General Fund	Amounts released from restriction from Specific		
	Purpose Funds		20,000
	To record research expenses from contribution.		

Illustration of Construction Grant with Eligibility Requirement

A federal agency makes a cash grant of $500,000 to finance a governmental hospital's acquisition of special equipment. The grant agreement contains an eligibility requirement; namely, the hospital does not qualify for the grant without first incurring allowable costs. In this situation, the hospital should report the grant as deferred revenue until it incurs expenditures under the grant. If the hospital spends $200,000 to acquire equipment and sends an invoice to the federal agency for that amount, it would make the following entries:

Entries to	Cash	500,000	
accounts for	Deferred revenue		500,000
Plant	To record receipt of grant for equipment acquisition.		
Replacement and	Amounts released from restriction to General Fund	200,000	
Expansion Fund	Cash		200,000
	To record capital expenditure.		
	Deferred revenue	200,000	
	Revenue—capital contributions		200,000
	To record revenue recognition		
Entry to accounts	Equipment	200,000	
for General Fund	Amounts released from restriction from		
	Plant Replacement and Expansion Fund		200,000
	To record purchase of equipment under federal grant.		

If the hospital does not receive an advance payment from the federal agency, it makes no entry until it incurs expenditures under the grant. When it incurs expenditures, it should recognize both receivables and revenues.

Financial Reporting Effect

Although the preceding illustrations assume the use of fund accounting for internal purposes, governmental hospitals prepare external financial reports on the entity as a whole, as illustrated in Tables 13-5 and 13-6 (pages 529 and 530). Therefore, when the hospital prepares its operating statement, amounts recorded in the funds as "released from restriction" are eliminated against each other. In the first illustration, the entire $50,000 contribution is reported as nonoperating revenue. At year end, the unspent portion ($30,000) of the contribution is reported as restricted net assets. In the second illustration, the $200,000 of recognized revenue should be reported as capital contributions after Income before other revenues and expenses. For illustrations of the reporting of transactions such as these, see the appropriate captions in Tables 13-5 and 13-6.

TABLE 13-3   Statement of Changes in Net Assets—Not-for-Profit Hospital

Hudson Valley Hospital Center
Statements of Changes in Net Assets
Years Ended December 31, 2005 and 2004

	Unrestricted Net Assets	Temporarily Restricted Net Assets	Permanently Restricted Net Assets	Total Net Assets
Balances, December 31, 2003	$15,502,408	$ 7,433,741	$ 669,163	$23,605,312
Changes in net assets				
Excess of revenues over expenses	5,421,919	—	—	5,421,919
Net assets released from restrictions for capital expenditures	3,126,250	(3,126,250)	—	—
Change in net unrealized gains and losses on investments	230,272	—	—	230,272
Change in interest in net assets of the Foundation of Hudson Valley Hospital Center	—	1,005,614	—	1,005,614
Total changes in net assets	8,778,441	(2,120,636)	—	6,657,805
Balances, December 31, 2004	24,280,849	5,313,105	669,163	30,263,117
Changes in net assets				
Excess of revenues over expenses	10,187,446	—	—	10,187,446
Cumulative effect of change in accounting principles	(146,854)	—	—	(146,854)
Change in net unrealized gains and losses on investments	(75,897)	—	—	(75,897)
Endowment transfer	—	—	1,005,456	1,005,456
Change in interest in net assets of the Foundation of Hudson Valley Hospital Center	—	227,646	—	227,646
Total changes in net assets	9,964,695	227,646	1,005,456	11,197,797
Balances, December 31, 2005	$34,245,544	$ 5,540,751	$1,674,619	$41,460,914

Source: Hudson Valley Hospital Center financial statements, December 31, 2005 and 2004. Reprinted with permission. (Accompanying notes, which are an integral part of these statements, are not shown here.)

FINANCIAL STATEMENTS

There are many similarities in the financial statements prepared by not-for-profit and governmental hospitals, but there are also some differences. The differences result from the differing standards of the FASB (and the AICPA's Health Care Organizations Guides) and the GASB. The financial statements of both not-for-profit and governmental hospitals focus on the hospital as a whole, rather than on individual funds. Not-for-profit hospitals report changes in net assets separately for unrestricted, temporarily restricted, and permanently restricted funds, and emphasize a performance indicator within the changes in unrestricted net assets. Governmental hospitals prepare an all-inclusive statement of revenues, expenses and changes in net assets.

TABLE 13-4   Statement of Cash Flows—Not-for-Profit Hospital

Hudson Valley Hospital Center
Statement of Cash Flows
Years Ended December 31, 2005 and 2004

	2005	2004
Cash flows from operating activities		
Change in net assets	$ 11,197,797	$ 6,657,805
Adjustments to reconcile change in net assets to cash provided by operating activities:		
Depreciation and amortization	4,488,172	4,962,198
Provision for bad debts	1,775,068	3,238,525
Realized losses and change in unrealized gains and losses on investments	(69,703)	(212,979)
Change in interest in net assets of the Foundation of Hudson Valley Hospital Center	(227,646)	(1,005,614)
Cumulative effect of a change in accounting principle	146,854	—
Endowment transfer	(1,005,456)	—
Changes in operating assets and liabilities:		
Patient accounts receivable	(3,435,555)	(5,775,078)
Other receivables, supplies and prepaid expenses, other assets	(1,569,271)	1,711,353
Accounts payable and accrued expenses	(432,487)	171,185
Accrued salaries and benefits	867,308	714,963
Estimated payable to third-party payers, malpractice, and other liabilities	2,979,235	3,975,848
Net change in due from Foundation of the Hudson Valley Hospital Center	(406,972)	85,339
Net cash provided by operating activities	14,307,344	14,523,545
Cash flows used in investing activities		
Acquisition of property, plant, and equipment	(4,302,565)	(2,085,717)
Net purchase of investments and assets whose use is limited	(9,610,279)	(3,403,170)
Net cash used in investing activities	(13,912,844)	(5,488,887)
Cash flows used in financing activities		
Principal payments on long-term debt and capital lease obligations	(2,379,907)	(2,421,721)
Proceeds from endowment transfer	1,005,456	—
Net cash used in financing activities	(1,374,451)	(2,421,721)
Net (decrease) increase in cash and cash equivalents	(979,951)	6,612,937
Cash and cash equivalents at beginning of year	10,524,715	3,911,778
Cash and cash equivalents at end of year	$ 9,544,764	$10,524,715

Source: Hudson Valley Hospital Center financial statements, December 31, 2005 and 2004. Reprinted with permission. (Accompanying notes, which are an integral part of these statements, are not shown here.)

Not-for-profit hospital financial statements are illustrated in Tables 13-1 through 13-4. The statements are the actual ones prepared by the Hudson Valley Hospital Center (HVHC) for the years 2005 and 2004. HVHC is a 120-bed acute care not-for-profit hospital, located in Cortlandt Manor, New York, that provides services to residents of Westchester and Putnam Counties. Governmental hospital financial statements are

TABLE 13-5   Balance Sheet—Governmental Hospital

County Hospital at Croton
Balance Sheets
December 31, 2005 and 2004
(Amounts in Thousands)

	2005	2004
Assets		
Current assets:		
Cash and cash equivalents	$ 8,300	$ 6,800
Short-term investments	3,100	2,600
Patient accounts receivable, net of estimated uncollectibles—$2,300 in 2005; $2,200 in 2004	16,700	17,500
Medical supplies and drugs	2,300	2,200
Total current assets	30,400	29,100
Assets limited as to use:		
Internally designated	15,000	15,000
Noncurrent assets:		
Restricted investments	1,500	
Land	6,200	6,200
Buildings and equipment	52,400	49,000
Less, accumulated depreciation	(16,700)	(13,000)
Total noncurrent assets	43,400	42,200
Total assets	$ 88,800	$ 86,300
Liabilities		
Current liabilities:		
Current maturities of long-term debt	$ 1,300	$ 1,300
Accounts payable and accrued expenses	4,800	4,000
Estimated third-party settlements	2,100	2,100
Total current liabilities	8,200	7,400
Noncurrent liabilities:		
Long-term debt, net of current maturities	27,000	28,300
Other noncurrent liabilities	4,700	4,700
Total noncurrent liabilities	31,700	33,000
Total liabilities	39,900	40,400
Net assets:		
Invested in capital assets, net of related debt	13,600	12,600
Restricted—research grants	800	800
Restricted—endowment funds (nonexpendable)	1,500	
Unrestricted	33,000	32,500
Total net assets	48,900	45,900
Total liabilities and net assets	$ 88,800	$ 86,300

See accompanying notes to financial statements.

TABLE 13-6 Operating Statement—Governmental Hospital

County Hospital at Croton
Statement of Revenues, Expenses, and Changes in Net Assets
Years Ended December 31, 2005 and 2004
(Amounts in Thousands)

	2005	2004
Operating revenues:		
Net patient service revenue	$62,300	$60,600
Premium revenue	13,900	12,900
Other revenue	2,500	3,600
Total revenues	78,700	77,100
Operating expenses:		
Salaries and benefits	43,600	42,800
Medical supplies and drugs	12,100	11,800
Insurance	5,800	5,600
Other supplies	9,700	9,300
Provision for bad debts	2,100	2,000
Depreciation of buildings and equipment	3,700	3,500
Total operating expenses	77,000	75,000
Operating income	1,700	2,100
Nonoperating revenues (expenses)		
Interest and investment revenue	300	400
Interest on long-term debt	(1,500)	(1,600)
Total nonoperating expenses	(1,200)	(1,200)
Income before other revenues and expenses	500	900
Capital contributions	1,000	0
Endowment contributions	1,500	0
Change in net assets	3,000	900
Total net assets—beginning	45,900	45,000
Total net assets—ending	$48,900	$45,900

See accompanying notes to financial statements.

illustrated in Tables 13-5 through 13-7. They are the statements of a fictitious hospital, County Hospital at Croton (Croton), prepared in accordance with GASB standards for business-type activities.

Balance Sheet

Notice the following items, in particular, about the balance sheets illustrated in Tables 13-1 and 13-5:

- Current assets and current liabilities are presented separately from other assets and liabilities.
- *Assets whose use is limited* are separated from other assets, and externally imposed limitations are shown separately (either on the face of the statements or

in the notes) from internal limitations. Notes to the HVHC statements show that the assets whose use is limited represent primarily resources that are externally restricted for plant replacement under bond indenture agreements, as well as resources escrowed in connection with certain capital lease agreements.

- *Interest in Foundation of Hudson Valley Hospital Center* (Table 13-1). Notes to the HVHC statements state the foundation's principal activity is soliciting,

TABLE 13-7 Cash Flow Statement—Governmental Hospital

County Hospital at Croton
Cash Flow Statement
Year Ended December 31, 2005
(Amounts in Thousands)

Cash flows from operating activities:	
Receipts from patients	$ 61,000
Receipts from insurance premiums, other	16,400
Payments to employees	(43,600)
Payments to suppliers	(26,900)
Net cash provided by operating activities	6,900
Cash flows from capital and related financing activities:	
Capital contributions	1,000
Purchases of capital assets	(3,400)
Principal paid on capital debt	(1,300)
Interest paid on capital debt	(1,500)
Net cash (used) for capital and related financing activities	(5,200)
Cash flows from noncapital financing activities:	
None	
Cash flows from investing activities:	
Purchases of investments	(3,100)
Proceeds from maturity of investments	2,600
Interest received	300
Net cash (used) for investing activities	(200)
Net increase in cash and cash equivalents	1,500
Cash at beginning of year	6,800
Cash at end of year	$ 8,300
Reconciliation of operating income to net cash	
provided by operating activities:	
Operating income	$ 1,700
Adjustments to reconcile operating income to net	
cash provided by operating activities:	
Depreciation expenses	3,700
Changes in assets and liabilities:	
Decrease in net patient receivables	800
Increase in inventories	(100)
Increase in accounts payable	800
Net cash provided by operating activities	$ 6,900

receiving, investing, and administering contributions primarily for HVHC. The interest in the foundation is included in temporarily restricted net assets because the resources are restricted to capital asset acquisition.

- *Net assets.* HVHC's net assets are separated among unrestricted, temporarily restricted, and permanently restricted, in accordance with FASB standards, discussed in Chapter 12. Croton's net assets are separated among invested in capital assets (net of related debt), restricted, or unrestricted, in accordance with GASB standards, discussed in Chapter 7. Purposes for which the restricted net assets may be used are shown either on the face of the statements or in notes.

Statements of Operations and Changes in Net Assets
Not-for-Profit Hospitals

FASB *Statement No. 117* permits differing formats for not-for-profit statements of activities, allowing entities to report information in what they consider to be the most meaningful way to financial statement users. For this reason, the *AICPA Guide* prescribes two statements of changes in net assets. One, called the statement of operations, covers only changes in unrestricted net assets and includes the details of revenues and expenses that constitute a *performance indicator.* The other, called a statement of changes in net assets, covers the changes in net assets for all three net asset classifications.

To emphasize the importance of the performance indicator within the statement of operations, the *AICPA Guide* calls for it to be clearly labeled, using terms such as *revenues over expenses, revenues and gains over expenses and losses, earned income,* or *performance earnings.*[10] The performance indicator should be presented in a statement that also presents the total changes in unrestricted net assets. To accomplish this purpose, changes in net assets other than those that affect the performance indicator are reported on the operating statement below the performance indicator line.

To illustrate, turn to Table 13-2 (see page 513). First, notice that this operating statement relates only to unrestricted net assets. Transactions affecting temporarily restricted and permanently restricted net assets are not included in a hospital's operating statement, except to the extent those net assets have been released from restrictions into unrestricted net assets.

Next, notice that patient service revenue is HVHC's main source of revenue. As discussed previously, Net patient service revenue is the excess of gross billings for services less provisions for charity care, contractual adjustments with third-party payers, and other similar items the hospital does not expect to collect. These adjustments do not include a provision for bad debts.

Other revenue is generated by normal day-to-day activities, other than patient care, that are related to the organization's central operations. Notice that in Table 13-2, all resource inflows that enter into the performance indicator (the performance indicator is the line captioned Excess of revenues over expenses) are reported under Operating revenues, except for investment income. Investment income, which is part of the performance indicator, could also be reported as part of Other revenue.

Notice also that the performance indicator *Excess of revenues over expenses* is separated from other factors causing the net increase in unrestricted net assets. Consider

---

[10]*AICPA Audit and Accounting Guide—Health Care Organizations* (2006), para. 10.20.

the difference in the nature of the transactions affecting the performance indicator from those presented below that line.

- *Change in Net Unrealized Gains and Losses on Investments.* As described earlier in this chapter, with regard to their unrestricted net assets, not-for-profit hospitals report realized gains and losses on investments separately from unrealized gains and losses on securities other than trading securities. Realized gains and losses are included with investment income as part of the measure of operating performance, while unrealized gains and losses are shown below that measure. (The notes show that interest income represents most of HVHC's investment income.)
- *Net Assets Released from Restrictions for Capital Expenditures.* Part of the resources held by HVHC's Foundation was used to acquire capital assets in 2004, resulting in reclassifying the net assets from temporarily restricted to unrestricted. Because the resources were used to acquire capital assets, the reclassification was reported *below* the measure of operating performance. If HVHC had net assets released from restrictions and used for *operations,* the reclassification in would have been shown as operating revenues and, therefore, as part of the performance measure. Why the difference? The answer lies in the matching principle of accounting. Reclassified net assets used for operations can be matched with related expenses. But only the current year's depreciation is shown as an expense when reclassified net assets are used to acquire capital assets; showing the entire amount released from restrictions as part of the performance indicator would overstate the hospital's performance.

The statement of changes in net assets is a summary reconciliation of the beginning and ending net assets of each of the three net asset classifications. Table 13-3 illustrates the statement of changes in net assets. Notice that, for the unrestricted net assets, the details constituting the performance indicator Excess of revenues over expenses—which were in the operating statement—are not repeated in the statement of changes in net assets. Notice also, that:

- For 2004, the amount shown as net assets released from restrictions for capital expenditures ($3,126,250) under Temporarily restricted net assets is the same as the amount reported as a reclassification in to Unrestricted net assets.
- For 2005 and 2004, Temporarily restricted net assets were increased by a change in the interest in the net assets of HVHC's foundation.

Governmental Hospitals

Governmental hospitals report in accordance with the GASB's standards for proprietary funds. GASB *Statement No. 34* requires that the proprietary fund operating statement take the form of an all-inclusive statement of revenues, expenses, and changes in fund net assets or fund equity, as illustrated in Chapter 7 (page 244). No provision is made in GASB *Statement No. 34* for separate "statements of operations" for unrestricted funds and "statements of changes in net assets" covering both unrestricted and restricted funds.

The statement of revenues, expenses, and changes in fund net assets, which distinguishes between operating and nonoperating revenues and expenses, requires a separate subtotal for operating income. It also requires that nonoperating revenues and expenses be reported after operating income, leading to a subtotal of Income before other revenues and expenses.

The GASB does not define "operating" and "nonoperating," but it allows each government to establish and disclose definitions appropriate to the activity being reported. However, revenues from capital contributions, additions to the principal of permanent and term endowments, special and extraordinary items, and transfers must be reported separately, after nonoperating revenues and expenses. Based on the types of items normally included in "nonoperating" (for example, interest income and interest expense) and the types of items that must be reported separately, it would be reasonable to use the subtotal Income before other revenues and expenses as a performance indicator.

Table 13-6 illustrates a statement of revenues, expenses, and changes in fund net assets for a governmental hospital. Notice the captions of the various subtotals and the items comprising nonoperating income and expenses, such as interest on long-term debt. Notice also that capital contributions and endowment contributions are reported toward the end of the statement, just before Change in net assets. Because this statements is all-inclusive, covering both unrestricted and restricted resources, reporting of amounts released from restrictions is not necessary.

Except for the net assets section, the governmental hospital balance sheet illustrated in Table 13-5 is similar to the not-for-profit hospital balance sheet shown in Table 13-1.

Statement of Cash Flows

Tables 13-4 and 13-7 illustrate the cash flow statements of not-for-profit and governmental hospitals, respectively. Cash flow statements describe the causes of increases and decreases in cash from the beginning of the year to the end of the year. Notice that the end-of-year amounts for cash and cash equivalents, shown in the last line of the cash flow statements, are the same as the amounts reported for cash and cash equivalents on the balance sheets.

Because of differences in the standards adopted by the FASB and the GASB, several major differences can be found in the details of these two statements:

1. The not-for-profit hospital cash flow statement is presented using the indirect method, whereas the governmental cash flow statement is presented using the direct method.
2. The not-for-profit hospital cash flow statement presents three major classifications of cash flows: operating activities, investing activities, and financing activities. The governmental hospital cash flow statement provides four classifications: operating activities, noncapital financing activities, capital and related financing activities, and investing activities.
3. The starting point for the operating activity portion of the not-for-profit cash flow statement is the change in net assets. Notice that the first line of HVHC's 2005 statement is $11,197,797, which is the increase in net assets for the year, shown in the statement of changes in net assets. The reconciliation point for the governmental cash flow statement, however, is operating income (loss) for the year.

Review Questions

Q13-1   Which major publications establish GAAP for health care organizations?

Q13-2   To what extent does the GASB permit government-owned health care entities that use proprietary fund accounting to apply FASB accounting standards?

Q13-3   Distinguish between the kinds of resources accounted for in the General Fund and the kinds accounted for in Restricted Funds.

Q13-4   Describe the four broad categories of resources included in the General Fund.

Q13-5   What is a contractual adjustment?

Q13-6   A hospital has contractual adjustments, takes charity cases, grants discounts to clergy, and has bad debts. How does each affect net patient service revenue?

Q13-7   How do prospective and retrospective payment agreements affect the amount reported as net patient service revenue?

Q13-8   A not-for-profit hospital invests a $10,000 restricted donation in equity securities. At the date of its financial statements, the securities have a fair value of $12,000. How would the hospital report the increased value in its financial statements? Would your answer be the same if it were a governmental hospital?

Q13-9   Under what circumstances, if any, would a not-for-profit hospital recognize donated services and donated drugs in its records?

Q13-10 Illustrate the difference between recording a hospital's expenses by natural classification and recording by function. Discuss which is more informative.

Q13-11 Describe the basic rule for recognizing expenses and liabilities for medical malpractice claims.

Q13-12 Describe the accounting process to record the segregation of resources by the managing board of a hospital.

Q13-13 Describe how the resources raised by a not-for-profit hospital's fund-raising foundation are reported in the hospital's financial statements.

Q13-14 If a governmental hospital receives a cash grant that contains a time requirement, when should the hospital recognize revenues for the grant?

Q13-15 Discuss the kinds of information a user of a not-for-profit hospital's financial statements can obtain from the statement of operations, the statement of changes in net assets, and the statement of cash flows.

Cases

C13-1   Several young doctors started a small not-for-profit out-patient-type hospital in a poor neighborhood in their spare time. Because the doctors received their education free from the state in the form of scholarships, they plan to work at the hospital without pay. The chief administrative officer does not believe that the value of the donated services should appear in the financial statements of the hospital. The controller feels that the conditions under which the services were donated require that they be recorded. The CEO feels that if the revenue associated with the services is recorded it will look like the hospital has a great deal more revenue than it actually has, which may cause it a problem when seeking donations and grants. The doctors do not want the value of their services recorded. How would you respond to this situation?

C13-2   The chief administrative officer of the East Jeff Hospital, Vera Thomas, is attempting to find resources to add a new wing to the hospital. For the past several years, many patients were turned away because of a lack of space. The hospital has a large endowment, but all earnings from these funds are restricted to various operating purposes; for example, providing continuing education for nurses and maintaining the parking lot. Thomas approached you and asked whether a recently received gift from T. W. Wealthy could be used to begin expansion. Wealthy donated $1 million to the hospital in his deceased wife's name. She recently died from cancer, and in her memory Wealthy established a cancer research fund. How would you respond to Ms. Thomas?

Ethics Cases

EC13-1 Rodney de Fine, the chief administrative officer of the First Street Hospital, is having an argument with Jane Bronson, the hospital's controller. De Fine recently received a gift of $100,000 from a benefactor. He wants to put money into a board-designated fund to allow the board to do whatever it wants with the money. Bronson, however, feels that the hospital should talk with the donor to determine whether he wishes any particular use for his donation. De Fine is concerned that if the donor wishes to use the money in a manner that does not meet the hospital's immediate needs, the hospital may have to turn away some patients because of a lack of facilities. How would you handle this dilemma?

EC13-2 A not-for-profit hospital is seeking a loan from a bank to finance a major acquisition of equipment. The hospital is preparing its financial statements for 2008, which the bank's loan officer wants to review before completing the loan agreement. Based on preliminary data, the hospital's treasurer thinks the loan officer will be troubled with the amount the hospital will report as "excess of revenues over expenses" in the hospital's statement of operations. The treasurer knows the hospital comptroller plans to report the allowance for bad debts at 20 percent of patient accounts receivable, the same rate used in preparing the 2006 and 2007 financial statements. The treasurer goes to the comptroller and says: "I'd really like to improve our bottom line a bit. Seems to me the economy is better than last year. I suggest you reduce the bad debts allowance to 12 percent." What should the comptroller do?

Exercises

E13-1 (Fill in the blanks—general terminology)

1. The AICPA publishes the _____ as a source of information on hospital accounting.
2. FASB standards (always, sometimes, never) _____ apply to governmental hospitals.
3. Board-designated resources are classified as (unrestricted, temporarily restricted, permanently restricted) _____ net assets.
4. Endowment Funds, Plant Replacement and Expansion Funds, and Specific Purpose Funds are _____ Funds.
5. The daily operations of a hospital are accounted for in the _____ Fund.
6. Hospitals use the _____ basis of accounting.

E13-2 (Use of funds)

The Brite-Hope Hospital uses the following types of funds:

GF   General Fund
EF   Endowment Funds
PREF Plant Replacement and Expansion Funds
SPF   Specific Purpose Funds

Using these codes, identify which fund or funds would be used to account for the following events:

_____ **1.** The operations of the cafeteria.
_____ **2.** A gift received from an individual for medical research (at this time consider only the receipt of the gift).
_____ **3.** Income is earned on investments of money donated by the Many-bucks Corporation (the original gift and all income earned must be used to provide up-to-date equipment for the hospital).
_____ **4.** The hospital received $1 million in securities from an individual. The principal of the gift must be maintained intact. (Consider only the receipt of the gift.)
_____ **5.** The managing board of the hospital decided to start a fund for cancer research. It transferred $30,000 into the fund. Which fund would be used to record the receipt of the money?
_____ **6.** The payment of salaries to the nursing staff.
_____ **7.** Depreciation is recorded on the equipment in use.
_____ **8.** The purchase of additional hospital equipment.

E13-3 (Identification of net asset classifications)

Assume that Brite-Hope Hospital, in E13-2, is a not-for-profit hospital. Using the following letters identify which net asset classification would be affected by the events listed in E13-2.
a. Unrestricted net assets
b. Temporarily restricted net assets
c. Permanently restricted net assets

E13-4 (Journal entries)

Prepare journal entries to record the following transactions of a not-for-profit hospital.

1. The hospital billed its patients for $250,000.
2. Nurses and doctors employed by the hospital were paid their salaries, $100,000.
3. The chief administrative officer was paid her salary of $10,000.
4. The hospital paid its utility bill, $5,000.
5. Depreciation on the equipment was $34,000.
6. Several adults donated their time (worth $5,000) selling merchandise in the hospital gift shop.
7. The hospital billed Medicare $100,000 for services provided at its established rates. The prospective billing arrangement gives Medicare a 40 percent discount from these rates.
8. An unrestricted donation of $4,000 was received.

E13-5   (Accounting for board-designated resources)
On January 1, 2009, the managing board of a not-for-profit hospital set aside $35,000 to upgrade the skills of its newly hired nurses. During January, the hospital spent $15,000 to train the nurses. Prepare journal entries to record the transactions.

E13-6   (Accounting for uncollectible patient accounts)
The Metro County Hospital could not collect the amount billed to a patient. The patient declared bankruptcy and had no assets with which to pay his debts. Assuming the patient owned the hospital $3,000, prepare the entry or entries necessary to record the uncollectible account if the hospital uses the allowance method. After preparing the necessary entry or entries, state what effect the write-off will have on the balance sheet.

E13-7   (Discussion scenarios)
Discuss the accounting and financial reporting principles in the following scenarios.

1. A governmental hospital does not carry insurance. Several patients have filed malpractice claims against the hospital, but the claims have not yet been adjudicated. Hospital attorneys think the hospital will probably lose one of the cases and have started settlement negotiations with the patient. The hospital is preparing its financial statements at year end.

2. A billing arrangement with a third-party payer provides for a retrospective adjustment. The hospital estimates it will need to refund $45,000 to the third party, but it has not started settlement negotiations on the amount of the adjustment. The hospital is preparing its year-end financial statements.

3. A not-for-profit hospital has just opened a gift shop. The merchandise for the gift shop is bought by a hospital employee, but all the selling is done by volunteers. The hospital comptroller estimates that, if she had to pay the volunteers for their services, it would cost the hospital $25,000 a year. She wants to know how to handle the donated services in the financial statements.

4. A hospital provides services to Medicare patients amounting to $40 million at its established billing rates. But the billing arrangement with Medicare provides for a contractual adjustment of 40 percent from the established rates. The hospital also provides charity care that has a value of $5 million at its established billing rates. A hospital board member wants to report the lost revenues as bad debts expenses.

E13-8   (Accounting for contractual adjustments)
A hospital arranges with a third-party payer to charge the third party 75 percent of its established billing rates. During January 2009, the hospital provided services amounting to $1 million at the established billing rates. Prepare journal entries to record the January billings.

E13-9   (Accounting for premium revenues)
A hospital arranges with an HMO to provide hospital care to the HMO's members at a specific rate per member, per month. During June, the HMO paid the hospital $850,000, in accordance with the agreement. The hospital's

cost accounting records showed that, if it had billed the HMO in accordance with its established billing rates, it would have billed the HMO $975,000. Prepare the appropriate journal entry (or entries) to record this transaction.

E13-10 (Accounting for net patient service revenues)

Shelley Marder Hospital had the following transactions during the year ended December 31, 2009.

1. The hospital provided services to third-party payer A amounting to $5 million at its established billing rates. The hospital's prospective billing arrangement with this third party stipulates payment to the hospital of 70 percent of its established rates for services performed. All billings were paid during the year.

2. The hospital provided services to third-party payer B amounting to $3 million at its established billing rates. Its retrospective billing arrangement with this third party stipulates that the hospital should receive payment at an interim rate of 90 percent of its established rates, subject to retrospective adjustment based on agreed-upon allowable costs. By year end, B had paid all the billings. Before issuing its financial statements, the hospital estimated that it would need to refund $250,000 to B based on allowable costs.

3. The hospital provided services to charity patients amounting to $1 million at its established billing rates.

Required: 1. Prepare journal entries to record these transactions.
2. State the amount that Shelley Marder Hospital would report as net patient service revenues in its operating statement.

E13-11 (Journal entries to record investment transactions)

A hospital purchased 100 shares of stock on June 30, 2009, for $3,100, intending to hold the stock until needed for plant expansion purposes. At December 31, 2008, the date of its financial statements, the stock's fair value was $3,200. On November 30, 2009, the hospital sold the stock for $2,800.

Required: 1. Assuming it is a governmental hospital, prepare journal entries to record all the transactions and events related to the investment.
2. Assuming it is a not-for-profit hospital, prepare journal entries to record all the transactions and events related to the investment.

E13-12 (Financial reporting of investment gains and losses)

Reread the material on reporting investment gains and losses in the section "Investment Returns" and consider the journal entries you made in E13-11. Which of the two reporting methods (if either) do you think is the more informative? Which of the two reporting methods (if either) do you think better expresses the hospital's financial performance? Give reasons for your answers.

E13-13 (Journal entries to record the receipt and use of contributions by a not-for-profit hospital)

Mary Milligan Hospital, a not-for-profit hospital, had the following transactions during the year ended December 31, 2008. Prepare journal entries necessary to record the transactions. The hospital does not use fund accounting.

1. Ed Glott, a high school senior, donated his services to the hospital for an entire summer, serving food to patients and performing general tasks. If paid for, these services would have cost the hospital $5,000.

2. D. Bean donated $20,000 to the hospital, stipulating that the resources be used only to update the skills of the nurses.

3. The hospital used D. Bean's donation for the stipulated purpose.

4. D. Lily Allen donated $500,000 to the hospital to help pay for new MRI equipment.

5. The hospital used D. Lily Allen's donation for new MRI equipment.

E13-14 (Use of funds)

The following transactions relate to the Tableaux Hospital, a not-for-profit hospital. Indicate which fund or funds would be used to record the data.

1. Collected $2,345 from a patient.

2. Received a $100,000 grant from Toosuups Drug Company for a study of the effects of morphine on female patients.

3. Received unrestricted gifts of $50,000.

4. Purchased equipment for $125,000 by using resources previously accumulated in the Plant Replacement and Expansion Fund.

5. Research expenses totaling $12,000 were incurred in studying the effects of morphine on female patients, using the Toosuups grant.

6. The board decided to begin a fund for nursing education. Initially $10,000 of general hospital resources was transferred to the fund.

7. Marketable securities with a fair value of $15,000 were donated by WFJ, Inc., to help the hospital acquire new equipment.

8. The securities in item 7 produced income of $5,000. Assume that the investment income is restricted in the same way as the original gift.

E13-15 (Transactions involving General Fund and restricted funds)

Using the same information given in E13-14, prepare the journal entries that would be used to record the data. Identify each type of fund used.

E13-16 (Financial statements)

Using the following codes, indicate which statement would be used to report each item for a not-for-profit hospital.

BS	Balance sheet
SO	Statement of operations
SCNA	Statement of changes in net assets only

_____ **1.** Land, buildings, and equipment

_____ **2.** Unrestricted contributions

_____ **3.** General services expense

_____ **4.** Contributions receivable

_____ **5.** Realized gain on sale of permanently restricted investments

_____ **6.** Assets limited as to use

_____ **7.** Change in interest in hospital foundation's temporarily restricted assets

_____ **8.** Estimated liability for malpractice costs

Problems

P13-1 (Matching)

Match items on the right with those on the left by placing the letter of the best match in the space provided.

a. Temporarily restricted net asset

b. Prepared for a not-for-profit hospital's changes in unrestricted net assets only

c. Permanently restricted net asset

d. *Audit and Accounting Guide— Health Care Organizations*

e. Used to account for resources that are donor-restricted for a particular operating purpose

f. General Fund

g. Assets whose use is limited

h. Reported on a not-for-profit hospital's statement of changes in net assets

_____ **1.** Used to account for day-to-day operations of a hospital

_____ **2.** Gift that must be used for a specific purpose, such as capital asset acquisition

_____ **3.** Resources set aside for a specific purpose by a hospital's governing board

_____ **4.** Revenues from restricted resources

_____ **5.** Resources donated to a hospital for which the principal must be maintained intact

_____ **6.** Specific Purpose Funds

_____ **7.** AICPA audit guide for hospitals

_____ **8.** Statement of operations

P13-2 (Multiple choice)

1. In accordance with its established billing rates, Alpha Hospital provided services amounting to $14 million during the year ended December 31, 2008. Included in the $14 million were contractual adjustments of $3 million and charity patient care of $1 million. What amount should Alpha report as net patient service revenue in its year 2008 financial statements?
   a. $10 million
   b. $11 million
   c. $13 million
   d. $14 million

2. Beta Hospital provided services to patients who were covered by the Eton Health Plan. Beta's arrangement with Eton called for interim billing rates at 25 percent less than the established rates, as well as a retrospective rate adjustment. Based on its established billing rates, Beta provided services amounting to $4 million to patients covered by Eton during the year ended December 31, 2008. At year end, Beta estimated that it would need to refund $150,000 to Eton in accordance with the cost standards set forth in the retrospective rate arrangement. What amount should Beta report as net patient service revenue in its year 2008 financial statements?
   a. $2,850,000
   b. $3,000,000
   c. $3,850,000
   d. $4,000,000

3. Gamma Hospital provided services amounting to $10 million at its established billing rates in the year ended December 31, 2008. Included in the $10 million were services of $8 million to Medicare patients. Medicare paid Gamma at 60 percent of Gamma's established rates. Also included in the $10 million were $2 million of services to self-pay patients. Gamma collected $1.5 million from the self-pay patients during the year and estimated that 40 percent of the uncollected amount would not be collected. What amount should Gamma report as net patient service revenue in its year 2008 financial statements?
   a. $6.3 million
   b. $6.6 million
   c. $6.8 million
   d. $10 million

4. On January 10, 2008, Delta Hospital received a bequest in the form of equity securities. Delta was required to hold the securities in perpetuity, but it could spend the income. The securities had cost the donor $2.7 million, but their fair value was $3.4 million when Delta received them. The fair value of the securities fluctuated during the year, and Delta's comptroller calculated that the average fair value during the year was $3.1 million. When Delta prepared its financial statements as of December 31, 2008, the fair value of the securities was $3.3 million. At what amount should Delta report the securities in its financial statements at December 31, 2008?
   a. $2.7 million
   b. $3.1 million
   c. $3.3 million
   d. $3.4 million

5. Abbott and Costello Labs donated drugs to Epsilon Hospital, a not-for-profit entity, in January 2008. If Epsilon had purchased the drugs, it would have paid $600,000. During the year, Epsilon used all the drugs in providing services to patients. How should Epsilon report the donation in its financial statements for the year ended December 31, 2008?
   a. Report nothing
   b. Report the donation in a note to its financial statements
   c. Report $600,000 as other revenues (or gains)
   d. Report $600,000 as a reduction of operating expenses

6. Omicron Hospital, a not-for-profit entity, received $6 million in premium revenue under an agreement with Zeta HMO to provide services to subscribing participants. Its internal records showed that Omicron spent $5.6 million in caring for Zeta's subscribers. How should Omicron report the transactions with Zeta in its financial statements?
   a. Report $400,000 as unrestricted premium revenue
   b. Report $400,000 as temporarily restricted premium revenue
   c. Report $6 million as unrestricted premium revenue
   d. Report $6 million as temporarily restricted premium revenue

7. Which of the following is the most likely description of the resources reported by Kappa Hospital on its balance sheet as assets limited as to use?
   a. A donation that can be used only for cancer research
   b. A donation that must be held in perpetuity in an Endowment Fund

   c. An investment of unrestricted resources that is not readily marketable

   d. An amount designated by Kappa's governing board for plant expansion

8. How should Phi Hospital, a not-for-profit hospital, report an increase in the fair value of its temporarily restricted investments?

   a. Only in the notes to its statements

   b. As part of nonoperating revenues (expenses) in its statement of revenues, expenses, and changes in net assets

   c. As a gain in its statement of changes in net assets

   d. As a direct addition to total net assets

P13-2 (Multiple choice)

1. A hospital has not transferred risk on malpractice claims to a third-party insurer. Which of the following statements best expresses the general rule regarding the reporting of liabilities for malpractice claims on the face of the balance sheet (or statement of net assets)?

   a. They should be reported only to the extent that judgments and settlements are due and payable.

   b. Outstanding claims should be described in the notes to the statements; adjudicated and settled claims should be reported if they have not been paid.

   c. They should be reported if it is highly likely that the disputes ultimately will be resolved in favor of the claimants.

   d. They should be reported if it is probable that a loss has been incurred and the amount of the loss can be reasonably estimated.

2. Historical experience shows that a hospital sometimes receives malpractice claims in the year after the incident occurs. Which of the following statements best expresses the general rule for reporting liabilities for such claims, if risk of loss has not been transferred to a third-party insurer?

   a. No mention is required to be made of these claims anywhere in the financial statements.

   b. A note should be prepared discussing the likelihood that claims will be received after the balance sheet date, but no estimate needs to be made of the possibility of loss.

   c. Liabilities should be recognized in the statements if it is probable that claims will be asserted for incidents occurring before the balance sheet date and the losses can be reasonably estimated.

   d. Liabilities should be recognized in the statements if claims have been received before the statements are issued; a note should be prepared discussing the likelihood of receiving additional claims after the statements have been issued.

3. A not-for-profit hospital receives a gift from a donor who specifies that the gift must be used only to further its research into the treatment of Lyme disease. When the hospital incurs expenses on this program, in which classification of net assets should the expenses be reported?

   a. Unrestricted net assets

   b. Temporarily restricted net assets

   c. Permanently restricted net assets

   d. Assets limited as to use

4. A not-for-profit hospital sells long-term bonds in the amount of $25 million to finance the construction of a hospital wing. The bond agreement requires the hospital to pay $1 million of this amount to a trustee as security until the debt is fully repaid. How should this payment be reported in the financial statements?
   a. As an expense, to be amortized over the life of the debt
   b. As assets limited as to use
   c. As noncurrent assets, with all other long-term investments
   d. As temporarily restricted net assets
5. A not-for-profit hospital creates a foundation whose sole purpose is to raise funds on behalf of the hospital. The hospital appoints all members of the foundation's governing board and directs its activities. The foundation raises $200,000 in unrestricted cash gifts during the year. The hospital does not need the cash, so the foundation continues to hold the cash at year end. How should the hospital report on the foundation's activities in its financial statements?
   a. Report an asset in its balance sheet and a "change in interest in the foundation" in its statement of operations
   b. Report an asset in its balance sheet and a "change in interest in the foundation" in the temporarily restricted net asset section of its statement of changes in net assets
   c. Report nothing on the face of its financial statements, but disclose the foundation's activities in a note to its financial statements
   d. Do not report anything on the face of its financial statements or in its notes
6. During the year ended December 31, 2008, a not-for-profit hospital had both unrealized and realized gains on investments made with its unrestricted net assets. How should these gains be reported in the hospital's statement of operations for the year 2008?
   a. Both the realized and the unrealized gains should be reported.
   b. Neither the realized nor the unrealized gains should be reported.
   c. Realized gains should be reported, but unrealized gains should not.
   d. Unrealized gains should be reported, but realized gains should not.
7. Under which of these circumstances would a not-for-profit hospital report restricted net assets?
   a. Whenever there are external limitations on using the resources
   b. When a donor places limitations on using the resources
   c. When the hospital's board of directors sets resources aside for plant expansion
   d. When a bond agreement requires the hospital to set resources aside

P13-4 (Multiple choice—governmental hospital)

1. What are the components of the net asset section of a governmental hospital's balance sheet?
   a. Unrestricted; temporarily restricted; permanently restricted
   b. Assets limited as to use; assets unlimited as to use
   c. Invested in capital assets, net of related debt; restricted; unrestricted
   d. Restricted; unrestricted

2. A county hospital receives grants from higher-level governments to construct and equip a special trauma unit. How should the hospital report the grants in its financial statements?
   a. As nonoperating revenues
   b. As a separate item after nonoperating revenues (expenses) are added to (deducted from) operating income (loss)
   c. As a direct addition to "invested in capital assets, net of related debt"
   d. As an item of extraordinary or special revenue

3. A county hospital receives $1 million from the county's General Fund to help cover the hospital's annual operating deficit. How should the hospital report that receipt of cash?
   a. As operating revenues
   b. As nonoperating revenues
   c. As a separate item after nonoperating revenues (expenses) are added to (deducted from) operating income (loss)
   d. As a direct addition to unrestricted net assets

4. A county hospital receives a grant of $250,000 from the state health department, which specifies that the grant may be used for any purpose the trustees wish, provided it is used at the rate of $50,000 a year for 5 years, starting the following year. How should the hospital report the gift in its financial statements in the year the cash is received?
   a. As deferred revenue
   b. As revenue in the amount of $250,000
   c. As revenue in the amount of $250,000, discounted at the government's borrowing rate over the 5-year period
   d. As a direct addition to unrestricted net assets

5. How is interest on long-term bonds issued by a county hospital generally reported?
   a. As operating expenses
   b. As nonoperating expenses
   c. As a separate item after nonoperating revenues (expenses) are added to (deducted from) operating income (loss)
   d. As a direct reduction of beginning net assets

P13-5 (Accounting for and reporting patient service revenues)
The Andrew Gorman Hospital had the following transactions regarding its patient service billings.

1. The total services provided by the hospital to all patients during the year amounted to $19 million at the hospital's established billing rates.
2. The hospital bills Medicare for services to program beneficiaries as included in item 1 at prospectively determined rates. Contractual adjustments under this program to the predetermined rates were $1.5 million.
3. An agreement with third-party payer X calls for retrospective final rates. Patient services included in item 1 under interim billing rates with X resulted in contractual adjustments of $1 million.
4. The hospital provided charity services included in item 1 valued at $500,000 under the established rates.
5. The hospital made a provision for bad debts in the amount of $300,000.

6. The hospital collected $13.5 million from third-party payers and direct-pay patients. The hospital also wrote off bad debts of $200,000.

7. The hospital estimated it would need to refund $100,000 to payer X in item 3, when retrospective rates are determined. (The hospital's receivables include no amounts due from payer X.)

Required: 1. Prepare the journal entries needed to record these transactions.

2. State (a) the amount of net patient service revenue the hospital will report on its operating statement, and (b) the amount of net patient accounts receivable the hospital will report on its balance sheet. Also, state how the estimated third-party payer settlements should be reported.

P13-6   (Accounting for medical malpractice claims)

Caire-Less Hospital carries no insurance for medical malpractice claims. Analysis of medical malpractice claims at year end shows the following:

1. Claim A is for $500,000. The hospital's attorneys are 90 percent confident that the hospital will win the claim if it goes to trial. The hospital will not settle the claim for any amount and is awaiting trial.

2. Claim B is for $400,000. The hospital's attorneys are not confident of winning if the case goes to trial. They believe the claim can be settled out of court, within the range of $100,000 to $200,000.

3. The hospital also has 20 outstanding smaller claims. The average claim is for $10,000. Experience shows that the hospital loses 60 percent of the claims, and the average loss on them is 30 percent of the amount claimed.

4. Experience also shows that two claims, each for $10,000, relating to incidents occurring before year end, are likely to be received during the following year.

Required: 1. Compute the amount, if any, that the hospital ought to establish as a liability on its balance sheet for malpractice claims. Discuss the content of any note disclosures that the hospital should make.

2. Describe the accounting principles leading to your conclusions.

P13-7   Comprehensive set of journal entries and financial statements)

Central Hospital was established as a not-for-profit organization on January 1, 2009, to take over the assets of an existing hospital. The hospital does not use fund accounting. It had the following transactions during 2009.

1. The hospital sold revenue bonds in the amount of $40 million. The hospital received $38 million cash from sale of the bonds. To provide security for payment of the debt service, the other $2 million was deposited in an escrow account with a trustee. The trustee immediately invested the cash in U.S. Treasury bills.

2. The physical assets of the existing hospital were purchased for $35 million cash. The appraised values of the assets were: land—$3 million; buildings—$28 million; and equipment—$4 million.

3. The hospital provided services of $20 million at its established rates to Medicare patients. Its agreement with Medicare provided for contractual adjustments of 30 percent against the established rates. By year end, the hospital had collected $12.5 million against the billings.

4. The hospital provided services of $10 million at its established rates to patients insured by a third-party payer. Its agreement with the third party provided for contractual adjustments of 20 percent from the established rates. It also provided for a retrospective adjustment, based on a cost submission by the hospital 30 days after the end of the year. By year end, the hospital had collected the entire amount that it was owed by the third-party payer. When it prepared its financial statements, the hospital estimated that it owed the third party $80,000, but the final settlement had not yet been negotiated.

5. The hospital provided services to members of an HMO at rates per member, per month, receiving cash premiums totaling $15 million for the year. The hospital's internal records showed that, if billings had been made at its established rates, it would have charged the HMO $18 million for these services.

6. The hospital provided care to charity patients amounting to $2 million at its established billing rates.

7. The hospital provided care to self-pay patients in the amount of $5 million at its established rates. The hospital collected $2 million against these billings. At year end, the hospital established an allowance for uncollectible receivables of 40 percent of the remaining amount due from the self-pay patients.

8. The hospital had the following functional expenses. Of the amounts shown, $29 million was paid in cash. Depreciation on building and equipment (included in each function) was $1.4 million and $600,000, respectively.)

Health care services	$22 million
Dietary services	4 million
Maintenance expenses	2 million
Administrative expenses	3 million

9. The hospital paid debt service of $4 million on its bonds ($1.6 million amortization of principal and $2.4 million interest). It also made a year-end journal entry, reclassifying $1.6 million of long-term debt as current.

10. The hospital recorded accrued expenses at year end, as follows:

Health care services	$2 million
Administrative expenses	5 million

11. The hospital paid $1 million for a claims-made policy for medical malpractice insurance through December 31, 2009. Because the policy did not transfer risk to the insurance carrier for incurred but not reported claims (IBNR), the hospital accrued $300,000 as a liability. (Note: Charge the expenses to the health care services function.)

12. The hospital received a check from the trustee for $100,000 representing earnings on the investment made by the trustee with the escrow moneys. The investment income is available for the hospital's general operations.

13. The hospital received equity securities from a donor who specified that the securities, together with any earnings thereon, be used for the purpose of upgrading the hospital's equipment. The securities had a fair

value of $250,000 when the donor made the gift. During the year, the hospital received dividends of $10,000 on the securities. At year end, when the hospital prepared its financial statements, the securities had a fair value of $270,000. (Assume the hospital's accounting policy provides for recording realized and unrealized gains and losses on restricted net assets in a single account.)

14. During 2009, the hospital created Central Hospital Foundation, whose sole purpose was to obtain donations for the hospital. At year end, the foundation advised the hospital that it had received cash donations of $300,000. Of this amount, $50,000 was unrestricted and $250,000 was restricted for upgrading the hospital's equipment. At the hospital's request, the foundation sent the entire $50,000 cash received from unrestricted donations to the hospital.

Required: 1. Prepare necessary journal entries to record these transactions.
2. Prepare a statement of operations for 2009.
3. Prepare a statement of changes in net assets for 2009.
4. Prepare a balance sheet as of December 31, 2009.

P13-8 (Journal entries and financial statements)
Following is a trial balance for the Metro General Hospital, a governmental hospital. The hospital does not use find accounting.

Metro General Hospital
Trial Balance
December 31, 2008

Cash	$ 6,000	
Patient accounts receivable	20,000	
Allowance for uncollectible receivables		$ 3,000
Inventories	5,000	
Land	300,000	
Building	2,000,000	
Accumulated depreciation—building		80,000
Equipment	500,000	
Accumulated depreciation—equipment		100,000
Accounts payable		8,000
Bonds payable		2,400,000
Net assets		240,000
	$2,831,000	$2,831,000

During 2009, the following transactions took place:

1. Services were provided to patients amounting to $3,300,000 at established billing rates. Following is an analysis of the billings:
   a. Medicare patients were billed for $2,000,000 at established rates. However, contractual allowances against these billings were $400,000.
   b. Billings under a retrospective arrangement with a third party were $600,000 at the established rates. However, the interim billing rates called for contractual adjustments of $100,000.

c. Billings to self-pay patients were $500,000 at established rates. Based on experience, the hospital anticipated that $25,000 of the billings would not be collected.

d. Services to charity patients were $200,000 at established rates.

2. Inventories of $56,000 were purchased on credit.
3. Operating expenses were incurred as follows:

Health care services	$2,140,000
General expenses	200,000
Administrative expenses	90,000

Assume that all the expenses were incurred on credit.

4. The board decided to set aside $30,000 cash in a separate account to provide for the continuing education of nurses.
5. The hospital entered into a capitation agreement with the county in which it was located, agreeing to provide hospital services to certain groups of county employees and their dependents. The agreement provided for the county to make a monthly payment for each covered county employee to the hospital. Cash payments received by the hospital under this agreement were $300,000.
6. Collections of patient receivables totaled $2,200,000. In addition, $13,000 of patient receivables were written off as uncollectible.
7. Payments of accounts payable totaled $1,900,000.
8. The use of inventories was recorded as follows:

Health care services	$30,000
General expenses	20,000

9. Depreciation was recorded as follows: building, $40,000; equipment, $50,000.
10. During the year, the hospital paid debt service of $220,000 on the outstanding bonds, consisting of interest of $120,000 and principal of $100,000. At year end, the hospital made an entry to report $100,000 of its outstanding long-term debt as current.
11. During the year, a self-pay patient instituted legal action in the amount of $200,000 against the hospital for medical malpractice. The hospital does not carry insurance. Hospital attorneys have started negotiations with the claimant and believe it is highly probable that the claim can be settled for $50,000. (Charge the expense to Health care services.)
12. At year end, the hospital reviewed its cost accounting records in connection with the retrospective billing arrangement made with the third-party payer in item 1, part b. The hospital believes it will need to refund $40,000 to that third party in accordance with that agreement. (The third party had paid all the billings made by the hospital in 1.b, above.)

Required: 1. Prepare all the journal entries necessary to record these transactions.

2. Prepare a statement of revenues, expenses, and changes in net assets for 2009.

3. Prepare a balance sheet at December 31, 2009.

P13-9 (Journal entries using funds and net asset classifications; preparation of financial statements)

Croton General Hospital, a not-for-profit organization, had the following transactions during 2009:

1. The hospital received a gift of $300,000 in equity securities from Elias Poulos. The terms of the gift specified that the principal amount of the gift and any investment gains must be maintained intact permanently. The gift terms also stipulated that the income from the investments could be spent only for cancer research.

2. Hudson Associates gave the hospital a cash gift of $50,000 and equity securities having a fair value of $150,000 at the date of the gift. The donor stipulated that the gift and all income derived from the gift (including proceeds from sale of the securities) could be used only for cancer research.

3. Sara Dawn promised to donate $50,000 to the hospital to provide equipment for the hospital's new gastroenterology unit, provided the hospital raised an equal amount of cash from other donors.

4. The hospital undertook a fund-raising campaign to purchase equipment for its new gastroenterology unit and raised cash of $80,000. Sara Dawn immediately sent the hospital a check for $50,000.

5. The hospital spent the entire $130,000 to buy equipment for its gastroenterology unit.

6. The hospital received interest and dividends totaling $20,000 on the gifts made by Elias Poulos and Hudson Associates.

7. The hospital sold some of the securities donated by Hudson so it could hire a well-known cancer researcher. It received $35,000 cash from investments that had a fair value of $30,000 at the time of the gift. (The hospital's accounting polices call for recording both realized and unrealized gains and losses on securities held in restricted net assets in a single account.)

8. The hospital spent $70,000 on cancer research, using the resources provided by the Poulos and Hudson gifts.

9. At year end, the fair values of the equity securities from the Poulos and Hudson gifts were as follows:

Poulos	$310,000
Hudson	$122,000

10. The hospital created the Croton General Hospital Foundation, over which it had full control. At year end, the foundation notified the hospital that it had received $25,000 in cash donations, to be used only to purchase equipment for its gastroenterology unit.

Required: 1. Prepare journal entries to record these transactions in the hospital's restricted and General funds. Identify the fund and, where appropriate, the net asset classification.

2. Prepare a statement of changes in net assets for the temporarily and permanently restricted net assets for 2009.

P13-10 (Journal entries for hospitals)

Following is a trial balance for Darwin Memorial, a not-for-profit hospital:

Darwin Memorial Hospital
General Fund
Trial Balance
July 1, 2008

Cash	$ 12,000	
Patient accounts receivable	40,000	
Allowance for uncollectible patient accounts		$ 4,000
Land	600,000	
Buildings	2,500,000	
Accumulated depreciation—building		650,000
Equipment	2,000,000	
Accumulated depreciation—equipment		400,000
Accounts payable		15,000
Notes payable		100,000
Bonds payable		2,000,000
Unrestricted net assets		1,983,000
	$5,152,000	$5,152,000

During the 2008–2009 fiscal year, the following selected transactions took place:

1. Darwin had capitation agreements with several HMOs, wherein the HMOs agreed to pay monthly premiums per member at the beginning of every month in exchange for Darwin's agreement to provide hospital services to the HMO members. Darwin received premiums of $2 million in cash during the year. In addition, Darwin billed its self-pay patients a total of $100,000.

2. Several self-pay patient accounts were classified as uncollectible and written off. These accounts totaled $2,000.

3. The MVT Corporation gave the hospital a grant for research into the use of a voice-activated microscope. The grant was for $500,000. The entire amount was immediately invested in marketable securities.

4. Operating expenses were incurred as follows:

Nursing services	$550,000
Other professional services	300,000
General expenses	300,000
Administrative expenses	175,000
Dietary services	100,000

Assume that all expenses were incurred on credit.

5. Self-pay patient receivables of $110,000 were collected.

6. Accounts payable of $1,400,000 were paid.

7. Several individuals in the community contributed a total of $1 million for the expansion of the burn unit of the hospital. This money was invested in marketable securities until the plans for the unit were completed. The fund was titled the Burn Unit Fund.

8. Debt service of $210,000 on the outstanding debt was paid in cash. Of this amount, $110,000 was for interest and the rest was for debt principal.

9. The managing board decided to establish a fund for the development of its professional staff. The amount transferred from general hospital resources was $25,000. The new fund was called the Professional Improvement Fund.

10. The construction and planning costs incurred on the new burn unit totaled $200,000. This amount was paid from the Burn Unit Fund cash account. To make these payments, investments that originally cost $190,000 were sold for $205,000. In addition, $10,000 cash income was received on the investments. Assume that the income from the investments has the same restrictions as the original donation.

11. During the year, the hospital received $25,000 cash income from the investment of the MVT grant money. Assume that the investment income is restricted in the same way as the original grant.

12. Research costs associated with the MVT grant were $20,000. These costs were paid with cash generated by the investment of the original grant.

13. Jane Doe gave the hospital $15,000, which must be maintained intact. The income from the gift can be used in any way the managing board feels is helpful to the hospital. The money was immediately invested in marketable securities.

14. Investments in the Jane Doe Fund earned $2,000 during the year. Of this amount, $1,900 was received in cash.

15. The fair value of the remaining investments in the Burn Unit Fund at the end of the year was $850,000.

Required: Prepare all the journal entries necessary to record these transactions and identify the fund or funds involved.

CHAPTER

14

ANALYSIS OF FINANCIAL STATEMENTS AND FINANCIAL CONDITION

Chapter Outline

After completing this chapter, you should be able to:

- Explain how financial statement format and content assist in financial analysis.
- Explain how using ratios facilitates analysis of financial data.
- Explain how time-series analysis and comparative analysis facilitate assessment of financial condition.
- Describe and calculate various indicators of an entity's liquidity.
- Describe and calculate various indicators of an entity's asset turnover or efficiency.
- Describe and calculate various indicators of an entity's budgetary solvency and operating results.
- Describe and calculate various indicators of an entity's debt burden and long-term financial flexibility.
- Describe the factors, other than ratios derived from financial statements, that are needed to assess an entity's financial condition.

Financial statements provide the primary source of data used by financial analysts and other interested parties in assessing an entity's operating results and financial position. For example, analysts for credit-rating agencies and other lenders use the data provided in the financial statements to help them reach conclusions about the creditworthiness of state and local governments and not-for-profit entities when these entities seek to borrow in the capital markets. Analysts for state governments also use financial statements in connection with their oversight of the finances of local governments.

Converting various elements of the statements to ratios (such as the ratio of current assets to current liabilities) or other useful formats (such as debt per capita) helps the analyst spot deviations either from industry norms or from previous-year entity patterns. When the trends in the ratios are considered in light of other data (such as economic and demographic statistics) that indicate the possible causes of the deviations, insight may be obtained into an entity's near-term future financial health.

The major purpose of this chapter is to discuss and illustrate some commonly used indicators of the operating results and financial position of state and local governments and not-for-profit entities. Some of the ratios used in analyzing the finances of for-profit business-type entities can be readily adapted to governmental and not-for-profit business-type activities, such as hospitals and water supply entities. Other indicators have been developed specifically for assessing the financial health of general-purpose governments.

When you read this chapter, keep in mind that analyzing an organization's financial health is an art, not a science. An analyst may be interested in knowing a particular ratio for a particular purpose, but no single ratio or indicator will suffice to reach a conclusion about an entity's overall financial condition. Instead, many ratios and other indicators—financial, economic, demographic, administrative, and political—must be considered.

INFORMATION CONTENT OF FINANCIAL STATEMENTS: A FINANCIAL ANALYSIS PERSPECTIVE

Before discussing the techniques of financial statement and financial condition analysis, let's reexamine the information content of the statements and related data covered in this text:

- *Statement of net assets,* also called the statement of financial position or the balance sheet
- *Statement of activities,* also called the statement of operations or the statement of revenues, expenses (expenditures), and changes in net assets (fund balances or fund equity)
- Notes to the financial statements and required supplementary information

Some differences in the financial statements and related data prepared by the various types of organizations covered in this text exist because of formatting differences and differing accounting standards. Nevertheless, a sufficient number of similarities allow the following general observations about the purposes served by the statements and the related data.

Statement of Net Assets

The statement of net assets (or equivalent designation) provides information about an organization's assets, liabilities, and net assets as of the date of the statement. Because of the way the statement of net assets is presented and its information content, the analyst can learn something about an organization's liquidity and its financial flexibility.

Assets are generally listed in order of *liquidity,* or their nearness to cash and nearness to being consumed in operations. Liabilities are listed in terms of nearness to being paid. To provide further emphasis on liquidity, assets and liabilities may be classified as *current* and *noncurrent.* Current assets include cash, those expected to be converted to cash in the following year, or those expected to be consumed in operations in the following year. Current liabilities are expected to be paid in the following year. For example, the portion of long-term bonds that is due to be paid in the following year is shown as current while the rest is reported as noncurrent.[1]

---

[1]As discussed in previous chapters, the term *current* has a shorter time frame in fund statements for governmental-type funds than it does for government-wide financial statements and not-for-profit entity and hospital financial statements.

Evidence of financial flexibility is provided by the captions attached to the various assets and liabilities, by the liquidity order in which the assets and liabilities are listed, and by the classifications shown in the net assets section of the statement of net assets. For example, both governmental and not-for-profit organizations show the extent to which the net assets are restricted as to use. When net assets are classified as unrestricted, they can be used for any purpose within the scope of the entity's charter that its management considers appropriate. When classified as restricted, the net assets are available only for the specific activity, function, or time period designated by law or by the party that restricted the use of the assets.

Obviously, management's financial flexibility is greater if its resources are relatively liquid and the level of its unrestricted net assets (or fund balance) is relatively high. How the analyst determines what is relatively liquid or relatively high will be discussed shortly.

Statement of Activities

The statement of activities (or equivalent designation) shows both the details and the totals of an organization's revenues, expenses, and other elements leading to the change in net assets for the year. Thus, depending on such factors as the measurement focus and basis of accounting used in preparing the statements and the level of detail provided in the statements, the analyst can discover the following:

- Whether the resources were sufficient to cover the costs of the services provided during the year
- The various sources of revenues obtained during the year
- The nature of the services provided during the year
- Whether unusual factors, such as significant "one-time" items, influenced the operating results for the year

Separating revenues by source provides a clue as to the volatility and reliability of revenue streams available to finance future activities. In financing governments, for example, property taxes tend to be more stable from year to year than personal income taxes and sales taxes, which are more heavily influenced by economic factors. Also, revenues from higher-level governments tend to be less reliable than own-source revenues. Heavily endowed not-for-profit organizations can experience volatile revenues because of stock market fluctuations, even though unrealized gains and losses on securities in a particular year may not affect the organization's long-run financial health.

Subtotals and formats play a useful role in conveying information on the statement of activities. For example, the not-for-profit hospital's statement of operations (Table 14-5 on p. 579) provides a measure of financial performance by separating the "excess of revenues over expenses" from other factors affecting the increase in unrestricted net assets for the year. The government-wide statement of activities (see p. 385) measures the relative burden each function places on the taxpaying public by showing both the gross functional expenses and revenues directly related to those functions. A not-for-profit organization's statement of activities (see p. 461) helps readers understand the sources and uses of resources by separating revenues into three net asset classifications, and by separating program expenses from administrative and fund-raising expenses.

A financial analyst needs to recognize that the statement of activities has limitations as an indicator of future events. Its limitations are particularly evident in government, where the statement of activities measures the cost of services provided but not the cost of unmet service needs. The fact that a governmental entity's net assets at year end increased over the previous year does not necessarily mean that its financial condition improved. Unmet service needs that cannot be readily financed must be considered in examining a government's financial condition.

Notes to the Financial Statements and Required Supplementary Information

As previously stated, notes are an integral part of the financial statements, providing information not shown on the face of the statements but nevertheless essential to fair presentation of the statements. Required supplementary information also provides information considered essential to financial reporting. Although all notes and required supplementary information need to be read, here are some of the more useful ones in assessing an organization's financial position and condition:

- *Property Tax Calendar.* Some governments obtain large amounts of revenues from property taxes. Although property taxes are generally collected twice a year, 6 months apart, the first payment may be due before the fiscal year begins, at any time during the year, or even in the next year. The tax calendar can therefore affect an entity's cash flows, producing either interest revenue or interest expenditure/expense, and it may help explain the size of amounts reported as cash, taxes receivable, deferred revenues, and notes payable.
- *Debt Service Requirements to Maturity.* Debt service requirements affect an entity's financial flexibility. An entity that can balance its current budget and simultaneously redeem relatively large amounts of debt has greater financial flexibility than one that needs to push its debt redemption off to the long-term future. Governmental entities are required to disclose their debt service requirements to maturity, showing amounts due each year for the next 5 years and amounts due in 5-year increments thereafter.
- *Pension Plan Obligations.* Defined benefit pension plans and other postemployment benefit plans create future debt-like commitments. As discussed in Chapter 8, governments with such plans are required to disclose funding progress (ratio of actuarial value of assets to actuarial accrued liability, or "funded ratio") and actual compared to required contributions. If all other factors are the same, an entity that has a high funded ratio and is contributing 100 percent of its annual funding requirement is likely to be in better fiscal health than one with a low ratio and that is not contributing the full requirement.

AN APPROACH TO FINANCIAL STATEMENT AND FINANCIAL CONDITION ANALYSIS

The extent to which one might analyze financial statements depends on the purpose of the analysis. One analyst might be concerned only about a particular data element, such as the size of a not-for-profit organization's year-end unrestricted fund balance and how it compares with the previous year end. Another analyst might be concerned with how a hospital's overall financial position at year end and results of operations for the year compare with the previous year. A third analyst might want to review the overall financial condition of a governmental entity to assess its long-term ability to finance anticipated debt and expanded services.[2]

The first analyst is interested in a single element of an organization's financial position at two points in time, which can be obtained by reading that data element in the statement of financial position. The second one needs to read the statements and related notes, select certain data elements from the statements, convert them to useful financial ratios, do the same with the previous year's statements, and interpret the results. The third analyst needs to use a longer time period, select additional data elements (including economic and demographic data obtained outside the financial statements), and develop a frame of reference based on other governments to aid in interpreting the results.

Converting Data to More Useful Formats

To aid in interpreting data for financial statement and financial condition analysis, the analyst needs to convert data elements to more useful formats. The numbers take on a different meaning when viewed in comparison with another relevant statistic. For example, an analyst may conclude that the accounts receivable collection process got worse if the accounts receivable balance at December 31, 2009, was $420,000, up from $400,000 at December 31, 2008. Considering the increase in revenues during 2009 by converting the accounts receivable balance to the number of days' revenue represented by the balance might show, however, that the collection process actually improved during the year.

Data formats used in financial analysis include ratios, per capita information, and common size statements. In addition, analyzing data can be made easier by developing percentage change information and location quotient information.

- *Ratios* are developed by relating one data element to another to produce an indicator of a particular characteristic. We just saw how relating the receivables balance to revenues provides the analyst with a good indicator of receivables collection efficiency. Using ratios also allows the analyst to assess trends for the entity itself and to compare the entity with other organizations—things that could not be done in a meaningful way using just the raw numbers.
- *Per capita information* is produced by dividing financial data elements by the entity's population. Converting financial data to per capita information also makes it easier to trace trends for the entity and to compare the entity with other organizations.
- *Common size statements* are obtained by converting financial statement elements to percentages of 100. Using common size statements allows the analyst to readily identify changes over time in the proportion that individual data elements bear to the total (for example, the share of total expenses represented by

---

[2]Robert Berne defines financial condition as "the probability that a government will meet both (a) its financial obligations to creditors, consumers, employees, taxpayers, suppliers, constituents, and others as they become due and (b) the service obligations to constituents, both currently and in the future." Robert Berne, *The Relationships Between Financial Reporting and the Measurement of Financial Condition* (Norwalk, CT: GASB, 1992), p. 17.

a government's public safety expenses, or a not-for-profit entity's fund-raising expenses).

- *Percentage change information* is obtained by comparing data elements for a later year with data elements for an earlier year. For example, if the cash balance increased from $200,000 in 2008 to $250,000 in 2009, the percentage change was plus 25 percent [($250,000–$200,000)/$200,000]. It provides another approach to showing comparisons over time within an entity or with other entities.
- *Location quotient information* is obtained by dividing a data element for the entity under study by the comparable data element for other entities, so that results revolve around 1. For example, if the cash balance for the entity under study was $200,000 and the cash balance for a comparison entity was $250,000, the location quotient would be 0.8 ($200,000/$250,000). It is a useful way of comparing data with other entities.

Time-Series Analysis

Financial statement and financial condition analysis require review of statements over a period of time for the organization under study, called *time-series analysis.* At a minimum, data (such as raw numbers, ratios, per capita information, or other formats) for the current year need to be compared with the previous year so that observations can be made about the nature and extent of improvement or deterioration. To assess financial condition, however, analysts generally study changes for 5 to 10 years. To ascertain the implications of trends in economic and demographic factors (such as population shifts), data for even longer periods are reviewed.

Comparative Analysis

Suppose the earnings margin (discussed later in this chapter) for a not-for-profit hospital increased from 2.2 percent to 2.5 percent from last year to the current year. The earnings margin improved, which seems to be a favorable factor. But, by what standard does 2.5 percent appear to be favorable? To answer this question, one might ask: "What is the median earnings margin of other not-for-profit hospitals of similar size and similar patient mix?" *Comparative analysis* is a valuable tool for the financial analyst because it provides an external reference point—a type of standard or norm—for assessing the data developed for the organization under study.

Analysts concerned with assessing operating results, financial position, and financial condition of individual organizations maintain extensive databases to facilitate comparative analysis among generally similar organizations. For example:

- Several state agencies, such as the New York State Comptroller's Office and the North Carolina Department of State Treasurer, publish annual reports containing comparative financial data on local governments within the state.
- Municipal bond-rating agencies maintain extensive nationwide databases to help in their bond-rating processes. These agencies often publish documents containing ratios that can serve as "rules of thumb" (general guidelines) for governmental entities seeking to compare their ratios with others.

Information obtained from sources such as these can help in assessing the implications of ratios developed for a particular entity. If such information is not readily available, analysts should construct their own "reference groups" or "peer groups" for comparison purposes. Nevertheless, rule of thumb and reference group data need to be developed and used with care because of the potential for distortion caused by environmental differences, such as nature of functions performed, mix of population served, size of entity, revenue sources, and location.

Although nationwide data may serve as good frames of reference for some ratios, it is often better to compare the organization under study with a reference group of similar organizations. For example, if an analyst is studying the financial condition of a city, a reference group of about 10 other *city* governments *within the state* might be developed, because all the cities are likely to perform the same functions and be subject to the same laws. They should also be of generally similar population size. For some ratios, data on all local governments within the state and available nationwide rules of thumb will serve as a useful check on the ratios developed for the 10-city reference group.

In summary, financial statement and financial condition analysis is helped by (1) converting data elements to more useful formats such as ratios, (2) tracing data over time within the entity, and (3) comparing the entity with other similar organizations.

FINANCIAL STATEMENT AND FINANCIAL CONDITION ANALYSIS INDICATORS

Many indicators used for analyzing financial statements and financial condition are developed entirely from financial statement data elements or from the relationship of a financial statement element to a demographic or economic element. These indicators may be classified as liquidity indicators, asset turnover or efficiency indicators, budgetary solvency and operating results indicators, and debt burden and other long-term financial flexibility indicators. Other indicators (used in the more extensive financial condition analyses) come from economic and demographic elements and other factors.

The indicators covered in this text are illustrative of the many ratios suggested by writers on this subject. We focus on indicators that we have observed in practice or that we consider particularly useful. Some indicators are used for analyzing all three types of entities covered in the text: governmental, general not-for-profit entities, and not-for-profit hospitals. Others have been adapted to or developed for the operating peculiarities of a particular type of entity.

In considering these indicators, keep in mind that no indicator taken alone can be used to measure an entity's financial position or condition. Also, ratios based on balance sheet information are as of a single point in time and may not be representative of what occurs throughout the year. Appropriate judgments can be made, however, when the indicators are considered as a group, examined over a period of years, and assessed in terms of a representative group of similar organizations.

Liquidity Indicators

New York City's fiscal crisis of the late 1970s was preceded by a sharp increase in short-term debt. Increased short-term borrowings and a buildup of unpaid bills are some of the first signs of fiscal stress. *Liquidity indicators* provide information on the ability of an organization to meet its short-term obligations.

Commonly used liquidity indicators are the *current ratio, quick ratio,* and *number of days' cash on hand.* The general formulae for calculating them are as follows:

$$\text{Current Ratio} = \frac{\text{Current Assets}}{\text{Current Liabilities}}$$

$$\text{Quick Ratio} = \frac{\text{Cash} + \text{Cash Equivalents} + \text{Short-Term Investments}}{\text{Current Liabilities}}$$

$$\frac{\text{Number of Days'}}{\text{Cash on Hand}} = \frac{\text{Cash} + \text{Cash Equivalents} + \text{Short-Term Investments}}{(\text{Total Expenses} - \text{Bad Debts} - \text{Depreciation}) / 365}$$

All three of these ratios are used in analyzing the financial statements of governmental business-type activities and not-for-profit entities, including not-for-profit hospitals. In these financial statements, current assets are cash and other assets as of the balance sheet date that will be converted to cash or consumed in operations in the following year. Current liabilities in both the current and quick ratios are obligations that are due to be paid in the following year.

Those who analyze general-purpose governments often concentrate on the quick ratio, using the governmental fund financial statements. As stated in Chapter 5, governmental fund liabilities are current liabilities with a short time horizon—generally payable in no more than 60 days; further, fund liabilities generally do not include accrued interest on long-term debt.

When calculating the quick ratio, current assets that are less readily convertible to cash are excluded from the numerator. At a minimum, the assets in the quick ratio are cash, cash equivalents, and other short-term (temporary) investments. *Cash equivalents* are short-term liquid investments readily convertible to known amounts of cash and are so close to maturity (having had an original maturity of 3 months or less) that there is little risk of loss in value. *Short-term investments* other than cash equivalents have slightly longer maturities and include certificates of deposit, money market assets, and U.S. Treasury bills.

Analysts of business-type activities often include accounts receivable in calculating the quick ratio. Analysts of general-purpose governments exclude taxes receivable in calculating the quick ratio, but consider them in assessing the implications of the ratio.

From the perspective of the financial condition analyst, higher current and quick ratios signify a greater ability to meet current obligations. Historically, many organizations (including business enterprises) have found that a current ratio of 2.0 and a quick ratio of 1.0 provide reasonable margins for safety in meeting current obligations. These historical rules of thumb, however, are not etched in stone. Many business enterprises have found more productive uses for their cash and have current ratios well below 2.0. Hospitals that carry large amounts of slow-paying accounts receivable may need a current ratio higher than 2.0 to meet current obligations.

A quick ratio of 1.0 says enough cash is on hand to pay currently due bills, but a lower ratio may suffice if some current liabilities are not due for immediate payment and if cash received early in the next year from the next year's activities will help pay them. Monthly cash forecasts help supplement the liquidity ratios. Increasingly large amounts of notes payable due early in the next year can signal an onset of liquidity problems.

Number of days' cash on hand, often used as a liquidity indicator by not-for-profit hospitals, provides another perspective on liquidity. It is a quick ratio converted to another form, because it shows how many days the entity can continue to pay its regular operating expenses without new inflows of cash. In making this calculation, bad debts and depreciation are removed from the total expenses because they do not require cash outlays. Some writers include debt principal repayments in the denominator.

Asset Turnover or Efficiency Indicators

Cash can be invested or used to pay bills, but accounts receivable cannot. Receivables can, of course, be sold or used as collateral to borrow cash, but both come at a price—the payment of interest. Generally, the more rapidly an entity can convert its receivables to cash, the more liquid it is.

You can express receivables collection efficiency in several ways. Hospitals and governmental business-type activities generally express *accounts receivable collection efficiency* in terms of number of days' revenue in receivables or average collection period. General governments measure property tax collection efficiency in terms of percentage of taxes collected (or *not* collected) in the year of the tax levy, or the ratio of property taxes receivable to property tax revenues. The general formulae for calculating these indicators are as follows:

$$\frac{\text{Days' Revenue in}}{\text{Receivables}} = \frac{\text{Net Patient Accounts Receivable}}{\text{Net Patient Service Revenue} / 365}$$

$$\frac{\text{Property Tax}}{\text{Collection Rate}} = \frac{\text{Current-Year Real Property Taxes Collected}}{\text{Current-Year Real Property Tax Levy}}$$

$$\frac{\text{Property Tax}}{\text{Receivable Rate}} = \frac{\text{Real Property Taxes Receivable}}{\text{Real Property Tax Revenues}}$$

The number of days' revenue in receivables also can be calculated using the *asset turnover* method. Accounts receivable turnover is calculated by dividing revenues by accounts receivable. Days' revenue in receivables (or average receivables collection period) is then determined by dividing 365 by the accounts receivable turnover.

Year-to-year changes in these rates may indicate weak administration, such as poor follow-up on slow payers or insufficient penalties for nonpayment of real property taxes. Increasing rates of real property tax delinquency, however, could also be a sign of the onset of fiscal stress, caused by an inability of property taxpayers to make their payments because of economic hardship. For example, referring again to the New York City fiscal crisis, analysis of the city's real property tax collection experience showed a gradual increase in delinquencies as the crisis of the 1970s worsened and better collections as the city emerged from the crisis.[3] Moody's suggests that a current tax collection rate of less than 95 percent or a declining trend is a potential sign of credit distress.[4]

Another common asset turnover or efficiency ratio is the *total asset turnover,* which is calculated as follows:

$$\frac{\text{Total Asset}}{\text{Turnover}} = \frac{\text{Unrestricted Revenues, Gains, and Other Support}}{\text{Unrestricted Net Assets}}$$

[3]Comparative Analysis of New York City's Financial and Economic Indicators," Office of the Comptroller, Bureau of Financial Analysis, The City of New York, January 1982.
[4]The Determinants of Credit Quality," Moody's Investors Service, May 2002, p. 8.

Total asset turnover is a good indicator of asset efficiency, particularly for hospitals. Assets used in producing revenues can be thought of as inputs, and the revenues can be considered as outputs. The greater the quantity of output for a given quantity of input (that is, the higher the asset turnover), the greater is the asset efficiency.

Budget Solvency and Operating Results Indicators

Budget solvency means being able to generate sufficient recurring revenues each year to meet recurring expenses (or expenditures) and having a sufficiently large "cushion" of unrestricted resources to weather unforeseen economic downturns and expenditure needs. Entities with relatively volatile revenue structures (such as governments that obtain large amounts of revenue from economy-sensitive taxes like personal income and sales taxes) should maintain a larger cushion than those with relatively stable revenue structures.

The general formulae for the ratios discussed in this section are as follows:

$$\text{Operating Margin or Earnings Margin} = \frac{\text{Excess of Revenues over Expenses (or expenditures)}}{\text{Total Revenues, Gains, and Other Support (or total revenues, or other corresponding item)}}$$

$$\text{or} \quad \frac{\text{Net Change in Fund Balances}}{\text{Total Revenues} + \text{Certain Transfers In}}$$

$$\text{Budgetary Cushion} = \frac{\text{Total Unreserved Fund Balance}}{\text{Total Revenues} + \text{Certain Transfers In}}$$

$$\text{Program Service Ratio} = \frac{\text{Program Expenses}}{\text{Total Expenses}}$$

One indicator of budgetary solvency is the excess of revenues over expenses/expenditures, which is used to determine the operating margin or earnings margin. The *AICPA Audit and Accounting Guide—Health Care Organizations* emphasizes the need for statements of operations prepared by health care entities to have clearly labeled operating performance indicators, using terms such as "revenues over expenses" and "performance earnings." This indicator should be presented in a statement that also presents the total changes in unrestricted net assets.[5] Significant transactions or events reported below the performance indicator also warrant scrutiny, however, in assessing financial health. An analyst might question, for example, whether unrealized securities losses might ultimately be realized.

For general-purpose governments, analysts generally measure operating margin by using only the General Fund or a combination of the General Fund and the Debt Service Fund, but some analysts add selected Special Revenue Funds. In this ratio, the numerator is the net change in fund balances and the denominator may be the revenues plus certain transfers in, or the expenditures plus certain transfers out. It is important to recognize, however, that the net change in fund balances is just the starting point for the calculation, because the net change is an all-inclusive number and may include items that seriously affect the *quality* of the net change. For example, the net change in fund balances might have been affected by "one-shot" financial inflows to the General

---

[5] *AICPA Audit and Accounting Guide—Health Care Organizations* (2006), para. 10–20.

Fund, such as (a) the proceeds of debt used to finance operating expenditures or (b) transfers in from closed-out funds. We will illustrate how these one-shot financial inflows are handled later in the chapter.

Operating margins need to be examined for a period greater than 1 year. A 1-year decline in operating results or even a negative net change in fund balances is not necessarily a cause for concern. For example, a government may budget deliberately for an operating deficit in a particular year to use up a small portion of its unreserved fund balance or to avoid raising tax rates. The analyst thus needs to understand the reasons for the year-to-year change and to examine the longer-term trends in the operating results indicator.

A significant indicator for analysts of general-purpose government financial statements is the ratio of unreserved fund balance to total revenues (or revenues plus certain transfers in). We call this ratio the budgetary cushion. Moody's writes that it "likes to see a General Fund balance sufficient to address *normal* contingencies, a level which, as a general guideline, is typically between 5–10 percent of annual revenues," but it emphasizes that an appropriate level of fund balance depends on each government's operating environment.[6] Other factors that need to be considered in assessing the level of fund balance include the amounts and reasons for interfund transfers, and the historical relationship between budgets and actual financial performance.

Trends in the composition of revenues and expenses are also important to the analysis of budgetary solvency. For example, an increasingly high level of revenues from economy-sensitive taxes may warrant an increase in the budgetary cushion. Review of expenditure details may help to identify why they increased over the previous year, so as to draw managerial attention to the need for remedial action.

Examination of the composition of expenses of not-for-profit organizations is useful to those concerned with how donations are being spent. The FASB requirement to show program expenses separately from administrative and fund-raising expenses enables the reader to calculate the percentage of total expenses devoted to program—the program services ratio. The BBB Wise Giving Alliance suggests that charities should spend at least 65 percent of their total expenses on program activities.[7]

Debt Burden and Other Long-Term Financial Flexibility Indicators

Credit-rating agencies, credit enhancers (such as bond insurers), and investors all are concerned with whether entities that issue long-term debt are likely to have sufficient resources to meet the interest and principal payments on the debt. The general citizenry is also concerned with the strain on resources caused by the need to meet those payments. Outstanding debt, however, is not the only potential drain on an entity's future resources. Pension and postemployment health care obligations also have an impact on an entity's long-term financial condition. Analysts for public and not-for-profit entity employee unions are concerned with the ability of these entities to meet such obligations.

---

[6]The Determinants of Credit Quality," Moody's Investors Service, May 2002, pp. 5–6.

[7]Web site at www.give.org/standards/newcbbbstds.asp.

Debt Issued by General-Purpose Governments

The general formulae for calculating a general-purpose government's debt and debt service burdens are as follows:

$$\text{Debt Burden} = \frac{\text{Outstanding Long-Term Debt}}{\text{Population (or full value of taxable real property or personal income)}}$$

$$\text{Debt Service Burden} = \frac{\text{Total Debt Service}}{\text{Total Revenues (or total expenditures)}}$$

As a general rule, governments issue long-term bonds to finance the acquisition of long-lived capital assets, although long-term debt may also be issued to finance operating needs in periods of fiscal stress. Governments that have a policy of financing a portion of their capital asset needs from tax revenues tend to have greater financial flexibility than those that finance all their capital asset needs by long-term borrowing.

State constitutions or statutes generally limit the amount of debt a local government can issue. Debt limits are usually expressed as a percentage of the full value of taxable real property. Therefore, the closer a government is to its maximum debt limit, the less flexibility it has to borrow for its capital needs. Further, even if it has the legal capacity to borrow, a government may still find it difficult to borrow at reasonable interest rates because of imbalances between its revenues and expenditures.

Common measures of a government's *debt burden* are those that relate outstanding long-term debt to bases that measure its ability to pay the debt and that can be tracked over time and compared with other governments. They include debt per capita and debt as a percentage of full value of taxable real property. Debt per capita is a simple measure, but it does not take account of the wealth of the government's citizens. Debt as a percent of full value of taxable real property provides a measure of the wealth of the community and is therefore a better measure. Debt as a percent of personal income is another excellent measure of debt burden because it takes account of a community's ability to pay the debt service.

Outstanding debt for purposes of calculating debt burden includes the *net direct debt* of the government itself and *overlapping debt,* which is the proportionate share of debt issued by other governmental units that provide services to the citizens of the government. Net direct debt includes both general obligation debt and lease-purchase debt of the government, but, depending on the circumstances, may exclude "self-supporting" debt, such as debt supported by the revenues of an enterprise fund. Overlapping debt includes debt issued by related entities, such as school districts, park districts, cities, and counties. These entities tax the same real property base taxed by the government, thus placing a burden on its stream of resources. For local governments, total direct and overlapping debt generally falls within a range of 2–5 percent of full value of taxable real property.[8]

A government's *debt service burden* is the portion of its revenues that is consumed by the annual payment of principal and interest on long-term debt and interest

---

[8]"Local Government General Obligation Rating Guidelines," FitchRatings, June 10, 2004, p. 2.

on short-term debt. Because refinancing outstanding debt may be costly, the annual debt service requirement is a relatively "fixed" expense. Therefore, the greater the portion of an entity's revenues that is consumed by its debt service requirements, the less flexibility it has to issue additional debt, to meet operating expenditure needs, and to weather the effects of an economic downturn. Credit-rating agencies generally consider a debt service burden of more than 10 percent to be the "level at which budgetary competition is a significant consideration."[9]

A factor closely related to the annual debt service burden is the rate of payback of debt principal. State constitutions or statutes generally limit the length of debt issuances. For example, some require that debt be issued for a period no greater than the useful life of the capital asset to be financed with the debt. Others require that debt be issued for no more than a specific number of years. To keep interest costs down, some governments repay their debt faster than is legally required. On the other hand, a government may decide to stretch its debt repayment schedule further into the future by refinancing its outstanding debt, which is often a sign of fiscal stress.

Municipal credit-rating agencies consider a debt repayment schedule "average" if 25 percent of the outstanding debt is paid off in 5 years and 50 percent is paid off in 10 years.[10] As long as it is not placing a strain on the operating budget, a faster rate of payback not only reduces interest costs, but also gives an entity greater flexibility in issuing additional debt to meet capital needs.

Debt Issued by Governmental Enterprises and Not-for-Profit Organizations

Debt analysis for governmental enterprises and not-for-profit organizations generally focuses on capital structure and on coverage. *Capital structure* concerns the extent to which the organization is leveraged; that is, the extent to which its assets are financed through the use of debt. Capital structure ratios are calculated in a variety of ways. The numerator in these ratios is often some formulation of outstanding long-term term debt, though some analysts prefer using total liabilities. The denominator is generally the net capital assets or some other expression of an asset base (resulting in a *debt ratio*) or the net assets (resulting in a *debt to equity* ratio). (In Moody's debt ratio, for example, the numerator is the "net funded debt" [long-term debt, plus the current portion of long-term debt, plus accrued interest payable, less the balance in the debt service funds] and the denominator is the sum of net capital assets plus net working capital.[11]) In any event, as the use of debt increases—and the ratio increases—the entity's financial flexibility tends to decrease.

Coverage analysis focuses on the entity's ability to repay the debt, as demonstrated by its level of net earnings. Coverage indicators measure the number of times debt service (or interest on debt) is covered by the earnings. Thus, the greater number of times debt service (or interest on debt) is covered by earnings, the greater is the cushion

---

[9]Ibid.

[10]Ibid., p. 3.

[11]Moody's, p. 13.

against possible nonpayment. The commonly used ratios are calculated generally as follows:

$$\text{Long-Term Debt to Assets} = \frac{\text{Long-Term Debt}}{\text{Net Capital Assets}}$$

$$\text{Long-Term Debt to Equity} = \frac{\text{Long-Term Debt, Net of Current Portion}}{\text{Net Assets}}$$

$$\text{Debt Service Coverage} = \frac{(\text{Excess of Revenues over Expenses}) + \text{Depreciation} + \text{Interest}}{\text{Principal Payment} + \text{Interest Expense}}$$

$$\text{Times Interest Earned} = \frac{(\text{Excess of Revenues over Expenses}) + \text{Interest Expense}}{\text{Interest Expense}}$$

Pension and Other Obligations

Pension benefit and postemployment health care arrangements create long-term debt-like commitments. To be adequately funded, these plans must receive annual employer contributions and employee contributions (if required) so that amounts contributed plus earnings on them will be sufficient to pay benefits earned by the employees as they come due. Failure to fund the plans appropriately each year as benefits are earned could place a future strain on an entity's operating budgets.

The most common measure of the adequacy of pension and postemployment health care funding is the *funded ratio,* discussed in Chapter 8. Another good measure, particularly where different measures of the actuarial accrued liability make comparisons difficult, is *payout coverage.* These indicators are calculated as follows:

$$\text{Funded Ratio} = \frac{\text{Fund Assets Available for Benefits}}{\text{Benefit Obligation (actuarial accrued liability)}}$$

$$\text{Payout Coverage} = \frac{\text{Fund Assets Available for Benefits}}{\text{Benefits Paid Last Year}}$$

Table 14-1 presents a summary of the indicators previously discussed.

FINANCIAL CONDITION ASSESSMENT

Financial statement analysis provides information about one or more aspects of the governmental entity's financial position and operations. *Financial condition assessment* uses financial statement analysis as a starting point for drawing inferences about the likely future ability of the entity to meet its financial obligations as they come due, to provide services to its individual and corporate citizens, and to maintain these activities in the face of periodic economic contractions. Financial condition analysis therefore has a longer time horizon and is broader in scope than financial statement analysis.

To assess an entity's financial condition, the analyst must consider not only the results of financial statement analysis, but also the numerous factors—economic, demographic, administrative, and political—influencing the entity's previous, current, and likely future finances.

TABLE 14-1   Summary of Financial Analysis Indicators

Liquidity Indicators

   Purpose: To help assess an entity's ability to meet its short-term obligations

   Common Indicators:

      Current ratio (current assets *divided by* current liabilities)

      Quick ratio (cash + cash equivalents + short-term investments *divided by* current liabilities)

      Number of days' cash on hand (cash + cash equivalents + short-term investments *divided by* cash needs per day)

Asset Turnover or Efficiency Indicators

   Purpose: To help assess an entity's efficiency in using its resources.

   Common Indicators:

      Number of days' revenue in accounts receivable (net patient accounts receivable *divided by* net patient service revenues per day)

      Property tax collection rate (current year property taxes collected *divided by* current year real property tax levy)

      Property tax receivable rate (real property taxes receivable *divided by* real property tax revenues)

      Total asset turnover (unrestricted revenues, gains, and other support *divided by* unrestricted net assets)

Budget Solvency and Operating Results Indicators

   Purpose: To help assess an entity's ability to generate sufficient recurring revenues to meet expenses and to meet unforeseen operating budget needs

   Common Indicators:

      Earnings margin (excess of revenues over expenses *divided by* total revenues, gains, and other support [or equivalent]) or (net change in fund balances *divided by* total revenues and certain transfers in)

      Budgetary cushion (total unreserved fund balance *divided by* total revenues and certain transfers in)

      Program services ratio (program expenses *divided by* total expenses)

Debt Burden and Other Long-Term Financial Flexibility Indicators

   Purpose: To help assess an entity's likelihood of having sufficient resources to meet its long-term obligations and to finance long-term capital and other needs

   Common Indicators:

     Debt issued by general-purpose governments:

        Debt burden (outstanding long-term debt *divided by* population or full value of taxable real property or personal income)

        Debt service burden (total debt service *divided by* total revenues or expenditures)

     Debt issued by governmental enterprises and not-for-profit organizations:

        Long-term debt to assets (long-term debt *divided by* net capital assets)

        Long-term debt to equity (long-term debt [net of current portion] *divided by* net assets)

        Debt service coverage ([excess of revenues over expenses] + depreciation + interest expense *divided by* principal payment + interest expense)

        Times interest earned ([excess of revenues over expenses] + interest expense *divided by* interest expense)

     Pension and post-employment health care obligations

        Funded ratio (fund assets available for benefits *divided by* benefit obligation)

        Payout coverage (fund assets available for benefits *divided by* benefits paid last year)

Financial condition analysis is undertaken for many reasons. For example:

- Credit-rating agencies provide an independent, objective assessment of the relative creditworthiness of state and local government debt obligations. These assessments, generally made before sale of a particular issue of long-term bonds or short-term notes, help the issuer raise capital and help the investor decide whether to invest in the obligation.
- Credit enhancers also assess the creditworthiness of debt obligations to decide whether to insure the payment of future debt service. Insurance lowers the net interest cost to the borrower and provides a guarantee of payment to the lender.
- Some state oversight agencies gather financial and other information from local governments within the state as part of their fiscal oversight responsibilities. The process is designed primarily to help both the state and local governments detect early signals of fiscal stress.

Here are some of the specific matters—beyond the ratios previously discussed—that one might consider in assessing municipal financial condition:[12]

- Behavior of the entity's *tax revenue bases*. The tax revenue bases are the specific sources tapped, such as real property values and general sales, to produce tax revenues. From a financial condition analysis perspective, previous-year growth in tax revenues resulting from increasing tax bases is preferable to tax revenue growth from increases in tax rates.
- Relative *tax bite*. Tax bite is computed as the ratio of tax revenues to the tax revenue base. The greater the entity's current tax bite relative to similar entities, the less flexibility it has to raise tax rates in the future.
- Trends in the economic and demographic base. Economics and demographics play a major role in tax revenue growth and expenditure needs. Therefore, the financial condition analyst examines such factors as trends in resident personal income; risk of tax revenue loss because of insufficient employer and taxpayer diversity; trends in poverty, labor skills, and population growth; and trends in the nature of employment within the jurisdiction.
- Managerial practices and political will. History shows that some governments with a strong economic base have encountered fiscal stress because of a failure of political will, while some with a weaker economic base have avoided fiscal stress because of strong financial management and conservative fiscal practices. In this context, a financial condition analyst might raise questions such as these: Does the entity prepare longer-term financial plans? Are its annual budgets routinely balanced both in form and in substance? What are its practices regarding expenditure control? Has it adopted a policy concerning the size of its budget cushion? Does it routinely finance some of its capital needs from tax revenues?

---

[12]For an extensive discussion of this subject, see Martin Ives, *Assessing Municipal Financial Condition,* Croton-on-Hudson, NY: Ives and Hancox, 2006.

FINANCIAL ANALYSIS IN PRACTICE
SEC Cites San Diego for Failing to Disclose Material Information

State and local governments are exempt from the registration and reporting provision of the Securities Act of 1933 and the Securities Exchange Act of 1934. They are, however, subject to the antifraud provisions of those acts—making an untrue statement of material fact or omitting a material fact—in the offer or sale of securities. A 2006 ruling by the Securities and Exchange Commission (SEC) regarding the City of San Diego, California, shows how the omission of certain data regarding pension and retiree health benefit costs could cause an analyst to reach an inappropriate conclusion.

According to the SEC, San Diego sold more than $260 million in five separate offerings of municipal bonds without disclosing significant problems regarding its future pension and health care obligations. The city made some disclosures about these obligations (such as its funding policy and funding status of the pension system) in its official statements and in presentations to credit-rating agencies. But it failed to "reveal the gravity" of its future funding problems regarding these benefits. When the city eventually disclosed its problems, the credit-rating agencies lowered the city's credit ratings.

The SEC stated that the city failed to disclose the following matters, among others, in presentations made to credit-rating agencies in connection with its bond offerings:

- The city was intentionally underfunding its pension obligations by increasing benefits but pushing the costs associated with those increases into the future. As a result, the unfunded liability of the plan was expected to increase dramatically, growing from $284 million at the start of 2002 to an estimated $2 billion in 2009.

- The growth in the unfunded pension liability resulted from the city's intentional underfunding of the plan, granting new retroactive pension benefits, using pension plan earnings to pay additional benefits, and earning less than anticipated.

- The city's annual pension contribution was expected to more than quadruple between 2002 and 2009.

- The city had been covering the annual cost of retiree health care with pension plan earnings from prior years that were expected to be depleted in 2006, after which these costs would have to be financed from its regular budget.

SOURCE: Order instituting cease-and-desist proceedings, in the matter of City of San Diego, California, before the Securities and Exchange Commission, November 14, 2006. Administrative Proceeding File No. 3-12478.

ILLUSTRATION OF ANALYSIS OF GOVERNMENTAL FINANCIAL STATEMENTS

This section illustrates some of the ratios used in analyzing the financial statements of general-purpose governments. To make the calculations we adapted the ratios shown earlier in this chapter to the government environment and to the data provided in the 2005 financial statements issued by the Village of Grafton, Wisconsin.

When analyzing the financial statements of general-purpose governments, analysts generally focus on the General Fund or on the total of the General and Debt Service

Funds. Some analysts include the Special Revenue Funds that account for normal, day-to-day operating activities of government, such as libraries. In developing or assessing the ratios, analysts also need to consider the data provided in the government-wide financial statements as well as the statistical data provided in the comprehensive annual financial report (CAFR). However, capital asset needs and enterprise funds are generally considered separately.

To simplify this illustration, most of our calculations are based on Grafton's General Fund and Debt Service Fund. For ease in tracing the numbers, we extracted the General and Debt Service Fund data from Tables 9-1 and 9-3 and have included them here (with memorandum totals for the two funds) as Tables 14-2 and 14-3.

TABLE 14-2 Excerpt from Governmental Funds Balance Sheet

Village of Grafton
Excerpt from Governmental Funds Balance Sheet
December 31, 2005

	General	*Debt Service*	*Total (Memo)*
Assets:			
Cash and Investments	$1,597,015	$ 383,070	$1,980,085
Receivables (Net)			
Taxes	4,531,504	995,082	5,526,586
Delinquent Personal Property Taxes	13,673		13,673
Accounts	169,026	14,032	183,058
Due from Other Funds	90,221		90,221
Prepaid Items	62,923		62,923
Total Assets	$6,464,362	$1,392,184	$ 7,856,546
Liabilities and Fund Balances:			
Liabilities:			
Accounts Payable	$ 154,680	$ 21	$ 154,701
Accrued Liabilities	139,358		139,358
Deposits	59,460		59,460
Due to Other Funds	2,193		2,193
Due to Plan Participants	3,625		3,625
Unearned Revenues	4,531,504	995,082	5,526,586
Total Liabilities	4,890,820	995,103	5,885,923
Fund Balances:			
Reserved	76,596	397,081	473,677
Unreserved	1,496,946		1,496,946
Total Fund Balances	1,573,542	397,081	1,970,623
Total Liabilities and Fund Balances	$6,464,362	$1,392,184	$7,856,546

Source: Excerpted from Table 9-1. Total column is a memorandum column to facilitate financial statement analysis.

TABLE 14-3 Excerpt from Governmental Funds Statement of Revenues, Expenditures, and Changes in Fund Balances

Village of Grafton
Excerpt from Statement of Revenues, Expenditures, and Changes in Fund Balances
For the Year Ended December 31, 2005

	General	*Debt Service*	*Total (Memo)*
Revenues:			
Taxes	$4,641,176	$ 959,693	$5,600,869
Intergovernmental	1,285,395	117,109	1,402,504
Licenses and Permits	346,166		346,166
Fines, Forfeitures, and Penalties	123,888		123,888
Public Charges for Services	224,821		224,821
Intergov't. Charges for Services	41,822		41,822
Investment Income	85,569	36,213	121,782
Miscellaneous	25,353		25,353
Total Revenues	6,774,190	1,113,015	7,887,205
Expenditures:			
Current:			
General Government	740,403		740,403
Public Safety	3,261,589		3,261,589
Public Works	1,906,633		1,906,633
Community Enrichment Services	363,459		363,459
Conservation and Development	137,982		137,982
Debt Service:			
Principle Retirement		1,309,479	1,309,479
Interest and Fiscal Charges		685,221	685,221
Debt Issuance Costs		26,850	26,850
Total Expenditures	6,410,066	2,021,550	8,431,616
Excess (Deficiency) of Revenues Over (Under) Expenditures	364,124	(908,535)	(544,411)
Other Financing Sources (Uses):			
Transfers In	48,959	842,648	891,607
Transfers (Out)	(401,310)		(401,310)
Total Other Financing Sources (Uses)	(352,351)	842,648	490,297
Net Change in Fund Balances	11,773	(65,887)	(54,114)
Fund Balances—Beginning	1,561,769	462,968	2,024,737
Fund Balances—Ending	$1,573,542	$ 397,081	$1,970,623

Source: Excerpted from Table 9-3. Table column is a memorandum column to facilitate financial statement analysis.

Liquidity Indicator (Quick Ratio)

The quick ratio provides a good, conservative measure of liquidity for general-purpose governments. In calculating Grafton's liquidity ratio, we did not include the unearned (deferred) revenues as a liability because the transaction resulting in recording unearned revenues produced no cash. (Grafton levies real property taxes in December for the following year and the amounts reported as unearned revenues and taxes receivable are the same.) Therefore, the liabilities figure used in this ratio is $359,337 (total liabilities [$5,885,923] − unearned revenues [$5,526,586]). Grafton's quick ratio, calculated from the data in Table 14-2, is:

$$\frac{\text{Cash and Investments}}{\text{Current Liabilities (net of Unearned Revenues)}} = \frac{\$1,980,085}{\$359,337} = 5.5$$

The calculation shows that Grafton has sufficient quick assets to cover its current liabilities 5.5 times. The quick assets of $1,980,085 are also sufficient to cover almost 3 months' expenditures. (Table 14-3 shows that Grafton's total General Fund and Debt Service Fund expenditures for the year were approximately $8.4 million, or about $700,000 a month.) A New York State Comptroller publication observes that cash balances tend to be lowest at year end, and suggests that year-end cash and investments generally should be about 50 percent of current liabilities.[13] The International City/County Management Association considers a quick ratio of less than 1 to be a negative factor.[14] Based on these rules of thumb, Grafton's quick ratio of 5.5 is very favorable.

Efficiency Indicator (Tax Collection Rate)

Grafton has only two types of taxes (real property and personal property) and records a relatively significant amount of them in funds other than the General Fund. To get a valid measure of tax collection efficiency, we need to take account of all the funds in which the taxes are recorded. Tax collection efficiency can be measured either as tax collection or tax delinquency rates. Based on the availability of data, Grafton's tax delinquency rate can be measured readily from Table 9-1 (see the caption delinquent personal property taxes) and Table 9-3 (see the caption taxes), as follows:

$$\frac{\text{Delinquent taxes receivable}}{\text{Tax revenues}} = \frac{\$13,673}{\$6,550,849} = 0.2\%$$

As stated earlier in the chapter, Moody's suggests that a current tax collection rate of less than 95 percent—or a delinquency rate of more than 5 percent—is a sign of potential credit distress. The foregoing calculation shows Grafton's tax delinquency rate to be well below 1 percent. Based on the Moody's rule of thumb, Grafton's tax collection efficiency is excellent.

Budgetary Solvency and Operating Results Indicators
Operating Margin

When calculating governmental activity operating margins, the analyst needs to use both the fund financial statements and the government-wide statements. Using only the fund statements can be misleading because they are prepared on the modified accrual basis of accounting and therefore lack certain accruals. Using only the governmental activities column of the government-wide statements also can be misleading, primarily because the requirement to reduce program expenses by program-related

---

[13]"Local Government Management Guide—Financial Condition Analysis," Office of the New York State Comptroller, Albany: 2003, p. 30.
[14]"Evaluating Financial Condition" by Sanford M. Groves and Maureen Godsey Valente, International City/County Management Association, Washington, DC: 1994, p. 77.

capital grants and contributions can overstate the margin resulting from operating activities; although these grants increase net assets, they are not "operating" revenues.

Many analysts assess operating results by starting with the fund financial statements and then considering the reconciling items in the reconciliation of the fund and government-wide operating statements. For example, the analyst might adjust the operating results shown by the fund statements if the reconciliation shows a large expense accrual or if depreciation expense reported in the government-wide statement significantly exceeds debt principal repayments. To simplify this illustration, we will make calculations using only Grafton's General Fund. (Grafton's Debt Service Fund is complicated somewhat by the large amounts of transfers in from tax increment funds and other funds).

When working with the fund statements, the analyst needs to focus particularly on the bottom part of the statement of revenues, expenditures, and changes in fund balances, starting with the caption "excess (deficiency) of revenues over expenditures." Notice the data in the General Fund column for Grafton in Table 14-3. It shows: $364,124 excess of revenues over expenditures, $48,959 transfers in, $401,310 transfers out, and $11,773 net change in fund balance for the year. We can start with the net change in fund balance and make an initial calculation of Grafton's General Fund operating margin as follows:

$$\frac{\text{Net change in fund balance}}{\text{Total revenues and transfers in}} = \frac{\$11,773}{\$6,774,190 + \$48,959} = 0.2\%$$

To assess the "quality" of the information content of the net change in fund balance, we might raise the following questions about the details entering into the calculation:

- What is the nature of transfers in and out? Should they be treated as the equivalent of revenues and expenditures for purposes of this analysis? Analysis of the note disclosures shows that $47,087 of the transfers in resulted from the nonrecurring closing of a Special Revenue Fund, but the entire $401,310 of transfers out represented recurring operating subsidies to Special Revenue Funds, primarily for the annual financing of the library. For analysis purposes, the *nonrecurring* transfer in should not be considered as revenues, but the *recurring* transfers out should be considered as expenditures. If we exclude the nonrecurring financing source, Grafton experienced a small "deficit" of $35,314 ($11,773 − $47,087), rather than a small "surplus"; its operating margin was a negative 0.5 percent, rather than a positive 0.2 percent.
- Does the additional information available from the reconciliation between the fund and government-wide financial statements materially modify the operating results shown in the fund statements? The reconciliation of the operating statements (Table 10-3) shows that the accrual-related adjustments are relatively small amounts and that they affected primarily funds other than the General Fund. So the answer to that question is No.
- What are the implications of the adjusted operating margin? By itself, the small negative ratio is not overly significant. But if it were, several questions need to be asked. Did the entity experience operating deficits in the previous year and the year before that? Did the entity budget for a deficit at the start of the year? If so, did it make efforts to keep the deficit to a minimum by

controlling operating expenditures? And, most important, is the unreserved fund balance at December 31, 2005, high enough to provide a reasonable budgetary cushion for the future?

The management discussion and analysis accompanying Grafton's financial statements points out that Grafton's 2005 budget contemplated a deficit of $328,000 and that the village decided to appropriate that amount from its existing fund balance to avoid raising tax rates. But the actual results of the year's operations were much better than anticipated. Actual revenues and other financing sources were greater than that budgeted, and expenditures and other uses were lower than budget. As a result, Grafton's General Fund fund balance increased by $11,773 (or would have decreased by $35,314 if not for the transfer in). This brings us to the key question: Is Grafton's budgetary cushion at December 31, 2005, high enough to cover temporary economic contractions and unanticipated expenditure needs?

Budgetary Cushion

The budgetary cushion—the availability of accumulated financial resources from previous years' activities to finance future years' activities—is a particularly important element of a governmental entity's financial condition. The larger the cushion, the more likely it is that the entity can withstand revenue shortfalls caused by economic contraction and meet emergency expenditure needs. The budgetary cushion is the ratio of unreserved fund balance to total revenues and transfers in. (Some analysts use total expenditures and transfers out as the denominator.) Grafton's General Fund budgetary cushion is calculated from Tables 14-2 and 14-3 as follows:

$$\frac{\text{Unreserved fund balance}}{\text{Total revenues and transfers in}} = \frac{\$1,496,946}{\$6,774,190 + \$48,959} = 21.9\%$$

As stated earlier in this chapter, Moody's considers a General Fund budgetary cushion of 5 to 10 percent as sufficient to address normal contingencies. Because most of Grafton's revenues are from real property taxes, which are less economy sensitive than sales and personal income taxes, a budgetary cushion at the lower end of the 5 to 10 percent scale would not be considered unreasonable. Fitch says that municipalites that consistently maintain a budgetary cushion of 10 percent or more are viewed more favorably than those that don't. Grafton's budgetary cushion of 21.9 percent is well above the 5 to 10 percent rule of thumb; further, analysis of recent trends shows that the cushion is similar to what it was 5 years ago. Therefore, the fact that it had a small operating deficit (after our adjustment) in 2005 is of no particular concern, and we regard Grafton's budgetary cushion as a favorable factor in assessing its financial condition.

Debt Burden and Other Financial Flexibility Indicators

Debt Burden

State laws generally limit the amount of long-term debt that their municipalities can have outstanding at any time. Wisconsin laws limit outstanding village long-term debt to 5 percent of the equalized value (full value) of taxable real and personal property within the jurisdiction. The equalized value of real and personal property in Grafton was $994.1 million in 2005, so its debt limit (at 5 percent) was $49.7 million. Against that limit, Grafton had total outstanding long-term debt of $27.4 million. Therefore, Grafton had a legal debt margin (the amount of additional long-term debt that it could legally issue) of almost $22.3 million.

To assess the relative amount of a local government's debt burden, analysts generally consider only the *tax-supported debt*. "Self-supporting" debt (that is, debt financed by user charges, such as debt sold to finance Grafton's water and wastewater utility plant) and amounts set aside in debt service reserve funds are excluded. Grafton's outstanding tax-supported debt at December 31, 2005, was $24,675,372. (This amount is part of the long-term obligations shown in the governmental activities column in Table 10-1 on page 382.) Grafton's tax-supported debt burden, using population and full value of property as the measurement bases, is therefore calculated as follows:

| | *Based on* | |
	Population	*Property Value*
Outstanding tax-supported long-term debt	$24,675,372	$ 24,675,372
Measurement base (population; property value)	11,310	$994,070,400
Ratio (debt/measurement base)	$ 2,182	2.48%

Grafton's outstanding tax-supported long-term debt at December 31, 2004, was only $16,328,718. However, its outstanding debt increased significantly in 2005 because it issued $9,615,000 of debt to continue redevelopment of its downtown and commercial districts and to acquire general capital assets. Grafton's 2005 CAFR did not report on its overlapping debt, but overlapping debt has added about 2 percent to Grafton's own direct debt in the past. So, for analysis purposes, let's assume that Grafton's overall debt (the total of its own direct debt plus the overlapping debt) is approximately 4.5 percent. As previously stated, Fitch observes that the average range of overall debt to full value of taxable real property is 2 percent to 5 percent. By that guideline, Grafton's 2005 ratio of overall debt to full value of taxable real property is at the upper end of average, but would not be characterized as "high."

Debt Service Burden

Debt service is a relatively fixed expenditure, which reduces the ability of a governmental entity to finance operating activities from taxes and other resources. Debt service burden can be calculated from the information reported in the statement of revenues, expenditures, and changes in fund balance (Table 14-3), as follows:

$$\frac{\text{Debt Service Expenditures}}{\text{Revenues and Transfers In}} = \frac{\$1,309,479 \text{ (principal)} + \$685,221 \text{ (interest)}}{\$7,887,205 \text{ (revenues)} + \$891,607 \text{ (transfers in)}}$$

$$= \frac{\$1,994,700}{\$8,778,812} = 22.7\%$$

As previously stated, credit-rating agencies generally consider a debt service burden of more than 10 percent to be the level at which competition among programs for tax resources is a significant consideration. Therefore, Grafton's debt service burden would be considered to be on the high side. It should be pointed out, however, that one reason why it is high is that Grafton tends to redeem its long-term debt in a relatively rapid manner. The note to financial statements on debt service requirements to maturity shows that Grafton will redeem 39 percent of its outstanding long-term debt in the next 5 years and 61 percent of its outstanding long-term debt in the next 10 years. As previously noted, credit-rating agencies look for debt principal payback of 25 percent in 5 years and 50 percent in 10 years, and consider a more rapid payback as a favorable factor.

Overall Assessment—Grafton's Credit Rating

We designed this illustration to provide an overview of some of the factors considered in analyzing state and local government financial statements. Analysis of financial condition for credit-rating purposes requires consideration of many factors beyond those covered here. As a point of information, the management discussion and analysis covering Grafton's 2005 financial statements states that Grafton maintains an A1 rating from Moody's for its general obligation debt. Moody's credit ratings range from Aaa (highest quality) to C (lowest quality). An A rating by Moody's means that the bonds possess many favorable investment attributes and are considered upper-medium-grade obligations—the factors securing principal and interest payments on the debt are adequate, but elements may be present that suggest a susceptibility to impairment sometime in the future. The symbol A1 means that Moody's believes the bonds possess the strongest credit attributes within the A category.

ILLUSTRATION OF ANALYSIS OF NOT-FOR-PROFIT HOSPITAL FINANCIAL STATEMENTS

To illustrate the calculations of several of the ratios used in analyzing not-for-profit hospital financial statements, we reproduced (as Tables 14-4 and 14-5) two of Hudson Valley Hospital Center's financial statements from Chapter 13. As you read the text, trace the numbers used in the calculations to the tables. Also, to provide a general frame of reference for understanding the size of the hospital's ratios, we have shown some national hospital medians, which are available at the Cleverley & Associates Web site.[15] (The national medians tend to vary year by year and by size of hospital, and they need to be used with care.) Our calculations show that, at December 31, 2005, the hospital was readily able to meet both its current financial obligations and its long-term debt obligations.

Liquidity Indicators
Current Ratio

The hospital's current ratio at December 31, 2005, was 2.70, calculated as follows, from the balance sheet in Table 14-4:

$$\frac{\text{Current Assets}}{\text{Current Liabilities}} = \frac{\$42,788,325}{\$15,820,110} = 2.70$$

The hospital's 2005 current ratio of 2.70 was higher than the previous year, when the ratio was 2.23 ($32,997,835/$14,829,293). As a broad frame of reference, the year 2000 median for hospitals with revenues between $60 million and $100 million was 2.22.

---

[15]The Cleverley & Associates Web site is at www.cleverleyassociates.com/resourcelibrary.html. Most of the national data we used in this section comes from "US Medians" (based on Medicare Cost Reports and other data for 2005, 2004, and 2003), a one-page document available at that site. The national current ratio is from the 2000 *Almanac of Hospital and Financial Operating Indicators,* provided to us directly by Dr. William Cleverley.

TABLE 14-4   Balance Sheet—Not-for-Profit Hospital

Hudson Valley Hospital Center
Balance Sheets
December 31, 2005 and 2004

	2005	2004
Assets		
Current assets:		
Cash and cash equivalents	$ 9,544,764	$10,524,715
Investments	17,665,267	9,570,503
Patient accounts receivable, less allowance for uncollectible accounts of approximately $4,240,000 in 2005 and $4,880,000 in 2004	12,317,650	10,657,163
Other receivables	1,516,119	576,110
Supplies and prepaid expenses	1,744,525	1,669,344
Total current assets	42,788,325	32,997,835
Interest in Foundation of Hudson Valley Hospital Center	5,947,723	5,313,105
Assets whose use is limited—externally restricted	6,692,714	7,064,422
Long-term investments	1,674,619	669,163
Property, plant, and equipment, net	32,436,683	30,516,903
Other assets	1,785,804	1,231,723
Total assets	$91,325,868	$77,793,151
Liabilities and Net Assets		
Current liabilities:		
Current portion of long-term debt	$ 645,349	$ 639,238
Current portion of capital lease obligations	904,412	1,421,699
Accounts payable and accrued expenses	6,419,826	6,852,313
Accrued salaries and benefits	6,089,351	5,222,043
Estimated payable to third-party payers	1,761,172	694,000
Total current liabilities	15,820,110	14,829,293
Long-term debt	17,321,911	18,120,671
Capital lease obligations	1,839,810	1,722,328
Estimated payable to third-party payers, malpractice and other liabilities	14,883,123	12,857,742
Total liabilities	49,864,954	47,530,034
Net assets		
Unrestricted	34,245,544	24,280,849
Temporarily restricted	5,540,751	5,313,105
Permanently restricted	1,674,619	669,163
Total net assets	41,460,914	30,263,117
Total liabilities and net assets	$91,325,868	$77,793,151

Source: Hudson Valley Hospital Center financial statements, December 31, 2005 and 2004. Reprinted with permission. (Accompanying notes, which are an integral part of these statements, are not shown here.)

TABLE 14-5 Statement of Operations—Not-for-Profit Hospital

Hudson Valley Hospital Center
Statements of Operations
Years Ended December 31, 2005 and 2004

	2005	2004
Operating revenues		
Net patient service revenue	$89,517,295	$84,542,802
Other operating revenue	2,342,573	2,415,522
Total operating revenues	91,859,868	86,958,324
Operating expenses		
Salaries	37,531,888	34,763,509
Physician fees	1,918,099	2,001,851
Fringe benefits	7,580,312	6,995,657
Supplies and other expenses	27,366,422	28,610,259
Provision for bad debts	1,775,068	3,238,525
Interest	1,341,181	1,518,418
Depreciation and amortization	4,488,172	4,962,198
Total operating expenses	82,001,142	82,090,417
Operating gain	9,858,726	4,867,907
Investment income	806,560	554,012
Loss on transfer	(477,840)	—
Excess of revenues over expenses	10,187,446	5,421,919
Change in net unrealized gains and losses on investments	(75,897)	230,272
Net assets released from restrictions for capital expenditures	—	3,126,250
Increase in unrestricted net assets before cumulative effect	10,111,549	8,778,441
Cumulative effect of change in accounting principle	(146,854)	—
Increase in unrestricted net assets	$ 9,964,695	$ 8,778,441

Source: Hudson Valley Hospital Center financial statements, December 31, 2005 and 2004. Reprinted with permission. (Accompanying notes, which are an integral part of these statements, are not shown here.)

Quick Ratio

The hospital's quick ratio was 1.72 at December 31, 2005, calculated from Table 14-4, as follows:

$$\frac{\text{Cash and Cash Equivalents } + \text{ Short-Term Investments}}{\text{Current Liabilities}} = \frac{\$9,554,764 + \$17,665,267}{\$15,820,110} = 1.72$$

The hospital's quick ratio of 1.72 is also better than it was at the end of 2004, when it was 1.36 ([$10,524,715 + $9,570,503] / $14,829,293).

Number of Days' Cash on Hand

Calculating the number of days' cash on hand requires reference to both the balance sheet and the statement of operations.

First, use Table 14-5 to estimate the average amount of cash needed each day to pay operating expenses. To do this, take the total expenses, subtract depreciation and the provision for bad debts (because they do not require cash outlays), and divide the result by 365. The 2005 calculation for the hospital is as follows:

$$\frac{\text{Total Expenses} - (\text{Depreciation and Amortization} + \text{Provision for Bad Debts})}{365}$$

$$= \frac{\$82,001,142 - (\$4,488,172 + \$1,775,068)}{365} = \$207,501$$

Then, to get the number of days' cash on hand, divide the cash and cash equivalents plus the short-term investments (from Table 14-4) by the average cash needs per day, as follows:

$$\frac{\text{Cash and Cash Equivalents} + \text{Short-Term Investments}}{\text{Average Cash Needs per Day}}$$

$$= \frac{\$9,554,764 + \$17,665,267}{\$207,501} = 131 \text{ days}$$

Thus, the hospital had sufficient cash and short-term investments at December 31, 2005, to pay operating expenses for about 131 days. This is an improvement over the previous year, when cash and short-term investments on hand covered operating expenses for 99 days. (First, $82,090,417 - [4,962,198 + \$3,238,525] / 365 = \$202,438$; then, $[\$10,524,715 + \$9,570,503] / \$202,438 = 99$). The hospital's number of days' cash on hand is also well in excess of the national hospital median, which was 38 days in 2005 and 36 days in 2003 and 2004.[16]

How much cash should a hospital have on hand? Cleverley suggests that most hospitals lack sufficient cash to cover all their short-term working capital needs, capital investment needs, and contingencies. He says that, in 2005, the average not-for-profit U.S. hospital held about 15 to 20 days' cash and short-term investments to cover working capital needs. But much more than that might be needed to finance capital investment needs, depending on projected levels of capital expenditures and the extent to which capital needs will be financed from debt.[17]

Efficiency Indicator (Number of Days' Revenue in Receivables)

Calculating the number of days' revenue in year-end receivables also requires using both the balance sheet and the statement of operations.

First, use Table 14-4 to determine the net patient service revenue per day. For 2005, the calculation is:

$$\frac{\text{Net Patient Service Revenue}}{365} = \frac{\$89,517,295}{365} = \$245,253$$

---

[16]Ibid.

[17]"How Much Cash Should Your Hospital Hold?" by William O. Cleverley, *Strategic Financial Planning*, Spring 2007, pp. 14–15.

Then, to get the number of days' revenue in year-end receivables, divide the net patient accounts receivable by the net patient service revenue per day, as follows:

$$\frac{\text{Net Patient Accounts Receivable}}{\text{Net Patient Service Revenue Per Day}} = \frac{\$12,317,650}{\$245,253} = 50.2 \text{ days}$$

Thus, the hospital had about 50.2 days of revenue tied up in accounts receivable at December 31, 2005. This indicator is slightly worse than it was at December 31, 2004, when there were 46.0 days' revenue in accounts receivable (first, $84,542,802 / 365 = $231,624 revenues per day; then, $10,657,163 / $231,624 = 46.0 days). The number, however, is better than the 2005 national hospital median of 57 days. (According to "US Medians," the median ranged from 57 to 59 days between 2003 and 2005.)

Operating Results Indicator (Earnings Margin)

The statement of operations (Table 14-5) provides the data for calculating the earnings margin. The hospital's earnings margin for 2005 was 11.1 percent, calculated as follows:

$$\frac{\text{Excess of Revenues over Expenses}}{\text{Total Revenues, Gains, and Other Support}} = \frac{\$10,187,446}{\$91,859,868} = 11.1\%$$

The hospital's 2005 earnings margin of 11.1 percent was significantly higher than the 2004 earnings margin of 6.2 percent ($5,421,919 / $86,958,324)—a favorable indicator. The hospital's earnings margin for 2005 also compares very favorably with the 2005 national hospital median of 3.9 percent. To determine the reasons for the improvement over the prior year (or the decline, if that had occurred), the analyst would compare the details of the revenue and expense components and determine the reasons for the major changes. In this situation, for example, the analyst might raise questions such as these:

- Net patient service revenue increased by 5.9 percent ([$89,517,295 − $84,542,802] / $84,542,802). What were the major reasons for the increase? Greater volume? Change in patient mix? Higher reimbursement rates? Is this rate of increase likely to continue into 2006?
- Although net patient service revenue increased by almost $5 million, total operating expenses were about the same in 2005 as in 2004. Salaries and related fringe benefits increased slightly faster than net patient service revenues, but there were reductions in other expenses. Why did the provision for bad debts decline by almost $1.5 million even though patient accounts receivable increased? Why did depreciation and amortization expenses decline almost $0.5 million even though the investment in capital assets increased?

Debt Burden and Other Financial Flexibility Indicators
Long-Term Debt to Equity Ratio

The hospital's long-term debt to equity ratio at December 31, 2005, can be computed from the balance sheet in Table 14-4, as follows:

$$\frac{\text{Long-Term Debt (Net of Current Portion)} + \text{Capital Lease Obligations}}{\text{Total Net Assets}}$$

$$= \frac{\$17,321,911 + \$1,839,810}{\$41,460,914} = \frac{\$19,161,721}{\$41,460,914} = 46.2\%$$

Debt Service Coverage and Times Interest Earned

Most of the data needed to calculate an entity's debt service coverage and number of times it earned its interest expense comes from the statement of operations (Table 14-4). The cash outflow for the principal portion of debt service can be found in the cash flow statement (see Table 13-4 on page 528.)

The denominator of these ratios shows what was covered: either the total debt service requirement or just the interest. The numerator is based on the hospital's earnings; to get the numerator, you start with the excess of revenues over expenses and add back either the depreciation plus the interest or just the interest. (Depreciation is added back because it does not require a cash outflow and because it is, in a sense, a surrogate for part of what was covered—the principal payment. Interest is added back because it is part of what was covered and because it had been deducted as an expense in determining the excess of revenues over expenses.)

The hospital covered its debt service 4.3 times in 2005, calculated as follows:

$$\frac{\text{Excess of Revenues over Expenses} + \text{Depreciation} + \text{Interest Expense}}{\text{Principal Payment} + \text{Interest Expense}}$$

$$= \frac{\$10,187,446 + \$4,488,172 + \$1,341,181}{\$2,379,907 + \$1,341,181} = \frac{\$16,016,799}{\$3,721,088} = 4.3 \text{ times}$$

The hospital covered its interest expense 8.6 times in 2005, as shown below:

$$\frac{\text{Excess of Revenues over Expenses} + \text{Interest Expense}}{\text{Interest Expense}}$$

$$= \frac{\$10,187,446 + \$1,341,181}{\$1,341,181} = \frac{\$11,528,627}{\$1,341,181} = 8.6 \text{ times}$$

The hospital improved its times interest earned performance in 2005 over 2004, when it was 4.6 times ([\$5,421,919 + \$1,518,418] / \$1,518,418). Its times interest earned performance in 2005 was also significantly better than the U.S. median for 2005, when it was 3.9. ("US Medians" indicates that the national hospital median for times interest earned was 3.1 in both 2003 and 2004.)

Review Questions

Q14-1   How does the organization of the statement of net assets help the reader assess an entity's financial position?

Q14-2   How does the organization of the statement of activities help the reader assess an entity's operating results?

Q14-3   How do the calculations of ratios and per capita amounts assist in assessing an entity's financial position and financial condition?

Q14-4   How do time-series analysis and comparative analysis help in assessing an entity's operating results, financial position, and financial condition?

Q14-5   What is the purpose of preparing common size financial statements?

Q14-6   What is the purpose of calculating the current ratio and the quick ratio?

Q14-7   What is the purpose of calculating the number of days' revenues in accounts receivable?

Q14-8   How is the budgetary cushion calculated and why should a governmental entity maintain such a cushion?

Q14-9   What can a potential donor to a not-for-profit organization learn by calculating the organization's program services ratio?

Q14-10   Discuss why an analyst might prefer to calculate a governmental entity's debt burden as a percentage of full value of property rather than on a per capita basis.

Q14-11   Describe the relationship, if any, between a governmental entity's debt service burden and the rate at which it pays off debt principal.

Q14-12   What is the purpose of calculating debt service coverage?

Q14-13   What is the purpose of calculating a pension plan's funded ratio?

Q14-14   Why is it necessary to consider the economic and demographic environment in assessing a governmental entity's financial condition?

Case

C14-1   Ken Mead, newly elected mayor of Bronson City, promised the citizens during his campaign that he would not raise taxes during his tenure as mayor. He asks his new commissioner of finance to analyze the city's financial statements to see whether the city has "any extra money lying around" to help keep taxes down. The commissioner of finance notices the caption "Unreserved fund balance" in the city's General Fund balance sheet. The commissioner shows the financial statements to the mayor and says: "See that unreserved fund balance? Looks like a slush fund to me. Why don't we just use it to help keep taxes down?" How would you advise the mayor about this matter?

Ethics Case

E14-1   Good Faith Hospital needs to sell bonds to finance major renovations and purchases of modern equipment. The hospital recently experienced difficulties, however, and its operating margin for the past 3 years fell below the median operating margin for hospitals of similar size. The hospital is preparing its financial statements, and preliminary indications are that its operating margin will continue its downward slide. The CFO is concerned that the bond-rating agency will lower the hospital's bond rating, resulting in an increase in the interest rate on the new bonds.

The CFO wants to report a higher operating margin than the previous year. He tells the chief accountant: "I don't want you to do anything you shouldn't do, but we both know that higher interest rates on the new bonds will reduce our operating margin even further. Just sharpen your pencil to see if you can reduce this year's provision for uncollectible patient receivables and estimated third-party settlements."

If you were the chief accountant, how would you react to the CFO's request?

Exercises

E14-1   (Multiple choice)

1. When common size statements are prepared, what do you do to the financial statement data elements?
   a. Convert them to amounts per capita
   b. Present them on a single page
   c. Show them as percentages of 100
   d. Show them in the form of location quotients

2. Which of the following is considered an asset in computing the quick ratio?
   a. Supplies inventory
   b. Prepaid insurance
   c. Investments in long-term bonds
   d. Certificates of deposit purchased with an original maturity of 30 days

3. Which of the following belongs in the numerator when computing the budgetary cushion of a municipal government?
   a. Infrastructure assets
   b. Unreserved fund balance
   c. Proceeds of bonds issued for capital construction purposes
   d. Deferred revenues

4. In computing the program services ratio, which of these expenses would *not* be considered part of the program service expenses?
   a. Donated services of an administrative nature, such as legal fees
   b. Depreciation of equipment used by a program
   c. Expenses of a program financed from temporarily restricted funds
   d. Donated services applicable to a program

5. What does the number of days' revenue in a hospital's receivables indicator reveal?
   a. Its bad debts expense for the year
   b. The amount of its charity services
   c. Its accounts receivable collection efficiency
   d. The amount of its net patient service revenue

E14-2 (Computation of current ratio and quick ratio)
The following information is extracted from Alpha Hospital's balance sheet:

Cash and cash equivalents	$ 2,432,000
Short-term investments	5,317,000
Long-term investments	15,641,000
Patient accounts receivable, net	12,903,000
Supplies inventory	3,815,000
Current portion of long-term debt	2,900,000
Long-term debt, net of current portion	22,600,000
Accounts payable and accrued expenses	4,615,000

Required: 1. Compute Alpha's current ratio.
2. Compute Alpha's quick ratio (without accounts receivable).

E14-3 (Computation of a hospital's debt service coverage and times interest earned)
The following information is extracted from Beta Hospital's financial statements:

Total revenues, gains, and other support		$78,458,000
Operating expenses	$62,490,000	
Depreciation and amortization	3,765,000	
Interest on long-term borrowings	2,200,000	
Provision for bad debts	3,000,000	71,455,000
Operating income		7,003,000
Investment income		2,000,000
Excess of revenues over expenses		$ 9,003,000
Principal payment on debt		$ 3,200,000

Required: Compute Beta's debt service coverage and times interest earned.

E14-4 (Computation of days' revenue in patient accounts receivable)

The following information is extracted from Gamma Hospital's financial records:

Patient accounts receivable, net	$14,710,000
Patient service revenues, gross	97,478,000
Provision for contractual adjustments	12,609,000

Required: Compute the number of days' revenue in patient accounts receivable.

E14-5 (Computation of a not-for-profit organization's program services ratio)

A voluntary health and welfare organization obtains contributions to perform various social services. The following information is extracted from its statement of activities:

Expenses:	
Youth services program	$ 89,000
Senior citizens health services program	312,000
Adult counseling services program	248,000
Management and general	156,000
Fund-raising	98,000
Total expenses	$903,000

Required: Compute the organization's program services ratio.

E14-6 (Computation and assessment of a city's budgetary cushion)

The following information is extracted from the General Fund column of a city's fund financial statements:

Fund balance:	
Reserved for encumbrances	$ 85,392
Unreserved	423,185
Total fund balance	$ 505,577
Revenues:	
Property taxes	$12,480,500
Sales taxes	14,325,700
Other revenues	1,683,800
Total revenues	$28,490,000

Required: Compute the city's budgetary cushion. Based on your computation and the textbook discussion of the budgetary cushion rule of thumb, assess the city's ability to withstand a potential near-term economic contraction.

E14-7 (Computation of a city's debt burden)

The following information is extracted from a city government's CAFR:

Net direct debt	$ 15,841,000
Overlapping debt	$ 12,142,000
Population	13,243
Full value of taxable real property	$484,481,000

Required: Compute the city's debt burden based on population and on property value. Make separate computations for (a) net direct debt and (b) combined net direct and overlapping debt.

E14-8 (Computation of a village's operating margin)

The following information is extracted from a village's governmental funds statement of revenues, expenditures, and changes in fund balances (amounts in thousands):

	General	Debt Service	Library
Total revenues	$ 8,640	$ 26	$ 15
Total expenditures	7,412	842	234
Excess (deficiency) of revenues over expenditures	1,228	(816)	(219)
Transfers in		850	225
Transfers out	(1,075)		
Net change in fund balances	$ 153	$ 34	$ 6

Required: Compute the village's operating margin (a) for the General Fund and (b) for the General, Debt Service, and Library Funds aggregated. *(Hint: The transfers out are routine transfers to the other two funds, and should be considered as expenditures in calculating the General Fund's operating margin. Because the transfers in are from the aggregated funds, they should be ignored in calculating the denominator for the aggregated funds operating margin.)*

Problems

P14-1 (Computation of financial analysis ratios for a hospital from a trial balance)

Following is a condensed trial balance of the accounts of Palindrome Hospital at December 31, 2009 (amounts in thousands).

	Debits	Credits
Cash and cash equivalents	$ 4,700	
Short-term investments	5,400	
Patient accounts receivable	14,700	
Allowance for uncollectible receivables		$ 2,600
Drugs and supplies inventories	2,100	
Buildings and equipment	72,000	
Accumulated depreciation, buildings and equipment		22,000
Accounts payable and accrued expenses		5,400
Estimated third-party payer settlements		2,300
Long-term debt		37,000
Unrestricted net assets, beginning of year		27,600
Patient service revenues (gross)		66,300
Provision for contractual adjustments	7,100	
Provision for charity care	1,500	
Operating expenses	45,300	
Depreciation expense	4,200	
Interest expense	2,400	
Provision for bad debts	2,300	
Other expenses	1,700	
Investment income		200
Totals	$163,400	$163,400

Additional information (amounts in thousands): (a) the amount of long-term debt principal paid during the year ended December 31, 2009, was $1,800; and (b) the current portion of the long-term debt payable at December 31, 2009, is $2,000.

Required: 1. In preparation for calculating ratios, compute the net patient accounts receivable, the net patient service revenues, the excess of revenues over expenses, and the unrestricted net assets at end of year.
2. Compute the following liquidity indicators: current ratio, quick ratio (without patient accounts receivable), and number of days' cash on hand.
3. Compute the efficiency indicator, or number of days' revenue in receivables.
4. Compute the operating results indicator, or earnings margin.
5. Compute the debt burden and other financial flexibility indicators: long-term debt-to-equity ratio, debt service coverage, and times interest earned.

P14-2 (Computation of financial analysis ratios for a hospital, using financial statements) Following are condensed balance sheets and statements of operations for Elias Hospital for the years ended December 31, 2009 and 2008. (Amounts are in thousands of dollars.)

Balance Sheets

	2009	2008
Assets		
Current assets:		
Cash and cash equivalents	$ 4,758	$ 5,877
Short-term investments	15,836	10,740
Assets limited as to use	970	1,300
Patient accounts receivable, net	15,100	14,194
Supplies inventory	2,670	2,856
Total current assets	39,334	34,967
Assets limited as to use, net of current portion	17,979	18,541
Long-term investments	6,695	6,570
Property and equipment, net	51,038	50,492
Total assets	$115,046	$110,570
Liabilities and Net assets		
Current liabilities:		
Current portion of long-term debt	$ 1,470	$ 1,750
Accounts payable and accrued expenses	7,787	7,496
Estimated third-party payer settlements	2,143	1,942
Total current liabilities	11,400	11,188
Long-term debt, net of current portion	23,144	24,014
Total liabilities	34,544	35,202

(*continued*)

	2009	2008
Net assets:		
Unrestricted	70,846	66,199
Temporarily restricted	2,115	2,470
Permanently restricted	7,541	6,699
Total net assets	80,502	75,368
Total liabilities and net assets	$115,046	$110,570

Statements of Operations

	2009	2008
Unrestricted revenues, gains, and other support:		
Net patient service revenue	$ 85,156	$ 78,942
Premium revenue	14,051	16,162
Total revenues, gains, and other support	99,207	95,104
Expenses:		
Operating expenses	88,521	80,585
Depreciation and amortization	4,782	4,280
Interest	1,752	1,825
Provision for bad debts	3,000	2,600
Total expenses	98,055	89,290
Operating income	1,152	5,814
Other income—investments income	3,900	3,025
Excess of revenues over expenses	5,052	8,839
Other items (not detailed)	(405)	(2,140)
Increase in unrestricted net assets	$ 4,647	$ 6,699

Required:

1. Compute the following ratios for both 2009 and 2008:
   a. Current ratio
   b. Quick ratio (without patient accounts receivable)
   c. Number of days' cash on hand
   d. Number of days' patient service revenue in receivables (Note: Do not include premium revenue in patient service revenue.)
   e. Earnings margin
   f. Long-term debt to equity ratio
   g. Debt service coverage (Note: Assume that $1,750 of long-term debt was redeemed in 2009 and $1,850 was redeemed in 2008).
   h. Times interest earned
2. Using the foregoing ratios and any other observations you make from reviewing the financial statements, discuss whether the hospital's financial position and results of operations improved or worsened in 2009, compared with 2008.

P14-3 (Computation of financial analysis ratios for a county government)
Following are extracts from the financial statements of Elisa County for the year ended December 31, 2009. The funds shown are the governmental operating funds; Capital Projects Funds are omitted. All amounts are in thousands of dollars.

Balance Sheet

	General	Special Revenue	Debt Service
Assets:			
Cash and cash equivalents	$ 6,700	$2,100	$100
Property taxes receivable (net)	19,500		
Other receivables	500	3,100	
Due from state government	3,500		
Total assets	$30,200	$5,200	$100
Liabilities:			
Accounts payable	$16,700	$1,100	
Accrued liabilities	1,800	300	
Matured bonds payable			$100
Total liabilities	18,500	1,400	100
Fund balances:			
Reserved for encumbrances	800	200	
Unreserved	10,900	3,600	
Total fund balances	11,700	3,800	
Total liabilities and fund balances	$30,200	$5,200	$ 100

Statement of Revenues, Expenditures, and Changes in Fund Balances

	General	Special Revenue	Debt Service
Revenues:			
Real property taxes	$ 46,000		
Sales taxes	45,000		
State and federal aid	36,500	$ 5,400	
Other revenues	27,200	9,400	$ 1,200
Total revenues	154,700	14,800	1,200
Expenditures:			
General government	15,100		
Public safety	26,600		
Public health	17,100		
Economic assistance	68,300		
Other expenditures	15,200	16,800	
Debt service:			
Principal			6,200
Interest	500		4,100
Total expenditures	142,800	16,800	10,300
Excess of revenues over expenditures	11,900	(2,000)	(9,100)
Other financing sources (uses):			
Transfers in		1,900	9,100
Transfers out	(11,000)		
Net change in fund balances	900	(100)	0
Fund balances—beginning	10,800	3,900	0
Fund balances—ending	$ 11,700	$ 3,800	$ 0

Note: The General Fund transfers out are routine transfers to finance county libraries (accounted for in a Special Revenue Fund) and debt service.

Required: Based on the data given, compute the following ratios for Elisa County:

1. Quick ratio (aggregated governmental operating funds)
2. Property tax receivable rate *(Note:* All taxes receivable are delinquent.)
3. Operating margin (separately, for General Fund and aggregated operating funds)
4. Budgetary cushion (separately, for General Fund and aggregated operating funds) *(Note:* Ignore transfers in when computing denominator.)
5. Debt service burden (aggregated General and Debt Service Funds)

P14-4 (Assessment of governmental financial analysis ratios)
The state in which Elisa County in P14-3 is located publishes certain financial analysis ratios for all counties within the state. To provide a reference group for assessing Elisa County's financial analysis ratios, the median county ratios are listed here:

Quick ratio	110%
Property tax receivable rate	47%
Operating margin	
General Fund	2.4%
Aggregated Funds	2.3%
Budgetary cushion	
General Fund	12.0%
Aggregated Funds	12.1%
Debt service burden	4.9%

Required: Based on the reference group ratios, prepare a brief report assessing the implications of the financial analysis ratios computed for Elisa County in P14-3.

P14-5 (Assessment of a government's results of operations and budgetary cushion)
You are assessing the financial condition of Teddy County. As part of your assessment, you obtain the following summary of the General Fund column of the statement of revenues, expenditures, and changes in fund balance for Teddy County for the year ended June 30, 2009.

Total revenues	$14,350,000
Total expenditures	4,755,000
Excess (deficiency) of revenues over expenditures	(405,000)
Other financing sources (uses)	
Transfer out to Library Special Revenue Fund	(235,000)
Proceeds of debt	650,000
Total other financing sources (uses)	415,000
Net change in fund balance	10,000
Fund balance — beginning of year	165,000
Fund balance — end of year	$ 175,000

Analysis of the county revenues shows that approximately 50 percent is from the sales tax. On inquiry, you learn that the county makes transfers every year to the Library Special Revenue Fund to finance the library's operations. You also learn that the county sold $650,000 of bonds during 2009 to finance a looming deficit for the year.

Required: Make a preliminary assessment of Teddy County's financial condition, based on the financial information provided in the problem. Consider the following factors in making your assessment: (a) the county's operating margin; (b) the quality of the operating margin; (c) the budgetary cushion; and (d) relevant credit-rating agency rules of thumb.

15

FUNDAMENTALS OF ACCOUNTING

Chapter Outline

Learning Objectives

The Accounting Equation: Transaction Analysis
  The Accounting Equation
  Effect of Transactions and Events on the Accounting Equation
  Changes in Equity
  Recording Business Transactions
  Review Exercise
  Solution

The Accrual Basis of Accounting
  Accruals, Deferrals, and Amortizations
  The Matching Process

Recording Transactions: Debits and Credits
  Journals, Ledgers, and Accounts
  Double-Entry Accounting—Debits and Credits
  Debit and Credit Analysis
  Transaction Analysis Using Debits and Credits
  Review Exercise
  Solution
  Completion of Review Exercise
  A More Complete Look at the Transaction Recording Process
  The Ledger and Posting
  Review Exercise
  Solution

Financial Statements
  The Accounting Cycle
  The Trial Balance
  Adjusting Entries
  Financial Statements
  Financial Statement Work Sheet

Closing the Books

Other Transactions and Other Matters
  Withdrawals by the Owner
  Control and Subsidiary Accounts
  Credit Sales and Bad Debts
  Buying and Selling Merchandise
Review Questions
Exercises
Problems

After completing this chapter, you should be able to:

- ■ Define and distinguish among assets, liabilities, and equity.
- ■ Explain the logic of the accounting equation.
- ■ Analyze transactions to distinguish between those that affect only assets and liabilities and those that affect equity.
- ■ Define and illustrate the accrual basis of accounting.
- ■ State the rules of debit and credit for assets, liabilities, equity, revenues, and expenses.
- ■ Record transactions in a general journal.
- ■ Post transactions from a general journal to a general ledger.
- ■ Prepare a trial balance from the general ledger.
- ■ Prepare adjusting journal entries.
- ■ Prepare an income statement, a statement of changes in owner's equity, and a balance sheet.
- ■ Prepare closing journal entries.

THE ACCOUNTING EQUATION: TRANSACTION ANALYSIS

The basic processes of accounting, whether they are done for governments, not-for-profit entities, or business enterprises, are similar.[1] They all must keep records of their resources, their use of the resources, and claims against the resources. These resources, commonly called *assets,* represent items of value that are either owned or controlled by the entity as a result of past transactions and events. Assets might be financial in nature (like cash and accounts receivable) or nonfinancial (like buildings and equipment). An entity's operations are centered on using its resources for the purpose for which the entity was established.

A business-type entity obtains assets primarily from three sources: (1) investing by its owners, (2) incurring economic obligations (commonly called *liabilities*), and (3) earning profits from its operations. These activities can be illustrated as follows. First, an owner might provide additional assets (such as cash) by investing to expand operations. Second, an asset (cash) is created when a business incurs a liability (called a note payable) by borrowing from a bank. Third, an asset (merchandise inventory) is created when a business incurs a liability (an account payable) by buying merchandise on credit from a supplier. Fourth, a net increase in assets (which might take the form of

---

[1]We used simple business enterprises in this chapter to introduce you to the basic accounting processes because the transactions and terminology are likely to be familiar to you.

cash or accounts receivable) occurs when merchandise inventory is sold or services are provided to a customer at a profit — a price that is greater than the cost of providing the goods or services.

The Accounting Equation

The difference between assets and liabilities is called *equity* or *capital.* Equity comes from investments in the business by its owners and from profits earned by the business. The relationship among these three elements can be expressed in the form of the following equation, known as the *accounting equation:*

$$\text{Assets} = \text{Liabilities} + \text{Equity}$$

This equation states that the assets (resources) of an entity are equal to the sources of those assets: liabilities and equity.

At any point in time, for example, at the beginning or at the end of the year, the assets, liabilities, and equity of a business can be presented in a financial statement. This statement is based on the accounting equation and is commonly called a *balance sheet.* The dollar value of the assets will always equal the dollar value of the liabilities plus the dollar value of the equity. The balance sheet is a status statement — a statement of financial position — at a particular point in time. In fact, most not-for-profit entities now refer to this statement as the statement of financial position.

Effect of Transactions and Events on the Accounting Equation

In the course of the year, an entity will engage in numerous transactions and be affected by many events that change one or more of the elements of the accounting equation: assets, liabilities, or equity. Changes that affect the equity of the entity are expressed in another financial statement, generally called an *income statement* or an operating statement. The income statement thus serves as a link between the balance sheet at one point in time (the beginning of the accounting period) and the balance sheet at a later point in time (the end of the period).

Some transactions or events affect only assets, only liabilities, or a combination of assets and liabilities. In those situations, no increase or decrease in the entity's equity occurs. Here are two examples of these types of situations: (1) If an entity buys equipment on credit, an asset (equipment) is increased and a liability (accounts payable) is increased; and (2) if an entity buys merchandise inventory for cash, an asset (merchandise inventory) is increased and another asset (cash) is decreased. Notice that, in both of these transactions, the accounting equation Assets = Liabilities + Equity is always in balance. In the first situation, an asset increase is offset by a liability increase; in the second, an asset increase is offset by an asset decrease. Equity is not affected in either case.

Other transactions may affect an asset or a liability and, at the same time, increase or decrease the entity's equity. For example, if an entity bills a customer for a service, an asset (accounts receivable) is increased and equity is increased because there is an increase in the entity's net assets. As a second example, if an entity pays an employee to provide the service just referred to, an asset (cash) is decreased and equity is decreased because of the decrease in the entity's net assets. If the price charged by the entity for the service is greater than the salary and other costs incurred by the entity, a net increase in the entity's equity will result.

Changes in Equity

Increases in assets generated through profit-oriented activities of a business (for example, by providing services to a customer) increase the owner's equity. These increases in equity are called *revenues*. On the other hand, assets used in or liabilities incurred through the profit-oriented activities of a business (for example, by paying an employee to provide the services) reduce the owner's equity. These decreases in equity are called *expenses*. When an owner adds capital to (or withdraws capital from) the business, however, it is neither a revenue nor an expense. It is a direct change in equity.

We can look upon revenues and expenses as temporary subsets of equity and thus broaden our equation to express both the point-in-time and the operating concepts:

$$\text{Assets} = \text{Liabilities} + \text{Equity [Opening Equity} + \text{(Revenues} - \text{Expenses)}$$
$$+ \text{(Owner Additions to} - \text{Withdrawals from Equity)]}$$

Recording Business Transactions

The process of accounting involves the following: first, analyzing economic transactions and events to see how they have affected assets, liabilities, and equity; and, second, recording the effects as changes (increases or decreases) to one or more of those elements. To understand this process, consider the following transactions of a computer service started on January 2, 2009, by Kyle Thomas. Thomas intends to provide computer education to individuals who purchase personal computers.

1. On January 2, Kyle deposited $10,000 of his personal cash into a bank account, to be used exclusively by the business.

2. On January 2, Kyle also purchased 10 computers. The computers cost $30,000. He made a down payment of $3,000 in cash and financed the remainder through the French Quarter bank. The agreement with the bank requires that Kyle pay back $9,000 on each succeeding January 2 for 3 years, together with interest of 10 percent a year on the unpaid balance of the loan.

3. In order to have an office for the operation of the business, Kyle rented office space on January 2 from the Mardi Gras Realty Company for $2,000 a month. Because the rental contract required payments at the beginning of each month, he immediately wrote a check for $2,000.

4. At the end of January, Kyle sent bills to his students. The amount due him for services performed in January was $5,000.

5. During the month, Kyle paid a salary of $1,500 to an employee who helped train his students.

6. Kyle received a utility bill for $300 for the month of January. Because the due date on the bill is February 10, the bill will not be paid until then.

Now, let us analyze each transaction and show how the accounting equation applies to it.

1. *The $10,000 Investment* The entity concept (which relates to the scope of the activities covered in financial reporting) requires that the operations of an organization be kept separate from the owner's personal financial records. Therefore, we will consider only those transactions that affect the assets, liabilities, and equity of the business. The $10,000 deposit causes an increase in the asset Cash. It also causes a corresponding increase in equity. To show the increase in equity, we will use the caption K. Thomas, Capital. This transaction is reflected in the accounting equation, as shown in Table 15-1.

TABLE 15-1 Effect of Owner Investment

		Assets	=	Liabilities	+	Equity
		Cash				K. Thomas, Capital
Owner invests cash in the business						
	+	$10,000	=		+	$10,000
		$10,000	=	-0-	+	$10,000

Two important observations about the transaction in Table 15-1 should be made:

1. The dollar amount of the items included in the transaction must balance in terms of the equation; that is, the net change in the assets must equal the net change in the liabilities plus (minus) the net change in equity.
2. The equation itself must balance after the transaction has been recorded.

2. *The $30,000 Purchase of Computers* Recording this transaction causes the accounting equation to expand, as shown in Table 15-2.

Several observations should be made regarding this purchase:

1 The assets of the business increased by $27,000: Cash decreased by $3,000 and computers increased by $30,000.
2. The business now owes the bank $27,000. Thus, a liability exists that must be reflected in the system.
3. The computers are recorded at their full cost, $30,000, even though Kyle borrowed $27,000 to purchase them.

In summary, the business now has assets totaling $37,000—that is, $27,000 contributed by creditors (the bank) and $10,000 contributed by the owner. Notice that the acquisition of the computers did not affect the owner's equity, because he did not contribute any additional assets to the business as a result of this transaction.

A simple method of analyzing a transaction in terms of its effect on the accounting equation is to ask four questions:

1. Did any asset increase or decrease?
2. Did any liability increase or decrease?
3. Did the equity increase or decrease?
4. Does the transaction have a balanced effect on the equation?

TABLE 15-2 Effect of Computer Purchase

		Assets		=	Liabilities	+	Equity
		Cash	Computers		Notes Payable to Bank		K. Thomas, Capital
Previous balances		$10,000		=			$10,000
The firm purchased computers	−	3,000	+ $30,000	=	+ $27,000		
		$ 7,000	+ $30,000	=	$27,000	+	$10,000

For example, consider the acquisition of the computers:

1. The asset Cash decreased by $3,000 and the asset Computers increased by $30,000.
2. The liability Notes payable to bank increased by $27,000.
3. No change in equity occurred.
4. The transaction increased assets by $27,000 and had a similar effect on total liabilities and equity. Therefore, the accounting equation is still in balance.

Although this type of analysis may seem cumbersome, it will be a great help when more complex transactions are encountered.

3. The $2,000 Office Rental Applying the four-step analysis, the transaction has the following effects on the accounting equation:

1. The asset Cash decreased by $2,000. Because the business now has "control" over the use of office space for the month of January, another asset has been acquired. This type of asset is usually called Prepaid rent, and it increased by $2,000. No other assets changed as a result of this transaction.
2. Because the business does not owe any more or any less as a result of this transaction, no liabilities changed.
3. Because the net effect of this transaction resulted in a decrease in one asset and an increase in another, the owner's share of the total assets did not change. Therefore, no change in equity took place.
4. The transaction had a balanced effect on the accounting equation. The decrease in one asset was offset by an increase in another asset. Liabilities and equity were not affected by this transaction.

The result of this analysis on the accounting equation is shown in Table 15-3. Notice that the total of the assets ($37,000) is equal to the total of the liabilities plus equity ($37,000).

4. The $5,000 Billings By applying the four-step analysis, we can determine the following:

1. Sending out the bills is a formal recognition that Kyle's customers owe $5,000 for services he rendered. As a result, he has a claim against each of them. These claims are assets because they give him the right to collect the amounts due. The title usually given to these assets is *Accounts receivable.* No other assets changed as a result of this transaction.
2. Because the business does not owe any more or any less as a result of this transaction, no liabilities changed.

TABLE 15-3   Effect of Office Rental

	Assets			=	Liabilities	+	Equity
					Notes		
			Prepaid		Payable		K. Thomas,
	Cash	Computers	Rent		to Bank		Capital
Previous balances	$7,000 +	$30,000		=	$27,000	+	$10,000
The firm paid the rent for the month	− 2,000		+ $2,000	=			
	$5,000 +	$30,000	+ $2,000	=	$27,000	+	$10,000

TABLE 15-4	Effect of Billing Customers					

	Assets				= Liabilities +	Equity
	Cash	Computers	Prepaid Rent	Accounts Receivable	Notes Payable to Bank	K. Thomas, Capital
Previous balances	$5,000 +	$30,000 +	$2,000		= $27,000 +	$10,000
The firm billed customers				+ $5,000	=	+ 5,000
	$5,000 +	$30,000 +	$2,000 +	$5,000	= $27,000 +	$15,000

3. Because the $5,000 net increase in assets was generated by Kyle's profit-oriented activities—services provided to customers—his equity increases by $5,000. (We can also "back into" this conclusion by noting that steps 1 and 2 produce an increase in assets without any change in liabilities. Because each transaction must have a balancing effect on the equation, an increase in equity must occur.)
4. The transaction has a balanced effect on the accounting equation: assets increased by $5,000, and liabilities + equity increased by $5,000.

The results of this analysis on the accounting equation are shown in Table 15-4. Notice that the total of the assets ($42,000) is equal to the total of the liabilities plus equity ($42,000).

5. **The $1,500 Salary Payment** Applying the four-step analysis, we find the following:

1. The asset Cash decreases by $1,500 as a result of the payment to the employee.
2. Technically, Kyle has a liability to his employee from the moment the employee starts to work. However, it is impractical to record that liability continuously. If he has not paid the employee, an increase in a liability rather than a decrease in an asset has occurred. But, because he has made the payment, there is no liability to record.
3. The salary is an expense of doing business and therefore a decrease in equity. (We can also "back into" this conclusion by noting that, because each transaction must have a balancing effect on the equation, and because steps 1 and 2 showed only a decrease in an asset, there must be a decrease in equity.)
4. The transaction has a balanced effect on the equation: assets decrease by $1,500 and liabilities + equity decrease by the same amount.

The result of this analysis is shown in Table 15-5. Notice that the total of the assets ($40,500) equals the total liabilities + equity ($40,500).

6. **The $300 Utility Bill** The four-step analysis results in the following effects on the accounting equation:

1. Because the business does not have title to or control over any items of value that it did not have before this transaction, no changes in assets occur.
2. The business now owes money to an additional creditor. The receipt of the bill is a formal recognition of this fact. It necessitates recording a liability of $300. The title normally given to this account is *Accounts payable*.

Table 15-5 Effect of Salary Payment

	Assets				=	Liabilities	+	Equity
	Cash	Computers	Prepaid Rent	Accounts Receivable		Notes Payable to Bank		K. Thomas, Capital
Previous balances	$5,000 +	$30,000 +	$2,000 +	$5,000 =		$27,000 +		$15,000
The firm paid salaries	−1,500				=		−	1,500
	$3,500 +	$30,000 +	$2,000 +	$5,000 =		$27,000 +		$13,500

3. The result of this analysis (steps 1 and 2) is an increase in liabilities with no corresponding increase in assets. Because each transaction must contribute to a balanced effect on the equation, a decrease in equity of $300 must occur.

4. The transaction had a balanced effect on the accounting equation: Assets did not change, and the net effect on liabilities + equity was zero (+ $300 − $300).

The result of this analysis on the accounting equation is shown in Table 15-6. Notice that the total of the assets ($40,500) is equal to the total of the liabilities plus equity ($40,500).

Although numerous other types of transactions could be illustrated for the operations of a business, those selected here should be sufficient to enable you to understand the process used for determining the effect of each transaction on the accounting equation.

Review Exercise

The following exercise should be completed by using the approach previously described. After completing a work sheet, compare it with the solution that follows so that you can determine how well you understand the concepts involved.

In this exercise, assume that Paige Keith is an independent tour guide who works for several large tour companies. Her income is determined by the number of

TABLE 15-6 Effect of Receiving Utility Bill

	Assets				=	Liabilities		+	Equity
	Cash	Computers	Prepaid Rent	Accounts Receivable		Notes Payable to Bank	Accounts Payable		K. Thomas, Capital
Previous balances	$3,500 +	$30,000 +	$2,000 +	$5,000 =		$27,000		+	$13,500
The firm received a bill for utilities					=		+ $300	−	300
	$3,500 +	$30,000 +	$2,000 +	$5,000 =		$27,000 +	$300	+	$13,200

individuals on each tour she hosts. To start the business, Paige had the following transactions:

2009

June 1   Paige placed $5,000 cash into a bank account to be used in the operations of her business, Kaki Tours.

2   Paige signed a contract with Tel-Ans, a telephone-answering service. The service cost $50 per month, payable at the beginning of each month. Paige paid Tel-Ans $50.

4   Paige paid Print Faster $55 for stationery and the various forms she needed.

5   Paige purchased office equipment for $250. She paid $25 down and will pay the remainder in 30 days.

7   Paige purchased additional office supplies costing $125. She paid cash for these supplies.

10   Paige billed several tour companies for tours she conducted during the month. The total billing was $300.

15   Paige received $250 from companies she billed earlier that month.

18   Paige hired an assistant and agreed to pay him 25 percent of her revenue from the tours that he helped to organize.

20   Paige deposited $130 in her bank account. This amount was collected from various walking tours she conducted.

25   Paige shared an office with someone and she paid $75 for her share of the June rent (including utilities).

30   Paige billed several tour companies for a total of $400 for tours she conducted during the month.

Solution

The solution is found in Table 15-7.

	Assets					=	Liabilities +	Equity
	Cash	Accounts Receivable	Prepaid Services	Office Supplies	Office Equipment		Accounts Payable	P. Keith, Capital
2009								
June 1	+$5,000							+$5,000
2	−$ 50		+$50					
4	−$ 55			+$ 55				
5	−$ 25				+$250		+$225	
7	−$ 125			+$125				
10		+$300						+$ 300
15	+$ 250	−$250						
18	No transaction—no assets, liabilities, or equity have changed.							
	Nothing is owed to the assistant until he completes some work.							
20	+$ 130							+$ 130
25	−$ 75							−$ 75
30		+$400						+$ 400
	$5,050	$450	$50	$180	$250		$225	$5,755

TABLE 15-7   Solution to Paige Keith's Transactions

Total Assets[a] = $5,980

Total Liabilities + Equity[a] = $5,980

[a]Cumulative totals after each transaction were omitted in order to conserve space.

THE ACCRUAL BASIS OF ACCOUNTING

Before moving on, you need to get a better understanding of the nature of assets, liabilities, expenses, and revenues, and of the purpose of accounting and financial reporting. Assume, for example, that you own a department store. You ask: "Can I find out how much profit I made last month just by seeing how much cash I had in the bank at the beginning of the month and at the end of the month?" If you think you can, then ask: "How about the unpaid bills for the merchandise I bought? What about the items I sold on credit for which customers have not yet paid? What about the new fixtures I bought that are likely to last 10 years?" Knowing your cash position is important, but it's not enough to let you know how much profit you made. It tells you nothing about your other assets and liabilities.

A major purpose of accounting is measuring performance (such as profitability) and financial position. To measure performance, an entity first needs to know what it is trying to measure, which is called its *measurement focus*. To achieve a particular measurement focus, accountants adopt what is called a *basis of accounting*. If an entity wants to measure inflows and outflows of cash, it uses the cash basis of accounting. But, as we have just seen, the cash basis of accounting will not provide a good measure of net income, because it recognizes the effect of transactions and events only when cash is received or disbursed. To measure net income, accountants use the *accrual* basis of accounting. Under the accrual basis of accounting, revenues are recorded when earned. Expenses are recorded when incurred, not necessarily when cash changes hands.

Accruals, Deferrals, and Amortizations

Accrual accounting is accomplished by certain processes known as *accruals, deferrals,* and *amortizations*. An accrual recognizes assets, liabilities, revenues, and expenses attributable to one period but not expected to be received or paid in cash until a future period. A deferral has just the opposite effect. In a deferral, cash has been received or paid in the past, but the economic benefit lies in the future. Thus, the recognition of the revenue or expense is deferred to a future period. Amortization includes recognizing an expense by periodically writing down an asset. In the examples that follow, observe that every accrual, deferral, or amortization affects equity (either an expense or revenue) and either an asset or liability:

- If employees earn their salaries in year 1 but will be paid in year 2, a salary expense and a liability are *accrued* (added to) in year 1.
- If revenues are earned in year 1 but the cash will be received in year 2, a revenue and an asset are *accrued* (added to) in year 1.
- If cash is paid in year 1 for a 3-year insurance policy, payment for the insurance creates an asset called "prepaid insurance." Recognition of insurance expense is *deferred* into the years actually covered by the insurance, some of which might be in year 1, some in year 2, and so on.
- If cash is paid in year 1 for equipment that will last 10 years, the payment creates an asset called "equipment." The expense of using the equipment is *deferred* and recognized by means of *amortizing* the asset over its 10-year life.

The Matching Process

The discussion of accrual accounting allows us to broaden our concept of the nature of assets. As previously noted, some assets either are cash or will soon be converted to cash, like accounts receivable. But buildings and equipment, previously described as nonfinancial resources, can also be described as unexpired bundles of future services, awaiting recognition as expenses as they are used up with the passage of time. Prepaid insurance and rent are also unexpired bundles of future services. So are inventories, which become expenses in the period they are sold. The notion of relating expenses to the same period of time that revenues are recognized is called "matching." Accrual accounting also helps broaden the notion of liabilities; that is, liabilities may result not only from borrowing and from not paying expenses, but also from receiving cash to provide services or products in the future.

Now, let us return to Kyle Thomas to see whether any of the transactions referred to previously require further consideration when applying the concepts of accrual accounting. Our analysis shows that, if Kyle requested financial statements to measure accurately his financial performance for January and his financial position at the end of January, these matters must be taken into account:

1. Interest of $225 would need to be accrued because, even though he did not pay it, Kyle incurred interest expense for January because of the loan from French Quarter Bank. The accrual decreases equity (Interest expense) and increases a liability (Interest payable). The calculation is $27,000 \times 10\% \times 1/12$.

2. The asset Computers (an unexpired bundle of future services) would need to be amortized to recognize an expense because 1 month of the computers' estimated useful lives has expired. Assuming the computers have estimated useful lives of 50 months, the expense for the month would be $600 ($30,000/50). This decrease in equity (an expense called *depreciation*) parallels the reduction in the asset Computers.

3. Rent expense of $2,000 would need to be recognized because the asset Prepaid rent (another unexpired bundle of future services) expired at the end of January. Recognizing rent expense decreases equity and also decreases the asset Prepaid rent.

The result of this analysis is shown in Table 15-8. Notice that the total assets ($37,900) equals the total of the liabilities ($27,525) plus equity ($10,375).

TABLE 15-8   Effect of Accrual Adjustments

	Assets				=	Liabilities			+	Equity
	Cash	Computers	Prepaid Rent	Accounts Receivable		Notes Payable to Bank	Accounts Payable	Interest Payable		K. Thomas, Capital
Previous balances (Table 15-6)	$3,500 +	$30,000 +	$2,000 +	$5,000	=	$27,000 +	$300		+	$13,200
Accrual of interest								+ $225	−	225
Using up of computers	−	600							−	600
Expiration of prepaid rent			− 2,000						−	2,000
	$3,500 +	$29,400	−	+ $5,000	=	$27,000 +	$300	+ $225	+	$10,375

RECORDING TRANSACTIONS: DEBITS AND CREDITS

Journals, Ledgers, and Accounts

In the previous sections we discussed how analysis of business transactions and events leads to the recording of increases and decreases to various components of assets, liabilities, and equity. The use of a work sheet to accomplish that procedure, however, is far too cumbersome. Consider, for example, the size of the work sheet that would be needed to record the huge number of transactions and the numerous kinds of assets, liabilities, revenues, and expenses of any large corporation.

Because of the awkwardness of the previously discussed systems of analysis and record keeping, a more efficient system has been developed. This system is based on the same concepts previously discussed: transactions and events are analyzed and recorded by increasing and decreasing components of the accounting equation. The actual recording of transactions, however, is accomplished through the use of journals, ledgers, and accounts. Transactions are analyzed and recorded in journals, from which they are then posted to a ledger that contains accounts. To explain these terms:

- *Journals* are books in which every transaction that affects the accounting equation is recorded in chronological order. Journals, often referred to as "books of original entry," are the permanent records of all the transactions of a business.
- *Posting* is the process of transferring information from the journals to the ledger.
- A *ledger* is a book with a separate page that accumulates transaction data (increases and decreases) for each account (component of assets, liabilities, or equity). For example, separate accounts are kept for cash, accounts receivable, and accounts payable. Each account is in the general form of a "T," with one side of the T representing increases to the account balance and the other representing decreases.

Double-Entry Accounting—Debits and Credits

Recall from the earlier sections of this chapter that every transaction resulted in changes to at least two components of assets, liabilities, and equity. For example, when Kyle Thomas sent bills to his students, an asset (accounts receivable) was increased and equity was increased. The practice of increasing or decreasing two or more accounts as a result of each transaction is known as double-entry accounting. We will now discuss how the T-form of the account facilitates the recording of increases and decreases.

As noted, rather than use columns on a work sheet, an *account* is used to accumulate the increases and decreases in assets, liabilities, and equity. It is much easier to accumulate changes if like items are grouped, so the increases are accumulated on one side of the account and the decreases on the other. Arbitrarily, the increases ($+$) in assets have been accumulated on the left and the decreases ($-$) on the right. As a result, it is much easier and faster to calculate the balance in an account at any point in time. This convention produces the following situation:

$$\frac{\text{Assets}}{+\mid-}$$

Because the system is based on the accounting equation the following relationship develops:

$$\frac{\text{Assets}}{+\mid-} = \frac{\text{Liabilities}}{\mid} + \frac{\text{Equity}}{\mid}$$

When the account form is transferred to the right side of the equation and is used to accumulate changes in liabilities and equity, the signs must change. The increases are accumulated on the right side and the decreases on the left side. This maintains the mathematical integrity of the transaction analysis and of the system:

$$\frac{\text{Assets}}{+\mid-} = \frac{\text{Liabilities}}{-\mid+} + \frac{\text{Equity}}{-\mid+}$$

Debit and Credit Analysis

In accounting terminology the left side of an account is referred to as the *debit side* and the right side is referred to as the *credit side.* Note that the terms *debit* and *credit* refer only to position. Without any association with a particular account, these terms do not mean plus or minus. When a particular type of account has been considered, however, the terms do refer to plus or minus. For example, when assets are considered (see the previous illustration), increases are accumulated on the left, or debit side, and decreases are accumulated on the right, or credit side. Liabilities and equity, however, are increased or decreased in the opposite manner: Debits represent decreases, and credits represent increases. These rules are summarized in Table 15-9.

To complete the system, revenues and expenses must be analyzed in terms of their debit/credit effect. At the end of each period, it is important that management study the relative size of the individual revenues and expenses incurred in operating an organization. In the previous illustrations, revenues and expenses were recorded as direct increases or decreases in equity. To make such an analysis easier, however, we will begin to accumulate the changes in each revenue and expense in a separate account. This practice will avoid the rather cumbersome task of sorting out the revenues and expenses after they have been combined in the equity account.

The debit/credit analysis of revenues and expenses is based on the relationship of each to equity. Remember that revenues and expenses were defined as temporary subsets of the equity of a firm. Because revenues cause equity to increase, they are recorded as credits. Any reductions of revenues are recorded as debits, as shown in the following illustration:

$$\frac{\text{Revenues}}{\begin{array}{c|c} \text{Debits} & \text{Credits} \\ \hline - & + \end{array}}$$

TABLE 15-9 Debits and Credits		
Type of Account	***Increases***	***Decreases***
Assets	Debits	Credits
Liabilities	Credits	Debits
Equity	Credits	Debits

Note the *direct* relationship with equity. Equity is increased with credits. Because revenues increase equity, *revenues* are increased with *credits*. Equity is decreased with debits. Because decreases in revenue are decreases in equity, revenues are decreased with debits.

Expenses follow the same logic. The analysis, however, is a bit more complex. *Expenses* have been defined as those decreases in equity associated with the profit-oriented activities of the business. Therefore, as expenses increase, the amount of equity decreases. A decrease in equity is recorded as a debit. Continuing with this logic, then, an increase in an expense must be recorded with a debit. This procedure reflects the decrease in equity that is taking place.

This analysis can be extended to include a decrease in an expense, which results in a credit to the expense account and reflects the increase in equity that is taking place, as shown in the following illustration:

Expenses	
Debits	Credits
+	−

To summarize, it is helpful to return to our earlier comment about considering revenues and expenses as temporary subsets of equity. In this context, revenues may be viewed as the increase side (credits) of equity and expenses as the decrease side (debits) of equity. Thus, an increase in expenses (a debit) is really a decrease in equity. This relationship is shown in the following illustration:

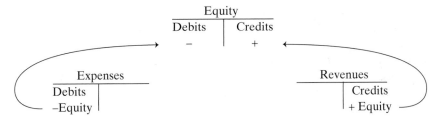

Notice that this system is based on the mathematical integrity of the accounting equation. As a result, the equality mentioned in the section "The Accounting Equation: Transaction Analysis" still exists—that is, the accounting equation must be balanced after the result of each transaction has been recorded. In terms of debits and credits, this equality can be stated as follows:

> The total dollar amount of debits for any transaction must EQUAL the total dollar amount of credits.

This rule is critical because it affects the integrity of the entire accounting system.

Transaction Analysis Using Debits and Credits

The effects of a transaction can now be recorded in terms of debits and credits that increase or decrease the accounts. Following are several examples taken from the Review Exercise in the previous section.[2]

---

[2]The effects of the transactions on the individual accounts are summarized in Table 15-10.

Transaction		Analysis	
June 1	Paige invested $5,000 cash into a bank account to be used in the operations of her business, Kaki Tours.	Debit:	Cash, $5,000—to record the increase in this asset.
		Credit:	P. Keith, Capital, $5,000—to record the increase in equity.
June 2	She signed a contract with Tel-Ans, a telephone-answering service. The service cost $50 per month, payable at the beginning of each month. She paid Tel-Ans $50.	Debit:	Prepaid services, $50—to record the increase in this asset.
		Credit:	Cash, $50—to record the decrease in this asset.
June 4	She paid Print Faster $55 for stationery and the various forms she needed.	Debit:	Office supplies, $55—to record the increase in this asset.
		Credit:	Cash, $55—to record the decrease in this asset.
June 5	She purchased office equipment for $250. She paid $25 down and will pay the remainder in 30 days.	Debit:	Office equipment, $250—to record the increase in this asset.
		Credit:	Cash, $25—to record the decrease in this asset.
		Credit:	Accounts payable, $225—to record the increase in this liability.

Review Exercise

Using the following information, prepare an analysis of the remaining transactions of Paige Keith's tour business similar to that presented previously. Compare your results with the solution that follows.

Transaction	
June 7	Paige Keith purchased additional office supplies costing $125. She paid cash for these supplies.
June 10	She billed several tour companies for tours she conducted during the month. The total billing was $300.
June 15	She received $250 from companies she billed earlier that month.
June 18	She hired an assistant and agreed to pay him 25 percent of her revenue from the tours that he helped to organize.
June 20	Paige Keith deposited $130 in her bank account. This amount was collected from various walking tours she conducted.
June 25	She shared an office with someone and she paid $75 for her share of the June rent (including utilities).
June 30	She billed several tour companies for a total of $400 for tours she conducted during the month.

Solution

June 7	*Debit:*	Office supplies, $125—to record the increase in this asset.
	Credit:	Cash, $125—to record the decrease in this asset.

June 10	*Debit:*	Accounts receivable, $300—to record the increase in this asset.
	Credit:	Tour revenue, $300—to record the increase in equity from profit-oriented activities.
June 15	*Debit:*	Cash, $250—to record the increase in this asset.
	Credit:	Accounts receivable, $250—to record the decrease in this asset.
June 18		No transaction: no assets, liabilities, or equity have changed. Nothing is owed to the assistant until he completes some work.
June 20	*Debit:*	Cash, $130—to record the increase in this asset.
	Credit:	Tour revenue, $130—to record the increase in equity from profit-oriented activities.
June 25	*Debit:*	Office rent expense, $75—to record the decrease in equity from profit-oriented activities.
	Credit:	Cash, $75—to record the decrease in this asset.
June 30	*Debit:*	Accounts receivable, $400—to record the increase in this asset.
	Credit:	Tour revenue, $400—to record the increase in equity from profit-oriented activities.

The results of these transactions in the accounts are summarized in Table 15-10.

Completion of Review Exercise

Table 15-10 covers each transaction in the Review Exercise in the section "The Accounting Equation: Transaction Analysis." Several transactions were omitted in that

TABLE 15-10   Paige Keith Transactions—Ledger Accounts

Cash		Accounts Receivable		Prepaid Services		Office Supplies	
5,000	50	300	250	50		55	
250	55	400				125	
130	25	700	250			180	
	125	450					
	75						
5,380	330						
5,050							

Office Equipment		Accounts Payable		P. Keith, Capital		Tour Revenue	
250			225		5,000		300
							130
							400
							830

Office Rent Expense	
75	

section, however, because we had not yet discussed accrual accounting. The items that follow are similar to those covered in the section "The Accrual Basis of Accounting":

1. The assistant was not paid for the services he performed. Because this amount is owed at the end of the month, the amount earned must be recorded. This entry will record the liability owed and the effect on equity of the services performed by the assistant. Assuming this amount is $40, the following entry is necessary:

Debit: Salary expense, $40—to record the decrease in equity from profit-oriented activities.

Credit: Salary payable, $40—to record the increase in liabilities.

2. By the end of June, the services performed by Tel-Ans for the month were "used up" and no longer had any value. The following entry, therefore, is necessary:

Debit: Telephone-answering expense, $50—to record the decrease in equity from profit-oriented activities.

Credit: Prepaid services, $50—to record the decrease in this asset.

Note: To save time, most companies record repetitive monthly payments for services such as answering services directly in an expense account. This practice eliminates the need for a second entry like the one described here. If this procedure had been followed here, the June 2 entry would have required a debit to Telephone-answering expense and a credit to Cash for $50. Notice that the effect of these two procedures on the accounting equation is the same: Assets decrease and Equity decreases.

3. Office supplies totaling $180 were purchased in June. During the month some of these supplies were used. Assuming the cost of the supplies used was $30, the following entry is necessary:

Debit: Office supplies expense, $30—to record the decrease in equity from profit-oriented activities.

Credit: Office supplies, $30—to record the decrease in this asset.

4. The final item that must be considered is office equipment. Whenever a business purchases an asset, it is really buying a "bundle of future services." As these services are used up, an expense is recorded. (This process is explained in the preceding entry for the asset Office supplies.) Using the services of an asset such as Office equipment is generally referred to as *depreciation.* Because it is the using up of an asset in the profit-oriented activities of the business, it is recognized as an expense. The following entry is, therefore, necessary (assume the amount is $5):

Debit: Depreciation expense—office equipment, $5—to record the decrease in equity from profit-oriented activities.

Credit: Accumulated depreciation—office equipment, $5—to record the decrease in the asset. Accumulated depreciation is credited instead of the asset itself because it is important to maintain the original cost in a separate account. The Accumulated depreciation account is treated as a negative, or contra, asset—the effect is the same as crediting the Office equipment account directly (see Table 15-15 on page 618).

After these transactions have been entered into the system, the accounts will appear as shown in Table 15-11.

TABLE 15-11   Paige Keith Transactions—Ledger Accounts

Cash			Accounts Receivable			Prepaid Services			Office Supplies	
5,000	50		300	250		50	50		55	30
250	55		400			-0-			125	
130	25		700	250					180	30
	125		450						150	
	75									
5,380	330									
5,050										

Office Equipment			Accumulated Depreciation— Office Equipment			Accounts Payable	
250				5			225

Salary Payable			P. Keith, Capital			Tour Revenue			Office Rent Expense	
	40			5,000			300		75	
							130			
							400			
							830			

Salary Expense			Telephone-Answering Expense			Office Supplies Expense			Depreciation Expense— Office Equipment	
40			50			30			5	

A More Complete Look at the Transaction Recording Process

Now that we have discussed the principles of recording transactions through the use of debits and credits, let us return to the actual process of maintaining accounting records by using journals and ledgers. We said that a journal is a permanent record of all the transactions of a business. The process of recording transactions in a journal is referred to as making journal entries or *journalizing*. Although there are various types of journals, the one we will illustrate is called a *general journal*. Exhibit 15-1 illustrates the form of a general journal. (To simplify the recording process, entities use separate journals—such as cash receipts, cash disbursements, sales, and purchase journals—to record similar types of transactions.)

Continuing the example used in the previous two sections, let us reconsider the first transaction illustrated. The following steps are used when entering information in the journal (follow each step by referring to the journal entry in Exhibit 15-1):

1. The year is written at the top of each page in the Date column.
2. The month of the transaction is entered. As additional transactions are entered, the month is usually not rewritten unless the same journal page is used for more than 1 month.

EXHIBIT 15-1   General Journal

		GENERAL JOURNAL			Page 1
Date 2009		Description	P.R.	Debit	Credit
June	1	Cash	101	5000 –	
		P. Keith, Capital	301		5000 –
		Owner invested $5,000 in the business			

3. The third item of information is the date of the transaction. Because this helps separate the transactions, the date for each transaction is usually entered—even if it is the same as that of the preceding transaction.
4. The debit account is entered next to the left-hand margin in the Description column. If more than one debit account is involved in a transaction, all the debit items must be entered before any credit items are entered.
5. Each debit amount is entered in the Debit money column.
6. The credit account or accounts are entered and are *slightly indented* to the right.
7. The respective credit amount or amounts are placed in the Credit money column.
8. The final part of the entry is the explanation. Here a brief description of the transaction is entered. It helps explain the event that was recorded. It can be useful when attempting to analyze the events that caused a particular account to change.
9. A line is usually skipped between journal entries to help separate the entries and to make the information included in the journal easier to read.

The Ledger and Posting

Changes in the accounting equation are accumulated in the journal by transaction. To provide information to decision makers, these data must be summarized in useful categories. This summarization is provided in the ledger. We said earlier that the ledger is a book with a separate page for each account. The traditional two-column ledger account is shown in Exhibit 15-2. We also said that posting is the process of transferring information from the journal to the ledger. The following steps are used when posting a debit entry to the ledger (follow each step by referring to the ledger in Exhibit 15-2):

1. The year is entered as the first item in the Date column on the debit side of the account. As in the journal, it is entered only once.

EXHIBIT 15-2 General Ledger

GENERAL LEDGER

Cash   Account No. 101

Date 2009		Item	P.R.	Debit	Date	Item	P.R.	Credit
June	1		1	5000 –				

P. Keith, Capital   Account No. 301

Date		Item	P.R.	Debit	Date 2009		Item	P.R.	Credit
					June	1		1	5000 –

2. The next item of information is the month. It is placed beneath the year and is entered only once unless the same ledger page is used for more than 1 month.

3. The date of the transaction is the next piece of information placed in the ledger.

4. The amount of the transaction is then entered in the Debit money column.

5. Finally, the P.R. (Posting Reference) column is used to enter the page number where the transaction is recorded in the journal.

6. The account number (for Cash it is 101) is entered in the journal in the P.R. column (see Exhibit 15-1). Thus the cross-referencing system has been completed. The journal entry can be traced to the ledger, and the ledger entry can be traced back to the original transaction in the journal.

These steps follow the posting of a debit to the Cash account. The process is the same for each credit entry except that the recording is made on the credit side of the account. (See Exhibit 15-2 for the P. Keith, Capital account, and follow the steps previously listed.) The ledger referred to in Exhibit 15-2 is a *general ledger*.

Review Exercise

Record the entries for Kaki Tours, following the format in Exhibit 15-1; post the entries to the appropriate accounts, following the format in Exhibit 15-2. (The entries are described earlier in this section. Don't forget the four entries used to "complete the exercise.") After performing these steps, compare your answer with the solution provided on pages 612–615. You should begin by recording the first transaction—the deposit by Paige Keith—in the journal.

Solution

GENERAL JOURNAL

Page 1

Date 2009		Description	P.R.	Debit	Credit
June	1	Cash	101	5000 –	
		P. Keith, Capital	301		5000 –
		Owner invested $5,000 in the business.			
	2	Prepaid services	102	50 –	
		Cash	101		50 –
		Paid Tel-Ans for telephone answering services.			
	4	Office supplies	104	55 –	
		Cash	101		55 –
		Purchased stationery from Print Faster.			
	5	Office equipment	107	250 –	
		Cash	101		25 –
		Accounts payable	201		225 –
		Purchased office equipment.			
	7	Office supplies	104	125 –	
		Cash	101		125 –
		Purchased office supplies.			
	10	Accounts receivable	103	300 –	
		Tour revenue	401		300 –
		Billed tour companies for tours conducted.			
	15	Cash	101	250 –	
		Accounts receivable	103		250 –
		Collected accounts receivable.			
	20	Cash	101	130 –	
		Tour revenue	401		130 –
		Collected cash for tours conducted.			
	25	Office rent expense	501	75 –	
		Cash	101		75 –
		Paid rent on office.			
	30	Accounts receivable	103	400 –	
		Tour revenue	401		400 –
		Billed tour companies for tours conducted.			

GENERAL JOURNAL

Page 2

Date 2009		Description	P.R.	Debit	Credit
June	30	Salary expense	502	40 –	
		Salary payable	202		40 –
		Recorded unpaid salary of assistant.			
	30	Telephone-answering expense	503	50 –	
		Prepaid services	102		50 –
		Recorded telephone answering services used.			
	30	Office supplies expense	504	30 –	
		Office supplies	104		30 –
		Recorded office supplies used.			
	30	Depreciation expense—office equipment	505	5 –	
		Accumulated depreciation—office equipment	108		5 –
		Recorded depreciation for June.			

GENERAL LEDGER

Cash   101

Date 2009		Item	P.R.	Debit	Date 2009		Item	P.R.	Credit
June	1		1	5000 –	June	2		1	50 –
	15		1	250 –		4		1	55 –
	20		1	130 –		5		1	25 –
		(5,050)		5380 –		7		1	125 –
						25		1	75 –
									330 –

Prepaid Services   102

Date 2009		Item	P.R.	Debit	Date 2009		Item	P.R.	Credit
June	2		1	50 –	June	30		2	50 –
		(Ø)							

Accounts Receivable   103

Date 2009		Item	P.R.	Debit	Date 2009		Item	P.R.	Credit
June	10		1	300 –	June	15		1	250 –
	30		1	400 –					
		(450)		700 –					

Office Supplies 104

Date 2009		Item	P.R.	Debit	Date 2009		Item	P.R.	Credit
June	4		1	55 –	June	30		2	30 –
	7		1	125 –					
		(150)		180 –					

Office Equipment 107

Date 2009		Item	P.R.	Debit	Date 2009	Item	P.R.	Credit
June	5		1	250 –				

Accumulated Depreciation — Office Equipment 108

Date 2009	Item	P.R.	Debit	Date 2009		Item	P.R.	Credit
				June	30		2	5 –

Accounts Payable 201

Date 2009	Item	P.R.	Debit	Date 2009		Item	P.R.	Credit
				June	5		1	225 –

Salary Payable 202

Date 2009	Item	P.R.	Debit	Date 2009		Item	P.R.	Credit
				June	30		2	40 –

P. Keith, Capital 301

Date 2009	Item	P.R.	Debit	Date 2009		Item	P.R.	Credit
				June	1		1	5000 –

Tour Revenue   401

Date		Item	P.R.	Debit	Date 2009		Item	P.R.	Credit
					June	10		1	300 –
						20		1	130 –
						30	(830)	1	400 –
									830 –

Office Rent Expense   501

Date 2009		Item	P.R.	Debit	Date		Item	P.R.	Credit
June	25		1	75 –					

Salary Expense   502

Date 2009		Item	P.R.	Debit	Date		Item	P.R.	Credit
June	30		2	40 –					

Telephone-Answering Expense   503

Date 2009		Item	P.R.	Debit	Date		Item	P.R.	Credit
June	30		2	50 –					

Office Supplies Expense   504

Date 2009		Item	P.R.	Debit	Date		Item	P.R.	Credit
June	30		2	30 –					

Depreciation Expense—Office Equipment   505

Date 2009		Item	P.R.	Debit	Date		Item	P.R.	Credit
June	30		2	5 –					

FINANCIAL STATEMENTS

The Accounting Cycle

Thus far, we have discussed the recording aspect of the accounting cycle, which consists of (1) analyzing transactions and events to see how they affect assets, liabilities, and equity; (2) recording the transactions and events by making entries in a journal; and (3) posting the journal entries to ledger accounts.

The ultimate purpose of accounting is to provide information to decision makers. Information about results of past operations and current financial position assists in making decisions about the future. Financial reporting organizes the mass of data that the accounting system has gathered into statements that can help users interpret the information. The financial reporting aspects of the accounting cycle are (1) preparing a trial balance, (2) adjusting the accounts as necessary, and (3) preparing financial statements. The final aspect of the accounting cycle is closing the temporary subsets of equity.

This cycle is repeated every accounting period. In specific cases, the cycle may be expanded or contracted to fit the particular circumstances facing the organization.

The Trial Balance

To help prepare financial statements and locate errors that may have been made in the recording or posting processes, a *trial balance* is prepared. The trial balance is a columnar listing of each ledger account, together with its balance. If the debit and credit columns equal each other, the system is in balance. (See Table 15-12, which was prepared from the ledger accounts on pages 613–615.)

TABLE 15-12 Trial Balance

Kaki Tours
Trial Balance
June 30, 2009

	Debits	*Credits*
Cash	$5,050	
Accounts receivable	450	
Office supplies	150	
Office equipment	250	
Accumulated depreciation—office equipment		$ 5
Accounts payable		225
Salary payable		40
P. Keith, Capital		5,000
Tour revenue		830
Office rent expense	75	
Salary expense	40	
Telephone-answering expense	50	
Office supplies expense	30	
Depreciation expense—office equipment	5	
	$6,100	$6,100

Errors can occur within the system even if the debit and credit columns in the trial balance are equal. Examples of such errors include (1) entries that are not recorded, (2) amounts debited (credited) to incorrect accounts, and (3) complete entries recorded for incorrect amounts.

The financial statements are usually prepared directly from trial balance data. In some systems, a formal adjusting process must be completed before the statements can be prepared. Such a process is discussed next.

Adjusting Entries

After the trial balance has been prepared, *adjusting entries* may be needed to bring the financial records up to date before statements are prepared. Adjusting entries, as discussed previously, are needed if the books have not been adjusted continuously to the full accrual basis of accounting. A good example is depreciation. Recall that in the Kaki Tours illustration depreciation was recorded to recognize the fact that the services of the asset Office equipment were being "used up."

Logic would indicate that the "using up" process is gradual and does not occur suddenly at the end of an accounting period. If the books were to be maintained on a current basis, an entry for depreciation would need to be made daily. Because financial statements are prepared only periodically, however, it is not necessary to have the books fully up to date until the statements are prepared. Therefore, adjusting entries are made at the end of each period before the financial statements are prepared.

In addition to depreciation in the Kaki Tours illustration, Prepaid services must be adjusted. Although the services were used each day, it was not necessary to record the using up (or gradual expiration) of the asset until the end of the period. In the illustration, note that adjustments were also made for using up Office supplies, as well as for salaries earned by an employee but not yet paid to him. The section "The Accrual Basis of Accounting" discusses other examples of accruals, deferrals, and amortizations for which adjusting entries might be needed if not otherwise recorded.

Financial Statements

After adjusting entries have been made, we are ready to prepare financial statements. Statements commonly prepared are (1) an income (or operating or activity) statement, (2) a statement of changes in owner's equity, (3) a balance sheet, and (4) a statement of cash flows.

An income statement compares the revenues earned with the expenses incurred in earning those revenues, and it reports the resulting net income or net loss. For a profit-oriented organization, this statement is called an *income statement.* An income statement for Paige Keith's business—Kaki Tours—is shown in Table 15-13.

The *statement of changes in owner's equity* provides a reconciliation of the beginning and ending owner's capital balance. Items that increase owner's capital include investments by the owner and net income for the period. Items that decrease the balance are owner's withdrawals and net losses. Owner's withdrawals are covered later in this chapter. A statement of changes in owner's equity is shown in Table 15-14.

The final statement that will be illustrated is the *balance sheet.* This statement reports the balances of the asset, liability, and capital accounts at the end of the period (see Table 15-15).

TABLE 15-13 Income Statement

Kaki Tours
Income Statement
For the Month Ended June 30, 2009

Revenue		
Tour revenue		$830
Expenses		
Office rent expense	$75	
Salary expense	40	
Telephone-answering expense	50	
Office supplies expense	30	
Depreciation expense—office equipment	5	200
Net Income		$630

TABLE 15-14 Statement of Changes in Owner's Equity

Kaki Tours
Statement of Changes in Owner's Equity
For the Month Ended June 30, 2009

P. Keith, Capital, June 1, 2009	$ -0-
Investment during June	5,000
Income for June	630
P. Keith, Capital, June 30, 2009	$5,630

TABLE 15-15 Balance Sheet

Kaki Tours
Balance Sheet
June 30, 2009

Assets			
Cash		$5,050	
Accounts receivable		450	
Office supplies		150	
Office equipment	$250		
Less: Accumulated depreciation	5	245	
Total assets		$5,895	
Liabilities and Equity			
Liabilities:			
Accounts payable		$ 225	Assets =
Salary payable		40	Liabilities +
Total liabilities		265	Equity
Equity:			
P. Keith, Capital		5,630	
Total liabilities and equity		$5,895	

An understanding of the accounting system requires an understanding of the relationship between the financial statements. Notice how the net income for the period is taken from the income statement and is used to determine the ending balance in the owner's capital account. Notice also how the ending balance in the owner's capital account is used to balance the balance sheet.

A *statement of cash flows* should also be prepared for a business, but a discussion of its preparation is beyond the scope of this text.

Financial Statement Work Sheet

To facilitate preparation of the financial statements, accountants use a *work sheet* that starts with the trial balance and spreads this information across columns for the income statement, the statement of changes in owner's equity, and the balance sheet. Often, the work sheet will contain 12 columns; the first two for the unadjusted trial balance, the next two for adjusting entries, the next two for the adjusted trial balance, and the last six for the financial statements. For Kaki Tours, a trial balance is shown in Table 15-12. This trial balance already contains the effect of the adjusting journal entries, so we will prepare an eight-column work sheet—starting with the adjusted trial balance. Preparing the work sheet requires an ability to distinguish between accounts that belong in the income statement and accounts that belong in the balance sheet.

When you review the work sheet (Table 15-16), notice the following:

- When you extend the income statement accounts from the adjusted trial balance columns into the income statement columns, the total of the credit amounts exceeds the total of the debit amounts by $630. This means that net revenues exceed net expenses, resulting in net income—an increase in owner's equity. To keep the statements in balance, the $630 net credit in the income statement columns is extended into the credit column of the statement of changes in owner's equity by putting a $630 debit in the income statement columns and a corresponding credit in the statement of changes in owner's equity columns.
- The next step is to extend the owner's equity accounts from the trial balance into the columns for changes in owner's equity. As a result of this year's net income, the owner's equity now shows total credits of $5,630. Because there were no debits, the new owner's equity amount is $5,630. Now extend that net credit into the balance sheet, by putting a $5,630 debit into the columns for the statement of changes in owner's equity, and a corresponding credit into the balance sheet columns.
- Finally, you should extend the balance sheet accounts from the trial balance into the columns for the balance sheet. Notice that the original balance for P. Keith, Capital has been changed by the net effect of the "temporary" revenue and expense accounts. If you made no errors in extending the amounts from the adjusted trial balance into the appropriate columns, the amounts of the total debits and the total credits in the balance sheet would "balance."

Now, trace the figures from each column of the work sheet to the corresponding financial statements illustrated in Tables 15-13, 15-14, and 15-15.

TABLE 15-16 Work Sheet for Preparing Financial Statements

Kaki Tours
Work Sheet for Preparing Financial Statements
June 30, 2009

	Adjusted Trial Balance		Income Statement		Changes in Owner's Equity		Balance Sheet	
	Debits	**Credits**	**Debits**	**Credits**	**Debits**	**Credits**	**Debits**	**Credits**
Cash	$5,050						$5,050	
Accounts receivable	450						450	
Office supplies	150						150	
Office equipment	250						250	
Acc. dep.—off. equip.		$ 5						$ 5
Accounts payable		225						225
Salary payable		40						40
P. Keith, Capital		5,000				$5,000		
Tour revenue		830		$830				
Office rent expense	75		$ 75					
Salary expense	40		40					
Tel. ans. expense	50		50					
Office supplies exp.	30		30					
Dep. exp.—off. equip.	5		5					
	$6,100	$6,100	200	830				
Net income			630			630		
			$830	$830		5,630		
P. Keith, Cap. 6/30					$5,630			5,630
					$5,630	$5,630	$5,900	$5,900

CLOSING THE BOOKS

The final step in the accounting process is closing the books and getting them ready for the next year.

In this chapter the accounting equation was originally used to account for the acquisition and use of the resources of an organization. Table 15-1, which explained how transactions affect the equation, contained only three types of accounts: assets, liabilities, and equity. These accounts are generally referred to as the *permanent* or *real accounts*. They are labeled *permanent* because they are carried from one period to another. Thus, for example, the ending balance of Cash of one period will be the beginning balance of Cash for the next period.

As the illustrations in this chapter became more complex, the changes in equity resulting from operations of the business were accumulated in separate accounts called revenues and expenses. The purpose of these accounts was to identify the particular operating items causing equity to change. Thus these accounts became the source of the data that were presented on the activity (income) statement. These data were used to help decision makers evaluate the effectiveness of the use of the resources available to management.

After such an evaluation has been made for the current period, however, the data lose their importance. The generation of revenue and the incurrence of expenses are relative to a certain period of time. It serves little purpose to know that a business that has been in operation for 100 years has generated $500 million in revenue. Information on revenues and expenses is useful only for evaluating the operations of an organization on a period-by-period basis. As a result, revenue and expense accounts are generally referred to as *temporary* or *nominal accounts*.

If temporary (revenue and expense) accounts are to be used to generate information relative to certain periods, they must be closed out (reduced to a zero balance) at the end of each period; and the balances in those accounts must be transferred to equity. The ledger in Table 15-11 shows a balance in the P. Keith, Capital, account of $5,000, the initial contribution by Paige Keith. Analysis of the balance sheet in Table 15-15, however, indicates a capital balance of $5,630. The reason for the difference between these two figures is that the former, the one found in the ledger, does not include the income for the period. Because the effects of operations have already been recorded in the asset and liability accounts, they must also be reflected in the capital account so that the balance sheet will balance.

In summary, the trial balance figure for capital does not include the effect of operating the business. Therefore, it must be updated. In addition, the revenue and expense accounts must be reduced to zero to begin accumulating data for the next period. The process of achieving these goals is referred to as *closing the books*. The closing entry for Kaki Tours at June 30, 2009, is shown in Exhibit 15-3.

The purpose of the closing process is to zero out the balances of the temporary accounts and transfer the net income for the period to the capital account. The steps involved in this process are as follows:

1. Debit each revenue account for the credit balance currently in the account.
2. Credit each expense account for the debit balance currently in the account.
3. Debit or credit the capital account for the amount needed to balance the journal entry—make the debits equal the credits—which provides the amount of the net income or loss.

EXHIBIT 15-3   Closing Entry

GENERAL JOURNAL   3

Date 2009		Description	Ref.	Dr.	Cr.
June	30	Tour revenue	401	830 –	
		Office rent expense	501		75 –
		Salary expense	502		40 –
		Telephone—answering expense	503		50 –
		Office supplies expense	504		30 –
		Depreciation expense—office equipment	505		5 –
		P. Keith, Capital	301		630 –
		Record closing the revenue and expense accounts			
		and transfer the net income to capital.			

After posting these entries to the accounts, the revenue and expense accounts will no longer have any balances. A double line should be drawn under the date and amount columns for each of those accounts, and the accounts are now ready for the next year's postings. The asset, liability, and equity accounts all have balances that will be carried into the next period as the beginning balances in those accounts.

OTHER TRANSACTIONS AND OTHER MATTERS

Withdrawals by the Owner

In the example just discussed, Kaki Tours had net income of $630 for the month of June. What if Paige Keith had decided—just before the end of the month—to withdraw $200 cash as compensation for her work? Withdrawals by the owner of a business are not treated as expenses. Instead, they are recorded as reductions of equity. An account called P. Keith, Withdrawals would have been debited for $200 and Cash would have been credited. (For financial reporting purposes, the withdrawal is reported not in the income statement, but rather in the statement of changes in owner's equity—Table 15-14.)

Control and Subsidiary Accounts

Until now, we have shown just single accounts for accounts receivable and for accounts payable. In practice, large entities will have thousands of individual accounts receivable and accounts payable, representing amounts owed by their customers and to their creditors. Maintaining separate accounts for each receivable and each payable in the general ledger would make the general ledger extremely unwieldy. To simplify record keeping, most entities maintain a separate accounts receivable ledger, with a page for each customer. They also keep a separate accounts payable ledger, with a page for each creditor. These ledgers are called *subsidiary ledgers* and the individual accounts are called *subsidiary accounts.*

To record individual receivable and payable transactions, postings are made to each affected account in the subsidiary ledger. Summary postings for the total of the amounts affecting the accounts receivable and accounts payable accounts are made to those accounts in the general ledger. The accounts receivable and accounts payable accounts maintained in the general ledger are referred to as *control accounts.* The totals of the control accounts must be equal at all times to the total of the individual accounts kept in the subsidiary ledgers.

Credit Sales and Bad Debts

The U.S. economy is basically a credit economy. Instead of paying cash immediately, customers are allowed a certain period of time to pay. Although this practice may stimulate sales, selling on credit also has a cost. Some customers may not pay their bills, resulting in an expense called *bad debts expense.* When should you record this expense: in the year of the sale or in the year the bad debt is written off?

To determine the answer, think about the question in another way: Is this expense attributable to the year the sales were made or to the year the customer failed to pay the bill? Remember that, under accrual accounting, expenses need to be matched with the revenues to which the expenses relate. Therefore, the bad debts expense should be recorded in the year the sales revenue was recorded.

Recording this expense raises a few questions:

- If specific bad debts have not yet occurred, how do you know how much to record as an expense?

Answer: Make an estimate, generally based on past experience and calculated as a percentage of the year's sales or as a percentage of the unpaid accounts receivable.

- If bad debts have not yet occurred, how do you reduce the balance of the Accounts receivable account? Which specific account in the accounts receivable subsidiary ledger should you reduce, if you don't know who the bad debt will be?

Answer: Don't reduce any specific account receivable at the time you record the bad debts expense. Instead, create another account, called Allowance for uncollectible accounts. This account stands in place of the credit to Accounts receivable until an actual bad debt becomes known. When an actual bad debt becomes known, reduce Accounts receivable, as well as the Allowance account.

To illustrate this process, return to the Kaki Tours illustration. Notice (from Table 15-13) that Kaki Tours had tour revenue of $830. Notice also (see Accounts receivable in Table 15-15) that some customers had not yet paid their bills. They owed Kaki a total of $450. These financial statements were based on the assumption that everyone would pay. Suppose, however, based on her experience, Paige Keith believes that not everyone will pay. She estimates that about 10 percent of the $450 owed to her on June 30, 2009, will not be paid. To record this estimate, the following entry is needed:

Bad debts expense	45	
Allowance for uncollectible accounts		45
To record estimated bad debts.		

The $45 bad debts expense would be reported as one of the expenses on the income statement, thereby reducing Kaki Tours' net income from $630 to $585. The Allowance for uncollectible accounts would be shown as a reduction of Accounts receivable on the balance sheet, so that the net accounts receivable would be reported as $405.

Now, assume one of the individuals included in Accounts receivable at June 30 goes bankrupt in August, after the statements are issued. Because he cannot pay, Accounts receivable must be reduced. Also, because the Allowance for uncollectible accounts had been set up for that purpose, that account is also reduced. The entry is as follows:

Allowance for uncollectible accounts	30	
Accounts receivable		30
To record write-off of bad debt.		

What is the financial reporting effect of these transactions? The account, Allowance for uncollectible accounts, is called a *contra-asset*. For financial reporting purposes, it serves to reduce the reported Accounts receivable balance, so that Accounts Receivable is stated at its net realizable value; that is, the amount expected to be realized in cash. A balance sheet prepared at June 30, 2009, would show Accounts receivable of $450, less Allowance for uncollectible accounts of $45, for a net asset of $405. A balance sheet prepared immediately after the write-off of the bad debt would show

Accounts receivable of $420, less Allowance for uncollectible accounts of $15, leaving the same net asset of $405.

Buying and Selling Merchandise

For simplicity, the illustrations in this chapter deal with the sale of services. Much of what takes place in the U.S. economy, however, concerns the purchase (or manufacture) and sale of products. How would a retail store, for example, account for the purchase and sale of clothing? Assume Sammi's Dresses purchases 12 dresses on credit at a cost of $100 each. She sells 5 of them for cash at $160 each.

You can tell from inspection that Sammi made a profit of $300 on the sale, because she sold five dresses and made a profit of $60 on each. You reached that conclusion because you "matched" the selling price of each dress ($160) with the cost of each dress ($100). The accounting process follows the same matching process, as the following entries show:

Merchandise inventory	1,200	
Accounts payable		1,200
To record merchandise purchases (12 dresses @ $100).		
Cash	800	
Sales revenue		800
To record sales of merchandise (5 dresses @ $160).		
Cost of goods sold	500	
Merchandise inventory		500
To record cost of sales (5 dresses @ $100).		

Consider the effect of these transactions. Merchandise inventory is an asset account. After the journal entries were made, that account has a balance of $700, representing 7 dresses that cost Sammi $100 each. Sales revenue and Cost of goods sold are equity accounts (a revenue and an expense account). Matching the Sales revenue ($800) with the Cost of goods sold ($500) shows that Sammi's gross profit was $300.

Review Questions

Q15-1　Define the following terms:
    a. Assets
    b. Liabilities
    c. Equity
    d. Revenue
    e. Expense

Q15-2　Write the accounting equation.

Q15-3　Must the accounting equation always balance? Why?

Q15-4　Describe the difference between the cash basis of accounting and the accrual basis.

Q15-5　Describe and illustrate the difference between an accrual and a deferral.

Q15-6　Identify the rules of debit and credit with respect to assets, liabilities, equity, revenues, and expenses.

Q15-7　A student of basic accounting made the following statement: "For each account debited, there must be another account credited for the same amount." Do you agree? Why or why not?

Q15-8   What is a journal and how is it used in the accounting process?
Q15-9   What is a ledger and how is it used in the accounting process?
Q15-10 How are journals and ledgers interrelated in an accounting system?
Q15-11 If the columns of a trial balance total to the same amount, the information included in the accounts must be correct. Do you agree or disagree? Why?
Q15-12 What are the three basic financial statements illustrated in the text?
Q15-13 Describe the interrelationship among the three statements in Q15-12.
Q15-14 Why is it important to put the appropriate date or time period on a financial statement?
Q15-15 What is the purpose of adjusting entries?
Q15-16 Which accounts are closed at the end of an accounting period? Why are these accounts closed?

Exercises

E15-1   (Preparing transactions)
For each of the following categories, compose a transaction that will cause that category to increase and one that will cause it to decrease:

1. Assets
2. Liabilities
3. Equity
4. Revenues
5. Expenses

E15-2   (Associating changes with specific accounts)
For each of the following transactions of the Kit-Kat Center, a not-for-profit entity, identify the accounts that would be increased and those that would be decreased:

1. The center borrowed $10,000 from a bank.
2. Rent for the month was paid to Jiffy Realty Company: $2,000.
3. A nurse was hired at a monthly salary of $4,000.
4. Customers were billed for day care services: $17,000.
5. The utilities bill for the month was paid: $350.

E15-3   (Calculating the change in equity from balance sheet data)
The beginning and ending balances in certain account categories of the Release Company are as follows:

Account Categories	*Beginning Balances*	*Ending Balances*
Assets	$318,000	$331,000
Liabilities	$107,000	$110,000

Based on this information, what was the change in equity for the period?

E15-4   (Associating accrual-type changes with specific accounts)
For each of the following events affecting the Kit-Kat Center in E15-2, identify the accounts that would be increased and those that would be decreased:

1. The month for which rent of $2,000 had been paid to Jiffy Realty Company expired.
2. The nurse worked for a full month and earned $4,000 but was not paid.

E15-5   (Associating accrual-type changes with specific accounts)
For each of the following events affecting Youth Services, identify the accounts that would be increased and those that would be decreased on April 30 in order to accurately measure the results of operations for the month of April:

1. Youth Services borrowed $10,000 on April 1 to provide working capital. It promised to repay the loan in 12 months with interest at 6 percent a year.
2. Youth Services did not plan to use the entire $10,000 immediately. On April 1, it invested $2,000 in a 90-day Treasury bill that would pay 4 percent interest.
3. Youth Services paid $1,800 on April 1 for a 3-year fire insurance policy.

E15-6   (Using debits and credits)
Identify the account(s) that would be debited and/or credited as a result of the following transactions:

1. The owner invested $10,000 in the business.
2. Supplies were purchased for cash: $800.
3. Service revenue of $1,000 was received in cash.
4. Customers were billed for services rendered: $500.
5. Employees were paid their salaries totaling $800.
6. Collections of accounts receivable totaled $300.
7. Rent for the month was paid: $350.
8. Salaries owed employees at the end of the month totaled $100.
9. Supplies costing $300 were used.

E15-7   (Associating debits and credits with account categories)
Each of the account categories listed in E15-1 is increased with either a debit or credit. Indicate which is used to record an increase in each type of account and identify the usual balance in that account category.

E15-8   (Associating transactions with their effects on the accounting equation)
Life Support, a not-for-profit nursing home, had the following transactions in 2009. For each transaction, state whether an asset increased or decreased, a liability increased or decreased, or equity (revenues or expenses) increased or decreased. (Each transaction has two answers.)

1. Borrowed $100,000 cash from a bank.
2. Bought equipment on credit.
3. Sent bills to Medicaid for care of residents.
4. Paid rent on January 1 for the 3-month period January–March.
5. Recorded depreciation on equipment it owned.
6. Paid salaries to its employees.
7. Made a year-end accrual for interest owed the bank on money it borrowed.

E15-9   (Recognizing asset, liability, revenue, and expense accounts)
Based on the following data, calculate the net income for the period and the balance in the account for Amy Norris, Capital after the closing entry has been posted.

Cash	$12,000
Accounts receivable	15,000
Prepaid rent	1,000
Office equipment	30,000
Accumulated depreciation, office equipment	14,000
Accounts payable	5,000
Notes payable to bank	10,000
Amy Norris, Capital	25,000
Service revenue	40,000
Depreciation expense, equipment	7,000
Rent expense	15,000
Salary expense	14,000

E15-10 (Using debits and credits)

Ken Cascioli and Bill Ryder, master painters and paperhangers, formed a partnership. They had the following transactions during their first month of business. Record the debits and credits, without making explanations.

1. Ken and Bill each invested $3,000 in the business. (*Note:* Use separate capital accounts for each.)
2. Ken and Bill acquired the following items of equipment for use in the business:
   a. Ladders and other equipment, for which they paid $1,800 cash. They estimated that the equipment would have an average useful life of 6 years.
   b. A pickup truck, which they bought for $10,000. They paid $2,000 in cash as a down payment and signed a note for the remainder, agreeing to pay $1,000 a month for the next 8 months, together with interest at the rate of 5 percent per annum on the unpaid balance of the loan. They estimated the truck would have a useful life of 4 years.
3. They took out a 3-year insurance policy related to their business activities, paying $1,200 cash.
4. They paid $380 for paint and other supplies, all of which was consumed on the various painting jobs they did during the month.
5. They paid $80 for gasoline for the pickup truck.
6. Ken and Bill expect payment from their customers every Friday for work done during the week. During the month they collected $9,380 in cash for their work.

E15-11 (Using debits and credits for adjusting journal entries)

Ken Cascioli and Bill Ryder (see E15-10) need to make adjusting journal entries to prepare financial statements based on their first month's activities. Make adjusting journal entries for the following events, referring to the transactions in E15-10 as necessary.

1. Record depreciation for 1 month on the ladders and other equipment.
2. Record depreciation for 1 month on the pickup truck.
3. Accrue interest for 1 month on the note referred to in transaction 2.b.
4. Record the cost of insurance for 1 month (transaction 3).

5. Ken and Bill worked on the last 2 days of the month and earned a total of $850, but they did not collect cash because the last day of the month fell on a Tuesday. Make an accrual for their earnings.

E15-12 (Preparing a trial balance and financial statements)
Ken Cascioli and Bill Ryder (see E15-10 and E15-11) want to know the net income for their first month's activities. Post the journal entries prepared for E15-10 and E15-11 to general ledger T-accounts and prepare a trial balance. From the trial balance, prepare an income statement, a statement of changes in owners' equity, and a balance sheet.

E15-13 (Recording transactions in a general journal)
Record the following transactions in general journal form for the Control Company, a private investigation service:

2009
January 2   Susan Bigger invested $10,000 in the business.

         2   Bigger paid the rent on office space for January: $500.

         4   Bigger purchased office supplies on credit for $200.

         5   Bigger billed customers for $5,000 for services performed.

      10   Bigger acquired an automobile for use in the business. The cost was $4,500. She paid $1,000 as a down payment and signed a note for the remainder.

      15   Customers paid Bigger $3,500 on their account.

      31   Depreciation of $100 was recorded on the automobile.

      31   Office supplies used during the month totaled $100.

      31   The utility bills arrived in the mail; they totaled $800. She will pay them in February.

E15-14 (Preparing a trial balance)
Using the following information, prepare a trial balance for the Forfeit Company at June 30, 2009.

Accumulated depreciation—equipment	$4,000
Taxes payable	200
Equipment	24,000
Cash	20,000
Utilities expense	1,000
Depreciation expense—equipment	600
Notes payable	24,000
Salaries expense	20,000
R. Key, Capital	15,800
Office supplies	2,000
Service revenue	32,000
Rent expense	8,600
Accounts payable	1,600
Office supplies expense	1,400

E15-15 (Computation of balance sheet amounts)
Based upon the following information, compute total assets, total liabilities, and total capital; in addition, determine whether all of the accounts are listed. (*Note:* This is the first month of operations of the business.)

Cash	$22,000
Accounts receivable	12,000
Accounts payable	15,000
Equipment	50,000
Rent expense	11,000
Service revenue	74,000
Notes payable	17,000
Accumulated depreciation	25,000
Depreciation expense	12,500
Office supplies	3,000
Office supplies expense	8,000
Salaries payable	4,000

E15-16 (Relating accounts and financial statements)
Identify the financial statement on which each of the following items would appear:

a. Bonds payable
b. Rent revenue
c. Owner's capital, beginning balance
d. Cash
e. Equipment
f. Supplies expense
g. Depreciation expense
h. Service revenue

i. Accounts receivable
j. Accounts payable
k. Owner's capital, ending balance
l. Rent expense
m. Accumulated depreciation
n. Net income
o. Salaries payable
p. Land
q. Supplies on hand

E15-17 (Matching accounts and financial statements)
Following are several financial statement classifications and accounts:

R	Revenue
E	Expense
A	Asset
L	Liability
C	Owner's capital (balance sheet)
SC	Statement of changes in owner's equity

Example: A Cash

____ **1.** Notes payable
____ **2.** Additional investment by owner
____ **3.** Automobile
____ **4.** Depreciation expense—automobile
____ **5.** Prepaid rent
____ **6.** Utilities expense
____ **7.** Consulting revenue
____ **8.** Accounts payable
____ **9.** Ending balance in owner's capital
____ **10.** Office supplies
____ **11.** Accumulated depreciation—automobile
____ **12.** Salaries payable
____ **13.** Office supplies expense
____ **14.** Service revenue

_____ **15.** Interest expense
_____ **16.** Accounts receivable
_____ **17.** Loans made to other companies
_____ **18.** Deposit made with utility company (This amount will be repaid to the company for which we are keeping the records in 5 years.)
_____ **19.** Cash held in a separate bank account from that mentioned previously (This money will be used to buy a building in a few years.)

Required: Identify the proper financial statement classification for each account by placing the appropriate key letter in the space provided. (Some items may appear in more than one statement classification.)

E15-18 (Fill in the blanks—definitions)
Match the items in the right column with those in the left column.

_____ **1.** Statement of changes in owner's equity

_____ **2.** Income statement

_____ **3.** Net income

_____ **4.** Additional investment by the owner

_____ **5.** Ending balance in owner's capital

_____ **6.** Balance sheet

a. A financial statement that presents the revenues and expenses of a business

b. A financial statement that presents a reconciliation of the beginning and ending owner's capital

c. An increase in owner's capital

d. A financial statement that presents the assets, liabilities, and owner's capital of a business

e. Can be found on a balance sheet and a statement of changes in owner's equity

f. An excess of revenues over expenses

E15-19 (Preparing closing entries and determining the ending balance in capital)
Prepare the appropriate closing entry based on the information in E15-14 and determine the ending balance in R. Key, Capital.

E15-20 (Accounting for uncollectible accounts receivable)
South Salem Daycare Center is a not-for-profit organization that provides daycare services. Prepare journal entries for the Center to record the following events. After making all the journal entries, calculate the net realizable value of the Center's accounts receivable.

1. The Center billed its clients $120,000 for daycare services during the year.
2. The Center received $105,000 from its Clients in payment of the bills.
3. The Center established an allowance for uncollectible accounts receivable in the amount of 10 percent of its outstanding receivables.
4. The Center could not locate three clients who owed a total of $800, and it decided to write off their accounts as being uncollectible.

E15-21 (Accounting for the purchase and sale of merchandise)
Nomoto Cars is an automobile dealership. Prepare journal entries to record these transactions:

1. Nomoto receives 10 automobiles from a manufacturer and puts them into its inventory for resale. Nomoto bought the autos on credit for $20,000 each.
2. During the following week, Nomoto sells four of the automobiles for $24,000 each. The customers pay in cash. (*Hint:* Prepare two journal entries, one to record the sale proceeds and one to record the expense of the sale. For the second entry, debit the account Cost of sales.)

Problems

P15-1   (Analyzing transactions on a work sheet)
Sally Golfo, a registered nurse, opens a business called Sally's Eldercare. Golfo plans to care for the elderly herself in a facility that she will rent. The following transactions occurred during July 2009, her first month in business:

1. Ms. Golfo invested $5,000 of her own money to start the business.
1. She borrowed $20,000 from the bank to provide her with additional cash. She agreed to repay the bank $1,000 on the last day of every month, starting July 31, with interest at the rate of 6 percent a year on the unpaid balance.
1. She rented the house next to hers for a 3-month period, paying a total of $6,000, to provide a facility to care for her patients.
1. She purchased furniture for the facility. She received an invoice for $4,800, payable in 10 days.
10. She paid the $4,800 invoice for the furniture.
18. She paid her assistant $800 for 2 weeks' work.
20. During the month, she billed her clients $12,000 for services rendered.
25. She received $9,000 cash from the clients who were previously billed.
30. At month end, she received a bill for electric service in the amount of $300. She will pay the bill in August.
30. During the month, she paid $500 for food to provide lunch to her clients. (*Hint:* For this problem, consider the food as an expense when it is purchased.)
31. She paid the bank $1,100 on the borrowing. Of that amount, $1,000 was for the principal payment on the loan and $100 was for interest.

Required: Analyze these transactions on a work sheet similar to that illustrated in the text. You will need columns for Cash, Accounts receivable, Prepaid rent, Furniture, Notes payable, Accounts payable, and Sally Golfo, Capital.

P15-2   (Analyzing accrual transactions on a work sheet)
Analyze the following accrual-type events and add them to the work sheet you prepared for P15-1.

1. Adjust for the expiration of 1 month's rent.
2. Adjust for the "using up" of the furniture during the month. (Assume the furniture will have a useful life of 4 years.)
3. Accrue for $800 of salary earned by the assistant during the last 2 weeks of the month but not yet paid to her.

P15-3 (Recording transactions in journals and ledgers)
Using the information given in P15-1 and P15-2, record the transactions in general journal form. Then, post the journal entries to ledger T-accounts, like those shown in Table 15-11. (To help keep track of your postings, give each journal entry the same reference number or letter shown in the problems, and insert that number or letter to the left of the amount recorded in the T-accounts.)

P15-4 (Preparing a trial balance and financial statements)
Required: 1. From the ledger accounts prepared for P15-3, prepare a trial balance.
2. Extend the trial balance into an eight-column work sheet like that shown in Table 15-16, and use the work sheet to prepare the following financial statements:
   a. Income statement
   b. Statement of changes in owner's equity
   c. Balance sheet

P15-5 (Preparing a closing entry)
Required: Based on the answers you obtained in P15-4, prepare the closing entry.

P15-6 (Analyzing transactions on a work sheet)
Dr. Harlan Elliott opened a magnetic resonance imaging (MRI) facility, to be known as Harlan MRI. These transactions took place during his first month of operation:

1. Dr. Elliott invested $80,000 in the business.
2. He purchased MRI equipment from the manufacturer for $1.8 million. To pay for the equipment, Harlan gave the manufacturer a note. He was required to repay the note in five annual payments of $360,000 each, together with interest of 6 percent a year on the unpaid balance.
3. He purchased supplies for $25,000 on credit. The supplies were received and put in inventory.
4. At the beginning of the month, he paid rent in the amount of $3,000.
5. He paid the bill for supplies in the amount of $25,000.
6. During the month, he incurred technician salaries of $12,000. Of this amount, he paid $11,000 in cash to employees. He withheld the other $1,000 from their salaries for taxes, which he will pay the government next month.
7. He billed his patients in the amount of $40,000 for MRI services.
8. On receiving the bills, the patients paid Dr. Elliott a total of $35,000.
9. During the month, he paid bills amounting to $4,000 for utility services.
10. He took inventory of the supplies and found that he had consumed $2,000 of those supplies in the course of the month's activities.

Required: Analyze these transactions on a work sheet similar to that illustrated in the text. You will need columns for Cash, Accounts receivable, Supplies inventory, Prepaid rent, Equipment, Notes payable, Accounts payable, Withholding taxes payable, and H. Elliott, Capital.

P15-7   (Analyzing accrual transactions on a work sheet)
Analyze the following accrual-type events and add them to the work sheet you prepared for P15-6.

1. Adjust for the "using up" of the MRI equipment during the month. (Assume the equipment will have a useful life of 10 years.)
2. Accrue for 1 month's interest owed on the note payable. (Add a column for Interest payable.)
3. Adjust for the expiration of the entire rent payment.

P15-8   (Recording transactions in journals and ledgers)
Using the information given in P15-6 and P15-7, record the transactions in general journal form. Then, post the journal entries to ledger T-accounts, like those shown in Table 15-11. (To help keep track of your postings, give each journal entry the same reference number or letter shown in the problems, and insert that number or letter to the left of the amount recorded in the T-accounts.)

P15-9   (Preparing a trial balance and financial statements)
Required: 1. From the ledger accounts prepared for P15-8, prepare a trial balance.
2. Extend the trial balance into an eight-column work sheet like that shown in Table 15-16, and use the work sheet to prepare the following financial statements:
a. Income statement
b. Statement of changes in owner's equity
c. Balance sheet

P15-10 (Preparing a closing entry)
Required: Based on the answers you obtained in P15-9, prepare the closing entry.

P15-11 (Analyzing transactions on a work sheet)
Ted's Ambulette provides services to and from hospitals and nursing homes. Ted, who went into business recently, keeps records on a work sheet similar to that illustrated in the text. At the start of the new year, his work sheet shows these balances: Cash—$30,000; Accounts receivable—$15,000; Fuel and parts inventory—$8,000; Vehicles—$192,000; Accounts payable—$12,000; Loans payable—$180,000; Ted Elias, Capital—$53,000. (You will also need columns for Investments, Prepaid rent, Prepaid insurance, and Withholding tax payable.) These transactions occurred in the first month of the new year:

1. Ted leased a garage to store his vehicles and to make minor repairs. He paid $6,000 for 2 months' rent.
2. Ted bought accident insurance for a 2-year period, paying $12,000.
3. He received $13,000 from charge-account customers he had billed last year.
4. During the month he purchased $10,000 of fuel and repair parts on credit.
5. He received $50,000 during the month from customers who paid in cash.

6. At month end, he sent out bills for $14,000 to charge-account customers.
7. He paid $12,000 to suppliers from whom he had purchased on account.
8. Ted's drivers and other employees earned $30,000. He paid them $28,000 and withheld $2,000 in taxes, which he will pay the government next month.
9. On the 15th of the month, Ted invested some of his cash in a 6-month $20,000 Treasury note.
10. During the month, Ted used $6,000 in fuel and repair parts from inventory.
11. Ted paid utility bills amounting to $3,000. He also received a utility bill for $1,000 that he had not paid at month-end.

Required: Record the opening balances on a work sheet similar to that illustrated in the text, and then analyze these transactions on the work sheet.

P15-12 (Analyzing accrual transactions on a work sheet)
Analyze the following accrual-type events and add them to the work sheet you prepared for P15-11.

1. Adjust for the expiration of 1 month's rent.
2. Adjust for the expiration of 1 month's accident insurance.
3. Adjust for the "using up" of the vehicles during the month. (Assume the vehicles have a useful life of 48 months from the beginning of the year.)
4. Accrue for 1 month's interest owed on the $180,000 loan. The interest rate on the borrowing is 8 percent a year. (Add a column for Interest payable.)

P15-13 (Recording transactions in journals and ledgers)
Using the information given in P15-11 and P15-12, record the transactions in general journal form. Then post the journal entries to ledger T-accounts, like those shown in Table 15-11. (To help keep track of your postings, give each journal entry the same reference number or letter shown in the problems, and insert that number or letter to the left of the amount recorded in the T-accounts.)

P15-14 (Preparing a trial balance and financial statements)
Required: 1. From the ledger accounts prepared for P15-13, prepare a trial balance.
2. Extend the trial balance into an eight-column work sheet like that shown in Table 15-16, and use the work sheet to prepare the following financial statements:
   a. Income statement
   b. Statement of changes in owner's equity
   c. Balance sheet

P15-15 (Preparing a closing entry)
Required: Based on the answers you obtained in P15-14, prepare the closing entry.

P15-16 (Recording debits and credits)
Joseph DeLapa, DDS, opened his practice on June 1, 2009. He had the following transactions during the 3-month period June 1–August 31.

1. Dr. DeLapa invested $20,000 of his own cash in the business.
2. He borrowed $80,000 on June 1 from the Vista Bank to pay for dental equipment and provide working capital.

3. He rented office space, effective June 1, agreeing to a 5-year lease. He paid the landlord $8,000 to cover the 4-month period June 1–September 30.
4. He received an invoice from a contractor for $20,000 for work done in April and May to get the office space in condition to receive patients and perform dental work. (Note: Debit an asset account called Leasehold improvements.)
5. He purchased dental chairs and related equipment, on credit, at a cost of $56,000. The chairs and equipment were delivered and installed on June 1.
6. He purchased dental supplies on credit at a cost of $5,000.
7. During the 3 months ended August 31, Dr. DeLapa performed dental services and billed his patients a total of $96,000. He received cash for the entire amount.
8. He paid his dental hygienist and his receptionist a total of $21,000 for work through August 29.
9. He paid creditors a total of $78,000.

Required: Record the transactions in general journal form. Then, post the journal entries to general ledger T-accounts.

P15-17 (Preparing adjusting journal entries)
Prepare adjusting journal entries for the following events related to the transactions in P15-16, and post the journal entries to general ledger T-accounts. (Use the T-accounts set up for P15-16 where appropriate, and set up new T-accounts as needed.)

1. Accrue interest for 3 months on the bank loan in P15-16, transaction 2. Dr. DeLapa had to repay the $80,000 loan in five annual installments of $16,000 a year, starting May 31, 2010, with interest at the rate of 6 percent per annum on the unpaid balance.
2. Adjust for the expiration of the prepaid rent in transaction 3.
3. Adjust for 3 months' amortization on the $20,000 leasehold improvement in transaction 4. The leasehold improvement should be amortized over the 5-year life of the lease.
4. Record depreciation for 3 months on the equipment purchased for $56,000 in transaction 5. The equipment has an estimated useful life of 7 years.
5. Dr. DeLapa took an inventory of the dental supplies purchased in transaction 6. The inventory totaled $4,100, the remainder having been consumed in providing dental care.
6. Accrue $700 for 2 days' salaries for Dr. DeLapa's employees.

P15-18 (Preparing a trial balance and financial statements)
    Required: 1. From the ledger accounts prepared for P15-16 and P15-17, prepare a trial balance.
           2. Extend the trial balance into an eight-column work sheet like that shown in Table 15-16, and use the work sheet to prepare the following financial statements:
             a. Income statement
             b. Statement of changes in owner's equity
             c. Balance sheet

P15-19   (Accounts receivable and sales transactions; comprehensive problem)
Camp Bryn Mawr, a summer camp, started the year with cash of $40,000,
land costing $300,000, and buildings and equipment costing $250,000. Because the camp had no liabilities, the assets were offset by the equity account
F. Jonas, Capital, in the amount of $590,000. The following transactions
occurred during the year:

1. Jonas sent bills in the amount of $150,000 to the parents of 75 campers.
2. Jonas purchased 80 camper packages (consisting of uniforms and supplies) from a vendor on credit. He received the packages and put them
   in inventory. He also received a bill for $4,800 (80 packages costing $60
   a package) from the vendor.
3. When they arrived at camp, each of the 75 campers received a camper
   package. Jonas sent bills in the amount of $6,750 to the parents, charg-
   ing them $90 a package.
4. Jonas received cash in the amount of $148,750 from the parents based
   on the bills sent out in transactions 1 and 3.
5. During the summer, Jonas paid employee salaries in the amount of
   $100,000 and food expenses of $8,000. (Assume all the food was consumed.)
6. Jonas paid the invoice for $4,800 for transaction 2.
7. Anticipating that several parents might not pay their bills, Jonas set up
   an allowance for uncollectible receivables in the amount of $4,000.
8. One of the parents, who owed $2,000, declared bankruptcy. Jonas wrote
   off the account as uncollectible.
9. Jonas made a provision for depreciation for the year, assuming that the
   buildings and equipment had a useful life of 20 years.
10. Jonas promised the camp director a bonus of $5,000, based on the excel-
    lent work she did during the year. Jonas, therefore, accrued a liability
    for that amount.

Required: 1. Prepare journal entries to record the preceding transactions.
(Among others, you will need accounts for Revenues—camper
fees, Revenues—uniform sales, and Inventory—uniforms.)
2. Post the journal entries to ledger T-accounts.
3. From the ledger accounts, prepare a trial balance.
4. Using the trial balance, prepare an income statement, a statement of changes in owner's equity, and a balance sheet.

Index